The Psychology of Human Development

THIRD EDITION

Franklin Ross Jones
OLD DOMINION UNIVERSITY

Raymond F. Morgan
OLD DOMINION UNIVERSITY

Stephen W. Tonelson
OLD DOMINION UNIVERSITY

KENDALL/HUNT PUBLISHING COMPANY
2460 Kerper Boulevard P.O. Box 539 Dubuque, Iowa 52004-0539

ISBN 0-8403-7405-4

Printed in the United States of America
10 9 8 7 6 5 4 3 2 1

CONTENTS

PART V. BEGINNING ADULTHOOD 361

PART VI. MIDDLESCENCE AND THE LATER YEARS 421

PREFACE

THE COMPLETION OF THIS TEXTBOOK, the third edition, and its compilation has been a cooperative effort representing important disciplines in the study of Human Development. The addition of a new author, Dr. Stephen Tonelson, has been especially salutary as he brings a depth of experience and information related to Early Childhood Development and Special Education. Dr. Ray Morgan is a language and children learning problem specialist. He was a co-author on the 2nd edition, and made an invaluable contribution to its success. Both Dr. Tonelson and and Dr. Morgan did their doctoral work at the University of Virginia. The senior author, Franklin Ross Jones, is a development psychologist with strong backgrounds in education and sociology. He is the author of a number of books and articles. Dr. Jones' doctoral work was done at Duke University.

This new volume has been organized in six parts and is designed to emphasize recent research on child, adolescent and adult development. Part I examines the theoretical overview and relevant ecological and environment issues along with the principles of development and pertinent research methodologies. The beginning of human development (Part II) includes new procedures and data dealing with the prenatal growth and related social issues. Part III begins with the infant and toddler and continues through the beginning prepubescent years. This section interrelates very closely the development of the infant, the early child, and later childhood period. The chapters enclosed in this framework discuss intellectual, social, physical and prosocial behavior, and the latest ideas for schooling for the handicapped, the average and the gifted. Adolescence (Part IV) features an examination of health problems, including AIDS, STD, and diet problems. Adolescent problems and issues are discussed, mainly vocational futures, morality, and the quest for meaning. Part V comprises the young adult; in this section the physical mode, the social and the psychological are highlighted in reference to a new theory of adult development. Finally, Part VI takes us through the development of the individual from middlescence to the last days emphasizing the positive aspects of the middle and later years supported by research projecting an upbeat theme "we're getting older but we're understanding it better."

ACKNOWLEDGEMENTS

THIS BOOK, like most others, would not have come to completion without the interest and assistance of many persons. The following persons reviewed the materials, chapters, the organizational outline, and/or the finished work: Dr. Dan Fowag, Chairman, Division of Social Science, Dekalb College; Dr. Katherine Wyatt, Department of Arts and Sciences, Danville Community College, Virginia; Dr. Gustave Kierwas, Department of Psychology, Piedmont Virginia Community College; Dr. Lucjan Mordjak, Department of Psychology, Greenville, S.C., Tech College; Dr. Gerald Rubin, Central Virginia Community College, Virginia; Professor Lanny Hampel, Nursing Education, Norfolk Sentara General; Professor Betty Henry, Department of Psychology, Old Dominion University; Professor William Noel, Durham, N.C.; Dr. Bernice Neugarten, Professor of Education and Sociology, Northwestern University, Chicago, Illinois; Karen Grauzlis, Public Schools, Newark, Delaware; Professor Pamela Herbert, Speech Therapist, Adjunct Professor, Washington University, Washington; and Dr. Allan Hurlburt, Professor of Education, Duke University.

Beyond the help of the subject matter specialists are others--Dr. Cynthia Duncan, Library Chief, Old Dominion University; Ms. Dawn Hall, Old Dominion University; Ms. Deborah Conn, Kendall/Hunt Publishers Copy Editor; the Libraries of University of North Carolina at Chapel Hill and Greensboro, North Carolina, and Duke University Library at Durham. Also a number of graduate students in Education and Counseling have contributed their ideas and criticisms to the manuscript. We are grateful for all the guidance provided by those listed above and the institutions who have generously assisted us.

F.R.J.
R.F.M.
S.W.T.

PART I

FOUNDATIONS OF DEVELOPMENT

Chapter 1

HUMAN DEVELOPMENT IN A CHANGING CULTURE

- ***The Process of Development***
  - Growth
  - Maturation
  - Learning
- ***The Context of Development***
  - Macrosystems
  - Microsystems
  - Mesosystems
  - Ecosystems
- ***Historical Timing and Cross Cultural Perspective***
- ***Life Span Development***
- ***Theoretical Overview***
  - Stage theories
  - Learning theories
  - Humanistic theories
- ***Human Development in Today's World***
  - Ecological systems
  - Resources
  - Environmental quality
  - Population growth
  - Economics and violence

HUMAN DEVELOPMENT IN A CHANGING CULTURE

Human beings have been favored in the development of adaptability, enabling them to improve their lives by means of creating symbols and developing tools and technology. The greatest evidence perhaps of human creativity is the development of language. According to White (1949), human behavior originates in the use of symbols. He states: "Human behavior is symbolic; symbolic behavior is human behavior." Anthropologists, educators, and psychologists have emphasized the role of language in education and socialization. Through a variety of experiences children come to know the meanings related to many conditions and situations. The two-year-old girl who calls the cow a doggie will at fifteen know the scientific classification of a cow. Why does the wind blow? The young boy, who does not know, later will learn about the uneven heating of the air. In this manner children use information to further their understanding.

In this work we will discuss this type of development and learning. In Chapter One we will describe the purposes for studying human development, theories, and the life span perspective in the dynamic socio-ecosystem of our earth. In addition, we will deal with physical development and tasks determined by society such as sex roles, morality, work responsibility, and an examination of the future of humanity in the age of science. We will discuss the forces that cause people to come to be what they are.

Arnold J. Toynbee has pointed out that humanity is astonishingly good at dealing with the physical world, but just as astonishingly bad at dealing with human nature. Human behavior is so complicated and its motivation so hidden that many believe it may be impossible to find valid principles to explain and predict the behavior of human beings. Though one may despair of constructing a precise science of human behavior, the attempt to do so goes forward even though we recognize that perhaps, as Heraclitus said in the sixth century B.C., "There is nothing permanent except change." And that's what development is about-- change.

Why Study Human Development?

The purposes of studying and understanding human development are based upon several broad assumptions:

1. Human culture is significant and worth studying, for knowledge of human psychology enhances individual understanding of the environment and serves as a basis for improvement of society.
2. A knowledge of the development of behavior provides a basis for assisting the young to reach the objectives and goals chosen first by society, and then partially modified by the young themselves. Do children learn appropriate behavior from models (through imitation, reward, or punishment), and in what proportions? The answer will improve family life and child-rearing practices.
3. Humanity can improve its condition by increasing its understanding of human development, which may aid in alleviating many existing inequities in society. The knowledge of the impact of poverty, prejudice, and ignorance on the developing person will produce changes in viewpoints that could effectively improve societal life.
4. Because modern humanity is deeply concerned with its own purpose and identity, it must seek the basic reasons and causes of human behavior. Is behavior fixed at birth to be unfolded with maturity, or is it modified in the environment; how much and in what ways? Knowledge bearing on this will be generally helpful.
5. Finally, a knowledge of the principles of behavior is a basic requirement for efficiently achieving humanly desirable ends. The impact of the needs and motives of human beings demands an understanding if society is to ultimately live in peace and to pursue cooperative goals.

STUDYING HUMAN DEVELOPMENT

Background

In attempting to reconstruct the lives of children in the middle ages, we are struck by the paucity of information. Our sketch of them comes from ancient paintings, an infrequent mention of a child in a story, or a fragment about school regulations. In the 18th and 19th centuries, many children died in infancy; the rest had brief childhoods. As soon as children reached seven or eight, they were given work as adults. The pictures of children depict them as miniature adults. Teen marriages were typical and early pregnancies the rule. The economic conditions accounted for the scenario noted by Aries (1962) in a scene where a mother with yet another baby was decrying the lack of food for her brood to a neighbor. The neighbor said, "Don't worry, before they are old enough to bother you, half or perhaps all of them will be dead." This characterized the callous but realistic view held of children, who were often treated like chattel. Even as late as the early 20th century, they were exploited in factories and on farms. In this century, increasing production levels, contraception, literacy, legislation, and information about child development have combined to change the way in which children are viewed and the status they enjoy. The interest in and concern about the child from the

1920s to the 1990s have resulted in this period being called the Century of the Child.

Early pioneers such as Rousseau in his *Emile* portrayed the child as being innately good, a God-given "good creative," untainted from the corruption of civilization. This contrasted with the belief of Calvin, the evangelical, that children were inherently evil after the nature of Adam. Darwin and Preyer wrote the first diaries and systematic accounts of children (Cairns and Valsinger, 1984). These were followed by the work of G. Stanley Hall, first president of the American Psychological Association, and John B. Watson. Hall utilized the questionnaire to get information on the child. He questioned children at length, arriving at averages; he also asked adults for retrospective information. He viewed the child as actively engaged with the environment and as developing through a series of stages. Watson, of John Hopkins, introduced the experimental method to gather facts on child development, utilizing learning theory and the stimulus-response connection as a basic construct. Following Watson's leadership, B.F. Skinner, after World War II, developed operant conditioning as another approach. Reinforcement of behavior was believed to determine conduct and its change.

The first books on children were written by physicians for parents about caring for babies. Some of their advice was ignorance personified: for instance, one 16th century work suggested mothers not nurse their babies right after being angry lest their milk prove fatal (Ryerson, 1961). Deciphering the mystery of conception in the 19th century, bringing with it debate about the influence of heredity and environment, encouraged study; along with the spread of protestantism, exhorting self-reliance made adults more concerned with their part in the way children grew up instead of viewing development as fate.

When Stanley Hall wrote his two-volume work on *Adolescence* in 1904, there was no such period of transition between childhood and adulthood. Later in 1922, he published *Senescence: The Last Half of Life*. Some universities such as Stanford University began the study of aging. In 1946 the National Institute of Health began large-scale research, collecting data and reporting information on aging. For the past 60 years a number of long-term studies bearing on development have been initiated. These include the Grant Study of Adult Development and the University of Chicago study under the leadership of Bernice Neugarten and her associates, who began studies of middle-aged people. Daniel Levinson and colleagues at Yale examined the lives of men and women in their middle years. The Gesell Institute and Child Study Center at Yale studied children. Life span studies of gifted children by Lewis Terman of Stanford University, beginning in 1921, were a landmark accomplishment. Other studies of note were the Berkeley Growth Study, the Oakland Growth Study, and those conducted by the Fels Research Institute. More recently, studies at Duke University on the aging process--social, sexual, and intellectual--have been important in the field of life span development.

Type of Development

Three areas of development are fundamental to human growth--the physical, the cognitive, and the psychosocial. The *physical* or *biological* relates to the changes that take place due to hereditary influences. This area has to do with the changes in the individual's body--including structure, height, weight, the brain, heart, muscle, and neurological and psychomotor functions. Following conception, change in development is rapid and dramatic. At 15 months, the infant can walk and talk a little; still he does not dress himself or control his bowels. However, at four years of age, he can run (mechanically) about as well as an adult, can talk a "blue streak" on occasion, and may resist any help with dressing. In contrast to the four-year-old, the adolescent is three times larger and stronger, can conceive, and can generally function as an adult.

Cognitive development involves those changes that occur in mental growth. This is an important domain in development, as it relates to a wide array of activities--memory, learning, thinking, reasoning, speaking, and imagination. These cognitive activities are tied to the psychomotor, personality, and emotional aspects of development. In Piaget's sensory-motor stages, the child develops object permanence (the knowledge that an object exists when out of sight). When this period is reached, the infant often becomes anxious when his mother leaves the room: she is an independent object.

Between 18 and 24 months, the infant develops mental representation, partly because of maturation and in part because of experience; the number of their fears is reduced and their control of bowels and urination improves. With growing insight, the young child's emotions are held in check often by remembering punishment received for past misbehavior. Later, the adolescents' ability for abstract thinking and problem solving will enable them to think about justice, truth, humanity, and democracy.

Psychosocial development involves personality and social development. The psychological aspect of a person interacts with the social environment and this determines his personality and often his future role. Relations with others are a significant part of social development. Social expectations are that children act their age. A child of six is expected to dress herself, help with chores, learn to read, etc., but not to talk to strangers or use foul language. If children are mature beyond their years in physique and mental ability, this usually affects social sophistication, but even so, limits are imposed on a child's conduct. Exterior circumstances can also affect socialization. For instance, devastating storms or earthquakes can affect the nature of growing up, the cultural expectations, and outcomes of development.

It must be recognized that the aspects of development we have discussed are not separate entities. Each of these domains has an impact on the other. They are related--one's cognitive development will affect socialization and physical factors; growth changes will affect both mental and social aspects. In the investigation of development, it is necessary for research to be done through each domain. Psychologists who focus on the cognitive study learning, language, perception, and memory. The major areas of social development are interaction with people, motivation, personality, emotions, and the environment. On the other hand, those interested in the physical study body systems, health, motor skills, nutrition, and fatigue. It remains for the developmentalists and human development specialists to bring cohesion and unity to the vast amounts of research from these domains to researchers in other fields, students, and the public.

Process of Development

Growth is the process of development which takes place under the aegis of the endocrine and metabolic systems. These systems process foods, utilizing them to develop the body. In time, the human body matures and growth slows and then stops at a certain height, usually about the time sexual adulthood is reached. Some qualitative changes, however, continue to occur, as in cognition, personality, emotion, and character.

In *maturation*, the map for development has been laid down by heredity. Maturation implies growth, which entails biological change. However, maturation is directly responsible for the functioning of such body parts as the legs and feet, sex organs, and the voice apparatus. These are only slightly affected by environmental conditions. For example, it takes extreme nutrition deprivation to throw skeletal growth off its pattern. The orderly changes we note in the child--sitting, crawling, standing, and walking--unfold in time. In the adolescent, sperm production in boys and ova in girls is directed toward reproduction--heralding a predetermined event--and all part of maturation.

Learning is an important aspect of development and an essential ingredient throughout one's life. Learning is change of behavior based upon experience; it is analogous to eating in that, once it begins, it has to continue. Unlike maturation, which does not require experience or rehearsal, learning depends upon growth and maturation. Certain structures must be present before learning takes place. For instance, in talking, the speech apparatus must be sufficiently developed for the experience to result in speech. We see the effects of nature's plan and timing in that talking typically is preceded by walking in the individual. The readiness to learn or psychological set requires certain growth and maturation potential. The organism has to adapt continually to changing conditions in the environment. How the person interacts with the environment accounts for who we are, our selves and our personalities. In effect, we become what we have been given by heredity and what has been shaped by our surroundings. The environmental, the social, and the psychological all make us what we are.

The Context of Development

The environmental influences on the developing person involve the social and the physical. The latter has to do with heredity, which sets limits--we grow only so tall and are made in a particular manner. The physical surroundings--the houses we live in, the geographical area (climate, topography, etc.)--and the social are determinants of development. In this manner, the individual interacts with environment to create ultimately the person. Bronfenbrenner and Crouter (1983) say that to study the influences on development you need to investigate the individual interaction with the environment, including ongoing physical and social changes. They list four levels of environmental influence: microsystems, mesosystems, exosystems, and macrosystems.

The *microsystem* consists of the social relationships and the physical settings a person is involved with each day (home, school, work place); for instance, how and when a child interacts with family members. Also important is the impact of the size and design of the home on children. The *mesosystem* represents the interaction between a person and various settings in which development takes place for them. For the 15-year-old, the mesosystem includes the home and school. It might also include the church, camp, club, and part-time work. The *exosystem* is the interplay between the major social structures that affect the individual. These can be both formal and informal, such as media, neighborhoods, agencies of government (state and local), transportation, Little League organizations, parks and playgrounds. The *macrosystem* is the prevailing institutional pattern of culture or subculture such as economic, social, educational, religious, legal, and political systems.

The following example depicts how these systems affect people in important ways. Mike, a boy of 13, has a sister of 10 named Susan, who is crippled and gets around in a wheelchair. Her education is often interrupted because the school system provides little help with transportation. Economic problems have forced severe cuts in special education programs. The father's work consists of a morning and evening paper route and much of the collection is made between deliveries. The route, a large one of 300-400 customers in a medium-sized city, provides enough income to support his wife, who is in poor health, and the children. The family also rents a room in their home to provide extra income. Mike is his father's assistant and is required to help twice a day except on Sunday, when the papers are combined into one edition. Mike gets up at 4:30 each morning and works until about 7:30. He has breakfast shortly thereafter and then goes to a nearby junior high school. After school he is picked up by his father for the evening route. Due to his job, he has little time to make friends, to play, or to be involved in school activities after classes. he does not belong to any group, and his family does not attend church. Because of his early rising schedule, he has little free time and hardly time to do his homework. He helps his mother some with errands, such as cleaning and strolling his sister on weekends to an ice cream store. His school work suffers but he doesn't worry about it, for his main task is to help his father. And there is little discussion of school with his parents. The family is close-knit and has few friends. Mike's leisure time is used in bicycle riding, making model planes, and seeing an occasional movie. The father and mother talk very little to neighbors across the street from them. On their side of the block the city has been zoned for business and, in fact, a cleaning establishment is located next to their yard. Encouragement is lacking for Mike to do well in school or to have friends; the parents believe the family is self-sufficient. The lower-middle-class surroundings give little stimulation for Mike. He is not being challenged to be creative or to explore, nor does he seem interested in being with other boys and girls his age. He apparently long ago decided it didn't fit in his schedule. His only wish for the future is to be like his father.

The neighborhood next to Mike's is a middle-class one made up mostly of adults who are college graduates. These parents are mainly in their thirties and forties and are upwardly mobile professionals and business managers. In one of these homes is Ruth, a girl of 15, who attends the same school as Mike. She knows Mike as the paper boy but that is all the contact she has with him. Though not the best of students (she repeated the first grade), she nevertheless is doing fairly well in the ninth grade. Her mother gives her great amounts of time, has sent her to summer school and camp, and gives her music lessons. Although Ruth isn't as pretty as some girls, she dresses well, is lively and interesting, and makes friends easily. She is often invited to visit other girls' homes and go to parties and outings with boys, and in general leads quite a successful social life.

Already plans have been made for her to take the College Preparatory Courses in High School. Ruth's father, a businessman, is very solicitous of her, frequently taking her to events and movies, and often checks on her homework. The relationship with her parents is exceedingly good. Ruth is self-confident and looking forward to going to college.

The outlooks for Mike and Ruth, reflecting the settings in which they live, are very different. In Mike's case, his home, a wooden frame, one-and-a-half story embedded in a partly commercial setting, is noticeably dreary. In contrast, Ruth's home is a two-story brick house with a spacious tailored lawn, expressing to her and others confidence, affluence, and optimism. Although they are of equal intelligence, Mike will probably only finish high school, whereas Ruth will graduate from college. Mike, unless something unforeseen happens, will do what his father does or something similar. There are no plans for college in the future and the necessity for work precludes Mike from developing many outside interests or friends and the care of the sister will be left in his hands.

Mike's interaction with his immediate environment--the home, school, and work place--is having a determining effect on his life. This is the microsystem. The interplay of major social structures--the exosystems--will also affect the lives of Mike and Ruth, though perhaps in different ways.

The Historical Timing

This aspect of development relates to one's particular age, a timing sometimes called normative age. Mike and Ruth are 13 and 15; they are consequently influenced by physical changes (growth spurts and sex characteristics) and cognitive changes when, as students of junior high school, they are introduced to more varied and concentrated work in such new fields as algebra, sciences, and language study. Social circumstances often open radically new vistas to them as larger and different groups of people challenge them to interact.

The *age cohort*, sometimes called birth cohort, is another kind of timing. This happening is a societal one, reflecting political and economic fluctuation which affects the group of infants who are born at the same time. The influences of the environment affects this cohort uniformly as it moves from childhood to adolescence. Children of the Depression (1930s) were affected by the lack of funds, both private and public. Children of the 1940s faced the fallout from the war. The silent generation of the 1950s and "me" generation of the 1960s created different sorts of developmental challenges. One can understand the importance of this when considering what it meant to grow up as a Jewish person in Germany in the 1930s or a black child in Alabama in the 1940s or 1950s.

It is normal for precipitous changes to occur in the lives of people that bring a significant effect. One person is hurt in a car accident in such a way that he can no longer walk. One inherits a great amount of money. A woman becomes pregnant and marries as a teenager. Someone changes from one profession to another. The care of a parent becomes one's responsibility in midlife. These types of events vary from person to person; almost everyone has some happening that affects his or her life in important ways. The advance of society in time affects the positions of people, with influence being altered as older cohorts are replaced by new cohorts. Culture loses some of its collected lore, customs and wisdom; then some is added and some modified as the generations move forward. Critical periods of time will be discussed in Chapter Two in connection with the developmental level.

The Life Span Approach

We divide the life span into infancy, childhood, adolescence, and adulthood. There are, however, divisions under each of these categories; for instance, infancy begins at birth. The days which follow are known as the neonatal; the closing time of this period is around two years of age. Overlapping infancy at 18 months is toddlerhood, which begins and lasts until around three. The infant by then has begun to walk and to talk--to acquire speech and mental representation--and is often thought of as a child, not a baby.

The table on *Types of Development* provides an outline for periods of life, chronology, and types of average development. These are rather definitive. Although years become increasingly less effective in describing characteristics of older adults, and there are overlaps in development themes, there are some similarities by 10-year cohorts that can be identified. We describe *Later Adulthood* in terms of Young-Old, a period Bernice Neugarten suggests is from 65-75; we now suggest 70-79 due to the increased longevity that is occurring. The projected life expectancy for women today on reaching 65 is 18 additional years and for men twelve. With this in mind, we have called the 80-89 group Old, but the Old Old not beginning until about 90. In some classification systems this begins at 85. People age differentially, many are old at 60; however, some 70-year-olds can be found jogging, playing tennis, and vigorously employed at work. Adolescence is usually defined as a period beginning with puberty, but its end is less conclusive. Some suggest extended adolescence goes to 25 or until one internalizes the world of work and accepts a societal role.

Margaret Mead (1968) suggests that in Samoa and some other societies there are only two periods of development--infancy and adulthood. The Western world has four phases (adding adolescence), in the chart noted under the physical, motor, cognitive, and psychosocial. Growth of the body in dimension is as important as is developing mental maturity. Biological maturation is the basis of many developmental advances in the early child. It is so uniform in most children that the time indicators are more appropriate than for adults. After childhood the passage of time does not

TYPES OF LIFE SPAN DEVELOPMENT

Periods of Life		Physical	Motor
Infancy	0 1	Homeostasis regular Weight 20-25 lbs Heights 27-31 in.	walking talking
Childhood	2		
Early	3	Weight 30-35 lbs. Height 34-41 in.	Rides tricycle & pushes wagon Plays and climbs.
Middle & older	5	Weight 32-54 lbs. Height 40-47 in.	Rides bicycle. Roller skates, learns to swim, plays variety of games.
	10	Weight 47-58 lbs. Height 50-100 in.	Has a number of playmates.
Adolescence	11	Puberty	Skills in games & athletics grow.
Early 11-13		Large increase in heart size and cardiovascular system.	Team & individual sports--tennis, softball, basketball, soccer.
Middle 14-16		Large gains in height and weight, sexual maturity for girls.	
Late 17-19		Considerable muscle growth & strength, sexual maturity for boys.	Learns to dance, plays touch football, team member.
Adulthood	20	Physical Maturity	Development of long-term interest in sports, golf, tennis, jogging, boating, hiking, camping, fishing, bicycling, swimming, walking, bowling.
Young 20-29			
Later Young 30-39		Weight gains, larger abdomen and thighs.	
Middlescence			
Younger 40-49		Waist expands, gains in weight. Arthritis onset for some. Hair recedes in men. Greyness occurs in both women and men.	Recreational varieties--traveling, visiting, games, swimming & walking.
Middle 50-59		Menopause in women. Lessening of potenia in men. Onset of diabetes for some.	Lessening of active sports--travel & vacations. Bicycling, walking.
Later 60-69		Most people have a chronic health problem. 30% of weight is fat for women & men. Many people exercise regularly.	Increase in sedentary activities. Card and game playing. Gardening and sewing, some play golf or tennis.
Later Adulthood	70	Cardiovascular or cancer problems for many/weight loss.	Walking, yard work, hobbies.
Young Old 70-79		Adjustment to less strength and to a slower pace.	Walking and visiting. Riding and walking.
Old 80-89		Problems with homeostasis.	Short trips, walking.
Old Old 90		Saving energy.	

TYPES OF LIFE SPAN DEVELOPMENT

Cognitive	Psychosocial/Personality
Sensory-motor. Object permanence. Mental representation.	Bonding, attachments expanded to siblings, others. Beginning autonomy.
Rudimentary sorting & puzzle solving. Number conservation. Learning to compute, communicate, and to comprehend--read concrete operations.	Develop a sense of self & initiative, has playmates, develops gender identity. Schooling--social activities in group and gangs, masters skills & social relationships, middle school/ junior high, meets new friends--boys & girls.
New subjects--computers--organizations.	
	Develops personal identity.
Formal operations--ability to see things in general, abstract ability.	
Completes high school & starts college or work.	Develops emotional independence.
Mastery of college work, technology or business skills. Adequacy in work life--economics decision making, ability to complete complicated forms--income tax, record keeping for insurance, mortgages & investments.	Developing economic independence. & awareness of the community. Becomes one's own person and assumes leadership roles
Understanding of people, children and spouse. Knowledge of government economic & social issues.	Increase in status and responsibility in the community and in helping children become emancipated.
Crystallized intelligence increases--fluid intelligence decreases.	General happiness for most men and women--many are grandparents.
Recall more difficult. Likes games and puzzles.	Emotional maturity. Retirement for many. Part-time work for some.
	Defensive styles shift from neurotic to mature ones for coping: suppression, altruism, sublimation, humor, anticipation.
Over learning becomes important in memory. Exchange of information & ideas among friends. Reading of newspapers, magazines, and the Bible. Watching TV movies. Talking over events of the past and present with friends & kin.	Reconsideration of social and personal goals. Interaction with select numbers of friends & relatives

parallel consistently significant changes--some achieve sexual maturity at 14, a few at 20. Some marry at 18, others at 30. A few men grow taller until they are 25; others complete their growth at 16. Nevertheless, most of the people share a common experience in change that leads to maturity and can be seen in phases that can be identified.

Cross-Cultural Perspective

Culture refers to the patterns we have learned from our social heritage. The mores and customs that we have internalized give us our views of life, a mode for thinking, concepts to be emotional about, and patterns of behavior. Culture makes a difference in the lives of people across the world. The suggested types and phases of development seen in the chart on pages 10-11 holds true in a general sense in the Western world. A girl of 14 in Uganda or Costa Rica will be married and assuming the adult role of child bearer. In America, a girl of this age will be in high school and will probably not bear a child until she is eight to 10 years older. As we noted, there is no adolescence in many countries, no period of transition between childhood and adulthood. Children work at an early age. The rural Russian child will be working on a collective farm as a teenager, and will typically have no opportunity to go to college. Even more extreme, the Ik tribes in Uganda (Turnbull, 1972) turn their children from home at three years of age to fend for themselves. They also treat their elders as badly as their young. Obviously because of these practices, this tribe is diminishing in number.

As the phases of life are determined by culture, so are other aspects of development, such as values and views about morality. Witness the Marind Anim culture of New Guinea, which encourages sexual activity among children, even homosexual relationships for boys. After marriage a wife may engage in extramarital sex with her husband's approval. In America this would be disapproved of vigorously (Van Baal, 1966), but among the Marind Anim culture, this has social approval.

Consider the varying views of old age--in America our consumer and youth-oriented society treats the aged as worthless. Youth reflects the dominant view of the culture and therefore the old are often treated with disrespect and scorn. In summer 1990 in Martinsville, Virginia, children 9 and 10 years of age were found throwing rocks at a helpless old lady who had done them no harm. In Eastern cultures, for example, among the rural Chinese and North Burmese (Amoss & Harrell, 1981), the elderly enjoy a premiere place in society. It is felt there that the aged have lived virtuous lives in a previous incarnation. Consequently, younger women in this culture often try to appear older. In the Russian province of Georgia claims are frequently made of ages running from 110 to 130; maybe the air, hard work, and diet increase longevity. In any case they are treated differentially. Gender also receives special attention within cultures. For instance in the United States, lower class families have often valued the girl child over the boy, whereas sometimes in the upper middle class, boys are valued over girls. The logic may be that a girl will bring economic betterment through the orientation of her husband to her family. In the case of the boys, they carry on the family line or father's name in business or a profession.

Culture is important in understanding human development. Culture determines the acceptable use of emotions, the importance of certain time periods and occupations. Also, culture determines the values of certain kinds of learning and information and what is considered an adequate life. To understand people is to know their background.

Theoretical Overview

Most societies have created various conceptual schemes to deal with the common experiences and cultural expectancies found in development. In the Western world these have been numerous. The theories of Freud and Erikson involve personality and psychosocial development, while Piaget's theories deal with cognitive development. Havighurst's cultural expectancies and Kohlberg's moral development play a part in the development of the maturing persons. All of these are stage theories. They are based upon a biological model. The stage concept is illustrated by the process of metamorphosis, as in the development of the butterfly through the cocoon, larva, pupa, and adult stages. Each stage is characterized by distinctive development, both mental and physical. The stage theory is allied with "critical periods" in development, in which certain times of life are viewed as providing favorable or unfavorable circumstances that have lasting consequences.

A second category represents a group of behavioral theories that approach development as mechanistic, in that no abrupt change occurs in development; it unfolds on a continuous basis between infancy and adulthood. The continuous nature of growth is typified by the leaf--it grows by expansion--a small young leaf to a larger one. The behavioral theories to be discussed are: (1) learning theories of conditioning of Pavlov and Watson, (2) social learning of Bandura, and (3) behavior modification of Skinner.

The third category of theories known as Humanism or Self Theories suggests that people are active in their development. They are not locked in by unconscious instincts the followers of psychoanalytic thought believe. Maslow and Rogers represent this compromise position, simply stating that the individual is not a pawn but a broker in determining the elements of his or her life.

Stage Theories

Psychoanalytic theory (Freud). Freud contends that the child's early formative stages must be successful to achieve a well-balanced adulthood. Development in life is affected by the basic system known as the psychic anatomy, which comprises the superego, ego, and id (See Figure 1.1). In a general sense they represent the biological (id), the psychological (ego), and the social (superego). The id in the newborn infant is activated purely by biological urges such as hunger, thirst, the need for warmth, and the need for sleep. Biological characteristics as well as reflexes are inborn, and they constitute the id, which is governed by the pleasure principle. It has no control and represents only impulse-seeking expression and satisfaction in an animalistic sense. It has no morality and was described by Freud as "a cauldron of seething excitement" (1933). The ego is governed by the reality principle in reacting to varying aspects of the environment. The id is gradually brought under greater control as the infant learns to develop a realistic view of the world. Recogni-

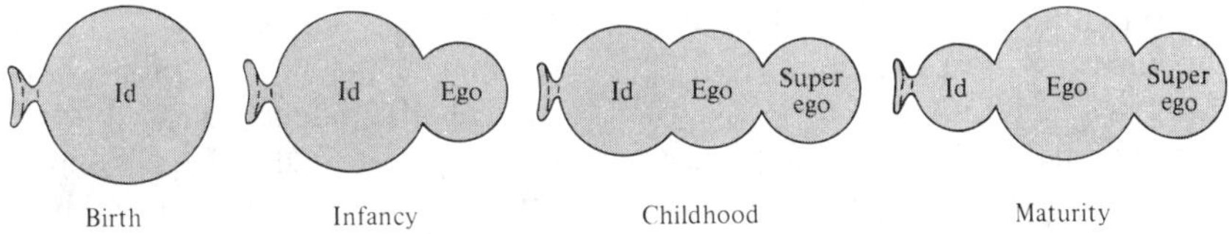

Figure 1.1 Normal development of the psychic anatomy.

tion of the reality principle is observed in the control exercised by the child when punishment follows disapproved conduct.

The superego, based on the model of parents, develops at four or five, and involves two divisions: the conscience and the ego-ideal. The conscience develops by threats (loss of love and status) and punishment as a way of discouraging aberrant behavior. The ego-ideal involves the encouragement by authority figures of behavior, such as when they say, "good boy," "you're smart," and "that's nice." Freud postulated five stages of early development: oral, anal, phallic, latent, and pubertal (genital).

Difficulties that will develop in solving conflicts during the early stages can have effects on personality. In the oral stage (approximately birth to 18 months) gratification comes through the mouth. Sucking is important. The absence or irregular presence of milk when demanded affects the ability to form interpersonal attachments. The infant may develop a lack of trust that later becomes manifest in excessive eating and drinking, a special interest in words, or sarcasm and arguing. Such a person represents the "oral character" type. During the anal stage (approximately 12 months to three years) gratification is received through the anus, that is, through defecation; toilet training is important. Conflict over control of the bladder and bowel may result in the "anal-retentive" type. This occurs when children resist parental efforts to toilet train by refusing to move their bowels. In consequence, they grow up to be stingy, obstinate, or very rigid adults. The implication for future development is that it may affect their ability to work and feel competent.

The major problem of development occurs during the phallic stage (approximately ages three to six) with the oedipal crisis. The Oedipus complex relates to boys who covet their mothers and have hostile rivalry toward their fathers. Girls experience the Electra complex, the reverse situation. Boys fear punishment through castration, and girls perceive that they have been castrated as they have no penis. Strong sexual feelings for the opposite-sex parent are worked out, and identification with the like-sex parent usually occurs. If unsuccessful, personality difficulties may occur later and have an effect on the development of conscience and guilt. The latency and genital periods, considered less important by Freud, cover the elementary school years, during which he thought children suppress most of their sexual feelings. The genital stage represents the period when hormone changes accompany puberty, bringing adult sexuality.

Mental life, according to Freud, has three levels of awareness: conscious, preconscious, and unconscious. The most significant aspects of mental life are unconscious. Sexual desire and the sensual are introduced as a primary unconscious determinant dominating much of life. The adult personality is a synthesis of the inborn id, ego, and superego as they have developed. The trend of development (birth to 14 years), according to the Freudian approach, is set by the individual's transition through oral, anal, phallic, latency, and pubertal stages. In each stage the child undergoes a different major conflict in the sexual realm and is subjected to unconscious motivation stemming from impulses below the level of awareness. If the conflict is unresolved, fixation at the stage occurs, affecting adult personality. In understanding the child's reactive behavior, the use of defense mechanisms such as rationalization, sublimation, repression, and compensation to insulate themselves from ego pain, is applied and is particularly insightful (see Chapter 7). Unconscious motivation cannot be observed nor studied objectively. Freud gave inadequate attention to adolescence and adulthood; further he constructed his theories on children mainly from inferences from his adult patients. Nevertheless common experience suggests the psychic anatomy has its counterpart in us all.

<u>Psychosocial theory</u> (Erikson). For Erikson, the road to maturity passes through eight psychosocial crises. Erikson's frame of reference is psychoanalytic but he gives principal atten-

tion to psychosocial crisis rather than to Freud's psychosexual stages. For Erikson there are three major aspects in understanding development:

- Somatic--physical strength and weakness.
- Personal--life history and the present developmental stage.
- Social--cultural, historical, and social forces.

Erikson believes these areas should be studied, not for the purpose of finding cause and effect, but to discover their relationships and interdependence. The resolution of each of the eight social crises is accomplished within the extreme "critical aspects" limits by most children and youths. During the first year (Freud's oral stage) there is a psychosocial crisis of *trust versus mistrust*, and its mode is to get or to give as determined by the mother's relationship. When security and love from the mother are satisfactory, a favorable outcome of drive and hope is provided. A feeling of security prepares the infant to enter the next phase and to develop self-control and willpower.

The first year of the child's life is involved principally with the mother or mother substitute in the family setting. It is during this time that children establish a sense of trust, provided they receive the love and attention characteristic of most mother-child situations. In the absence of these, children develop mistrust. From ages one to three, they establish a *sense of autonomy* (Freud's anal stage) through associations with different family members, including close kin and friends. It is essential for the child to identify himself or herself as a person and to develop a favorable self-concept in order to develop successfully in the next stage of initiative and responsibility. Failure to establish autonomy results in shame and doubt. As children mature, developing the ability to walk, dress, and feed themselves, they push their own autonomy. This accounts for the "terrible two's," often observed as negativism. Parents need to provide behavior limits and a safe haven for the child to come back to for reassurance. A balance between encouraging exploration, experimentation, and maintenance of proper control is needed during this period. However, parents should be aware that no society prepares for the future so well that our children are without problems (Smelser & Erikson, 1980).

The social conflict for children of four and five is one of *initiative versus guilt*, with the social setting being the family. The motor and mental abilities of children greatly expand, involving them in activities such as jumping, running, and roughhouse play, and these develop initiative. Parents who restrict the freedom or criticize their children excessively often give them the idea that they are nuisances, and they may become passive recipients of whatever the environment brings.

From the sixth to the eleventh year the crisis is one of *industry versus inferiority*, involving being successful in school--learning how things work, how they are made, and what they are called. Children gain a sense of industry when their achievement is recognized by teachers and parents. They may, however, acquire a sense of inadequacy if they are ignored or derided for their efforts. Praise and support have a positive effect on children in encouraging industry. The principal setting for this achievement is the neighborhood and school. If the children fail in school, a sense of inferiority will surely follow. The question then becomes what type of defense mechanisms they will use to combat psychic pain. It is important for society to understand why children often turn to drugs, violence, and crime; often to forget lives of failure.

Identity and *role confusion* represent aspects of the social crisis from ages 12 to about 18. The social situation exerts pressure between peer groups and other group models as children enter adolescence. Examples are the greatly expanding roles involving physical growth, new insights, and widening social experiences. On the question of identity ("Who am I?"), adolescents try out many roles as they grope with vocational choices, choose physical relationships, and ponder their status relative to the adult world. A core identity, which according to Erikson includes acceptance of a value system and commitment to work, is essential, for otherwise a negative identity or self-confusion is likely to occur.

Intimacy and *isolation* are crisis points for young adults, with the social setting revolving around partners in friendship and sex. Intimacy finds expression in deep friendship involving sharing and caring for others. Rejection of intimacy often brings painful emotional experience, so that some individuals are afraid of deep commitments and opt for relationships that are shallow or from which they may withdraw into isolation.

The middle years are characterized by the problem of *generativity versus stagnation*. A productive person reaches beyond his or her own needs and immediate concerns to embrace the welfare of society. The social setting is one of work and family. In contrast, stagnation is a situation in which individuals are caught up with material possessions or physical well-being.

In old age, *integrity* and *despair* mark life. If a sense of accomplishment and satisfaction is felt by an individual, integrity usually characterizes the person's life in its summation. Others, who lack the feeling of integrity, despair, for there is not enough time to repeat the life struggle. They end their lives embittered, self-engrossed, and caring little for humankind.

<u>Cognitive theory</u> (Piaget). Four stages characterize Piaget's cognitive development. For him children are engaged in a continual interaction with their surroundings. They act upon it, change it, and modify the world in which they live. During the sensory-motor period (birth to two years), development by the child of object permanence (usually around 8 to 10 months) and hand-eye, hand-mouth coordination is important. Piaget's theory on the development of cognitive structure details the manner in which conceptual ability develops in the child. The first stage in the development of intelligence is the sensory-motor, in which the infant's first schema is reflexive--that is, learned from such activities as touching its mother or sucking a nipple. By interacting with their environment during play and other activities, children construct a series of schemas (schema-models) for coping with their world. The schema becomes more complex in its organization as the increased number of experiences demand a system for relating these data. This is assimilation. The filing of different experiences requires some adjustment (accommodation) and constant reorganization of the information system, so that the child's model conforms more readily to the real world. A balance or equilibrium between assimilation and accommodation is necessary for normal progression in development--that is, making a new model or scheme: New assimilation will create disequilibrium, and accommodation will occur and then equalize. This fluctuation causes cognitive development.

From two to seven, the child in the pre-operational stage (begins to use symbols, is highly egocentric) progresses in intuitive thought. At this point children use symbols to represent an external world internally; for example, they talk about water and form a mental image of it. Between 7 and 11 years of age concrete operational tasks are learned; the child begins to understand and use concepts that help to deal with the immediate environment. The child masters logical operations, including arithmetic, class, and set relationships, and has a growing ability to conserve mass, weigh numbers, and so on. Following this the period of formal thought (12-18) occurs, during which the individual can think in abstract terms and deal with hypothetical problems. In the concrete operation stage the child's thoughts remain fixed upon visual evidence and concrete objects and events, but in the final stage they free themselves from our "physical givers" and are abstractions. According to Piaget, the child's cognitive development depends upon maturation, physical experiences, social interaction, and the balance between experience and organizing it into usable patterns. It is obvious that a majority of adults never achieve the formal operation stage, whereas others build new cognitive structure into their later years.

Moral development theory (Kohlberg). Kohlberg outlines six stages in moral development that roughly reflect Piaget's view on the steps to formal or mature thinking. The *premoral* or *preconventional level* of Kohlberg's theory represents Stages 1 and 2. Stage 1 runs from four to seven years of age (Kohlberg, 1976). Morality at this level is based upon fear of punishment. In Stage 2, behavior is based upon the reward system: the child conforms to obtain rewards. The basis of morality at this stage is reciprocity: "I'll be good if you're good to me." The *conventional level* encompasses Stages 3 and 4. The first is characterized by the good boy/good girl stage, in which behavior may conform to whether it pleases or helps others. This period usually occurs when children are between 10 and 13 years of age. In Stage 4, fixed rules to maintain the social order are motivators of behavior. Doing one's duty, and respecting authority to avoid censure and resultant guilt, usually dictate conformity. Most individuals at this stage are adolescents 12 to 14 years of age. The *postconventional level*, representing Stages 5 and 6, involves social contracts (Stage 5), and may begin as early as age 13, during adulthood, or never. Here the individual believes in individual rights and democratically accepted laws; right actions are those agreed upon by society. In this stage, people are under contract to legally obey the law. If they disagree with laws, people have the right to change them through referendum, the courts, or representation. The final stage, Number 6 seldom reached by most adolescents or adults--is known as the universal ethical principle orientation. Individual principles that appeal to logical comprehensiveness, universality, and consistency give impetus to conduct.

Kohlberg's stages, like those of Piaget, are invariant and therefore progressed through in order. He also maintains that all cultures employ the same basic moral concepts, including justice, love, respect, and authority. They are not concrete rules but abstract ethical principles like the Golden Rule.

The use of a standard procedure makes it possible to judge the level of morality an individual has reached, the person's reaction to a moral dilemma. An often-used illustration is in the situation in which a man, Henry, steals a drug to keep his wife alive. He cannot secure the necessary funds to purchase it, and consequently the druggist refuses to give him the drug, and so Henry steals the medicine. Response to this indicates the moral level of development--conventional, preconventional, or postconventional. A step-by-step application of this is discussed in Chapter 8.

Developmental tasks theory (Havighurst). According to Havighurst (1972) and Erikson (1968), a pattern of expectations for development appears as a result of biological changes and cultural influences. Socializing agencies, such as the home and the school, reward the child for attainments and punish the child for failures to achieve developmental milestones in harmony with expectations. These developmental tasks and critical aspects are closely related to social expectations of the individual at different age levels in society. Some of the tasks by stages are:

Infancy (biological tasks). Walking, talking, eating, and controlling body waste.

Early childhood (biosocial tasks). Learning sex differences, simple concepts, right and wrong, motor skills, and simple concepts of social and physical reality.

Late childhood (psychological and cultural tasks). Developing skills in reading, sex roles, personal independence, conscience, and getting along with age mates.

Adolescence (psychosocial and biological tasks). Achieving mature relations with age mates, selecting an occupation, selecting a set of values, achieving emotional independence from parents and other adults, and using the body effectively.

Young adulthood (psychosocial tasks). Selecting a mate, working, managing a home, carrying out civic responsibilities, and finding a suitable social group.

Middle adulthood (psychosocial tasks). Relating to one's spouse as a person, developing leisure-time activities, accepting physical changes, assisting teenage children become adults, and adjusting to aging parents.

Late adulthood (psychosocial and biological tasks). Adjusting to moving to smaller quarters, loss of a spouse, declining health, and reduced income.

The development tasks concept occupies middle ground between two opposing theories of education: permissiveness and constraint. The first theory suggests that the child will develop best if left as free as possible, and the latter theory postulates that the child must be taught to become a worthy, responsible adult through restraints imposed by society. A developmental task is positioned between an individual need and a societal demand. It assumes the individual is an active learner interacting with a dynamic social environment. In this aspect it is like the organismic approach, which will be presented later.

A number of factors influence successful handling of the societal expectancies, such as accelerated physical development, abundant energy for one's age, an enriched environment, superior intelligence, and a strong motivation to learn. A number of obstacles to success with the tasks unfortunately exist, such as less than average physical and mental development, chronic illness, a defect or health problem, lack of opportunity for social interchange, and an impoverished environment, including poor parenting and lack of motivation. It should be understood that failure to adequately learn and achieve competency in a given task generates a type of developmental arrest that may remain for years and prevent the child from coping with his or her environment at a later time. For example, the child handicapped by a crippling disease during the adolescent period may be thwarted in developing self-determination and independence.

The nature of some tasks is closely related to specific cultures, periods, and social classes. The age of choosing an occupation and entering the working world varies from culture to culture. The longer period of schooling required in present-day Western culture has resulted in a delay of the time when individuals enter different vocational pursuits, whereas in the underdeveloped nations it comes earlier. Marriage and homemaking in most Western nations are reserved for the young adult ages of 20 to 24, whereas in underdeveloped nations this is typical of the adolescent ages of 15 to 18. However, in lower socio-economic classes in the United States, the marriage age parallels that of other cultures. The task approach is a useful concept for students who would relate human development and understanding of behavior to such problems of development as child care and adjustment of individuals.

Learning Theories

Conditioning. A second basis for exploring human development is derived from conditioning theories, largely behaviorism (Watson, 1913). Early theorists assumed man's learning to be neural and passive (people are neither good nor bad; they simply respond to the environment), with development of growth in structure by the stimulus-response patterns that make each set of responses that are learned necessary in making the next response. Such linkage is the function of the two laws of readiness: practice and effect. Modern theorists believe that the learner is actively involved because of internal motives that provide purposes for the accomplishment of goals.

The behaviorists hold that development is based on conditioning, and as a consequence certain behavior at different ages can be expected. The behaviorist believes that most behavior can be measured precisely. Human beings, according to the behaviorist, are neural-passive beings who can be constantly reinforced and programmed through conditioning and shaping. Institutions and society have some natural operants that serve this function--for example, cutting off electricity at prescribed times when the bill is unpaid, or giving rebates for earlier payment.

Human behavior is believed to fall into one of two general categories. Either we behave voluntarily under our own impetus or we react involuntarily when an outside agent forces us to act. Respondent (involuntary) behavior exists when a stimulus or set of conditions elicits a specific response (we blink when something gets in our eye). In operant conditioning the person operates on the environment (the man calls his dog). Both respondent and operant behaviors may be seen in the performance of a single act. The baby may put a finger in its mouth eliciting a sucking reaction, but can slow or speed it up by voluntary control.

In *classical conditioning*, it is assumed that if there is to be a response, a stimulus must precede it. Hence, if there is no stimulus, there will be no response. In responding through involuntary reflex, reinforcement precedes the response because it is associated with a stimulus that comes from the environment. Learning takes place through the pairing of conditioned stimulus and unconditioned stimulus due to the contiguity of the stimuli. The behavior is respondent as seen in Pavlov's famous experiment. This conditioning accounts for much of the fear, anxiety, or pleasure that we acquire, and it is the basis of many positive and negative emotional reactions in infancy. An example of this occurred when Watson (1920) conditioned Albert B. to fear a white rat, and then other furry things that formerly were not associated with fear. Watson paired a loud startling noise with Albert's attempt to reach for the rat. Soon Albert responded with avoidance and fear to the rat he earlier enjoyed. Pairing positive consequences with the appearance of the feared stimulus may extinguish the conditioning.

In *operant conditioning*, the response produces the stimulus, which cannot be elicited without the behavior occurring that is being sought. Then it can be reinforced. Such behavior comes from the person, not the environment. Since the behavior does not happen automatically, the problem is to get the desired behavior to occur initially. Skinner's (1953) pigeons were reinforced at the first point of a step in making the figure eight, and subsequently for making the right moves until the circles were complete. Thereafter, it was a matter of learning the pattern. Thorndike (1949) utilized the same approach in getting cats to lift a latch. This he called the law of effect. In the case of a boy who comes into the house with muddy shoes, his mother will have to wait until the shoes are cleaned off before entering to reward him. This conditions him to repeat the behavior until it is regularized. Applying operant conditioning principles to change or initiate learning is behavior modification. Tokens frequently are given as rewards to children in special language instruction for correct verbal and pronunciation response. The earned tokens may be exchanged for gifts and prizes. Token economies work with autistic and retarded; also in classroom and for therapy by psychologists and psychiatrists.

The teaching of a complicated act is accomplished step by step through shaping. Here, as in the case of Skinner's pigeons, rewards are given for successive approximations of the desired behavior until it is completed. The father uses a reinforcement method when he helps his daughter with a model airplane, completing parts of the steps while leaving more and more to be done by the daughter. Each time the daughter needs less help, and can finally do everything herself. The token reward or reinforcement is used in school in encouraging children to perform or be disciplined.

Obviously some conditioning is involved in most learning situations. The learning theorists argue for the importance of environmental shaping of behavior. Conditioning theorists study the human being as the dependent variable (the variable that is under experimental control--the environment) whose measured changes are attributed to changes in the independent variable. To the behaviorist and other learning theorists the stimulus is the principal cause of human action. They begin with some small aspect of a problem, such as what situation exists to cause a child to complete a puzzle. When enough parts have been put together (motivation, ability, conditions, and so on), the larger picture of human motivation and conduct will be understood. The distinction between classical and operant conditioning has been blurred by experiments conducted by DiCara (1970) in modifying visceral responses by operant learning.

Social learning. Bandura and Walters (1963) believe, as do social learning theorists, that observational learning plays a considerable part in human adaptation. Children identify with their parents, who shape their behavior by reinforcement and punishments. Identification is important in learning language, appropriate gender behavior, and morality and controlling aggression. Behaviorists believe the environment makes the child. Social learning theorists believe there is an interaction in that children act on the environment--may even change it or make a new one. In watching TV, children select models they believe to be like themselves. In this way, children form standards of what their behavior should be like. The child, adolescent, and adult avoid tedious and perhaps harmful trial-and-error experimentation by imitating the behavior of socially competent models. They believe that operant conditioning fails to explain many changes in behavior that result from interaction with people in a social situation. They contend that if we only learned from direct experience--by reward and punishment in consequence of our behavior--most people would not survive to adulthood. They question whether the skills involved in driving a car, solving a mathematical equation, or preparing a meal would ever develop if a person were limited to direct reinforcement. Bandura (1963) contends that a great deal of learning takes place as a result of imitation and the observation of people in the environment who serve as models. The process he describes in observational learning includes attention, retention, motor reproduction, and reinforcement or motivation. Children must first pay attention, for if they do not they cannot imitate. If they see, they also need to retain what they have seen, or no learning can take place. If a child pays attention and remembers a modeled behavior, he or she still may not reproduce that behavior if the necessary motor skills are lacking, for example, to ride a bicycle. A child can also acquire information, retain it, and have the appropriate motor skills, but rarely have this activated into overt performance if reinforcement for the act does not exist. Positive reinforcement is assured when certain behaviors or acts are approved and rewarded by parents, teachers, or peers. When this occurs, good results (learning) can generally be expected.

Learning through instruction is an important mode for the child as development takes place. A discussion of this view in relation to aggression and pro-social behavior is presented in Chapters 8 and 9. The modeling of violent behavior seen on television or in movies often occurs, demanding parental and societal concern.

Organismic and Humanistic Models: A Compromise

Organismic theory. A third approach to the investigation of human development lies in the organism. This theory directly counters the mechanistic model (behaviorism), in that people are viewed as active organisms who by their own actions determine their development in a major way. The organismic approach considers insight the unifying agent that determines the developmental direction of the individual (Lewin, 1942). A person's cognitive input is highly important. These psychologists do not believe that the well-defined stimulus necessarily establishes the pattern of response, but is determined by the individual's perception of the entire field of circumstances through insight. Responses are meaningless unless they serve to fulfill a goal that comes from the perceiver. Human development is not atomized to the degree behaviorists believe, but rather involves the whole-field environments. Therefore there is more to meaning than judging isolated acts of behavior. That is, the whole of an individual's behavior (mental life, social activities, physical growth, environmental deficits, and so on) is greater than the sum of the parts that go to make it up.

For example, a symphony is constructed from musical notes, melodic tones, variation in pitch, a combination of instruments, and other parts. An analysis of these parts will not provide the sensations enjoyed when all are combined. In the same manner, behavior cannot be understood through analysis of the separate components. We cannot break behavior down into its individual elements. This follows the law of *pragnanz* (goodness), which states that the tendency is for human beings to work to achieve a state of equilibrium.

The organismic view is very concerned with the internal and external forces that affect the individual in a particular situation (configuration). It is concerned with process rather than product, with how individuals come to believe certain things and to act as they do, rather than with the specific act of behavior. Life experiences do not determine development but are factors that speed or retard it. Development takes place in a structured sequence (organization) of qualitatively different stages that are not necessarily continuous. The principal contribution of field theorists is found in their emphasizing the importance of goals as a directing force in human development. They maintain that children must be provided with those goals that are most important and based upon reality or they will have a distorted view of the real world.

Humanistic approach. While the humanistic approach accepts many theoretical aspects of organismic theory, it emphasizes that people can direct their life course: human consciousness is placed at the center of human drama. Understanding human behavior demands the equal importance of studying people both as subject and object. As Severin (1974) has suggested, human beings in reaching for goals experience themselves always by spontaneous self-determination. Humanists argue that both psychoanalysts and behaviorists are mistaken in characterizing people as passive beings acted upon by forces outside their control. Abraham Maslow and Carl Rogers portray people as capable of actively fashioning their personalities and lives deliberately and insightfully.

Two important psychologists who exhibit a humanistic viewpoint are Maslow and Rogers. Maslow's view is conceptualized by the term *self-actualization*. According to Maslow, people have an innate need to develop their potentialities but are frequently concerned with "lower" needs--food, safety, companionship, and shelter --rather than higher-order needs of developing to the fullest capacity of one's ability (see Figure 1.2). Rogers believes psychology should help people to realize their potential ability. Teachers, social workers, ministers, and counselors need to accept people as they are and to communicate positively with them. The goal of the humanist is to focus on the improvements of the human condition.

We have reviewed a number of theories about the development of the individual. Generally speaking, they can be placed into three categories. These categories explain the nature of development through the psychologi-

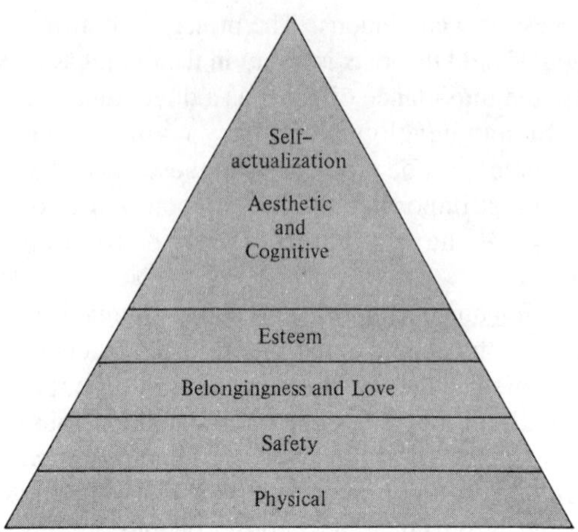

Figure 1.2 Maslow's hierarchy of needs.

cal-biological (stages theory), the cultural-learning (cognitive), and the organismic-humanistic models.

The psychological-biological model holds that individuals are neither passive nor active but reactive, always in flux between their natural instincts and the pressure of society to make them conform. The nature of these conflicts depends upon the stage of physical development that a child has reached at a particular time. The instinctual energy shifts from one body zone to another--from mouth to anus to genitals. The child at each stage undergoes a different major conflict either in the sexual realm (Freud) or the social realm (Erikson). The degree of ability to resolve these problems determines the future personality of the individual. In criticism of Freud's views, his clients were upper middle class *adults* in therapy, not normal children from a typical population. The sexual origin of conflict of a psychological nature is too limited and subjective. Testing his theories is difficult by standard research. Blame the times and setting, but Freud demeaned women and seemed to hold them accountable for maladaption of children. A problem with his theory is that it ends at adolescence, leaving the rest of life in question.

Erikson emphasized social influences on development over the life span. He did not, however, take into account social and cultural factors that influence the attitudes and conduct of the sexes. The tenets of his theory are too broad to easily assess objectively.

Some critics say Piaget overlooked the effect of education and culture upon performance. He also down-played emotion and personality development except as they related to cognition. He used little standardization in his interviews and experiments with children. Nevertheless his careful observations gave us the notions that an object or person didn't exist out of sight and that rearranging a group of objects can change their number. In short, he taught us that the child thinks very differently than an adult. He provided a framework for knowing the approximate times for introducing certain subjects to children. In Piaget's theory, cognitive development is affected by physical experience, maturation, social interaction, and equilibration.

The cultural-learning model states that quantitative and developmental change are continuous. This approach views people as machines mechanically reacting to stimuli and environmental forces rather than initiating behavior or action, and attempts to identify the discrete factors in the environment that make people behave in certain ways. It focuses on early experience that affects later behavior. This theory tries to account for the effects of experience by breaking down complex stimuli and complex behavior into their detailed elements. Classical conditioning directed to sensory stimulus was used by Watson and operant conditioning by Skinner in programming behavior.

Learning theorists have contributed to the science of human development through their demand for rigorous experimentation and the clear definitions of terms. However, such theorists have given little time to study of behavior in the natural setting. They underestimate the importance of biological influence or unconscious factors in behavior. They spend little time examining what children and adults are like in various periods in the life span. The behaviorists have given effective programs of therapy (like quitting smoking or stuttering) but have spent a paucity of time looking for origins of the difficulties. Social learning has emphasized the part the social milieu plays in development and cognitive mediation.

The organismic-humanistic view is opposed to the mechanistic model in that people initiate their own action and thereby control their development. Both qualitative and quantitative change are inherent aspects of life, though internal rather than external. Life experiences are factors that can speed or delay development. The proponents of this view are more interested in how individuals come to believe what they do and how they act in certain ways than in the specific operation of an act. The humanists contend that human beings have a need to be self-actualized; both Rogers and Maslow believe people are capable of actively fashioning their lives and personalities through personal insight.

Humanistic theories emphasize the unique element in human behavior that, unlike animals, humans are capable of fashioning their own lives. Such theory is criticized for turning people inward, encouraging love affairs of the self. Critics also contend that humanism is very amorphous and its tenets too vague to research.

HUMAN DEVELOPMENT AND TODAY'S WORLD

The child born at the present time faces an unknown future. The environment for the developing human is not static. What significant shifts in resources, in populations, in

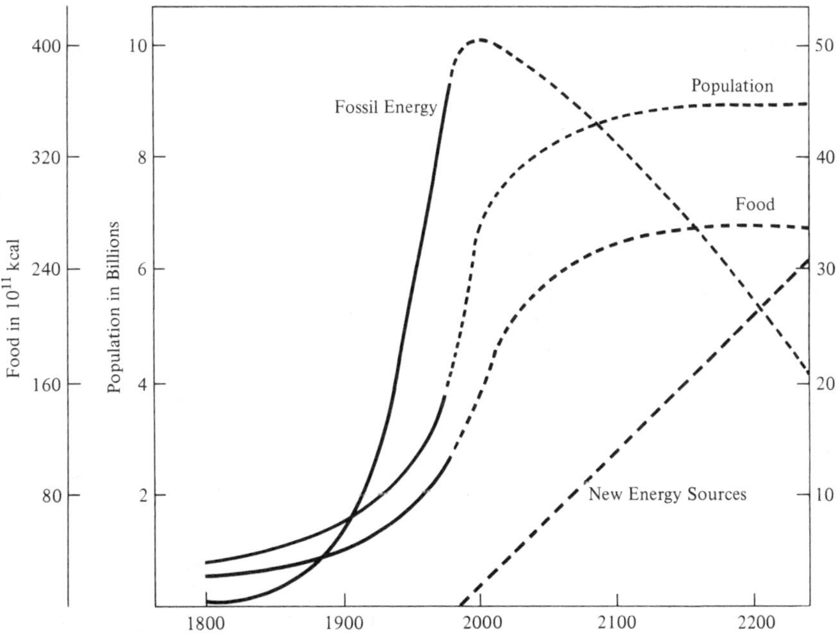

Figure 1.3 Estimated trends in world population, fossil fuel consumption, food production, and new energy sources. (*Source*: Biswas & Biswas, 1979, p. 100).

psychological concerns, and in societal objectives will shape human development? A brief discussion of this is relevant, for it deals with the very core of our existence--survival and improvement of life--in short, with human development.

Ecological Systems

We are seeing scientific developments that are destined to change our way of life. Prospects for effective intervention in the lives of children who are handicapped by genetic predisposition (Chapter 3), impoverished environments, and other circumstances are clearly envisioned. Will the struggle for resources, which creates the possibility of war, or universal distrust and greed among people, which create a society hobbled by lawsuits and adversary relationships, effectively abort this promise?

Resources

One should remember that whatever theoretical approach one holds regarding development, life events do not happen in the abstract (purely in mental or psychological terms) but against the realities of the historical and ecological times. The United States is consuming 27 percent of the world's energy, yet has only 5 percent of the population (*U.S. News & World Report*, 1984). The Presidential Task Force on Global Resources and Environment (1980) projected the following for the year 2000:

World population	up 59%
Food production	up 15%
Farmland	up 4%
Food prices	up more than 100%
Energy prices	up more than 100%

There is no evidence in 1990 that this will change for the better.

Environmental Quality

In a decade assessment from 1969 to 1979, the National Wildlife Federation measured seven environmental areas and found a general deterioration of the environment. Although the National Wildlife Federation suggested a comprehensive plan for the next decade, there has been a drop in quality in every category, except for air quality, which improved slightly after 1972. In its latest assessment, the National Wildlife Federation (1990) noted that in each of the categories there is no improvement. This is incredible considering the massive interest in earth watch and environmental issues.

The following is an overview of its latest findings:

	1980 to 1990	
Air	Worse	Toxic pollutants are a far greater threat now than before. Three hundred twenty emissions have been identified, of which 60 are cancer causing.
Wildlife	Worse	Wetlands losses, oil spills spell trouble for water fowl.
Water	Worse	Sixty-six percent of the nation's 15,600 waste water treatment plants have documented quality or public health problems.
Forests	Same	From six Appalachian forests and others the Forest Service envisions 200 million of board footage to be out by 1996.
Energy	Same	The United States' reserve represents 4 percent of the world's total. Drilling is at its lowest level since 1940. At the last count, oil pumping has dropped 400,000 barrels per day. Fossil fuel is running out at a rapid rate.
Soil	Same	The 1988 drought and wind damage ruined 4.7 million acres of land in the Great Plains states. Six hundred million acres of land in the public domain are unhealthy. Even the Bureau of Land Management admits that 94 million acres are in unsatisfactory condition.

Quality of life	Worse	Toxic chemicals in the ocean and pollution of urban drinking water. The United States produces twice as much garbage as the next greatest consumer. Violations get only a wrist slap. The EPA has detailed 15 violations in the 1980s whose levels exceeded the 1988 fall-out in Bhopal, India.

SOCIAL PROBLEMS

In addition to environmental problems, the world is facing unprecedented population growth. Currently the world population is estimated to be 5.3 billion. If by 2000, 75 percent of couples practice family planning, the population would result in a stable count of 9.3 billion (World Population Council, 1990). If the current birth and death rates continue as in the "high variant" graphic (Figure 1.4), the population of the world will double by the year 2040. In the U.S. there is a mounting immigration problem with heavy demand from abroad and illegal entry from neighboring countries. It is anticipated that, because of this, the country's population could increase dramatically in the coming years.

Population Growth

Improved medical care, nutrition, sanitation, and other health measures have done much to alleviate suffering. However, improvement in life conditions is related to population growth. A 33 percent increase in the birthrate over the death rate of the world's population is anticipated for the next 25 years. In 1980, however, an upturn was noted, as 3.6 million children were born, and the fertility rate of women aged 15 to 44 was 69.2 per 1000 population (Vital Statistics Report, p. 1; 1981).

Economics and Violence

The future of the nation's youth is undetermined. Although world peace seems to be more of a possibility, the search for power can effect radical changes in a brief time. The armed forces will certainly need fewer men, heavy industry has lost much of its great need for thousands of new workers. The Bureau of Labor has projected that there will be less need in the near future for child-care employees, garment workers, general laborers, and farm workers. Electronic assembly is being affected by automation. It would appear that most of the jobs in the next decade will certainly come from the service sector. When college preparation becomes the rule for youth, how can they find fulfillment with a job at a fast-food restaurant or delivering pizza? Most professional fields are over-supplied today, although high school teachers and computer analysts are two notable exceptions. Because of the possibility of fewer high-paying jobs, life may be affected by reduced standards of living.

Already the "baby boomers" are seeing an effect on their affluence. Two-income families are the norm today. Even so, a number of comforts of the good life often go begging.

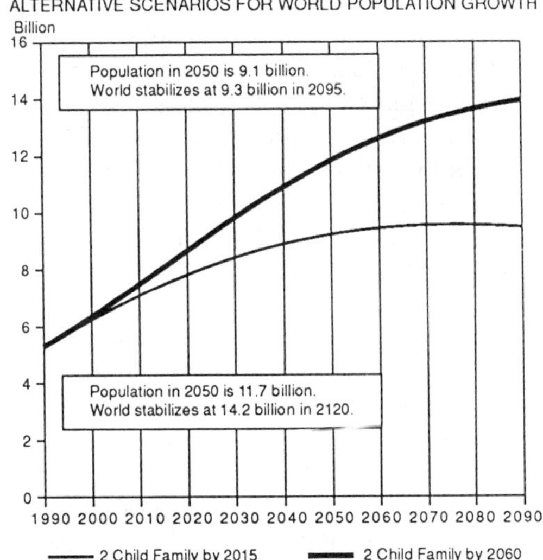

Figure 1.4 Alternative Scenarios for World Population in 2000. (*Source:* Population Crisis Council, 1989).

A society in which a surplus of workers increasingly appears may require changes in our concept of the individual's place in society. Abrogation of law is commonplace, with persons resorting to physical violence when they are directly affected by the current social and technological changes. Terrorism may be spreading from Europe to America (*U.S. News & World Report*, 1984). Churches, homes, and trains have been bombed, and kidnapping and hijacking are commonplace. When people dislike an event or consequence, more and more frequently they turn to violence. An emerging task of psychology, sociology, and education is the handling of violence. If our society fails in this task, the traditional patterns of violence as a tool will prevail--our world is well-schooled in these techniques.

It is possible that we will have fewer problems of delinquency and crime as the population of youth decreases in the coming years; 15-24 year olds account for a disproportionate number of criminal acts. Teenage and adult crimes of violence in the streets continue, and there is general unrest due to unemployment, inflation, foreign policy, hunger, the issue of abortion, the ecology, mass immigration, and withdrawal of funding by the government from many programs. These programs have helped minorities by providing education and jobs. They aid youth who are often without goals, without controls, and without religious convictions. Understanding of human development will be essential to help alleviate some of the difficulties.

On the positive side, East-West tensions are receding, democracy is expanding, medical advancements are being made, longevity of life increases, and recognition that brotherhood is an essential element in a stable world is a priority among most nations. Even race relations are improving in some unexpected places (*U.S. News & World Report*, 1990), along with expanded documents detailing civil and human rights for people around the world.

SUMMARY

Human beings have been favored in the development of adaptability and the ability to create tools. These were accentuated by the development of language, science, technology, and human socialization patterns. An understanding of human development must take into consideration the cultural forces that impinge upon us. Culture in the United States today is characterized by rapid and significant changes. Our greatly expanded knowledge is reflected in the vast amount of research in progress, and also by the growing acceptance of the dignity of human beings and the need to study human development. There has also been a sharp rise in the percentage of high school and college students who graduate, and an increased number of scholars engaged in scientific and other types of scholarly research. The study of human development has profited from this progress. The study of human development and its psychology serves (1) to enhance the individual's understanding of his or her environment, (2) to assist the young to reach objectives and goals chosen by society and then modified by themselves, (3) to aid in improving humanity's conditions, (4) to assist the search for identity, and (5) to efficiently achieve humanly desirable ends. This text follows the life span approach, beginning with the prenatal stage and continuing through old age. A variety of theories are incorporated throughout the text, representing the views of Freud, Erikson, Piaget, Havighurst, Kohlberg, and others.

There has been an enormous growth in the world's population, with more and more of it concentrated in large urban areas. As the world's population continues to multiply, environmental protection is more urgent, and the work-force requirements in the industrialized areas are rapidly decreasing as a result of automation. This has brought forth important vocational changes as well as social changes involving family structure and life activities. Thus, cities, governments, and families alike are beset with difficult problems such as recession, environment, inflation, energy shortages, and lack of money. These factors also require that we examine the impact of the historical times and ecology on human development. They also create a demand for reassessment and the need to set national priorities. Though rapid change may be occurring now, to despair--as C.P. Snow put it--is not only a sin but unwarranted.

KEY WORDS

operant conditioning

ecology

classical conditioning

social learning

ego

super ego

id

humanism

mesosystem

macrosystem

exosystem

microsystem

maturation

sensory-motor

concrete operations

pre-operational

formal operation

hierarchy of needs

conditioning

psychosocial

pre-conventional stage

conventional stage

post-conventional stage

cross cultural perspective

REFERENCES

Amoss, P.T. and Harrell, S. (eds.). *Other Ways of Growing Old: Anthropological Perspectives.* Stanford: Stanford University Press, 1981.

Aries, P. *Centuries of Childhood.* Translated by R. Baldrick. New York: Random House, 1962.

Bandura, A., and Walters, R. *Social Learning and Personality.* New York: Holt, 1963.

Bayley, N. The life span as a form of reference in psychological research. *Vita Humanus*, 1963, *6*:125-139.

Bayley, N., and Schaefer, E.S. Consisting of maternal and child behavior in the Berkeley growth study. Symposium of personality consistency and change. *American Psychologist*, 1963,*18*(7).

Biswas, A.S., and Biswas, M.R. *Food, Climate, and Man.* New York: Wiley, 1979.

Block, J. Some enduring and consequential structures of personality. In A.I. Ruben et al. (eds.), *Further Explorations in Personality.* New York: Wiley, 1981.

Brim, O.G., Jr., and Kagan, J. (eds.). *Consistency and Change in Human Development.* Cambridge, Mass.: Harvard University Press, 1980.

Bronfenbrenner, U. Toward an experimental ecology of human development. *American Psychologist*, 1977, 513-531.

Bronfenbrenner, U., and Crouter, A.C. The evolution of environmental models in development research. In P.H. Mussen (ed.). *Handbook of Child Psychology*, 4th ed., vol. 11. New York: Wiley, 1983.

Cairnes, R.B. and Crouter, A.C. The evolution of environmental models in developmental research. In P.H. Mussen (ed.). *Handbook of Child Psychology*, 4th ed., vol. 1. New York: Wiley, 1983.

Cairnes, R.B. and Valsinger, J. Child psychology. *Annual Review of Psychology*, 1984, *35*:553-577.

DiCara, L.V. Learning in the autonomic nervous system. *Scientific American*, 1970, *222*:30-39.

Energy Information Administration. *1982 Annual Energy Review.* Washington, D.C.: U.S. Department of Energy, 1983.

Erikson, E. *Identity, Youth, and Crisis.* New York: Norton, 1968.

Exploring Energy Choices. Washington, D.C.: Ford Foundation, 1974.

Freud, S. *New Introductory Lectures on Psychoanalysis*. New York: Norton, 1933.

Gutmann, D.L. Parenthood: A key to the comparative study of the life cycle. In N. Datan and L.H. Pinsberg (eds.). *Life Span Developmental Psychology: Normative Life Crises*. New York: Academic Press, 1973, pp. 167-184.

Havighurst, R.J. *Developmental Tasks and Education*. New York: McKay, 1972.

Kagan, J., and Moss, H.A. *Birth to Maturity*. New York: Wiley, 1962.

Kohlberg, L. The stability of passive and dependent behavior from childhood and through manhood. *Child Development*, 1960, *31*:577-591.

_____. Early education: A cognitive-developmental view. *Child Development*, 1968, *39*:1014-1062.

Maslow, A.H. *Motivation and Personality*, 2nd ed. New York: Harper & Row, 1970.

National Wildlife. 1969-1979: A decade of revolution. *Tenth Annual Environmental Quality Index*, 1979.

Population Crisis Committee. *Population Pressures Abroad and Immigration Pressures at Home*. Washington, D.C., 1989.

Presidential Task Force on Global Resources and Environment. The Global 2000 Report to the President, vol. 1: *Entering the Twenty-First Century*; vol. 2: *Technical Report*. Washington, D.C.: U.S. Government Printing Office, 1980.

Reese, W.H., and Overton, W.F. Models of development and theories of development. In L.R. Goulet and P.B. Baltes (eds.), *Life-Span Developmental Psychology: Research and Theory*. New York: Academic Press, 1970.

Rogers, C. *On Becoming a Person*. Boston: Houghton Mifflin, 1961.

Ryerson, A.J. Medical advice on child rearing, 1550-1900. *Harvard Educational Review*, 1962, *31*:302-323.

Severin, F.T. What humanistic psychology is all about. *Newsletter* feature supplement. San Francisco: Association for Humanistic Psychology, 1974.

Skinner, B.F. *Science and Human Behavior*. New York: Free Press, 1953.

Smelser, N., and Erikson, E. *Adult Themes of Work and Love*. Cambridge, Mass.: Harvard University Press, 1980.

Thomas, A., Chess, S., and Birch, H.G. The origin of personality. *Scientific American*, 1970, *223*:102-109.

Thorndike, E.L. *Selected Writings From a Connectionist's Psychology*. New York: Appleton-Century-Crofts, 1949.

U.S. News & World Report. January 9, 1984, *53*:24-31.

U.S. News & World Report. Race and the South. July 23, 1990, *109*(4):22-30.

Van Baal, J. *Derna: Description and Analysis of Married Anim Culture, South New Guinea*. The Hague: Martinus Nuhoff, 1966.

Virginian Pilot/Ledger Star. Children rock old lady. June 15, 1990. Norfolk, VA.

Vital Statistics Report. *Annual Summary for the United States, 1975*. (HRA) June 30, 1976, *24*(13):76-1120.

Vital Statistics Report. National Center for Health Statistics, vol. 29, No. 12, March 18, 1981.

Vogel, M.L. Warning: Auto fumes may lower your kid's I.Q. *Psychology Today*, 1980, *13*(8).

Watson, J.B. Psychology as the behaviorists view it. *Psychological Review*, 1913, *20*:158-177.

Watson, J.B., and Raynor, R.R. Conditioned emotional reactions. *Journal of Experimental Psychology*, 1920, *3*:1-4.

White, L. The concept of culture. *American Anthropologist*, 1949,*61*:227-251.

Chapter 2

HUMAN DEVELOPMENT: PRINCIPLES, ISSUES, AND RESEARCH METHODOLOGY

- ***Introduction to Growth***
  - Biosocial
  - Motor growth
  - Neuromuscular coordination
  - Language
  - Personal social
- ***Principles of Growth***
  - Proximo-distal
  - Cephalo-caudal
  - Rate growths
  - Progression of response
  - Differential growth for areas parts
  - Various areas of growth correlated
  - Nature and nurture positively affect growth
  - Rate of growth consistent for the individual
- ***Research***
  - The scientific method
  - Experimental
  - Case study
  - Cross section study
  - Longitudinal study
  - Clinical study
- ***Correlation***
  - Standard deviation
  - Significant level
  - Hypotheses
  - Confidence level
- ***Protection of Human Subjects***
  - APA standards for research
  - Briefing and honesty in using subjects

HUMAN DEVELOPMENT: PRINCIPLES, ISSUES, AND RESEARCH METHODOLOGY

Developmental psychology is concerned with change in behavior or psychological functioning as it relates to the individual. From this point of view, the present chapter will discuss aspects of growth, nature and nurture, principles of growth, research approaches, and the use of statistics.

The Growth Process

Human beings have the longest period of development of all animals--nearly 30 percent of the life span is devoted to it. This may be due in part to the fact that human beings are principally learning creatures. They are designed to be adaptable, to change their behavior--in brief, to learn. The child has a double inheritance of the biological and the social. The child is first a physical being and then an interacting one at the personal-social level. Krogman (1972) suggests that in the biosocial complex there are four major aspects of growth: (1) motor growth, involving gross body control and the finer motor coordination including all bodily movements and postural responses such as balance, sitting, and walking; (2) adaptive responses relating to the neuromuscular coordination of the whole body--for example, eye-hand coordination directed to the performance of a specific task; (3) language, which includes all forms of communication, verbal and nonverbal use of symbolism; (4) personal-social development, which involves the biological and cultural conditions in which the child lives.

NATURE AND NURTURE INTERACTION

In the past some people believed that nature (inborn hereditary factors) accounted for all development, whereas others believed that nurture (environment) was the determiner of what we are. Today most experts feel that somewhere between these extremes lies the truth.

The question of which--heredity or environment--plays the greater part in human development, points up the importance of the interaction that takes place. How much weight each should be given remains in doubt. An example is seen in the controversy surrounding the inheritance of intelligence. California psychologist Arthur Jensen (1969, p. 42) contends that approximately 80 percent of measured intelligence is accounted for through heredity. This suggests that the reaction range (that which is accounted for through environmental and cultural differences) is about 20 percent, placing the main emphasis on heredity or nature in explaining mental development. However, Kagan (1969) and Gottesman (1968) take exception to this viewpoint, believing that similar environments would tend to produce a more uniform spread in intelligence.

Jensen (1969) himself has provided a striking example of how environmental influences can operate in the testing situation:

> When I worked in a psychological clinic, I had to give individual intelligence tests to a variety of children, a good many of whom came from an impoverished background. Usually I felt these children were really brighter than their IQ would indicate. They often appeared inhibited in their responsiveness in the testing situation on their first visit to my office, and when this was the case I usually had them come in on two to four different days for half-hour sessions with me in a "play therapy" room, in which we did nothing more than get acquainted by playing ball, using finger paints, drawing on the blackboard, making things out of clay, and so forth. As soon as the child seemed to be completely at home in this setting, I would retest him on a parallel form of the Stanford-Binet. A boost in IQ of 8 to 10 points or so was the rule; it rarely failed, but neither was the gain very often much above this. (p. 100)

How much of human behavior, then, should be attributed to maturation (biological unfolding), and how much to learning that provides stimulation from the environment? The infant will, in time, walk or talk due in large part to maturation; but the effective use of potential skills for making a living will have to be learned. How this is accomplished will depend upon timing, opportunity, environmental conditions, and perhaps other things. Timing may be thought of as being the critical instant when a specific environmental factor can have effect. The effect of timing on development was seen in the use of Thalidomide, a sedative and tranquilizer, on prenatal infants. Thalidomide was used by pregnant women during the embryonic stage (the critical time, running from the second to the eighth week). It resulted in the birth of babies without limbs and created a great furor everywhere. The deleterious effect of German measles on the pregnant mother is another matter of timing. Most investigators believe imprinting on ducks occurs as a matter of timing, with the critical time being the first few hours after hatching. The baby ducklings will then become attached to almost any animal, including a human. Once the critical time is past, imprinting, even with the mother duck, will not take place. Environmental timing is the crucial aspect to human and animal development. Kolata (1975) reports of sewing shut the eyes of animals shortly after birth. The animals were allowed to see in two to three months. Animals such as monkeys, cats, and rabbits could not see. The absence of stimulation affected the way visual stimuli were processed in the young animal's brain. The genes, then, interact with the environment in complex ways; rather than being opposing forces, they interact in complementary ways.

There are periods of time when it is most appropriate, in terms of economy and efficiency, for something to be learned. This has been called *readiness*, psychological set, or preparation. Others have called this a sensitive period when certain learning can take place with greater effectiveness and ease. During this time the individual has developed and matured sufficiently to learn a given thing--for example, to ride a bicycle, swim, or roller skate. It is held by many that readiness to learn to read on the average appears at about age 6, although readiness may occur earlier or later in some children. Both physical maturation and environmental stimulation are needed for children to begin this difficult task. Most youngsters, by the age of six, are ready biologically, socially, and physically to begin reading instruction.

There may be a best or most appropriate time to learn certain skills. To become the ultimate performer in tennis, swimming, or ballet usually requires not only arduous practice and talent but an early beginning or readiness. When maturation is appropriate to the experiences that present opportunity for learning, this is not suddenly lost, though some things depend upon memory and flexibility for the greater return. Still, one can learn to swim, ride a bicycle, or complete a medical education at 45 years of age or older.

The exact relation of timing to human development is only partly understood. We do know that in general the developmental level reached by an individual can be represented by the following formula.

Heredity X Environment X Time =
The Developmental Level

The interaction between heredity and environment is a fundamental aspect of human development. The boy's voice becomes lower due to thickening of his vocal cords by a change in the functioning of the ductless glands. Timing is important. Critical time in human development may be an extended period, as in a situation where a child receives improper care--too little food, too little care, too little intellectual stimulation--which over time can result in deprivation. White (1975) believes infancy is critical in cognitive development, contending that "if you do a lousy job of nourishing the child's basic intellectual curiosity this essentially wipes him out."

Heredity influences personality through such traits as physical characteristics, motor skills, intelligence, and sensory acuity. Studies at the University of Minnesota involving 348 pairs of identical twins, including 44 reared apart, who were put through extensive testing--medical, psychological and preference data--revealed the information found in Figure 2.1.

THE ROOTS OF PERSONALITY

The figure shows the extent to which traits of personality are estimated to be inherited, as gauged by tests with twins. The traits were measured by the Multi-dimensional Personality Questionnaire, developed by Auke Tellegen at the University of Minnesota.

In summary, the environment provides a twofold function: first, it supplies the stimulus

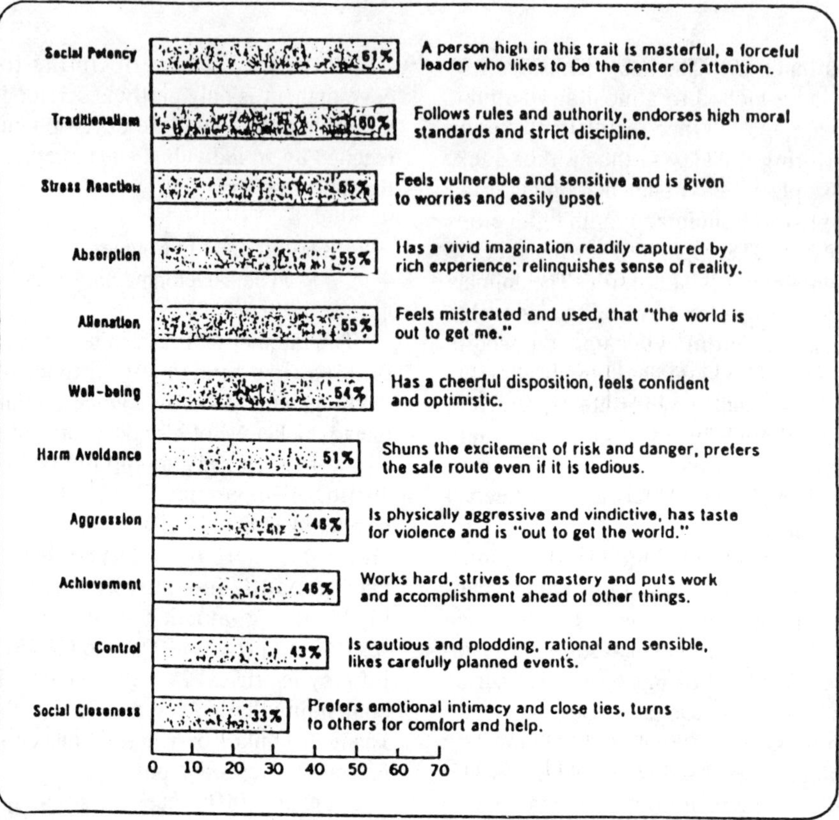

Figure 2.1 *New York Times*

that sets the pattern of response already prepared by maturation, and second, it provides situations conducive to the person's learning new patterns or altering old ones.

SOME PRINCIPLES OF GROWTH

Every species, whether human or nonhuman, follows a pattern of development peculiar to that species as laid down by the DNA genetic code. This pattern extends from the beginning of a new life, with the fertilized egg, through the various stages, and ends with senescence and death. Since human development during the fetal period is orderly, it is possible to give a timetable of the development of structures and functions. This timetable may be altered by unusual or abnormal conditions within the uterus. The study of mice by Ginsberg and Hovda, presented in Chapter 3, shows that the same genes under different environmental conditions will produce different results. Thus we note that developmental irregularities may result either from faulty genes or from unfavorable environmental conditions in the uterus (Pasamanick & Knobloch, 1966). Genes influence the kinds of environment we seek, what we attend to, and how much we learn (Plomin & Daniels, 1987). Scarr and McCartney (1983) suggest psychological development is given impetus through biological maturation. These researchers contend that children fashion their environment in passive, evocative, and active ways with their genetic predispositions. Parents not gifted in social relationships, who tend to be loners, are not likely to give children an outgoing response to society. Children of such parents may be more passive. In the evocative relationship, the child elicits from others more social interaction than do passive children. Active children seek out environments that they find suitable to their temperaments and genetic dispositions.

The notion of Super Children or "invulnerables" reflects a particular kind of heritage allowing them to succeed in a hostile environment. They have been found to:

1) be at ease with other people;

2) extract support from teachers, relatives and other adults;

3) actively attack their environment with a sense of competence;

4) minimize their emotional involvement with a sick parent and acquire independence; and

5) show a good deal of creativity and originality.

The pattern of mental growth is predictable. Longitudinal studies of intelligence forecast patterns of development. Studies covering segments of the life span up to 50 years of age show that mental growth parallels the rapid physical growth period of the first 18 years of life (Schaie, 1972). Longitudinal studies of Terman and coworkers (1925, 1947) indicate that early promise among bright children is fulfilled. Predicting development is important in educational guidance in order to assist children, in selecting orphaned children for home placement, and later in giving vocational direction.

Development is Continuous

Growth and development begin with the fertilization of the egg, with significant changes taking place predictably throughout life until senescence or death. For example, the child's vocabulary growth the first year seems of little consequence. Actually the child is experimenting with making sounds that can later be used in building a comprehensive vocabulary for associating words with objects and certain kinds of experiences in the everyday environment. The normal child growing up in a stimulating environment will develop a considerable vocabulary by age 6. There is a continuous rapid development of the vocabulary throughout the elementary school years. This growth proceeds at a decelerated pace through high school, college, and later adulthood.

The appearance of baby teeth seems to occur suddenly. They may be observed in the jaw during the fifth fetal month, but do not mature to the point that they are ready to cut through the gums until around the fifth month after birth. The apparent growth spurts are not as irregular in nature as they appear, especially when we take into consideration the more subtle aspects of different growth features.

Growth Follows a Pattern Toward Maturity

The curve of growth may be undulating, but its direction is always toward maturity. The pattern of growth is evidenced in the acquisition of new features and the discarding of old ones. The fetus discards the umbilical cord, baby teeth give way to permanent ones, crawling falls into disuse as a way of locomotion, and fine hair and skin give way to pubic hair and a coarser quality skin. Tanner (1970, 1973) undertook research that validates that growth is a continuous and gradual process. To be sure, there are great growth changes that cover a year or two, but if one looks at a variety of differences among children, as indicated by standard deviation in weight and stature, they are not impressive.

The most obvious thing about maturing is change, which fundamentally occurs in these five ways: (1) change in body size--height, weight, and so on; (2) change in dimensions--that is, body proportions; (3) change in features such as face contour; (4) acquiring new features--that is, sex characteristics; and (5) mental change, as observed in the increased use of logic and the ability to abstract. Thinking and language affect a variety of socio-personal issues such as morals, sex, and society

Change is necessary to growth. Children are not as troubled with change as their parents, though it is true that many parents may try to speed the process of growth in their children. Children typically view change positively, for it allows them to gain a new status with each achievement. John, a neighbor's youngster of two or so, called one morning from an upstairs apartment, "I do my B.M. in the potty," proud to announce this change toward boyhood.

Individual Consistency

The growth rates of individuals tend to remain constant within their pattern; growth remains consistent for a given person. Figure 2.2 illustrates this tendency.

Growth of Physical and Mental Areas is Uneven

Differential rates of growth at specific stages of development contribute to the physical differences observable in our population. For instance, the length of the head of the newborn is about one-fourth the length of the body; in the adult, it is about one-eighth (Figure 2.3). The average neonate is approximately 20 inches tall, and the head represents approximately 5 inches of this, or one-fourth of the total. If the person grew to be 6 feet tall and the head grew at the same rate, it would be 18 inches in length at age 21. Conversely, the length of the legs of the newborn is relatively short compared to the length of the arms and total height. Thus, differences in growth rate at different stages of development lead to significant changes in proportion of different parts of the body during the growing years.

The parts of the body and its system can be seen through the relationship of the four fundamental body tissues and organs: (1) the lymphoid type, composed of the thymus gland,

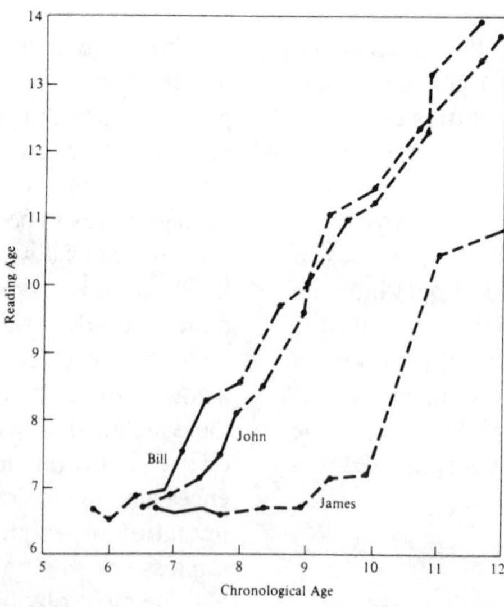

Figure 2.2 Differences in growth in reading ability among children who are similar in reading ability at age 6. (*Source:* Olsen, 1959).

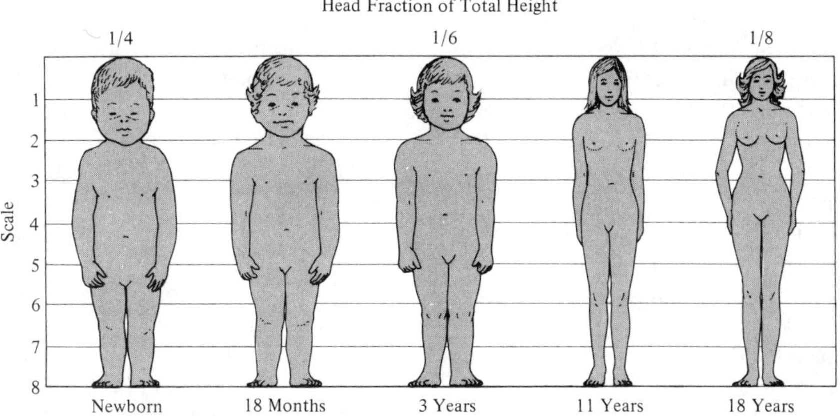

Figure 2.3 Changes in female body proportions from birth to physical maturity. (*Source*: Marlow, 1988, p. 172).

lymph nodes, and intestinal lymphoid masses; (2) the neural type--brain tissue, dura, spinal cord, and certain dimensions of the head; (3) the general type of the body as a whole, its external dimensions (except the head), respiratory and digestive organs, musculature as a whole, and skeleton as a whole; and (4) the genital type--testes, ovary, epididymis, uterine tube, prostate, urethra, seminal vesicles, and the structures associated with reproduction. The nervous system (neural) is largely complete at age four, and the brain at 10 (Tanner, 1970). The genital system is later in maturing. These basic systems are depicted in Figure 2.4 as curves whose foundation is based on the principle that maturity for all dimensional sizes is

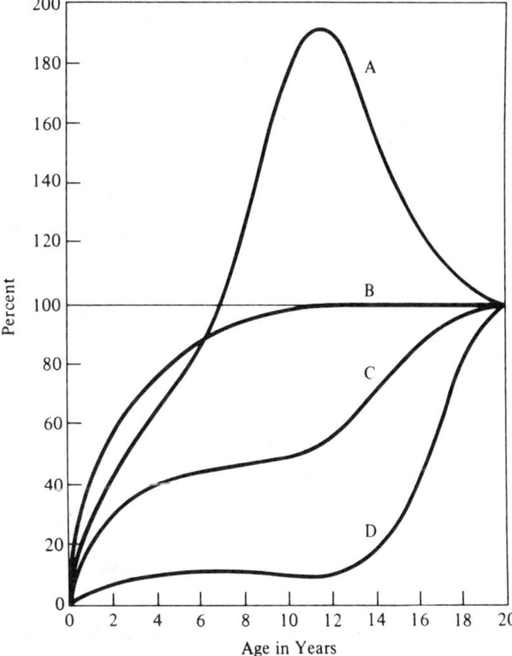

A. Lymphoid type: Thymus, lymph nodes, intestinal lymphoid masses.

B. Neural type: Brain and its parts, dura, spinal cord, optic apparatus, many head dimensions.

C. General type: Body as a whole, external dimensions (with exception of head and neck), respiratory and digestive organs, kidneys, aorta and pulmonary trunks, spleen, musculature as a whole, skeleton as a whole, blood volume.

D. Genital type: Testis, ovary, epididymis, uterine tube, prostate, prostatic urethra, seminal vescicles.

Figure 2.4 Basic curves of postnatal growth. (*Source:* Scammon, 1927).

adult at age 20 (Scammon, 1927). These curves represent uniform characteristics of human beings. Krogman (1972) states that "the curves are so basic that it is reasonable to conclude that they are genetically entrenched with equal vigor in all children the world over" (p. 7).

The point in Figure 2.4 where the general and genital types curve and turn from concave to convex marks the circumpubertal growth acceleration.

The educational and psychological aspects of growth are also uneven. The individual's maturational level at a particular time will vary with the different characteristics or abilities being tested. In learning, creative imagination enjoys early and rapid development, rote memory reaches its peak in the early relationships, and the reasoning ability comes later and slower.

uneven. Some possible variations are seen in Table 2.1. It is important for teachers, parents, and social workers to understand individual differences in growth rate. Parents frequently overlook this basic principle when they make comparisons of the development of their own children. They should realize that James, who is a late maturer and will develop physically more slowly than his older brother, may actually end up being taller.

The failure of teachers and parents to recognize these differences in rate of growth and timing of certain growth features is often a source of misinterpretation and faulty guidance. Variations in children are genetically induced, affected by the socio-physical environment and the interaction between them. Parents need to understand this, although attempts to direct young children may lead to problems for an

Table 2.1 PROBABLE READING ABILITIES IN THE SECOND, FOURTH, AND SIXTH GRADES OF A TYPICAL ELEMENTARY SCHOOL CLASSROOM

	Approximate number of pupils (class of 30)	Beginning-year reading grade level		
		Grade 2	Grade 4	Grade 6
120 up	2	3.0–5.0	6–7	8–10
110–119	5	2.5–3.0	5–6	6–8
100–109	8	2.0–2.5	4–5	6–7
90–99	8	1.5–2.0	3–4	5–6
80–89	5	1.0–1.5	2–3	3–4
Below 80	2	Readiness	Readiness 1	Readiness 2–3

Individual Differences in Rate of Growth

Although children follow a similar pattern in their development, each grows at his or her own unique rate. Bayley's study (1971) of individual patterns of development in height and weight presents evidence for differences in rate of maturation. Many children who enter school at age six are too immature to begin reading or to deal successfully with other educational tasks that confront first-grade children. Various growth curves show that some children develop faster than others, so that the growth rate is uneven. (continued above)

individual child who likes close supervision and another who likes less control. Ways of accommodation must be found to forward the development of each.

All Growth is Interrelated

There is a continuous interaction among the various aspects of growth. Although we speak and write of physical growth, mental growth, emotional growth, and other aspects of growth, we should realize that it is a total individual who is growing. Tanner (1973, p. 41) indicated that the rate of growth at any age is clearly the outcome of the interaction of genetic and environmental factors. The child inherits possible patterns of growth from his parents. The environment, however, dictates which (if any) of the patterns will become actual. In an environment where nutrition is always adequate, where the parents are caring, and where social factors are adequate, it is the genes that largely determine differences between members of the population in growth and in adult physique. In an environment that is suboptimal and perhaps changes from time to time, as in the periodic famines characteristic of much of the world, differences between members of the population reflect the social history of the individuals as much as their genetic endowment.

Emotional development has a direct effect on social development, and physical strength usually correlates positively with other aspects of growth--that is, with mental ability and personality. The old cliche that the star athlete lacks academic ability needs close scrutiny. Although usual growth patterns show the various areas (mental, social) normally to be positively related, it can be the reverse. The sick child confined for a long period of time is stymied in the struggle for independence. This illness may result in the slowing down of intellectual development due to lack of experience, exercise, and social interaction. As a result, a low fatigue level could also develop that will never be entirely compensated for. It is generally true that those who start behind stay behind, where chronic sickness or handicap conditions prevail. If the developmental tasks (achieving independence is such a task for adolescents) suggested by Havighurst are inadequately learned, they become gaps to be filled in during the next period. The complexities of the cultural and personal demands placed on the individual may be one reason why it can be said with some justification that no one is 100 percent adult or grown-up.

METHODS OF RESEARCH

Through research methods we can obtain information about human behavior. If the methods are scientific and appropriate for the area of investigation, then we will gain valid data for the confirmation or rejection of a hypothesis. Research that relates to human development is designed to obtain data about infants, children, adolescents, and adults. Research as defined in its broadest sense is an attempt to use scientific methods to gain insight into the status and developmental aspects of people.

Getting Information

Information about a given situation is obtained through two channels which, used together, account for reasonably accurate data or facts being obtained. First, we get information through use of logic: reflection and the ability of the mind to uncover principles, rules, and underlying structure from sensory data. This process, called rationalism (thinking), often utilizes the thought of great people as sources of truth. In former times it represented the principal source of knowledge. One effect of this was such that centuries after Aristotle lived, people disdained looking through the telescope of Galileo because the ancient Greek had failed to mention it.

The second basis for knowledge came in the seventeenth century. Empiricism is a method that emphasizes the importance of experience and use of the senses, especially in the role of observing phenomena. This approach uses inductive logic in investigation. Investigators try to find from observation general principles by isolating and cataloging specific data which, when repeated enough, justify a conclusion. Hence, to discover the general direction of the wind, one would erect a weather vane, taking many readings at different times of day for a period of months. The conclusions then would be based upon the general results. These two approaches are not mutually exclusive, but are used together in the scientific method of inductive-deductive reasoning.

The scientific method has five generally recognized steps:

1. The problem. In this initial stage, a problem for investigation is identified and precisely defined. The scope of the problem should be carefully described, including what is to be covered and how it relates to other investigations.

2. Formulation of the hypothesis, which involves the use of assumptions, hunches, or guesses. The precise hypothesis might not be forthcoming until some preliminary research is undertaken. The problem is clarified as the study proceeds.

3. Collection and analysis of the data. The data are gathered during this stage, and then organized into categories that provide a basis for analyzing the statistics and research information.

4. Formulation of the conclusion from the study.

5. Verification or rejection of the hypothesis, a result of the conclusion which in turn is the result of the analysis made of the data. Thus, the hypothesis is tested through the experimental situation. Analysis of the results leads to a conclusion confirming or rejecting the hypothesis.

Many feel that an unfortunate tendency exists today to accept studies at face value if they yield statistically significant results. Repetition of experimental investigations under the same and different circumstances is required and should be completed before we judge studies to be valid or invalid. When the results from many studies are available, careful and systematic evaluation should be made to synthesize them. The results should conclude with an adequate presentation of the dissenting viewpoint (Pillemer & Light, 1980).

Observations

Observation is important in constructing new theories for human development. There are two kinds: naturalistic and contrived. In naturalistic observation, individuals (usually children) are interpretively observed in their natural setting. No attempt is made to alter their behavior. Usually normative information relating to certain behavior is provided by this approach. One can gather more detailed data and receive a greater depth of insight by this method than from a social survey. It is more costly than the survey method and does not provide the variety of subjects, though rich material and ideas for further study are provided by such natural observation. The resultant theorizing is often highly speculative.

Two types of naturalistic observation are time sampling and event sampling. In time sampling, observation is made of certain class behavior: aggression, quiet, talking, quarreling, etc. The observer usually has a checklist of behaviors to note. Generally, no structuring of the situation is arranged. In event sampling, one observes specific behaviors rather than records of sequential events. For instance, one might ascertain how much time children in a classroom spent in disruptive behavior or interrupting the teachers.

Contrived observation, the kind often utilized in clinics, provides a special arrangement and structure, as in the research conducted by Bandura. Children usually are introduced to a situation, like viewing television, playing at home, or making a group decision, and then left alone. Often covert videotaping is conducted to study the interaction and behavior of children or youths. Contrived observation occurs when individuals are placed in restrictive environments (clinics) or problem situations to elicit responses that are carefully noted. Such observation stimulates many new hypotheses and ideas because the observer has noted something different, raised questions, and challenged old assumptions, all of which serve to generate new premises of research. Observing very young children who cannot talk may be the principal method of gathering information on their activity. Animals are studied for their own sake, as well as when they present possible danger to people. In typical cases, rats, cats, monkeys, and other animals may be observed in experimental situations.

Steps to Effective Observations

There are a number of aspects to good observation such as an open mind, willingness to search for background information, and the ability to put into proper perspective whatever we observe. The observer must bring a new viewpoint to the familiar situation in order to be effective, whether observing children at play or in the classroom. One's prejudices, biases, and feelings must be controlled in order not to unduly influence observations. If we watch Johnny, for example, doing his homework half-heartedly and infer the reason is due to his hunger because we ourselves are hungry, our conclusions may be wrong. Our hypotheses about causative factors must be adequate to encompass the detail elements in terms of the larger context. Using anecdotal records for insight into behavior patterns of children must be made at varied times, under varying conditions, and recorded immediately after an observation session. Researchers must limit their observation to a period of one-half hour, in order to be alert enough to remember simultaneous and sequential occurrences. Some practice in observation and use of a systematical recording plan is important. In summary, effective observation must safeguard itself from bias (such as a dislike of older adults or young children). The purpose of observation should be kept clearly in mind, and the commonplace should be closely observed for unsuspected clues to understanding behavior or the situation. Hypotheses must be scrutinized for being too broad or too narrow, in order to avoid the errors of the marketplace (including or accounting for too much) or the cave (taking a local view or reflecting one's heritage). The following summarize guidelines for observing children:

Observing Children

1. Organize a form for recording the data you wish--time, place, name, sex, ages, circumstances, events, times of behaviors, interpretation, and notes.

2. Observe the children in multiple settings--at play, in parks, on the street, and at home.

3. Clearly define the purpose of your research, how many will be involved, which sex, number, place, type of behavior, etc. In this manner, a researcher will not make the research too limited.

4. Describe the behavior in context. Record expression, actions, body language, and anything else that bears on the situation.

5. Make your observation in brief shorthand or codes, transcribing them shortly after the observation period is over.

6. Limit the period of observation to 20 to 30 minutes; longer periods of time create proactive inhibition and confusion as too many events crowd into the picture and muddy the report.

7. Remember to focus on the actual occurrences in a general context, not allowing your prejudices and biases to sway the interpretation.

8. Use time sampling and event sampling in some observations. Timing various behaviors in intervals is important. For instance, the researcher might observe inattention, or the number of times reading or seat work is inter-

rupted. Careful observation might bring insight as to the cause of the behavior.

Developmental Research Approaches

One major change in the development of research is the use of mechanical devices to aid in the monitoring of conduct and behavior, such as filming, videotaping, and recording. These have improved observations involving research in the everyday setting. Nevertheless, imprecision still exists in the measurement of behavior. The principal kinds of research approaches are described in the following sections.

Experimental Studies This type of study is usually thought of as the most rigorous technique available to science. An experimental study is an approach in which the investigator manipulates one or more variables, termed independent variables, and measures others, called dependent variables. These experiments serve to "put questions to nature," and are thought to be the most effective way of establishing a cause-and-effect relationship. The better the control one has over the independent variables, the more certain one can be about the results. For instance, in an experimental setting for the study of the reading speed among children, any variables (X variables) can be manipulated, such as the climatic conditions (temperature and humidity), mental ability, and level of reading difficulty. The dependent variables (Y variables) might be measurement of rates and effectiveness in reading, tension level, and other associated factors. In a simple experiment on learning, utilized in students' projects and theses, the question is raised whether one method of teaching is superior to another. Experimental and control groups are organized, with the experimental group taught with the new method and the control group the usual method. To ensure equal representation of the groups, a random sampling is made with a likelihood that one could as easily have been chosen for the control of the experiment. Both are tested at the beginning and ending of the teaching period. Comparisons are then made. The following schema illustrates this approach. Though simple, it represents the basic experimental method.

Groups	Initial test	Teaching	Final test
Control	Y_1		Y_2
Experimental	Y_1	X	Y_2

If the two groups are matched or are similar to each other, as with two second-grade classes homogeneously distributed so that traits and chance factors likely to affect the results are kept to a minimum, then testing the groups with the same test will provide a baseline for comparison as to the effect of a particular method. Using this approach, we could compare reading methods between these two groups. If we teach the control groups by a traditional method and the experimental groups by a nontraditional method (X experimental treatment), then the results of final testing give one an answer or partial answer to the question of method. Gains of one method over the other can be statistically examined in order to see whether they rule out chance factors at the 1 percent or 5 percent level of confidence (leaving chance as a factor in 1 out of 100 or 5 out of 100), utilizing the *t*-test statistic or some other formula. In such an experiment, small gains are not conclusive. Such a gain would call for further investigation as to the superiority of one method over the other.

Charles Judd divided students for an experiment into two groups (experimental and control) and measured their ability to shoot at rocks under water (Figure 2.5). After getting the baseline data, Judd taught principles of light refraction to the experimental group and then repeated the measurement of shooting accuracy. He found that teaching of the physics principles greatly affected the accuracy of shooting. From this and similar experiments Judd advanced a theory of general transfer of training.

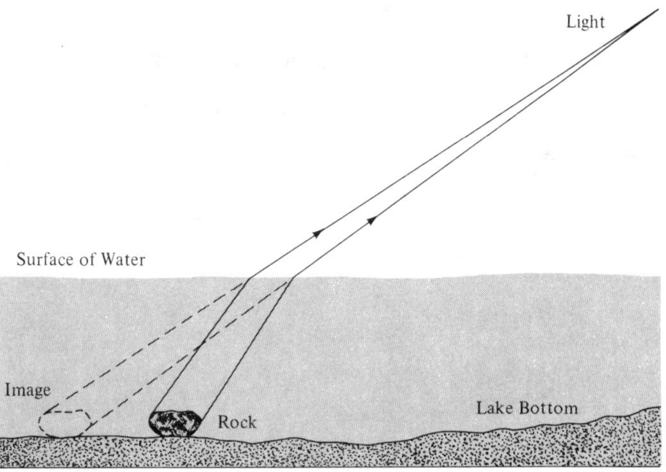

Figure 2.5 Light refraction.

We should remember that in environmental situations (the natural setting), lack of control and imprecision mar the results. Many experimental investigations are limited by "hothouse" artificiality (repetitious use of the same subjects), which precludes wide validity and generalization. Automobile manufacturers that test their cars for mileage on mechanical treadmills are certainly going to find the actual road test of cars to be another matter. A treadmill does not have the built-in shocks, breaks in the pavement, mud, snow, and undulating surfaces found on highways and streets.

Longitudinal and Cross-sectional Studies

Longitudinal study involves the continuing observation of the same person or persons over an extended period of time. Investigators study the same individuals at different times in their lives, noting changes that occur and how these characteristics compare with those in the general population. Nancy Bayley's study on the intellectual development of girls over a 20-year period is an example of a longitudinal study. By correlating the scores on a given year with those of other years, a projection of the relationship to future scores was known. The Terman Study of the Gifted (IQs of 135 and higher) begun in 1921 in California is still underway in the Psychology Department of Stanford University, with the original subjects now mainly in their 70s and 80s. The longitudinal results have revealed that their achievement-measured tests of intelligence have remained generally consistent with age and that the mortality rate of the least successful was twice that of the most successful. It did not possess a representational sample, as no Chinese were included, and other groups were underrepresented (Goleman, 1980).

Unlike the longitudinal method, which takes measurements of the same individuals over a period of time, the *cross-sectional* study examines at the same time varied groups of persons who differ in age. For example, Roger Gould examined the attitudes and life histories of men and women in seven age groups, ranging from 16 to 60, to ascertain which aspect of their lives was the most significant factor (Smelser & Erikson, 1980). Another example may be observed by noting weight variations of subjects in the HEW study summarized in Table 2.2. One can note from the data given in Table 2.2 certain developmental aspects of growth, such as the prepubertal spurt showing girls heavier than boys at 12 years of age, and vast differences in weight range.

A variation of the cross-sectional and the longitudinal study is seen in Figure 2.6. In this situation a number of cross-sectional studies by

Table 2.2 CROSS-SECTIONAL WEIGHT STUDY OF CHILDREN 4 TO 12 YEARS OF AGE

Age in years	Sex	Mean in pounds	Standard deviation variability	Range in pounds
4	Boys	38.2	4.5	25.3– 57.5
	Girls	37.3	4.8	26.3– 55.8
5	Boys	43.2	5.5	29.7– 66.5
	Girls	42.0	5.9	27.9– 73.9
6	Boys	47.6	6.3	30.0– 79.0
	Girls	46.4	6.8	30.0– 78.1
7	Boys	52.5	7.1	25.0–114.0
	Girls	51.2	7.5	30.0– 99.0
8	Boys	58.2	8.7	35.0–109.0
	Girls	56.9	9.4	35.0–109.0
9	Boys	64.4	9.8	39.6–134.0
	Girls	53.0	11.1	35.0–119.0
10	Boys	70.7	11.5	44.0–129.0
	Girls	70.3	13.2	50.0–154.0
11	Boys	77.6	13.1	45.0–169.0
	Girls	79.0	15.5	45.0–209.0
12	Boys	85.6	15.8	50.0–174.0
	Girls	89.7	17.8	45.0–239.0

Source: HEW, 1953.

age have been collected to form a longitudinal study of growth of groups, yielding average gains in growth at successive year periods from ages 4 to 17.

The longitudinal study has the advantage of allowing us to study development over a long period of time. On the other hand, it is expensive in terms of time and money. In the case of children who are being studied, there is much attrition through children changing schools. Another problem is to project in advance what is pertinent to be observed over time. Cross-sectional studies have the advantage of faster completion with less cost and fewer lost subjects. However, there exists the uncertainty of the lack of comparable subjects. Even if age categories are used, one may not be able to eliminate environmental differences or cohort influences.

Case Studies In this type of study an accumulation of data is collected on one adult or child over a long period of time. Its aim is the same as longitudinal approaches: the accumulation of developmental information. The biography of the young child kept by investigators, clinicians, or sometimes parents was the earliest kind of case study. A notable diary was kept by Darwin on his son. Various pieces of information are collected on an individual in the case study, such as developmental, physical, and social changes, experiences, test results, projective techniques, self-reports, sociograms, and dates of first accomplishments. The case study provides explanations of behavior by helping to place the individual in a structured setting that yields comparative data. It is an important diagnostic tool in education, psychology, and psychiatry and as an instrument in the clinical treatment of maladjusted or disturbed children and adults. Unfortunately, unless there are numerous collections of individual cases (as in Piaget's studies) that have been structured to seek similar information, its general application is uncertain. Drawing inferences from one or a few studies, as perhaps in Freud's generalization of the castration complex through which he alleged the Oedipus complex was resolved, may not allow the researcher to generalize.

Clinical Method This approach is not technically a research method, though like the case study, it seeks to collect data. Jean Piaget, the renowned psychologist, used the clinical method to study his own three children and hundreds of other children, utilizing the results as the basis for constructing his cognitive theory. The clinical method combines observation with careful, individualized questions. The interviewer can probe more deeply into interesting and fruitful problems. A criticism of this approach is the heavy reliance placed on the interviewer's ability to pose good questions and to interpret them correctly.

Survey Method This approach to data-gathering is usually reserved for the study of behavior of large, often widely distributed groups. Public opinion polls, such as those of Harris and Gallup, utilize this method, although they do not necessarily poll millions of persons to find out their opinions. They usually select small (100 to 1200) representative samples and apply statistical techniques in analyzing the results, which are generally fairly accurate. Considerable useful data can be gathered on attitudes, practices, and beliefs. Interviews are often combined with intelligence tests, physical examinations, and personality measures in some studies. One needs to remember that a *Playboy* sex study may be colored by a liberal readership as well as by possible conservative purchasers of the magazine. Asking the "right questions" can distort the information.

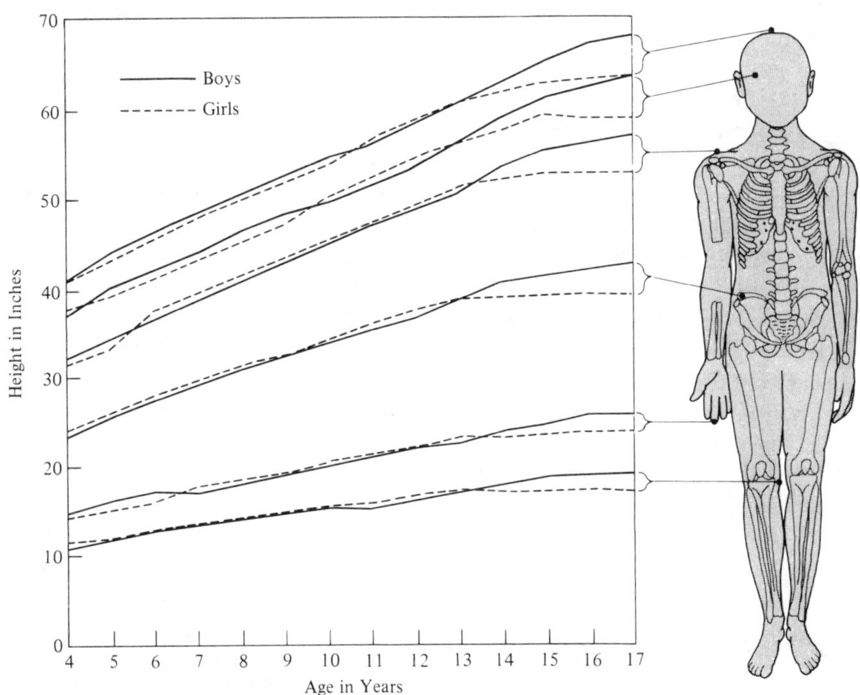

Figure 2.6 A cross-sectional and longitudinal study. (*Source:* HEW, 1953).

Another method is the interview-questionnaire survey. In this survey researchers interview people and question them from a questionnaire in hand. This is the type of research done by Kinsey, Pomeroy, and Gebhard in their study of male and female sexual behavior. The kinds of questions involved in these studies were often complex, requiring some elaboration and interpretation, so that a trained interviewer was needed to clarify questions and elicit more precise data.

Cross-cultural research, utilizing careful observation, lends itself to this kind of questioning. Typically the samples are small and are gathered from adjacent lands and cultures. An example in the U.S. is research in child rearing practices among Japanese Americans, Mexican, Indians, and Black Americans. In such studies, scientists seek more information from various cultures because they are interested in finding commonalities among people.

Questionnaires can be quite simple and still be useful for gathering information. Many questions of the "Who am I?" variety are designed to get a perception of an individual's self-concept and can be quite productive. These types of social surveys have their limitations, especially with younger children before they learn to read. Results can be biased by respondents' lack of insight, fear of revealing their true selves, or portraying themselves in what they perceive to be a socially desirable manner. The survey can gather data from older subjects, however, that would otherwise be unobtainable. A legislator can conduct a poll of constituents through the mail in a matter of days and get their reactions to an issue, thereby helping decide on a course of action.

USE OF STATISTICS IN RESEARCH

Investigators utilize two kinds of statistics: descriptive and inferential. Descriptive statistics are used to organize and present data in a concise and understandable manner. Though their form may vary, three kinds are important in psychology: (1) central tendency, which means roughly "average" (for example, average test scores, salary, height); (2) measures of variability, which indicates the degree a score varies from the mean; and (3) correlation, the degree of association between two sets of measures or scores. Central tendency will be illustrated in this section through the data on the heights of school children. Correlation and variability are presented next.

Correlation

Correlation* is the degree of association between two variables. Any characteristic--height, weight, intelligence--that can vary from time to time or place to place, individually or in a group, is a variable. If one variable, such as weight, changes together with a change in another variable, such as height, in the same direction, the correlation is said to be positive (+) (see Figure 2.7 for another example). This is the case with height and weight. The taller a person is, usually the heavier the person is. When two things are positively correlated, it means something is generally true, though not in every case, for a person of average height can weigh more than a tall person.

The coefficient of correlation (*r*) is the numerical expression of how closely two sets of measurements correspond. For example, the correlation by the IQ scores of two unrelated children reared apart is -.01, basically, .00 or no correlation. The number (coefficient) implies that knowing the IQ score of one child tells us nothing about the IQ of the unrelated child. Perfect correlation is either -1.00 (negative or inverse)--for example, snow and summer time--the more into summer time, the less snow. Body weight (measured with a spring scale) on the moon and Earth, although different, would be +1.00 (perfect) as are birth and death. Most

* The correlation (*r*) formula is $r = (XY/N - XY)/(Sx)(Sy)$

correlations are in between -1.00 and +1.00. For instance, a .00 or close to zero correlation exists between eye color and age.

As another example, one can note the interest of 12th grade boys working in skill trades correlates about -.34 with their information on theater and ballet, suggesting that the higher one's interest in skilled trades, the lower one's knowledge of theater and ballet.

relationships; .20-.40, slight correlation; .40-.70, substantial; and .70-1.00, very high relationship. Correlations do not of themselves imply causal relationships between variables, but covariance, as the following illustration of the northeast European storks shows. A correlation has been found to be high between the number of storks and human birth rates, but obviously this doesn't confirm that the stork brings the

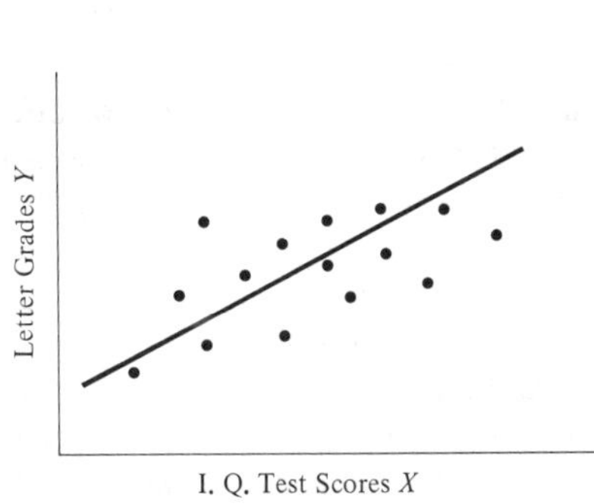

r = Positive Relationship

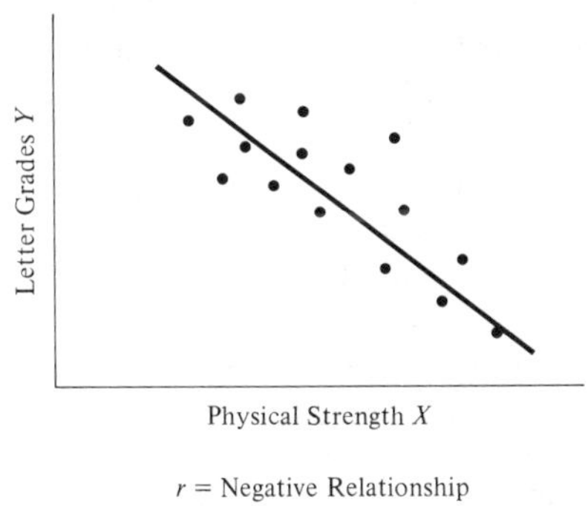

r = Negative Relationship

Figure 2.7 Scattergram indicating relationships.

Remember, correlation coefficients are not percentages. To establish a percentage for prediction, the following formula can be used.

$$E = 1 - \sqrt{1 - R^2}$$

If you substitute a correlation of .50 in the formula ($.50^2$), you will get an answer of 13 (percent) for E. This represents how much better chance (50-50) a .50 correlation is. Half of 13 is 6.5. Add this to 50. It means 56.5 chances out of 100 exist in predicting future behavior; or 43.5 out of 100 of not being able to predict. Correlations have to be very high--on the order of .80 or better--to be good cross-predictors, but even low ones (.10-.20) express some relationship. A correlation (r) of .80 represents a 70 to 30 percentage chance using the formula above; an r of .98 gives a 90 to 10 predictive efficiency. Correlations can be interpreted as follows: .00-.20, denotes negligible

baby--the figures simply covary. Correlations help predict relationships between variables, not necessarily to understand or control them (Gage & Berliner, 1988). Most behaviors when measured relate in some degree, however small.

Testing the Significance in Experimental Research

Investigators often have a need to examine the differences between groups and to know to what extent they can be confident of this relationship. Statistics that are used to judge whether the differences between two groups is significant or not are called inferential. A statistic, such as the student's t (t-test), is one of many vehicles (a formula) designed to tell what difference would occur (a ratio) if any experiment were repeated or another population were used. What differences would occur by chance or as a result of uncontrolled variables? A fundamental question for experimenters is the degree of reliability that could be predicted from another time or population.

To illustrate this concept we examine the following hypothesis, that boys with high self-esteem (n=50) earn better grades than those boys with lower self-esteem (n=50). In such a study it was found that the boys in a certain college with higher self-esteem did score higher in quality point average in a semester; they had a 3.0 average, to a 2.3 for those with lower self-esteem. To what degree can we put confidence in this mean difference? In order to test this we formulate a hypothesis as follows:

> There is no difference between the grades of boys with high self-esteem and the grades of boys with low self-esteem.

The students' t* will allow us to test this assertion. If, in completing the formula, the t value turns out to be of a certain size (2.58 or above) with a sample of 10 or more, we find by reading a "table of t" from most books on statistics a significance at the .01 level. This means that 99 out of 100 times the hypothesis made originally was realistic; only 1 percent of the time or less would this result occur by chance alone. A value of the t between 1.96 and 2.58 with an N of 10 or more indicates a .05 level of confidence (attributing the results to chance only 5 times or less out of 100).

Researchers in the behavioral sciences (psychology, sociology, and education) typically use a probability of 95 percent as a reasonable standard. The significance of a correlation can be obtained by checking a correlation table with .05 and .01 levels of significance indicated.

Many experiments are more complex than those just illustrated. In some instances there are many variables among and between groups that need to be analyzed; in this case, an ANOVA (analysis of variance) is appropriate, or a computer program such as the SPSS (Statistical Package for the Social Sciences) can be utilized to obtain this information.

Standard deviation (also called sigma or σ for the Greek letter for s) is used in computing the correlation formula as well as the student's t. By definition, σ is the distance from the mean that is needed to take in approximately 68 percent of the cases.† For two SDs or sigmas it would be 95 percent of the cases. The SD is used to compare the variability of scores of different groups or individuals; it gives an indication of how much alike or different two groups may be. They may be, for instance, the same in mean (average), but if one has a smaller (less) standard deviation, it is more homogeneous. An illustration given in Figure 2.8 involves the height of third-grade children who were the same in mean (48 inches) as those of the entire school population of kindergarten to sixth grade (Janda & Klenke-Hamel, 1982, p. 557). The third-grade children on the curve show that they are more alike (as expected) than the entire school (K-6) for which the comparing mean was taken, ranging over a wider age and development period. The shorter kindergarten children and the taller sixth graders undoubtedly helped to balance the means. Sixty-eight percent of the children of the third grade were found between 44 and 52 inches in height--that is, 1 SD. For the school, one standard deviation was a wider range (40 inches up to 56 inches), therefore less homogeneous. The SD is applied to both sides of the curve (plus and minus). Theoretically, the typical curve (Gaussian) has five sigmas.

Other Considerations in Doing Research

Ethical considerations have increasingly become an issue in carrying out research. Investigations dealing with human subjects that utilize mock circumstances, such as locking a person in the luggage compartment of a car and having him scream for help in order to gauge the reaction of the passerby, are questionable. Another example is to have the person feign injury, such as one experiment carried out in a New York subway, to ascertain the effect on those present. An experimental study by Stanley Milgram (1974) that involved having subjects give increasingly higher level electric shocks (no electricity was used) to others who believed they were being shocked invoked negative responses from a number of professional groups and became a center of controversy.

The American Psychological Association (1973) formulated a series of research guidelines. The preamble suggests among other things that:

> The responsible psychologist weighs alternative directions in which personal energies and resources might be invested. Having made the decision to conduct research, psychologists must carry out their investigations with respect for the people who participate and with concern for their dignity and welfare. (p. 1)

The Society for Research in Child Development in its 1972 guidelines notes that children are more vulnerable to stress than adults and are unable to evaluate as well as adults the effects of participation in experimental research. Therefore, it suggests that both the parents and the children involved must give permission in order to have them included in research. The highest kinds of ethical considerations should be provided, and a thorough briefing and debriefing of the subjects should be held before and after their participation in the study.

The Health and Human Services guide for "Human Subjects" experimentation requires that subjects not be forced into participation and that any participation be with informed consent. Also, having begun participation, subjects must be allowed to withdraw at any time. In addition, experimenters must assume responsibility for psychological harm, and they must give full explanations concerning the research procedures prior to and after the experimentation. Researchers should not distort the facts, even if they are unpleasant to the subject. Personal data should remain strictly confidential and the

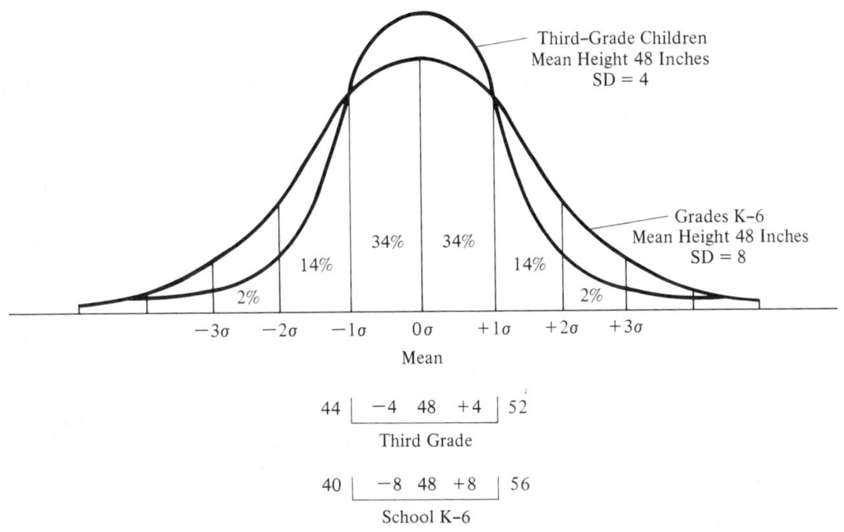

Figure 2.8 Height distribution and standard deviation. (*Source:* Janda & Klenke-Hamel, 1982).

experiment should be of some positive benefit to the participants.

Evaluation of research should be an ongoing concern of institutions and individuals. There are those who believe that some of what appears in journals and professional magazines is rarely scrutinized with adequacy. Too little replication is required before publicizing results, so that sometimes the least probable conclusions are often given as much publicity in the popular periodicals and press as those of more serious and better controlled kinds of research. Students should learn to thoroughly review the literature and to fully check out their ideas on initial research attempts, discussing their theories freely with professors and colleagues. Such an approach can only result in improved evaluation and understanding of behavior.

SUMMARY

Learning and maturation are interwoven in all aspects of the child's development, especially during the early years. Learning depends upon opportunity and stimulation as well as maturation. Where opportunities are limited, children will not develop their full potentialities. The development of a culture depends upon learning, with many institutions and individuals making contributions.

The interaction of heredity and environment may be observed in certain principles of growth. Some of these principles are (1) growth tends to follow a cephalo-caudal pattern and a proximodistal pattern; (2) development is continuous toward the aim of maturity; (3) the direction of growth is always toward maturity; (4) growth rates of individuals tend to remain consistent; (5) growth of physical and mental areas is uneven; (6) individual differences in children's rates of growth exist; and (7) all growth is interrelated. The social and cultural influences are important and pervasive in their effect upon development.

Information-getting is the objective of research. The most significant method of gathering information is the scientific method, which is composed of five steps: (1) statement of the problem; (2) formation of the hypothesis; (3) collection and analysis of data; (4) formation of a conclusion; and (5) verification of the initial hypothesis. Effective observation is important to research. The major types of data-gathering approaches are important in research. Cross-sectional research design provides base amounts of data from a variety of sources of people who differ on a specific dependent variable. Longitudinal research design allows us to measure the same subjects more than once, to see what changes take place.

The clinical or case study, where not flawed, through painstaking yet definitive examination of individuals adds some validity to other types of research. As important as a research method is, it is usually best undertaken with other methods, for no single approach has been sufficient to satisfy all questions and the demands of validation. The chapter illustrates that human development must be an eclectic study requiring extensive use and knowledge of various disciplines and fields. Highest ethical consideration is imperative in dealing with human subjects so that confidentiality, proper briefings, and stringent scholarly standards are adhered to in undertaking research.

"Silly, eh son? After a few years you won't think so. Then when you get old you'll think it foolish."

KEY TERMS

standard deviation

correlation

confidence level

significant level

case study

clinical study

experimental study

longitudinal study

cross-sectional study

survey

neuromuscular coordination

cephalo-caudal

proximo-distal

normal curve

biosocial

experimental design

environmental interaction

control

personal social

motor growth

language

REFERENCES

American Psychological Association. (1973). *Ethical Principles in the Conduct of Research with Human Participants.* Washington, D.C., 1973.

Bayley, N. Consistency and variability in the growth of intelligence from birth to eighteen years. In Jones et al. (eds.), *The Course of Human Development.* Waltham, Mass.: Xerox Publishing Co., 1971, pp. 106-117.

Gage, N.K. I.Q. hereditibility, race differences, and educational research. *Phi Delta Kappan*, 1972, pp. 227-307.

Gage, N.L., and Berliner, D.C. *Educational Psychology*, 4th ed. Boston: Houghton-Mifflin, 1988, p. 26.

Goleman, D. 1528 little geniuses and how they grew. *Psychology Today*, 1980, *13*(9):28-67.

Gottesman, I.I. Severity/concordance and diagnostic refinement in the Maudsley-Bethlem schizophrenic twin study. In D. Rosenthal and S.S. Kety (eds.), *The Transmission of Schizophrenia.* New York: Pergamon, 1968.

Health, Education and Welfare (HEW), U.S. Department of, Office of Education. *Basic Body Measurements of School Age Children.* Washington, D.C., 1953.

Honsik, M.P., MacFarlane, J.W., and Allen, L.A. The stability in mental test performance between two and eighteen years. In Jones et al. (eds.), *The Course of Human Development.* Waltham, Mass.: Xerox Publishing Co., 1971, pp. 117-123.

Hunt, C.E., and Brouillette, R.T. Sudden infant death syndrome: 1987 perspective. *Journal of Pediatrics*, 1987, *110*(5):669-678.

Janda, L., and Klenke-Hamel, K. *Psychology: Its Study and Uses.* New York: St. Martin's, 1982.

Jensen, A. How much can we boost IQ and scholastic achievement? *Harvard Educational Review*, 1969,*39*(1).

Kagan, J. Inadequate evidence and illogical conclusions. *Harvard Educational Review*, 1969, *39*:274-277.

Kolata, G.B. Behavior development: Effects of environment. *Science*, 1975, *189*:207-209.

Krogman, W.M. *Child Growth.* Ann Arbor: University of Michigan Press, 1972.

Land, G.T.L. *Grow or Die*. New York: Random House, 1973.

Marlow, D.R. *Textbook of Pediatric Nursing*, 5th ed. Philadelphia: Saunders, 1977.

Marlow, D.R., and Redding, B.A. *Textbook of Pediatric Nursing*, 6th ed. Philadelphia: Saunders, 1988, p. 172.

Milgram, S. *Obedience to Authority*. New York: Harper & Row, 1974.

Olsen, W.C. *Child Development*, 2nd ed. Boston: Heath, 1959.

Pasamanick, B., and Knobloch, H. Retrospective studies on the epidemiology of reproductive causality. *Merrill-Palmer Quarterly*, 1966, *12*:7-26.

Pillemer, D.B., and Light, R.J. Synthesizing outcomes: How to use research evidence from many studies. *Harvard Educational Review*, 1980, *50*(2).

Plomin, R., and Daniels, D. Why are children in the same family so different from one another? *Behavior & Brain Sciences*, 1987, *10*:1-16.

Scammon, R.E. The first seriatim study of human growth. *American Journal of Physical Anthropology*, 1927.

Scarr, S., and McCartney, K. How people make their own environments: A theory of genotypes--environments effects. *Child Development*, 1983, *54*:424-435.

Schaie, K.W. Limitations on the generalizability of growth curves on intelligence: A reanalysis of some data from the Harvard growth study. *Human Development*, 1972, *15*:141-152.

Smelser, N., and Erikson, E. *Adult Themes of Work and Love*. Cambridge, Mass.: Harvard University Press, 1980.

Society for Research in Child Development. *Ethical Standards for Research with Children*. Chicago, 1972.

Tanner, J.M. *Growth at Adolescence*, 2nd ed. Oxford: Blackwell, 1962.

_____. Physical growth. In P.H. Mussen (ed.), *Carmichael's Manual of Child Psychology*, 3rd ed., vol. 1. New York: Wiley, 1970, pp. 75-155.

_____. Growing up. *Scientific American*, 1973, *229*(3).

Terman, L.M., et al. *Genetic Studies of Genius*. Stanford, CA: Stanford University Press, 1925.

Terman, L.M., and Oden, M. *The Gifted Child Grows Up*. Palo Alto, CA: Stanford University Press, 1947.

Wegman, M.E. Annual summary of vital statistics. *Pediatrics*, 1986, *80*(6):817-827.

White, B.L. *The First Three Years of Life*. Englewood Cliffs, NJ: Prentice-Hall, 1975.

PART II

ORIGIN OF LIFE AND INFANT DEVELOPMENT

Chapter 3

THE BEGINNING OF HUMAN DEVELOPMENT

- ***Conception***
  - In-vitro fertilization
  - Artificial insemination
  - Surrogate mother
  - Donor eggs
  - Adoption
- ***Operation of Heredity***
  - Mendelian laws
  - Dominant and recessive characteristics
- ***Genetic Problems in Men and Women***
  - Genotype and phenotype
- ***Range of Reaction***
  - Twin study
  - Nature and nurture
- ***Prenatal Development***
  - Ovum
  - Embryonic
  - Fetal
  - Examination of progress
  - Genetic counseling
- ***Prenatal Influences***
  - Drugs and alcohol
  - Malnutrition
  - Infections and viruses
  - Teratogenic agents
  - Radiation and Rh influence
  - Physical health of mother

THE BEGINNING OF HUMAN DEVELOPMENT

Findings from studies in the biological sciences have furnished us with answers to many questions regarding the beginning of life and the growth processes. This has required the coordination of efforts by students of biology, genetics, endocrinology, medicine, psychology, and related fields of study. The conquest of disease and the study of the structure of living cells provide hope for the future amelioration of many problems related to the beginning, growth, and nature of living human organisms.

CONCEPTION

Life for an individual begins at the time the sperm cell from the male penetrates the ovum of the female. The ovum is one of the largest cells, about 0.1 millimeters in diameter. The sperm is one of the smallest cells, about 0.05 millimeters in diameter.

The role of the ovum in fertilization is (1) to provide the female complement of genes to the nucleus of the fertilized egg, (2) to reject all sperms but one, and (3) to furnish nutrients until the embryo begins to feed upon exogenous materials. There are thousands of rudimentary ova in the human female at birth--perhaps over 400,000--and many of these atrophy prior to puberty. Approximately 400 will mature, one at a time, usually prior to menopause, over the fertility life span of a woman. During each menstrual cycle one ovum breaks out in the form of a blister from one of the pair of ovaries. Ovulation is said to have occurred when the estrogen fluid washes the ovum through the ruptured ovary. This is made possible through the action of the hormones from the endocrine glands, which regulate the sequence so that usually only one egg is released from the ovary at each menstrual cycle. The egg can be fertilized for 24 hours and sperm is viable for 48 hours.

The role of the sperm in the fertilization process is (1) to penetrate the egg, (2) to activate the egg to nuclear and cytoplasm division necessary to the development of the embryo, and (3) to contribute the paternal (male) complement of the genes to the nucleus of the fertilized ovum. As many as 20 million sperm that are needed to make fertilization likely are released at the time of ejaculation during intercourse. However, usually only one sperm makes contact and penetrates the ovum. This sperm, containing 23 chromosomes of the male, moves toward the nucleus of the ovum, which contains 23 chromosomes of the female. Fusion takes place and a new cell of 46 chromosomes is formed.

At the moment of conception the biological potential of each parent is brought to bear on the beginning offspring (Glass, 1969). The sex-determining chromosomes are called X and Y. The other 22 pairs are autosomes (non-sex chromosomes). Males carry both X and Y chromosomes (sex chromosomes), while females carry only X chromosomes. The Y chromosomes are smaller and have fewer genes. When an ovum (X) combines (Figure 3.1) with an X-carrying sperm, it is called a gymnosperm (zygote--XX, a female). An ovum (X) fertilized by a Y-carrying sperm is called an androsperm (zygote--XY, a male). Many sex-linked genetic defects are related to the X chromosomes. They

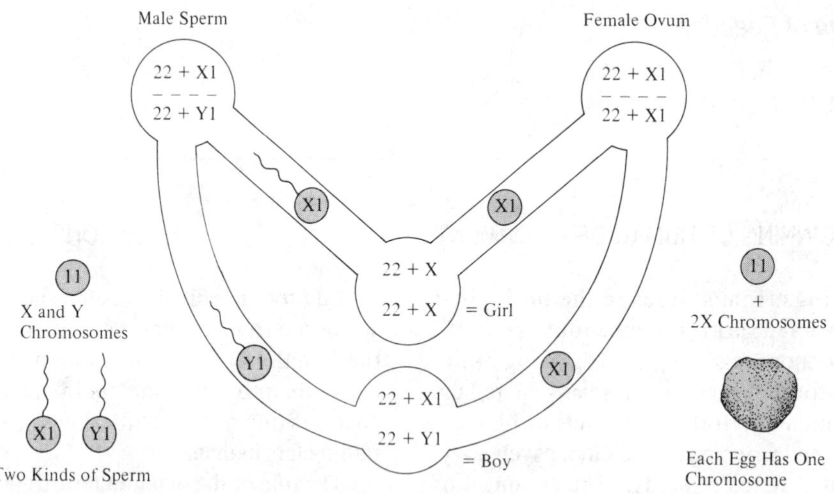

Figure 3.1 Sex Determination.

are transmitted by the female and are expressed in the male. Discussion of these follows in this chapter.

There are two kind of cells found in the body, somatic cells and germ cells. Although all cells contain the same combination of chromosomes, only the germ cells--which are the reproductive cells--are transmitted at the time of conception. Somatic cells make up the organs, brain, and body itself. These cells are the ones that respond to learning. They develop acquired traits. Since somatic cells are not transmitted in the reproductive process, acquired learning is not passed on by heredity. A bright mother and father's learning is not passed on to the child--only potentiality is transmitted.

Qualities subject to inheritance, based upon twin studies that utilized correlation, include physical features, strength of tissue, time of puberty, predisposition to heart disease and diabetes, maintenance function in the storage of energy, rate of release of energy, maleness and femaleness, and physical characteristics of the brain and nervous system.

Getting Pregnant

Men and women marry at a later age than ever before in this century: 23 years of age for women and 25 years of age for men. Although most pregnancies are conceived in marriage, a growing number, particularly among younger females and blacks, take place outside of marriage or are aborted. Over one million abortions occur every year in the United States. Because of late marriages and changing lifestyles, couples are delaying the decision to have children--although the majority of births come to those in their twenties to the late thirties. Many women find by their mid-thirties that conceiving is difficult. Infertility, the inability to conceive after a year of trying, has tripled in the past 25 years. At least 10-15 percent of couples who want a baby cannot conceive (Francoeur, 1985). Fertility declines with age (Figure 3.1). Acquired Immune Deficiency Syndrome (AIDS) and other diseases, birth control methods, and lack of sperm count all play their part in this problem. However, many who receive treatment eventually conceive.

Artificial Insemination

Possibilities of conception are seen in artificial insemination, in-vitro fertilization, donor eggs, and surrogate motherhood. And, of course, there always exists the possibility of adoption. In artificial insemination a woman either receives an injection directly into the cervix of her husband's sperm or sperm of an anonymous donor whose background and physical characteristics resemble the husband. The information of this latter pregnancy is never revealed to anyone, including the children. Conception through in-vitro fertilization occurs outside the mother's body, beginning with the act of taking an ovum from her. The dish is placed in an incubator and fertilized with the father's sperm. After the zygote divides into four cells, the physician implants the embryo in the mother's uterus, where development takes place. If the mother's fallopian tube is blocked, this becomes a viable way to have a child.

Donor Eggs

In this procedure another woman furnishes the ova and the husband furnishes the sperm. An ovum is taken from the body of a fertile woman, allowed to mature and be fertilized, and the embryo implanted in the uterus of another woman. Then the donor's ovum is fertilized through artificial insemination while it is still in the donor's body. After five days the embryo is removed from the uterus and inserted into the uterus of the recipient.

Chromosomes and Genes

Each cell contains a nucleus rich in a highly complex nucleoprotein called deoxyribonucleic acid (DNA). DNA appears to be a basic living substance capable of duplicating itself so as to form more DNA. In the nucleus of every cell is a number of rodlike, darkly stained bodies called chromosomes, the agent for transmission of heredity. Within each cell genes coalesce into beadlike strings called chromosomes. The gene always appears at the same place on the same chromosome. "The DNA of a chromosome is a linear array of many genes. Each gene, in turn, is a chain of about 1,000 nucleotides in a precisely defined sequence which, when translated into amino acid, spells out a particular protein of enzyme" (Kornberg, 1968). Parents transmit specific traits and tendencies to their children through genes. Each sex provides around 100,000 genes. Gene pairs provide units of information for the blueprint for heredity.

Surrogate Motherhood

The surrogate is impregnated by the father (artificially) and carries the baby to birth. After a few days, the surrogate gives the baby to the couple to raise. The surrogate mother takes all the risks for a fee, usually high. As is well known, as in the recent Baby M case, the surrogate mother sometimes does not want to give the baby up. The Baby M case was settled giving the custody to the couple, but the surrogate mother was allowed visiting privileges.

Genetic Counseling

A couple planning to have a child can learn about the risk of having a child through genetic counseling. Taking the family history and conducting laboratory tests are part of the assessment made concerning the implications of having a child. By examination of the karyotype, the couple can provide the genetic blueprint to uncover chromosome abnormalities. Risks (odds) are discussed with the couple. A 25 percent risk means that there is one chance in four that the child will inherit the disease. If the disease is not too disabling, the couple may decide to take a chance. Depending upon the problem, the wife might decide on sterilization or consider artificial insemination if the father has a defective gene. They may also consider adoption.

GENETIC INFLUENCES IN DEVELOPMENT

The beginnings of the human organism are initiated at the time of fertilization. In the process of development, the fertilized cell divides and redivides until thousands of cells are formed. It is estimated that from the time of conception until birth, weight increases two billion times. The materials making up the fertilized cell are most important. Environmental forces and conditions during the nine-month period before birth are significant in determining the development of the child.

Watson and Crick, Nobel Prize winners, discovered that with the DNA molecules the pattern of the chromosomes is in the shape of a twisted ladder, called a helix. A sugar alternates with phosphate to form the sides of the ladder. The rungs of the ladder are formed by combinations of cytosine (C), guanine (G), adenine (D), and thymine (T). A sequence of CG, GC, AT, GG, TA may indicate eye color, and scrambled in another order might represent hair color. The genetic code for a characteristic may consist of hundreds of rungs. Sickle cell anemia, for example, is the result of only one change in the sequence of 574 amino acids that makes the protein hemoglobin. These, in various combinations, seem to be capable of encoding all the characteristics that an organism transmits from one generation to another. Watson and Crick discovered further that DNA carries the blueprint for proteins and that RNA (ribonucleic acids) does the work of making them. The structure and replication of DNA is shown in Figure 3.2.

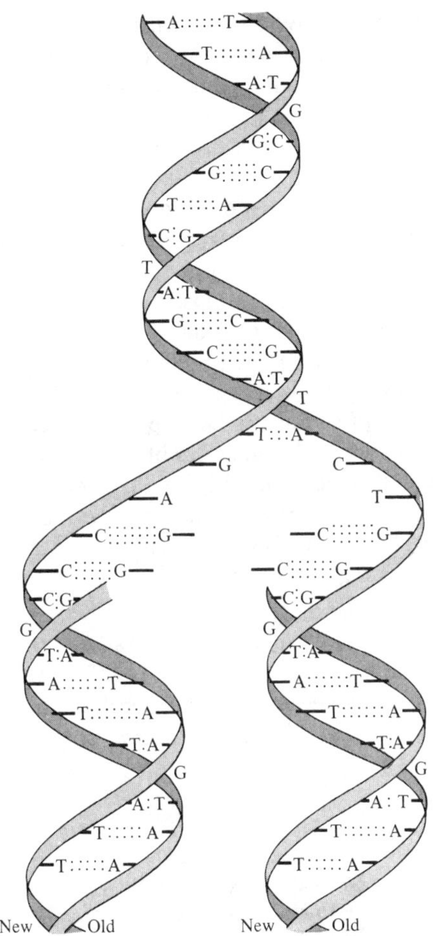

Figure 3.2 The double helix sugar phosphate backbones twists on the outside with the flat hydrogen-bonded base pairs forming the core symbols: T (thymine), C (cytosine), A (adenine), and G (guanine).

The Operation of Heredity

The combination of genes received by a child is a matter of chance, although each gene from the mother's chromosome is paired with a corresponding gene from the father's. Perhaps the most important difference between modern genetic concepts and earlier viewpoints of heredity is that today we conceive of the transmission of individual particles of hereditary material from parents to offspring; earlier viewpoints postulated a blending of the hereditary elements of the pairs of chromosomes. In heredity the genes control single characteristics, and they exist in pairs, one from each parent. The term *allele* is used to note each of the alternate genes in a pair. When the allele is dominant, the characteristic that is obvious is called the phenotype (among people, physical and behavioral traits). The genotype represents the genetic makeup of a pair of genes. The term *heterozygous* refers to a genotype that contains contrasting alleles in a gene pair. Like alleles for a trait are called *homozygous.*

Types of Inheritance

In polygenetic inheritance, where dominance is not clear-cut, multiple genes are involved, interacting to produce certain traits. The result, as seen in human mating of blacks and whites, is a blending of incomplete dominance in terms of skin color ranging from light to dark. Multifactorial inheritance involves interaction between genetic (such as intelligence and stature) and environmental factors. A child deprived of nutrients could have his height affected (Ehrman & Probber, 1983).

Mendel: Father of Hereditary Principles

Mendel's first law of heredity points out that the paired genes derived from the two parents, which influence the development of traits, retain their individuality and segregate unaffected by each other to pass into different gametes (sperm cells and egg cells), and are able to enter into new combinations when they unite to form a new pair. Mendel's second law of heredity, dominance and recessiveness, arose out of his discoveries in experiments with peas.

When the two genes (one from each parent) are different, one may dominate the other. A striking illustration of this in human beings is the characteristic of red hair. If a red-headed woman marries a man with dark hair, the children resulting from this marriage will all have dark hair. Such children will, however, carry a recessive trait for red hair. The results of this in the grown children, marrying those whose inheritance is the same (homozygous) would be (for children resulting from the marriage of a red-haired woman and a dark-haired man):

1/4 dark hair
1/2 dark hair (red hair recessive)
1/4 red hair

Since the pure dark hair and the homozygous types are indistinguishable, three-fourths of the children should have dark hair and one-fourth red hair. In the chromosome pair, the genes of one member may differ in some ways from those of the other. This difference is attributable to the fact that the two chromosomes come from different people with unlike genetic backgrounds. Often the pair of genes determining a particular characteristic is alike. In the case of eye color they may both be genes for blue eyes. It is then said that these chromosomes are homozygous for eye color. If the genes for eye color are different--that is, blue and brown--the chromosomes are designated as heterozygous for eye color. The gene for brown eyes is dominant; the gene for blue eyes is recessive. The recessive gene can be transmitted to offspring. In the case of blue (recessive), if paired with a gene for blue eyes, this color will be inherited. The recessive genes are then alike (homozygous) and determine the eye color. A list of dominant and recessive human genes is given in Table 3.1.

Table 3.1 DOMINANT AND RECESSIVE HUMAN GENETIC CHARACTERISTICS

Dominant	Recessive
Full head of hair	Baldness*
Skin pigmentation	Albinism
Curly hair	Straight hair
Brown eyes	Blue or hazel eyes
Drooping eyelids	Normal
Near or farsightedness	Normal vision
Skin and brain cancer	Normal
Glaucoma	Normal
Normal color vision	Color blindness*
Normal hearing	Congenital deafness
Free earlobes	Attached earlobes
Normal metabolism	Phenylketonuria
Polydactylism (extra fingers and toes)	Normal number of digits
Dark hair	Light or red hair
Hereditary cataract	Normal vision
Long eyelashes	Short eyelashes
Broad lips	Thin lips
Ichthyosis (scaly skin)	Normal skin
Achondroplasia (dwarfism)	Normal
Huntington's chorea	Normal
Freckles	Unspotted skin
Normal blood clotting	Hemophilia*

*Sex linked.

Often, paired genes differ and the results are a compromise--for example, the black-and-white gene presented in the Andalusian fowl. The progeny of these fowls have a slate blue color. An individual trait (a distinct and enduring characteristic determined by the gene), such as height in human beings, shows no Mendelian ratio such as the typical simple 1:2:1. This trait seems to be determined by multiple genes; its inheritance is inferred to be polygenic, and the color dominance is incomplete. Sometimes one gene is not completely dominant over the other. The resulting circumstance represents a blending of the phenotypes of the parents. It is not produced by a blending of the genotype. Penetrance, another factor in inheritance, manifests itself in expression. Interaction with other genes and the environment plays a part in the outcome. Manic depressive illness may not always result in the disorder due to reduced penetrance (Kolata, 1986).

Among the important modifications of the law of segregation discovered since Mendel's time is the law of linkage. When a trait is affected by a gene lying within the X chromosome, it is said to be sex-linked (three such genes are noted in Table 3.1). This means that the X chromosome carries genes for characteristics other than those that determine sex. Such characteristics will be linked by sex in heredity; they are not linked to a particular sex, but such characteristics follow the distribution of the X chromosome in both sexes. It has been estimated that as many as 150 traits are sex-linked. Almost all sex-linked genetic defects occur in men, since they have only one X chromosome. In women the defective gene action on one chromosome is muted by a dominant gene on the other chromosome. Perhaps the best known sex-linked traits are color blindness and hemophilia. "Among whites, two men out of every 25 suffer from some lack of ability to recognize

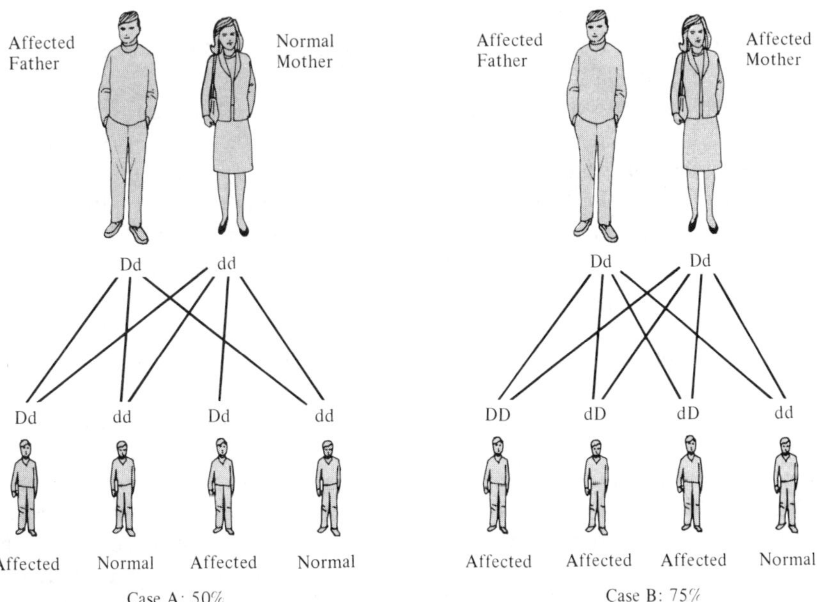

Figure 3.3 Dominant single gene in heredity. (*Source*: National Institute of General medical Sciences, 1975, p. 13.)

red and green. Less than one woman out of 200 suffers from a similar defect" (Montague, 1963, p. 187). A man can receive from his mother alone an X chromosome with a genetic defect. Sons receive only Y chromosomes from their father but daughters receive X chromosomes from their father.

Hereditary Factors and Related Circumstances

The characteristics usually closely associated with inheritance are color of the eyes and hair, pigmentation of the skin, blood types, body build, and other physical features. The rapidly accumulating knowledge of cytogenetics (the study of chromosomes) reveals the wide diversity of ways in which heredity operates. The Duke University School of Medicine reported that although three to five genetic defects exist in everyone, most of these are benign (for example, birth marks). Dominant autosomal single gene defects can be transmitted by one affected parent. One thousand such disorders so far have been identified; every pregnancy involves a 50 percent risk of transmitting the defect if one parent is affected, and a 75 percent risk if both are affected (see Figure 3.3).

Hereditary disorders of metabolism such as phenylketonuria (PKU), transmitted by a single recessive autosomal gene, have been detected through modern biochemical techniques within 48 hours if the milk intake is normal, and otherwise by the sixth day. This is a disorder resulting from an inborn error of metabolism (lack of a liver enzyme). The disease, according to Lyght (1966), caused only about 15 percent of the cases of mental retardation. Prior to comparatively recent use of the low phenylalanine diet, most PKU cases were severely retarded inmates of institutions. With the development of treatment procedures, increased efforts have been made to identify PKU cases as early as possible. Early treatment (in the first three months) tends to prevent irreversible brain damage. In some cases the special diet can be discontinued after three years (Emery, 1975). If mental deficiencies become established, the outlook for improvement is poor. Children discovered early have their intelligence quotients affected within ten points of unaffected siblings (*British Medical Journal*, 1963).

Genetic loadings causing metabolic disease such as PKU, galactosemia, albinism, sickle-cell anemia, and other nutritional and infectious diseases are largely under control (see Table 3.2). Insulin has been developed to protect diabetics, blood-clotting drugs to help hemophiliacs, and alternative food for babies unable to tolerate galactose.

Investigation through successive generations on rats introduced to equivalent amounts of radiation from atomic explosions does show noticeable effects. Cataracts, sterility, and shortened life are in considerable evidence. Rats are not humans, it is true, but one investigation shows incidence of cancer in radiologists over non-radiologists in a 12 to 4 ratio (Lewis, 1963).

Genetic Problems in Men

More males than females are born with genetic defects, and as infants fewer survive than their sexual counterparts. Those with chromosomal abnormalities more often are males, as in the case of Klinefelter's syndrome (affects only males), which occurs about 1 out of 400 times (Mertens, 1975). Unfortunately, this syndrome cannot be diagnosed at birth due to the lack of specific characteristics (Nielsen et al., 1982).

Patients with Klinefelter's syndrome have a general male appearance, are tall and thin, with small male external sex organs, but are sterile, frequently mentally retarded, and have nuclear chromatin bodies characteristic of females. The sex chromosomal pattern of XXY has a (45, XXY) schema and is found in the majority of individuals with this syndrome (Pennington, Bender, Puck et al., 1982). The typical human being transmits 23 chromosomes, 22 of which

Table 3.2 SELECTED BIRTH DEFECTS AND PROGNOSIS

Defect	Incidence	Etiology	Amelioration
Birthmarks	Common	Cause is unknown, seen as winecolored patches made up of many small blood vessels	Plastic surgeon can remove many marks, skin grafts are used and tattoo of normal skin color over area
Congenital heart	1 in every 160	Caused generally by German measles during pregnancy	Repair by surgery is commonplace
Diabetes	1 in 4 carried in heredity. 1 in 50 persons over 60 clinical cases	Cause of marked hereditary, enzyme defect possible	Special diets, use of insulin
Rh-negative blood (erythroblastosis)	10% of Rh-negative mothers married to Ph-positive fathers. One of 7 Americans have Rh-negative	Rh blood factor is inherited. Effects are seen in often yellow color of baby, anemia; is a cause of stillbirth or can cause retardation	Early detection, transfusion of blood with compatible blood. Risks in subsequent pregnancies can be avoided by injection of immunoglobulin to mothers within several days of delivery of the current infant
Fingers and toes (polydactyl), Fused fingers and toes (syndactyl)	1 in 100 among blacks. 1 in 500 among whites	Cause unknown; frequently hereditary	Amputation of the extra digit by 3 years of age. Surgery in syndactyl cases improve function. Artificial limbs are sometimes necessary
Sickle-cell anemia	Low among whites—40% in blacks of Africa, 10% in American blacks	Heredity defect seen in sickle-shaped cells. Carries some immunity from malaria	Little can be done to relieve this defect, but when anemia is present this can be treated if not severe

Adapted from National Foundation, March of Dimes (1973).

are called autosomes and carry genes for general body characteristics and functions. The other chromosome is the sex chromosome.

A number of male prisoners have been found to have XYY or double YY syndrome (47, XYY) phenotypical chromosomes. They are fertile males. However, it is not the heredity that makes criminals; it is a matter of criminals having a higher incidence of chromosomal abnormality (Witkin et al., 1976). Chromosomal aberrations, especially the XYY type, may predispose one to crime but are not a cause of crime. The estimated incidence of the XYY is 1 in 800; among the other abnormalities discussed above, the incidence is 1 in every 400 to 500 births (Janda & Hamel, 1980).

Genetic Problems in Women

Turner's syndrome usually occurs in persons who appear to be females but who are sterile, fail to show breast development, are broad chested, and have webbing of the neck. Most of them also have a congenital heart defect, and some are mentally retarded and have abnormal shortness. In most cases, the sex-chromatin pattern is negative and the karyotype analysis reveals 45 chromosomes, only one sex chromosome X (45, XO) being present (McCauley, Kay, Ito, & Tredet, 1987). However, sex-chromatin-positive cases of Turner's syndrome have been reported (Nielsen et al., 1982).

Cases of females with a triple X syndrome cannot be diagnosed at birth due to lack of characteristics--(47, XXX) or even (48, XXX) patterns have been reported (Janda & Hamel, 1980). Such women are usually fertile and their offspring normal. Abnormalities of sex chromosomal patterns have also been found in a few patients with a confusion of sexual organs.

The most common chromosomal error in girls is Turner's syndrome (affects only females), which occurs once in 3,000 female infants (Kennedy, 1971). In 50 percent of the

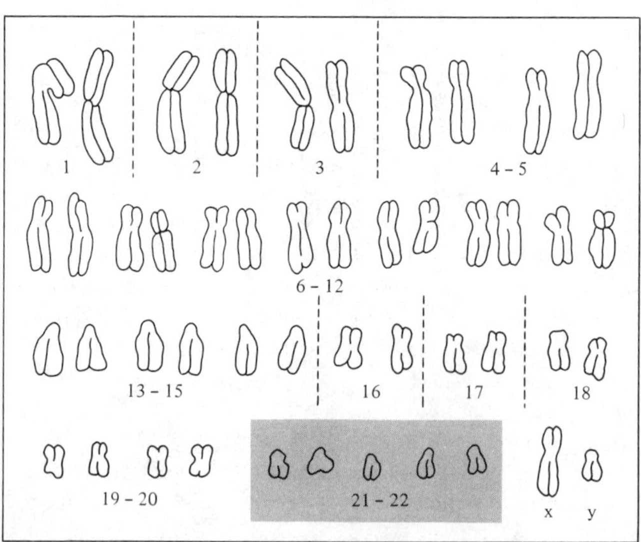

Figure 3.4 Chromosome karyotype of a male afflicted with Down's syndrome. (*Source*: Kang, 1966.)

cases, diagnosis is possible at birth due to the puffing (pseudo-oedema) of the back of the hands and feet (Nielsen et al., 1982). Clubfoot is more often seen in boys than in girls, as are hemophilia, color blindness, Hunter's disease, muscular dystrophy, juvenile glaucoma, and pyloric stenosis (overgrowth of the intestinal muscles) (Omenn, 1978).

Another chromosome variation is the case of Down's syndrome, presented in Figure 3.4. The Down's syndrome child normally has 47 chromosomes and is characterized by specific abnormalities in physical structure and mental retardation (Snyder, Freifelder, & Harte, 1985). Cases of Down's syndrome have been reported where the normal complement of 46 chromosomes was abnormal, with an extra chromosome in one group and a deficiency in another (Polani et al., 1960).

Since females cannot transmit Y chromosomes, as they are carried only by males, there are no uniquely female hereditary diseases; consequently it is extremely rare for a girl to have X-linked genetic disease (*National Institute of General Medical Science*, 1975). Most genetic problems come from recessive rather than dominant genes. Huntington's chorea (a progressive degeneration of the nervous system) is dominant and caused the death of Woody Guthrie, the well-known folk singer who wrote "This Land Is Your Land." His son, Arlo Guthrie, also a singer, has a 50-50 chance of having inherited this disease. More male embryos are likely to be miscarried or to abort spontaneously than females, reflecting the genetic situation.

Range of reaction is a concept used to indicate the possible genetic variations for which the genotypic base can be altered, resulting in a variety of phenotypic examples (Figure 3.5). The reaction range refers to the upper and lower limits within the environmental circumstance to determine the outcome of the phenotype. Even intelligence, which is closely linked with heredity, is affected by environmental conditions (as discussed in Chapter 7). The genetic factor influences human behavior through its effect upon enzymes, hormones, and the nervous system, which mediates the pattern laid down by the genes and the psychosocial aspects of behavior observed in personality. In order to understand human development, it is necessary to recognize the potential given in the genotype and fulfillment opportunity that is provided by the environment and then seen in the phenotype.

The Nature-Nurture Investigation

How much influence does environment or heredity have on development? Motor development in the infant unfolds in sequential chronology: creeping, crawling, walking, and running. This shows the importance of maturation. The hereditary timetable is interfered with only when it takes an extreme form such as long-time deprivation. In one study, children in an Iranian orphanage who received little attention and exercise were found to sit up and walk late compared with Iranian children who received excellent attention (Dennis, 1960).

In language development, maturation is a clear requirement before children begin to talk, as a certain level of neurological and muscular development must be attained. No matter how superior the child's home is in enrichment, a child will not speak in complete sentences, read, or write before one year of age. Still, the environment plays a large role in language development, for if parents encourage their children's first efforts to make sounds by babbling back to them they will speak earlier than if their early attempts to make sounds are ignored.

Blood type and hair color are inherited, and health, intelligence, and personality are subject to interaction between heredity and environment. Studies of personality, including those on twins, provide evidence that many personality traits are strongly influenced by genetic factors (Plonin, 1989). How much does each matter? If we know a certain birth defect is hereditary we can better advise caretakers and parents. If a child's intelligence is affected by environment

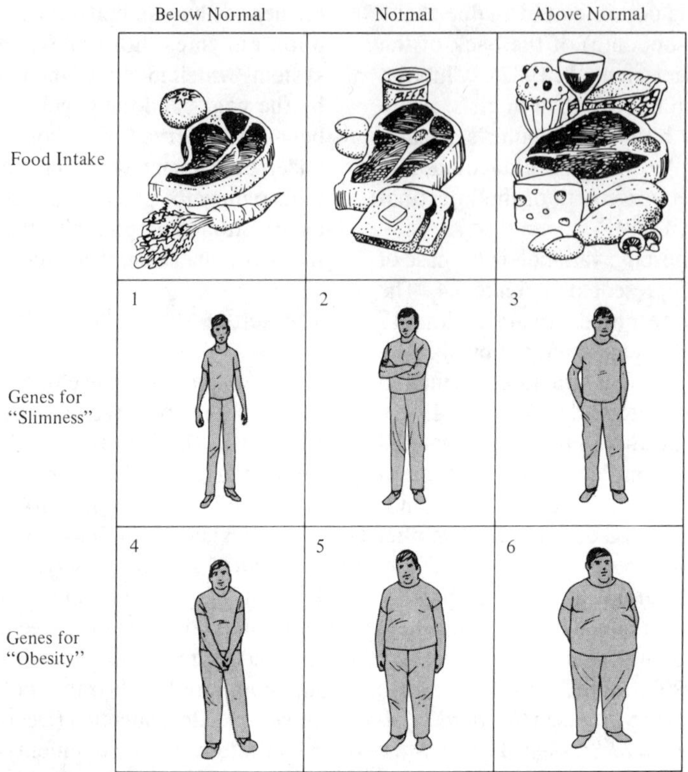

Figure 3.5 Environmental conditioning and its impact on heredity.

we can enrich it as much as we can. We can study the relative effects of heredity and environment through twin studies (identical and fraternal) and comparison with adopted children, full and half siblings, and the manipulation of the environment of such laboratory animals as mice. A study of the latter follows.

The difficulty of ascribing all behavior tendencies to either heredity or environment is well illustrated by a series of experiments by Ginsberg and Hovda (1947) on autogenetic seizures in mice. The fact that susceptibility to fatal seizures is high in some strains and low in others supports the conclusion that seizure incidence is genetically determined. However, there is scientific evidence that the incidence of seizures can be significantly altered without changing the genetic constitution.

In these studies the investigator implanted the fertilized eggs recovered from the tubes or uteri of females of one strain into the uteri of a different strain. This was accomplished by using seizure-susceptible females as donors and seizure-resistant females as hosts. In this way the genetic characteristics of the fetal rates were unaltered. Their susceptibility to fatal seizures, however, was found to be lower than that of those of their own genetic strain produced in a normal manner, but higher than that of the "foster" mothers in whose uteri they developed.

Twin Study An important way to examine heredity and environment is by the use of the correlation of many of the traits and behaviors of twins. Research has shown that the correlation of parent IQ to identical twins is .87

(Loehlin et al., 1975) when reared together. For fraternal twins, the correlation of parent IQ is .56 for twins of the same sex and .49 for twins of different sex. This information provides the fundamental rationale for why the study of twins provides insight on the effects of heredity and environment. Identical twins (monozygotic) come from one egg, whereas fraternal twins (dizygotic) come from two eggs, and are simply siblings born at the same time, although treated as identical by many parents. Although identical twins are usually raised together by their natural parents, in some cases they are separated in infancy and adopted by different families. A study of these twins reared in different environments approximates the botanist's approach to plant cuttings placed in different settings (seashore, mountains, and so on) to judge the effect of the environment. Comparing the average differences in the characteristics of identical and fraternal twins, such as performance on intelligence tests, provides important information. Whether they are reared apart or together gives insight into the relative contributions of environment and heredity to a particular trait of behavior. In the study of adopted children we see the influence of heredity; when they resemble their adoptive parents more we see the influence of environment. We can compare half and full siblings--for example, blood relationship among groups of people--to see what characteristics are shared, whether or not close relationships affect the degree of similarity for specific traits, and what environmental influences are in evidence. Studies of identical twins reared apart show these twins to be more alike than those reared together; being apart suggests they need not try to be dissimilar (Reed, 1982).

The question of nature or nurture is a false dichotomy. The question of which is the most fundamental in development depends upon how much each contributes to a given trait. If we speak of personality in general, heredity appears to be the most important element in development. If we speak of obesity, the environment plays a part with the range reaction being significant. Stern (1956) provides insight into the possibilities for viewing the range of interaction between inherited potential and environment.

According to Weinberg (1989), genetics establish a range of possibilities. Genetics not only limit but provide latitude.

MENTAL DISORDERS AND HEREDITARY LINKAGE

Schizophrenia

Schizophrenia is a common type of psychosis evidenced in individuals through perceptual difficulties such as anomalous views of reality, hyper-emotional responsiveness, and illogical thinking. Research has shown the kinship of parents to be a major determinant of schizophrenia (Kessler, 1975). Heston (1970) found the risk for this disorder to rise in direct proportion to the closeness of the genetic relationship with the affected relative. The environmental factor is also important in this situation. For this reason, some researchers in genetics (Shields, 1976) believe that genotypes for schizophrenia may not result in psychosis because of lessened penetration or because of a supportive environment. It is known that a specific genotype may express different phenotypes by alteration of the environment. It might be that a genetic predisposition is not transmitted through disease, but triggered by a stress factor.

Alcoholism

A study of alcoholism as determined by the biological relationship was carried out by Schuckit (1987). The findings of this study of half siblings suggest that the best predictor of alcoholism is having an alcoholic biological parent. Biological children are four times as likely to become alcoholics even when they are adopted soon after birth and raised by non-alcoholics. On the other hand, children of non-alcoholic parents brought up by alcoholics are not at unusual risk.

This is not to say that environment is not a contributing factor. Even when a gene or genes predispose certain traits, they do not always emerge to express themselves in penetrance (the ability of a gene to manifest itself in the phenotype of the person who carries it). Mendel's experiments produced 100 percent penetrance. If the dominant gene is expressed in only 80 percent of the individuals that possess the gene, then the penetrance is only 80 percent. Some animals (such as Asian mountain rabbits) exhibit different coloring patterns when raised outside their natural habitats (in cold rather than warm conditions).

Research in Genetics

Research is accelerating in the area of the identification of additional genetic defects; already some 2,000 have been identified (McKusick, 1986). Refining genetic screening programs is a priority, as is cloning, a process which allows an entire duplication of an animal, like the frog, from one somatic cell. Gene splicing, another developing technique, has created a strain of bacteria for producing the human growth hormone. Genetic engineering with its implications for selective and restrictive breeding of human beings will make possible some interesting future choices for society.

Undoubtedly the major emphasis is on the new field of molecular biology, barely a decade old. Already we can examine chromosomes by isolating the sequences of DNA molecules and thereby identify chemical components which help in locating those segments that parallel the gene.

Researchers have found in recombinant DNA research that the use of certain enzymes (proteins that catalyze biochemical reactions) penetrate through sequences of DNA fragments, producing microscopic DNA fragments. Using the fragments (called restriction fragment length polymorphisms, or RFLPs) the scientists can in time identify specific genes on specific chromosomes that are associated with the presence or absence of some phenotypic characteristic. These genes, called marker genes, have been found for all chromosomes (Plonin, 1987). Discoveries are continuing, such as the marker gene for Huntington's disease on chromosome 4 and some forms of schizophrenia on the A0 locus of the HLA complex on chromosome 6 (Loehlin, Willerman & Horn, 1988). As of 1989 nearly 5,000 genes have been identified. The national government has organized a 15-year study which will result in the mapping of the entire genetic landscape (termed genome) of the human being. James Watson, principal discoverer of DNA "double helix," is chairing the task force in conjunction with specialists at the National Institutes of Health and universities. The federal government is providing the basic funds which will be augmented by the private sector and many foundations. Scientists are on the threshold of being able to detect genetic problems. Beyond this they may be capable of altering genetic patterns for the betterment of humankind. Recombinant DNA techniques will result in new medicines, the manufacturing of unheard of products, and the creation of new ways of doing things. A troubling question, however, is the potential dangers that exist in the experiments. There may be changes and new life forms that we cannot now know but only imagine. Society will have to address the following issues: (1) the morality of altering genetic codes, (2) what will be controlled and who will control, (3) the legality of surrogate motherhood, (4) the moral issue of ending or continuing life, and (5) the question of artificial insemination and who should have a right to be born. If the issue of abortion alone can generate such diversity of reaction, as it has in recent years, what will result from these advances? We need the courage of awareness that our new knowledge will also produce the character needed to deal with the concomitants of ethical, legal, and societal considerations.

PRENATAL DEVELOPMENT

Conception occurs in the fallopian tube, where the sperm cell encounters the ovum. Once conception has occurred, the fertilized ovum is referred to as the *zygote*. Within a period of 24 to 36 hours after conception, cell division of the zygote takes place. Embryologists usually divide prenatal life into three periods, each with its own growth characteristics. The first period is called the germinal, or the period of the zygote.

Germinal Period

This developmental period usually occurs in the first several weeks after fertilization, the time of union of the nuclei of the two parent cells. Once conception takes place, the fertilized egg begins to divide and make its way down the fallopian tube to the uterus (Figure 3.7). The zygote usually will divide within an hour or two, and within another 10 to 12 hours these two cells will divide into four, and so on. During most of this period the ovum remains a free organism. It is not attached to the mother and does not get any sustenance from her. It does not increase in size, although important internal changes take place. During this period the task in development relates to making clusters of specialized cells. The entire sphere of cells is called a blastocyst (zygote). Some of the blastocyst cells do not become a part of the human being. The covering of the fertilized egg does not become the child, but a part of the chorion, the outside embryonic membrane, and later the placenta (Figure 3.8). The outer layer of cells of the zygote is called the trophoblast. It will develop roots with which to attach itself to the uterus and finally become the chorion. An inner mass of cells will develop from the center in the sphere; within this inner cell mass two hollow areas will be formed with a wall separating the two. The area next to the outer wall becomes the amnion, or water sac, and the other hollow area will become the yolk sac. The wall of cells between the two cavities is the embryonic disc. It is this disc that becomes the child. This is accomplished in several steps. First, the amnion encloses the embryo in a protective bag of fluid in which the developing fetus moves and later swallows. The amniotic

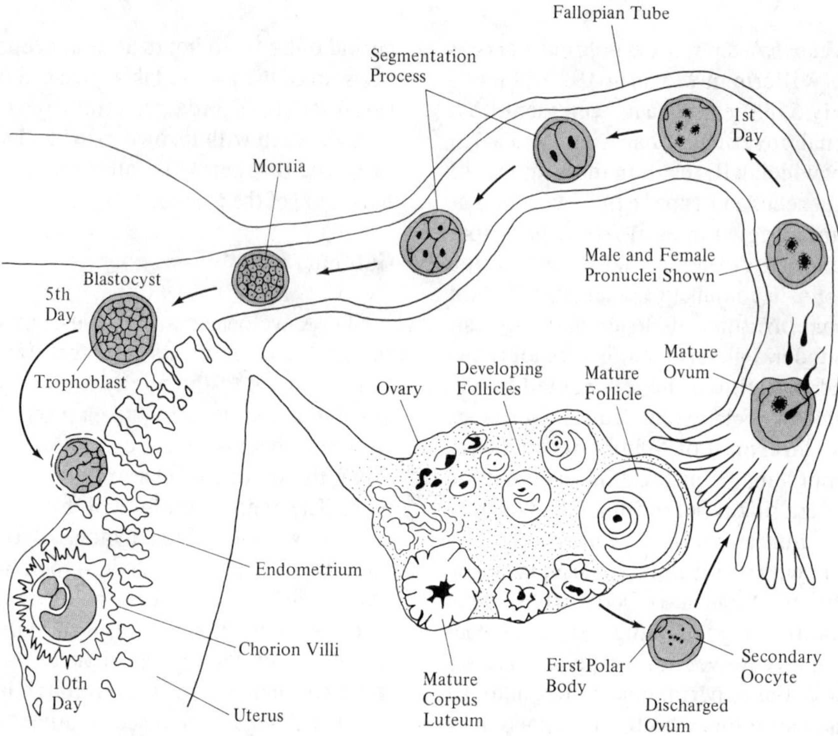

Figure 3.7 The first ten days of ovulation, fertilization, and implantation.

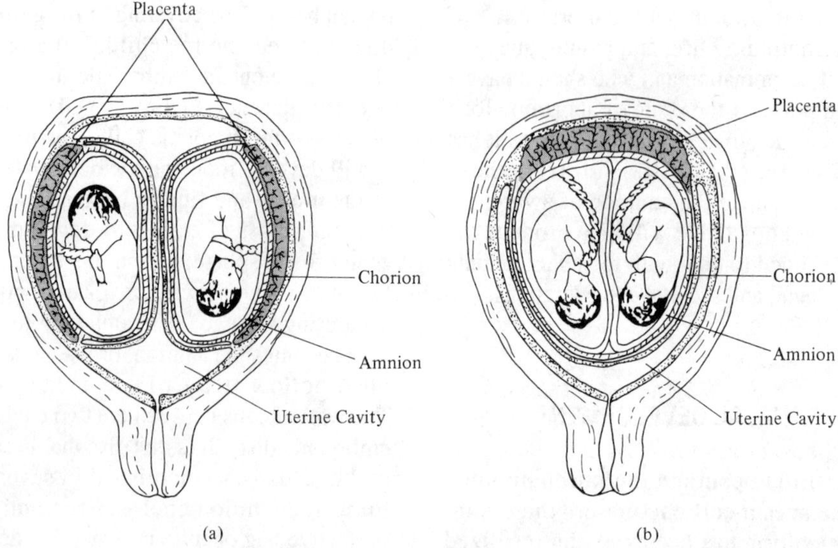

Figure 3.8 (a) Fraternal twins with separate placenta. (b) Identical twins with a common placenta.

fluid provides protection from bumps or shocks and aids in the regulation of the embryo's temperature. The amniotic and yolk sacs, along with the embryonic disc, separate from the outer layer of cells by the formation of a connecting stalk that becomes the umbilical cord. The zygote moves down the fallopian tube to the uterus in three to five days, where it attaches itself to the uterine wall. The uterus prepares in each menstruation period for the fertilized egg and is ready for implantation of the zygote. The lining is rich and thick with nourishment in its cells, and the chorion will develop a series of fine roots known as villi, which spread into the uterus lining (endometrium). These villi contain blood vessels that are connected with the fetus. Oxygen and food are received from the mother through this source, since the placenta is not completed until some time in the third month. By the eleventh day after conception, implantation is completed; the ovum is about the size of a pinhead. If the ovum fails to reach the uterus and remains in the tube, ovary, or abdominal cavity, the pregnancy is called an ectopic one. Figure 3.9 (Moore, 1988) has charted this period day by day.

the periphery. During this period organs along the central axis develop first with the extremities developing later. In the early three or four weeks the organism is all head and heart, the progression of growth is from head to foot. Descriptively, this details the time from the implantation of the ovum to the embryo's development into an obvious human fetus. It is during the early part of this period that the placenta, the umbilical cord, and the amniotic sac are formed for nourishing and protecting the embryo in preparation for birth. At full growth (seventh month, usually) the placenta is around 8 inches in diameter and 1 inch thick. A baby's brain begins to form about the second week after conception; the most critical period lasts until about the 11th week. Factors that cause birth defects during the critical first few months of pregnancy frequently result in mental retardation. During this period there is a very rapid growth in size, and the differentiation of the bodily parts is about 95 percent complete. By the end of this period a truly human being is formed that can be differentiated by the trained observer from the monkey and the other forms of mammals that may resemble humans.

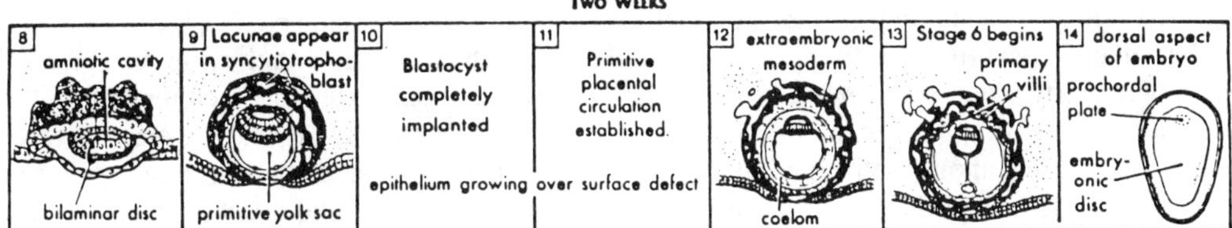

Figure 3.9 The second week scenario. (*Source:* Moore, 1988).

Embryonic Period

This period usually covers the time span of 6 weeks from approximately two weeks after conception to around 8 1/2 weeks later (see Figure 3.9). The two principles which control development in this period are proximo-distal and cephalo-caudal. Development generally progresses from the center of the body toward

However, the new life is very different in body proportions from the adult, the child, or even the newborn baby.

The placenta's fundamental purpose is to supply the growing organism with food, oxygen, and hormones, which are passed to the embryo through the placenta via the umbilical cord. There is, however, no direct circulation or neural connections between the mother and the

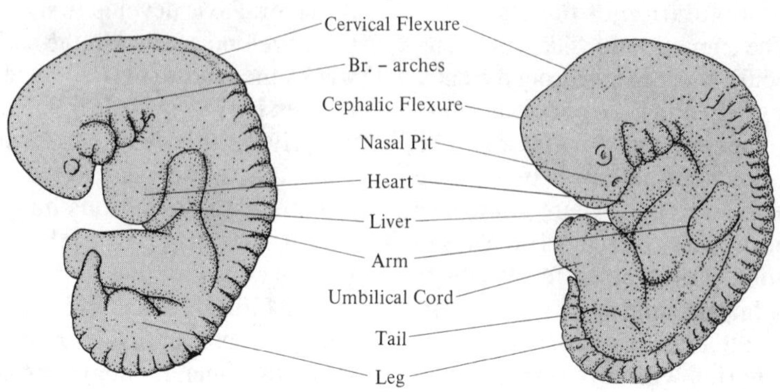

Figure 3.10 Development of body parts during embryonic period.

fetus. The placenta is a partially permeable membrane preventing intermixing of the mother's blood with the embryo. The transfer between the placenta and the embryo takes place across the web of fingerlike villi that extend into the blood spaces in the maternal uterus. Waste products are circulated back through the cord and eventually dispelled by the mother. The cord itself is a whitish rubbery tube containing one vein and two arteries. It has no nerves and at full growth is usually around three-fourths of an inch thick and 20 to 22 inches long. The blood pressure and a jelly substance (Wharton's) in the cord keep it somewhat stiff like a soft garden hose. The cord keeps itself straightened out through constantly swimming about in the amniotic fluid. Because of this it is unlikely the growing baby will be choked.

By 18 days the embryo has begun to take shape. The heart, at this period a single tube, begins to beat at around 25 days, though at this point there is no blood to circulate. Its operation becomes much more regular and smooth after several months. The nervous system by this time has started to develop, beginning with a neural plate and groove and eventually forming a tube with two projections for the brain. The brain and spinal cord develop in order to provide control and a monitoring system for the growing organism. During this period of development the body parts are 95 percent complete, although at the one-month stage the embryo is only about one-fifth of an inch long or half the size of a green pea. The mother may not recognize that she is pregnant. Although her menstrual cycle is behind by two or more weeks, she has no discomfort.

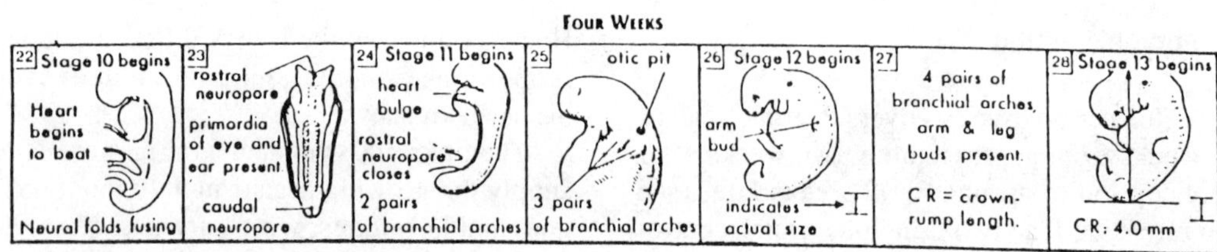

Figure 3.11 The fourth week scenario. (*Source:* Moore, 1988).

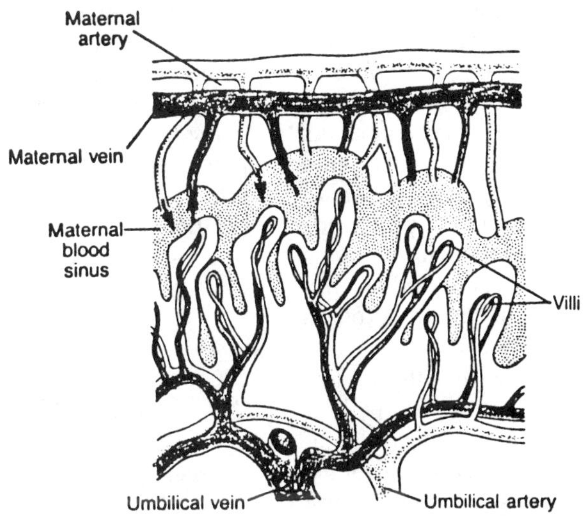

Figure 3.12 Diagram of placental circulation. Note that maternal and fetal circulations are completely separate.

By 2 1/2 months, all the basic buds for teeth are made. The stomach, intestines, pharynx, lungs, and organs of elimination and sex are in evidence. The ductless glands (endocrine glands) take shape, and some begin to function, such as the adrenal medulla, which secretes epinephrine, and the testes in the male, which begin to emit androgen. The end of the embryonic period is marked by the development of bones that begin to replace cartilaginous materials and can be differentiated from those of infrahumans or other chordates. This represents the most critical period in the pregnancy for a mother and her embryo. Most abortions, natural or induced, take place during this period. Many disturbances occur in the first two months of development and, significantly, at a time mothers are least aware of imbalances. This point will be discussed later in this chapter.

Fetal Period

Most mothers reach the initial part of this period simultaneously with a visit to a physician to verify their suspected pregnancy. By the end of the third month, the genitals are clearly defined in the fetus and the muscles of the arms and legs are capable of responding to tactile stimulation.

Bones are beginning to take the place of cartilage around the jaw, cheeks, and nose, giving greater shape to the head. The fetus becomes more active at this time, becoming able to turn the head, bend the arms, close the hand, and make a strong fist. These movements cannot be felt by the mother, but by the third month the fetus is 3 inches long and weighs 7/8 ounces. The fourth month finds the fetus increasing its length to over 6 inches on the average, and increasing its weight to about 4 ounces. It is during this time that the first observable movements of the fetus will be noticed by the mother. The toes and fingers have separated, with the curls and patterns emerging on the fingertips that mark the uniqueness of the individual at this early age.

By the fifth month the fetus has established regular periods of sleep and has discovered a favorite position. Hair begins to grow on the head, the sucking reflex is present, and the heartbeat is regular and strong enough to be heard by the physician through a stethoscope via the mother's abdomen. In the sixth month the fetus opens its eyes, and the skin becomes covered with a whitish, oily, fatty substance called vernix caseosa, designed to protect the skin from the long immersion in the amniotic fluid. The fetus during this period usually weighs around 2 pounds and is over a foot in length.

Sometimes birth takes place in the seventh month. The chance for survival in such births is about one in two, depending upon the ability of the nervous system to effectively control the vital organs and functions of the body. The control of the concentration of oxygen through use of an *isolette* is indicated for the prevention of blindness due to retrolental fibroplasia (a high concentration of oxygen causes spasms of the retinal vessels) and as a precaution against infections (Marlow, 1988). The myth exists that the seven-month-old fetus is better off than the eight-month-old. Obviously, the maturity attained with an additional month is significant, improving the chances of normal birth to about 90 percent (McCary, 1973, p. 115). During the final two months the fetus puts on 4 to 5 pounds on the average. In the eighth month the development of nearly all the organic systems is completed, and the downlike hair that has covered the fetus begins to disappear. From 36 weeks until birth, 99 percent of infants born will survive. The birth date of a child can generally be computed by adding 280 days to the date of the last menstruation start or 266 days within the mother's body.

Nearly three-fourths of all babies are born within one week on either side of that date (Schifferes, 1970, p. 315). Women who are very athletic usually deliver 20 days earlier than their opposites, and brunettes deliver a few days sooner than blondes. Girls are born five to nine days earlier than boys (McCary, 1973). The extremes in weight that have survived range from 26 pounds to 1 1/2 pounds. Very large infants must usually be delivered by Caesarean section. The usual birth position is longitudinal (99 percent), and most births are cephalic (head presentation), with some 4 percent breech presentation. If the fetus lies crosswise with arm or shoulder entering the birth canal, the position must be altered or Caesarean section performed. This occurs in about 1 out of 200 cases.

PRENATAL INFLUENCES

Many factors and conditions present during the mother's pregnancy can have an adverse effect on the developing offspring. These factors have frequently been confused with hereditary factors; it is not possible to draw a clear line of demarcation between the operation of heredity and environment, especially during the prenatal life of the organism. Detecting the cause of birth defects and of prenatal and natal birth injuries has become a promising field of medical research. Discoveries have shown that there is much the expectant mother can do to improve her chances of having a healthy, normal baby with an undamaged brain. Obstetricians have within their power the prevention of many crippling conditions if they can care for the expectant mother during this period.

Fetology--Diagnosis of Defects and Assistance in the Prenatal Period

Fetology, the new branch of medical science dealing with the fetus, is developing techniques for diagnosing and treating fetal imperfections, making it possible to prevent many birth defects and to ensure normal response in the infant. It is possible through amniocentesis (Figure 3.13) to draw off amniotic fluid during the first three months, grow cells from the fluid in a tissue culture, and upon analysis discover genetic defects such as Down's syndrome. This is done

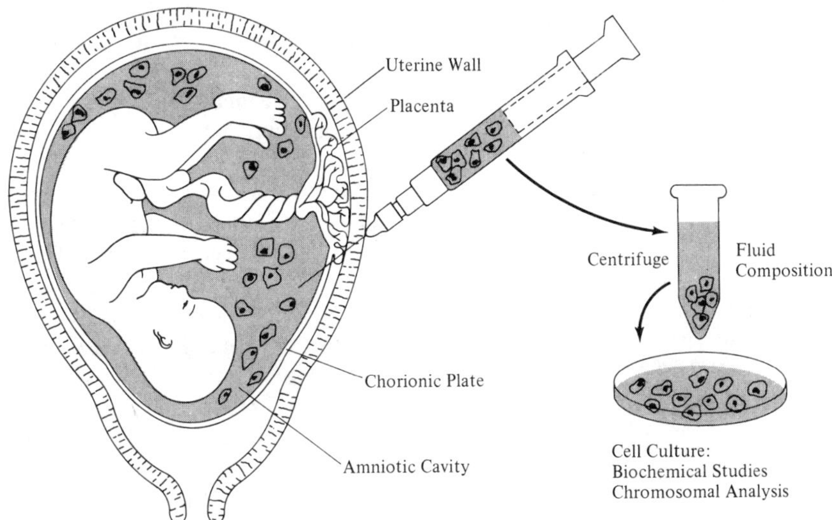

Figure 3.13 Amniocentesis.

usually in the 15th or 16th week of pregnancy and it is recommended for women over 35 if they and their partner are known carriers of Tay Sachs disease, sickle-cell disease, or other maladies such as Rh factor, spina bifida, and muscular dystrophy. The sex of the baby and important indicators of sex-linked defects such as hemophilia can also be determined. Fetal surgery is performed by insertion of a catheter into the fetus through the mother's abdomen and uterus, allowing corrective measures to be taken and observations made.

Ultrasound is a procedure utilizing high-frequency sound waves directed to the abdomen of the woman. It is used to judge the progress in development of the fetus, i.e. detect gross structural abnormalities, evaluate uterine problems, find whether a fetus has died, and act as a guide in connection with amniocentesis. The sound waves can yield a sonogram showing the placenta, fetus, and uterus. Still another procedure is the chorionic villi sampling. In this test tissue is taken from the end of the hair-like villi of the membrane around the embryo that are made up of rapidly developing fetal cells and tested for the presence of various conditions. It can be performed in the first trimester and results can be known in a week. Maternal blood tests performed from the 14th to the 20th week can ascertain the amount of alpha fetoprotein (AFP) it contains. Low levels of AFP have been associated with Down's syndrome and high levels have indicated for women with risks for spina bifida and anencephaly that further investigation through amniocentesis or other screen be applied. Electronic fetal monitoring is most often used to check up on the labor and delivery of the baby. This approach provides valuable information during high-risk births, premature deliveries, and fetal distress. Routine use is likely to result in Caesarean delivery without improved prognosis; hence, continuous routine use is contraindicated with pregnancies that are seemingly uncomplicated.

Maternal Age

The optimal age of the mother for the development of the offspring is the period of the 20s. Crippling conditions, unhealthy states, and the mortality rate rise sharply as mothers deviate in age from this optimal range. In younger and older women, the reproductive system is often inadequate, so that the functional ability of the system is problematic. The natural fertility of a woman decreases with age, as noted in Table 3.3.

Table 3.3 Fertility and Age

Age	Rating
20-24*	100
25-29	93
30-34	85
35-39	69
40-44	35
45-49	5

*Highest assignment. Rating of 100 represents most optimal time for fertility. Source: Henry (1961).

Emotional State of Mother

That the emotional state of the mother may have significant influences on the child during the prenatal period is borne out by a number of studies. Sontag (1950) indicates that babies born to mothers suffering from emotional disturbances tend to have more difficulties in the weeks following birth, including gastrointestinal upsets and other illnesses. In addition, infants of mothers who were emotionally disturbed during pregnancy frequently exhibit behavior characteristics of an irritable and hyperactive autonomic nervous system. Sontag points out that feeding difficulties of a motor or secretory nature present from birth have their origin in basic disturbances during intrauterine life. Anxiety among pregnant women is inevitable, however, and seldom harmful.

Malnutrition

Malnutrition of the mother deprives the fetal organism of necessary food in the maternal bloodstream; the effects are worst in the last trimester of pregnancy. The effects of this were shown in studies reported by the Milbank Memorial Fund (1962) comparing the offspring of 120 pregnant women on a poor diet with 90 pregnant women of the same socio-economic status on a good diet during the last four months of their pregnancies. In every comparison the mothers and their babies who were on a good diet did better than the mothers and their babies who were on a poor diet. The results set forth in Table 3.4 show that an inadequate diet seriously interfered with the efficiency of the pregnant mother as well as the welfare and development of the fetus. Malformations including congenital blindness and other visual abnormalities frequently appear where the mother's diet is deficient in carotene and vitamins. Control of weight is important in preventing unnecessary complications in delivery, backaches and pains, and retention of toxic body wastes. Weight gain during pregnancy runs from 15 to 40 pounds. A gain of 15 pounds is divided as follows: baby 7, afterbirth 1, amniotic fluid 1/2, increases in uterus 2, blood 3, weight of breasts 1 1/2 (Janda and Hamel, 1980). These findings have expanded on the earlier studies by Naeye (1979) and Brody (1970). Weight gain recommendations are usually individualized; many physicians suggest gains between 20 and 28 pounds for the typical pregnant woman.

One major purpose of prenatal care is to check for the likelihood of toxemia and other complications and to prevent them if possible. The maternity and infant legislation enacted in 1963 and revised in later years has done much to reduce crippling conditions that originate during the prenatal period among poverty-stricken families. Teratogenic agents are any substance, environmental circumstance, or inherited condition that cause a change in the genetic code. These agents affect genes and the production of protein. Susceptibility is highest during the embryo period. Table 3.5 suggests some of these agents.

Infections and Viruses

Growth in recognition that maternal virus infection can damage the fetus is one of the

Table 3.4 COMPARISON OF THE EFFECTS FOR EXPECTANT MOTHERS WITH A POOR AND GOOD DIET

		Diet	
		Poor	Good
Prenatal maternal record	Poor–Bad	36.0%	9.0%
Condition during labor	Poor–Bad	24.0%	3.0%
Duration of the first stage of labor	Primapara	20.3 hr	11.1 hr
	Multipara	15.2 hr	9.5 hr
Convalescence	Poor–Bad	11.5%	3.5%
Record of babies during first 2 weeks	Poor–Bad	14.0%	0.0%
Illness of babies during first 6 months			
Frequent colds		21.0%	4.7%
Bronchitis		4.2%	1.5%
Pneumonia	5.5%	1.5%	
Rickets	5.5%	0.0%	
Tetany	4.2%	0.0%	
Dystrophy	7.0%	1.5%	
Anemia		25.0%	9.4%
Deaths		3.0%	0.0%
Miscarriages and infant deaths			
Miscarriages		7.0%	0.0%
Stillbirths		4.0%	0.0%
Deaths			
Pneumonia		2.0%	0.0%
Prematurity		1.0%	0.0%
Prematures		9.0%	2.0%

Source: Milbank Memorial Fund Quarterly (1962, pp. 35–36).

dramatic developments of the mid-century. The fetus does not develop antibodies, and immunization does not become active until some time after birth. Interest in maternal viral infection has been acute since it was first demonstrated that German measles in the mother during the early months of pregnancy can result in malformation and mental defect in the fetus. According to Nash (1970), if the mother contracts rubella (German measles) during the first three months of pregnancy, the chances are that she will give birth to a congenitally defective child. Contraction of rubella in the later stages of pregnancy will not have such pernicious effects. Immunization against rubella is now possible, but it must be done three months before the beginning of pregnancy. Also, smallpox, chicken pox, mumps, scarlet fever, erysipelas, and recurrent fever in the pregnant mother can have a deleterious effect upon the developing fetus.

Infection from the parent, especially syphilis (after the 18th week of life) in its active phase, affects the fetal nervous system, although the results of such an infectious condition may not become apparent until some time after birth. There are thought to be 1.2 to 1.5 million untreated cases of syphilis in the United States. A wasting disease in the mother such as cancer or tuberculosis may deny the fetus necessary food. Maternal toxemia and/or eclampsia (attack of convulsions) may cause insufficient oxygen in the blood (anoxia) of the infant. There is no known cause in at least half the cases of all children born each year with birth defects and with brain damage.

AIDS (Acquired Immune Deficiency Syndrome)

Women who are exposed to the AIDS virus are at risk in giving the disease to children. The blood of the mother is shared through the placenta with the fetus and blood acting as a transmitter of the virus. The abnormalities accompanying the virus in children are small heads, big eyes, protruding lips, short and flat noses. The disease weakens the immune system of the victims and makes them prey to a number of infections and forms of cancer (Iosub et al., 1987). Women who are intravenous drug users, particularly those who share needles with others, are at risk to get AIDS. Over half of the abnormalities are in the head and face suggesting, since the craniofacial structures are developed in the first trimester, the abnormal feature is generated by the virus early in fetal life. Genital herpes is a growing cause of concern due to the difficulty of controlling some forms of this malady. Infants delivered through an infected birth canal stand some chance of getting the disease. A large number die and others are subject to brain damage. Delivery by Caesarean section is an attempt to counter the problem. Miscarriage often accompanies genital herpes.

Drugs

In addition to diseases that are closely related to birth defects, many drugs may be harmful to the fetus. At one time it was thought that the placenta--the organ that forms inside the uterus to nourish the unborn infant--filtered out infectious agents, drugs, and other substances that could harm the unborn child. It is now known that injurious as well as nourishing substances can pass through the placenta into the developing child. Some of these materials, especially certain viruses and drugs, have far greater effect on the immature tissues of the unborn child than they do on the mother (Beck, 1968).

The terrible effects of thalidomide in 1961 and 1962 alarmed the medical profession about the possible dangers of other drugs and medicines. Mothers, mostly in England and Germany, who had used the drug as a tranquilizer from the 34th to the 46th day of pregnancy, gave birth to 8,000 deformed babies (Schardein, 1976). More recent research suggests ulterior

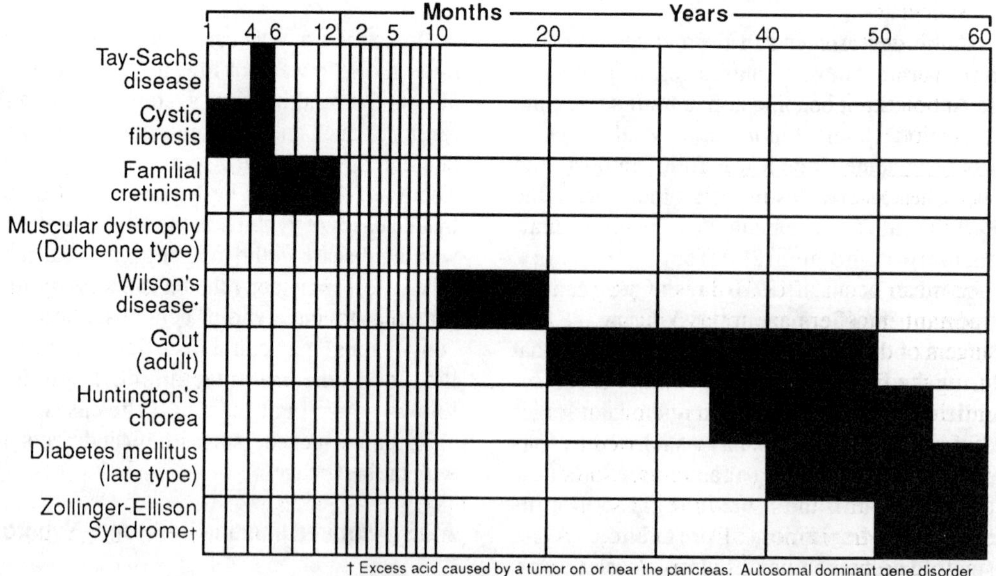

Figure 3.14 Selected genetic problems and their time frame.

Table 3.5 SUBSTANCES--HAZARDOUS AND NON-HAZARDOUS

DRUG	CLINICAL FINDINGS
Alcohol	Fetal alcohol syndrome
Accutane (Isotretinoin)	
Hormones	
Androgens	Labial fusion and clitoral hypertrophy
Folic acid antagonists	
(aminopterin, methotrexate)	Cranial and skeletal abnormalities; microcephaly
Anticoagulants (Coumadin)	Nasal hypoplasia; fetal hemorrhage; stippled epiphyses; psychomotor delay
Anticonvulsants	
Dilantin	Fetal hydantoin syndrome
Tridlone	Craniofacial abnormalities
Thalidomide	Craniofacial, skeletal (limbs), and cardiac abnormalities
Diethylstilbestrol	Genital cancer
Estrogens/progestins	VACTERL syndrome
Amphetamines	Cardiac malformations
Lithium	Cardiac malformations
No Evidence of Teratogenic Effect:	
Salicylates	
Antihistamines	
Heparin	
Antibiotics (penicillins, sulfonamides)	
Narcotics	

Adapted from Knuppel, Drukker, 1986

effects can occur after 21 days of pregnancy. Pregnant mothers are today warned of the dangers of drugs as simple as aspirin, especially during the first three months of pregnancy. In addition, after three months of pregnancy, alcohol and addictive narcotics carried by the mother are transferred to the fetus. Some affected newborn babies show the classic symptoms of withdrawal not unlike adult alcoholics and drug addicts. Even excessive use of vitamins (A, B^6, C, D, and K) is suspected to be detrimental to the growing embryo, the same as some antibiotics, depressants, and hormones (Brody, 1973). Obviously, the physician's advice is the safest guideline.

Radiation and Rh Influences

Radiation has been found to be an important influence on offspring (Yamazaki et al., 1954), particularly when an expectant mother is exposed to X-rays during the first several weeks of conception between the fertilization period and attachment of the ovum to the uterus through the embryonic period (sixth week). Brain damage, mutations, and certain cancers can result. Physicians using X-rays on pelvic or abdominal regions of women should do so only when pregnancy is not in evidence (Apgar & Beck, 1974). The effects of the atom bombing in the Hiroshima and Nagasaki areas during World War II have revealed considerable incidence of skin cancers, leukemia, and other diseases. Women who watch a video display over 20 hours per week have twice the rate of miscarriage in the first trimester than women doing other kinds of office work (Goldhaber, et al., in Altman, 1988).

The Rh factors, so named because they were first discovered in the blood of a rhesus monkey, may produce an incompatibility in the blood of the mother and child. Berrill (1968) says 85 percent of whites and 92 percent of blacks have the Rh substance (Ziegel et al., 1972, pp. 725-726). About 16 percent of mothers in Western societies are believed to be Rh negative. The mating of an Rh positive male with an Rh negative female occurs about 12 times in 100, but not all offspring will have hemolytic disease (Ziegel). When a mother with no Rh factors (Rh negative) has a baby who has Rh factors (Rh positive), a substance from the baby stimulates the development of a substance in the mother that, in time, may act upon the blood cells of the baby and prevent them from distributing sufficient oxygen. This deprivation of oxygen leads to an alteration of the infant's development. The Rh disease has been found in about 1 in every 105 to 200 full-term deliveries. However, medical advancements have virtually eliminated this as a factor producing brain damage or other damaging conditions when adequate services and safeguards are provided. A serum (Rho GAM), has been developed to prevent the production of antibodies in mothers who have not already formed antibodies. If a child with the Rh factor is born anemic, an exchange transfusion can be given to remove sensitized blood.

Smoking

Among drugs found in clinical and animal studies to retard physical growth, one that has received attention because it is so widespread is nicotine. It has been noted that high incidences of premature birth, spontaneous abortion, and low birth weight accompany heavy smoking of mothers during pregnancy. Smith (1975) attributes low birth weight to nicotine, as it constricts the blood vessels in the uterus, cutting the amount of blood supply and nourishment to the placenta.

Yerushalmy, however, studying 18,000 women under the aegis of the National Institute of Health, found that although many smoking women bore low-weight babies, they also bore low-weight babies before they began to smoke. But a surprising revelation was that smoking mothers had substantially fewer perinatal stillbirths or dead babies within the first month of the final semester (Goodall, 1972, p. 25). Among mothers who smoked during pregnancy, their children when aged 4 to 11 were more hyperactive, had poor attention spans, had problems in reading, experienced difficulty with math perceptual skills, and had poor social adjustment. Such children were more often than normal diagnosed as having minimal brain damage (Naeye & Peters, 1984).

SUMMARY

The development of the individual begins with the fertilized egg, which consists of 46 chromosomes, 23 from the male and 23 from the female. The chromosomes are most important in that they furnish the blueprint and the means by which potentialities are transmitted. Abnormalities of the chromosomes are the bases of many disorders and anomalies. The genes of a special pair of chromosomes determine the sex of the individual: a fertilized egg that receives a Y chromosome from the sperm produces a male baby, while a fertilized egg that receives an X chromosome from the sperm produces a female baby. Males have X and Y chromosomes while women have only X and therefore there are no uniquely female transmitted diseases. Methods of getting pregnant and having children are accomplished through the traditional manner, or by less traditional means such as a donor, surrogate motherhood, artificial insemination, and adoption.

The first law of heredity is that of segregation. In polygenetic inheritance the trait appears to be determined by multiple genes. Mendel's discovery of dominant and recessive traits led to further discoveries, including the law of linkage. More recent studies have shown that genes are not unalterable, indicating that environmental factors may operate from the time of the fertilization of the egg cell. The rate and pattern of growth can be altered at all stages of life. These alterations may result from (1) the interaction of the genes, (2) chemical imbalance in the mother during pregnancy, (3) interference with fetal development, (4) brain damage, (5) prenatal accidents, (6) accidents at birth, and (7) an environment unfavorable to optimum growth and development.

The chief importance of the chromosomes is that they provide the means by which potentialities are transmitted, for it is in the chromosomes that the genes are found, and these furnish the basic hereditary materials. A gene is a small region in a chromosome composed of a giant nucleic acid molecule or part of a molecule, which consists mainly of deoxyribonucleic acid, or DNA, containing four nucleotides held together in varying sequences by twisting sugar-phosphate strands. These four bases in various combinations are capable of encoding all the characteristics that an organ transmits from one generation to another. In some organisms there may be more or less than 46 chromosomes, as with Down's syndrome or an XXY sex-linked aberration. These are due to abnormal chromosome development in the ovaries or in the sperm, and result in many disorders in children.

The prenatal period and infancy provide the foundation for subsequent development. Embryologists divide prenatal life into three periods: germinal, embryonic, and fetal. Some 2 to 3 percent of expectant mothers in the United States receive no prenatal care; the most obvious effect of this is the probability that the offspring will be born prematurely or that other troubles will ensue. The pre-term and low weight baby is much more vulnerable to difficulties than the full-term. Many factors and conditions present during the mother's pregnancy can have an adverse effect on the developing fetus; these include (1) the emotional status of the mother, (2) malnutrition, (3) infection, (4) drugs, (5) radiation and Rh influence, (6) smoking, (7) position, (8) glandular factors, (9) age of the mother, and (10) genetic anomalies.

Research in the use of recombinant DNA is mapping the genome and already 5,000 have been identified. Help for modifying defective genes is already being accomplished. Genetic counseling, the use of ultrasound, amniocentesis, and chorionic villi sampling are improving our knowledge and effecting a better life for many infants.

KEY TERMS

amniocentesis

ultrasound

chorionic villi sampling

karyotype

dominance

recessive

in-vitro fertilization

fetoscopy

blastocyte

germinal disc

embryonic

fetal

mendelian laws

genotype

phenotype

anoxia

Apgar scale

phenylketonuria

Caesarian delivery

isolette

vernix caseosa

teratogenic

chromosome

gene

range of reaction

labor

afterbirth

Turner's syndrome

Klinefelter syndrome

Down's syndrome

REFERENCES

Apgar, V. A proposal for a new method of evaluation of the newborn infant. *Anesthesia and Analgesia*, 1953, *32*:260-267.

Apgar, V., and Beck, J. *Is My Baby All Right?* New York: Pocket Books, 1974.

Beck, J. Guarding the unborn. *Today's Health*, 1968, *46*:38-41.

Berrill, N.J. *The Person in the Womb*. New York: Dodd Mead, 1968.

British Medical Journal. Medical research council report: 1961. 1963.

Brody, M.E. How a mother affects her unborn baby. *Woman's Day*, 1970, *33*:12.

_____. Most pregnant women found taking excess drugs. *The New York Times*, March 18, 1973.

Dennis, W. Causes of retardation among institutional children: Iran. *Journal of Genetic Psychology*, 1960.

Ebbs, J.H., Brown, A., Tisdall, F.F., and Scott, W.A. *The Milbank Memorial Fund Quarterly*, 1942, *20*:35-36.

Ehrman, L., and Probber, J. *Fundamentals of genetics and evolutionary theories in behavior genetics.* In J.L. Fuller. Hillsdale, NJ: Lawrence Erlbaum Assoc., 1983, Chapter 3, 1-32.

Emery, A.E.H. *Elements of Medical Genetics*, 4th ed. Berkeley: University of California Press, 1975.

Francoeur, R.T. Reproductive technologies: New alternatives and new ethics. *SIECUS Report*, 1985, *14*:1-5.

Frankenberg, W.K., and Dodds, J.R. The Denver Developmental Screen Test. *Pediatrics*, 1967, *71*:181-191.

Ginsberg, B.E., and Hovda, R.B. On the physiology of gene-controlled audiogenic seizures in mice. *Anatomical Record*, 1947, *99*:65-66.

Glass, B. Evolution in human hands. *Phi Delta Kappan*, 1969, *50*:506-510.

Goodall, K. One rap removed from smoking--maybe. *Psychology Today*, 1972, *5*(10):25.

Goldhaber, in Altman, L.K. Pregnant women's use of VDTs scrutinized. *The New York Times*, June 5, 1988, p.22.

Henry, L. *Eugenics Quarterly*, 1961, *8*:81-91.

Heston, L.L. The genetics of schizophrenic and schizoid disease. *Science*, 1970, *167*:249-256.

Iosub, S., et al. More on human immunodeficiency virus embryopathy. *Pediatrics*, 1987, *80*:512-516.

Janda, L.M., and Hamel, K. *Human Sexuality*. New York: Van Nostrand, 1980.

Jost, H., and Sontag, L.W. The genetic factor in autonomous nervous system function. *Psychosomatic Medicine*, 1944, *6*:308-310.

Kang, E.S. The genetic basis of some abnormalities in children. *Children*, 1966, *13*(2):6-62.

Kennedy, W.A. *Child Psychology*. Englewood Cliffs, NJ: Prentice-Hall, 1971.

Kessler, S. Psychiatric genetics. In D.A. Hamburg and K. Brodie (eds.), *American Handbook of Psychiatry*, vol. VI: *New Psychiatric Frontiers*. New York: Basic Books, 1974, pp. 352-384.

Knuppel, R.A., and Drukker, J.E. *High Risk Pregnancy: A Team Approach*. Philadelphia: W.B. Saunders, 1986.

Kolata, G.B. Manic-depression: Is it inherited? *Science*, 1986, *232*:575-576.

Kornberg, A. The synthesis of DNA. *Scientific American*, 1968, *219*:68-69.

Kraemer, H.C., et al. Obstetric drugs and infant behavior. *Journal of Pediatric Psychology*, 1985, *10*:345-353.

Leichtman, L.A. A conversation with the Director of the Genetic Division, Medical College of Hampton Roads, Norfolk, Virginia Convention, July 27, 1990.

Lewis, E.B. *Science*, December 13, 1963.

Loehlin, J., Willerman, L., and Horn, J. Human behavior genetics. *Annual Review of Psychology*, 1988, *39*:105-133.

Loehlin, J., Gardner, L., and Spuhlery, J. *Race differences in intelligence*. San Francisco: Freeman, 1975.

Lyght, C.E. (ed.) *The Merck Manual of Diagnosis and Therapy*, 11th ed.Merck, Sharpe and Dohme Research Laboratories, 1966.

Marlow, D.R. *Pediatric Nursing*. Philadelphia: Saunders, 1973, pp. 112-123.

_____. *Pediatric Nursing*. Philadelphia: Saunders, 1988, p. 41.

Maziade, M., Boudreault, M., Cote, R., and Thivierge, J. Influence of genetic birth procedures and other circumstances on infant temperament. *Journal of Pediatrics*, 1986, *108*(1):134-136.

McCary, J.L. *Human Sexuality*. New York: Van Nostrand, 1973.

McCauley, E., Kay, T., Ito, J., and Treder, R. *The Gene Hunt*, 1987.

McKusick, V.A. *Mendelian Inheritance in Man*, 7th ed. Baltimore, MD: Johns Hopkins University Press, 1986.

Mertens, T. *Human Genetics*. New York: Wiley, 1975.

Milbank Memorial Fund Quarterly, January 1962, p. 20.

Montagu, A. *Human Heredity*, 2nd ed. Cleveland: World, 1963.

Moore, K.L. *The Developing Human: Clinically Oriented Embryology,* 4th ed.Philadelphia: W.B. Saunders, 1988.

Naeye, R.L. Weight gain and the outcome of pregnancy. *American Journal of Obstetrics and Gynecology*, 1979, *135*(3).

Naeye, R.L., and Peters, E.C. Mental development and children whose mothers smoked during pregnancy. *Obstetrics & Gynecology*, 1984, *64*:601.

Nash, J. *Developmental Psychology*. Englewood Cliffs, NJ: Prentice-Hall, 1970.

National Centers for Disease Control. Press release on breast feeding. March 22, 1984.

National Foundation, March of Dimes, 1973.

National Institute of General Medical Sciences. *What Are the Facts About Genetic Disease?* Washington, DC: U.S. Government Printing Office, 1975.

National Institute of Health. Conversation with Dr. Paul Maton, Clinical Center, Bethesda, MD. June, 1990.

Nielsen, J., Krag-Olsen, B., Dirdal, M., Holm, V., Hadhr, J., Rasmussen, N., Videbech, P., and Yaregiswa, S. Chromosome abnormalities in children in two Danish counties, born during 1967-1978. *Heridatas*, 1982, pp. 209-210.

Omenn, G.S. Prenatal diagnosis of genetic disorders. *Science*, 1978, *200*:952-958.

Pennington, B.F., Bender, B., and Puck, M., et al. Learning disabilities in children with sex chromosome anomalies. *Child Development*, 1982, *53*:1182-1192.

Plonin, R. Environment and genes: Determinants of behavior. *American Psychologist*, 1989, *44*:105-111.

_____. Developmental genetics and infancy. In J.D. Osofy (ed.), *Handbook of Infant Development*, 2nd ed. New York: John Wiley, 1987.

Polani, P.E., Briggs, J.H., Ford, C.E., Clark, C.N., and Berg, J.M. A mongol girl with 46 chromosomes. *Lancet*, 1960, *1*:1721-1722.

Reed, S.C. A survey of identical twins reared apart. *The Journal of Heredity*, 1982, *73*(4).

Schardein, J.L. *Drugs on teratogens.* Cleveland, OH: Chemical Rubber Co. Press, 1976.

Schifferes, J.J. *Healthier Living*, 3rd ed. New York: Wiley, 1970.

Schuckit, M. Biological vulnerability to alcoholism. *Journal of Consulting and Clinical Psychology*, 1987, *53*(3):301-309.

Schuckit, M., Goodwin, D., and Winokur, G. A study of alcoholism in half siblings. *American Journal of Psychiatry*, 1972, *128*(9):1132-1135.

Shields, J. Genetics in schizophrenia. In D. Kemalie, G. Bartholini, and Richter (eds.), *Schizophrenia Today*. New York: Pergamon, 1976.

Snyder, A., Freifelder, D., and Hartl, A.L. *General Genetics.* Boston: Jones and Barlett, 1985.

Sontag, L.W. The genetics of differences in psychosomatic patterns in childhood. *American Journal of Orthopsychiatry*, 1950, *20*:479-489.

Watson, J.D. *The Double Helix*. New York: Atheneum, 1968.

Weinberg, R. Intelligence and IQ. *American Psychologist*, 1989, *44*:98-104.

Yamazaki, I.N., et al. Outcome of pregnancy in women exposed to the atomic bomb in Nagasaki. *American Journal of Diseases in Children*, 1954, *87*:448-463.

Ziegel, E., Blarcom, V., and Conant, C. *Obstetric Nursing*, 6th ed. New York: Macmillan, 1972.

Chapter 4

BIRTH AND NEONATAL LIFE: DELIVERY, PROGNOSIS, MOTOR AND SENSORY RESPONSES

- ***Phases in Birth Labor***
  - Head moves to the cervix
  - Crowning
  - Afterbirth

- ***Types of Labor***
  - Breech
  - Caesarean
  - Medicated
  - Natural
  - Gentle birth

- ***Setting for Birth***
  - Birthing center
  - Hospital
  - Midwife nurse at home

- ***Premature Infants--Outcomes and Effects***
  - Low weight--prognosis
  - Socio-economic status and child-bearing

- ***Early Response***
  - Motor activity and the neurological
  - Emotional responses
  - Reflexes--blinking, ocular, tonic neck, moro, grasping, startle and gagging

- ***Sensory Responses***
  - Auditory, sleep, smiling, taste and smell, vision, nursing and suckling
  - Differences in activity and sensitivity

BIRTH AND NEONATAL LIFE: DELIVERY, PROGNOSIS, MOTOR AND SENSORY RESPONSES

There is at the present time no sure way to determine the trigger which precipitates labor. There are events that may suggest a correlation but causation cannot be proved for what provides the impetus for the beginning of labor. Many Jewish women find labor often begins after a 24-hour fast associated with Yom Kippur holy day. Less blood flow, due to the lack of food, perhaps causes the uterus to contract, and it may be that blood flow decreases just before labor begins. Fetus and uterus size may be connected. As an example, twins come earlier than singletons, and triplet and quadruplets come even earlier. One idea suggests urine from the fetus stimulates the action of the prostaglandins (hormones related to a number of body functions) which may initiate birth labor. Some substance released into the urine of the fetus might be the alarming stimulus. Perhaps even the placenta is genetically programmed to begin the labor. It is a mystery how this momentous event occurs.

In this chapter we will discuss the types of birth deliveries along with the process of birth beginning with the muscle contractions which force the head or buttocks downward and outward. The setting for giving birth will be reviewed, whether through the use of a midwife in the home or a birthing center. The length of the term in carrying the fetus will be examined as to its effect on development and prognosis for normal growth. A discussion of early responses will be presented as they are important as developmental milestones that lead to neurological and motor control coordination. Finally, the various kinds of sensory responses evidenced in the early days following birth are noted.

Birth

The process of birth is frequently referred to as a traumatic event. This viewpoint is hardly in line with careful observations of the reactions and behavior of newborn infants. As the fetus nears full term, the supply of oxygen within the mother's womb becomes progressively less adequate for the fetus's needs. Intrauterine life becomes more intolerable because of the limited space and oxygen, and the constant threat of asphyxiation. Birth furnishes the neonate an opportunity to breathe a greater supply of oxygen, stimulate the development of the sense organs, and make use of developing muscles. Birth makes it possible for mental growth to take place at an accelerated pace.

Leboyer (1975) believes birth is a traumatic experience amid the noise, arc lights, and bustle of the delivery room. He suggests that the lights should be dimmed, the neonates bathed immediately in warm water, and placed on the stomachs of their mothers. Critics contend that the dim lights may cause the physician to miss signs of distress and infection from the water or mother's body. Another method, the Lamaze, using principles of conditioned reflexes, offers a variety of breathing and muscular exercises designed to facilitate labor, and the use of a "coach," usually the husband, for support.

Birthing Methods

Increasingly hospitals, social welfare workers, and physicians are providing preparation for birth through the use of instruction, pamphlets, and short courses. Still it is believed that most births occur in conjunction with some medication. Recent research has found that medicated delivery where the mother was given anesthesia occurred in 95 percent of all deliveries in 18 teaching hospitals (Brackbill & Broman, 1979). Some women receive general anesthesia, making them unconscious, while others receive only local spinal blocks designed to impede the nerve passage to the brain. Others receive analgesics for pain killing and assisting in relaxation. The placenta does not screen out these drugs and it is believed by some that the high rate of infant mortality in the U.S. is due to the routine use of obstetric medication (Haire, 1972). In medicated deliveries sometimes the effects of the drug make the baby less than normal in motor and physiological response, perhaps affecting the mother's view of the baby. The "mother instinct" at best is questionable; probably most of the feeling for the infant comes from the response the mother receives from the baby--the baby who nurses eagerly or is alert elicits love and attachment. Studies by Brackbill and Broman (1979) of 3,500 healthy full-term babies found that those whose mothers had received no obstetric medication demonstrated the most progress in sitting, standing and moving around. The babies of mothers who received locals showed less progress and those of mothers who had general anesthetics showed the least. Studies of the effect of medicated births were examined by Kraemer and colleagues (1985) with the conclusion that such studies often were ill-designed and misleading.

These researchers suggested that other factors should be examined: birth order, maternal age and health, socio-economic status, length and difficulty of labor, position of the fetus, and other conditions. Their own research showed no difference between medicated and non-medicated babies on strength and tactile sensitivity, activity and irritability, and sleep. Still the American Academy of Pediatrics (1978) has said where behavior might be affected the mother should receive the minimum effective dose for relief of pain.

Natural Childbirth

Dr. Granly Dick-Read, a British physician, in 1914 suggested the pain in childbirth was largely created by fear. He visited Russia where this idea was being reacted to through the use of Pavlovian methods. To eliminate this fear, he developed the concept of natural childbirth. He explained to women the physiology of reproduction and delivery and trained them in breathing, relaxation, and physical fitness. The Lamaze method popularized in America consists of the following aspects:

1. Instruction in anatomy and physiology of childbirth.

2. Training in respiration techniques such as rapid breathing and panting.

3. Use of a labor "coach." The coach's voice becomes a conditioned stimulus helping the woman relax or tense her muscles as required.

4. Cognitive restructuring for helping a woman concentrate on feelings other than muscle contractions.

5. Social support given by the coach and others who attend classes and help with the exercises, which reduces the sense of loneliness and fear. Many hospitals now allow the fathers to be in the delivery room. This, along with the other support routines, gives the mother a sense of worth.

The Leboyer method we discussed elsewhere finds little or slight support for temporalimprovement over conventionally delivered babies (Maziade, et al., 1986). The Caesarean delivery is a breech presentation where the baby is lying crosswise in the uterus or the legs and buttocks emerge before the head. The operation involves the surgical removal of the baby. It is sometimes required when the baby's head is too large to pass through the mother's pelvis, the mother is experiencing vaginal bleeding, or the baby is in trouble. The U.S. has more Caesarean births than any other industrialized country; 18 of every 100 births are by this method. The stress hormones (catecholamines) may trigger the need for some of these operations. This method has its disadvantages, among them a higher risk of infection, longer hospital stays and recovery period, greater expense, and physical and psychological impact.

Some births may be overseen by midwives or nurse-midwives. Among out-of-hospital births it is estimated that such persons attend 15 percent of the blacks and 47 percent of the whites (Wegman, 1987). Many hospitals and centers have developed special birthing rooms where the baby stays with the mother for much of the day and is family-centered. They are designed for low-risk and uncomplicated births, but have access to medical facilities and physicians.

The Birth Process

The birth process involves three stages: labor, delivery, and afterbirth. In labor the muscles of the uterus rhythmically contract, pushing the infant downward toward the birth canal, easing the mother's pain and strain as the fetus rests on the pelvis. The muscle tissue forces the lower opening of the uterus (the cervix) to relax, becoming shorter and broader and allowing the infant to emerge. For first birth labor usually requires 14 hours and subsequent ones average 8 hours. The uterine contractions usually occur 15 to 20 minutes apart and last 25 to 30 seconds. When the interval shortens to three to five minutes, the contractions become stronger and last 45 seconds. The amniotic sac bursts during labor--sometimes at its beginning. Delivery begins as the infant's head passes through the cervix (neck of the uterus) and is completed when it passes through the birth canal. This stage usually requires 20 to 80 minutes. The contractions last from 60 to 70 seconds and come at two to three minute intervals. The mother aids the delivery by bearing down--pushing with her abdominal muscles. Crowning occurs when the baby's head is at the mother's vulva (the outer entrance to the vagina). After this occurs, the rest of the body of the baby follows quickly.

Following the baby's birth the afterbirth takes place. The uterus commonly stops its contractions for a short interval; contractions resume in about five minutes and the placenta separates from the uterus. The placenta is forced into the vagina and is finally totally expelled. This process, termed the afterbirth, lasts for about 20 minutes.

The baby's condition at birth is usually appraised today by use of the Apgar Scoring System, a method developed by Virginia Apgar (1953). The infant is assessed at one minute and again at five minutes after birth for heart rate, respiratory effort, muscle tone, reflex irritability (the infant's response to a catheter placed in its nostril), and body color. Each of the conditions is rated 0, 1, or 2. The ratings of the five conditions are added, with a highest possible score of 10. Most babies score from 7 to 10. A score of less than 5 indicates the need for prompt diagnosis and treatment. Table 4.1 summarizes the Apgar Scoring System.

Mothers over 35 have a more difficult pregnancy and delivery, along with a higher incidence of congenital malformations and chromosomal aberrations (deviation) in their offspring than do younger mothers. Difficulty in birth delivery is high among mothers of the poor and other disadvantaged groups. Prolonged or difficult birth resulting in physical injury or oxygen depletion may cause problems that persist years after birth. Birth palsies and spastic paralysis occur more frequently in instrumental deliveries than in young spontaneous births. When spontaneous births are prolonged, asphyxia may result, causing a degeneration of the brain cells.

The mental and physical health of the mother are important factors affecting the birth and survival of the infant. It is thought that the optimum weight for humans at birth is between 7 and 9 pounds (Blakaslee, 1969, p. 10), slightly more for males and less for females. Two-thirds of full-term infants weigh between 6 and 8 1/2 pounds. The first few days after birth, infants tend to lose 6 to 10 ounces (Marlow, 1988). Chances for survival decrease the more the baby is under or above this norm. Thus, normal birth and the optimum development of the baby depend upon many factors, and the competent obstetrician must be well aware of these.

THE APGAR SCORING SYSTEM

Score	Heart rate	Respiratory effort	Muscle tone	Reflex irritability	Appearance
0	Absent	Absent	Limp	Absent	Pale or blue
1	Below 100	Slow, irregular	Fair flexion	Grimace	Blue extremities
2	100–140	Good (crying)	Active motion	Vigorous cry	Pink all over

Source: Adapted from Apgar 1953.

Premature and Low-Weight Infants

An infant is usually considered premature if it is born before the 37th gestational week. Additional signs of prematurity are a birth weight of less than 5 1/2 pounds (2,500 grams) or a head circumference of less than 33 centimeters. It is estimated that 7 to 10 percent of all births are premature or full-term low weight (Wegman, 1987). It is especially common among first-born infants, and among boys more than girls. As of 1966 it was estimated that 30 percent of all expectant mothers in the United States received no prenatal care. If this was true, a dramatic drop has occurred, since only 1.0 percent of white and 2.7 percent of black mothers are listed as having no prenatal care in 1980 (HEW, 1982). In 1980, 99.0 percent of all babies were delivered by physicians (HEW, 1982). Also the educational levels of all parents, black and white, had risen; the median years of education ranged between 12.1 and 12.7. The most obvious effect of lack of prenatal care is the likelihood of the offspring's being born prematurely and therefore of low weight. The potential effects of prematurity can be offset by an enriched environment during the first year of life, which includes prior medical, nutritional, and care-giving attention (Zeskind & Ramey, 1978).

Prognosis of Prematurely Born Infants

The main hazards to the survival of the premature baby, both at the time of birth and during the weeks that follow, appear to be the lack of development of the respiratory, thermoregulatory, and gastrointestinal functions, as well as the immune responses, which make the baby more susceptible to infection. The leading cause of death, approximately 10,000 a year, in the premature is respiratory distress syndrome (RDS). The cause is usually the lack of surfactant, a lubricant found in the amniotic fluid that helps inflate the air sacs in the lungs after birth and prevents the lungs from collapsing and sticking together after each breath. The fetus normally doesn't develop surfactant until the 35th week. Lung failure can be avoided when this substance is given to the infant. Infants weighing less than 5 1/2 pounds are 40 times more likely to die in the first four weeks than babies who are over this weight. Those under 3 1/2 pounds are 200 times the normal risk. We can be optimistic over a study in Victoria, Australia, where 351 babies who weighed from 1 to 2 pounds were observed. Even though 75 percent died, 72 percent of the survivors had no handicaps at all at age five and only 19 percent had severe disabilities (Kitchen et al., 1987). A number of children who had been diagnosed at age two as having cerebral palsy had outgrown the condition by the age of five. The establishment of adequate respiration requires the maturity of the nervous centers regulating respiration and adequate development of the lungs and associated muscles. If premature babies survive the first few days after birth, they may continue development in the incubator apparently as well as if they had remained in the mother's uterus.

It should be noted that the premature infant's response to sensory stimulation is highly important (Field, 1987). Ruth Rice, reporting on research (1975) designed to ascertain the effect of tactile stimulation and stroking on the development of pre-term infants, found significant differences favoring the experimental group of prematurely born infants. Thirty prematurely born infants 37 weeks or less in gestational age, whose birth weight was 2,500 grams or less, were randomly placed in experimental and control groups. There was an equal distribution of low socio-economic status white, black, and Mexican-American infants. For the experimental group, treatment consisted of sequential caudocephalic progression of a precise method of stroking and massaging the infant's entire body. To ensure adequate nutrition, a four-month supply of formula was provided for each baby.

The results of the assessment after four months indicated that stroking and rocking can accelerate maturation of cellular components insofar as neurological development can be measured by functional behavior. There were statistically significant differences ($p=.05$, which means that only 5 times out of 100 would there be a chance of this conclusion being false) in favor of experimental infants in the assessment of the phylogenetic reflexes, labyrinthine and Landau reflexes, weight gain, mental functioning, and certain endocrine hormone increases. There were no significant differences in head circumference, body length, or motor development, though the raw scores for each of these variables were greater for the experimental group.

Subjective findings indicated that the infants receiving the stroking and rocking were more socially adaptive and aggressive. Further, the nature of the treatment was such that the mother/father relationship was enhanced and nurtured. This phenomenon could have far-reaching effects on the infant's continuing psychosocial-cognitive development and functioning. Rose, et al. (1981), studying cognitive lags in pre-term infants, found that giving extra sensory stimulation during the early weeks of life gave long-term benefits resulting in performances equal to full-term infants on visual recognition memory.

Socio-economic Status and Childbearing

Risks for women bearing low-weight babies may be summarized as socio-economic status--age, race, income, education, etc.; medical risks--previous low-weight babies, diabetes, miscarriages, etc.; lifestyle--smoking, poor health (diet and exercise), drugs, etc.; and current pregnancy status--weight gains of less than 14 pounds, prenatal care, twin presence and infections. Each of these is closely tied to the social circumstance which exists for the woman.

There seem to be many variables which make it difficult to draw specific conclusions about the relation of prematurity and later development, although there is considerable evidence for the conclusion that the smaller the premature baby at birth, the greater the likelihood of brain injury and associated conditions. Intellectual retardation is morc common among lower-class than middle-class children, even when there is no evidence of prenatal or perinatal problems (toxemias, infections, prematurity, or anoxia) (Smith, et al., 1972). The phenomena of lower class membership, prenatal and perinatal complications, and poor performance on measures of intellectual capacity are positively related. The difficulties forecast for premature children should be tempered somewhat with several illustrations indicating that many premature children grow up to be normal. One investigator reported that Laura, who had a gestation period of 36 weeks and a birth weight of 4 1/2 pounds, could suck and swallow and showed normal neonatal reflexes. As a young child, she had a speech defect that was cured by a few weeks of speech therapy. At 22 she was successful as a businesswoman, graduate student, and wife, and was also a member of Phi Beta Kappa. In another case, Susan, 17, was pre-term by several weeks and had a birth weight of 3 pounds and 13 ounces; nevertheless, she had the normal reflexes expected of the typical baby. Following birth she was placed in the isolette for a month, allowed to be brought home when her weight reached 5 pounds. She needed iron added to her diet, had a small hernia which was summarily taken care of through the use of a makeshift truss, and by two years of age had equaled the levels on the Gesell Developmental Charts for her age. She is average in height, though slightly overweight, is an honor-roll student, first-class Girl Scout, and student council member, plays the piano and the flute, swims, and shows no signs of the early effects of deprivation. It must be noted, however, that these children were nurtured in optimal environments with parents from upper middle socio-economic circumstances.

Early Responses

Neonates have little awareness of their environment in the first two or three days of life, although their senses are fairly well developed at birth. Nevertheless, it might well seem to them like William James described the times--one of a booming, buzzing confusion. Piaget suggested the final months were ones of exercising reflexes. Neonates lack the capacity for interpreting stimuli they receive. Important early responses of the neonate are discussed in the following sections.

The Nervous System

The neurological system of the neonate is immature. Bodily functions and responses to external stimuli are carried on by the midbrain and by reflexes of the spinal cord. The cerebral control is lacking at the neonatal stage. When the nerve fibers become myelinated and are connected to one another, control from the higher cerebral centers begins and more complex behavior emerges. Most reflexes disappear after three or four months as maturity of the neurological system takes place.

Body Movement and Motor Activity

The motor activity of the neonate is rapid, as observed in kicking a leg and flailing about with the arms, and the neonate displays a diverse array of reflex behavior. Early postnatal movements represent a very generalized type of activity (Marlow, 1988). These motor activities are under subcortical control. Around the fourth month, voluntary movements are controlled by the cortex. When the infant feels irritated, it reacts with the whole body by attempting reflex movements associated with relief. The infant does not connect the breast or the bottle with relief from hunger, but makes sucking movements with its lips and will try to suck anything it touches. Responses to specific stimuli are an outgrowth of this generalized activity. In time, useless movements will be discontinued and useful ones practiced to perfection. Maturation is most responsible for improved motor control as bones, muscles, and the nervous system undergo developmental change.

At birth the infant can raise the head slightly when lying on the abdomen, but not when on its back. If pulled to a sitting position, generally the head falls back and the spine is curved in a bow from the shoulders to hips. The leg movement is characterized by jerking, flexing, extending, rolling, rotating, and trembling. However, evidence from the study of 350 Ugandan infants (Frankenburg et al., 1967) revealed that two days after home delivery without anesthetics the infants had the ability to sit upright. In addition, the babies were expert crawlers by two months of age. This is an indication that experience drastically affects capabilities of motor movement.

Emotional Responses

Emotion in infants falls into two categories, quiescence and distress. The distorted face and vocalization show emotion in the infant. Crying that is evident at birth serves a twofold function: (1) to supply the blood with oxygen, and (2) to inflate the lung sac. Crying in a short time comes to be the major avenue for the expression of discomfort. Oswald and Peltzman (1974) analyzed tape-recorded cries of abnormal and normal infants. The spectrograph (which analyzes complex sounds into component frequencies) showed that the cries of abnormal infants were different from those of normal infants, the abnormal being more irregular and higher pitched. When there is no obvious physical need to be met (hunger, pain, wetness, exercise), the infant who cries and is cuddled is usually quieted. If this action fails to still the neonate, then a careful watch should be instituted for symptoms of sickness.

The neonate cannot maintain homeostasis due to the underdeveloped nature of the autonomic nervous system. Body temperature fluctuates widely from subnormal to above normal, its pulse rate is rapid, and respiration is double and more that of the typical adult (18 per minute). Vomiting, urination, and defecation are frequent, and periodic sleeping is light and easily disturbed. Control of motor activity is involuntary, and coordination of sucking and swallowing is not well developed due in part to lack of synchronization with stomach emptying. In summary, the human infant is exceedingly vulnerable.

In time, the infant's homeostatic mechanism will maintain a relatively calm, balanced state. Involuntary actions of bodily mechanisms help the child realize a remarkably stable internal temperature and supply certain elements essential for meeting internal and external emergencies.

Reflexes

The reflexes are part of the homeostatic system that protects the infant from harm and overstimulation, and assists in initiating activity. The infant comes equipped to have his reflex system activated. The first responses of the neonate are characterized by excitation and general mass activity. Some of the responses of the newborn are designed for protection and survival, although some may no longer be necessary for survival and are holdovers from the distant past. Included here are the following:

1. Blinking reflex and eyelid operation, as seen in the opening and closing of the eye, with variation in the size of the pupil in response to light.

2. Ocular reflex, operating when the head is moved quickly and the eyes move in a compensatory direction.

3. Mouth and face response, such as opening and closing the mouth, or the lip responding to touch.

4. Swallowing and gagging response, essential to establish nursing, to emit fluid taken in the trachea by coughing, and to vomit.

5. Tonic neck reflex, as indicated when the infant lying on its back turns the head to one side and extends the arm and leg at right angles.

6. Grasping reflex, shown by closing and opening the hand. The grip at birth may allow it to pull up holding the fingers of the mother.

7. Genital reflex, as seen in the raising of testes and penile erection.

8. Prancing, as exhibited when the infant is held up with its feet touching a surface and prances and kicks, simulating walking.

9. Startle (Moro) reflex, indicating the awareness of the neonate of sudden loud noise or loss of support, and also the presence of equilibrium.

10. Abdominal response, as seen in the twisting and drawing in of the stomach.

SENSORY RESPONSES

The senses of touch, taste, hearing, and smell are better developed than sight at birth. Although they do not approach adult ability, nevertheless they give information about the world. An infant shows by general discomfort--the grimace, the cry, and the accelerated motor activity--the effect of pressure, temperature, change, and pain. The sense of touch is the most highly developed of the special senses, and is most acute on the lips, tongue, ears, and forehead. Failure to grasp the nipple is one indication of brain damage. At the time of birth, sensitivity to pain is lessened, so that the body will not feel its effects while passing through the birth canal. Munn (1974) contends there is no clear evidence of pain at birth, although Lipsitt and Levy (1959) observed toe reflexes and withdrawal of the foot from electrodermal stimulation. Pinpricks elicit little or no response the first few days of life. Over the first days of life the threshold of such response to electrical stimulation is greatly lowered. The neonate also appears to be sensitive to organic stimulation, since hunger and thirst are the most common causes of crying. The newborn is not likely to have pain from gas in the intestines, but the infant of a few weeks of age appears to suffer intensely if feeding produces colic (sharp abdominal pain).

Hearing

Hearing may be difficult at birth due to fluid in the external auditory canal, unequal pressure within and without the auditory apparatus, and the fact that the sense cells in the inner ear are only partially developed. Nevertheless, the presence of the Moro (startle) reflex in response to loud sounds indicates that the infant is able to hear immediately after birth. According to Birtholz and Benacerrof (1983), the fetus can hear three months before birth. Hence the fluid in the ear no doubt affects early hearing. The newborn will turn its head to sound within an hour after birth (Wolff, 1973). The neonate appears to be predisposed to respond to certain auditory stimuli (pattern, pitch, and volume) that come from human caretakers--especially their mothers and other females (Eisenberg, 1978). Infant crying is often soothed by the calm, directed human voice, and attempts to find the source of comfort will be made. Studies indicate that by three to eight days the neonate will respond differently to the mother's voice repeating his or her name as opposed to other words or to other voices repeating his or her name. Such voice contact can modify the emotional quality of the relationship between mother and child in ways which can be detected as much as one year later (Klaus & Kennell, 1976). In the study of habituation infants have been observed to alter their sucking pattern to listen to voices or sound. Discriminative sucking observed in three-day-olds indicates babies know their mother's voice (DeCasper & Fifer, 1980).

Vision

The cones of the retina in the eye are small and underdeveloped at birth; the rods are more developed but limited to a small area, restricting the visual field. The vision of the neonate is like a still camera; both eyes cannot focus on one object at the same time. The eyes are not coordinated and may turn inward or outward at a given time. Eye fixation is noted by the end of the first week, and the use of eye muscles by four weeks. The results of Fantz's studies (1963) have shown conclusively that the infant's visual equipment is much better developed in the early months of life than had previously been believed. Fantz noted that infants make visual discrimination between patterned stimuli within 48 hours after birth. By four months they can discriminate between bright colors, and by six months their color perception is equal to that of adults (Bornstein, 1978). There is more evidence from the results of Brazelton's 1973 study that the neonate has greater capacity to respond to its environment than had previously been assumed. It may even perceive three dimensions and have depth perception in the first weeks of life. The infant responds to flashing lights, is able to differentiate between colors (maybe by three weeks), and moves the eyes to follow a light (Hartup & Yonas, 1971). As Gesell has said, the infant takes hold of the world ocularly long before it grasps it manually. Fine coordination of the sense requires a period of about a year to occur (Gottfried, Rose, & Wagner, 1977). The senses work in some coordinative fashion earlier than a year.

Taste and Smell

The taste cells, located on the surface of the

tongue, are numerous and relatively well developed at birth. The infant's reactions to sweet tastes are positive, while reactions to salty, sour, and bitter tastes are negative. The infant will suck sweet fluid harder and drink more of it (Haith, 1986). In fact, by two or three months children react to changes in their food formula (Breckenridge & Murphy, 1961).

Research has shown that the gross sense of smell is well developed at birth, at least judged by reaction to strong odor. The cells for smell are located in the upper part of the nose and are well developed. Studies by Lipsitt, Engen, and Kaye (1963) found acetic acid to be stimulating, and obtained evidence of response to, and differentiation of, odors without tactile-imitating aspects. These were anise, asafetida, and phenylethyl alcohol. The percentage of responses to the odorous as compared with the odorless stimulus was used to gauge the presence or absence of olfactory sensitivity. Differences in the percentages gave clear evidence of olfactions. MacFarlane (1978) pursued the question further, finding babies could differentiate between clean breast pads and the smell of breast pads with some milk drippings on them. After 6 to 10 days the infants could distinguish their mother's milk smell from others.

Sleep

Sleep in the newborn can hardly be distinguished from tranquil rest. The neonate sleeps from 15 to 20 hours a day. By six months this typically has been reduced to 14 hours. Brief waking periods occur every two hours, but are fewer and shorter during the night probably due to fewer stimuli. During the first month the infant takes four naps each of about two hours duration. The infant is aroused by internal discomfort caused by hunger or pain. Hunger is by far the most common cause of its waking before need for sleep has been satisfied. As the infant matures, the length of unbroken periods of sleep decreases and, at the same time, wakefulness increases. With increasing age (six months), active sleep (REM, for Rapid Eye Movement) increases and clusters toward the end of the night, whereas quiet sleep (non-

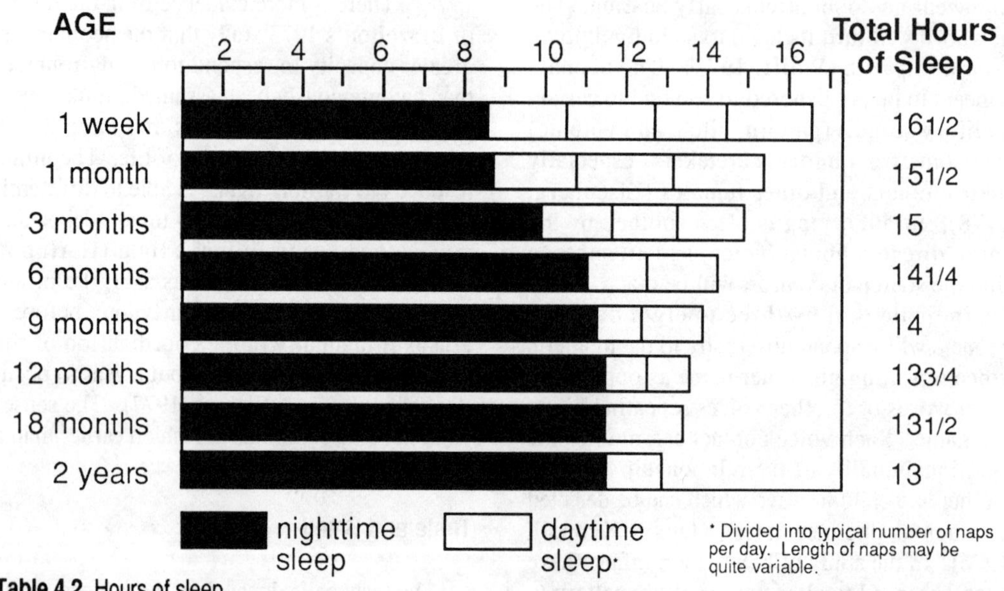

Table 4.2 Hours of sleep.

REM) increases toward the beginning of the sleep period (Hoppenbrouwers et al., 1982). By six months, most infants can sleep through the night, with sleep being easiest to achieve after meals. Although the baby becomes used to household noise, the best sleeping condition is a room away from family traffic and on a mattress that is firm. A study by Hartman (1981) indicates that some young children have their REM or dreaming sleep interrupted by what he calls "night terror." This occurs about an hour after falling asleep. Hartman suggests this may be due to the immaturity of their nervous systems. It should be remembered that the infant will sleep as much as it needs to sleep and at the time it needs to sleep; culturally approved patterns will be learned in time. Table 4.2 summarizes sleep habits from birth to 18 years (after Ferber, 1985).

Nursing and Sucking

The child's tongue, cheeks, hard and soft palate, gums, and lips are sufficiently developed at birth to participate in the important life function of sucking and nursing. However, the act of sucking, like other functions, is developmental; the premature infant is considerably less efficient than the full-term baby. Siqueland (1968) points out that infants as young as three months of age can control the visual input that is received by sucking on an automatic nipple linked to a slide projector.

In 1956 only 21 percent of mothers left the hospital with a nursing baby. Since this time breast feeding has gained greater acceptance. An early 1980s survey by the National Centers for Disease Control (1984) found 51 percent of white mothers and 25 percent of black mothers fed their babies by the breast. Advantages are numerous aside from emotional and sensual experiences. Breast milk has been called the "ultimate health food" (Eiger & Olds, 1987). Breast-fed children are protected against a number of illnesses such as diarrhea, respiratory infections, pneumonia and bronchitis (Fallot, Boyd & Oski, 1980). The American Academy of Pediatrics (1982) states that the best food for every newborn infant is breast milk unless the mother has some physical condition that makes nursing impossible. They also advise Vitamin D supplements, fluoride, and iron be given the infant. Many women report that the physical act of nursing is a sensually pleasurable experience. Others believe that the intimate contact involved in breast feeding creates a sense of security and love that has a lasting effect on the child.

Disadvantages are namely that it requires more time, limits the physical freedom of the mother, and, of course, in the case where the mother works, often is prohibitive. Breast feeding is less popular with poor, minority, and younger women. This despite the fact that breast milk is much more economical than commercially bought formula. Certainly bottle feeding is acceptable, and many babies thrive on it. Also, the psychological aspects of closeness can be duplicated by holding the child while feeding with the bottle. Mothers who breast feed and do not wish to might well pass on the resentment and unhappiness to the infant (Eiger & Olds, 1987).

Differences in Activity and Sensitivity

The skin, as a general sense organ, is affected by touch, temperature, and pressure. The nerve system involved lies close to the surface of the skin and is well developed at birth. Therefore, sensitivity to cold is greater than to heat. The face, especially the lips, is more sensitive to touch and pressure than other regions of the body. Also, pain sensitivity develops slowly, and the threshold for pain goes down in the first four or five days.

The human heartbeat as a significant sound has been studied in Salk (1962). An experimental group of newborn babies was exposed continuously to a heartbeat recording. Though there were no significant differences in food intake between the control and experimental groups during the first four days of life, they differed significantly in weight gain, a mean gain of 40 grams for the experimental group (see Table 4.3).

It is possible that the prenatal experience of feeling the mother's rhythmic heartbeat has the effect of calming, along with lullabies and even the clock. The Japanese developed a heartbeat machine some years ago, which has been used in some hospitals to soothe babies (Lily, 1967), but this has been questioned by Wolff (1966), who recommends caution in the use of artificial devices.

Although infants make differential responses involving the senses, whether they experience organized sensations is still unknown (Munn, 1974). Nativists (Gestalt theorists) infer that the perceptual world of the infant is to a certain degree organized from the beginning, whereas empiricists (behaviorists) believe that organization and meaning depend upon experience or conditioning and on what the individual learns. That perception begins with inborn sensitivity and a degree of innate organization can hardly be denied. Development during infancy and childhood then proceeds based on this innate endowment. The effect of environment is closely contingent upon the limits of growth as laid down by heredity.

Infants also differ in sensitivity to varying kinds of stimuli. In a study by Birns (1965), 30 healthy full-term babies were tested and observed during four sessions. The first session always occurred on the first day of life, and the last session on the fourth or fifth day. The stimulation applied to each baby consisted of a soft tone, a loud tone, a cold disc applied to the baby's thigh, and a pacifier inserted in the baby's mouth. The major finding was that babies could be differentiated within the first five days of life in terms of a consistency of their reactivity to external stimuli. Some neonates consistently responded moderately, and others were characterized by mild intensity responses. In general babies who responded to one stimulus responded vigorously to all stimuli, and thus stability from day two to day five was established.

SUMMARY

The birth process involves three stages: (1) labor, which begins when the muscles of the uterus contract to push the fetus downward toward the birth canal; (2) delivery, which begins as the infant's head passes through the cervix and goes through the birth canal; and (3) crowning, which occurs when the baby's head is at the mother's vulva (the outer entrance to the vagina). In breech or Caesarean delivery (the baby is surgically removed), the presentation of the baby is crosswise in the uterus and the legs and buttocks emerge before the head.

In medicated deliveries the mother receives an anesthetic to ease the pain. In western societies, most women get this relief. In natural childbirth, such as in the Lamaze Method, training is provided the husband in respiration techniques and assistance in providing social support. Another type is gentle birth, called the

WEIGHT CHANGES IN NEWBORN BABIES WITH AND WITHOUT EXPOSURE TO HEARTBEAT RECORDINGS

	Gained weight		No gain or loss in weight	
Group	Number	Percent	Number	Percent
102 neonates exposed to heartbeat sound	71	69.6	31	30.5
102 neonates not exposed to heartbeat sound	27	33.0	75	67.0

Source: Salk (1962).

Leboyer method, which occurs in a dimly lighted, quiet room, without the use of forceps and a general anesthetic. Following birth, the baby is bathed in warm water and immediately placed on the belly of the mother.

The setting for birth historically has occurred in homes and hospitals. Now birthing centers or maternity centers are available in hospitals or other facilities which are designed to allow a more natural setting, one where the infant can be with the mother and the surroundings are home-like. A midwife, trained as a registered nurse, is an option where an uncomplicated pregnancy exists. In this situation, the delivery may be done at the home of the mother.

Low-weight and pre-term babies (those born before the 37th gestational week) are typically less than five pounds. Today medical advances make it possible for babies before the 26th week of gestation to survive. Many of these are less than two pounds. Babies under three pounds are considered at risk and account for two-thirds of the infants who die in the first month of life. Women who are characterized under the following conditions are at risk for having low-weight babies: low socio-economic status, medical problems such as diabetes, weight gains of less than 14 pounds, rubella, presence of twins and lifestyles, including smoking, drug abuse, malnutrition, and poor prenatal care. Due to an immature homeostatic mechanism, the newborn infant maintains only a relatively calm and balanced state. The reflexes are part of the homeostatic system that protects the neonate from harm and over-stimulation and assist in initiating activity. The first responses of the neonate are characterized by excitation and general mass activity and movement. Crying at first is a response to distress, whereas cries become increasingly differentiated as the infant matures. The responses of the newborn, designed basically for protection, are reflex systems that are readily activated, such as the blinking reflex, the swallowing reflex, tonic neck and ocular response, gagging response, the grasping reflex, and the startle reflex.

In addition to these reflexes, many special senses are present: touch, taste, vision, hearing, smell, skin sensations, and organic sensations. The genetic factors and the environment of the neonate are destined to determine the development of the organism and its impetus into childhood. This process is charted in Chapter 5.

AVERAGE GROWTH LEVELS OF INFANTS - 1 MONTH TO 1 YEAR

Psychosocial	Intellectual, Moral Development	Language Development	Physical	Motor	Sensory
	12 MONTHS		12 MONTHS		
PSYCHOSOCIAL • Sense of Trust theoretically achieved. If not, a sense of mis-trust predominates • Infants emotion, such as fear, jealousy, anger, can be more clearly interpreted • Attachment developed to primary caregiver(s) • Clings to caregiver, usually mother, when fearful • Explores away from caregiver if secure • Responds to requests for affection such as a kiss or a hug • Has established begin-ning view of self as a seperate person • "Security blanket" or favorite toy begins to provide comfort • Cooperates in dressing: puts arms through sleeves, feet into shoes. Takes off socks • Drops objects on purpose so someoone can pick them up	INTELLECTUAL Sensorimotor Stage Substage IV: • Coordination of secondary schemas (8 to12 months) • Has learned that objects continue to exist even when out of sight (object permanence) • Beginning perception of cause and effect relationships • Early beginning of anticipatory and intentional behavior • Problem solving beginning to develop, although the infant has not learned to "think" per se MORAL Preconventional Morality Stage 0 (0 to 2 years)	RECEPTIVE LANGUAGE Responds with gestures or actions to more com-plex verbal requests, such as "Please give it to me" EXPRESSIVE LANGUAGE • May speak two or more words besides "ma-ma" and "da-da" • Understands meaning of many more words than can be spoken • Knows names of increasing number of objects • Imitates sounds animals make • Intonation becomes more like adult speech • Continues using jargon • Indicates "no" by shaking head • Beginning voluntary control over responses to sound: may or amy not respond or may delay response to another's voice • Vocalization decreases as walking increases	• Weight 10 =± 1.5kg (22 ± 3 pounds); has tripled birth weight • Length 74.5 ±3 cm (29 ± 1.5 inches); length has increased by almost 50 percent from birth • Head circumference 46 cm (18 inches); head circumference has increased by one third since birth • Brain weight has increased rapidly since birth, resulting in sig-nificant developmental achievements • Head and chest are equal in circumference • Pulse 115 ± 20 • Respirations 30 ± 10 Blood pressure 96/66 ± 30/24 • Teething has 6 to 8 deciduous teeth • Lumbar curve and the compensating dorsal curve develop as walking continues • Physiologic stability achieved and maintained during first year	GROSS MOTOR •Stands alone for variable length of time • Sits down from standing position alone • Walks in few steps with help or alone hands held at shoulder height for balance • Improves competence in motor skills through practice FINE MOTOR • Good pincer grasp • Picks up small bits of food and transfers them to mouth • Enjoys eating with fingers • Turns pages in a book but usually not one at a time • Drinks from a cup and eats from a spoon but still requires some help • Holds crayon adaptively to make a stroke or a amrk on a piece of paper	• Listens for recurring sounds • Full binocular vision well established • Follows fast-moving object with eyes • Discriminates simple geometric forms: square, circles • Visual acuity: 20/100 to 20/50

KEY WORDS

Caesarian section

crowning

tonic neck

birthing room

ocular response

moro response

preterm

isolette

stillbirth

vernix caseosa

rooting

Babinski

visual cliffs

anoxia

neonate

fetal monitoring

breech position

transverse position

obstetrician

Lamaze method

midwife

Apgar scale

lanugo

habituation

sudden infant death

neonatal behavioral

apnea

REFERENCES

American Academy of Pediatrics Committee on Drugs. Effects of medication during labor and delivery on infant outcome. *Pediatrics*, 1978, *62*(3):402-403.

Birns, B. Individual differences in human neonates' responses to stimulation. *Child Development*, 1965, *36*:249-256.

Birtholz, J.C., and Benacerrof, B.R. The development of human fetal hearing. *Science*, 1983, *222*:516-518.

Blakaslee, A.L. Today's health news. *Today's Health*, 1969.

Bornstein, M.H. Visual behavior of the young infant: Relationship between chromatic and spatial perceptions and the activity of underlying brain mechanisms. *Journal of Experimental Child Psychology*, 1978, *26*:174-192.

Brackbill, Y., and Broman, S.H. *Obstetrical medication and development in the first year of life*. Unpublished manuscript.

Brazelton, T.B. Neonatal behavioral assessment scale. In *Clinics in Developmental Medicine*, No. 50, Philadelphia: Lippincott, 1973.

Breckenridge, M.E., and Murphy, M.N. *Growth and development of the young child*. Philadelphia: Saunders, 1961.

DeCasper, A., and Fifer, W. Newborns prefer their mothers' voices. *Science*, 1980, *208*:1174-1176.

Eiger, M.S., and Olds, S.W. *The Complete Book of Breastfeeding*. New York: Bantam, 1987.

Eisenberg, R.B. Stimulus significance as a determinant of infant responses to sound. In E.B. Thoman and S. Trotter (eds.), *Social Responsiveness of Infants*. New Brunswick, NJ: Johnson & Johnson Products, 1978.

Fallot, M.E., Boyd, D.L., and Oski, F.A. Breastfeeding reduces incidence of hospital admission for infection. *Pediatrics*, 1980, *65*(6):1121-1124.

Fantz, R.L. Pattern vision in newborn infants. *Science*, 1963, *140*:296-297.

Ferber, Richard. *Solve Your Child's Sleep Problems*. New York: Fireside Book--Simon & Schuster, Inc., 1985

Field, T. Interaction and attachment in normal and atypical infants. *Journal of Consulting Clinical Psychology*, 1987, *55*(6):853-859.

Frankenberg, W.K., and Dodds, J.R. The Denver developmental screen test. *Pediatrics*, 1967, *71*:181-191.

Gottfried, A.W., Rose, S.W., and Wagner, H.B. Cross-modal transfer in human infants. *Child Development*, 1977, *48*:118-123.

Haire, D. The cultural warping of childbirth. *International Childbirth Education Association News*, 1977, 35.

Haith, M.M. Sensory and perceptual processes in early infancy. *Journal of Pediatrics*, 1986, *109*(10):158-171.

Hartmann, E. The strangest sleep disorder. *Psychology Today*, 1981, *15*:14-20.

Hartup, W.W., and Yonas, A. Developmental psychology. *Annual Review of Psychology*, 1971, *22*:337-392.

Health, Education and Welfare (HEW). National Center for Health Statistics, *Monthly Vital Statistics Report*, 1981, *31*(8).

Hoppenbrouwers, T., Hodgman, J.E., Harper, R.M., and Sterman, M.B. Temporal distribution of sleep states, somatic activity and autonomic activity during the first half year of life. *Sleep*, 1982, *5*(2):131-143.

Klaus, M.H., and Kennell, J.H. *Maternal-Infant Bonding*. St. Louis, MO: Mosby, 1976.

Leboyer, F. *Birth Without Violence*. New York: Random House, 1975.

Lilly, H.B.I. *Modern Motherhood.* New York: Random House, 1967.

Lipsitt, L.P., Engen, T., and Kaye, H. Developmental changes in the olfactory threshold of the neonate. *Child Development*, 1963, *34*:371-376.

MacFarlane, J.A. What a baby knows. *Human Nature*, 1978, *1*(2):74-81.

Maziade, M., Boudreault, M., Cote, R., and Thivierge, J. Influence of genetic birth procedures and other circumstances on infant temperament: Development and social implications. *Journal of Pediatrics*, 1986, *108*(1):134-136.

McKenry, P., et al. Adolescent pregnancy: A review of the literature. *Family Coordinator*, 1979, *28*:17-18.

Munn, N.L. *The Growth of Human Behavior*, 3rd ed. Boston: Houghton Mifflin, 1974.

Oswald, P.F., and Peltzman, P. An infant's cries may signal physiological defects. *Scientific American*, 1974, *230*:84-90.

Rice, R.D. Premature infants response to sensory stimulation. *APA Monitor*, 1975, pp. 8-9.

Roffwarg, H.P., et al. Ontogenic development of the human sleep cycle. *Science*, 1966, *152*:604-619. Data revised based on personal conversation with Franklin Ross Jones, author, September 21, 1982.

Rose, S.A., Gottfried, A.W., and Bridger, W.H. Crossmodal transfer in 6-month-old infants. *Developmental Psychology*, 1981, *17*:661-669.

Rosen, M., et al. Differences between mothers of low-weight and term-size infants. *Obstetrics and Gynecology*, February 1968.

Salk, L. *Transactions of the New York Academy of Science, Ser. II*, 1962, *24*:753-763.

Siqueland, E.R. Reinforcement patterns and extinction in human newborns. *Journal of Experimental Child Psychology*, 1968, *6*:431-442.

Smith, A.C., Flick, G.C., Feriss, C.S., and Sellman, A.H. *Child Development*, 1972, *43*:495-507.

Wegman, M.E. Annual summary of vital statistics. *Pediatrics*, 1987, *80*(6):817-827.

Wolff, P.H. The causes, controls and organization of behavior in the neonate. *Psychological Issues*. New York: International University Press, 1966.

_____. Observations on newborn infants. In L.J. Stone, H.T. Smith, and L.B. Murphy (eds.), *The Competent Infant: Research and Commentary*. New York: Basic Books, 1973.

Zeskind, P.S., and Ramey, C.J. Fetal malnutrition. An experimental study of its consequences on infant development in two care giving environments. *Child Development*, 1978, *49*:1155-1162.

PART III

THE COURSE OF DEVELOPMENT

Chapter 5

THE INFANT AND TODDLER: PHYSICAL, COGNITIVE, PERSONALITY, AND HEALTH CARE

- ***Abilities of the Infant and Toddler***
  - Physical
  - Motor
  - Perceptual
- ***Cognition and Language***
  - Piaget's sensory-motor stage
  - Language
  - Milestones in development
- ***Personality, Social and Emotional Growth***
  - Theories of personality
  - Emotions
  - Bonding and attachment
  - Parenting practices
  - Development of self-control
  - Day care
- ***Health and Preventive Practices***
  - Immunizations
  - Diets for infants and toddlers
  - Hazards

PHYSICAL, MOTOR AND PERCEPTIVE ABILITY

The task of the child during this period is to develop the competencies that have been laid down by heredity. At one year of age a child is poised for fundamental development in social skills and language. Children are constantly seeking stimulation from and interacting with the environment. How quickly they become toddlers and then children!

The rate of growth during the first years of life is rapid in comparison to later years (see Table 5.1). Weight at birth for normal nine-month babies will vary from 5 to 12 pounds; the weight at six months will be approximately twice that of birth. Body length at birth will usually vary from 18 1/2 to 23 inches. During the first year, a healthy child grows about 1 inch a month during the first six months and by age one has an average increase in body length of about 50 percent (28 1/2 inches). Additionally, infants usually double their birth weight by six months of age and triple their weight by age one (21 pounds). Of all the body organs, the brain, at birth, is closer to its eventual gross weight than any other organ, and the skull at birth is very malleable in order to allow this relatively large brain to pass through the birth canal.

By age two, adult height and weight can be predicted with some degree of success by using the following procedures. For boys, the formula is two times height at age two = adult height; five times weight at age 1 1/2 = adult weight.

PHYSICAL GROWTH, BIRTH TO AGE 3
(Fiftieth Percentile)

	Length (inches)		Weight (pounds)	
Age	**Boys**	**Girls**	**Boys**	**Girls**
Birth	20	19¾	7½	7½
1 month	21¼	21	10	9¾
6 months	26	25¾	16¾	15¾
12 months	29½	29¼	22¼	21
18 months	32¼	31¾	25¼	24¼
24 months	34½	34	27¾	27
30 months	36¼	36	30	29½
36 months	38	37¾	32¼	31¾

For girls, the formula is two times height at 1 1/2 years = adult height; five times weight at 1 1/4 years = adult weight (Krogman, 1972).

Despite the great variability in growth, there is considerable homogeneity and stability between the sexes relative to sequence of development and change in the growth process. A formula for postnatal growth has been developed suggesting that head and neck dimensions increase by two times, trunk by three, arms by four times, and legs by five.

The control of body temperature downward is a matter of maturity. The baby generates increasing amounts of heat until the second year. At this time the baby generates more heat per body weight than at any other time. Heat in body temperature drops an average of 1 1/2 degrees from birth to adolescence, as shown in Table 5.2.

Neuromuscular Development

During infancy maturation provides children with enhanced connection between various parts of the brain as well as the central nervous system and the muscles. Such maturation, along with interactions with the environment (development) allow the infant greater and greater motor abilities which appear to proceed in two directions: (1) cephalo-caudal--head to tail or top down--leading to the ability to stand and walk, and (2) proximo-distal--near to far or center of body outward--leading to the ability of the hands to perform in more and more sophisticated ways.

With regard to learning, brain research provides support for some aspects of early childhood education, but challenges other aspects. It has been determined that the brain does not act as a "black box" with learning a simple input/output system. Siegel (1976) suggests that the brain or cognition within the brain serves to organize, to extract relevant information, and to reduce uncertainty in the environment.

A number of brain models that facilitate cognitive processing have been suggested. The "up and down" model or RAS (reticular activating system) model theorizes that (1) components of the brain have structure with higher and lower functions, and (2) these brain components are interrelated. In this model, the RAS acts as a gate channeling an individual's experience to the correct part of the brain. Maslow's hierarchy would support this model.

The side-by-side model suggests that the different hemispheres of the brain control different cognitive and body functions. Side-by-side models agree that individual differences may be due to (1) processing styles, (2) prior

AVERAGE BODY TEMPERATURE IN INFANCY AND CHILDHOOD

Age	Temperature		Standard deviation	
	F	C	F	C
3 months	99.4	37.5	0.8	0.4
6 months	99.5	37.5	0.6	0.3
1 year	99.7	37.7	0.5	0.2
3 years	99.0	37.0	0.5	0.2
5 years	98.6	37.0	0.5	0.2
9 years	98.7	36.7	0.5	0.2
13 years	97.8	36.6	0.5	0.2

These rules apply only to children who at a given age up to 2 years are within the normal range of variation (M ± 1 standard deviation).

experiences which enhance or inhibit processing, and (3) interaction of experience and processing style.

MacLean's (1978) triune model states that the brain consists of three components. These components include (1) the Reptilian Complex (R Complex), which controls primary survival instincts, (2) the limbic system, which includes some survival components, but also tells the body what to do, and (3) the cortex or neocortex, which differentiates humans from other higher-order primates and controls future and abstract thought. This model is supported by the concept of evolution.

Although the question of whether motor development is a result of only maturation or only experience still is debated, the research suggests that both components of development and the interaction between them play a role. An early study (Gesell & Thompson, 1929) suggests that motor development is maturational. These researchers compared the chair-climbing ability of children with and without prior stair-climbing experience. Identical twins, 46 weeks of age, were used to control for heredity. In this experiment, one twin was given daily practice climbing stairs for six weeks. In four weeks this twin could climb stairs without help and at 52 weeks the twin could climb the stair in 26 seconds. The second twin who had never climbed stairs began the stair climbing protocol at 53 weeks. This twin, without prior experience could climb the stairs in just 10 seconds with two weeks of practice (age 55 weeks). These results suggest that maturation, rather than experience, is the key factor in motor development. However, one could argue that both twins had similar motor experiences, other than stair climbing, prior to the experiment and that these experiences were generalized to the stair-climbing behavior.

A later study (Dennis, 1960) suggests that environmental practices played a large part in motor development. Dennis's research with Iranian orphans suggests that if infants are not stimulated or allowed free movement, their motor development is delayed. Also, Kaplan and Dove (1987) suggested that Ache children in Paraguay are delayed in walking as a result of parents who keep them from exploring the environment. However, even though this research has wide ranging effects for children today, additional research indicates that children are resilient and that even when an infant is deprived at a young age, the retarded development can be overcome by placing the child in more appropriate conditions. The typical times of development are outlined below for various groups in terms of percentiles.

The average scores for the black infants included in Table 5.3 were found to be consistently superior to those for the white infants throughout the age range. This could indicate a genetic difference in which blacks are more precocious than whites in their motor coordination. However, these results also could be explained by the fact that the black infants who, in this study, came from a predominantly lower socio-economic class, were left to move about more freely with fewer restrictions. Thus, the nature versus nurture question in motor development remains to be answered. It seems that neuromuscular development appears to depend both on maturation and on experience. Although it is true that training and experience can play a role in the early appearance of motor skills, the child without early experience catches up quickly when age appropriate.

Prehension

At birth infants are unable to use their fingers as separate units since they are controlled by the cortical regions of the brain which at that time are poorly developed. However, the hand is a useful conductor of sensations and is an effective medium for children to explore the world about them. In the early stages of development, children examine their fingers and toes and reach into space, touching objects within the reach of their poorly coordinated arm and hand movements. Children explore the unique properties of objects about them and begin to differentiate between themselves and the things in their environment. However, infants less than three months old rarely succeed in grasping an object when it touches their palms (Bower, 1977).

The development of prehension is very important to the child's early intellectual and motor development. White and Held (1966) conducted research which suggests that at one month an infant simply will stare at an attractive object placed in his field of vision. At this age, he will make no purposeful attempt to grasp it. At approximately 2 1/2 months an infant will reach or swipe at the object, but will be unable to make contact (or make contact purely by chance). At approximately four months the child will reach closer and closer to the object, look at his hand and at the object alternately and may even touch the object through trial and error. By five to six months the infant will be able to make contact with the object on the first try.

Table 5.3 MOTOR DEVELOPMENT

Skill	25 Percent	50 Percent	90 Percent
Rolling over	2 months	3 months	5 months
Grasping rattle	2 1/2 months	3 1/2 months	4 1/2 months
Sitting without support	5 months	5 1/2 months	8 months
Standing while holding on	5 months	6 months	10 months
Grasping with thumb and finger	7 1/2 months	8 1/2 months	10 1/2 months
Standing alone well	10 months	11 1/2 months	14 months
Walking well	11 months	12 months	14 1/2 months
Building tower of two cubes	12 months	14 months	20 months
Walking up steps	14 months	17 months	22 months

Perception and Development of Vision

As may be evident, the majority of physical maturation discussed previously is related to an infant's use of motor abilities and senses. Perception is the process by which the brain interprets sensations generated through motor actions and sensory stimulation. Vision is a prominent sense through which perception occurs. The four-month-old infant's vision is 20/150 (Salapatek et al., 1976), which means that the infant can see at 20 feet what an adult with normal vision can see at 150 feet. The infant's visual sensitivity is assessed by its response to such visual stimuli as pupillary reflex, visual pursuit, binocular fixation, or convergence and adjustment of objects at varying distances (accommodations). By the age of four months, infant accommodation approaches that of adults.

Historically, it was believed that a newborn was unable to see. This is not true, as the basic equipment for vision is present at birth. Cells in the retina, called rods, register black and white only. These cells are so sensitive they can detect light as feeble as a 100-trillionth of a watt. Other retinal cells, called cones, are affected by color. These cells are found most abundantly at the fovea in the back of the eye at the place where the image falls when the eye focuses. This is near the blind spot; the place the optic nerve leaves the retina carrying the picture to the brain to develop.

Illingworth (1972) presents the following schedule of visual development in infants:

4 weeks:	Watches mother intensely when she speaks to the infant. Opens and closes mouth. Follows dangling objects when brought to midline less than 90 degrees.
6 weeks:	When supine, follows many objects from side to midline (90 degrees).
8 weeks:	Fixates eyes. Converges. Focuses.
12 weeks:	When supine, watches movements of hands (until 24 weeks). Follows dangling objects from side to side.
20 weeks:	Smiles at mirror images.
24 weeks:	Does not regard hand.
28 weeks:	Pats image of self in mirror.
40 weeks:	Looks around corner for object in mirror.

Responses to Faces and Contours

From the onset of life infants will respond to light, its contour (black line on a white background), and its intensity. They also respond to color, preferring red and blue over yellow and green (Bornstein, 1975), and moving rather than stationary objects (Milewski & Siqueland, 1975). Contour or movement cannot explain all attention, for at three months of age the infant tends to prefer a solid round shape like a bull's-eye to the striped pattern of an earlier period. Infants attend longest to complexity involving the number of elements, the amount of variety, and perhaps even variation in texture and color of the stimuli. In general, moderate amounts of complexity stimulate attention, but meaning and discrepancy also are important (Figure 5.1). Within the process of attentional response behavior of infants, some difference appears for males and females, with the latter holding longer fixations on some patterns (Mitchell, Ivinski, & Finlay, 1982). In general, infants three months old could discriminate smiling from frowning expressions based on previous experience (Barrera & Maures, 1981). Also, Labarbera, Izard, Vietze and Parisi (1976) found that infants four to six months of age gazed at joyful faces longer than they gazed at angry faces. Their research suggests that infants, very early in life, are aware of adult emotional states.

Depth, Spatial, and Three-Dimensional Perception

Like all aspects of development mentioned previously, depth, spatial, and three-dimensional perception are both learned and innate, and are probably a result of the interactions of heredity and the environment. At the age of 10 weeks infants look longer at a three-dimensional sphere than a two-dimensional circle of the same area. Up to 10 weeks the infant will react similarly to two- or three-dimensional faces and to a photo of a face or an actual face of a person. At three months infants will smile and coo more to an actual face.

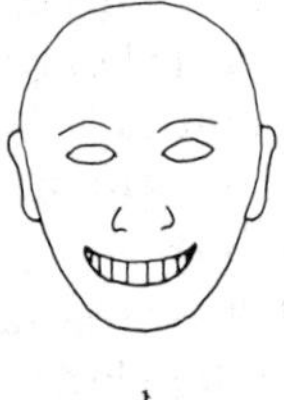
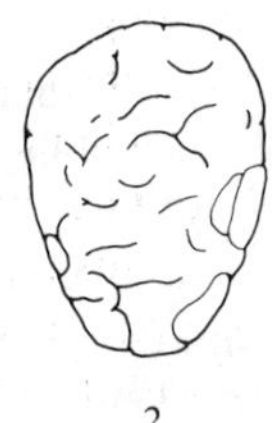
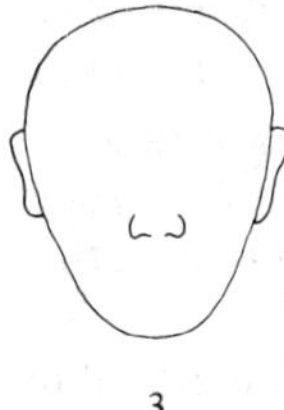
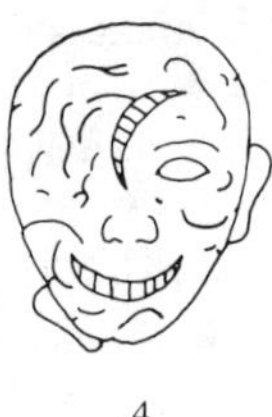

Figure 5.1 Stimulus faces used in studying discrimination in infants.

Theorists historically believed that the visual world of the child was two-dimensional and that children had to learn to perceive in three dimensions. Other theorists suggest that depth perception begins at birth, as revealed by the experiments with "visual cliffs" constructed on a table covered with glass extending outward on either side. On one side a textured pattern was placed far below the glass, giving the illusion of depth (Figure 5.2). Six-month-old infants and other land animals avoided the side on the apparent drop-off even though entreated by the mother (in the case of the infants) to cross. The infants refused to cross even though they could feel the heavy glass that meant they could cross safely (Fantz & Fagan, 1975).

Also indicative of an infant's visual perception was a study by Acredolo and Evans (1980). In their research an infant's ability to keep track of its relationship to a place in space was assessed under four conditions varying the presence, salience, and location of landmark information. These researchers studied infants who were placed first in one position, then rotated to the opposite side of the room. The direction of search was interpreted as an indication of whether the event's location was being coded by the child egocentrically or objectively. Investigators found that in the absence of landmarks, a high proportion of egocentricity was shown by 6-, 9- and 11-month-olds trained to expect an event at one or two windows to their left or right. According to Piaget, young infants tend to rely on the action-based, egocentric reference system resulting from their past experience to locate an object. However, when the windows were lighted or had stripes around them, the 9- and 11-month-old subjects became more objective. The six-month-olds were unsure as to which reference system to use. Though egocentric approaches were stubbornly utilized to locate an object, landmarks became increasingly important with maturation in keeping track of position in space.

Memory and Conditioning

The development of the cortex at birth is not advanced sufficiently to assume that the newborn remembers the birth experience or the experiences during the early period after birth. Memory depends upon the neurological development of infants whose mental apparatus functions as a sense impression recording. However, infants in the first weeks of life retain information. For example, an infant fixates on a

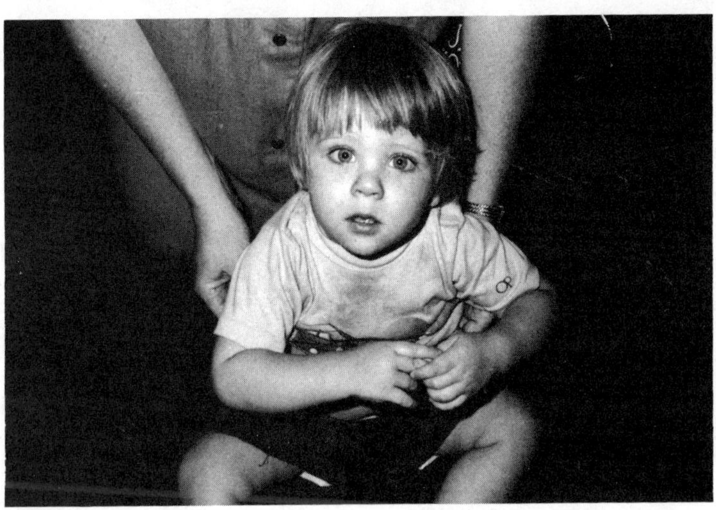

An early start on toilet training and being a "big boy" (usually 18-24 months).

visual pattern. Later, when the same pattern is shown along with another pattern, the infant fixates on the new pattern for a longer period of time than the original. This suggests that the infant has retained information about the original pattern (McCall, 1971).

Memory serves to make learning possible. Behavior learned by the infant stems from certain reflexive behaviors that are innate such as crying, sucking, and grasping. Learning, in its simplest form, is change in behavior based upon experience with events that have occurred in the environment. Modification in behavior begins with the first day of an infant's life. The sucking reflex can be altered on the first day of life, as indicated by Schaffer (1977) who found that an infant's suck varied when exposed to different stimuli--milk, corn syrup solution, or a pacifier. This ability to adapt behavior suggests that learning has occurred.

Patterns of response are ingrained in the neural traces and become increasingly numerous as the cortex matures. According to behavioral theory, the two basic mechanisms of learning are classical conditioning and operant conditioning. The former is illustrated by Pavlov's experiment with dogs who were taught to associate feeding, a reflexive act, with the sound of a bell ringing. With repeated pairing of the bell with food, the bell sound elicited salivation by itself--even in the absence of food, thus providing evidence that an association had been formed. This type of conditioning explains a small component of human behavior.

Operant or instrumental conditioning is believed by many to play a much larger role in human behavior and complex learning. In operant conditioning the consequences of a behavior cause it to increase or to decrease. Major concepts associated with operant conditioning include positive and negative reinforcement, both of which cause an increase in behavior. An example of positive reinforcement would be a praise statement (or less ideal, a piece of candy) after a child successfully has completed his math. The praise statement or candy as a consequence makes it more likely the child will complete his next math assignment (desired behavior). Negative reinforcement also causes the likelihood of a behavior to increase. Negative reinforcement can be thought of as relief from an unpleasant situation. An example of negative reinforcement is the seat belt buzzer in a car. This buzzer buzzes (unpleasant situation) until you buckle up your seat belt (desired behavior). The negative

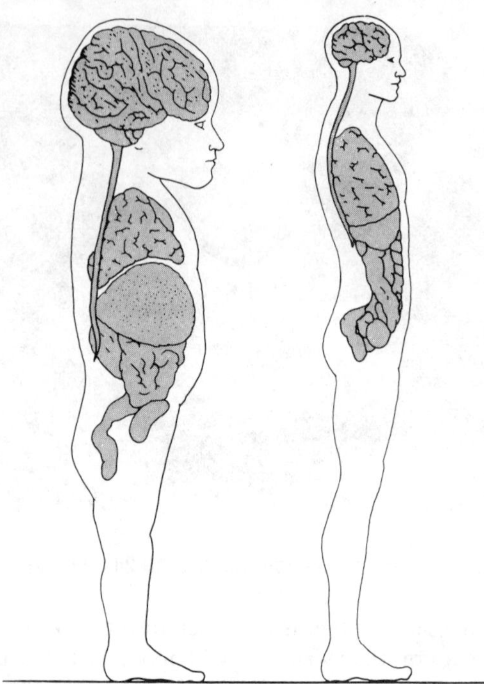

Figure 5.2 Neonate and adult drawn to same height showing early development of central nervous system.

reinforcement makes it more likely that you will continue to buckle your seat belt.

Negative reinforcement often is confused with punishment. The difference is that punishment decreases the probability that a behavior will occur while negative reinforcement increases the probability that a behavior will occur. A problem with punishment, even though it may suppress a behavior and cause it to decrease in frequency, is the possible side effects. A more appropriate solution to address inappropriate behavior is to withhold reinforcement. Ignoring the inappropriate behavior, when possible, is a way to withhold reinforcement and will cause a behavior to become extinct without the negative side effects of punishment.

Sensory and Motor Integration

Piaget (1972) has called the first one and a half to two years of life the *sensory-motor period* (Piaget's entire cognitive development theory is discussed in detail in Chapter 7). During the sensory-motor period all learning stems from motor activity and the senses. The infant learns to control its own bodily movements. Figure 5.2 shows the advanced early development of the central nervous system, which supports a growing sensory capacity.

Cognition and Language

The infant learns to integrate its various sense impressions into schema (a mental representation of an event) and learns to respond differently to each type of sensory input. Only during the latter part of the sensory-motor period can an infant combine these sensations into a perceptual motor function. As previously stated, at birth and in the first month of life all learning is based on reflexes. Innate reflexes quickly are modified as indicated by different "sucks" on different objects. After a few weeks this "sucking" reflex becomes differentiated. A nipple will be sucked differently than will a finger or blanket. This concludes the first stage of Piaget's sensory-motor period which is called appropriately the Reflexive Stage.

The second stage of Piaget's sensory-motor period is called Primary Circular Reactions (one to four months). In this stage, the infant is learning about his body (primary) and tends to repeat, in a trial and error fashion, pleasurable actions (circular reactions) that were discovered by chance. These amorphous movements are designed to aid in development of hand-mouth, hand-eye coordination.

From about the fourth to the eighth month (Piaget's Secondary Circular Reactions Stage) infants begin to concentrate on objects other than their own bodies (secondary). This idea suggests that the environment and the concept of circular reactions remains, as stated previously. In this stage a child will accidentally kick his crib, making a mobile move and dance about. This pleasurable trial-and-error event will occur again and again until the child forms a scheme (organized pattern of behavior) for it and is able to repeat it at will.

From 8 to 12 months of age the infant is in the stage called Coordination of Secondary Schemes. In this stage the infant first manifests true intelligence (according to Piaget) through the use of goal-directed behavior. In this stage the infant will put two intact schemes together in order to obtain a goal. For example, the 10-month old infant will open an adult's hand in order to get a ball or pick up a pillow while reaching for a ball with the other hand.

The fifth stage of the sensory-motor period is called Tertiary Circular Reactions or "Directed Groping." During this stage one sees the infant beginning to experiment with his schemes. A common example of this is the infant who, although previously able to get oatmeal from a bowl to his mouth on a spoon will, all of a sudden, begin to fling the oatmeal about. At this point, the infant is trying to understand what will happen when he changes his scheme. Although obnoxious to the parent, this behavior is a developmental milestone and should be expected. During this stage, the child can follow sequential displacement.

Piaget's last stage of the sensory-motor period is termed the Beginning of Representational Thought (18 to 24 months). At this stage, the infant begins to manifest behaviors that suggest an ability to represent various objects and situations mentally and to solve problems through mental representation. Deferred imitation, or the ability to conjure up images of past experiences, is indicative of this stage of development. This ability reduces the child's need for the use of trial and error. The infant can remember pictures of experiences of what his father or mother did to fix his wagon so it would run.

During this entire period of early development and all later human development, Piaget argues that motivation is internal and caused by a child trying to understand discrepancies between old and new experiences. In seeking to understand the difference between what he knows and a new stimulus, the child is motivated to learn. The ability to recall depends upon the clues an infant can find to activate the classification (schemata) that he has. The infant's memory ability to store and to retrieve information develops from the neonatal period onward at a rapid rate. Object concept (important in Piaget's theory) partially begins as early as four to five months, as the infant develops some recognition of familiar objects. This is indicated by the infant's excitement and pleasure when it sees a bottle or its mother. By four months, experiments indicate that babies, when reaching for projected images of objects on a screen, were surprised and frustrated when they grasped for empty air. However, when the actual objects were dangled before them they showed no surprise. In other words, they expected them. Object identity (another important Piagetian concept) is recognition of an object, the nature of which an infant comes to understand (develop a schema for the concept), and in some way use, play with, or gaze at it. Object permanence (the last important Piagetian concept, for now) is obtained when objects continue to exist in the mind of an infant even when they cannot be perceived through any of the infant's senses. As early as four months the infant appears to realize on some level that a moving object exists even when it is out of sight. At six or seven months, the baby seems to know it has only one mother. During the period of four to eight months, babies do not have a schema for object permanence. They will look for an object, like a ball, may kick at it if they see it, but if it is entirely hidden they seem to forget about it as if it never existed. By eight months, the schema for object permanence begins to develop. However, if the object is moved from one hiding place to another while the infant watches, he or she will look for it in the first hiding place. Piaget's experiment with all three of his children from the age of nine to ten months showed they would look behind a screen for an object if they had seen it hidden, but would not search for an object out of sight until around one year.

Evaluation of Piaget's Theory

Nearly four decades have passed since the publication of the *Origin of Intelligence in Children* (1952), and much debate and research has accumulated since then. Piaget took children seriously and studied them persistently with a careful, naturalistic approach. Although he emphasized the infant as being responsible through an active, adaptive, and constructive role for his own learning, many investigators believe he overstated the place of motor development in overall development. On the other hand, some say he underrepresented the place of perceptual development. Many skills and acquisitions in the child's intellectual progress come earlier than Piaget suggested. Object permanence may come earlier than nine months according to Baillargeon (1987), who believes other approaches to testing show an earlier acquisition of this ability. He and others think the infants may know the object is behind the pillow but not have the ability to perform the sequences of movement--that is traverse the distance to the pillow, stand, or pull up and reach for the pillow.

Deferred imitation, which shows long-term memory, occurs at about 18 months according to Piaget, but research by Melzoff (1988) finds it occurring at 14 months or earlier--maybe nine or ten months. Number concept emerging at two years of age has been challenged, suggesting at least rudimentary knowledge of numbering comes as early as seven months (Starkey et al., 1983). Piaget says achievement of conservation (weight) comes at about nine years of age. This has been countered by Bowers (1976), who did research on infants, picking up a piece of clay shaped one way and then another, and how they reacted by moving their arms in a way which suggested the weight remained the same. This seems to be highly speculative. Can the ideas of evaluation be transmitted to the infant--that is, are the two shapes the same weight? Bowers said at three or four years of age children had lost this ability, to have it return at seven or eight. The sensory-motor stages themselves have been validated by the research of Uzgiris (1972). Piaget's object permanence sequence also has been reproduced by Kramer et al. (1975). And the idea of infants being active participants in their own learning finds a parallel in the research by Benson and Uzgiris (1985). Ten-month-old infants allowed to crawl around in a box where a toy had been hidden were more successful in finding the toy after they had been around the hiding area. More definitive research will continue to alter some specifics of Piaget's theory. Nonetheless, the major framework seems generally intact. The massive work generated by his theories has been salutary and he will continue to hold a significant place in science.

The Development of Language

Language, as a communication system, allows a child (1) access to information and (2) control over his environment. Piaget writes that language evolves and is controlled by thought. For example, a child first thinks about an object and then develops the appropriate word or language to communicate about the object. Vygotsky and Luria believe that thought evolves from language and that an individual's thought processes are limited if there is a language limitation. According to Vygotsky and Luria, a child could never think about anything that transcended his language ability at any point in time.

There are two important elements in language development during infancy: receptive and productive language. The former has reference to the understanding of the spoken word and latter has importance for the child's written work and talking out what he writes. The receptive is usually a little bit in advance of the productive. The beginning of language is initiated with the cry, undifferentiated at birth, but in the first weeks, cries that mean a variety of things--calls for help, hunger, attention, etc. At about six weeks, cooing is added to the repertoire of the infant. The left hemisphere of the brain has developed to the point that allows the child to listen and respond to speech from the beginning (Brooks and Obrzut, 1981). In the second and third month, the infant is oriented to speech and is able to distinguish between *b* and *p* and *d* and *t*. The baby has used nonverbal aspects of communication from the earliest days--it has learned to signal, to take turns, to gesture, and play peek-a-boo (Ross and Lollis,

TABLE 5.4

MONTHS	LANGUAGE IN INFANCY AND TODDLERHOOD
0.25	Makes some response to sound
1.25	Smiles in response to stimulation
1.6	Coos; makes long vowel sounds
4	Turns toward speaker; says "ah-goo"; makes razzing sound
6	Cooing changes to babbling, with introduction of consonants
8	Says "dada" and "mama" but does not use them as names
9	Plays gesture games like peekaboo; understands word "no"
11	Uses "dada" and "mama" as names; responds to one-step command and gesture indicating activity
12	Says gibberish "sentences" without real words; says first word; imitates sounds
13	Says third word
14	Responds to one-step command without gesture
15	Says four to six words
17	Says gibberish sentence with some real words; points to body parts; says 7 to 20 words
18	Patterns of sounds sound like speech
19	Says two-word combinations
21	Says two-word "sentences"; has 50-word vocabulary
24	Uses pronouns (I, me, you) indiscriminately; two-word phrases are most common; more interested in talking; no more babbling

Adapted from Capute, Shapiro, & Palmer, 1987

1987). Skillful parents or caretakers at playing social games with their infants help them to take turns and learn give-and-take. By one year of age, the infant is aware of people around him and will respond to emotional expressions of others, by facial expression and body movement.

At six months the baby has learned a variety of sounds and frequently practices them. It repeats sounds generalized under the term babbling, though sometimes called iteration. Its echoing of the sounds of others is called echolalia. The infant's use of expressive jargon is observed in its inflection and mimicry of adults. Some words are understood before talk. This is known as receptive vocabulary and begins with pseudo words, those seen in a range of vocalizations that are often paired with gestures and have a specific meaning. Words like "bye-bye" and instructions like "put the cup down" or "give me the spoon," when acted upon, are clear signs of understanding.

Around the first birthday, the child says its first words, usually adding single words at first, then rapidly others by two years of age. Most first words are nouns and often holophrastic--conveying a sentence or idea in a single word such as "Dada" may mean "I want my daddy!" We should not, however, put too much meaning in simple utterance. Another aspect of language development is overextensions by children. These are numerous, such as "moo" for any kind of animal or "fly" for dust, small insects, crumbs or their toes. Around two years, telegraph speech begins; children put words together as "sock off" or "more milk." Additional information addressing language can be found in Chapter 6.

EMOTIONAL AND SOCIAL BEHAVIOR IN INFANCY

Becoming a sociable human being is a learning process fostered by society; it is not innate but results from interactions between the child and other humans. This process is known as socialization. During the first year of the infant's life, the mother or primary caregiver is the central influence on social behavior. According to Senn and Solnit (1970), this process begins at four to eight weeks, with the mother using her special language and sounds to elicit a smile from the infant. A happy exchange or positive reciprocal relationship between the mother and infant provides a good foundation for social development throughout life.

Ainsworth (1964) postulated four phases of socialization, including:

1. Infant responds indiscriminately to everyone (0-4 months);

2. Attachment in the making; babies smile and babble more to the mother but also to others (2-4 months);

3. Babies show clear-cut attachment to the mother and less friendliness to others (6-7 months); anxiety and fearfulness of strangers appear during this stage;

4. Infants develop multiple attachments to sisters, brothers, or father.

Ainsworth (1973) also stated that the same phases of socialization appear in all infants, regardless of cultural influences. However, in Uganda she found babies somewhat more accelerated in their social development on the Gesell Development Schedules than other babies she studied. She hypothesized that African babies were breast-fed and experienced more interaction with adult figures than infants in the Western world.

Smiling

Smiling frequently is regarded as the beginning of social development that occurs once the

First Smile	Percentage
Before 2 weeks	0
2-3 weeks	11
3-4 weeks	49
4-5 weeks	21
5-6 weeks	19

infant has distinguished between objects and persons. The smile is at first indiscriminating. At four months, however, a discriminating social smile clearly is directed to the mother and accounted for by the infant's having developed a schema for the mother's face and recognizing an object bringing pleasure. Soderling (1959) observed the age of the first smile in 40 normal full-term infants and noted the smiling and ebullience in the growing infant gives some indication of well-being.

Attachment

At approximately six months, the young infant has established a firm emotional bond with the mother or primary caregiver. During the early months, there is a close relation among love, food, and relief of discomfort. Food brings the child and mother, or primary caregiver, into close contact. Also, this person continually provides the infant with relief from discomfort. The attitudes and manners of the caregiver in feeding and caring for the infant when it is uncomfortable often determines the quality of later affections. During the first year, the child develops a sense of trust. A happy, loving, understanding caregiver provides a climate in which the baby feels secure, comfort-

Table 5.5 PHASES IN THE DEVELOPMENT OF INFANT ATTACHMENT

Preattachment	First month	Crying, smiling, rooting, clinging, sucking, looking at; movements synchronized with adult speech; discrimination of mother's voice.
Attachment-in-the-making	Into second half of first year	Singling out objects of primary attachment; selective social smile--directed more toward attachment objects or persons than toward the unfamiliar.
Clear-cut attachment	Second half of first year	Continued use of behaviors designed to draw attention--smiling, crying, squirming; use of newly developing locomotor skills to approach attachment object or person.
Goal-corrected attachment	Second year	Begins to adopt mother's point of view and to make inferences about mother's behavior; manipulation of mother's behavior in more subtle ways following gradual recognition of cause-and-effect relationships.

Source: Based on *Attachment and Loss* (Vol. 1) by J. Bowlby, 1969, New York: Basic Books able, and friendly; an impatient, hostile caregiver provides a climate of fear, suspicion and distrust.

Family Influences and Parenting

Research shows that infants form their strongest attachment to their mothers. But when fathers frequently and consistently interact with the baby, the child also will form a strong bond with them. The early closeness by the father also means that he will have considerable influence later on the child's socialization. Even among siblings many more close relationships develop than do life-long rivalries. Sisters and brothers usually maintain the longest ties of all relationships. Often others in the wider family have great influence on the infant's growth and progress. Grandparents see the baby often and in many cases do regular or considerable baby-sitting for the parents; also uncles, aunts, and cousins are influential. In some cases such relationships compensate for the inadequacies in the nuclear family. Also, important in the child's life is the relationship between the father and mother. If it is a poor one, the children will suffer.

Fathers and mothers differ in their interaction with infants. Fathers are usually more physical and spontaneous, and they are more occasionally involved in high intensity activities with their children. They may have periods, though, of little interaction with their children. Fathers are most influential with their infants when they spend time with them, respond to their wants and needs, are responsive to their cries, and show interest in them (Parker, 1981). Mothers are thought to be naturally responsive to their children, though this is not automatic. Simply having a child does not confirm bonding. Even separation of the mother from the child after birth for a period of time may influence the development of bonding. Perhaps, however, mothers have inherited more nurturant traits from the animal ancestry. In addition, strong emotions are aroused by breast-feeding, and in our society women have been socialized to be caretakers.

In the case of handicapped infants, such as in deafness, there are often difficulties which need to be overcome. Sometimes such difficulties arise in establishing good relations and rapport because of neglect and physical or mental abuse. Infants often are at risk due to the absence of love and support, which often parallels inadequate care in feeding and poor medical and psychological attention.

As one might expect, research continues to support the notion that mothers spend more time with infants than do fathers. However, changes are occurring (Pedersen, 1980). Ricks (1985) indicates that newborns form attach-

Adapted from "Dennis the Menace."

ments with fathers that are almost as strong as the mother/infant attachment. It appears that infants, when given the chance, talk, smile, and play with their fathers at a very young age. In addition, fathers appear to be able to feed, bathe, and change their children as well as can mothers.

In infant monkeys such a relationship was shown in a series of studies by Harlow and Harlow (1962, 1970). The investigators examined the infant/mother affectional bond, contrasting hard wire mesh and soft terry cloth mother surrogates. The infants became attached to the cloth mother surrogates, showing a distinct preference for them over the wire mother substitutes, which were equipped with nursing bottles. It would appear that the comfort afforded by bodily contact was valued more highly by the monkeys than was the food.

Also related to attachment is stranger anxiety. Kagan (1973) noted that stranger anxiety typical of American children 8 to 12 months old did not occur in a tribe of Guatemalans until they were 18 months old. He attributed this to physical confinement and lack of verbal interaction with mothers. The infants were fed and held close, but adults did not talk with or to them. Thus, anxiety toward strangers seems to be the product of both the maturation process and experience.

The occurrence of such anxiety appears to parallel cognitive development at the point where object permanence is being solidified. This suggests that objects such as the mother have an existence of their own that the child cannot control (Kagan, 1976). The disappearance of stranger anxiety also parallels the growth of language abilities in that once the infant begins to talk, the number of fears decreases (Figure 5.3).

The social smile, fear of strangers, and separation anxiety all are positive signs of development and constitute important steps during the first years of infancy. Clarke-Stewart and co-workers (1980) studied 60 infants with their mothers and strangers at 12, 18, 24, and 30 months. Their behavior was analyzed to reveal sociability, cluster of smiling, vocalizing, and playing. It was found that when the mother and stranger behaved similarly the infant's behavior was the same to both. Sociability to the mother was not consistently related to physical contact with her, whereas social and physical contact with strangers consistently was correlated. Sociability to the mother was more related to maternal behavior than was sociability to the stranger, which was associated with non-parental care. The older the infant, the more it attempted to be social. The development of social behavior of the infant has been

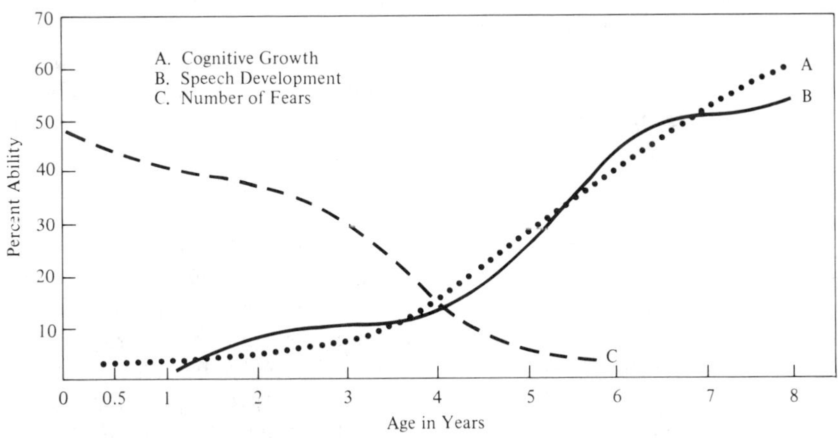

Figure 5.3 Relationships in development of speech, cognition, and fears.

summarized by Illingworth (1972) as follows:

8 weeks: Vocalizes and smiles. Shows interest in surroundings, follows dangling toy from side to the point past the midline.

12 weeks: Is excited when presented a toy. "Talks" a great deal as a response.

20 weeks: Smiles at mirror image. Discovers his or her own body.

24 weeks: Holds arms out to be picked up. May show fear of strangers and be coy.

28 weeks: Imitates. Tries to attract attention by cough; responds to name.

32 weeks: Tries persistently to get hold of toys out of reach. Responds to "no."

40 weeks: Pulls mother's clothes to draw attention. Waves "bye-bye," "pat-a-cakes." Repeats performance when laughed at. Can say two or three words like "dog" and "cat."

44 weeks: Drops toys deliberately to be picked up.

48 weeks: Anticipates body movement in nursery rhyme. Is interested when shown simple pictures in book.

Personality

Heredity plays a major role in the development of personality in that parameters are set for how a child might react to a situation. However, the range of reactions within these parameters is subject to environmental influence. Thomas, Chess, and Birch (1981) suggest that a large percentage of infants can be classified with regard to temperament. However, all children even within temperament listings may not react similarly to an event (see Table 5.6).

Theories of Personality

In the first chapter we looked at a number of important theories of development--two of these, Freud's and Erikson's, we will discuss here. It is frequently said that no theory will cover all bases, or like the example of the procrustean bedcover in mythology, all the necessary parts. These two theories, however, do touch on two important aspects of development. First, there is the aspect that the hereditary and the physical nature of a person provides a basis for study, as in Freud's psychosexual theory. Second, there is the aspect that the environment with its caretakers impact heavily on the child, as seen in Erikson's psycho-social theory. The caretaker is principally the mother. One readily admits that others besides the mother play a large part in the development of the infant and its future direction. Certainly the environment of places, people, and things affect development, as do family and kin and the given uniqueness of the person. Nevertheless, the mother is the crucial element in the early life of the child, for usually "as the twig is bent, so grows the tree."

An often-heard criticism of these theories is that they are difficult to test in research. What is "anal personality" or what is "basic trust"? For a short answer, the anal personality has been seen by countless caretakers whose infant and toddler's maturity directs their attention away from sucking to toileting--resisting training or being cooperative with it. Parents have seen the immediate effects on the child; of course, this does not guarantee the long-term effects suggested by Freud. Do infants become obsessively precise and tied to routines if the toilet training is too severe? As to basic trust, the security of the infant in the first year and a

Table 5.6 CLASSIFICATION AS TO TEMPERAMENT

Temperament	Description	Approximate Percentage
Easy	Regularity in eating and sleeping (high rhythmicity); high approach tendencies in novel situations; high adaptability to change; preponderance of positive moods; low or moderate intensity of responses.	40
Difficult	Irregularity in eating and sleeping (low rhythmicity); withdrawal in novel situations; slow adaptation to change; preponderance of negative moods; high intensity of reactions to stimulation.	15
Slow-to-warm-up	Low activity level; high initial withdrawal from unfamiliar; slow adaptation to change; somewhat negative mood; moderate or low intensity of reaction to stimulation.	10
Varying mixtures	Unclassified	35

half is seen easily in the infant's attachment to, and openness toward, others. Research doesn't pinpoint the precise degree of lack of trust and what follows, but it is accepted that most children inadequately cared for in the early years have difficulties easily traceable to a lack of security in these years.

According to Freud, children must transit through the stages of oral/anal in a reasonable manner to be successful children and adults. If the infant receives too little or is forced to move on too quickly, oral gratification becomes fixated. This fixation remains a problem until alleviated via some substitute--pleasure, maturity, or understanding. The infant operates principally under the influence of the pleasure principle through Freud's first two stages. Growing cognitive development and socialization forces the infant to increasingly accept the reality of society and control. Therefore, in general Freud's theory appears to have some validity in assessing the experience of the child.

Inadequate mothering can make infants dependent and reduce their creativity. Erikson's theory makes the first critical social aspect in infancy--that of developing security. This is accomplished through good care such as feeding the child when it is hungry, stroking and holding the infant, changing diapers regularly so children won't wallow in their excrement and are not chafed by wet clothes. This social crisis, according to Erikson, is largely between mother and infant. A good experience leads the infant to feel secure and trust people, providing an entree into the next stage that is favorable. Autonomy versus shame and doubt is the next social crisis for the infant between 18 to 30 months of age. This parallels the increased prowess of its motor skills, movement ability, and cognitive growth. The child's exertion of self and the attempt at creating self concept results in a challenge to parental control. The parent will often judge the child's behavior by adult standards. The idea of the "terrible twos" comes from this phenomenon. It is probably essential that all children need to express self-will in order to become independent. Toddlers will often "try" their parents, become negative, and frequently resent the parental dictum of "clean up your room" to the extent of putting on a temper tantrum. They may refuse to eat because they have been rebuffed or told to come to supper. Some suggestions about dealing with this follow:

1. Let children play out, if possible, what they are doing. Interruption is the worst thing the three-year-old can face. If you have to interrupt, give a warning; say, "In 10 minutes we have to eat."
2. Be flexible. Parents who are inflexible teach less flexibility to their children.
3. Make choices available, even if they are limited; for instance, "Which do you wish to do now, take your bath or eat?"
4. Be consistent in following regulations, requests, etc.
5. Use time-out; remove the child or yourself from the situation. If you leave the room, the authority crisis may resolve itself and the child become more docile.
6. Don't agitate over thumb-sucking or use of a pacifier, blankets, or toys. They are used by most infants. Most will stop by age five or six. Damage to teeth will, if it comes, be at six to eight when second teeth are coming.

The self-control of infants and toddlers develops typically beginning at 1 1/2 years. By two, mental representation has been accomplished and infants can remember what has been said to them, as in staying away from electrical outlets and plugs. When they want to do something very badly, they usually do it, such as getting into dessert mother has warned them to stay out of because it's for dinner. At three, children will develop self-regulation and learn to postpone gratification and remember what has been told them. Parents can help by suggesting alternative activities and reminding the child often of what is expected. They can pair commands with nice social consequences, such as, let's stop watching the TV so we can go to the drugstore. Also, the parent needs to recognize the child's stress, be considerate, and refrain from expecting perfect behavior.

Emotions

The development of emotions and personality are interrelated. Emotions are evident at

Fun at the party!

birth, delineated by Bridges (1932) as undifferentiated excitement; then by three months, into distress and delight. We know now a number of emotions are in operation at birth (Izard, 1982). Excitement, interest, startle response, distress, disgust, and perhaps a half-smile (which some believe is a grimace or reflex) have all been isolated. Certainly it would appear that emotions are precursors of behavior; those used frequently effect a pattern of behavior. For example, expressions of pain at two months brings help. Later, at seven or eight months, the same experience may generate activity designed to rid one's self of an annoyance, like pushing the cat away. Infants who have been abused show fear earlier than typical infants, perhaps because of traumatic experience (Gaensbauer and Hiatt, 1984). Mothers show a greater range of emotions to girls than to their sons. This may account for the fact that generally girls are better than boys in recognizing the meaning of emotional expression (Trotter, 1983).

Self-recognition develops at about 18 months paralleling the autonomy and doubt stage of Erikson. Image self-recognition via the mirror is accomplished at about 18 months. It has been frequently observed that most infants, though fearful of strangers at eight or nine months, are not usually afraid of other infants, apparently thinking they are like themselves. An experiment, by Lewis and Brooks (1974), in placing coloring--rouge--on the faces of babies 6 to 24 months and then placing them before a mirror, resulted in considerably more touching to the nose than babies without the coloring. Apparently infants know the rouging is not their normal color. From self-awareness, infants develop preferences for playmates, like same-sex playmates and children rather than adults. They also can empathize and think about their own feelings. Perhaps by three years of age they recognize that no one else knows what they are thinking--not even Mommy--so telling a lie seems reasonable and normal. Learning about self determines interaction with others and undergirds social competence, peer relations, and identity. Some say self-recognition generates out of maturation exclusively; this is partly true. For just as mental representation has a correlation with physical development, self-awareness means the child is developing neurologically through experience. Regardless of the degree of environment or maturation, some rudimentary knowledge of self comes early and is a factor in social and personality growth.

Psychological and Emotional Deprivation

The need for warmth, security, love, and the abundance of mothering has been well researched. Years ago, it was demonstrated that if babies admitted to pediatric hospitals were not returned to their mothers immediately upon recovery, they tended to develop marasmus, a condition characterized by loss of muscle tone, low-grade fever, hemoglobin deficiency, and lethargy. The cure for this condition was to return these children to their homes as quickly as possible so that each child would receive the stimulation and attention normal in most families, but lacking in the typical hospital ward. In these infants, the child was responding to the lack of stimulation essential for its health and well-being (Lemkan, 1961). The classical studies by Spitz (1949), Bowlby (1956), and Fralberg (1967) found that infants go through critical periods. One such period may be a long separation from their mothers, and if unsolicitous caretakers do not provide attention, contact, and love, damage can result in many types of stress symptoms. This deprivation can lead to the development of problem children and neuroticism. Lourie (1970) stated that a critical period begins at the age of five months and that the failure to provide appropriate mothering results in the inability of the infant to thrive physically. Some human beings, however, may have weak instincts for mothering. Zalba (1971) estimated that 250,000 children suffer physical abuse each year. More recently gathered data indicate that the incidence of abuse is an ever-escalating problem. The child abuser destroys the expectations of love, trust, and dependence essential to the child.

Influences Affecting the Development of the Infant

It was suggested earlier that unfavorable influences during the prenatal period will have a detrimental effect upon the offspring. Metcaff (1978), Dobbing (1976), and Scrimshaw (1965) have delineated and summarized the effects of diet in pregnancy and its subsequent relation to the development of the offspring. Numerous other factors besides diet also affect the development of the infant. These are cultural expectations, socio-economic differences, psychological care, homeostasis, and health care.

Cultural Expectations

Although the biology (size, sex, and so on) of the infant largely determines the expectations set forth for it, each culture envisions its own ways of inducting the child into the particular society. Many non-Western societies expect a child to assume adult responsibilities early in life and consequently provide less latitude in terms of play and permissiveness. In some cultures where considerably more experimentation is allowed with regard to sex play prior to marriage, less expectancy exists regarding schooling. Where the culture does not emphasize schooling, family solidarity often is closer, because the family performs more functions of both a primary and a secondary nature.

The Western world following World War II imposed its way of life on many developing countries. Presently, many Third World countries show a decline of maternal nursing of infants. Breast feeding is important everywhere, but even more so in developing countries, for it usually meets the nutritional needs of the infant for the first four to six months and can furnish up to three-quarters of a child's protein requirement during the second six months of life. Shortening the lactation period increases the chances of illness during infancy for many Third World children. Also, many water supplies from which infant formula is prepared are polluted and are a primary cause of infant illness in developing countries.

As with breast feeding, cultural expectations are also different with regard to toilet training, aggression, punishment, and the mother's relation to the child. The transmission of the cultural content of a society to the growing child begins in the home. The family is influenced by wider aspects of culture: its race, ethnic origin, and religion. Children's concepts concerning the world, either real or unreal, are absorbed, and their development is affected accordingly.

Day Care

Prior to 1970, only about 25 percent of U.S. mothers with children under one year of age were in the work force. In 1988, the figure was 53 percent (Hymes, 1989). This tremendous increase has occurred contiguously with a multitude of societal changes. The question is no longer whether infant day care is appropriate or not, but how to make infant day care a positive experience.

Infant day care usually can be broken down into three areas. The first is home care by extended family. The pros and cons of this type of care are rather obvious. Some family members may provide care in the same manner as would the mother; other family members may ignore, or even abuse the infant. A second type of infant care would be home care by a stranger. This second category has similar pros and cons with the added problems of initially not knowing the individual with whom you leave your child. The third type of care is institutional care. This type of care, unlike categories one and two, is usually regulated and although there are problems with abuse and neglect, these problems are statistically insignificant. In fact, most child abuse is perpetrated by a family member or acquaintance. Ideally,

Table 5.7 TODDLER'S DAILY DIETARY INTAKE

FOOD GROUP	SERVINGS	AVERAGE SIZE OF SERVINGS
Milk (Cheese, yogurt, milk beverages, and desserts)	4	1/2 to 3/4 cup each
Meat Group	3 or more	
Egg		1
Lean meat, fish, poultry (liver once a week)		2 Tbsp
Peanut butter		1 Tbsp
Fruits and Vegetables	4 at least	
Vitamin C source (Citrus fruits, berries, tomato, cabbage cantaloupe)	1 or more (Tomato has only half the vitamin content of citrus fruit)	1/2 cup citrus
Vitamin A source (Green or yellow fruits and vegetables)	1 or more	3 Tbsp
Other vegetables	2	3 Tbsp
or		
Other fruits		1/3 cup
Cereals (Whole grain or enriched)	4 at least	
Bread		1 slice
Ready-to-eat cereals		3/4 oz.
Cooked cereal, rice, or pasta		1/3 cup
Fats and Carbohydrates	Sufficient to meet caloric needs	
Butter, margarine, oil 1 Tbsp = 100 calories (kcal)		1 Tbsp
Desserts and sweets (100-calorie portions)		1 1/2 portions

Adapted from Behrman and Vaughan, 1987.

an infant care center should be licensed by the National Association for the Education of Young Children.

Child-Care Checklist

Questions to ask at day care centers:

1. What are the educational and training backgrounds of staff members?

2. What is the child-staff ratio for each age? Most experts say it should be no more than 4:1 for infants, 5:1 for eighteen months to two years, 8:1 for two to three years, 10:1 for three to four years and 15:1 for five to six years.

3. What are the disciplinary policies?

4. Are parents free to visit at any time?

5. Are the center's facilities clean and well maintained?

6. Are child-safety precautions observed? Such as heat covers on radiators, childproof safety seals on all electrical outlets?

7. Are staff members careful about hygiene? It's important to wash hands between diaper changes in order to avoid spreading diseases.

8. Are there facilities and staff for taking care of sick children?

9. Is there adequate space, indoors and out, for children to play?

10. Most important of all, do the children look happy and cared for? Trust your instincts.

Research results addressing the issue of infant care are ambivalent. However, most studies suggest that it is the quality of such care that is important and not necessarily where the care is provided.

HEALTH CARE AND PREVENTIVE PEDIATRICS

Checkups and Immunization

In an age where scientific research bears on all aspects of life, it may be easy to overlook the value of routine checkups, good nutrition, and proper immunization during the first years of life. These can have a lasting effect upon the child's physical, cognitive, and emotional development. For example, Michaelson (1972, p. 32) points out:

> Diphtheria, once the most dreaded disease of childhood, is now held in check by immunization. Polio is a crippling disease of children that also is controlled by immunization. However, if babies born today don't receive diphtheria and polio vaccinations, we will be faced with epidemics within the next decade. There is, however, a real danger in complacency and neglect on the part of many parents in particular and the public in general. It has been pointed out that immunization levels for measles are still low enough to permit extensive spread of the measles virus in this country.

A mother may be immune to certain diseases, but antibodies for diseases such as smallpox, mumps, diphtheria, and measles pass through the placenta from mother to infant. A mother's temporary immunity provided for the child lasts from a few weeks to several months. It does not include chicken pox and pertussis (whooping cough), so that infants may contract these diseases. Unfortunately, immunization is not possible for young infants, as their immaturity preempts their ability to form effective antibodies (Marlow, 1973, p. 31).

Another enemy to the health of children is tuberculosis, and there is no vaccine for this.

Table 5.8 RECOMMENDED SCHEDULE FOR ACTIVE IMMUNIZATION OF NORMAL INFANTS & CHILDREN

Recommended Age	Immunization(s)	Comments
2 months	DTP,[1] OPV[2]	Can be initiated as early as 2 weeks of age in areas of high endemicity or during epidemics
4 months	DTP, OPV	2-month interval desired for OPV to avoid interference from previous dose
6 months	DTP (OPV)	OPV is optional (may be given in areas with increased risk of polio virus exposure)
15 months	Measles, Mumps, Rubella (MMR)	MMR preferred to individual vaccines; tuberculin testing may be done
18 months	DTP,[4,5] OPV[5]	
24 months	HBPV[6]	
4-6 years[7]	DTP, OPV	At or before school entry
14-16 years	Td[8]	Repeat every 10 years throughout life

[1]DTP--Diphtheria and tetanus toxoids with pertussis vaccine.
[2]OPV--Oral poliovirus vaccine contains attenuated poliovirus types 1, 2, and 3.
[3]MMR--Live measles, mumps, and rubella viruses in a combined vaccine.
[4]Should be given 6 to 12 months after the third dose.
[5]May be given simultaneously with MMR at 15 months of age.
[6]*Haemophilus* b polysaccharide vaccine.
[7]Up to the seventh birthday.
[8]Td--Adult tetanus toxoid (full dose) and diphtheria toxoid (reduced dose) in combination.

For all products used, consult manufacturer's package insert for instructions for storage, handling, and administration. Biologics prepared by different manufacturers may vary, and those of the same manufacturer may change from time to time.

From American Academy of Pediatrics, 1986.

The disease is still common enough in certain parts of the world to present a problem. A program of regular checkups by the pediatrician can help in identifying at an early age not only the symptoms of tuberculosis, but also many other potentially handicapping conditions, some of which can be cured or ameliorated if observed at an early age.

Frequent visits to the doctor or health clinic should be made for reviewing progress and general health conditions during the first 18 to 24 months. It is important to know which immunizations are required (Table 5.8) and about other aspects of health care.

SUMMARY

The post-natal development of the infant is most rapid during the first year of life. The physical size in weight triples for most by the first birthday and, by nine months, the sitting height is 50 percent of what it will be at 17 years of age. The brain at birth is closer than any other organ to its eventual gross weight. By 12 months, considerable neuromuscular development has occurred in most infants. They have the ability to stand alone and to pull up and walk, prehension is developed, and they have depth perception. Infants also can utilize a frame of reference for spatial location, and other sensory abilities (vision, hearing, taste, smell) have been functioning since birth.

Memory serves to make learning possible, which enables conditioning to take effect. According to Behavioral theory, the two kinds of conditioning are classical (respondent) and operant (instrumental). In the latter type (operant), behavior changes occur as a function of the consequences of a behavior that is voluntary.

The cognitive theorists believe cognitive structures begin to develop in the infant in what Piaget calls the sensory-motor period (birth to age 18 months or two years). A mental construct, called a schema, is associated with such processes as sucking, looking, listening, vocalizing, and prehension. Coordination of the schema sucking with vision calls for anticipatory action, such as seeing the feeding bottle and making some adjustment. New experiences and learning require either utilizing an old schema (assimilation) or modifying schema to incorporate new information (accommodation). Language is composed of receptive and productive language. Receptive is initiated first. Language starts with crying and non-verbal communication. Infants distinguish between *b* and *p* and *d* and *t* early. They babble at six months, say "bye-bye" at nine months, and use a full word at one like "mama."

Emotional development begins in early infancy as undifferentiated excitation. Distress and delight are noted by three months, with the further differentiation of fear, disgust, and anger occurring by six months. Discrepant faces and loud noise stimulate the emotion of fear under certain conditions.

Researchers often regard smiling as the first sign of social development. Fear of strangers develops at the seventh or eighth month, followed by separation anxiety. All are milestones in social development. A major aspect of normal development is the attachment of the infant to the mother. In the absence of love and attention, the prognosis for an infant is very poor, affecting all areas of development.

The following influences affecting the individual child during infancy were described in this chapter: (1) cultural expectations, (2) socioeconomic differences, (3) psychological needs--love and affection, (4) day care, and (5) health and pediatric care. All were shown to have significant ability to facilitate or to inhibit the development of an infant.

KEY WORDS

attachment

bonding

self-regulation

object permanence

primary circular reactions

secondary circular reactions

directed groping

reflexive

coordination of secondary schemes

mental representation

visual cliffs

anal & oral personality

psychosocial

psychosexual

deprivation

schema

holophrastic

positive reinforcement

proximo-distal

cephalo-caudal

reticular activating system

prehension

binocular fixation

accommodation

retina

cones

operant conditioning

negative reinforcement

babbling

cooing

autonomy & doubt

echolalia

self-recognition

diphtheria-tetanus-pertussis (DTP)

overextension

REFERENCES

Acredalo, L.P., and Evans, D. Developmental changes in the effects of landmarks on infant spatial behavior. *Developmental Psychology*, 1980, *16*(4):312-318.

Ainsworth, M.D. The development of mother-infant attachment. In B.M. Caldwell and H.N. Riccent (eds.), *Child Development Research*, vol. 3. Chicago: University of Chicago Press, 1973.

_____. Patterns of attachment behavior shown by the interaction with his mother. *Merrill-Palmer Quarterly*, 1964, *10*:51-58.

Aldrich, C.A., and Norvall, M. A developmental graph for the first year of life. *Journal of Pediatrics*, 1946, *29*:51-58.

American Academy of Pediatrics. *Active Immunization Procedures: Report of the Committee on Infectious Diseases*, 17th ed. Evanston, Ill., 1974.

Baillargeon. Object performance in 3-1/2 and 4-1/2 month old infants. *Developmental Psychology*, (1987)*23*(5):665-676.

Barrera, M.E., and Maurer, D. The perception of facial expressions by the 3-month old. *Child Development*, 1981, *52*:203-206.

Bayley, N. Comparison of mental and motor test scores for ages 1-15 months by sex, birth order, race, geographic section, education and education of parents. *Child Development*, 1965, *36*(2):379-411.

Benson, J.B., and Uzgiris. Effect of self initiated locomotion on infant search activity. *Developmental Psychology*, 1985, *21*:923-931.

Bernard, H.W. *Human Development in Western Culture*, 4th ed. Boston: Allyn & Bacon, 1975.

Bornstein, M.H. Qualities of color vision in infancy. *Journal of Experimental Child Psychology*, 1975, 401-419.

Bower, T.R.G. *A Primer of Infant Development*. San Francisco: Freeman, 1977.

Bowlby, J., et al. The effects of mother-child separation: A follow-up study. *British Journal of Medical Psychology*, 1956, *29*:211-247.

Bregman, E.D. An attempt to modify the emotional attitudes of infants by the conditioned response technique. *Journal of Genetic Psychology*, 1934, *45*:169-198.

Bridges, K.M.B. Emotional development in early infancy. *Child Development*, 1932, *3*:324-341.

Brooks, R.L., and Obruzut, J.E. Brain lateralization: Implications for infant stimulation and development. *Young Children*, 1981, *26*:9-16.

Buhler, C. *The First Year of Life*. New York: Day, 1930.

Burke, B.S. Maternal nutrition during pregnancy. In H.C. Stuart and D.G. Prugh (eds.), *The Healthy Child*. Cambridge, MA: Harvard University Press, 1960.

Campos, J.J., Hiatt, S., Ramsey, D., Henderson, C., and Svejda, M. The emergence of fear of the visual cliff. In M. Lewis and L. Rosenblum (eds.), *The Development of Effect*. New York: Plenum, 1978, pp. 149-182.

Clarke-Stewart, K.A., Umeh, B.J., Snow, M.E., and Pederson, J.A. Development and prediction of children's sociability from 1 to 2 1/2 years. *Developmental Psychology*, 1980, *16*(4):4290-4302.

Costello, C.G. Dissimilarities between conditioned avoidance responses and phobias. *Psychological Review*, 1970, *77*:250-254.

Crowell, D., Blurton, L., Kobayashi, L., MacFarland, J., and Yang, R. Studies in early infant learning: Classical conditioning of the neonatal heart rate. *Developmental Psychology*, 1976, *12*(4):373-397.

Dennis, W. Causes of retardation among institutional children: Iran. *Journal of Genetic Psychology*, 1960, *96*:47-59.

_____. Infant development under conditions of restricted practice and of minimum social stimulation. *Genetic Psychology Monographs*, 1941, *23*:143-191.

Dobbing, J. The later development of central nervous system and its vulnerability. In A.V. Davison and J. Dobbing (eds.), *Scientific Foundations of Pediatrics*. London: Heinemann, 1976.

Fantz, R.L., and Fagan, J.F. *Child Development*, 1975, *46*:3-18.

Flavell, J.H. *Cognitive Development*. Englewood Cliffs, NJ: Prentice-Hall, 1977.

Fralberg, S. The origin of human bonds. *Commentary*, 1967, *44*(6):51-57.

Gaensbauer, T., and Hiatt, S. *The Psychology of Affective Development*. Hillsdale, N.J.: Erlbaum, 1984.

Gerber, M. Test de Gesell et Terman-Merrill appliques en Uganda. In *The Growth of the Normal Child During the First Three Years of Life: Modern Problems in Pediatrics*, vol. 7. Basel, Switzerland: S. Karger, 1962.

Gesell, A., and Ilg, F.L. *Child Development: Introduction to the Study of Human Development*. New York: Harper & Row, 1949.

Gesell, A., and Thompson, H. Learning and maturation in identical twins: An experimental analysis by the method of co-twin control. *Genetic Psychology Monographs*, 1929, *6*:5-124.

Goodenough, F.L. The expressions of emotions in infancy. *Child Development*, 1931, 2:96-101.

Halverson, H.M. An experimental study of prehension in infants by means of systematic cinema records. *Genetic Psychology Monographs*, 1931, *10*:107-286.

Harlow, H.F., and Harlow, M.K. Social deprivation in monkeys. *Scientific American*, 1962, *207*:136-146.

Harlow, H.F., and Suomi, S.J. Nature of love simplified. *American Psychologist*, 1970, *25*:161-168.

Harris, B. Whatever happened to Little Albert? *American Psychologist*, 1979, *34*(21):151-160.

Harris, F.R., Wolf, M.M., and Baer, D.M. Effects of adult social reinforcement on child behavior. *Young Children*, 1964, *20*(1):8-17.

Hebb, D.O. *A Textbook of Psychology*, 3rd ed. Philadelphia: Saunders, 1972.

Hineline, D.N. Negative reinforcement and avoidance. In W.K. Honig and E.R. Stoddon (eds.), *Handbook of Operant Behavior*, vol. 2. Englewood Cliffs, NJ: Prentice-Hall, 1977.

Hymes, J. *Early Childhood Education, The Year in Review: A Look at 1988*. Washington, DC: National Association for the Education of Young Children, 1989.

Illingworth, R.S. *The Normal Child*, 5th ed. Edinburgh: Churchill Livingstone, 1972.

Irwin, O.C. The amount and nature of activities of the newborn infant under constant stimulating conditions during the first ten days of life. *Genetic Psychology Monographs*, 1930, *8*:1-92.

Izard, C.E. The young infants' ability to produce discrete emotional expression. *Developmental Psychology*, 1982, *16*:132-140.

Jones, M.C. The elimination of children's fears. *A Journal of Experimental Psychology*, 1924, *7*:382-390.

Kagan, J. Do infants think? *Scientific America*, 1972, *226*(3):74-82.

_____. Conversation with Jerome Kagan. *Saturday Review of Education*, 1973, *1*(3):41-43.

_____. Emerging theories in human development. *American Scientist*, 1976, pp. 186-196.

Kagan, J., Kearsley, R.B., and Zelazu, P.R. *Infancy: Its Place in Human Development*. Cambridge, MA: Harvard University Press, 1978.

Kaluger, G., and Heil, C.L. Basic symmetry and balance: Their relationship to perceptual-motor development. *Progressive Physical Therapy*, 1970, *1*:132-137.

Kaplan, H., and Dove, H. Infant development among the Ache of eastern Paraguay. *Developmental Psychology*, 1987, *23*:190-198.

Krogman, W.M. *Child Growth*. Ann Arbor: University of Michigan Press, 1972.

LaBarbera, J.D., Izard, C.E., Vietze, P., and Parisi, S.A. Four- and six-month old infants' visual responses to joy, anger, and neutral expressions. *Child Development*, 1976, *47*:535-538.

Lawick-Goodall, J. Some aspects of mother-infant relation. *The Origin of Human Social Relations*. New York: Academic Press, 1971.

Lemkan, P.V. The influence of handicapping conditions on child development. *Children*, 1961, *2*:43-47.

Lewis, M., and Brocks, J. Self, other, and fear: Infants' reaction to people. In Jim H. Lewis and L. Rosenblum (eds.), *The Origins of Fear: The Origins of Behavior*, Vol. 2. New York: Wiley, 1974.

Lipton, E.L., Steinachmeider, A., and Richmond, J.B. Autonomic function in the neonate. VII. Maturational changes in cardiac control. *Child Development*, 1966, *37*:1-16.

Lourie, R.S. Pica as a disturbance in socialization. In *Issues in Human Development*. Washington, D.C.: National Institute of Child Health and Human Development, 1970.

Lowrey, G.H. *Growth and Development of Children*, 7th ed. Chicago: Year Book, 1978.

Luria, A.R. Cultural differences in thinking. In M. Cole and S., *Soviet Psychology*. Cambridge: Harvard University Press, 1979, p. 195.

Marks, I. Phobias and obsessions: Clinical phenomenon in search of a laboratory model. In J.D. Maser and M.E. Seligman (eds.), *Psychopathology: Experimental Models*. San Francisco: Freeman, 1977.

Marlow, D.R. *Textbook of Pediatric Nursing*, 4th ed. Philadelphia: Saunders, 1973.

Marquis, D.P. Can conditioned response be established in the newborn infant? *Journal of Genetic Psychology*, 1931, *39*(4):479-492.

Masland, R.L., Sarason, S.B., and Gladwin, T. *Mental Subnormality*. New York: Basic Books, 1958.

McCall, R.B. Attention in the infant: Avenue to the study of cognitive development. In D.N. Walcher and D.L. Peters (eds.), *Early Childhood: The Development of Self-Regulatory Mechanisms*. New York: Academic Press, 1971, pp. 107-140.

Meltzoff, A.N. Infant imitation and memory: Nine-month-olds in immediate and deferred tests. *Child Development*, 1988, *59*:217-225.

Metcoff, J. Association of fetal growth with maternal nutrition. In F. Falkner and J.M. Tanner (eds.), *Human Growth: Vol. 1. Principles and Prenatal Growth*. New York: Plenum, 1978.

Michaelson, M. Physicals and shots your kids must have. *Today's Health*, 1972, *50*(9).

Milewski, A.E., and Siqueland, E.R. Discrimination of color and pattern novelty in one-month human infants. *Journal of Experimental Child Psychology*, 1975, *19*:122-136.

Mitchell, M., Ivinski, A., and Finlay, D.C. Visual attention in infants: A study of stimulus complexity, habituation and sex differences. *Perceptual and Motor Skills*, 1982, *54*:15-21.

Montagu, A. *Touching*. New York: Columbia University Press, 1971.

Mostiller, F., and D.P. Moynihan, (eds.) On equality of educational opportunity: Paper from the Harvard law faculty seminar on the Coleman report. *Harvard Educational Review*, 1972, *42*(1):109-125.

National Academy of Sciences, Food and Nutrition Board, National Research Council. *Recommended Daily Dietary Allowances*. Washington, D.C, 1974.

New York Times. Violence is occurring in the best of families. March 1977, p. E6.

Pedersen, F.A. (ed.) *The Father-Infant Relationship: Observational Studies in the Family Setting*. New York: Holt, Rinehurt and Winston, 1980.

Piaget, J., and Inhelder, B. *The Child's Conception of Space*. London: Routledge & Kegan Paul, 1958.

Piaget, J., and Inhelder, B. *The Science of Education and the Psychology of the Child*. D. Colman, Trans. New York: Viking, 1972.

Plutchik, R. *Emotion: A Psychoevolutionary Synthesis*. New York: Harper & Row, 1980.

Ricks, S.S. Father infant interactions: A review of inspirical research. *Family Relations*, 1985, *34*:505-511.

Ross, H.S., and Lollis, S.P. Communication within infant social gaines. *Developmental Psychology*, 1987, *23*:241-248.

Salapatek, P., Bechtold, A.G., and Bushrell, E.W. Infant visual acuity as a function of viewing distance. *Child Development*, 1976, *47*:860-863.

Schaffer, R. *Mothering*. Cambridge, MA: Harvard University Press, 1977.

Scrimshaw, N.S. Infant malnutrition and adult learning. *Saturday Review*, 1965, *50*(64).

Sears, R.R., Rau, I., and Alpert, R. *Identification and Child Rearing*. Stanford, CA: Stanford University Press, 1965.

Senn, M.J., and Solnit, A.J. *Problems in Child Behavior and Development*. Philadelphia: Lea & Febiger, 1970.

Siqueland, E.R., and Lipsitt, L.P. Conditioned head turning in human newborns. *Journal of Experimental Child Psychology*, 1966, *3*:356-376.

Smith, C.V., and Henry, J.P. Cybernetic foundations of rehabilitation. *American Journal of Physical Medicine*, 1967, *46*: Suppl. 117.

Soderling, B. The first smiles. *Acta Poediat*, 1959, *48*:Supplement 117.

Solomons, G., and Solomons, H.C. Factors affecting motor performance in four-month-old infants. *Child Development*, 1964, *35*:1283-1296.

Spitz, R.A. The role of ecological factors in the emotional development of infancy. *Child Development*, 1949, *20*:145-156.

Starkey, P., Spelke, E.S., and Gelway, R. Deletion of intermoded numerical correspondences by human infants. *Science*, 1983, *10*:179-181.

Thomas, A., and Chess, S. The role of temperament in the contribution of individuals to their development. In R.M. Linger and N.A. Bunch-Rossnagel (eds.), *Individuals As Producers of Their Development*. New York: Academic Press, 1981.

Trotter, R.J. Baby face. *Psychology Today*, 1983, *20*(8):14-20.

Vygotsky, L.S. *Thought and Language*. (Translated and revised by A. Kozulin.) Cambridge, Mass.: M.I.T. Press, 1986.

Watson, E.H., and Lowery, G.H. *Growth and Development of Children*, 7th ed. Chicago: Year Book Medical Publishers, 1978.

Watson, J.B., and Morgan, J.J. Emotional reactions and psychological experimentation. *American Journal of Psychology*, 1917, *28*:163-174.

Watson, J.B., and Rayner, R. Conditional emotional reactions. *Journal of Experimental Psychology*, 1920, *3*:1-14.

Weiner, I.B., and Elkind, D. *Child Development: The Core Approach*. New York: Wiley, 1973.

Werner, J.S., and Perlmutter, M. Development of visual memory in infants. Unpublished manuscript. Brown University, 1978.

White, B.L., and Held, R. Plasticity of sensory-motor development in the human infant. In J.F. Rosenblith and W. Allinsmith (eds.), *The Causes of Behavior: Readings in Child Development and Educational Psychology*, 2nd ed. Boston: Allyn and Bacon, 1966.

Wise, J.A., and Jones, F.R. Development of visual perceptual tests for normal and neurologically handicapped children. *Perceptual and Motor Skills*, 1972, *34*:429-430.

Zalba, S.R. Battered children. *Trans-Action*, 1971, *8*:58-61.

Chapter 6

DEVELOPMENT IN EARLY CHILDHOOD: PHYSICAL, COGNITIVE, AND SOCIAL

- ***Introduction***
  Physical, social and personality, cognition, and types of schooling and care
- ***Physical and Motor Development***
  Motor skill advances among the three- to five-year-old
  Large and small muscle use among the three- to five-year-old
  Sleep patterns
- ***Cognitive and Language Development***
  Obstacles to cognitive development
  In defense of children
  Language of the early child
  Intellectual development in early childhood
- ***Personality and Social Development***
  Theories of development
  Fears of children
  Early social behavior
  Self concept
  Play and young children
  Development of sexual identity
  Television
  Hazards in child development

DEVELOPMENT IN EARLY CHILDHOOD: PHYSICAL, COGNITIVE, AND SOCIAL

The early childhood years (two through six) are important in the life of the child. These are the foundation years for later childhood and adolescence. A typical girl will grow from a height of little more than 37 inches to somewhere around 46 inches--almost 4 feet. Her weight during this period will increase from about 31 pounds to 47. Typically, boys' height will increase from 38 inches to 46 inches and they will gain an average of 16 pounds. Children lose their roundness during this time, become more slender and athletic--the trunk, arms, and legs get longer. Boys have slightly more muscle per pound than girls, but even so they are less well coordinated and cannot match girls in small muscle control. Stamina for both sexes improves, as does the development of the immune system.

These years are characterized by cognitive development beyond that of the sensory-motor stages of Piaget and the inactive stage of Bruner. Children are now into the pre-operational stage, facing the obstacles of egocentrism, centration, failure to conserve, and inability to perform reversibility; they also have difficulty transforming and transposing concepts. In the Piaget experiment, where a pencil is held at a

90-degree angle to a table and the child is asked to describe what takes place after the pencil is dropped, a child can only tell where it starts and ends, saying nothing of the intervening stages. Such thinking is neither inductive or deductive, but transductive.

Language development assumes an adult similarity once the child is three. Three-year-olds will use plurals and the past tense. They also know the difference between persons; e.g., you, we, and I. By the time they are four their sentences include four or five words. They can use prepositions like over, under, in, on, and behind. Whereas earlier they used more nouns than verbs, they now use more verbs than nouns. At age five or six, sentence length increases to six to eight words, with more use of conjunctions, prepositions, and articles. At ages six to seven, children speak correct compound and complex sentences.

One of the most important aspects of socialization is recognition of gender. This is called gender identity and is accomplished when children recognize their sex and differences between the sexes. The little girl may understand that men shave their faces but women may shave their legs. Culture influences gender differences--in America and other countries like Pakistan more attention is paid to boys (Maccoby and Jacklin, 1974; Shepard-Look, 1982). Mothers and fathers act differently toward boys than they do girls, increasing the cleavage between them. We will discuss the theories of personality that bear on social development following the section on physical and cognitive growth.

PHYSICAL AND MOTOR DEVELOPMENT

Children have matured a great deal by the time they enter the first grade. Much of their physical development and motor growth relates to the sensory, emotional, and cognitive areas of development. Children utilize their bodies in expressive ways to learn, such as through play, discovery, sensory exploration, and experimentation. All these activities form the basis for later ability to handle more complex cognitive tasks. Sensory exploration leads to understanding the relationships of "up and down," "straight and crooked," "wide and thin." When children climb a ladder they may recognize fear and in time, sense the meaning of confidence. For instance, playing in a tree and hanging upside down develops a special perspective. Sometimes girls are not as active in such climbing activities and vigorous play. Consequently they sometimes lag behind boys in this special ability. Times are changing, however, as many girls do hang upside down in trees or on bars on playgrounds and in gyms.

In the three- and four-year-old, cartilage turns to bone faster than in the previous years, making the child's body increasingly firmer. By three years of age all the primary or deciduous teeth are in place, allowing full chewing. By five, the permanent teeth are beginning to mature and most will be in place at six. Thumb sucking behavior at this time can have an effect on how straight the teeth will be and their direction.

The eating pattern of children three to six varies, with many boys or girls disdaining food. Typically they do not eat as much as they did earlier in proportion to their size. According to Williams and Calendo (1984), two glasses of milk and a serving of meat (eggs, cheese, seafood, etc.) each day plus a serving of carrots, spinach, greens, green beans, or asparagus will provide enough nutrients for a growing child. Beyond this, vitamin C can be represented by juices, citrus fruits, tomatoes and dark green vegetables. Lack of a proper diet has been the main factor associated with illness in children. This parallels lack of care--immunizations, check-ups, and suitable clothing (Brown, 1987).

Health for the three- to six-year-old is usually very good, with only colds and minor sicknesses. Large families have more problems than smaller ones, along with those who have children attending child-care programs. Major illness and contagious diseases--measles, whooping cough, mumps, diphtheria, and poliomyelitis--are problems due to lack of immunization. The U.S. Department of Health reported that 90 percent of the children in the first grade were immunized in 1982. In Chapter 4, we suggested the timetable for various shots and the types needed for the young child. Most of these are available free through social and health services. Pneumonia and influenza still take their toll but, due to advances in treatment, death rates from these illnesses and from cancer (largely leukemia, lymphoma, and Hodgkin's disease--forms of cancer that strike children) have dropped by 84 percent since 1950. Accidents, mostly automobile accidents, are the leading cause of death of children aged three to six. Causes of fatal accidents in the home include poisoning, drowning in the bathtub or pool, electrocution, fire, suffocation, etc. Childproofing has become a must for parents and caretakers.

MOTOR DEVELOPMENT OF PRESCHOOL CHILDREN

3-YEAR-OLDS	4-YEAR-OLDS	5-YEAR-OLDS
Keep legs closer together when walking and running.	Can vary rhythm of running.	Can walk a balance beam.
Can run and move more smoothly.	Skip awkwardly; jump.	Skip smoothly; stand on one foot.
Reach for objects with one hand.	Have greater strength, endurance, and coordination.	Can manage buttons and zippers, may tie shoelaces.
Smear and daub paint; stack blocks.	Draw shapes and simple figures; make paintings; use blocks for buildings.	Use utensils and tools correctly.

LARGE MUSCLE MOTOR SKILLS IN EARLY CHILDHOOD

3-YEAR-OLDS	4-YEAR-OLDS	5-YEAR-OLDS
Cannot turn or stop suddenly or quickly.	Have more effective control of stopping,	Start, turn, and stop effectively.
Jump a distance of 15 to 24 inches.	Jump a distance of 24 to 33 inches.	Can make a running jump of 28 to 37 inches.
Ascend a stairway unaided, alternating the feet.	Descend a long stairway alternating the feet, if supported.	Descend a long stairway unaided, alternating the feet.
Can hop, using largely an irregular series of jumps with some variations added.	Hop 4 to 6 steps on one foot.	Easily hop a distance of 16 feet.

Source: Corbin, 1973.

Sleep Patterns

One of four children between the ages of three and eight suffer from nightmares or night terrors. The former are terrifying dreams usually brought on by heavy eating, overexcitement, or staying up beyond bedtime. Night terrors are due to a sudden awakening and being scared by a shadow or noise and/or imagination. Children may scream upon wakening and sit up or get out of bed, but they usually go back to sleep almost immediately, often before the parents reach them. Sleepwalking (usually older children and those in adolescence) is a matter of concern, as is talking (usually in childhood) in one's sleep. This is an incomplete waking from deep non-dreaming sleep considered harmless (Ferber, 1985). From five years of age until pre-adolescence, one in six or seven children sleepwalk. After making the home "sleepwalking-proof" the exercise may be considered harmless.

One problem noted by parents is a child's resistance to go to bed. These occasions reach their peak between the ages of two and four. Probably as many as 30 percent of all children resist bedtime at some time. Some causative factors have been noted by Lozoff et al. (1985) such as a mother's sudden absence during the day, depressed or indifferent mothering, stress from an accident, or illness. Accompanying the resistance is sometimes the desire of the child to sleep with his or her parents. The typical sleep requirements are presented in Figure 6.1 below. Most authorities feel children should have naps up until five, although Ferber (1985) does not include naps for the four-year-old in his data. If children miss their naps, they are much more irritable at suppertime, often too sleepy to eat their meal, and frequently have to be put to bed early. Bed-wetting is sometimes a problem. Enuresis runs in families; about 75 percent of bed-wetters have kin who wet the bed. By age five only 7 percent of boys and 3 percent of girls wet the bed; at age ten, 3 percent of boys and 2 percent of girls. Parents should be reassured that this is a common problem and not serious unless continued into adolescence (DSM III-R 1987).

Sleep Requirements in Children

Age in Years	Hours of Sleep	Hours Napping	Total Sleep
2	11	2	13
3	11	1	12
4	11.5	—	11.5
5	11	—	11
6	10.75	—	10.75

COGNITIVE AND LANGUAGE DEVELOPMENT

Children are impressed with loud noises, bright colors, masks, and costumes. They hide their faces when viewing a ghost movie or dragons, attributing to them magic powers or animistic ability. For three-year-olds, sorting out reality can be confusing--they might think, for instance, that the steam shovel is angry when it blows steam and makes a grating noise as its machinery clanks. The cloud moves because someone is pushing it and anything that moves is alive! The child at three is in Piaget's pre-operational stage, having developed to the point of deferred imitation and symbolic representation; this is the preconceptual stage highlighted by the increased use of symbols. It gives them the ability to communicate even though the things they can name, such as elephant, giraffe, or drum, are absent. Since egocentricity marks this period of development they fail to recognize the differences between the real--physical, wanting, and willing--and the social and mental--thinking, imaging, and remembering. By five most children will enter the transitional stage (typically five to seven). The child begins in rudimentary ways to realize there are multiple points of view and relational concepts--larger and smaller, north or south. Maybe at age five or six, boys and girls will be successful at conservation-of-number experiments and a few dealing with mass conservation. Development of symbolic representation is the main aspect of growth at this period.

Children in the pre-operational stage understand identities to a degree. They may recognize that at four they are different from when they were a baby, and mother is still mother although dressed in a formal gown instead of slacks. They understand functions partially, at least enough to turn on the TV or radio and perhaps work the VCR--realizing that with a cassette placed in the VCR they can see a movie. These are simple accruals for the child, but important, as such development allows them to increasingly understand the nature of everyday activity.

Obstacles to Cognitive Development

There are generally several obstacles to Piaget's stage of concrete operations--egocentricity, irreversibility, centration, and the focus on isolated states. Egocentricism is seen in the classic Piaget experiment of the mountains. Children are seated facing three mountains, with a doll in place opposite the mountains. They are asked to describe the mountains by use of photographs, from the doll's viewpoint. They rarely choose the right photo until they are seven, and many not until age eight. Flavell (1978), however, contends that when the child understands the motives and actions of the requestor, he or she can often perform this problem correctly at an earlier age.

Children are hobbled by centration; that is, they cannot decenter, focusing on one aspect of the problem while ignoring others. In one problem, there are 20 wooden beads in a glass container; 18 are white and two are brown. If the child can separate the white from the brown he or she has demonstrated color classification. When asked to separate the wooden from the brown beads, the typical child has difficulty performing the operation at the pre-operational stage. Tied closely to centration is *reversibility*. In this, the pre-operational child cannot trace the results back to the original circumstance. Philips (1969) cites an example of this when he asks a four-year-old boy, "Do you have a brother?" Yes, the child replies and says that his name is Jim. "Does Jim have a brother?" "No, he doesn't have a brother," will be the answer. This demonstrates that the child cannot take the part or perspective of another. Concerning the focus on states rather than transformation, as in the earlier exercise of the perpendicular pencil, children cannot reconstruct the various intervening positions as the pencil falls to the table. In transductive reasoning children cannot use deductive or inductive logic. Causes and effects are usually ascribed to two unrelated events. "I had mean thoughts about my brother and this made him sick." "Mother and Daddy are getting a divorce and I caused it." These couple transductive logic with egocentricity, whereby the child believes he or she caused the sick brother and the divorce of the parents.

In Defense of Children

In a number conservation experiment (rows of coins are matched; then one row is spread apart and the child is asked whether all the rows still have the same number of coins) Gelman (1979) found that if he used five or fewer coins or M & M's, the pre-operational-stage child could conserve. Some of the stories used by Piaget have been challenged by Mandler (1983) who read them and had difficulty reciting them from her memory. She rewrote the stories, simplifying and clarifying cause-and-effect relationships and presented them to first-graders, typically six years of age. The result was that they had no difficulty retelling the stories correctly. We must remember that Piaget's children and others involved in his experiments were Swiss, generally with very high socio-economic backgrounds, and the stories were often somewhat complex.

Cumeo (1980) found three- and four-year-olds using both the height and width rule to judge physical area. Piaget's idea that centration causes the child of three to focus on and utilize information from only one salient stimulus does not hold true in this experiment. The height-width experiment showed that children's judgments and response capacity for quantity represent a simple algebraic combination of relative stimulus cues. Cumeo also found a similar result in using an adding rule--length and density--in three- and four-year-olds' estimates of the number of beads in a row. This would support a general-purpose integration rule in a child's quantity judgment utilizing a combination of cue stimuli.

It is possible that training can effect an acceleration in children's cognitive capacity (Field, 1981). Field showed children various items--candies, rods, sticks, etc.--and asked them to pick rows that had the same number or objects that were the same length. The objects were then changed and the children were asked if they were similar. Three rules were utilized to help the child with identity, reversibility, and compensation. *Similarity* or *equivalence* emphasized that no matter where you place the objects they number the same. In *reversibility* items can be put back into their original position and have the same length as before. In *compensation* the child is told that change in one direction can be balanced by change in another. The water is higher in this container but the other container is wider (has a greater radius). Obviously, modifications have been validated in Piaget's theory. Flavell suggests that there is overlapping and disappearance of skills as children transit the stages. But the major thrust of Piaget, that the child in important ways helps create his knowledge of the world, still goes mainly unchallenged.

The Language of the Early Child

Children of three typically can use four words in a sentence and most of the time ask "Why" questions. They can also use plurals, give their full names, and name their sex. They can name figures in a picture and have a vocabulary of 800 to 1,000 words. They can obey at least two commands with such prepositions as "on" and "under." The child's language is intelligible 90 percent of the time. When children are four they have learned past tense. Often, though, in such words as "hold," "hold-ded" is likely to result rather than "held." "He hurted me." These are generalizations. Expressive language development is such that children can count to five, name one or two colors correctly, and may use profanity mainly to get attention. The use of "I" is evidence of a new skill; also sentences have expanded to three to seven words and the vocabulary has grown to 1,500 words. Understanding in receptive language improves, with the child understanding directions such as under the table, on the chair, in back of the sofa, and in front of the mirror.

At five years of age the boy or girl can receive and carry out such three-task instructions as "Wash your hands, Mary, dry them, and then sit down at the table." Five-year-olds can name the basic colors, as well as pennies, nickels, and dimes. Now the child will ask the meaning of words: "What does 'forget' mean?" Preschoolers of five can count to 10 or beyond and have a vocabulary of 2,000 or more words. Also they can repeat sentences of around 12 syllables. Bolles (1982) summarizes the characteristics of the development of social speech as follows:

Age	Characteristics of Speech
2 1/2	Beginnings of conversation: Speech is increasingly relevant to others' remarks. Need for clarity is being recognized.
3	Breakthrough in attention to communication: Child seeks ways to clarify and correct misunderstandings. Pronunciation and grammar sharply improve. Speech with children the same age expands dramatically. Use of language as instrument of control increases.
4	Knowledge of fundamentals of conversation: Child is able to shift speech according to listener's knowledge. Literal definitions are no longer a sure guide to meaning. Collaborative suggestions have become common. Disputes can be resolved with words.
5	Good control of elements of conversation.

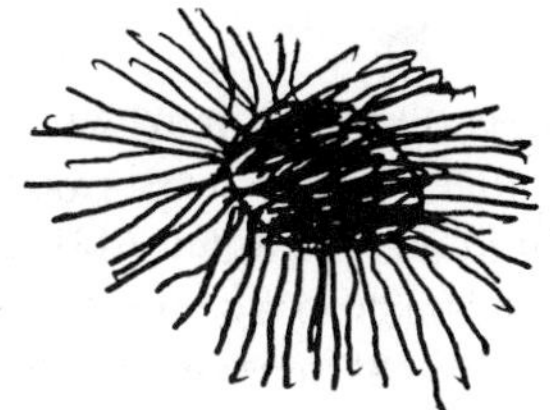

Kyle, 4 years old, drew this. Most children can name each of the items.

Private speech is defined as speech not intended for anyone else or for communication. In early childhood (two to six), it is normal and quite common, accounting for 20 to 60 percent of what children say. The behaviorist Watson viewed private speech as an unnecessary activity. Piaget thought it was the result of egocentricity, but believed it was of value because it helped children integrate language and thought. Vygotsky (1962) believed talking to one's self was positive, a special communication. Berk (1986) and others found among middle class children ages four to ten that private speech rises and falls with age; also the most popular and sociable children used it the most. It should be remembered that children may be trying to sort out problems in their schoolwork and would like some help. Teachers should be alert to this and not summarily think of this as misbehavior. Boys in some subcultures are taught to talk little. This can be found among low-income groups in Appalachian subcultures; consequently their self-talk continues until 10 or so. Berk and Garvin (1984) suggest private speech may have the following relationships:

Type	Child's Activity	Examples
Repetition, word playing.	Repeating words and sounds, often in a playful, rhythmic way.	1) Ray wanders around the room, repeating in a singsong manner, "Plate on your on the table, put in on the floor, out the place on your..."
Repetition, solitary fantasy play and speech addressed to material objects.	Repeating words and talking to objects, pretending, producing sound effects for objects.	1) Tom wanders around the room, pretending to be a paratrooper, saying, "Ka-powee, ka-powee," aiming his finger like a gun. 2) Jane says in a high-pitched voice while playing in the doll corner, "I'll be better after the doctor gives me a shot. Ow!" she remarks as she pokes herself.
Emotional release and expression	Expressing emotions or feelings to one's self.	1) The girl is given a new box of crayons and says to no one in particular, "Wow! Great!" 2) Rachel is sitting at her desk with an anxious expression on her face, repeating to herself, "My mom feels bad."
Egocentric communication.	Communicating with a person, but incompletely or peculiarly that it can't be understood.	1) Jack and Bill are sitting next to one another on the rug. Jack says to Ray, "It broke," with no explanation. (Bill may have known.) 2) Susan says to girl at the art table, "What are the brushes?" Girl says, "What brushes?" Susan shrugs and walks off.
Describing or guiding one's own activity.	Reciting one's actions, thinking out loud.	1) Bob sits down at the art table and says to himself, "I want to draw something. Let's see. I need a piece of paper. I want to draw my dog." 2) Working in his arithmetic workbook, Michael says to no one in particular, "Six." Then, counting on his fingers, he continues, "Seven, eight, nine, ten. It's ten, it's ten. The answer's ten."
Reading aloud, saying the words.	Reading aloud.	1) While reading a book, Tim begins to sound out a difficult word. "Sher-lock Holm-lock." he says slowly and quietly. Then he tries again. "Sher-lock Holm-lock, Sherlock Holme," he says, leaving off the final "s" in his most successful attempt.

(cont'd)

Unintelligible	Speaking so quietly that the words cannot be understood.	1) Tommy mumbles inaudibly to himself as he works a math problem.

Intellectual Development in Early Childhood

The measurement of intelligence by an individual IQ test of children between three and six is not precise. At eight or nine years of age scores may be much more accurate. Two well-known individual tests are the Wechsler Children Intelligence Scale and the Stanford-Binet. The latter has been revised, (4th edition, 1985) modifying the scales in important ways. In response to the heavily weighted verbal aspect of the test the constructors have attempted to balance verbal and nonverbal, and memory and quantitative. The publishers of the test claim now to have made it effective in measuring practical judgment in real situations, memory, and spatial relations. The Stanford-Binet takes around 35 to 45 minutes. The examinee is asked to string beads, to give meaning to objects, to name the parts in a picture that are missing, and to do puzzles and numbers. A departure from the 3rd edition is the emphasis on "developed abilities" and the isolation of various kinds of cognitive abilities. The results of the test still yield a single-score IQ. Its developers have made an attempt to restandardize the test by balancing it in terms of geography, minorities, socio-economic levels, gender, and the disabled.

The Wechsler Preschool and Primary Scale of Intelligence (WPPSI) is used with children 4 to 6 1/2 years old. It takes about one hour to complete, however, and is often given in sections. The WPPSI yields a verbal IQ, performance IQ, and a full-scale IQ. The verbal subtest assesses children's basic information, arithmetic, comprehension, vocabulary, and similarities. The performance scale utilizes mazes, completion of pictures, code pictures of animals with different colored cylinders representing their houses, and copying geometric and block designs. An 11th test is provided as a substitute for one of the verbal tests; it asks the child to repeat words after the examiner. Both of these tests, the WPPSI and the Stanford-Binet, offer validity and reliability to a degree; nonetheless the predictive element in projecting to 16 to 18 years of age is limited, as early experiential development is an important factor that confounds the issue.

. Parents and teachers can greatly influence the growth of knowledge and intelligence. Teachers can do this by stimulating children to be curious. The teachers themselves can be cheerful and provide evocative materials and learning activities, thereby generating enthusiasm for study.

Schooling for the Preschooler

Structured school learning for the four- or five-year-old has been an issue in the past but now is generally viewed as positive for children. The objection has been that previewing materials to be used in the first grade, as when the child hears or reads a story, kills the interest in those stories or similar ones. The fear also exists that teacher preparation will not be sufficient to provide adequate preschool programs (State Certification does not exist for many programs). The likelihood in some cases is that such programs will be detrimental. The developmental aspects of children's growth has changed in the past 30 or 40 years, thanks to improved health care, diet, and improved living standards. Because of these changes, the 12-year-old of the 1940s and 1950s is equivalent in many ways to today's 11- or 10 1/2-year-old.

Day Care

Sixty percent of mothers work by the time their youngest child is four years old. Sixty percent of working mothers with children under five use some kind of day care outside of the home. The demand for day care is increasing and agencies providing subsidized programs have long waiting lists with no end in sight.

(National Institute of Health, AAP, 1986). Arrangement for day care is distributed as follows:

Table 6.1 Arrangement for Day Care for Children Five and Under

Form of Care	Percent of Mothers Making Arrangement
Care in child's home:	31.0
By father	15.7
By grandparent	5.7
By other relative	3.7
By nonrelative	5.9
Care in another home:	37.0
By grandparent	10.2
By other relative	4.5
By nonrelative	22.3
Organized child-care facilities:	23.1
Day or group care center	14.0
Nursery school or preschool	9.1
Kindergarten or grade school	0.7
Parent caring for child	8.1

Source: The U.S. Bureau of Census, 1987

Good day care is characterized by licensure by a state agency, trained staff, sensitivity to children's needs, spacious facilities, small groups with high ratio of staff to children, controlled but not too restrictive environment, and a planned, effective program.*

Head Start and Compensatory Programs

Head Start, begun in 1965 under President Johnson's Great Society, was designed to help in the war against poverty. Intellectual embellishment, a supportive environment, and health care were provided to the children of low-income families. These programs were organized to focus on improving social competencies, everyday practical competencies, and future outcomes. Twenty-five years later (past programs have given assistance to 8 million children) Head Start is providing assistance for some 20 to 25 percent of poor children ages three to four. Before the advent of kindergarten, the focus was on five-year-old children.

Assessments of the effect of this schooling are generally positive:

1) Improvement on tests of motor control and physical development.

2) Success where parents participate, small groups are enrolled, and good teachers and extensive services are procured.

3) Gain in self-confidence and motivation.

4) Substantial gains in areas of language and intelligence (Collins & Deloria, 1983).

This child can name these items--Andrew, 6 years old.

Nevertheless, the Westinghouse Study (1969) reported that initial IQ progress of up to 12 points in children during the first four or five months was lost by the time they were six years old. This study, however, evaluated many different kinds of programs together. One of the authors had an early experimental Head Start grant and worked with five-year-olds with some success, judging by pre-and-post tests on readiness for reading and other variables. However, there were only eight or ten children and eight people worked with them, most of whom were full-time.

Bloom (1964) believes that 50 percent of the mental development has taken place by four years. Research on the effectiveness of early intervention generally confirms this, with earlier work with children having more positive results. The work of Heber (1977) and others who have provided enrichment, health care, etc., for very young infants has been quite successful (Heber began with one-year-olds). This research, although subject to debate, indicated that the mothers of these infants had projected IQ's of approximately 75, but the ten-year follow-up showed these same children had an average IQ of around 110 to 115. Children need to be nurtured early if significant progress is to be made--stimulation, interest, assistance, and a helpful environment are important elements in this enterprise.

Montessori Method

This method was originally developed to teach the mentally retarded and poor Italian children in Rome. The founder of this method, Dr. Maria Montessori, was a physician concerned about these disadvantaged children; as a response she constructed a child-centered curriculum (see Figure 6.2). The setting, use of equipment, and materials are designed to elicit the full potential in children. The program uses methods that are self-correcting. Children select tasks to work on, and when they are finished they return the materials to the shelf. One kind of task would be to arrange in sequence a set of graduated cylinders, weights, or smooth- or rough-textured pieces of cloth. Practical tasks are also dealt with, such as painting a real wall, gardening, washing dishes, and making soup. Classrooms have children of mixed ages (typically three to seven) and gender. Teachers interject themselves infrequently into the learning process and do not praise or criticize the children. The focus of the curriculum is to develop sensory-motor skills and classification abilities as the forerunners of reading and mathematics. This method has been popular in the United States among middle classes for normal children and others who can afford the private education utilizing this approach. Other types of schools have adopted some Montessori methods, such as individually paced progress, real-life tasks, and self-teaching materials (cuisenaire rods, etc.).

Individualizing instruction.

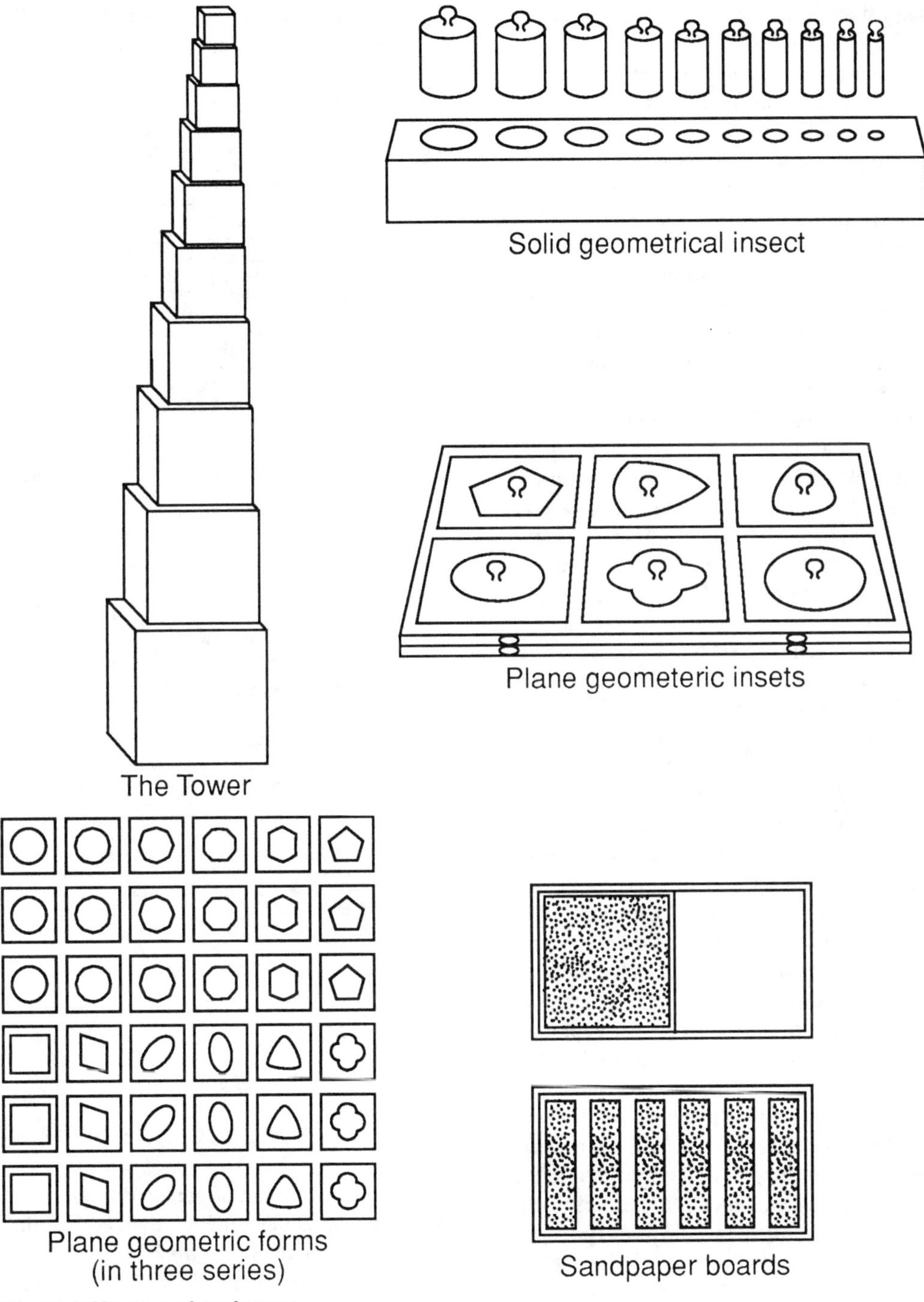

Figure 6.2 Montessori equipment.

Open Education

In many ways this approach to education has been patterned after the British Infant School. The purpose of the British School was to help children prepare for formal schooling at eight or nine years of age. The term "open" belies the nature of the curriculum, which is structured and entails considerable planning and preparation. This type of education is characterized mainly by an *integrated day*. Discrete periods do not exist and children work on a project such as running a store--writing for goods, keeping records, visiting farms to see produce, discussing the operation in groups, doing art work, and using visual aids as part of the program. Another aspect is *vertical grouping*--children of different ages are in the same classrooms, allowing the youngest child in time to become a leader among those younger than himself. Finally, children choose from among a number of alternatives the kind and duration of the project in which they wish to be involved. The child's decisions are respected and little punishment and reward are given. Where planning has been sufficient and community support forthcoming, schools of this kind have been successful. In some instances lack of intensive planning and lack of support have doomed this approach.

It is generally felt by most educators that we should include in a school program all the areas involved in the child's development: physical, emotional, social, cognitive, and expressive. The curriculum in so far as possible should be individually adapted to the child's progress and interests in a setting that allows for exploration and interaction with teachers and children. The use of workbooks, dittoes, etc., should be minimized and emphasis placed on the use of concrete materials and activities relevant to their lives. Finally, it is thought that adults, parents, and caretakers should adapt to children's needs and respond quickly to their messages, styles, and abilities. The National Association for the Education of Young Children in 1986 proposed the following view of education for four- and five-year-olds.

Component	Appropriate	Inappropriate
Curriculum Goals	All developmental areas, such as physical, social, emotional, and intellectual, are stimulated. Individual abilities and interests determine the activities, which are designed to encourage self-esteem and the desire for learning on the part of children.	Academic excellence is the only quality that is developed. Children are measured solely by how well they perform on standardized tests.
Teaching Strategies	Teachers prepare the learning environment for children, who select the activities they are interested in, such as math, games, puzzles, science, music, blocks, books, art, or dramatic play. The children are expected to be physically and mentally active, working individually or in small groups most of the time.	Teachers follow highly structured, teacher-directed lesson plans almost entirely. Children are expected to sit quietly and pay attention to the teacher. They do as the teacher instructs and work most often with commercially manufactured material, such as ditto sheets and flashcards.
Guidance of Social and Emotional Development	Teachers encourage self-control in children by exhibiting this quality themselves, rewarding expected behavior, redirecting children to a more acceptable activity, and setting clear limits. Children are encouraged to develop social skills, such as cooperating in activities and negotiating differences among themselves.	Teachers enforce rules and punish deviations from them and other unacceptable behaviors by making a child sit in a corner or stand isolated from class activity. Children may not relate to one another in class, but if a dispute arises between children in the classroom, the teacher steps in and settles the disagreement.
Development of Language and Literacy	Children engage in a variety of activities that call for language skills, such as listening to poems and stories, dictating stories about their experiences, reading, and experimenting with writing.	Instruction in reading and writing focuses on such skills as reciting the alphabet and recognizing separate letters.

Source: NAEYC, 1987.

PERSONALITY AND SOCIAL DEVELOPMENT

The development of personality and social development is theoretically divided into three groups; the *psychodynamic*, representing Freud's view and, partially, Erikson's psychosocial view. The difference lies in their emphasis on feelings, drives, and conflicts in growing up. Freud's drive theory sees innate aggression giving impetus to the pleasure principle as a main element in behavior patterns; whereas Erikson sees drive mainly to resolve the social crises that arise at each stage of development. In the *social learning* view, personality development is based principally upon environment. Punishment, rewards, reinforcement, and models determine the behavior patterns of the child. *Cognitive* theory suggests that these areas of development are realized as maturation and the environment interact. Some behavior may come from models, but most stems from children's own interpretation of experience and their insight. Children learn gender roles and expectations; as they get older they learn moral precepts--they come to know the difference between being fair and cheating.

Freud's Phallic Stage

Having passed through the oral and anal stage, the three- to five-year-old is confronting the Oedipus and Electra complexes, which are part of the phallic stage. Girls (in the Electra stage) have strong feelings for the opposite-sex parent. Girls want their father exclusively, creating worry and tension for a period of time. In time girls identify with the mother, becoming close to father through the mother. This helps develop an identity of femaleness. Boys desire their mothers (Oedipus complex) but at the same time are fearful of the father and, according to Freud, believe they may get castrated because of their feeling. In the Greek myth an oracle foretold a boy would be born to kill his father and grow up and marry his mother. The father of Oedipus, the king, ordered him killed; he was, however, left in a far away place. He grew up and killed the king not knowing it was his father and then, in ignorance, married the queen, his mother. When he found this out he killed himself. Freud assumed every boy falls in love with his mother but this is remedied by thoughts of possible castration which drives it out of mind. In this manner children inhibit their emotions and in time identify with their fathers.

Children during this period (ages three to six) are very much interested in the anatomy of the opposite sex. They also engage in sharing information about nakedness, body parts, and "dirty tales" (mainly about the bathroom rather than the bedroom, as many of them are not ready for that connection). Freud thought little girls develop penis envy; the denial of envy can cause neurosis in adulthood because hatred for this lack is attributed to the mother. Unconsciously the little girl hopes for a penis and to become a man. The normal girl turns this desire into wanting a child, and when she gets a boy baby her satisfaction is complete.

The role of the superego is first played by the parents by granting proofs of affection and threats of punishment, which to the child mean a loss of love. This is to be feared for its own sake. According to Freud this anxiety (objective anxiety) is the forerunner of the later moral anxiety; when the former anxiety is dominant the superego or conscience has not developed. It is only later that the secondary situations arise, which are frequently regarded as normal. External restrictions are so interjected that the superego takes the place of the parents, observing, guiding, and threatening the ego as the parent formerly did. The feeling of guilt is the tension between the ego and the superego. When the Oedipus complex/Electra complex fate is settled, the superego becomes heir of that emotional tie. To compensate for this loss greater identification with parents occurs. The superego must overcome the Oedipus complex and become strong if it is to be an independent person (Freud, 1933).

The social crisis for the child of three to six relates to *initiative* and *guilt*. This third stage of Erikson involves sense of direction. Following the earlier autonomy-versus-shame stage the child begins to develop a self concept and is determined to pursue a plan--a purpose! It may be to construct something, build a playhouse, or paint the fence. Children's motives may be challenged and radically controlled by their parents. Children must learn to control how far they push their initiatives, considering their parents' views about them. If parents refuse to allow children to express originality and creativity, they may become slavish to parental wishes, thereby reducing independence and creativity. Children may feel guilty when denied initiative, due to their constant challenge for expression.

If the guilt feeling is strong enough they may connect this with loss of their parents' love. If so, they may become moral absolutists parroting their parents' views, becoming self-righteous and intolerant of other people's opinions. They also may come to suffer from inhibitions and psychosomatic illnesses. Parents and caretakers need to allow children to play house, try to use the vacuum cleaner, wash the dishes, bake a cake, and "mess up" to some degree, but provide some guidance along the way.

These theories are highly speculative, to be sure, but were postulated by men who were first-rate thinkers. True, their views are not easily subjected to scientific experimentation. Castration anxiety and penis envy has hardly been validated--the phallus notion sounds like a male projection; penis envy is probably the result of females' noting the power of men to create such a thought. Nevertheless the general ideas of the psychic anatomy seem validated by common experience, and the Oedipus complex has often been observed by investigators and parents.

Erikson fused the sexes in their cultural influences on the development of children. He did not provide enough differentiation between men and women, placing greater emphasis on the impact of women. His stages are nearly universally accepted, particularly as they describe the social crises that usually occur in the various periods of life. But again no scientific check tells us his work is accurate.

Social Learning Theory

This theory, enunciated by Bandura and Mischel, suggests that social behavior and personality are reflections of the environment. The kinds of rewards and punishments the child receives along with models of good and bad behavior eventually shape them. Erikson thought that preschool children became socialized mainly by imitation; later identification allows them to imitate a variety of models. Bandura believed that the principal aspect of initiation is the information given by the model as interpreted by the child or youth. This is important as to how the observer views or understands. Imagination and expectation enter into this learning through imitation. It is behavioral in nature and involves three kinds of effects. The *model effect* is seen by learning new behavior--John, having observed his brother talk to their parents, decides to use this information as his own. In *inhibition* and *exhibition effects*, punishment serves to inhibit negative behavior; rewards reinforce a positive model. The *eliciting effect* is where the model's behavior stimulates a similar or related action in the child.

Social tendencies to be cooperative and competitive are undoubtedly learned by imitation. Research suggests that much of socialization relative to cooperation and competition comes from our immediate environment. Close cooperation in native tribes, the primary group, probably occurs because families and kin are role models. For instance, rural Mexican children have been found to be more cooperative than urban Mexican children.

Cognitive Theory

Children come to have increasingly complex concepts as they develop. These become the structure through which the patterns of social behavior occur. They learn gender, brother-sister relationships, fairness, and give-and-take. Early in the pre-operational period children confuse the object and the symbol. Right and wrong are judged by the amount of punishment for a given offense. As stated by Kohlberg, mental maturity parallels moral development. At six or seven, girls are becoming conventionally oriented and conformist. The child learns toward the end of this period that language is flexible and that a word can easily represent one concept as another. Punishment becomes less of a guide to behavior and intention begins to be considered. Aggression among boys is beginning to be controlled and channeled into games and sports. Children are increasingly taught to inhibit hostility and anger. Jealousy, a frequent companion of the child of two and three, gives way to the inhibition of these feelings. Some children will develop defense mechanisms to assist with this; some examples are running away or withdrawal and denial (see Chapter 7). As children mature they will use reaction formation and/or rationalization. These techniques are sometimes learned from their parents, other kin, or their brothers and sisters. Parents can help their child who demonstrates considerable tension (i.e., by acting out, temper tantrums, loud talk, and excessive arguing) by simplifying their lives for a few days, helping the child to anticipate upcoming stressful events, calming them with quiet talk, and explaining what is expected of them. Continual use of a defense mechanism, if ingrained strongly enough, can distort reality and become a problem for the future. For instance, if children establish a pattern of denial and running away, then trouble may ensue in later life. Certainly withdrawal can be a good defense mechanism for us adults (as when we get angry with the boss and want to "tell him off" but instead bow out). But the constant use of escape may lead to a personality difficulty.

The Fears of Children

We may know that a child is fearful of the dark but if you ask a five- or six-year-old, the response will usually be "no." They have been socialized to know that fear is not to be admitted. Increasingly as children grow older and begin to reason, they understand that the goblins are not going to snatch them away. But young toddlers beginning to expand cognitive skills have developed mental representation, and partly for this reason, their imagination expands. Their fears are multiplied--loud noises, the dark, separation from parents, people, places, large and grotesque objects create "scary" feelings. Morris and Kralochwill (1983) charted fears in children in this adaptation of their work:

2 years	A multiple of stimuli, including loud noises (vacuum cleaners, sirens and alarms, trucks, and thunder), animals, dark rooms, separation from parent, large objects or machines, changes in personal environment, strange peers
3 years	Masks, dark, animals, separation from parent
4 years	Separation from parent, animals, dark, noises (including noises at night)
5 years	Animals, "bad" people, dark, separation from parent, bodily harm
6 years	Supernatural beings (e.g., ghosts, witches, Darth Vader), bodily injury, thunder

At four to six some children are fearful of people or animals that look ugly. As they get older, at 10 or so, they fear physical danger and personal injury. Increased understanding of cause and effect may account for this. Girls are more fearful than boys, poor children more than middle class. Parents may encourage boys to be fearless (Dupont, 1983), and for the poor, this may parallel the realism of their lives and surroundings. Parents should avoid making fun of fearful children with such remarks as "You're a big boy now, don't be such a sissy!" Reassurance and encouragement are the key element in reducing fear and tension. One cannot ignore fear or avoid it--sooner or later it has to be faced. Talking about fears with sympathetic parents probably helps. Some children have phobias, irrational, involuntary fears that are out of reason to the situation. The child may say that a dog is trying to bite him or her when the dog is actually shut off by a fence. Inner anxiety is usually the basis of this inordinate fear. A small number of children do not lose these fears until the late teens (Dupont, 1983). Security and comfort from parents can help remedy this problem.

Early Social Behavior

During the preschool years the child develops into a distinctly socialized individual. Most of the important types of social behavior begin to develop in infancy and are expanded and enriched during the preschool years. The ill effects of an inadequate social environment have been recognized; a step forward would be the encouragement of nursery schooling on a national basis to provide children from such environments with a richer and broader experience.

Passivity and Dependence

Based on observations of 2-, 2 1/2-, and 3-year-olds, Craig and Garney (1972) traced early developmental trends in expressions of dependency. Two-year-olds spend more time with their mothers and want to remain in the same room with them. They frequently look at their mothers for approval and disapproval. Older children make use of verbal rather than physical contacts in seeking attention and approval of their mothers.

Passive behavior develops during the early years, dependent in part upon the cultural environment. There is evidence from studies reported by Kagan and Moss (1962) that early passivity may be linked with direct forms of passivity during late childhood and adolescence. The investigators state:

> Intensive study of the observations of the school-age children who fell at the behavioral extremes of this dimension suggested that the tendency toward passivity during preadolescence was already apparent during the first two years of life. Passivity during the first three years was significantly associated with a consistent cluster of school-age behavior (ages six to ten); avoidance of dangerous activity, absence of physical and verbal aggression, conformity to parents, and timidity to social situations (p. 79).

It seems that the essential aspect in the early childhood development of personality (Jacklin, 1979) is dependency on others, such as for food, help with dressing, and help with cleaning the house or oneself. These behaviors are observed and imitated by the child. The attempts the child makes to be autonomous are important for the two-year-olds. In pursuit of this they try to operate the vacuum cleaner or brush their teeth; if frustrated, aggressive rivalry with siblings and expression of discouragement occur. Physical maturity and socialization will soon change much negative behavior.

THEORIES OF DEVELOPMENT AND AGGRESSION

Several theories attempt to explain the development of childhood behavior. Social learning theorists stress the effect of observational learning and reinforcement on developing childhood behavior patterns. Such theorists feel that children learn much vicariously and internalize the proper behaviors by a process of self-regulation, setting their own criteria for behavior. Prevalent social learning theory rejects the idea of aggression as an instinct or as the result of frustration. It is viewed as a response designed to ensure getting one's own way. It is learned through observation or modeling, like other responses. The degree of support for a particular behavior of aggression is directly related to its recurrence. The kind and degree of aggression relate to patterns of adjustment found successful by an individual. Such responses may include running away, seeking comfort and help, striking out in violence, attempting to induce euphoria by drugs, or engaging in furious activity. Usually, the type of behavior will conform to the pattern that has been most successful. Cognitive factors such as knowledge of the consequences of past behavior and weighing the positive and negative incentives involved in the current situation enable the child to anticipate the consequences of certain behavior and to alter it.

In psychoanalytic theory the instinct of aggression is expressed through the death instinct, whose energy builds up until there is harsh conflict. In the early life of the infant when pleasure is denied or interrupted, extreme agitation often results, with crying, self-flagellation, and accelerated motor movement. Aggression in the child finds an outlet through biting, fighting, kicking, roughhousing with schoolmates in games, sibling rivalry, and play. Due to prohibition against these forms of behavior by parents and teachers, they are repressed; however, they remain fertile and lively as unconscious motives.

A third approach, drive theory (Dollard et al., 1939), rejects the idea of innate drives of instincts, proposing instead that frustration produces drive. Thwarting a person's attempt to reach a goal induces aggressive drives that in turn motivate behavior designed to injure the persons or objects causing the problems.

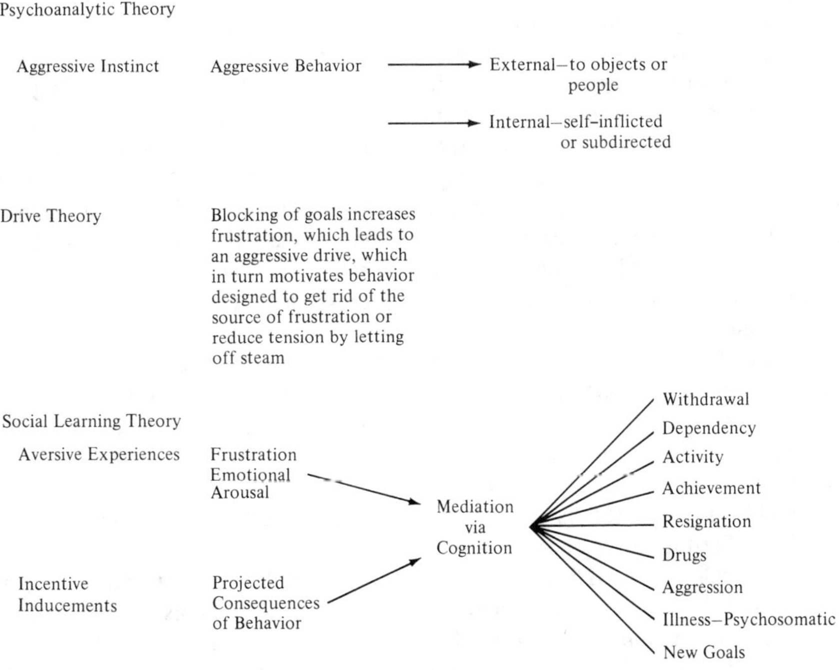

Figure 6.3 Determinants of aggression. (*Source:* Bandura, 1973.)

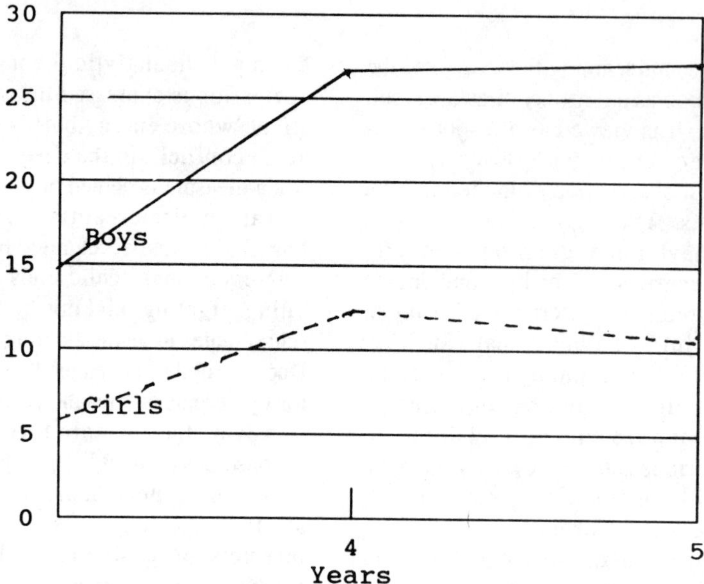

Figure 6.4 Sex differences in aggression during the preschool years (after Sears, 1951).

Expression of the drive reduces the tension. Since frustration is a universal condition, the aggressive drive needs an outlet.

Preschool and beginning schoolchildren have their aggression increasingly controlled by socialization, for interacting with others in games and other activities requires cooperation, play, and exercise, which tend to reduce tension. By the time older children reach the stage of mental maturity, they have learned a variety of strategies with which to handle or to work off aggressive drive. Research has been conducted to validate the existence of discrete social cognitive-related stages (Ellis, 1973). A conceptualization of how these theories deal with aggression is presented in Figure 6.3.

Observations reveal that aggression appears during infancy and develops as a result of maturation and learning. It can appear when the child's normal behavior pattern is blocked. A study by King (1966) involving a small group of kindergarten children showed that the ratio of unfriendly acts to the total number of actions made by one child to another during free play was strongly related to the mean distance maintained by the second child from the first. The mean distances, however, were found to reduce in most cases when a prized toy was juxtaposed with the first child.

Boys are usually more aggressive than girls (Sears, 1951; Maccoby and Jacklin, 1974). This is examined in Figure 6.4. Aggression varies according to the time of the day, the setting of the play situation, and the degree of familiarity with the other children. The better the child knows the other children in a play group, the more likely the child is to display aggressive behavior. The potential for conflict over aggression is greater for females than for males, since the pattern of social rewards and traditional sex-role standards of behavior act to discourage direct aggression in girls, even during the preschool years. We would accordingly expect that aspects of aggression would be more stable for males than for females. Kagan and Moss (1962) found this to be true.

According to Rule, Nesdale, and McAra (1974) children as young as five regard personal aggression, such as hitting another child, as more wrong than socially motivated aggression, such as forcing a playmate to return something that he or she has taken. The authors note that at an early age children adopt the distinctions that their society makes concerning right and wrong in aggressive behavior. However, wide differences exist among children of the same sex at all ages in the amount of aggressive behavior displayed, in the motivations for such behavior, and in its extent and persistence.

Effects of Divorce

Young children may manifest aggressive behavior especially during the period when their parents are getting divorced. During this period the basis for trust that underlies prosocial behavior is temporarily shaken. Among children aged 2 1/2 to 5, regression can occur to such earlier habits as thumb-sucking, bed-wetting, and excessive crying. Children from ages five to eight fantasize about the return of their parent, are often excessive eaters, are anxious, feel guilty, and are aggressive.

The Self Concept

Children of two have seen their reflection in the mirror and also recognize that they are separate from their mother. They are constantly comparing themselves with other children--hair color, height, likes, and dislikes. Children define their boundaries and possessions by "this is my house, my ball, my doggie," etc. During the preschool years they have broad attitudes about themselves--they are good, have positive attitudes of self, or are naughty. Ideals are developed by children who tend to measure themselves by the standards derived from what parents or sisters or brothers have said about them. Some nicknames and monikers stick, not always with positive connotations, as when a clumsy child is called "stumble bum" or one who breaks things often is named "sore fingers" or called "bull in a china closet." In an effort to understand who they are, young children ask parents a lot of questions, such as: "Where did I come from?" "Why do I have red hair?" A child's self-concept rises in an interpersonal setting, and feelings about the self are established early in life and modified by subsequent experience. The significant people in the life of the child provide standards, and with their pressures, attitudes, and demands, shape the elements of the child's self-concept. The growing child and later adult will have guideposts to measure up to or rebel against. Experiences set standards and prospects, and the child comes to know that a certain kind of behavior will bring a certain kind of response. If this were not so, life would be chaotic, for there would be no patterns to which people could accommodate themselves. Children with high self-concepts feel they will be successful with tasks and interrelationships with other people. Therefore, they tend to be more assertive and express their convictions more readily. Children with low self-concepts avoid attention, tend to listen more, and actively participate less (Patterson, 1976).

Identification With Parents

Preschool children frequently perceive their parents as ideal. During late childhood they often look to figures outside the home as their ideal, but tend still to identify closely with their parents. Children identify with the parent whom they perceive as being the more rewarding and affectionate (Payne & Mussen, 1956); the relationship is closer when children see themselves as being similar to the parent of the same sex. The nature of the identification is very important to the socialization of the boy, since peers are more likely to favorably regard the boy who sees himself as similar to his father (Gray, 1959).

According to psychoanalytic theory, the identification process for girls is more complex than for boys. The reason seems to be that the role of the girl is less well defined. Working with upper middle class pupils in the fifth through the eighth grades, Gray found that there was no significant difference in the adjustment of girls with high or low mother identification.

The reason for these differences seems to lie in the masculine prestige factor in Western culture; the feminine role of the mother or the work role of women often lacks this prestige factor (Feinman, 1974).

Working Mothers

The question has been raised about the effects on the adjustments and behavior of elementary schoolchildren of the mother's employment outside the home. A number of factors must be considered in evaluating this situation. A study by Woods (1972) showed that mothers who had favorable attitudes toward their work scored high in measures of personal and social adjustment. This naturally affected the psychological atmosphere in the home and their relations with their children. Most studies seem to agree that working mothers have a more favorable attitude toward children than nonworkers. They further indicate that adjustment to children improved the longer the mother worked. In a recent study, Meyer (1980) found mothers' employment had no effect on girls' perceptions of the adult female role or their sex-role attitudes. Lois Hoffman (1979), in reviewing studies of maternal employment, found that boys of working mothers have been rated above average in social and personality adjustment. But boys from lower class families may experience a problem in father-son relationships when the mother works, particularly if the father doesn't work. Some evidence exists to show that sons of middle-class working mothers may be somewhat below average in academic achievement, with the nature of this deficit undetermined (Hoffman, 1979). It should be pointed out that the quality, not the quantity, of interaction between mother and child is of most importance to the child's personal and social development. The issue of child care, particularly for the early years (birth to age five), has been raised by some as a factor that creates problems in the development of the child--that is, interferes with early bonding with the mother, causes insecurity, and accounts for other problems. Many research studies have established that children with a history of day care do as well later on in life as home-cared children (Maier, 1982). In 1979, 6.2 million infants, toddlers, and preschoolers attended day care centers on a part- or full-time basis. In a report to Congress (National Day Care Study, 1979) on an evaluation of the Federal Interagency Day Care Requirements, the following was revealed:

1. For economically disadvantaged children, day care may have enduring positive effects.

2. Paramount in importance is whether day care affects the emotional bond between mother and child.

3. No differences were found in the mother-child bond for children in day care and home-reared children.

4. Day care stimulates the development of adult friendships, natural helping networks that support families in their child-rearing roles.

5. The effects of day care, whether center or family based, are mediated by the children's experiences at home.

6. Coordination attempts in children's socialization processes by the home and center are often minimal and should be improved. However, negative effects of this have not been demonstrated.

7. With infants and toddlers, the ratio of staff to children in a center is the most significant indication of a better experience (Belsky & Steinberg, 1979).

Many children, both preschool and school-aged, will suffer from poor caretaking, but recent evidence points to improvement. Bron-

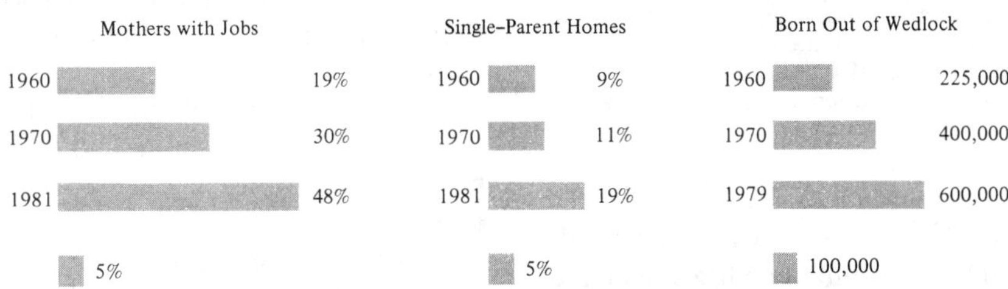

Figure 6.5 Working mothers and single parents. (*Source:* U.S. Department of Labor, 1982.)

fenbrenner (1977) says, "Every child needs at least one person who is really crazy about him or her." However, *U.S. News & World Report* ("Teenagers in trouble? Youths speak out," 1982) raises the issue of "neglected" children. They point to three danger signals for children: more mothers with jobs, more single-parent homes, and more children born out of wedlock. Also, 35 percent of single-parent households headed by a female are below the poverty level. A review of data from the U.S. Department of Labor (1982), shown in Figure 6.5, confirms this.

Interactions at School

The three important variables in a classroom situation are the individual learner, the teacher, and the other pupils. Each has unique characteristics. Different patterns of communication between teacher and pupils appear in the various classrooms. Magoon and Garrison (1976) point out:

> How a teacher interacts with pupils depends largely on what he believes is expected of him in various roles. Some of these expectations are poorly defined; others, relat-

> ed to teacher personality, are vague; others are affected by the character of the community and school. The way the teacher interacts with the pupils will affect the interests, motives, social development, and academic outcomes of instruction (pp. 328-329).

A classroom group of pupils may be relatively homogeneous or highly differentiated, and this will have an important bearing on the interactions between pupils. Studies conducted by Schmuck (1962, 1963) show the effects of classroom structural organization on the child's self-perceptions and academic performance. Two kinds of sociometric structures--central and diffuse--were differentiated. Schmuck explains them this way:

> Centrally structured peer groups are characterized by a large number of pupils who agree in selecting only a small cluster of their classmates as pupils they like. Along with this narrow focus on a small number of pupils many other pupils are neglected entirely. Diffusely structured peer groups, on the other hand, are distinguished by a more equal distribution of liking choices; by no distinct subgroups whose members receive a large proportion of preference; and by fewer entirely neglected pupils (Schmuck 1963, p. 341).

Playmates During the Preschool Years

Self-concept may be affected by association with friends. The young child's friends will consist of the adults in the family, siblings, and children in the immediate neighborhood. Only if children attend Sunday school, nursery school, or kindergarten does the circle of their companions enlarge. Young children's relationships at home play an important role in their adjustment to children outside the home. Only children or those with siblings widely separated in age, or of a different sex, are likely to be withdrawn when they are with other children. When the siblings are of the same sex, the child has more difficulty in associating with peers of the opposite sex. Children younger than the available playmates strive to keep up with them and become dominated by them. Children older than playmates and siblings generally are "bossy" and become the leaders. This early play experience with siblings and companions outside the home has a marked influence on how successfully the child makes the transition to school.

Young children show far less stability in their friendships than older children. Because their companions are, in reality, playmates rather than true friends, children are likely to lose interest in their companions when their own play interests change. Kindergarten children sometimes change friends many times during a weekend. Boys usually change their friends more often than girls. Children's need for friends is best met by those who like to do the same things. Similarity in interests facilitates expressions of affection and provides an outlet for self-expression. In a study of Oriental and Caucasian children, McCandless and Hoyt (1961) observed that the children preferred as their companions children of their own race and sex, since they felt more "at home" with children from a background similar to theirs, not because of prejudice at an early age. A study by Rubin (1980), however, found that children who made friends across age lines were better able to cooperate and learn from adults and other children.

Play and Young Children

Play is the most important thing the young child does. Its ramifications are very broad. Some have called it the work of children, essential and constructive. Others have noted its effect as a tension reducer, a socializer done first for pleasure, and an activity allowing for creativity. Some have identified several types of play: *Sensory play* involves stimulating the senses--beating on a pan, picking a flower, chewing on a stick, or kicking a can. This kind of play helps children to know about things in the environment and their bodies. *Motion and rough-and-tumble play* relates to climbing,

Surviving school. (*Source:* Virginian Pilot.)

swinging, running, skipping, hiding, and wrestling with each other. Most of these activities begin around three years of age. *Language play* involves manipulating words, sounds, and patterns . The very young child likes "I'm barefoot all over" or "the little dog meows, the little cat bow wows." What makes others laugh is enjoyed by the child. *Dramatic play* consists of taking parts, making believe--I'm mother or a repair man--which tends to embellish social relationships and help the child understand how to get along with others.

Children by four or five begin to play simple games. As they grow older, these games become more competitive in nature--baseball, football, soccer, etc. Often rituals are involved in making up special rules or modifying them in playing tag, hide-and-seek, kick the can. These can be cognitive in nature--dealing with cause and effect, sequences, and consequences--and therefore deal with learning. Types of cognitive play have been noted by Piaget and others as presented below.

COGNITIVE PLAY

Category	Description
Functional play	Any simple, repetitive muscle (sensory-motor play) movement with or without objects. Rolling a ball or pulling a toy.
Constructive play	Manipulation of objects to construct or to "create" something.
Dramatic play (presented play)	Substitution of an imaginary person or thing to satisfy the child's personal wishes and needs. Pretending to be someone (doctor, nurse, Superman), beginning with fairly simple activities, then developing more elaborate plots.
Games with rules	Any activity with rules and a goal (such as winning), like tag, hopscotch, marbles. Acceptance of agreed-upon rules and adjusting to them.

Social types of play described by Parten (1932) are *unoccupied play*, where the child simply watches what is going on around him. He may play by himself by gyrating around on a chair. This may not be social play, for there is no interacting with others. In *onlooker play* the child observes what other children are doing, may ask questions of them and take a position in relation to the others, but does not directly participate. *Solitary independent play* is the child playing alone, making no effort to join with other children. *Parallel play* involves the child who plays next to or near other children without interaction.

In *associative play* the child plays with other children. The child acts independently and follows other children in a parade of scooters, wagons, and toys, but the child may drop out at any time. This is not organized play. There is some sharing of toys, and frequently one or more children will just watch the others. The final type of social play is *organized activity*. One or two children, usually the oldest and/or the best liked, decide the format, method, and goal of their play: dramatic events, games, building a tree house or something else. An interesting element of play is the location children choose for their endeavors. Adapted in part from R.C. Moore (1986) by order of preference, here are some typical play locations:

Their own lawns and yards
Playgrounds--school yards
Own home
Parks
Trees
Through streets
Friend's home

These choices for place of play are principally those of older children, ages 9 to 12. When younger children four, five, or six are queried, they prefer mainly their own yards and homes followed by playground, school yard, and parks with their parents or older brothers and sisters.

Imaginary playmates are common among young children, especially when parent-child relationships are unfavorable or when the child has few opportunities for real playmates. It is a natural development phenomenon in many children and is especially characteristic of the age period from 2 1/2 to 4 1/2 years. This is the time when the craving for friendship with other children begins to appear. The child who is unable, for one reason or another, to satisfy this craving frequently compensates with imaginary companions. This, however, is not a satisfactory solution to the problem of only children. Having learned to play with an imaginary companion, the child does not get the training in social cooperation essential to satisfactory adjustment to real children. Such children are likely to acquire the habit of dominating their playmates, which is possible with an imaginary playmate but frequently not with a real child. When they discover that the technique that worked so successfully with imaginary playmates does not work with real children, they may become maladjusted members of the group.

Middle-class children in the United States do not have much peer contact until after age two, and in some instances not until nursery school or kindergarten. In a study (Lewis & Brooks, 1975) it was shown that only 22 percent of middle-class children under age one, and 28 percent of those 18 months of age, encounter peers consistently.

Friends may be formed at many places outside the school environment, such as at recreation centers, during travels and visits, in work activities, and at church, where many youth activities are frequently promoted. Although friendships sometimes may be tense during childhood, there is rarely any jealousy displayed when one member of a pair forms other attachments. Likewise, there is little grief for any long period when a friend moves away. The notion that "you may never see the friend again" has little significance to the child. New friendships are easily formed, and at this age there is no apparent reason for selecting a friend of a particular type. Friendships are formed on the basis of mutual responsiveness.

Social Acceptance--Popularity

When children begin to play with other children, acceptance or rejection by them soon becomes apparent. Whether children are popular is not necessarily determined by their activity in the group. Sometimes aggressively bossy children who push themselves into everything are thoroughly disliked by other children. The outstanding trait that makes for popularity among children is the acceptance of a situation, such as willingness to do what others do, complying with requests, and graceful acceptance of certain events. Popular children are conscientious in their conformity to group ways. Girls at this age are more popular than boys with members of both sexes. Bright children are generally more popular than less bright. Children who are less dependent on adults and who participate more in social activities are more popular than dependent children. However, as children learn to function in a group, they become less dependent on adults.

Helping Children Make Friends

Roopnarine & Honig (1985) believe parents can do a number of things to assist their boys and girls improve relations with other children. They recommend that parents praise the child often and reward them for cooperative behavior. Also, parents need to set a good example for being friendly with children and adults. This will help enhance a son's or daughter's self esteem. Parents can also read stories to children about shy and lonely animals and people who learn to make friends, and encourage children to join groups of two or three people rather than large ones. Playing with children in such games as cut-outs, puppets, and role-playing demonstrates social skills. Finally, a parent can start a group for the child who does not have an opportunity to play with other children.

DEVELOPMENT OF SEXUAL IDENTITY AND GENDER

The results of studies of widely different cultures show that sexually defined roles follow different patterns. Primitive tribes differ in defining the roles of the male and female; however, there is in all cases a clear delineation of the tasks that are the responsibility of the male and of the female. Children reared in certain foreign cultures that clearly structure the roles of males and females at different age levels have very little responsibility for their sexual determination. Their responsibility is that of accepting and fulfilling as best they can certain long-identified roles such as sewing, cooking, and keeping house. Children reared in the United States, where sex roles are less clearly structured, have some discretion and responsibility about their sexual identity at different stages of development.

Quest for Sexual Identity

Sexual identity (the identification of one's self as a particular sex--female or male) is not settled at birth, for some children choose to play the opposite-sex role. Studies of individuals who choose a different sex role conclude that the cause is not clear. Psychoanalysts, psychologists, and physiologists, as well as other students of human development, have developed theories concerning this phenomenon.

According to psychoanalytic theory, early childhood experiences may determine gender identity, as noted in early views set forth by Freud. He thought the child "was aware that humans along with other mammals, have primordial male and female anatomic structures before birth, and postulated that they develop gender identity as they become aware of genital differences between males and females" (Green, 1974, p. 44). Sex-role identity is thought to be the result of identification with the same-sex parent, occurring as part of the resolution of the Oedipus conflict.

It is difficult to test by experiment the theory of Freud, but according to Stangor and Ruble (1987) research does not support it. In children, girls and boys alike are more similar to their mothers than to their fathers--socially, psychologically, and somewhat physically. Also others--friends, kin, teachers, etc.--influence the children's gender view of themselves.

Identification, a term introduced by Freud, indicates the process through which the child comes to believe that he or she is like another person who in some way serves as a model. The child shares some of the attributes of the model, acting as if he or she had the model's characteristics--strength, appearance, and thoughts. Identification is important in developing security in children, since through identifi- children feel that they have taken on the qualities of the parent's power and competence.

Identification is more than observational learning, for it requires emotional ties. Children may imitate a person they are casually involved with, but in the process of identification children absorb the wholesale qualities of the parent--views on a variety of subjects, ways of doing things, and value systems. The establishment of identification requires two things: (1) the child must perceive some likeness to the parent--that is, a similarity of body, ways of talking, and so on; (2) sexual identity is affected by socialization--that is, what is reinforced, observation of others, and the object of identification. The latter is a very important element in the sex-role decision.

The social-learning psychologists contend that parents teach children their gender by rewarding appropriate sex-role behavior and punishing cross-gender behavior. Boys are encouraged to engage in activities involving strength, endurance, and motor coordination. Girls are similarly rewarded for pursuing so-called feminine activities, although they receive less stereotyped conditioning than boys. The question of sex-role models in the development of children is of prime importance to the child's development of his or her sex role.

The cognitive theorist, Piaget, introduced the term gender schema, or the idea that gender is the outgrowth of the organized information of concepts of boy and girl centered on their sex. The visitor says to the mother, "My you have a big boy here," as the two-year-old tries to evade her grasp! "What a pretty little girl," "Oh, she looks like her daddy." The young child hearing these expressions and others will begin to act out these designations. In time girls learn female language and ways and boys learn male language and ways of acting. Bem (1985) contends that children pick up the schema because society identifies people more often by gender than anything else--in clothes, toys, work, activities, and separate toilet facilities.

Other students of human development have sought a biological basis for sexual identity. Although no specific cause for cross-sexual identity appears, a striking relationship has been noted among gonadal hormones, anatomical behavior, and sexual behavior. Concerning such studies, Green (1974) states that:

> Scientists have found evidence that girls who are exposed to high levels of prenatal androgenic hormones (male sex hormones) show much less interest in playing with dolls than other girls, and more interest in boys' toys. They express less satisfaction with their femininity; people call them "tomboys." We have also learned that males exposed to excessive female hormones before birth may be less aggressive and athletic than other boys. These signposts point to possible prenatal influence on later sexuality (p. 46).

It would appear, therefore, that in the quest for gender role identity both biological and historical-cultural factors are in operation.

The major sources of sexual identity that determine people's concept of themselves and others as male or female are believed by Josselyn (1967, p. 38) to be (1) the inherent biological characteristic of each sex, (2) the conceptualization and mores of the culture in which one lives, and (3) the attitudes and behavior of those people who are emotionally meaningful to the individual during childhood--the parents or in some cases other persons with whom the individual was closely identified during childhood.

THE PROCESS OF SEX IDENTIFICATION

During the preschool period children identify with their own sex, which is, of course, dependent upon their ability to discriminate sex differences. In a study by Katcher (1955), four- through six-year-olds readily assigned the correct sex to adults based upon clothing, hair style, genitals, and breasts, in that order. In an earlier study, Rabban (1950) compared the sex discrimination ability of nursery and lower-elementary schoolchildren from two different social classes. He concluded:

(1) Three-year-old boys and girls of both groups show incomplete recognition of sex differences and as a group are unaware of any appropriateness of sex-typed toy objects.

(2) The fourth and fifth years are periods of growth in clarification of sex roles for working-class boys, while the sixth year is particularly significant for middle-class boys.

(3) Working class girls accept the sex-appropriate pattern by six years of age, but middle-class girls do not fully acquiesce to the definition of appropriate sex patterning

even by the eighth year, when all other groups have accepted the social expectation (p. 141).

An investigation by DeLucia (1963) made use of a toy preference test for studying sex-role identification. The subjects were from kindergarten through the fourth grade. Photographs of 52 familiar toys were judged by a panel of young adults and rated on a 9-point scale from 1 (masculine) to 9 (feminine). From these were taken 24 pairs that were used in this study. Then a pair of pictures was presented to the child and the child was asked which toy shown in the pictures he or she would like to play with. Sex differences were manifested in toy preference.

Gender Role Behavior

Sex roles, sometimes called gender roles, are defined as sets of cultural expectations that define how members of each sex should behave. In the early grades at school, girls frequently show a preference for aspects of the masculine role. In contrast to this preference by girls, boys at all grade levels beginning at kindergarten show a predominantly masculine preference (Hartup, 1974). In the fifth grade a decided shift may be observed among girls toward a more pronounced acceptance of the feminine role. This is a likely result of (1) greater segregation in playground activities and competition and (2) the beginning of puberty and changed attitudes toward the sexual self. The discrepancies of strong preferences by girls for the feminine role are almost exclusively products of cultural demands and expectations transmitted through the parents to the child.

Theoretical attempts have been offered to account for sex differences in personality. Maccoby and Jacklin (1974) conducted a vast survey of a body of literature to determine what we know and do not know about sex differences. Their study revealed no conclusive evidence for the following widely held views:

(1) Girls are more "social" than boys.

(2) Girls are largely lacking in achievement motivation.

(3) Girls are more susceptible to suggestion than boys.

(4) Girls are superior to boys in rote learning.

(5) Boys are superior to girls in reasoning and "analytic" learning.

(6) Boys have a higher self-esteem than girls.

(7) Boys are better at high-level tasks, including mathematics.

(8) Girls are primarily "auditory"; boys are primarily "visual."

(9) Girls set up more rules when playing, boys are more aggressive.

(10) Girls have a more cooperative relationship with parents, boys resist and challenge their parents more and resist being called "sissy." Girls do not like to be labeled "tomboy" (Maccoby 1980).

The investigators include that there is little evidence based upon research for early gender-based differences in behavior. More recent studies (Klein & Roddy, 1979; Brodzinsky, Messer, & Tew, 1979; and Liss, 1979) support the view of Maccoby and Jacklin.

Gender and Socialization

Gender-role stereotypes are observable in different cultures, indicating the importance of culture to the establishment of sex roles. In the socialization process (parents' developing and influencing the behavior of children in ways considered appropriate) girls are usually closely associated with the activities of their mothers; boys relate more closely to their fathers. It is possible to recognize deeper sex-role issues that affect the socialization of boys and girls. Kagan (1971) reports that mothers respond more physically to their boys and more verbally to their girls, even during the infant babbling stage. These differences are detectable by the time a child is six or seven months of age and are discernible in the treatment of 18- to 20-month-old children. An observational study by Fagot (1974) of toddlers' behavior and parental reaction revealed some interesting sex differences in harmony with stereotyped roles played by men and women. The results, shown in Table 6.2, reveal significant sex differences in behavior and socialization on the part of 11- to 24-month-old children in their home environment when they were observed over a period of several months.

Table 6.2 SIGNIFICANT FREQUENCY DIFFERENCES BETWEEN BOYS AND GIRLS

	Frequency	
Activity	Boys	Girls
Play with soft toys, dolls	21	72
Dance	10	24
Play with blocks	36	5
Ask for help	61	132
Manipulate objects or toys	324	240
Dress up in adultlike clothes	1	28

Source: Fagot (1974), p. 556

Birth Order

Birth order means the position of a person among his or her siblings with respect to order of birth. Many students of child and adolescent development have studied the effects of birth order on development. The studies indicate that firstborns are bossy (Sutton-Smith & Rosenberg, 1966; Hilton, 1966; Oberlander & Jenkins, 1966), since in their first childhood experiences they frequently display dominant behavior in their relations with younger siblings.

Differences in family environment for the second children as opposed to the first children seem generally known. Firstborns, for some period during their early life, have only adults in their family and are free of competition for other brothers or sisters. Later-born children find more competition for parental attention. The attitude of the mother tends to be more relaxed and less anxious with later-born children (Warren, 1966).

The results of a study of mother interaction with firstborns and later-borns by Rothbart (1971) support those by Lasko (1954) and Hilton (1966). Two groups of mothers were observed for their interaction with their five-year-old children. In one group the child was a firstborn, in the other group a second-born. In all cases the family consisted of two children. The mother was given five tasks to engage in with her child: general conversation, explaining a cartoon, showing the child 20 pictures, supervising the child on a difficult geometric puzzle, and explaining how a water tap works. Rothbart observed that mothers of firstborns displayed more anxious intrusiveness. This greater interference on the part of mothers was particularly marked for girls. Although these studies deal with the attention given by mothers, it seems likely that somewhat similar results might prevail for fathers. Knight (1982), in examining the interaction of birth order and competition-cooperation involving sex and economic class, found that second children, if they are girls, seem to receive less attention from their mothers. They seem to develop preferences for rivalry outcomes and less preference for altruistic outcomes. No difference in attention--time given to social, affection, and caretaking activities--was observed when the second child was the first boy in comparison to the firstborn.

In relation to socialization, it has been noted that oldest and only children have the most exclusive contacts with their parents and lack the socializing influences of siblings. Most studies have concluded that the closeness and intimacy of parent relationships with firstborns tend to produce greater anxiety, conformity, and achievement motivation (Sutton-Smith & Rosenberg, 1970). However, a study by Howarth (1980) found anxiety was lower in firstborns, although persistence was higher. The child's sex, ordinal position, and siblings' sex must be considered in an evaluation of birth order. A boy with a much older sister tends to be more dependent, withdrawn, and tenacious than a boy with a much older brother, and children with brothers tend to be more competitive and ambitious than children with sisters. Boys with only sisters are, according to a study by Brown (1956), somewhat more feminine in their preferences and activities than boys with both male and female siblings.

Social Class

Children growing up in modern suburbia have the advantages of developing in a middle-class home where middle-class values exist. As they move from the home to institutions they come into contact with other children from middle-class homes. Thus, their early middle-class ways of behaving and middle-class values are practiced throughout their childhood. Miel and Kiester (1967) present a fairly complete description of a shoreline suburb of New York City, which is relatively self-sufficient, with advantages, both material and otherwise, to offer its children. The study centered primarily on children in the elementary schools. But this suburb is sorely lacking in providing these children with opportunities to learn about life and "ways of living" outside their own sheltered world. The investigator concluded that growing up in an American suburb today fails the child in certain ways. The suburban child tends to be (1) materialistic, (2) slightly hypocritical, (3) competitive in school, (4) rigid in certain social distinctions, and (5) conformist. The child's attitude toward disadvantaged families, like that of the parents, is likely to be condescending and patronizing.

Television

The extent of television's involvement in the daily lives of children is very impressive. The television ownership rate in families where there are young children is estimated at 99 percent (Murray, 1973). Furthermore, it has been estimated that television sets are turned on an average of six hours each day. One estimate is that children see 18,000 murders and 300,000 commercials on television before they enter school at age six (Laffey & Morgan, 1980). According to Gerbner (1972), children's cartoons have been among the most violent fare.

These disturbing facts, coupled with the rising crime rate among children and adolescents, have fostered serious concern about television viewing by children and adolescents. This concern by parents, teachers, and others interested in the welfare of children has led to attempts at legislation on the part of some groups. Commissions have been formed to study this problem.

Many studies have been conducted on the impact of television on aggression and violence by children and adolescents. A crucial study conducted by Lefkowitz and others (1972) was designed to study the development of aggressive behavior in children by studying the same boys and girls over a 10-year period between ages 8 and 18. Ten years after the children were evaluated for aggressive behavior, these individuals were evaluated for progressive preference and aggressive behavior. Results from this study, as reported by Murray, were as follows:

> For boys, the results indicated that preference for violent programs at age 8 was significantly related to aggressive and delinquent behavior at age 18. For girls, the relationship was in the same direction but less strong. Thus, one general interpretation of the result of this study is that preferring violent televi-

> sion at age 8 is at least one cause of the aggressive and antisocial behavior these young men displayed 10 years later (Murray, 1973, pp. 476-477).

More recently the National Institute of Mental Health (1982) reviewed more than 3,000 studies completed in the 1970s, finding that television is a major influence in the lives of children. Television encourages aggression in two ways: (1) children initiate what they see and (2) they learn that aggression is appropriate behavior when one is frustrated, offended, or aroused. Certainly television also inculcates prosocial behavior; children who watch "Sesame Street" and "Mister Roger's Neighborhood" are going to be affected, generally in positive ways. But the effect of televised aggression may endure for years. A study of 427 third-graders' (girls and boys) viewing habits was made, and it was found that the single best indicator of aggression at 19 was the amount of violence watched from age 8 (Eron, 1982). From 1982 to 1987 war cartoons were televised 1 1/2 hours per week, but by 1987, 48 hours per week. The average child saw 250 episodes over a year and the purchase of war toys in the nation increased 700 percent (Papalia and Olds, 1990).

Many experts like J. Singer and D. Singer (1979) believe fast-paced cartoons and action reduce the attention span and reflection ability of children, causing an inability to retain new information. The American Psychological Association calls for parents to monitor programs their children watch.

Singer and Singer (1983) believe that children who view considerable amounts of television and who live in an overstimulating environment are not helped by the programs; on the other hand, children from families with fewer opportunities seem to get useful information and be more motivated to learn. Some think that television hinders language development. Certainly the television menu contrasts invidiously with the classroom's usually quiet, dull routine and therefore may make it more difficult for the child to concentrate.

The studies of Bandura (1973) and Hicks (1965) indicate that children who observe adult aggression in various forms imitate many of their actions. Liebert and coworkers (1973) found that a preference for viewing violent TV programs at an early age is positively correlated with aggressive behavior in the teenage years. No consistent relationship between TV habits of girls and their aggressive behavior at either 9 or 19 emerges. Girls are seldom reinforced for behaving aggressively, but an increase in such TV dramas as "Cagney and Lacy" and "Police Woman" could change this. Hilgard and Bower (1975) conclude that watching films showing aggression or viewing live models in socially unacceptable aggressive acts increases the likelihood of their repetition by children. Figure 6.7 presents comparable results from another study.

The observation of live models produces more imitation of specific aggressive acts, whereas viewing filmed models instigates more aggressive responses of all kinds, whether real-life or cartoon. Bettelheim (1981) suggests that children often keep the TV set running when they are not watching it, for it blocks out fantasies or ideas they do not wish to consider. Making noise is one of the oldest methods of blocking out the devil. One child said the TV is a comforter, so perhaps hi-fi, radio, and TV noise serve to drive away evil and scary thoughts. Bettelheim does not, however, approve of these practices.

There are, nevertheless, positive aspects of television. Regarding television and its pervasive nature, over 30 years ago Shayon (1951) called it:

> the most accessible window to the grown-up world...TV never shuts children out because it has to prepare dinner. Television plays with children, and goes to any length to get and keep children's attention.

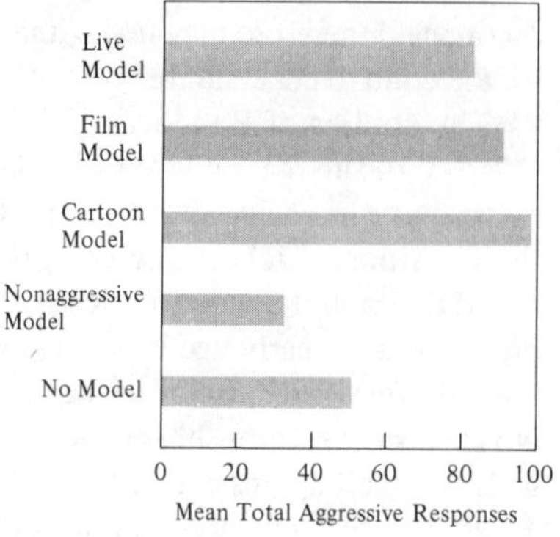

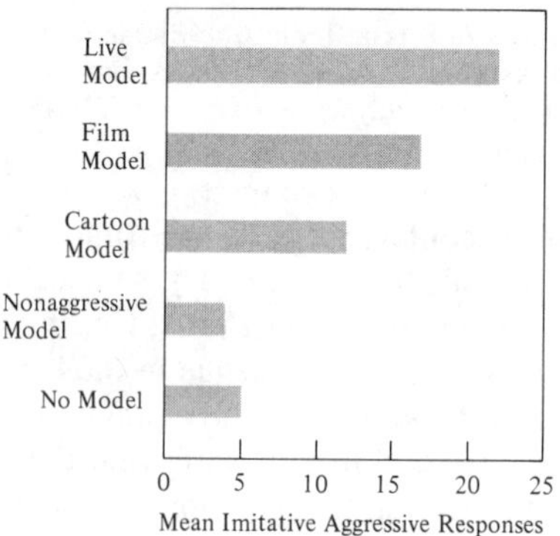

Figure 6.7 Modeling and aggression. (*Source:* Bandura, 1973.)

Since almost all children in the United States are able to view television, this medium might have a leveling influence on class and/or cultural differences in general information, vocabulary, and the appreciation of the arts. Much of the effects of television will depend upon the guidance and rules in the home regarding its usage.

Continuity and Stability of Social Development

Two questions may be raised about social development: (1) Does a pattern of social behavior appear during the preschool years? (2) If so, to what extent is this a continuous and somewhat stable pattern? Results from studies by Kagan and Moss (1962), cited earlier in this chapter, indicate that passivity and aggression (especially among males) tend to persist from the preschool years into the adult years.

In a short-term longitudinal study of continuity and stability of early social development, Emmerich (1966) used as subjects 53 middle-class children who attended four consecutive semesters of nursery school. The average age of the children at the beginning of the first semester was 3.1 years. The children were rated at the end of each semester by the head and assistant teachers independently on 34 social behavior scales. Through the application of statistical procedures, the number of factors was reduced. The same basic factor structures emerged in all four time periods. These were aggression-dominance, dependency, and autonomy. These factors exhibited considerable individual stability as well as behavioral continuity through the four semesters. This is suggested by the stability coefficients presented in Table 6.3. Emmerich concludes:

> Aggression-dominance, dependency, and autonomy are salient personality dimensions having high stability from ages three to five, supporting the view that personality differences arise early in life and are maintained in essentially their original form. However,

FACTOR-STABILITY CORRELATIONS

Semester	Aggression-dominance				Dependency				Autonomy			
	Semester				Semester				Semester			
	1	2	3	4	1	2	3	4	1	2	3	4
1												
2	.84				.83				.78			
3	.47	.64			.61	.56			.44	.63		
4	.47	.66	.81		.48	.45	.69		.54	.67	.80	

Source: Emmerich (1966).

because of certain methodological limitations, these generalizations should be accepted with caution (p. 26).

Hazards in Child Development--Failure to Meet Basic Needs and Abuse

Most parents and caretakers attempt to do the best they can for their children. Many, however, do not foster the child's development nor do they recognize in many instances children's special talents or, if they do, fail to encourage them. Some parents do not feed or clothe their children, letting them starve or freeze to death. They are not concerned about their safety, their whereabouts, or comfort. Other parents give no emotional support or praise to their children, contributing to their failure to thrive. Misuse of children is seen in child abuse where physical injury is involved. Often this is active perpetration, with the child being battered, burned, kicked, strangled, suffocated, beaten, tied up, or locked in closets. This is the battered child syndrome. Worst yet is child sexual abuse, referring to any kind of sexual contact between child and an older person. The incidence of its rise in America is shown in Figure 6.8.

CAUSATIVE FACTORS IN NEGLECT AND ABUSE

In our times sexual abuse is highly publicized, particularly when its origin is institutional. The publicity concerning the California day care center created consternation and fear among day care entrepreneurs, parents, and outraged public and congressional leaders. However, according to the Child Welfare League of America (1986), 90 percent of sexual abuse is committed in the home. Typically women have been the greater abusers of children, mainly physical, but men are considered

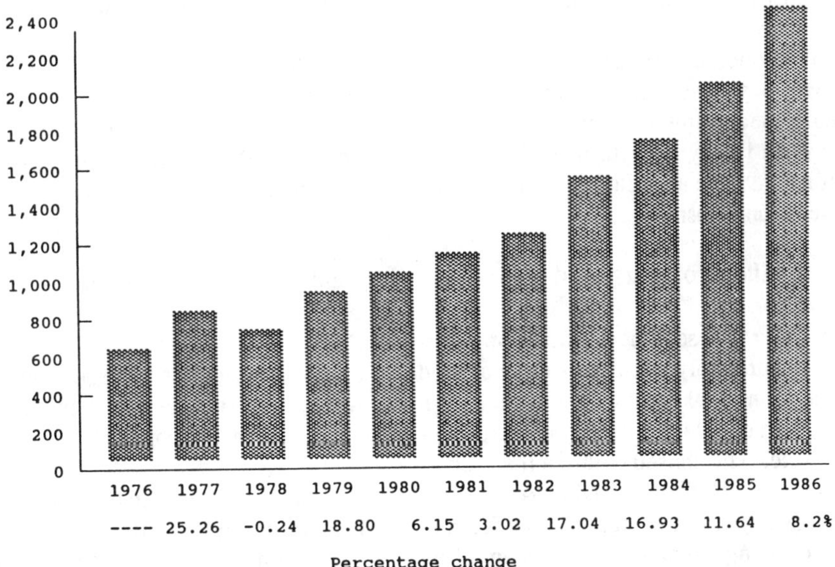

Figure 6.8 Reports of child abuse and neglect. Between 1976 and 1986, reports have more than tripled, from 669,000 reported cases in 1976 to nearly 2.2 million cases in 1986. This may represent a greater willingness to report mistreatment, or it may indicate that mistreatment is increasing, or both. (*Source:* American Humane Society, 1987.)

to be the main abusers today, particularly in sexual abuse and in causing fatal injuries to children. Most abusers are not deranged, psychotic, or criminal but possess one or more of the following attributes: are lonely, under stress, unhappy, or have health problems.

Unfortunately, abusers are likely to have been abused themselves as children. Many are ignorant of principles and knowledge of development; for instance they do not know how to toilet train a child, cannot quiet an infant who has been crying for a long period of time, do not understand nutrition and health care needs, may feed an infant when it is sick and become outraged when it vomits the food (Kropp and Haynes, 1987). The neglectful parent is frequently apathetic and not responsible and therefore may find it easy to ignore the child (Wolfe, 1985).

The victims of mistreatment are most apt to be these type of vulnerable children: low-weight, preterm, hyperactive, mentally retarded, or physically disabled (Reid, 1982). The parents of children who are abused are often stressed, for they are usually having marital problems, economic difficulties, or the mother may have a boyfriend who joins the household, frequently becoming an abuser. Also these families are likely to withdraw from their neighbors and have a limited support network from friends and kinsmen.

Long-Term Effects of Abuse and Help

According to researchers (Kaufman & Sigler, 1987), probably two out of three abused children go on to take good care of their own children, with one-third of the group perpetuating the cycle. The abused children themselves often grow up to be fearful, having low-esteem, anger, hostility, anxiety, aggressiveness, and feelings of being stigmatized. They are often sexually maladjusted. Beyond this they are self-destructive, often engaging in drugs and antisocial behavior and are likely to have been raped or sexually assaulted.

Most communities have volunteer or public social and health agencies that provide escapes from abuse, counseling, education, and care for children. Many programs, designed to help mothers (particularly young mothers), give them information about how to manage their children's behavior. Such agencies explain about reinforcement and rewards to help encourage good behavior, and often help with organizing the family routine and home responsibilities. It's important that parents and others such as school teachers and Sunday school personnel identify the clues that suggest physical and sexual abuse. Changes in behavior, signs of not wanting to be around a person, torn or stained clothing (undergarments), vaginal or rectal bleeding, itching, swollen genitals, unusual interest in sexual matters, or trying to tell about an incident can indicate sexual abuse (USDHHS, 1984). Children at a very early age (three to five) should be counseled to not allow anyone to touch them against their will. They need to know that their bodies belong to them, and if an adult or other child or youth fondles them, they are not to blame for it. Such children, however, should be counseled to tell their parents and/or caretakers.

One also needs to recognize that there is considerable psychological abuse of children, including the following types:

Rejection - implying strong dislike for the child by refusing to meet the needs or requests of the child.

Lack of Emotional Responsiveness - Passive withholding of affection. Coldness, aloofness, no warmth (no kissing, hugging, or talking)

Degrading - humiliating the child in public, low-rating their mental ability, calling them such names as "stink pot," "dummy," or "stupid."

Terrorizing - forcing the child to witness violence, "I'll slap the living fool out of you."

"If you don't stop crying, I'm going to stop the car and put you out."

Isolating - keep children from the family and friends. Making them stay in a closet or outside or a room for long periods of time.

Exploitation - taking advantage of children's weakness to use them in such ways as sexual molestation or having them participate in crime or view pornographic materials. Requiring tasks, chores, or works beyond their ability to perform them.

Since corporal discipline is used by an estimated 93 percent of all parents in America, it is no wonder that many parents and caretakers go beyond civility. Those who use psychological abuse are just as culpable as physical abusers, for the effects are similar and devastating. The old adage, "sticks and stones may break my bones but words will never hurt me" is not true. Words can kill the human spirit and, perhaps even more effectively than physical punishment, destroy the promise of a normal life.

SUMMARY

Physical development is characterized by rapid growth between the ages of two and six. Boys typically are somewhat taller and heavier than girls. The protective system is developing along with cardiovascular and the muscular/skeletal system. Minor illnesses mark this period in the child's life as well as a reduction in eating; consequently they need to pay attention to their diets. Immunizations are important; such contagious diseases as measles are still widespread, because caretakers think there is no danger. Accidents are the leading cause of death in the two- to six-year-old child. Care of teeth is important as the permanent teeth emerge. Sleep patterns are changing; during the first part of this period sleep through the night is usual with one nap, while toward the end of the period the nap is let go. Continued sleep problems may indicate health or emotional problems.

Motor skills are developing at a fast pace. Girls are better at small manipulations than boys and about their equal in most areas. They usually skip rope and hop earlier than the average boy. Some anatomical differences may account for variations in games with boys, for instance, most boys throw balls overhand, but fewer girls do it that way. Language is important; at age three the child has a vocabulary of 1,000 words.

Intellectual development begins this period with the transit completed through the sensory-motor stage, finally achieving mental representation. Children enter the pre-operational stage of Piaget and the iconic stage of Bruner. They begin to learn about the social local culture. Problems of this period are egocentrism, centration, perceptual domination of logic, and a lack of understanding of transformation and conservation. Yet some investigators say conservation can be achieved. New measurements of intelligence by the Stanford-Binet (revised in 1985) have more practical items and are providing for levels of cognitive development analysis, with new norms including more ethnic groups and the handicapped, increasing validity and reliability.

Socialization is a lifelong task, beginning in early childhood. It is the process by which the individual acquires attitudes, beliefs, customs, values, and role expectations of social groups. Socialization as expressed through personality has been explained variously by psychoanalytic, biological, psychosocial (critical aspects), and social learning (limitation of models) theories.

Although infancy may be characterized as a time of dependence, aggressive behavior is in evidence. Its manifestation is explained by psychoanalytic theory as instinctual, by social learning theory as feedback from observation, and by drive theory as based on frustration.

Imitation of models, live or portrayed, influences children's conduct.

The increased employment of mothers has spawned thousands of day care centers enrolling millions of children too young for school. Research studies indicate that there are generally no negative effects--in fact, children and mothers often both benefit. Generally, disadvantaged children profit from the experience of attending day care centers, and children with long histories of day care do as well later in life as home-cared children. However, child care should be chosen carefully.

Children's self-concepts, begun as others' views, are internalized and result from interaction with their own ideas about themselves. School experiences frequently modify the self-concept, and children learn to face certain realities about themselves. During the school years children frequently develop an ideal self, which may be a teacher or some important adult. The ideal is closely related to the values in the culture that the child regards as important. The relative position of these values remains fairly stable into and through adolescence.

It is during childhood, particularly ages five and six that less time is spent in the home. It is during this period that the developmental task of learning to get along with others must be learned. Boys and girls also learn a great deal about their sex roles. The girl identifies more closely with girls; the boy with boys. Guidance and opportunities to learn acceptable social roles are most important during this period if juvenile delinquency is to be avoided during the adolescent years. Children tend to identify with their parents during childhood. The identification process for girls is more complex than that for boys; it is important for the boy to identify with the father or some male authority figure. Identification is an important element in determining sex roles, along with training and observation of others.

Throughout the nursery years, kindergarten, and the first school grades there is a progressively greater tendency to form close ties with members of one's own sex. However, there is no evidence for a natural antipathy to members of the opposite sex during this period. Sexually defined roles will vary with culture. These roles are manifested during the preschool years in American culture.

Home influences as a socializing force appear to diminish when the child enters school, although there is a relationship between deviant behavior at home and behavior problems at school. The child's sex, ordinal position in the family unit, and siblings' sex are important socializing influences. Preschool experiences are important to learning and socialization at school. Later, the teacher and classmates will have significant roles in this process. The child in suburbia is likely to be competitive, materialistic, conformist, and rigid in social distinctions. Membership in a minority frequently disposes the child to conflicts and frustrations, while the lower-class child is often disadvantaged in school and in socialization involving middle-class values.

KEY WORDS

Montessori

open education

Head Start

enuresis

night terrors

Stanford-Binet Test

Wechsler Preschool & Primary Scale

psychoanalytic theory of personality (Freud)

Erikson's psycho-social theory

social learning

drive theory

transformation

conservation

transductive

private speech

centration

mental representation

reversibility

aggression

passivity

identification

self concepts

gender

socialization

sexual abuse

physical abuse

motor development

immunization

over-regulation

REFERENCES

Aggression in childhood: Developmental perspectives. *American Psychologist*, 1974, *29*:336-341.

American Humane Society. *Child Abuse Statistics*. Denser: Author, 1987.

Bandura, A. *Aggression*. Englewood Cliffs, NJ: Prentice-Hall, 1973.

Belsky, J., and Steinberg, L.D. Follow-up of the National Day Care Study. *Children Today*, July/August 1979, *8*(4):21-26.

Bem, S.L. Androgeny & gender schema theory: A conceptual and empirical integration. In T.B. Sodereggen (ed.), *Nebraska Symposium on Motivation, 1984, Psychology and Gender*. Lincoln: University of Nebraska Press, 1985.

Berk, L.E., and Garvin, R.A. Development of private speech among low-income Appalachian children. *Development Psychology*, 1986, *20*(2):271-286.

Bettelheim, B. Our children are treated like idiots. *Psychology Today*, July 1981, *15*(7).

Bloom, B.S. *Stability and Change in Human Characteristics*. New York: Wiley, 1964.

Bolles, E.B. *So Much To Say*. New York: Martins, 1982.

Brodzinsky, D., Messer, S., and Tew, J. Sex differences in children's expression and control of fantasy and overt aggression. *Child Development*, 1979, *50*:372-379.

Bronfenbrenner, U. The fracturing of the American family. *Washington University Daily*, Seattle, Washington, October 5, 1977.

Brown, D.G. Sex role reference in young children. *Psychological Monographs*, 1956, *70*(14):1-19.

Brown, J.L. Hunger in the U.S. *Scientific American*, 1987, *256*(2):37-41.

Child Welfare Leagues. *Born to Run: The Status of Child Abuse in America*. Washington, DC: Author, 1986.

Collins, R.C., and Deloria, D. Head Start research: A new chapter. *Children Today*, 1983, *12*(4):15-19.

Corbin, C.B. *A Textbook of Motor Development*. Dubuque, Iowa: Brown, 1973.

Craig, G.J., and Garney, P. Attachment and separation behavior in the second and third years. Unpublished manuscript, University of Massachusetts, 1972.

Cumeo, D.O. A general strategy of quantitative judgments: The height and width rule. *Child Development*, 1980, *51*:299-301.

DeLucia, L. The toy preference test: A measure of sex-role identification. *Child Development*, 1963, *34*:107-118.

DSM 111-R *Diagnostic and Statistical Manual of Mental Disorders*, 3rd ed. rev. Washington, DC: American Psychiatric Association, 1987.

Dollard, J., Doob, L., Miller, N., Mowrer, O., and Sears, R. *Frustration and Aggression*. New Haven: Yale University Press, 1939.

Dupont, R.L. Phobias in children. *Journal of Pediatrics*, 1983, *102*(6):997-1002.

Ellis, M.J. *When People Play*. Englewood Cliffs, NJ: Prentice-Hall, 1973.

Emmerich, W. Continuity and stability in early social development: Teacher ratings. *Child Development*, 1966, *107*:295-308.

Eron, L.D. Parent child interaction, television violence, and aggression in children. *American Psychologist*, 1982, *37*(2):197-211.

Fagot, B. Sex differences in toddler's behavior and parental reaction. *Developmental Psychology*, 1974, *10*:554-558.

Feinman, S. Approval of cross-sex role behavior. *Psychological Reports*, 1974, *35*:643-648.

Ferber, R. *Solve Your Child's Sleep Problems*. New York: Fireside Books, Simon and Schuster Inc., 1985.

Field. Can pre-school children really learn to conserve? *Child Development*, 1981, *52*:326-334.

Flavell, J.H. Developmental stage: Explanous or explanandum? *Behavioral and Brain*, 1978, Sciences 1: 187.

Freud, S. *New Introductory Lectures on Psychoanalysis*. New York: Norton & Co. Inc. Publication, 1933.

Gelman, R. Preschool thought. *American Psychologist*, 1979, *34*:900-905.

Gerbner, C. Violence in television drama: Trends and symbolic functions. In G.A. Comstock and E.A. Rubenstein (eds.), *Television and Social Behavior*, vol. 1. Washington, DC: U.S. Government Printing Office, 1972.

Gray, S.W. Perceived similarities to parents and adjustment. *Child Development*, 1959, *30*:91-107.

Green, R. Children's quest for sexual identity. *Psychology Today*, February 1974, *7*(9):44.

Handbook of Development Psychology. Englewood Cliffs, NJ: Prentice-Hall, 1982.

Heber, R. Conversation by F.R. Jones with Director Heber of the Milwaukee Project on the completion of the ten-year follow-up, 1977.

Hicks, D. Imitation and retention of film mediated aggressive peer and adult models. *Journal of Personality and Social Psychology*, 1965, *2*:97-100.

Hilgard, E.R., and Bower, G.H. *The Theories of Learning*, 4th ed. Englewood Cliffs, NJ: Prentice-Hall, 1975.

Hilton, I. Differences in the behavior of mothers toward firstborn and later-born children. Paper read at the Annual Meeting of the American Psychological Association, New York, 1966.

Hoffman, L.W. Maternal employment: 1979. *American Psychologist*, 1979, *34*(10):859-865.

Howarth, E. Birth order, family structure and personality variables. *Journal of Personaltiy Assessment*, 1980, *44*(3):299-301.

Jacklin, C. The growing years film series, No. 9, *Emerging Personality*. New York: McGraw-Hill, 1979.

Josselyn, I.M. Sources of sexual identity. *Child and Family*, Spring 1967, *6*(2):38-45.

Kagan, J. *Change and Continuity in Infancy*. New York: Wiley, 1971.

Kagan, J., and Moss, H.A. *Birth to Maturity: A Study in Psychological Development*. New York: Wiley, 1962.

Katcher, A. The discrimination of sex differences by children. *Journal of Genetic Psychology*, 1955, *87*:131-143.

Kaufman, J., and Sigler, E. Do abused children become abusive parents? *American Journal of Orthopsychiatry*, *57*(2):186-192.

King, M.G. Interpersonal relations in preschool and average approach distance. *Journal of Genetic Psychology*, 1966, *109*:109-116.

Klein, H., and Roddy, J. Sex role expectations and adjustment to early childhood group care.

Knight, G.P. Cooperation-competitive social orientations: Interaction of birth order with sex and economic class. *Child Development*, 1982, *53*(3):661-667.

Kropp, J.P., and Haynes, O.M. Abusive and nonabusive mothers' ability to identify general and specifications signals of infants. *Child Development, 58*:187-190.

Laffey, J., and Morgan, R. Sociocultural bases of reading instruction. In P. Lamb and R. Arnold (eds.), *Reading: Foundations and Instructional Strategies*. Belmont, CA: Wadsworth Publishing Co., 1980.

Lasko, J.K. Parent behavior toward first and second children. *Genetic Psychology Monographs*, 1954, *49*:97-137.

Lefkowitz, E.L., Walder, L., and Huesmann, L. Television violence and child aggression: A follow-up study. In G.A. Comstock and E.A. Rubinstein (eds.), *Television and Social Behavior*, vol. 3. Washington, DC: U.S. Government Printing Office.

Lewis, M., and Brooks, J. Infants' social perception: A constructivist view. In L.B. Cohen and P. Salapatek (eds.), *Infant Perception: From Sensation to Cognition*, vol. 2. New York: Academic Press, 1975.

Liebert, R., Neale, J., and Davidson, E. *The Early Window: Effects of Television on Children and Youth*. New York: Pergamon Press, 1973.

Liss, M. Variables influencing modeling and sex-typed play. *Psychological Reports*, 1979, *44*:1107-1115.

Lozoff, B., Wolf, A.W., and Davis, N.S. Sleep problems seen in pediatric proactive pediatrics. 1985, *75*(4):477-483.

Maccoby, E. *Social Development*. New York: Harcourt, Brace, Jovanovich, 1980.

Maccoby, E., and Jacklin, C. *The Psychology of Sex Differences*. Stanford: Stanford University Press, 1974.

Maccoby, E., and Jacklin, C. What we know and don't know about sex differences. *Psychology Today*, 1974, *8*:109-112.

Madsen, M.C., and Lancy, D.F. Cooperative and competitive behavior: Experiments related to ethnic identity and urbanization in Papua New Guinea. *Journal Cross-Cultural Psychology*, *12*:389-409.

Magoon, R.A., and Garrison, K.C. *Educational Psychology*. Columbus, Ohio: Merrill, 1976.

Mandler, J.M. Representation. In J.H. Flavell and E.M. Markman (eds.), *Handbook of Child Psychology: Cognitive Development*, vol. 3. New York: Wiley, 1983.

McCandless, B.R., and Hoyt, J.M. Sex, ethnicity, and play preference of preschool children. *Journal of Abnormal and Social Psychology*, 1961, *62*:683-685.

Meyer, B. The development of girls' sex-role attitudes. *Child Development*, 1980, *51*:508-514.

Miel, A., and Kiester, E. *The Shortchanged Children of Suburbia.* New York: American Jewish Committee, 1967.

Moore, R.G. *Childhood's Domain: Play and Place in Child Development.* London: Groom Helm, 1986.

Morris, R., and Kralochioll, T. *Treating Children's Fear and Phobias: A Behavioral Approach.* Elmsford, NY: Pergamon, 1983.

Murray, J.P. Television and violence: Implications of the surgeon general's research program. *American Psychologist*, June 1973, *28*(6):472-478.

National Day Care Study. Executive Summary of Volume 1: *Summary Findings of Policy Implication of the National Day Care Study.* Cambridge, Mass.: Agt. Associates, 1979.

National Association for the Education of Young Children (NGEYC), 1987.

National Institute of Health (AAT). *Positive Approaches to Daycare Dilemmas: How to Make It Work.* Elk Grove Village, 1986.

National Institute of Mental Health (NIMH). *Television and Behavior: Ten Years and Scientific Progress and Implications for the Eighties*, vol. 1, Summary Report (DHHS Publication No. ADM82-1195). Washington, DC: Government Printing Office.

Oberlander, M., and Jenkins, N. Birth order and academic achievement. Paper read at the Annual Meeting of the American Psychological Association, New York, 1966.

Papalia, D.E., and Olds, S.W. *A Child's World.* New York: McGraw-Hill, 1990.

Parten, M. Social play among pre-school children. *Journal of Abnormal and Social Psychology*, 1932, *27*:243-269.

Patterson, G.R. The aggressive child: victim and architect of a coercive system. In L.A. Hamerlynch, L.C. Handy, and E.J. Mash (eds.), *Behavior Modification and Families: 1. Theory and Research.* New York: Brunner/Mazel, 1976.

Payne, D.E., and Mussen, P.H. Parent-child relations and father identification among some adolescent boys. *Journal of Abnormal and Social Psychology*, 1956, *52*:358-362.

Phillips, J.L. *The Origin of Intellect: Piaget's Theory.* San Francisco: Freeman, 1969.

Rabban, M. Sex role identification in young children in two diverse social groups. *Genetic Psychology Monographs*, 1950, *42*:81-158.

Reid, J.R., Patterson, G.R., and Locker, R. The abused child: Victorian instigator or innocent bystander? In D.J. Berstein (ed.), *Response Structure and Organization*. Lincoln: University of Nebraska Press, 1982.

Roopnarine, J., and Honig, A.S. The unpopular child. *Young Children*, 1985, pp. 59-64.

Rothbart, M. Birth order and mother-child interaction in an academic situation. *Journal of Personality and Social Psychology*, 1971, *17*:113-120.

Rubin, Zick. Breaking the age barrier to friendship. *Psychology Today*, March 1980, pp. 96-99.

Rule, B., Nesdale, A., and McAra, M. Children's reactions to information about the intention underlying an aggressive act. *Child Development*, 1974, *45*:794-798.

Schmuck, R.A. Sociometric status and utilization of academic abilities. *Merrill-Palmer Quarterly*, 1962, *8*:165-172.

_____. Some relations of peer liking patterns in the classroom to pupil attitudes and achievements. *School Review*, 1963, *71*:337-359.

Sears, P.S. Doll Play aggression in normal young children: Influence of sex, age, sibling status, father's absence. *Psychological Monographs*, 1951, *65*(6).

Shayon, R.L. *Television and Our Children*. New York: Longman and Green, 1951.

Shepard-Look, D.L. Sex differentiation and the development of sex roles. In B.B. Wolman (ed.), *Handbook of Developmental Psychology*. Englewood Cliffs, NJ: Prentice-Hall, 1982.

Singer, J.L., and Singer, D.G. Come back, Mr. Rogers, come back, Mr. Rogers, come back. *Psychology Today*, March 1979, pp. 56-60.

Singer, J.L., and Singer, D.G. Psychological break at television: Cognitive, developmental, personality and social policies implications. *American Psychologist*, 1983, *38*(71):826-854.

Stangor, C., and Ruble, D.N. Development of gene role knowledge and gender constancy. In S. Liben and M.L. Signorelle (eds.), *Children Gender Schema*. San Francisco: Jossey Bass.

Sutton-Smith, B., and Rosenberg, R.G. Sibling consensus on power tactics. Paper read at Annual Meeting of the American Psychological Association, New York, 1966

U.S. Bureau of Census. *Who's Minding the Kids? Child Care Arrangement: Winter 1984-1985*. (Current 1987 Population Reports: Household Economic Studies Series, p. 70, no. 9) Washington, DC: U.S. Government Printing Office

U.S. Department of Health Human Services (USDHHS). *Child Sexual Abuse Prevention: Tips to Parents*. Washington, DC: Office of Human Development Services for Children, Youth and Families, National Center on Child Abuse and Neglect, 1984.

U.S. Department of Health and Human Services. *Prevention, 1982* (DHHS) (PHS) Publication No. 82-50157, Washington, DC: U.S. Government Prevention Office, 1982.

U.S. Department of Labor, Commerce and Health and Human Sciences. *Working Mothers and Single Parents*. Washington, DC: U.S. Government Printing Office, 1982.

U.S. News & World Report. Teenagers in trouble? Youth Speaker, 1982, *92*(1).

Vygotsky, L.S. *Thought and Language*. Cambridge, Mass.: MIT Press, 1962.

Warren, J.R. Birth order and social behavior. *Psychological Bulletin*, 1966, *65*:38-50.

Webb, W.B. Self-evaluation compared with group evaluations. *Journal of Consulting Psychology*, 1952, *16*:305-307.

Westinghouse Learning Corporation. *The Impact of Head Start: An Evaluation of the Effects of Head Start on Children's Cognitive and Effective Development*. Columbus: Westing Row Learning Corporation, Ohio University, 1969.

Whiteley, Elaine. Every mother's nightmare. *Ladies Home Journal*, October 1990, *15*:1-153, 219-225.

Williams, E.R., and Caliendo, M.A. *Nutrition: Principles, Issues and Applications*. New York: McGraw-Hill, 1984.

Woods, M. The unsupervised child of the working mother. *Developmental Psychology*, 1972, *6*:14-25.

Wolfe, D.A. Child-abusive parents: A nespirical review and analysis. *Psychological Bulletin*, 1985, *97*(3):462-482.

Chapter 7

PHYSICAL AND SOCIAL DEVELOPMENT IN MIDDLE AND UPPER CHILDHOOD

- ***Physical Growth***
  Height and weight
  Body types
  Metabolism
  Vital factors--blood pressure, respiration, etc.
  Nutritional needs
  Health care and hazards
- ***Motor Growth***
  Development of strength
  Coordination
  Learning motor skills
- ***Social Development***
  Types of role playing
  Peers and groups
  Parenting styles
  Stress and children

PHYSICAL AND SOCIAL DEVELOPMENT IN MIDDLE AND UPPER CHILDHOOD

The growth of the individual from birth to complete physical maturity constitutes a long period of time--almost one-third of the normal life span. The social growth of the person never ceases, but nowhere do more things change than they do in the middle childhood stage. Social and physical development interact with each other. One axiom among the principles of development is that normally the areas of growth--intellectual, physical, and social--are positively related. Views of self and social roles are tied closely to self-concept and body image. Whether learning social skills or motor skills the impetus among children is largely from society, their peers, and their families.

PHYSICAL DEVELOPMENT

In investigating the relationship between self-worth and perceived inadequacies, Harter (1987) found high correlations (.66 and .57) in elementary (grades three through six) school children and middle school children (sixth through eighth grades) with physical appearance. The second highest correlations were with social acceptance--.36 for elementary and .45 for the middle school students. These were correlated with inadequacies to a greater degree than behavioral conduct, athletic competence, and scholastic competence.

The meaning of body types has an early recognition among children. Staffieri (1967, 1972) asked 90 boys from ages 6 to 10 which body type they would like to be and asked subjects to apply a selected list of adjectives to silhouettes of fat, thin, and muscular boys. Obviously for older youth and even adults, the body affects one's view of self. Certainly future health is more likely to be affected by the endomorphic build, assuming more obesity (30 percent over normal weight) and therefore, by the age of 40 more diabetes, hypertension, and cardiovascular problems. It is believed that as many as 30 percent of North American children are overweight or obese (Cusack, 1984). Children's inadequate diets and lack of exercise and health knowledge heighten the chance of poor mental health and the absence of a sense of well-being. It has long been thought that status and vocational success have been linked to body builds, and personality has often been associated with physical shapes.

Morphological Differences and Personality

The structure of the physique has been of interest since ancient times, mainly because it was always assumed that the body type and behavior, including mental disorders, are related, as formulated by Kretschmer (1925). W.H. Sheldon and coworkers (1940, 1954) examined 4,000 photographs of adolescents for a criterion in classifying human physiques; he subsequently identified three primary body types (Figure 7.1).

These correlations above, though attempted are not accepted by many psychologists, according to Suinn (1975, p. 91) and others. They say Sheldon's body trait correlations were too high, whereas the replications have not been as high. The problem is that the concepts are simply too nebulous to describe the complex nature of personality. Sheldon's original appraisal of types was later refined to include in each of the three categories a continuum scale for rating 1 (minimum) to 7 (maximum), recognizing that no one represented a pure type but each was a composite. For example, a person with a 7 (endo) -1 (meso) -1 (ecto) would be seen as an extreme endomorphy with a 7-1-1 rating. A 4-4-4 assessment would be a somatype in moderation of all three components. Sheldon found the typical Harvard student to have a 3-4-4 physique.

Support for Sheldon's view comes from research of Walker (1963), who indicated sig-

Somatotype	Physical Characteristics	Personality Type
Endomorphy 	Digestive viscera large and predominant Body soft and round Bones and muscles underdeveloped	Visceratonia Love of physical comfort, relaxation, sometimes gluttonous Relaxed, tolerant, complacent Sociable, dependent, needs affection Seeks others when troubled
Mesomorphy 	Muscle and bone predominant Body hard and rectangular Strong body resistance to injury	Somatotonia Vigorous physical exertion, active, bold, adventurous Assertive, aggressive, energetic Much self-expression, direct, competitive Needs action when troubled
Ectomorphy 	Delicate form Body linear and thin Lightly muscled	Cerebrotonia Restrained, light posture and movements Tense, inhibited, poor sleep habits, more thought than action Introverted, keeps to self Needs solitude when troubled

Figure 7.1 Body types in children and personality characteristics.

nificant relationships between morphological types and corresponding temperamental types from his study of nursery school children. Obviously the body type does confer advantage or disadvantage, in addition to that discussed earlier, of some kind on the individual. The endomorphic child (broad hips and relatively short legs) matures earlier than the average child. The ectomorph (long legs, slender, and broad shoulders) matures later than any other group, while the mesomorph (compact build) matures somewhat earlier than the average. Wiggins, Wiggins, and Conger (1968), studying correlates of heterosexual somatic preferences, found in young men some relation to being "breast men," "buttocks men," and "leg men" to their personalities. Some psychologists say this is as reasonable as Sheldon's types.

Boys as a group show a greater tendency to have mesomorphic builds than girls, while girls tend to have either ectomorphic or endomorphic builds at the time of puberty. Black children differ from white children in that their trunks are shorter, hips and chests are more slender, and lower legs are longer (Malina, Hamill, & Lemeshaw, 1974). Although the question of body type is open, no one questions the meaning of body type for the individual. It can be disturbing for a young woman to be ectomorphic above the waist and endomorphic below the waist. In a study by Staffieri (1972), 60 girls were asked to select adjectives relating to looks. Judged by the adjectives used, mesomorphs were the most-liked body builds. Body shape and size, let alone attractiveness, have significant effects upon the way children see themselves and each other. Children's bodies from ages 4 to 10 are more alike than they will be in adolescence; even so, differences appear. Elementary school children are usually thinner and taller than they were as preschoolers.

Physical attractiveness is important in how children are treated. Investigations show that pictures of "good looking" children elicited many more positive comments than negative (Dion, Berscheid & Walster, 1972). Late maturing boys seem more often to have negative self-concepts. Early maturing boys more often get respect, since a premium is placed upon athletic and physical maturity. Leadership roles attributed to these boys make for self-confidence and the opportunity to become leaders. Early maturing girls are desirable to older boys for physical reasons. Late maturing girls, according to adult observers (Jones, 1949), have more prestige and leadership qualities than their early maturing counterparts.

GROWTH AND BODY SIZE

Growth of the body--its ultimate size in height and weight potential--is largely predetermined. Weight is more readily influenced by environmental conditions and by variations in nutrition and health, but it is still useful to keep in mind body types and timing differences. Growth changes involve not only dimensional aspects but also proportion and shape. Tanner (1973) says that the shape of the body is under closer genetic control than is size. Identical twins may be so nearly the same in shape that they are indistinguishable, yet at the same time one may be taller even from the time of birth. Also, nutrition may influence size. Tanner found Japanese reared in California grew up to be larger than their kin in the earlier, poorer nutritional circumstances of Japan; nevertheless, their facial characteristics and trunk-limb proportions did not change.

The essential aspects of the physical growth of the body are as follows: (1) the development of the skeletal system, which affects the weight and height of the child; (2) the endocrine glands, which regulate the process of growth controlling the maturation of the body parts and tissues; and (3) the sex changes, which are stimulated by the sex chromosome that accounts for the manufacture of testosterone and the Y chromosome. Specific action on the hypothalamic section of the brain is required to translate

EXPECTED INCREASE IN HEIGHT PER YEAR

Age	Both sexes	
	Inches	Centimeters
Birth to 1 year	9.8	24.9
1–2	4.8	12.2
2–3	3.6	9.1
3–4	2.9	7.4
4–5	2.7	6.9
5–6	2.7	6.9
6–7	2.4	6.1
7–8	2.2	5.6
8–9	2.2	5.6
9–10	2.0	5.1

	Boys		Girls	
	Inches	Centimeters	Inches	Centimeters
10–11	1.9	4.8	2.3	5.8
11–12	1.9	4.8	2.5	6.4
12–13	2.2	5.6	2.6	6.6
13–14	2.8	7.1	1.9	4.8

it into a male hypothalamus. Developmental and maturational age is calculated by a number of indications: age at eruption of teeth, amount of pubic hair, breast and penis size, age of menarche onset, amount of water in muscle cells, and the degree of calcification of the bone.

Growth in Height and Weight

Growth in body size is controlled by the growth hormones. Growth in height and weight are the most obvious changes in body size; the development of the bones, genitals, and secondary sex characteristics furnish a good basis for evaluating physical development. Growth of the bones is affected by the thyroid glands and hormones produced by the gonads--testosterone is mainly responsible for the adolescent spurt in boys; it is aided by the growth hormone (somatotropin). The growth hormone and androgenic hormones from the adrenal gland account for the adolescent girl's spurt. The female sex hormone (estrogen) does not give rise to general body growth, but only to growth of the breasts and reproductive tract. These hormones act as retarding forces or influences on the growth hormones by stimulating the manufacture of calcium, which causes the bones to ossify and produce the closure of the epiphyses (ends) of the bones.

Change in height and weight is the most conspicuous feature of growth during middle childhood (Table 7.1), and although there is considerable variation in growth in height and weight of children, the pattern is similar. Children of the same age show such variation in height that if a child who was of exactly average height at his or her seventh birthday did not grow at all for two years, the child would still be within the normal limits of height attained at age nine. If growth deficiencies exist, children can be helped to approach average height through treatment with growth hormones (Lowrey, 1978).

Since girls reach pre-puberty earlier than boys, they grow taller and are heavier for the same age. Many young boys of 11 or 12 who

WEIGHTS OF GIRLS AND BOYS 10 TO 15 YEARS OF AGE

	Age in years	Sex	Mean in pounds	Variability: Standard deviation in pounds	Variability: Number of cases	Range in pounds: Reported in studies	Range in pounds: Computed at ± 1 sigma from mean	Number of cases
	10	Boys	70.7	11.5	8,573	44.0–129.0	59.2– 82.2	15,264
		Girls	70.3	13.2	7,936	40.0–154.0	57.1– 83.5	14,696
	11	Boys	77.6	13.1	8,449	45.0–169.0	64.5– 90.7	15.527
		Girls	79.0	15.5	7,824	45.0–209.0	63.5– 94.5	14,936
girls exceed boys (ages 11–14)	12	Boys	85.6	15.9	8,677	30.0–174.0	69.8–101.4	15,091
		Girls	89.7	17.8	7,678	45.0–239.0	71.9–107.5	14,761
	13	Boys	95.6	18.2	8,419	59.4–194.0	77.4–113.8	13,488
		Girls	100.3	19.0	6,947	30.0–234.0	82.3–118.3	13,920
	14	Boys	107.9	20.1	6,942	60.0–224.4	57.8–128.0	13,954
		Girls	108.5	17.2	5,393	53.0–239.0	91.3–125.7	12,204
	15	Boys	12.7	20.6	6.320	50.0–254.0	101.1–142.3	13,281
		Girls	113.0	16.2	5,394	70.0–239.0	98.8–131.2	12,072

Source: HEW (1953).

HEIGHTS OF GIRLS AND BOYS 9 TO 14 YEARS OF AGE

	Age in Years	Sex	Mean in inches	Variability: Standard deviation in inches	Variability: Number of cases	Range in inches: Reported in studies	Range in inches: Computed at ± 1 sigma from mean	Number of cases
	9	Boys	54.2	2.5	13,571	43.0–60.9	51.8–56.8	15,266
		Girls	54.2	2.6	13,015	47.4–52.7	51.6–56.8	14,697
girls exceed boys	10	Boys	56.2	2.6	13,921	49.0–63.2	53.6–59.3	13,325
		Girls	56.5	2.8	13,269	49.1–64.8	53.7–59.3	14,539
	11	Boys	58.2	2.9	14,485	50.8–58.0	55.3–61.1	16,091
		Girls	59.0	2.9	13,106	51.3–66.8	56.1–61.9	14,781
	12	Boys	60.5	3.2	13,889	52.0–71.4	57.3–62.7	15,494
		Girls	60.6	2.6	12,212	53.4–68.9	58.0–53.2	13,919
	13	Boys	63.0	3.4	12,346	54.0–72.6	59.6–66.4	13,959
		Girls	62.3	2.4	10,510	55.2–71.7	59.9–64.7	12,304
	14	Boys	65.6	3.1	11,726	54.3–74.8	62.5–68.7	13,286
		Girls	63.2	2.3	10,473	57.0–70.2	60.9–65.5	12,071

Source: HEW (1953).

are beginning to become interested in sports are disturbed to find their sisters of the same or younger age are taller and weigh more than they do. The fact is that girls weigh more than boys on average for the years 11 through 14 and are taller from 10 through 12 than boys, as seen below in the Health and Human Services data (1953) (Tables 7.2 and 7.3). Because of this and earlier maturation girls can compete with boys on equal terms in some sports. Girls at six or seven usually are ahead of boys in agility and coordination.

MOTOR DEVELOPMENT

A summary of physical and motor development along with self-care abilities are presented in Table 7.4. These represent averages for children 6 to 12. The self-care development parallels social development; increasingly the child is socialized by his family, school and church and in time receives considerable pressure from peers. Peers influence children's preferences in clothes, popular pastimes, sports, and games. The years from 6 to 12 are the prime years for learning both social and physical skills. Though both of these skills continue at a high rate of growth through the adolescent years, these are the times when the imprint of interest and the desire to practice and learn are germinal. In the past, low expectations for girls' achievement in motor skills and sports have served to preclude participation and reduce drive to excel in these areas of physical activity. Research by Hall and Lee (1984) with boys and girls in the third through fifth grades in excellent co-physical education programs indicated girls do about as well as boys in shuttle run, dashes, broad jump, and 600-yard run. Girls also showed continued improvement each year of the study. Some examples of motor development levels among girls and boys 6 to 12 are suggested by Cratty (1979).

Age 6 Girls are superior in accuracy of movement; boys are superior in forceful, less complex acts. Children can throw with proper weight shift and step.

Age 7 Balance on one foot without looking. Can walk a 2-inch wide balance beam. Can hop and jump accurately into small frames. Most can do the jumping jack exercise.

Age 8 Both sexes participate in a variety of games. Grip strength permits steady 12-pound pressure. Girls can throw a ball 40 feet. Children can engage in alternate rhythmic hopping in a 2-2, 2-3, 3-3 pattern.

Age 9 Girls can jump vertically to a height of 8.5 inches and boys 10 inches. Boys can run 16.5 feet per second and throw a ball 70 feet.

Age 10 Girls can run 17 feet per second. Children can judge and intercept the path of small balls thrown from a distance.

Age 11 Broad jump for boys, 5 feet; for girls, one-half foot shorter.

Age 12 Standing high jump of 3 feet possible for both sexes.

Perceptual-Motor Development

A number of skills involving the ability to see accurately and to control muscles (or produce writing or manipulate objects) are fundamental in development. These skills tend to come with maturation. Vision, hand movement, and their coordination are basic to learning to read, write, and use instruments. Figure 7.2 gives a schematic representation of the development of hand manipulation.

Table 7.4 PHYSICAL, MOTOR AND SELF-CARE DEVELOPMENT IN MIDDLE AND UPPER SCHOOL CHILDREN 6-12 YEARS

Measures	Ages 6-8	Ages 8-10	Ages 10-12	Age 12
Pulse Rate	90± 15 beats per minute	85± 10 beats per minute	90± 20 beats per minute	Boys 90-20 Girls 85-20
Respiration	21± per minute	20± per minute	19± per minute	
Blood Pressure	100/60± 16/10	102/60± 16/10	109/56± 16/10	113/59-18/10
Weight	39.5-55.5 lbs.	48-70 lbs.	57-85 lbs.	Girls 68-108 Boys 73-97 lbs.
Height	43.5-48.5 inches	47.5-53.5 inches	52-58 inches	Girls 57-63 inches Boys 56-62 inches
Teeth	First permanent molars, medical incisors, and lateral incisors	-----	-----	Cuspids, first and second premolars
Motor	Rides bicycle without training wheels, climbs, jumps, runs, hops, moves constantly though awkwardly, knows right hand from left hand, can draw a person with 16-20 parts, learns cursive writing.	Performs tricks on bicycle, participates in sports, throws a ball skillfully, uses hands independently, can draw a person with 18-20 parts, prints fluently.	Participates in all physical activities, can roller skate, plays tennis and soccer, swims. Fine motor development continues with better coordination and control.	Athletic sports coordination accelerates.
Self Care	Eats with fingers, stuffs food in mouth, at 7 & 8 table manners improve, talkative when eating, may need help with dressing, usually wears clothes suggested by parents, can comb hair, has to be reminded to bathe and wash hands, leaves clothes where they are removed, dawdles in bathtub.	Handles eating utensils well, dresses alone and selects clothes, needs to be reminded to bathe and wash hands. Increased speed and smoothness in fine motor control.	May criticize parents' table manners, may hesitate to take off clothes they like to wear, leaves clothes where they fall, enjoys current fads in clothes.	Bathes frequently, prefers showers, selects own clothes.

Adapted from Marlow (1988)

Children at five or six are usually farsighted; they see better at a distance than close up. Their eyes are not mature enough to focus on a line of normal-sized print, nor can they usually scan from one word to another in one direction (Vurpillot, 1968). The child is more likely to guess at a word based on the first letter than to see the whole word. Though they can focus fairly well, they often lack reliability. By age eight most children are able to read small print. Size constancy for known objects is present by the sixth month, adult competency is not achieved until around 10 years of age. Object constancy develops slowly; by eight years of age most children can isolate *u* from *o* or *m* from *w*. Before the first grade, eye examinations should be given that consider any evidence of eye strain, binocular vision, and nearsightedness. Reading involves more than just seeing the word plainly, for the child must see the connection between letters and sounds in a word by scanning it correctly. Larrabee and Jones (1980) found "low plus lenses" effectively aid some children with vision problems. Many poor readers, however, do not have vision disabilities. Chapter 8 has a section on the reading task.

Most infants are both left- and right-handed. By age two, preference for the right hand is demonstrated. Hardyck and Petrinovich (1977) suggest that between two and five one child in ten chooses the left hand as an obvious preference. Genetic and prenatal environments perhaps account for hand preference (Fincher, 1977). Left-handed persons are as capable as right-handed ones and perhaps more advantaged by the tendency to be ambidextrous. Left-handed children are handicapped in learning to write, due to the added difficulty of writing legibly and in writing such languages as English that read from left to right, for the paper will be soiled as the hand moves. Left-handed children should not feel this is wrong. Skills in reading, scanning letters or words, and writing are important; some claim fine motor skills are important links to these skills and they come after crawling, hopping, and balancing (Hallahan & Cruickshank, 1973).

Skull and Brain Growth

Although the gross brain properties averaged over many individuals are highly unlikely to exhibit possible special growth periods,

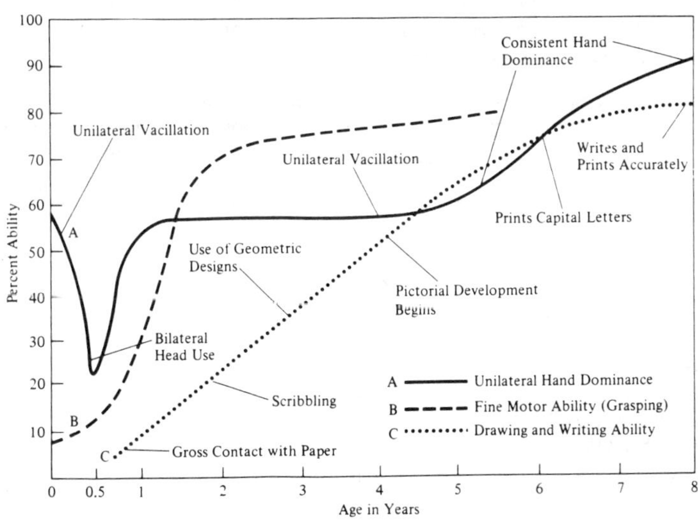

Figure 7.2 Hand manipulation in children.

information pertaining to spurts in brain growth can be ascertained to some extent from average data by computing multi-year weight increments (Epstein, 1974). Since brain weight correlates with skull circumference, similar spurts may be found in the two areas. Characteristic spurts in brain and skull occur roughly in the years 6 to 8, 10 to 12, 14 to 17, and possibly 2 to 4. Phrenoblysis (spurts in brain growth) research collated by Epstein gives credence to the brain spurt hypothesis (see Table 7.5). It might be that the phrenoblysic age is correlated with spurts in mental abilities. The spurt at age 14 to 15 is correlated with the Piagetian stage of formal operations, which is generally supposed to be initiated after age 12. The spurt at age 11 is correlated with the rapid growth of conceptualization about concrete objects that exist in the environment and are used in schools to build concepts, such as fractions or geometrical objects. The spurt at age seven coincides with the start of formal learning normally associated with the acquisition of reading and writing skills by the average child.

Learning New Motor Skills

The best time for learning motor skills is childhood, because children are more flexible. They have learned fewer skills that will conflict with a newer skill. In addition, they are more curious, so they will readily try new things. Also, repeating exercises does not bore them as it does adults. Physical fitness, motor coordination, and acquisition of motor skills are closely associated with an individual's physical development; children taught such complex motor skills as jumping rope, hopping, throwing, and catching will nevertheless be superior to those who receive no training (Seils, 1951).

Between ages 6 and 12 there is a pronounced growth in children's ability to run, jump rope, climb, play hopscotch, skate, ride bicycles, swim, and slide. Also, during this period more complex motor skills are acquired through special training. Growth in the ability to perform motor acts reaches its maximum around age 13 1/2 or 14 for girls and around 17 for boys. Speed of voluntary movement increases continually from early childhood at a progressively slower rate (Espenschade & Meleny, 1961).

The necessary essentials in learning motor skills include the following:

Sufficient maturational levels - The child must be developmentally ready to learn the skill. Eye-hand coordination is important, depending upon many things, such as neural-muscular maturation.

AGES OF PEAKS IN BIENNIAL INCREMENTS IN BRAIN AND SKULL

Researcher	Age at midpoint of biennial span					
	3–5	6–7	8–10	11–12	13–14	15–17
Boas (1912)						
Hebrews		+	−	+	−	+
Central Europeans			+	+		+?
Sicilians		+		+		+
Coppoletta-Walbach (1933)		+	−	+		
Shuttleworth (1939)		+	−	+	−	+
Vickers-Stuart (1943)	+					
Simmons (1944)		+	−	+	−?	+
Reynolds-Schoen (1947)		+	−	+	−	+
Westrop-Barber (1956)	+					
Dokladal (1959)	+	+	+	+		+
Bayley-Eichorn (1962)		+	−	+	−	+
Dullemeijer (1971)	+	+	−	+	−	+

Source: Epstein (1974).
? indicates marginal evidence of peaks; − indicates troughs; + indicates evidence of growth peaks.

RECOMMENDED DIETARY ALLOWANCES FOR CHILDREN AND YOUTH

	Males and females		Males		Females	
Age (years)	**4–6**	**7–10**	**11–12**	**15–18**	**11–14**	**15–18**
Energy (kcal)	1,800	2,400	2,800	3,000	2,400	2,100
Protein (g)	30	36	44	54	44	48
Vitamin A (I.U.)	2,500	3,300	5,000	5,000	4,000	4,000
(R.E.)	500	700	1,000	1,000	800	800
Vitamin D (I.U.)	400	400	400	400	400	400
Vitamin E (I.U.)	9	10	12	15	12	12
Ascorbic Acid (mg)	40	40	45	45	45	45
Folacin (mcg)	200	300	400	400	400	400
Niacin (mg)	12	16	18	20	16	14
Riboflavin (mg)	1.1	1.2	1.5	1.8	1.3	1.4
Thiamine (mg)	0.9	1.2	1.4	1.5	1.2	1.1
Vitamin B_6 (mg)	0.9	1.2	1.6	2.0	1.6	2.0
Vitamin B_{12} (mcg)	1.5	2.0	3.0	3.0	3.0	3.0
Calcium (mg)	800	800	1,200	1,200	1,200	1,200
Phosphorus (mg)	800	800	1,200	1,200	1,200	1,200
Iodine (mcg)	80	110	130	150	115	115
Iron (mg)	10	10	18	18	18	18
Magnesium (mg)	200	250	350	400	300	300
Zinc (mg)	10	10	15	15	15	15

Source: Food and Nutrition Board (1974).

Opportunity to learn and practice - A chance to learn is fundamental. Parents afraid to teach, delaying teaching, or an environment that does not provide an opportunity to learn a skill will eliminate the acquisition of a new motor ability. Regular practice is important in learning a new skill; uneven hit-or-miss means poor and irregular performance.

Models to pattern after and direction - Imitation of a skill is important and a good model provides inspiration and perhaps direction. Guidance helps eliminate mistakes and missteps before they are difficult to correct.

Adequate motivation - Interest sufficient to keep a child trying is essential for sustaining practice until the skill is learned. Once learned, the joy of doing, the independence, and the prestige of the "group" give satisfaction, serving as an impetus to greater achievement. Whatever the skill--jumping rope, riding a bicycle, or skating--it is a great compensation for failures in other areas of life, such as at school or work.

Skill differentiation and proper timing - General skills do not exist. Holding a tennis racket is not transferable to holding a golf club. Trying to learn several skills at a time is self-defeating. Children are particularly confused by attempting new skills that use the same muscles. One skill should be mastered before others are introduced.

Nutrition and Energy Requirements

The amount of energy needed in terms of calories will vary considerably from individual to individual, since it is dependent upon a number of variables. It differs with the age and size of the individual, as is indicated from the calorie requirements set forth for different age groups in Table 7.6

The calorie requirements will also depend upon the rate of activity of the body processes while at rest--the basal metabolism rate. The faster the metabolic rate--heart beat, respiration--the greater will be the number of calories used in a given period of time. Children aged 7 to 10 years require 80 calories per kilogram of body weight. After age 11 boys require more protein whereas girls need more protein and iron. Of the four food groups, school-age children (6-12) need 2 to 3 cups of milk (the milk group), 2 to 3 servings of meat or other protein (the meat group), 4 to 5 servings of fruits and vegetables (fruit and vegetable group), and bread and cereal. The calorie distribution consists of 50 percent carbohydrates, 35 percent fat and 15 percent protein.

Children often forget to eat, as play and school interfere with good eating habits. Such habits are largely learned through imitation of adult family members. School children prefer starches and sugars above meat and vegetables. Mother and Daddy have to be consistent models in eating, not disdaining broccoli while demanding their son or daughter eat it. Little purpose is served in harassing children about their eating. A friendly atmosphere and enjoyment of meals is the best climate to reinforce cooperation and proper digestion.

Poor nutrition slows growth and also has some social implications. Results from the research of D.E. Barretts et al. (1982) showed the long-term effects on Guatemalan children who were deprived and malnourished in the first two years of life. The child's diet was a good predictor of social behavior at six to eight. Of 138 children aged six to eight who were given supplementary vitamins and extra calories, only some had received protein. Those who did not receive protein tended to be passive, more dependent on adults, and more anxious. Malnourished children unfortunately are generally not responded to by mothers as well as those who are better nourished (Lester, 1979).

Health Care

Although the middle years of childhood are the safest period in life in terms of mortality, it is a period where 90 percent of children have acute (short term) medical conditions (Starfield, 1984). Starfield found the following maladies: eczema, upper respiratory infections, viruses, nearsightedness, bed wetting, phobias, and headaches.

Parents and caretakers must see that their children are on programs designed to check their health progress regularly. This can be done through regular medical and health care systems. For instance, parents should arrange to have their children's eyes and vision checked. Ten percent of children aged six have eye problems. There were 25,000 cases of measles expected in the United States in 1990; many among 6 to 12 year olds had devastating effects. Immunization is a serious matter (*U.S. News & World Report*, 1990). Many children have dental problems which parallel the beginning of first grade. This is the time that the basis (baby) teeth begin to be lost and the permanent teeth come in, at the rate of about four teeth per year. School age children should be taught to floss their teeth. A general physical examination or regular check-up for the child is necessary to keep weight control and prevent loss of appetite that might signal anorexia or bulimia or developing obesity, and any other unusual anomalies that might be observed. Teachers can assist parents by observing poor health habits, signs of health problems such as persistent coughing, listlessness, chronic tiredness, nervousness, or repeated inappropriate behavior. Parents should know that there is a 2 percent greater chance of obesity for every hour children spend watching television daily. During TV time children eat more snacks and exercise less (Dietz & Gortmaker, 1985).

Protection of Children: Accidents and Hazards in Development

Many parents/caretakers and some teachers think that when children reach the age of six or seven, they have enough judgment and foresight to take care of themselves and stay out of trouble. This is often not the case; accidents are the principal cause of death among children 6 to 12, and injuries are counted in the thousands among this age group. Parents and teachers need to be aware of the risk of accidents among young children, since caution on the child's part is often the exception and forethought is largely momentary. The child's chances of having an accident depend upon (1) supervision, (2) a safe location for play, and (3) the activity level of the play. Of accidents resulting in death, poisoning most often is the cause in the first year. Drowning most likely is the cause at age two, and at age three the most frequent accident is being struck by a motor vehicle. About one of every 3,000 children dies of an accident, and, by age 10, most children have required stitches or a cast (National Council of the Organization for Children and Youth, 1976). In addition, 10,000 to 20,000 crib deaths occur every year in the United States (Lipsitt, 1978). A profile of the circumstances surrounding childhood accidents reveals that boys have more accidents than girls and that firstborn children have fewer accidents (usually because they have more supervision and are trained to be more cautious). In addition, accidents are most likely to occur from Thursday through Saturday, on poor weather days, and at home (Spock, 1974; Roberts, 1973; Woods, 1972). Accidents leave both physical and psychological scars that may leave a child handicapped or make a child feel unattractive or self-conscious, thereby limiting oral expression and affecting self-concept. Allied with this is the fact that many parents never see that their children have physicals--general teeth or eye examinations. This is important, for improper maintenance may lead to glandular and diet problems, illnesses, and low-grade infections.

Childhood is not always a period of euphoria. The problems are many, and parents need to understand the process of growth in order to provide love and direction during difficult developmental stages. In addition, a survey by Bernback (1982) published in *Health* reported that 65 percent of 500 parents aged 25 to 49 were reluctant to give up their happiness for the good of the family. Although parents' educational levels were not reported, a study by Wolfe and Vander der Gaag (1982) found the mother's educational status to be the most significant factor in a child's health.

SOCIAL DEVELOPMENT OF CHILDREN 6 TO 12

Social competence is a period of development that begins with birth. Its major stages of progression, however, are in the middle childhood years. The socialization process starts at the neonatal stage when the mother cares for the infant--strokes, talks, sings to, and elicits responses from the baby. Eventually attachment and bonding occur. During the first five or six years the child's orientation is egocentric. That is, there is no other view but their own and contrary evidence is ignored. Role-taking relates to the development of social abilities, among them morality. Selman (1973) presents four stages in role-taking as follows:

Stages	Age	Characterization	Development
0. Pre-role Absolutism	4-6	Egocentric	One view is possible--mine
1. Differences in situations	6-8	Informational	Your view is different but if you were me, it would be like mine
2. Reciprocal awareness	8-10	Reflective	We have different views, you have one and I have one
3. Varied perspectives	10-12	Mutuality	There are other possible views
4. Adolescence	12-	Conventional	Perspectives on role are based on social and conventional system

Selman's ideas came from those of Piaget and Kohlberg paralleling cognitive development. He links role-taking closely to moral development. Kohlberg's first two levels coincide with Piaget's though his third level goes beyond Piaget's. Selman's Stage 3 suggests that in the story of Heinz (who stole a drug to cure his dying wife), a judge would listen to him validate his action in the "need to save a life." Even so, in Stage 4, the law must be upheld and therefore the theft of the drugs will not be excused. Selman (1981) investigated the nature of role perspectives by having children respond to stories such as a kitten caught in a tree. The most adequate rescuer, a young girl, has been asked by her father to promise not to climb a tree. The father had observed his daughter fall from a tree earlier without being hurt, but was nevertheless worried about her. The stages of Selman reflect typically these views about the positions taken.

Stage 0 This level reflects the feelings the children experience: "Her daddy will be happy for he likes the kitten."

Stage 1 He'll be mad for he doesn't want her to climb the tree.

Stage 2 Her father will understand why she had to climb the tree.

Stage 3 The girl and her father can talk it out and understand each other.

Stage 4 How much is the cat worth? Obedience and risk are factors to be taken into consideration.

Role-taking relates to cognitive development, self-concept, peer influence, morality, experience, and cultural circumstances. Any answers to the dilemma reflect the nature of the child's developmental level and therefore role-taking. To be socially competent one must demand recognition of self, have a conscience, understand social expectancies, and have adequate mental health.

Recognition of Self

To develop a sense of others, one must develop a sense of self. Self-concept is part of the Erikson stage of Autonomy versus Shame and Doubt occurring as early as 18 months. It begins with the recognition of one's abilities--to talk, to walk, to coordinate movement and activities. It reflects, in the infant, the treatment and the accord shown during this period. This period is sometimes referred to as self-recognition: children see themselves in mirrors but beyond this, at about three years of age, they know about special names for people--nicknames--and also special attention. Probably at six or seven, children are able to think of the "real me" and also the "ideal me." The "ideal me" begins to understand what is desirable behavior. What is expected by teachers, friends, and significant others becomes important. Children begin to enlarge their knowledge of self and try to learn what it means to be a friend in a club or to play on a team. They start to understand how life works--how Dad can be pleasant at one point and critical and demanding at another. Incorporating society's expectations, the ideas and ways of their peers, into acceptable conduct is another necessary step of growth. The elementary school child learns to control his or her own behavior, fitting their own set of principles into society's. Self-image develops as children come to evaluate themselves. Coopersmith (1967) contends people base their self-image on four criteria: (1) significance--their importance to others, the degree of love they feel; (2) competence--how able they are to complete important tasks; (3) virtue--how well they meet ethical standards; and (4) power--how much they influence others and their own lives.

Peers and Their Influences

The peers are those equal to the child. The peer group is a group of equals, usually of the same sex among children 6 to 12, often from the same neighborhood and socio-economic level. The main source of the peer group is the classroom. Peers might be friends, but those who are not frequently influence self-worth to a greater degree than friends or teachers (Harter, 1987). A measure of assessing peer acceptance or rejection is through the use of the sociogram. This information is variously obtained. One method is to ask children in a classroom or group to select the person they would like to be with on a study committee, go to a party with (indicating same and opposite sex), and be with on a camping trip. The individual choices can be plotted with arrows running to the boys and girls chosen. Mutual choices can be designated with arrows in both directions. See Figure 7.4 below. This type of exercise might be effective in discovering who is often left out and treated as an isolate. Perhaps it would tell the attributes associated with popularity. On the other hand, sociometric measurement might easily convey the wrong notion; for instance, unless varied types of reasons for choosing a classmate are provided, it would not validly tell whether the person is rejected in the general sense. A child may be rejected as a person to go to a party but be picked to help build a basketball goal. Most of those selected in these exercises are the most attractive. Boys are particularly fond of choosing the most athletic and daring. Maturity and social skills are more important to girls (Langlois & Stephan, 1977). Attractiveness is important to both girls and boys (Hartup, 1983). Most of the social isolation uncovered through the use of sociograms are not children who have been entirely rejected but those who do not interact with others; another isolate is one not chosen as best friend by anyone and/or one who might be picked as someone "I don't like" (Gottman, 1977). Gottman has suggested five categories of social status which he contends characterize isolation of children.

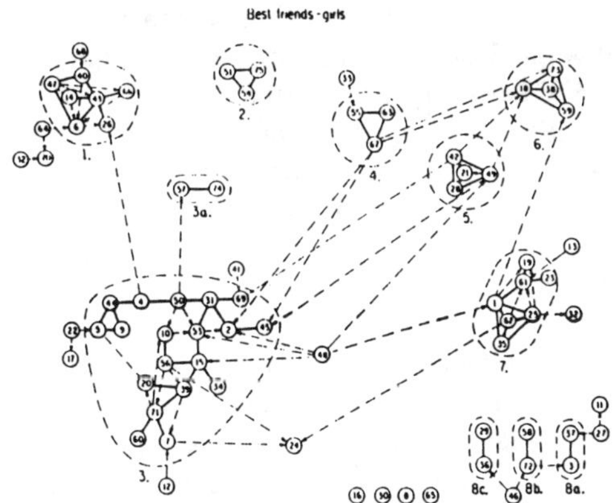

Figure 7.3 Sociogram for girls based on the California Adolescent Growth Study. (From Harold E. Jones.)

CATEGORY	ATTRIBUTE
Sociogram Star	Well liked by most peers
Mixers	High peer interaction. Some well liked; others not liked
Teacher negatives	In conflict with teachers; some liked; others not
Tuned out	Does not interact; ignored but not rejected
Rejected in sociometry	Not liked; rejected, not simply ignored

Adapted from Gottman, 1977

The function of peers is to provide a reflection of self-worth. This will become increasingly important as children grow into adolescence, for typically the peer group does not reject a person once accepted, nor does it fail to give answers to a member on complex questions and ultimately it provides a shelter. Another function is normative--the peer group transmits the culture and norms of society--it teaches and reinforces. Peers help in the formation of values and attitudes. The negative aspects associated with peer groups are often the pressure to conform and the group's imposing values on children who have low status and may be too weak to resist.

Friendships

In early childhood, ages three to five years, a friend is simply a playmate. The notion of an enduring relationship is to play together always. By the time a child is 11 or 12, the idea of friendship has expanded to being one of sharing mutual experiences, opening trust, making mutual plans, and getting to know the other person. Girls have fewer friends than boys, but the ones they have are more intimate (Berndt, 1981). Many of the friendships, whether girl or boy, are mutual choices. Even best friends will be competitive with each other, although in most instances friends will be very supportive.

Selman and Selman (1979) define the stages of friendship as follows:

STAGE	AGE	ATTRIBUTES
I Incidental playmates	3-6	Friends are those who live close to me. She lives behind me and we play together.
II Unilateral friend	4-9	He lets me play with his erector set. I don't like her anymore; she won't let me ride her scooter.
III Reciprocal friend	6-12	Involves give and take, but serves also separate interests rather than common ones. He plays with me when I want him and I play with him when he wants me to play.
IV Intimate friend	9-15	This is a relationship that is committed to sharing time, resources, ideas, and the future. Girls develop one or two close friendships, fewer than boys but more intimate.
V Autonomous interdependence	12+	Respect for the other person's interdependence and autonomy. You give trust and risk losing because you make a commitment.

A number of social competencies are involved in making friends. Certain social skills are needed to form friendships (Gottman & Mettetal, 1987). First, one needs to have a way to initiate a friendship. To do so children need to exchange information and decide on a common activity. If both are already playing with a toy or a game, a decision on who will continue has to be made. Children who make friends easily approach others slowly and are not demanding; they communicate well and demonstrate a reciprocity that is positive. Finally, according to Gottman and Mettetal (1987), children who make friends easiest are able to resolve conflicts with other children; they are less argumentative.

The importance of friendships in children cannot be underrated. They serve the purpose of satisfying certain needs in each child, providing a setting where one can be dominant and the other submissive. One may use the other as a model, or they may be egalitarian in their relationship. The friends may share fears and give support to a wide variety of feelings. When children are paired, it offers opportunity for self-expression with little criticism, less competition, and cooperation in sharing personality traits that neither alone could demonstrate. In addition, friendship pairs provide a structure for a child's activity in ritualized games and other activities. They solidify group norms, attitudes, and values. They provide a training group for in-and-out-group competition.

The Influence of the Family

Of all the socializing agencies which influence the child, the family is the most important. Even though school and religious institutions, governmental agencies and quasi-organizations, and such informal groups as friendships and peers are all important, none equals the home and its effect on a child's social and personal development.

From the home, children acquire values, learn what is expected of them and the limits placed on their behavior. They learn by example what and whom they should model, how they should interact with their siblings and others and, in general, internalize a pattern for displaying their lives. Children reflect the kind of parenting they receive. Most parenting can be generalized in three categories: restrictive-permissiveness, warmth-hostility, and anxious emotional involvement-calm detachment. It is possible, for example, for two parents to use a permissive approach. Both may be calm, nevertheless discipline their children sometimes with coldness and at other times with warmth. Permissiveness may also involve parents who negotiate with their child but then hold the child to strict accountability. We will discuss the three types.

Restrictiveness and Warmth In the past girls have been more passive than boys; they are more dependent and then stay that way over the years. This may be changing to some degree as cultural determinants are effecting a greater independence in women. Permissiveness does not necessarily produce independent children; if this style is utilized with detached warmth, positive characteristics are likely to result. Where permissiveness is defined as non-controlling, lacking pressure, and undemanding, children have been found to be active, creative, and constructively aggressive in their behavior (Watson, 1957). On the other hand, permissive approaches accompanied by hostility on the part of parents result in non-compliance and aggressiveness. It should be noted that over the years a number of juvenile delinquents have been the product of permissiveness, neglect, and/or hostility.

Authoritative, Authoritarian, and Permissive Family Styles The authoritative parents frequently combine a high degree of control with considerable warmth. Typically these parents are flexible. Though they set limits for their children, they also discuss the reason why. For instance, if a child wants to stay out longer and play, a recital of the child's responsibilities will probably be in order and the child may or may not be allowed to stay longer.

In the authoritarian approach, the parents are very inflexible and absolute. If the question of permission to modify a stipulation came up such as, "Can I stay and play with Mary 30 minutes longer?" the answer would ordinarily be no. This parenting position is usually accompanied by low to moderate warmth. Little discussion takes place with children and a child struggling to gain some measure of control or compromise with their parents might well give up in frustration. The permissive type of parenting is the direct opposite from the authoritarian style. The child wishing to play longer would be granted permission or need not report in until later. The youngster is in control and makes the decision. Many of these types of parents are warm toward their children but believe the child is mature enough or if not, that they will learn to be more capable, to make their own decisions even if they make mistakes. What children often lack is guidance and they may receive the impression that their parents do not care for them. Research by Baurind (1972) indicates that the authoritative parent's children are the most self-reliant, self-controlled, self-confident, and socially competent of the three groups. Authoritarian parents produced children who were fearful, showed little independence, were moody, and generally unassertive. Permissive parents had children, according to the study, who were rebellious, impulsive, aggressive, and socially inept. The ideal situation would be where neither child nor parent dominated the family, but where they shared goals. Certainly the younger the child, the more direction and supervision will be needed. Children need emotional support and frequent counseling concerning their projects, problems, and fears.

Children are often unable to handle stress, whether such stress arises from economic, social, or psychological problems encountered by the family. After both mother and father are working, there is the need to mesh schedules for several children at different ages for schooling, there is often little care after school and poor transportation. This can be so perplexing to children that it can lead to the frequent problem of "overload." Common to this generation of children is the "hurry hurry" syndrome named by Elkind (1981) and described as being under the gun--there isn't much time!

Overload can take a number of forms. First there is overload through constant change, where children in mobile families are shunted from home to home, school to school, caregiver to caregiver with subsequent emotional and nervous consequences. Responsibility overload occurs where children in a family of several children are given the task of looking after the younger sisters and brothers; they may also be required to prepare them a meal, shop for the food, even see that they get from school or the day care center. Several months of this will create severe stress in many children, who must do their own work in preparing for school, doing their homework, and finding time for relaxation. Finally, there is information overload, brought on by the tremendous amount of ideas and information coming from television and the classroom.

Clearly, children need to be protected from too much stress; many parents, however, do not understand the fragile nature of the child's neurological make-up nor the symptoms that arise of attempts to maintain balance while they are under considerable strain. Elkind has organized a stress chart similar to an earlier one of Rahe and Holmes' called the Stressful Events List. When the child's stress events total up to 300, serious problems are a high probability. Some of the events listed are:

Events	**Score**
Parent Dies	100
Parents divorce	73
Parents separate	65
Parent remarries	47
Parent fired from job	45
Personal illness or injury	50
School difficulties	39
Family financial troubles	38
Starts a new extracurricular activity	36
Change in number of fights with siblings	31
Threat of violence at school	30
Move to another city or part of town	26
Trouble with teacher	24
Go to a new school	20

Divorce

Divorce, which is high on this list, is the most common dramatic and stressful event for the child. About 1,000,000 children a year in the United States are living in a family going through divorce. Nearly half of all children will live with only one parent some time before they are 18. When parents divorce and one moves to another state, this effectively cuts that parent's ties to the children. Emotional impoverishment follows for a time and creates emotional difficulties for children. Even though older children have some insight into the nature of the problem, they still suffer feelings of worthlessness and depression. Children usually have to adjust to new roles and change at least somewhat their relations with their parents. For young children five to seven, rules that they have experienced often break down and the security afforded by routine and consistency is lost. Parents are typically overburdened with emotions and stimuli; they are giving most of their energy and attention to immediate problems and cannot be the best caretakers.

The effect on children depends on the nature of the breakdown. How much venom and hate is generated before the last straw of divorce? What is the nature of fights over custody, property, turf, and ego, and how much of this is discussed with the children? Also, the effect of change is important. Does the daily routine change? Do the children stay in the same home? Do they move to a new place and enter a new school, etc.? And, finally, what is the nature of the relationship of the parent to the child? A child who has a good relationship with both parents may not lose the opportunity to see one parent, but divorce will still create sadness, apathy, and disturbances that likely militate against doing good school work or paying attention to chores and playing the usual part in the family. It has been said that the important thing in divorce is the quality of the one parent who has custody, but where there have been two quality parents, superior child rearing is likely to be compromised. More often than not, other aspects enter the equation of caring for the children; one of these is finance. Most women, as heads of household, suffer considerably in the division of money, at least until after the period of reorientation to work and the final settlement is made.

Defense Mechanisms

Psychological mechanisms designed to protect the child's ego often arise in greater ferocity under the impact of family stress and divorce. In the normal growing up process very few children escape the use of some support to help them cope with fears and anxieties. By the time children are six years of age, they have learned to hide and disguise their fears. The fears of children should not be made fun of; many can be handled by teachers and parents through sympathetic discussion and talk. Others may require therapy of some sort. But for most when the crisis period is past, many of the mechanisms for reducing tensions will vanish. As children mature, they will reduce the number of defenses they use and will develop more appropriate ways and mechanisms to handle stress.

Everything is not negative that happens in the life of a child. A typical scenario in terms of psychosocial development proceeds like this. For the six-year-old child in the school years, this is the beginning of Erikson's industry stage of industry, as opposed to the negative counterpart of inferiority. Continuing from early childhood, such children are bossy, egocentric, and usually have a "know-it-all" attitude. They frequently insist on being first in everything. They often return to "temper tantrums" or may use verbal or physical attack to get their way or their point across. The observed tension released is seen in wiggling, picking the nose, chewing on their nails or hair. They have good days and bad days, are jealous of siblings, and fearful of bodily harm. They want other children to play with them. Little thought is given to sex specifically, but to body growth (Freud's latency stage).

Psychosocial development in the 8-to-10-year-old represents a continued interest in school and learning, as children wish to be thought of as competent. They are ready for anything--curious about everything! Relationships with others become important and they are oriented to peers; are easy to get along with at home, although increasingly they consider peer opinion more important than parents. They begin to worship heroes; they still have fears but are more realistic, i.e., about dragons and spooks. At this period, children have improving relationships with siblings and enjoy running errands and helping Mom and Dad around the house. Finally, they are aware of the sexual role they are designed to carry out. Most children of this age will not think sex in a sensual way, but a few boys and some girls of ten may know about intercourse.

The 10-to-12-year-old child is usually at the conventional level of morality as described by Kohlberg as Stage 3, the good-girl and good-boy stage. Such children have greater self-control, confidence, and are generally congenial and sincere. They respect their parents and their roles. Hero worship of adults continues; they join groups--formal and informal; begin to have cliques and gangs. They have short bursts of temper but are able to control their anger better than a year or two earlier. Often these children still fear the dark and the unknown but worry little about goblins and ghosts. They know about sexual intercourse and some girls may be having intercourse with an older boy or man. Unfortunately, some may be having relations with kinsmen--fathers, uncles, and cousins. According to Kinsey (1953), many of the first encounters with sex for girls is with kinsmen--uncles and cousins. He didn't isolate fathers in this data.

There is evidence from clinical studies that excessive anxiety may have its basis in rigid socialization, with the imposition by parents and others of unreasonable standards for children, unequal treatment, and negative assessment of their worth. The following are a list of some common defense mechanisms learned by children.

Regression Children often regress in order to recapture the remembered security of an earlier pleasant time. An illustration of this might be the child who has entered school for the first time and returns to thumb-sucking or bed-wetting after these habits have been broken. The arrival of a new baby or the divorce of parents might also precipitate this problem. Such regressions are generally short-lived and vanish after the crisis is passed.

Sublimation Children who feel guilty and uncomfortable about their sexual feelings and their maturing body often channel their energy into games, schoolwork, and family activities. This expunges the unacceptable impulses, which are expressed in a socially desirable manner.

Displacement In children displacement represents a fear that results in an appropriate response to anxiety but one not related to the real basis of the problem. Fear of a parent may be translated into a substitute symbol, such as fear of a teacher. To express fear of a parent seems highly unreasonable, so in order to hide this emotion, the fear is displaced to another person.

Repression Anxiety and worry that occur in the child are often blotted out or repressed in the memory. Feelings that children may formerly have expressed are so uncomfortable that they must keep them from coming to consciousness. Children's use of repression does not mean a denial of anxiety or the refusal to remember but that they have banished the memory of the event from consciousness, at least temporarily.

Projection Projection is a method for a child to handle an unacceptable thought or impulse by attributing it to another child. Children attribute their thoughts to another in an effort to deny their existence in themselves. So children may talk about the older brother who says bad words or the sister who took the candy.

Rationalization This defense is used by almost everyone, typically after the occurrence of an unpleasant situation, when people provide rational and logical reasons that account for their conduct. For example, the person who fails to gain admittance to engineering school may explain that he or she didn't want to study that hard anyway.

Reaction Formation Children may say the opposite of what they really feel. Schoolchildren often play exclusively with one child of the same sex for fear of rejection by others. They may contend, "I don't want to play with them," meaning exactly the opposite. In this mechanism, threatened feelings are repressed and an opposite feeling is expressed. Overconcern with cleanliness, psychoanalysts suggest, may be to cover a strong desire to be dirty or soiled.

Denial This is the refusal of a child to admit something has happened. A significant event may be denied such as the death of an uncle or aunt. The child says the aunt "comes to visit me every night and we're going to the zoo soon."

The lives of children are varied and not all experience highly negative situations. But children from the lower socio-economic status are affected by a number of assaults on their psyche and bodies. Child abuse is a general problem for all classes of children but the advent of early sexual experience and its aggrandizement is more likely to occur with minority and economically deprived children.

Children cannot frame the attributes they need in their parents that enable them to be successful and reasonably happy; but when they grow up they would probably list the following:

(1) Proper clothing, housing, and food;

(2) Protection and guidance;

(3) Emotional warmth and rapport with the family;

(4) Assistance on their projects and activities whether recreational or work;

(5) Help in the development of values to live by, a structure for feeling comfortable about themselves and their parents;

(6) A chance to be oneself--to explore, be curious, and make mistakes;

(7) Presence of strong, steady, and uncompromising love by others.

A lack of well-adjusted parents is the start of many children's problems. Parents must set standards, show firmness, be consistent, and be concerned. It is important that parents do not over-assess the meaning of their children's behavior as they develop.

SUMMARY

Physical development is the most obvious aspect of development and has an important bearing on the child's total development. There is a pattern of growth in height and weight of children. The most rapid period of growth is in the early years following birth. This is followed by a continuous deceleration of the rate of growth until the onset of puberty. From ages 10 to 12, girls are taller on the average than boys and on the average weigh more from 11 to 14. At this time there is a spurt of growth for girls which is about one-and-a-half years ahead of that for boys. The timing and pace of growth during childhood is dependent upon the operations of the hypothalamus-pituitary-gonadal axis.

Significant physiological changes appear during childhood; the most important of these are those related to the endocrines. There is a continuous decrease in basal metabolism throughout the teen years, with that of boys being higher than that of girls. There is a gradual and continuous growth of the blood vessels during childhood; during puberty, there is a rapid rate of growth for the heart. Also, a marked change in both blood pressure and pulse rate occurs with physiological maturity. Body types are important in childhood because they have social, occupational, and health connotations. Few investigators see relationships between physical types and personality types; however, the physical does allow for certain opportunities otherwise precluded.

Nutritional needs increase as the child nears adolescence. A number of factors account for differences in nutritional needs. Most cases of obesity can be traced to consuming more calories than the body needs for growth, energy, and the metabolic processes. Girls and boys of 7 to 10 need approximately 2,400 calories; 11 to 12, 2,600. Girls from 11 to 14 need 2,400 calories.

The development of strength, coordination, speed, and precision in the use of body muscles follows the principles of growth set forth earlier. Children who receive training in the acquisition of motor skills such as hopping, throwing, and catching will be superior to those who receive no training. The acquisition of motor skills during early childhood, however, is limited by maturational level. In addition to readiness, the essentials involved in learning motor skills are (1) opportunity to learn and to practice; (2) good models and some help; (3) motivation; and (4) focusing on one skill at a time.

Motor performances reach their peak during the teen years, except for complex performances requiring years of practice. There is a decline in motor performances for girls after age 11 or 12, depending upon cultural norms. Most authorities in physical education feel increased attention should be paid to motor skill development in children.

Social development relates to role-taking in the school years. The stages can be characterized as the egocentric stage (4 to 6), the informational stage (6 to 8), the reflective stage (8 to 10), the mutuality stage (10 to 12), and adolescent stage (12 upward). Important in social development is self-concept, which originates in the recognition of self. Relationships with peers assume a critical role in social growth as the child proceeds through the middle years. Peers provide a reflection of self-worth and help in the transition of the culture and norms of society; negative aspects involve the imposition of values on weak members of a peer group who may not be able to resist being dominated.

Friendships are important elements of social life for the child 6 to 12. They serve to share fears, give support to ideas, and allow self-expression. Friendships develop from the playmate stage through recognizing the other person's autonomy to the point where a commitment to the relationship is made. Family affects the nature of the child's life depending upon whether the parent-child relationship is authoritarian, authoritative, or permissive in style. Stressful events create fear and anxiety and have an unsettling influence on the child. Notable among these events are divorce, death, parental remarriage, school difficulties and family economic problems. Due to these and other needs to sooth the ego from assaults, defense mechanisms are learned such as denial, rationalization, withdrawal, reaction formation, etc. Beyond the obvious problems, there may be the general ones imposed upon them as rigid socialization, unreasonable standards for children, unequal treatment, and negative assessment of their worth.

Children should expect to be clothed properly, protected and guided in health matters, and helped in their psychological lives. Emotional warmth should be afforded by the family as well as assistance on children's projects, whether in recreation or school. Help in clarifying values should be given and a structure of home life should be maintained that gives a feeling of self-worth. Children should be given a chance to be creative, to explore, and be curious--to be themselves. Finally, they should be given strong, steady, and uncompromising love. Parents set the standards, showing firmness, consistency, and concern. The child's behavior should not be over-assessed, with the well-adjusted parent being the key to success for the child.

KEY WORDS

sociogram

mesomorph

endomorph

ectomorph

obesity

peer group

authoritative

authoritarian

denial

rationalization

regression

phrenoblysis

self-concept

role taking

socialization

repression

displacement

defense mechanisms

sublimation

projection

reaction formation

permissive

REFERENCES

Barretts, E.B., et al. Chronic malnutrition and child behavior: Effects of early calorie supplementation on social and emotional functioning at school age. *Developmental Psychology*, 1982, *18*:541-556.

Baurind, D. Socialization and instrumental competencies in young children. In W.W. Hartys (ed.), *The Young Child: Review of Research*, vol. 2. Washington, DC: National Association for the Education of Young Children, 1972.

Bernbach, D.D. Survey of parent willingness to give time for the good of the family. *Health*, 1982, *14*(7):58.

Berndt, T.J. The features and effects of friendship in early adolescence. *Child Development*, 1982, *52*:1447-1460.

Blakeslee, A.L. Today's health news. *Today's Health*, 1971,*7*.

Coopersmith, S. *Antecedents of Self-Esteem*. San Francisco, CA: Freeman, 1967.

Corbin, C.B. *A Textbook of Motor Development*. Dubuque, IA: Brown, 1973.

Cratty, B. *Perceptual and Motor Development in Infants and Children*, 2nd ed. Englewood Cliffs, NJ: Prentice-Hall, 1979.

Cusack, R. Dieting management of obese children and adolescents. *Pediatric Annals*, 1984, *13*:454-464.

Dietz, W.H., and Gortmaker, S.L. Do we fatten our children at the television set? Obesity and television viewing in children and adolescents. *Pediatrics*, 1985, *75*:807-812.

Dion, K.K., Berscheid, E., and Walster, E. Physical attractiveness and peer perception among children. *Sociometry*, 1972, *37*:1-12.

Elkind, D. *The Hurried Child*. Reading, Mass: Addison-Wesley, 1981.

Epstein, H.J. Phrenoblysis: Special brain and mind growth periods. II Human mental development. *Developmental Psychology*, 1974, 7(3):207-217.

Espenschade, A.S., and Meleny, H.E. Motor performance of adolescent boys and girls today in competition with those of twenty-four years ago. *Research Quarterly*, 1961, *32*:186-189.

Ferris, B.G., Whittenberger, G., and Gallagher, J.R. Maximum breathing capacity and vital capacity of male children and adolescents. *Pediatrics*, 1952, *9*:559-570.

Fincher, J. *Sinister People: The Looking-Glass World of the Left-Hander--A Shaggy Dog Story*. New York: Putnam, 1977.

Food and Nutrition Board, National Academy of Sciences--National Research Council. *Recommended Dietary Allowances*. Washington, D.C., 1974.

Gottman, J.M. Toward a definition of social isolation in children. *Child Development*, 1977, *48*:513-517.

Gottman, J., and Mettetal, G. Speculations about social and affective development: Friendship and acquaintanceship through adolescence. In J.M. Gottman & J. Parker (eds.), *Conversations of Friends*. New York: Cambridge University Press, 1987.

Greulich, W.W. The growth and developmental status of Guamanian school children in 1947. *American Journal of Physical Anthropology*, 1951, *9*:55-70.

Greulich, W.W., and Pyle, S.I. *Radiographic Atlas of Skeletal Development of the Hand and Wrist*, 2nd ed. Stanford: Stanford University Press, 1959.

Gutteridge, M.V. A study of motor achievements of young children. *Archives of Psychology*, 1939, *244*.

Hall, E.G., and Lee, A.M. Sex differences in motor performances in young children: Fact or fiction? *Sex Roles*, 1984, *10*:217-230.

Hallahan, D.P., and Cruickshank, W.M. *Psychoeducational Foundations of Learning Disabilities*. Englewood Cliffs, NJ: Prentice-Hall, 1973.

Hardyck, C., and Petrinovich, L.F. Left-handedness. *Psychological Bulletin*, 1977, *84*:385-404.

Harris, R.E. Some observations on blood pressure in children. In J.P. Ambuel (ed.), *Physical and Behavioral Growth, Report of the 26th Ross Pediatrics Research Conference*. Columbus: Ross Laboratories, 1958, pp. 49-52.

Harter, S. The determinants and mediational role of global self-worth in children. In N. Eisenberg (ed.), *Contemporary Topics in Developmental Psychology*. New York: John Wiley, 1987.

Hartys, W.W. The peer context in middle childhood. In W.A. Collins (ed.), *Development During Middle Childhood: The Years From Six to Twelve*. Washington, DC: National Academy, 1984.

Health, Education and Welfare (HEW), U.S. Department of, Office of Education. *Basic Body Measurements of School Age Children*. Washington, D.C., 1953.

Johnston, J.A. Adolescence. In I. McQuarrie (ed.), *Brenneman's Practice of Pediatrics*, vol. 1. Hagerstown, MD: Prior, 1957.

Jones, H.E. Adolescence in our society. In *The Family in a Democratic Society: Anniversary Papers of the Community Service Society of New York.* New York: Columbia University Press, 1949.

Kinsey, A.C., et al. *Sexual Behavior in the Human Female*. Philadelphia: Saunders, 1953.

Kretschmer, E. *Physique and Character*. New York: Harcourt, 1925.

Krogman, M.W. *Child Growth*. Ann Arbor: University of Michigan Press, 1972.

Langlois, J.H., and Stephan, C. The effects of physical attractiveness and ethnicity on children's behavioral attributions and peer preferences. *Child Development*, 1977, *48*:1694-1698.

Larrabe, P., and Jones, F.R. Behavioral effects of low plus lenses. *Perceptual and Motor Skills*, 1980.

Lester, B.M. A synergistic process approach to the study of prenatal malnutrition. *International Journal of Behavioral Development*, 1979, *2*:377-394.

Lipsitt, L.P. Perinatal indications and psychophysiological precursors of crib death. In Frank Degen Horowitz (ed.), *Early Development Hazards: Predicting and Precautions*. Boulder, CO: Westview Press, 1978.

Low, W.D., Chong, S.T., Chong, K.S.F., and Lee, M.M.C. Skeletal maturation of southern Chinese children. *Child Development*, 1964, *35*:1313-1336.

Lowrey, G.H. *Growth and Development of Children*. Chicago: Year Book Medical Publishers, 1973, pp. 79-89.

_____. *Growth and Development of Children*, 7th ed. Chicago: Year Book Medical Publishers, 1978.

_____. *Life Science Library*. New York: Time, 1964.

Marlow, D.R., and Redding, B.A. *Textbook of Pediatric Nursing*. Philadelphia: Saunders, 1988, pp. 1005-1015.

Mayer, J. *Overweight--A Problem for Millions*. Public Affairs Pamphlet No. 364, 1973, pp. 5-6.

_____. Regulation of food intake and the multiple etiology of obesity in weight control. In E.S. Eppright, P. Swanson, and C.A. Iverson (eds), *A Collection of Papers Presented at the Weight Control Colloquium*. Ames, IA: Iowa State College Press, 1955.

Meredith, H.V. Standing heights of young children in different parts of the world. In H.W. Reese and L.A. Lipsett (eds.), *Advances in Child Development and Behavior*, vol. 12. New York: Academic Press, 1978, pp. 2-59.

Metcalf, H.G. Physical education. *Collier's Encyclopedia*, vol. 16, 1954, pp. 33-34.

Minerbrook, S., and Kritz, F.L. *U.S. News and World Report*. Aug. 20, 1990, pp. 63-64.

National Council of the Organization for Children and Youth. *America's Children 1976: A Bicentennial Assessment*. Washington, DC: Bicentennial Conference on Children, February 1-4, 1976.

Nourse, A.E. The body. In R. Dubos, H. Morgenau, and C.P. Snow (eds.), *Life Science Library*, New York, 1964.

Roberts, J. *Examination and Heart History Findings Among Children and Youth 6-17 years*. Rockville, MD: Health Resources Administration, National Center for Heart Statistics, 1973.

Seils, L.G. The relationship between measures of physical growth and gross motor performance of primary-grade children. *Research Quarterly of the American Physical Education Association*, 1951, *22*:244-260.

Selman, R.L. A structural analysis of the ability to take another's social perspective: Stages in the development of role-taking ability. Paper presented at the Society for Research in Child Development, Philadelphia, PA.

Selman, R.L., and Selman, A.P. Children's ideas about friendship: A new theory. *Psychology Today*, 1979, *13*(4):71-80, 114.

Seltzer, C.C., and Mayer, J. Body build and obesity: Who are the obese? *Journal of the American Medical Association*, 1964, *189*:677-684.

Sheldon, W.H., Dupertuis, C.W., and McDermott, E. *Atlas of Men: A Guide for Somata-Typing the Adult Male at All Ages*. New York: Harper & Row, 1954.

Sheldon, W.H., Stevens, S.S., and Tucker, W.B. *The Varieties of Human Physique: An Introduction to Constitutional Psychology*. New York: Harper & Row, 1940.

Spock, B. *Raising Children in a Difficult Time*. New York: Norton, 1974.

Staffieri, J.R. A study of social stereotype of body image in children. *Journal of Personality and Social Psychology*, *7*:101-104.

Staffieri, R.J. Body build and behavioral expectancies in young females. *Developmental Psychology*, 1972, *6*(1):125-127.

Stuart, H.C., and Stevenson, S.S. Physical growth and development. In W.E. Nelson (ed.), *Textbook of Pediatrics,* 7th ed. Philadelphia: Saunders, 1959.

Suinn, R. *Fundamental Behavior Pathology*. New York: Wiley, 1975.

Vurpillot, E. The development of scanning strategies and their relation to visual differentiation. *Journal of Experimental Psychology*, 1968, pp. 632-650.

Walker, R.N. Body build and behavior in young children. II: Body build and parents' ratings. *Child Development*, 1963, *34*:1-23.

Watson, G. Some personality differences in children related to strict or permissive parental discipline. *Journal of Psychology*, 1957, *14*:227,249.

Weil, W.B. Infantile obesity. In M. Winick (ed.), *Childhood Obesity*. New York: Wiley, 1975, pp. 61-70.

Wiggins, J., Wiggins, N., and Conger, J. *Journal of Personality and Social Psychology*, 1968, *10*(1):82-90.

Wolfe, B.L., and Gaag vander der, G.J. What influences children's health. *Children and Youth Services Review*, 1982, *4*(12):195-208.

Woods, M.B. The unsupervised child of the working mother. *Developmental Psychology*, 1972, *6*(1):14-25.

Zakas, G., and Solomon, M. The family situations of obese adolescent girls. *Adolescence*, 1972, *8*(29):33-42.

Chapter 8

MIDDLE AND LATER CHILDHOOD: COGNITIVE AND MORAL GROWTH

- ***Cognitive Understanding***
  - Concept formation
  - Types of concepts
  - The role of language
- ***Stages in Cognitive Development***
  - Piaget's cognitive structure
  - Schema
  - Assimilation
  - Accommodation
  - Equilibrium
- ***Piagetian Periods of Cognitive Development Pertaining to Middle and Later Childhood***
- ***Pre-Operational Thought***
  - Egocentrism
  - Transformation
  - Centration
  - Reversibility
  - Conservation
  - Space, sequence and time
- ***Formal Operations***
  - Combination
  - Scientific approach
  - Verbal problems
  - Conservation of movement
- ***Reconsidering Piagetian Theory***
- ***Bruner's Information-Processing Theory of Cognition***
  - Enactive stage
  - Iconic stage
  - Symbolic stage
  - Logical thinking
- ***Flavell's Interface Stage Theory***
- ***Intelligence***
  - Its measurement
  - Intelligence quotient
  - Stanford-Binet intelligence scale
  - Wechsler tests
  - Group tests

(*continued*)

- ***Intelligence*** *(continued)*
  - Intelligence and school achievement
  - Cattell's types of intelligence
  - Gardner's multiple intelligence theory
  - Sternberg's contextual intelligence
  - Feuerstein's instrument enrichment
  - Basis of intelligence
  - The stability of mental growth
  - Cultural impoverishment
  - Parent-child relationships
  - Improving cognitive development
  - Motivation and intelligence
  - Sex differences in intelligence
  - Racial differences in intelligence
  - Differences in intelligence due to birth order

- ***Intelligence and Schooling: Cognitive Styles, Giftedness, and Creativity***
  - Intelligence and cognitive styles
  - Creativity
  - Creativity and problem solving

- ***Schooling and Informational Processes***
  - Cognitive learning
  - Metacognition
  - Memory strategies
  - Computers and learning

- ***Children With Special Needs***
  - Learning disabilities
  - Policies for handicapped youngsters

- ***Moral Reasoning in Middle and Later Childhood***

- ***Theories of Moral Development***
  - Social learning theory
  - Piaget's stages of moral growth
  - Kohlberg's levels of morality
    - Preconventional level
    - Conventional level
    - Postconventional level
  - Assessment of theories

COGNITIVE UNDERSTANDING

Flavell (1977) suggests that viewing cognition as the "higher mental processes" has limited value. He would expand this to include consciousness, awareness, discovery, intelligence, thinking, imagining, creating, generating plans and strategies, reasoning, symbolizing, inferring, problem solving, conceptualizing, classifying, relating, and perhaps dreaming. Other processes important in the study of knowing are motor skills, perception, memory, attention, and imagery. Intelligence is the function of cognition; its application is seen in the activities of children and youth.

Perception in the very young is essential for more complex aspects of cognitive development. For instance, the development of the child's eye-hand coordination depends partially upon ability to identify the object, enabling the hand to touch and to judge the distance between the hand and the object. This perceptual-motor coordination takes a long time to develop, often as much as four or five months. If the perceptual development is thwarted, other cognitive processes will be impaired, as Kaluger and Heil

Figure 8.1 Acquiring a concept.

(1970) found in their work with school-age children. Some of these children (with average to better ability) were having difficulty in learning and were found to lack the ability to execute basic motor patterns that children normally develop during the first year of life.

Concept Formation

Sensory input initiates perception and becomes the basis of conception. A concept is a classification of stimuli having certain common characteristics requiring both abstraction and generalization. According to McDonald (1965), two processes are involved in acquiring a concept: discrimination and generalization. These may be observed in the child's acquisition of the concept of "airport." To repeat the definition is not enough. The formation of the concept must be extended to other examples of airport. The child needs first to make a discrimination, and secondly to generalize the concept to examples (see Figure 8.1).

Most concepts are statements that refer to common properties such as blue, square, velocity, and beauty. Pseudoconcepts depend upon an overlapping common property such as honesty or virtue (Verplank, 1957). Symbols are not concepts; they represent one specific event. Concepts, on the other hand, represent something common to several events.

Types of Concepts

Bruner, Goodnow, and Austin (1956) have identified four types of concepts: (1) simple, (2) conjunctive, (3) disjunctive, and (4) relational. The simple concept is a condition where objects to be classified have one element in common, as in groups of figures (squares, circles, triangles, and so on); discrimination of a square from the other figures indicates formation of the concept square. The conjunctive concept is one where all the attributes must be present in order for the object to be included in the category. A baseball team is such a concept, typically having nine players as opposed to five for basketball. A disjunctive concept is one that embraces different items that are either/or; they need not have all the attributes of the category. The legal term felony includes rape, arson, and murder, even though they seem very different. Relational concepts represent relative circumstance, such as direction, size, and temperature.

The Role of Language

There is a close relationship between language and thinking, especially in the more complex types of thinking involving abstractions and in making finer distinctions. Language includes the most complex organization of perceptual and motor skills (muscle coordination and in the use of the tongue, throat, mouth, and so on, for making sound), and the most abstract, symbolic processes of which the human being is capable. The interaction of language and thought with the environment appears in all types of concept building, problem solving, and creative thinking.

The role of language in the development of thought is as yet unresolved. Piaget has taken the general position that language is merely another reflection of thought, that the language the child uses can be only as abstract as his or her thinking is. He says that in a conservation experiment (where the quantity of something stays the same whether or not its shape changes), the child who is not able to conserve may say, "This ball is wide; this ball is thin." The child who is able to conserve may say, "This ball is wider but thinner." Both children know the words wide and thin, but they are using them differently in sentences.

Bruner suggests that language and thought are essentially separate until about age six or seven, at which time they come together; children are then able to use language as an aid in memory, problem solving, and analysis. Bruner also notes that in a child's language, classifications are used even though thinking remains simple. This disparity to children is an original dichotomy--language is rooted in the biological, and thinking primarily extends from interaction with the environment. Vygotsky (1962; 1986), a Russian investigator, notes that language plays a role in the development of internal representation at about two years of age. For him the discovery that each object has a name is a crucial point in the child's developing intelligence. Yet Furth (1971), through his work with deaf children, showed that children develop internal representation without the aid of spoken language. In young children (ages two to seven) the first manifestation of operational knowledge of symbolic behavior appears in the form of gestures and play in the linguistic comprehension. The one-year-old child, Piaget says, will imitate people unloading heavy steel bars from a truck by spreading his or her fingers as if holding the bars and swinging the arms like the workers do. Observation and imitation are important in development of both language and cognition. Dale (1972) says linguistic competency should not be equated with putting such competency to work. "Language is not used," he points out, "for many functions--memory, classification, inner speech--until a point of development considerably later than the essential mastery of structure" (p. 215). Piaget suggests that "language does not appear in children until the sensory-motor intelligence is more or less achieved" (1970, p. 42).

Like Bruner, Vygotsky (1978) felt that language and thought first develop independently. Children express simple thoughts and emotions before age two. After two, language and thought are increasingly intertwined. Vygotsky felt that after age two language could actually begin to control behavior in young children. He saw children developing in a series of spiral stages, with conceptual awareness becoming more controlled at each higher level. Vygotsky also felt children displayed a zone of proximal development. This refers to children being able to complete tasks when an adult is present to help with difficult concepts, as opposed to what he can do independently of an adult. The zone of maximal development is the difference between the child, his success working independently (actual development), and what can be accomplished with an adult (potential development). A child may be able to make cereal (cooked) for breakfast with an adult's help but not alone. After a period of adult supervision, the child should then be able to make cereal unaided. Vygotsky also felt with adult help children could perform tasks meant for older children. Some researchers (Palinscar & Brown, 1984) have used Vygotsky's principles in teaching schoolchildren to comprehend and remember material better through much interaction between teacher and student. There is much promise for Vygotsky's work in American schools today, which have an abundance of at-risk youth in need of greater rapport and interaction with teachers.

STAGES IN COGNITIVE DEVELOPMENT

Developmental psychologists are becoming increasingly skeptical of the use of the "cognitive-developmental stage," whether in the Piaget model, Bruner model, or some modification of these (Flavell, 1977). The question of qualitative change is an issue, as in Piaget's theory (Brainard, 1978), and others relating to socialization, moral development, and cognition (Kohlberg, 1969). Stages seen as hierarchical models--Havighurst's developmental tasks, the social crises of Erikson, and the sexual development levels of Freud--have also come under attack (Phillips & Kelly, 1975). One prime example of the stage theory is the structural theory of Piaget, which has assumed in the past three decades a major place in the psychological and educational literature.

Piaget's Cognitive Structure

The Swiss investigator Piaget, a biologist and genetic epistemologist, was concerned with uncovering the ontogenesis (individual developmental changes) of cognitive functioning from birth through adolescence. Functioning as a biologist, he was aware of and impressed by the interaction of mollusks with their environment. Mollusks, like all living organisms, he noted, are constantly adapting to changes in environmental conditions. From this study Piaget came to believe that biological acts are those of organization and adaptation to the physical environment. Cognitive acts are acts of organization and adaptation to the perceived environment. Organization and adaptation are complementary processes. As Piaget states (1952):

> From the biological point of view organization is inseparable from adaptation: They are two complementary processes of a single mechanism, the first being the internal aspect of the cycle of which adaptation constitutes the external aspect. (p. 7)

Cognitive functioning and intellectual activity are inseparable in the operation of the person. Intellectual and biological activities are both part of the general process by which an organism adapts to the environment and organizes experience. Children construct reality out of their experiences with the environment in much the same way that artists paint a picture from their immediate impressions. When children are acting on the environment they are handling objects and searching with their eyes and ears. In effect, they are digesting just like the physical body and assimilating the raw materials out of which the cognitive structure develops.

The heart of the Piaget theory is the acquisition of operations, which is a cognitive activity, allowing for reversibility to take place. Every operation has a logical opposite or can be reversed; for example, the square of 8 is 64 and the square root of 64 is 8. The rules for lying by a seven-year-old to his parents are not operations according to this view. The boy does not know what to do since the rule (action) is not reversible unless it is obtained when he tells the truth. However, knowing all actions have reactions or opposites makes possible the comprehension of a continuum schema and seeing the lie in perspective--lie and nonlie. On this continuum all classes of conditions, behaviors, and observations are somehow recognized by passage through time, existing in space, and are reducible to contrast--in short, a schema. Truth-falsehood and past time-infinity are continuums.

Behavior is not an isolated entity but lies somewhere on a continuum--for example, ranging from positive (good) behavior to negative (bad) behavior--and other gradients of behavior lie somewhere in between.

The child, in Piaget's theory, passes through stages, acquiring different classes of operations until arriving at the most mature stage. The stages of development are sequential, invariant, irreversible, and qualitatively different. Progressive development leads to the ability to reason abstractly, to think about hypothetical circumstances in a logical way, and to organize schema or operations into higher-order structures. Schemata are developed, through the mechanisms of assimilation and accommodation, and affect the mental growth of the child. The adaptation that results from assimilation and accommodation is known as equilibration, representing a level of growth that has been reached. A description of these Piagetian concepts follows.

Schema

Schemata are the cognitive structures by which individuals intellectually adapt to and organize the environment. These structures are the mental counterparts of the biological means of adapting. The structures are mental constructs, as is the psychic anatomy of Freud (superego, ego, and id). The schema is a way of organizing environmental stimuli much the same as the animal utilizes its stomach to assimilate food, adapting the food for its use. An analogy suggested by Wadsworth (1979) to represent the categories or concepts is that of an index file. Each card in the file represents a schema. Adults have many cards; children have few.

The schemata of the adult evolve from the schemata of the child through adaptation and organization. It is logical for the child, for instance, to describe the cow as a dog where a schema for cow is as yet unmade. In this case the child has not made an error, as the only available schema has been to identify a dog. Schemata are reflected in the overt behavior of the child, though they are more than behavior: they are the structures from which behaviors generate. The behavior patterns that recur often in the course of cognitive activity are conceptualized as reflecting schemata. "Every schema...coordinated with all other schemata and itself constitutes a totality with differentiated parts" (Piaget, 1952). Since schemata are structures of cognitive development that do change, allowance must be made for their growth; the processes responsible for this are assimilation and accommodation.

Assimilation

The cognitive process by which a person integrates new perceptual matter or stimulus events into existing schemata or behavior is known as assimilation. The child who sees a cow and says "That's a dog" has in sifting through his or her schemata found the most appropriate one. Assimilation then can be looked upon as the cognitive process of placing new stimulus events into existing schemata; it is a part of the process by which the individual cognitively adapts to and organizes the environment or growth of schemata. Theoretically it is like putting air into a tire--the tire gets larger (growth by assimilation) but does not change its general shape. To account for change, the idea of accommodation is introduced by Piaget.

Accommodation

The creation of new or modification of old schemata is accommodation. It has been thought of as the interjection of the element of tension--adjustment to new experiences, ideas, and stimuli that demand recognition. Mental growth involves resolution of the tension between assimilation and accommodation, the conflict between using old responses for new situations and acquiring new (or modifying old) responses to fit new problems. Cognitive growth occurs as the child adapts to new situations and events. The young child has global schemata; compared to adults they are very imprecise and often inaccurate; however, in time improvement is noted. In the process of assimilation the child imposes available structure or schemata on the stimuli being internalized; the opposite is true in accommodation as the child is compelled to change the schemata to coincide with the new stimuli. Accommodation accounts for development that represents a qualitative change, whereas assimilation accounts for growth that is a quantitative change.

Equilibrium

A balance between assimilation and accommodation is called equilibrium. The child constantly strives for the necessary condition of equilibrium. The child ultimately assimilates all stimuli or stimulus events with or without accommodation. When an imbalance occurs, the child is motivated to seek a balance--equilibrium, that is, to further assimilate or accommodate. If there were no balance it is conceivable that, in mental development, a child who constantly assimilated stimuli but never accommodated would end up with only global schemata, unable to detect definitive differences in things. If the reverse were true and only accommodation occurred without assimilation, the child would have an infinite number of minute schemata. The biological analogy suggests the axis ingestion--digestion--egestion. In terms of food utilization this means stimuli (new ideas) received, stimuli appropriated (placed in categories), and stimuli discarded (old ideas, discordant facts or information).

To summarize, in assimilation the child fits stimuli into schemata that already exist, while in accommodation a child modifies schemata to fit the stimulus. Accommodation results in a qualitative change in intellectual structures, while assimilation adds to existing structures, generating quantitative change. The child who pretends a chip of wood is a boat is, in Piaget terms, assimilating the wood chip to his or her mental concept of boat. Accommodation (wood--to tree, to boat, to chair) means taking account of the various real properties and relationships among aspects (wood) that external objects and events possess--that is, the knowledge of the structural attributes of environmental data (Flavell, 1977).

PIAGETIAN PERIODS OF COGNITIVE DEVELOPMENT PERTAINING TO MIDDLE AND LATER CHILDHOOD

In his work *The Psychology of Intelligence* (1963), Piaget summarizes the periods of cognitive development that are most important to middle and later childhood as:

- The period of concrete operations (ages 7 to 11). In these years the child develops the ability to apply logical thought to concrete problems.
- The period of formal operations (ages 11 to 15). In this period the child's cognitive structures reach their greatest level of development with the ability to apply logic to all classes of problems.

As in the earlier Piagetian stages, progress through these two stages is not automatic as in maturational theory or philosophical naturalism. Mentally superior children may go through the stages rapidly and dull children never complete formal operations. There is one thing that is invariant with Piaget's theory: the stages must be passed through in sequential order and a stage cannot be skipped. Factors affecting the transition are:

1. Maturation, particularly relative to the development of the growth of brain tissue and the endocrine system.

Table 8.1 PIAGET'S COGNITIVE DEVELOPMENT

STAGE AND TIMEFRAME	BEHAVIOR ATTRIBUTES	CHANGES IN COGNITIVE STYLE
	Sensory-Motor	
Birth-24 months		
Stage I 0-1 month	Reflex activity with no differentiation (i.e., sucking, gasping, blinking, gagging).	
Stage II 1-4 months	Primary circular reactions--hand-mouth coordination, differentiation in sucking reflex, waving, and general interest in activity.	
Stage III 4-8 months	Secondary circular reactions--interest in the results of activity.	Development proceeds from reflex activity to representation and sensory-motor solutions to problems.
Stage IV 8-12 months	Coordination of secondary schemata--object permanence obtained, attempts to understand relations between objects, pull and push stage.	
Stage V 12-13 months	Directed groping--experiments with the environment, follows sequential displacements.	
Stage VI 18-24 months	Internal representation--internal schemata, begins less use of trial and error.	
	Pre-operational	
2-7 years	Problems solved through representation--language development (2-4 years). Thought and language both egocentric; cannot solve conservation problems.	Development from sensory-motor representation to prelogical thought are solutions to simple problems.

Table 8.1 *(Continued)*

STAGE AND TIMEFRAME	BEHAVIOR ATTRIBUTES	CHANGES IN COGNITIVE STYLE
	Concrete Operational	
7-11 years	Reversibility attained. Can solve conservation problems--logical operations developed and applied to concrete problems. Cannot solve complex verbal problems.	Development from prelogical thought. Logical solutions to concrete problems.
	Formal Operations	
11-15 years	Logically solves all types of problems--thinks scientifically, solves complex verbal problems, cognitive structures mature.	Development from logical solution to concrete problems to logical principles and to all classes of problems.

2. Physical experience, which involves the interaction of the child with the environment, enabling assimilation and accommodation to take place.

3. Social interaction, which refers to interchange of ideas between people. The concept of honesty, for example, does not have a physical reference independent of others, so the child would have difficulty in developing a socially acceptable concept of honesty.

4. Equilibration, the state of balance between assimilation and accommodation. It ensures that children are protected from being overwhelmed by new experiences and information and from overreaching themselves in an attempt to adjust to rapid changes in the environment (Pulaski, 1971). It provides experience and social interaction.

Table 8.1 summarizes the principal stages of development and the behavior attributes and changes in cognitive ability that take place during this period according to Piaget. A discussion follows.

PRE-OPERATIONAL THOUGHT (Ages Two to Seven)

The period corresponding to the chronological ages of two to seven is when the child is increasingly able to internally represent events and become more sophisticated in thinking. The most important development during this period is that of language--the use of symbols to represent objects. In the early part of this period the child's speech is egocentric in nature, whereas toward the end of this stage the child begins to use socialized speech in which intercommunication is evident. Children frequently talk out loud when they are with other children, with no intention of communicating. They are speaking to themselves--this is egocentric. Cooperation in games and play will usually develop in the pre-operational stage. This is an

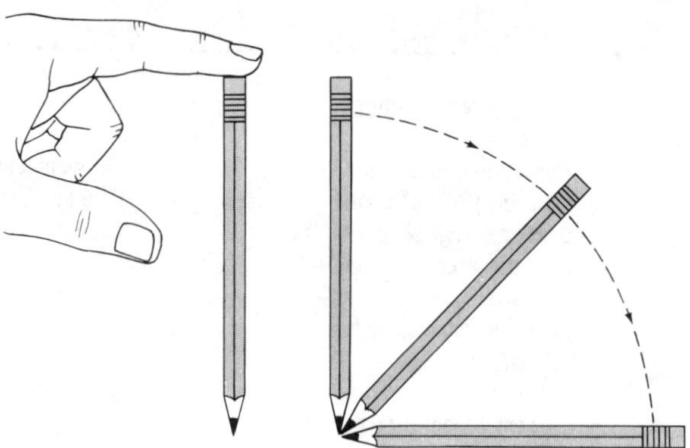

Figure 8.2 Transformation

indication of developing social behavior. At four or five, if a child plays marbles, the child plays by the rules he or she knows; when other children accept these rules the child can sometimes win this way. By seven or eight, children become concerned with winning by the rules. Obstacles to logical thought during this period besides egocentrism are transformations, centration, conservation, and reversibility.

Egocentrism

Pre-operational children do not question; what they think are only true thoughts. They think everyone thinks the way they do. This egocentricity is not stubbornness on the part of children; they cannot conceive of a view by another person. Around six or seven children's thoughts increasingly come into conflict with peers, forcing accommodation to occur more often. Social interaction, which has been the origin of conflict, becomes the point of verification as they compare ideas with peers and begin to accommodate. Egocentricity tends to limit cognitive development, inhibiting accommodation in the pre-operational stage.

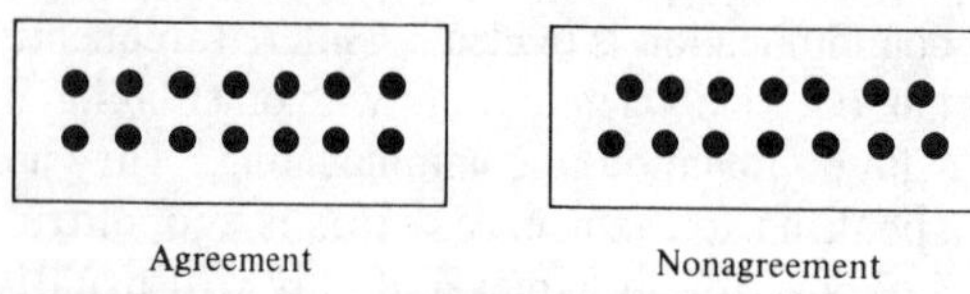

Figure 8.3 Agreement and nonagreement.

Transformation

A characteristic of the pre-operational child's thinking is the failure to understand the process of transformation. In observing the sequence of change or successive states, the typical child focuses primarily on the elements in the sequence rather than the transformation by which one state is changed to another. In Figure 8.2, the child in the pre-operational period can draw the final stages of the pencil but cannot reproduce the successive stages. The child's thought is neither inductive nor deductive, but rather is transductive, referring to the tendency to associate only the start and finish in viewing a transformation operation. The intermediate steps are lost on the child.

Piaget discovered another type of transformation when walking in the woods with one of his children who, upon seeing different snails along the trail, tended to think they were the same snail. The child cannot reconstruct transformation from object to object, place to place, and time to time. Development toward logical thought is thwarted until he or she has adequate transformation insights.

Centration

During the years from 1 1/2 to about 7 the typical child, upon being presented with a visual stimulus, tends to center on some specific aspect of the picture or scene rather than take in various particulars (decenter). The cognitive activity of this period seems to be dominated by the perceptual; seeing two rows with equal numbers of checkers, though in one the checkers are spread farther apart, inevitably leads the child to say that the longer row has more checkers in it. And this is generally true whether or not the child can count.

Reversibility

According to Piaget, reversibility is the most clearly defined attribute of intelligence. This represents the ability to follow the line of reasoning back to its origin or where a process started. The child who does not yet possess this characteristic of cognition, if shown two rows of candy with the same number of pieces in them, agrees that they contain the same number of candies. However, if the candies in one row are lengthened, the child will no longer agree they contain the same number of candies (Figure 8.3). The child is not able to reverse the process of lengthening. Here again the perceptual dominates the reasoning process. The thought of the child is dominated by egocentrism--centration, and closely tied to reversibility. When decentering develops, under the effect of socialization, skill at tracing operations from initial point to culmination will be accomplished. Phillips (1969, p. 61) cites this example of another type: A four-year-old is asked, "Do you have a brother?" "Yes. His name is Jim." "Does Jim have a brother?" The child answers, "No."

Conservation

Conservation of matter, a principle of physics, is the cognitive expression that the substance of matter irrespective of form change remains the same in weight, size, and so on. The child in proceeding toward maturity (logical operation) must come to understand that most matter, regardless of its shape, is always the same. Number, volume, and area are important aspects of conservation. The typical child during the pre-operational stage cannot hold one dimension invariant in reference to change in another dimension. Piaget thought that the conservation operation could not be learned through direct teaching or reinforcement techniques. Some research that disputes this will be presented later in this chapter. Usually by age seven the child has developed the conservation operation sufficient to proceed toward logical operations. The crucial element is action; change is the function of the child's interaction with the environment.

In achieving area conservation the child has the usual centering problem. In response to the situation where the child is presented with a marked area on a floor with a box such as A or B on it (Figure 8.4), and questioned as to which has more space in which to play, the child will respond, "they have the same." But when the boxes are separated, as in C, the pre-operational child who is nonconserving will say the area where they are together (D) provides the most space. Conservation of area is usually attained around the age of seven or eight; until then perception dominates logical thought.

Another type of problem involves the conservation of volume. The child's thinking is closely tied to visual perception, so the child does not conserve. The average child in the pre-operational period faced with two identical short beakers containing equal amounts of water will say they contain the same amount of water in them (Figure 8.5). Yet if the water is poured from one of the beakers into a tall, thin glass (showing a higher water level), the child will

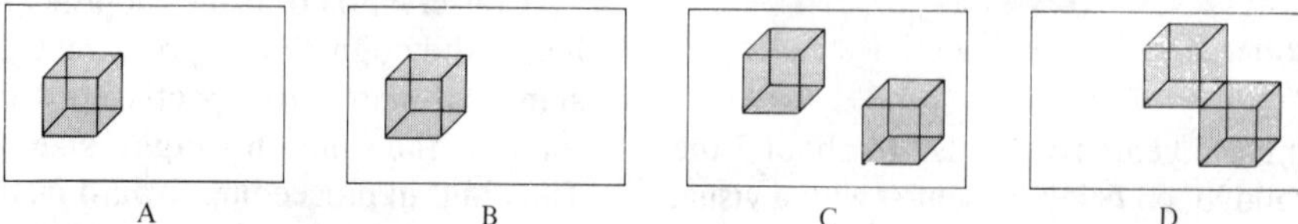

Figure 8.4 Area conservation example.

credit it with having more water. At a later age the child may be disturbed by the discrepancy; in time, with considerably more experience, the child will come to recognize why the water levels are different. Wadsworth (1979) maintains that "conservation concepts are acquired slowly after much experience and subsequent assimilation and accommodation." Qualitatively new patterns of responses are interpreted by Piaget to reflect recently formed cognitive structures. The construction of structures allowing for the development of conservation with all types of problems is not acquired at parallel times. The use of conservation principles in different kinds of problems, however, typically follows a sequential order, with those related to volume attained last. The following represent the usual ages in which children develop the cognitive structures for conservation.

	AGE
Number	5-7
Substance (solids)	7-8
Length	7-8
Area (level)	7-8
Weight	9-10
Volume	11-12

Space, Sequence, and Time

The four-year-old child may well announce that "grandpa" is coming to visit next week and perhaps also say that he lives "far away." But observation of this age child reveals that often upon wakening from an afternoon nap, the child will not know what day it is. Indeed, a specific date--even December 25th--is a difficult abstraction for a child. Actually, time concepts

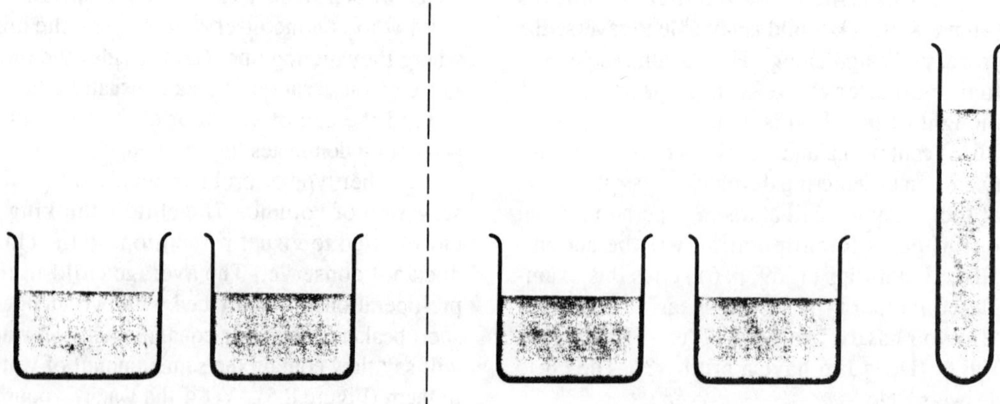

Figure 8.5 Volume conservation example.

are late arrivals as schemata. Uka (1956), investigating the understanding of time by children aged 6 to 11, found most could not name the months of the year until they were 11 years of age. Most (90 percent), however, knew in which month Christmas occurred. This has probably changed since this research was conducted.

With limited chronological understanding, the notion of cause and effect is lost on the five-year-old. Nonetheless the child of this age is likely to repeat over and over again the question "Why?" In response to "When can we get ice cream?" the mother replies, "Later" or "I'm busy," and then gets the oft-used word, "Why?" Action other than a verbal response may ensue. The child actually may be attempting to comprehend the meaning of "later" or "busy," but since the child is not yet able to grasp concepts of cause and effect such as on-time or later, he or she is unable to ask the precise questions that will elicit the information needed. However, the child knows the question will bring some sort of answer.

Piaget contends that children do not understand the relationship between time and speed--velocity equals speed/time--until beyond the pre-operational period well into the concrete operation stage of 10 to 11 (Piaget & Inhelder, 1969). The pre-operational child presented with the problem illustrated in Figure 8.6 and told that the cars reach point B at the same time, in answer to the query which car went fastest, will answer that they both traveled at the same speed. It is not until eight or nine years of age, according to Piaget, that the child develops a ratio concept of speed in terms of the relationship between time and distance.

Children in the pre-operational stage have difficulty with sequences, as seen from the situation where they are presented with six sticks. Four-year-old children can pick out the shortest and longest stick but are unable to line up the sticks in correct order like a staircase. The problem lies in the fact that the task requires a simultaneous judgment that each stick is longer than another one but at the same time is shorter than another one (Flavell, 1963).

Spacial relations are another set of concepts that may be developed during the preschool period. The meaning of such words as from, near, far, in, out, up, and down are learned with the child's body. Weikert and coworkers (1971) stated that the usual occurrence is for a child to learn a concept first with his or her body (crawling under the table), and then with objects (pushing a toy truck under a table).

CONCRETE OPERATIONS (Ages 7 to 11)

During the stage of concrete operations, children from 7 to 11 develop cognitive structures enabling them to reason in a logical

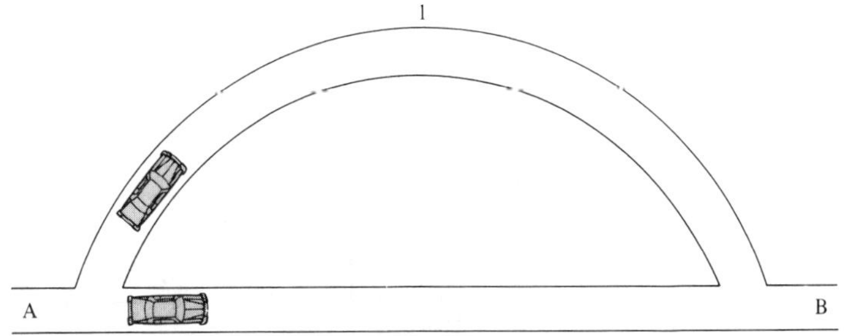

Figure 8.6 Shortest distance between two points.

manner. The children during this period are no longer dominated by the perceptual; they decenter, perform transformations and attain reversibility. The ability to assume another person's viewpoint and seek validation from peers is a characteristic of this stage.

Logical Operations

Four characteristics of an operation for Piaget are (1) it is an action that can be internalized; (2) it is reversible; (3) it always presupposes some conservation and some invariance; and (4) it never exists alone--that is, it is always related to a system of operations (Piaget, 1970).

Seriation Seriation is a logical operation acquired during the concrete operation stage. Children in the pre-operational period, if shown two sticks of slightly varying lengths (A and B), can compare them and perceptually determine that A is shorter than B. If then shown sticks B and C, where B is shorter than C and where A is hidden, children can visually determine that B is shorter than C. If children are then asked to compare A to C while A is hidden, they cannot make the right deduction (A < B, B < C, therefore A < C). Children first learn seriation of length at around age 7, of weight (same size but differential weight) at around age 9, and seriation of volume at around age 12. The concept of equivalence (A=B; B=C; therefore A=C) of length, weight, and volume is learned about the same time as seriation and conservation. Length equivalence develops before volume equivalence does. Seriation is also an important skill for children to use in following the structure of a story. Children who cannot seriate will have difficulty in elementary school years following the events that unfold in a story.

Classification A well-known Piagetian procedure was used to establish ability to classify. The pre-operational child can accomplish simple classification, as Figure 8.7 indicates, but cannot add classes and subclasses. The child is shown a bowl of 20 wooden beads, 18 of which are brown and the other 2 white. The child is told to place the brown beads in a separate bowl. When the child does this, he or she has performed the brown classification. The child is then asked to separate the beads according to white and wooden, which the child can usually do. However, when asked if there are more wooden beads than brown, most children at the pre-operational level say there are more brown beads than wooden. In the operation of addition of another class most children after 8 understand the relationship between class and subclass.

Causality Piaget and Inhelder asked children what happens after lumps of sugar are dissolved in a glass of water. For pre-operational children, the sugar is melted and disappears and its taste vanishes like an odor; for children who have passed through the pre-operational stage, the sugar is retained without its weight or

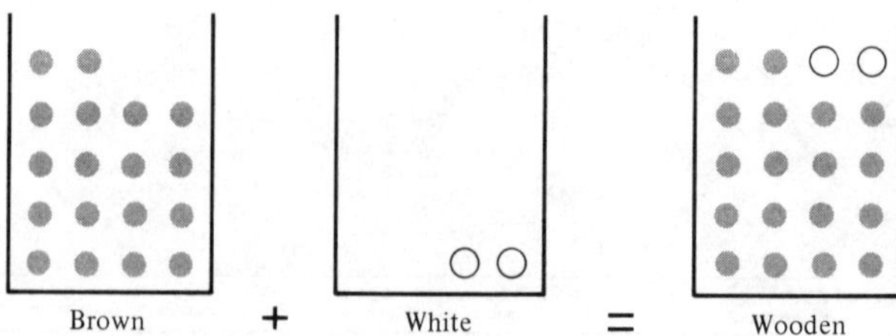

Figure 8.7 Classification example.

volume. At 9 or 10, conservation of weight is present, and at 11 or 12 there is also conservation of volume. This is seen in the fact that the level of water is lightly raised when the sugar is added and does not return to its original level after the sugar is dissolved.

FORMAL OPERATIONS (Ages 11 to 15)

The period of formal operation is characterized by the utilization of the scientific method, hypothesis projection, and testing that reflects an understanding of causation. The principal difference between the child in the concrete operational stage and in the formal is that the child in the former cannot deal with complex verbal problems, or those futuristic ones involving the hypothetical. Piaget believes that preoccupation with thought is the principal element in the period of formal operations. Some 12-year-olds will attain this level, but average American children will be 14 or 15 years of age, and even then not the majority.

There are several aspects of the formal operations period in solving problems: hypothesis testing, proportion, combinational thought, verbal problems, and conservation of movement. The hypothetical problem for the adolescent is solved by separating the argument from the content. For a question that begins, "If coal is green," the child in the concrete stage says, "coal is black." and therefore cannot answer the question about coal being green. The youth in the formal category can extract the structure of the argument from its content (and present the structure in isolation) to logical analysis. The child of eight or nine typically cannot deal with the argument independent of its content.

In the *proportion problem* the typical child in the concrete operational stage will learn to equalize weight and length in a systematic manner. To balance a seesaw the child uses a smaller weight to balance a larger one by placing it farther from the pole (fulcrum) on which it rests. The child has not, however, learned to coordinate the two functions of weight and length as a proportion. At approximately age 13 the proportion principles (W/L = 2W/2L) is known as the relation between distance and weight, which are compensatory when placed in the proper ratio.

Ability to utilize the principle of *combination* is revealed in the example of Piaget and Inhelder (1969) in getting the child to produce a yellow color from five colorless liquids. The combination of three of the five liquids produces a yellow color; the child is shown the colored liquid but does not see how it is obtained. Children from 7 to 11, when asked to produce the yellow color, proceed by combining two liquids at a time; following this their systematic search stops. They may then mix all five together but fail to give a yellow color. By the age of 12 most children will test all possible combinations of one, two, and three liquids until the yellow color is found.

In the *scientific approach* the adolescent uses the deductive logical method to solve problems. A hypothesis may be presented that is unreal, such as "They found an old boat that had five sides and two paddle wheels on different sides. What is funny about that?" The preoperational child might react to this problem by saying there are no boats with five sides and two paddle wheels on different sides, thereby dismissing it. The adolescent could accept this hypothesis, ridiculous or not, and ferret out a suitable answer.

Verbal problems are not usually solved by children without formal operational skills, as in the following: "Jane is fairer than Susan; Jane is darker than Ross. Who is the darkest of the three?" This is a problem similar to the one of lining up the serialized sticks mentioned earlier.

The problem of the pendulum was utilized by Piaget to illustrate *conservation of movement* through regulating the length of the string to vary speed. Concrete operational children typically, when asked to adjust the speed of a pendulum, insist on adjusting the weight. They have a problem in differentiating weight and length. By the period of formal operation, adolescents have learned to separate weight and length; at 15, they are usually aware of the effect of the string's length in regulating the speed.

The adolescent (15 years of age for Piaget) is able to think logically in relation to all classes of problems, including the ones above. Egocentrism, however, is still present, as seen in the inability of the child to separate the real world from idealistic thought. Piaget and Inhelder (1969) maintain that the adolescent will become an adult only when he or she undertakes a real job, and is then transformed from an idealistic reformer into an achiever.

RECONSIDERING PIAGETIAN THEORY

A number of researchers (Brainard, 1978) have reevaluated and even questioned many of Piaget's basic principles of learning. Although Piaget's theories are still in the forefront of cognitive psychology, a number of studies have had results that point to discrepancies in them. Researchers have noted that children can often display complex behaviors not called for at a particular age or stage (Carey, 1985; Gelman, 1985). Studies have also questioned Piaget's definition of formal operations (Boden, 1980) and whether children and adults really do think differently in certain content-specific situations (Carey, 1985). Probably most damaging to Piaget's ideas, a number of studies have trained children in concrete or formal operational thought long before Piaget maintained such thought could occur (Case, 1978; Scandura & Scandura, 1980). These problems with Piagetian theory have encouraged those opposed to his theories who maintain that children can be taught more complex tasks at very early ages, such as reading and writing. Whereas Piagetian theory is still vital, researchers are questioning various aspects of his theory more frequently.

BRUNER'S INFORMATION-PROCESSING THEORY OF COGNITION

Jerome Bruner (1968; 1985) has enunciated some information-processing systems through which to construct a model of the world: (1) action, (2) sensation (smell, touch, sight), and (3) language (symbolic).

The Enactive Stage

This period is the time when the infant is encoding and coding events in the world and reacting (reflexive thinking) in terms of motor response or physical activities. In exploring the world the infant grasps objects, places things in its mouth, pushes and pulls, and learns certain rules about life. The infant acts (enacts) out in physical ways its understanding of the environment, as when it makes a sucking sound indicating hunger. With no language, this is one way to point to discomfort.

The Iconic Stage

A form of thought that begins at about age one is the iconic or ikon (meaning "image") stage. The child is able to process information by organizing images or perceptions. Motor response plays less a part in this period, for infants begin to represent objects and events with visual perception. The iconic representation helps the child think about objects and events not actually or physically present. Though this is progressive development, it represents only physical qualities of an object, not the function or the properties. The four-year-old, for example, says that an orange, a tangerine, and a satsuma are alike because they are orange in color and similar in size; the typical adult would probably group these to-

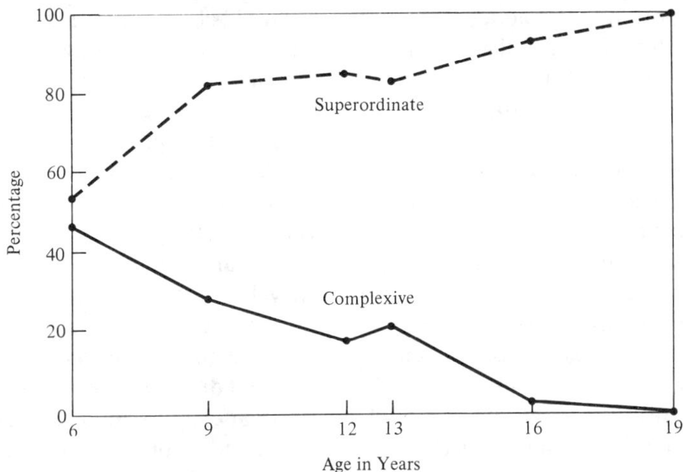

Figure 8.8 Student classification using two types of structure. (*Source:* Bruner et al., 1963)

gether as citrus fruit or food. Children in the iconic stage are dominated by their perception, like the pre-operational child of Piaget (Bruner, 1977).

Symbolic Representation

By about age three, the child has begun to use language to interpret and represent the world. With words, children can think almost anything, not just visualize objects. For Bruner, classification ability is important. He studies superordinate and complexive grouping among 6- to 19-year-olds (Figure 8.8). Superordinate grouping is based on common attributes, such as fruit--lemons, grapefruit, or oranges. They are common because they all have skin or all can be eaten. Complexive categorizing is more primitive for the common characteristics only partially identified or is subsequently used to form the superordinate group. For example, a banana and a peach are both yellow, a peach

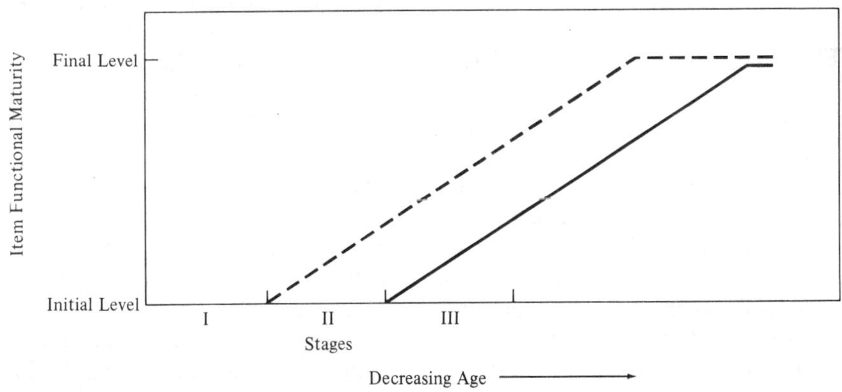

Figure 8.9 Overlapping of stages in cognitive development. (*Source:* Flavell, 1977)

and potato are both round, and a potato and meat are both eaten. Because they represent color, shape, and can be eaten, they are a simple grouping. Bruner (1968) found that while superordinate and complexive groupings were used by 52 percent and 48 percent respectively at age six, the percentages were about 78 percent and 22 percent at age nine. These results do not support the successive stage theory, since there is only a gradual increase in superordinate categorizing during this period and a gradual decrease in complexive categorizing. Klausmeier (1975) suggests that stage theorists would expect a greater break at 12 years of age, heralding formal operations, than Bruner reported.

Logical Thinking

At approximately age six upward, thinking is processed according to rules of logic. The mature preadolescent can utilize two pieces of information to process a third element. Take, for example, the following syllogisms: "All men are mortal, John is mortal, therefore John is a man"; or "A is larger than B, B is larger than C, therefore A is larger than C." The latter fact of these syllogisms is known without having examined or experienced the former together. Once the rules are learned they can be applied to many classes of problems.

FLAVELL'S INTERFACE STAGE THEORY

Flavell, the main promoter of Piaget in America (also Smedslund, 1964, and in the *Scandinavian Journal of Psychology*, and Wohlwill and Lowe, 1962), is perhaps the most knowledgeable critic of this pioneer. Stages could be conceived, according to Flavell (1985), as similar to metamorphosis in insects where the butterfly develops from an egg, to a larva, to the pupa, to an adult butterfly. Flavell thinks this idea is useful as a general approach in studying cognitive development. The analogy, Flavell believes, fails in that development is not marked by discrete stages; the sequential route to maturity in cognition varies considerably among individuals. In addition, not all major cognitive acquisitions, according to Flavell, look as if they come from equilibration. He contends that in order for development to take place via Piaget's theory, certain prerequisite skills are needed, and how these are to be developed is not explained. The views of this theorist, presented graphically in Figure 8.9, imply a qualitative change that is overlapping and not discrete in the maturing child's repertoire of classification skills, concepts, principles, and so on. Although research suggests that egocentricity is a characteristic of preoperational thinking, preschool children are capable of perceiving other people's viewpoints (Flavell, 1977). At the beginning of each stage, children's ability to use the concepts mature very gradually rather than abruptly.

Admittedly, cognitive structures develop, but many major cognitive-developmental changes appear to be qualitative rather than quantitative at some level of analysis. That is, the initial appearance of various cognitive skills (transformation, seriation, and so on) do not completely mature until a later time. According to this view, cognitive skills of the pre-operational (Piaget) level may still be achieving ripeness during or after the concrete stage of operation. Cumeo (1980) found three- and four-year-olds using both the height and width rule to judge physical area. Piaget's idea that centration causes the child of three to focus on and utilize only information from salient stimulus does not hold true in this experiment. The height-width experiment shows that children's judgments and response capacity for quantity represent a simple algebraic combination of relative stimulus cues. Cumeo also found a similar result in using an adding rule--length and density--in three- and four-year-olds' estimates of the number of beads in a row. This would support a general-purpose integration rule in a child's quantity judgment utilizing a combination of cue stimuli.

Skills, then, may emerge at the same time but develop at different rates and draw apart. Others may emerge at different points in time and reach their maturity at the same time. For example, classification seems to cut across several Piagetian stages, according to Kofsky (1966). Her research on hierarchical classification revealed links between resembling sorting and consistent sorting, whereas there was only probablistic linkage between exhaustive classes and conservation and conservation with multiple class membership. She also noted that the order of mastery overlaps, as seen in Figure 8.10.

Research on the question of acquisition of conservation skills in the period of concrete operations raises a question about variance of sequence. Children in Western society, Iran, and Papua, New Guinea, display the Piagetian pattern (Elkind, 1961; Ashton, 1975). Thai children appear to develop conservation of quantity and weight simultaneously (Boonsong, 1968). Further, some Arab, Indian, Somali, and Australian aborigine children conserve weight but not quantity (DeLemos, 1969; Hyde, 1959). Ashton (1975) also reports some other cultural differences, such as children of pottery-making families in Mexico performing better on conservation substance tasks than their peers from non-pottery-making families.

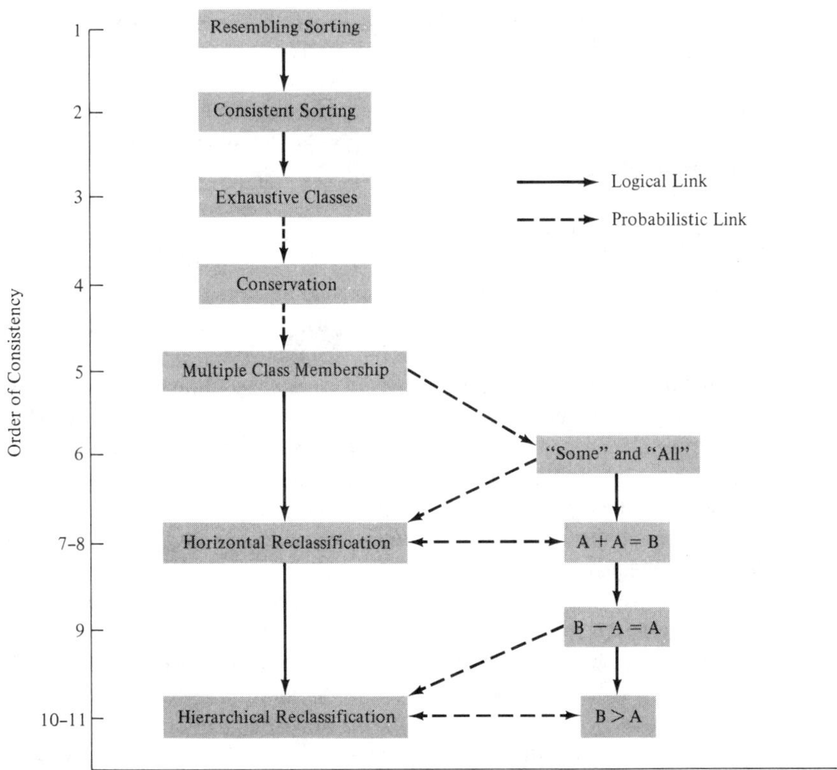

Figure 8.10 Sequence of classificatory skills. (*Source:* Kofsky, 1966, p. 194)

The views of Flavell (1985), Brainard (1978), Dagenais (1973), Feldman and Toulmin (1975), and others suggest ideas about cognitive development that differ from the metamorphosis analogy. Researchers such as Klausmeier (1975) have noted important implications for assimilation of developmental theory relating to teachers, nurses, and child development personnel. Klausmeier maintains that if people do not know the extent to which there is gradualness and continuity versus abruptness in development, and if they do not know the rate of maturation of the specific skill or concept in which they are interested, they cannot use a stage concept to draw implications concerning when to start teaching any particular skill or concept. He could, however, use the descriptions of stages by Piaget and others to understand the child in the child's frame of reference, as opposed to those of an adult. Duckworth (1979) says the natural activity of children utilized by Piaget serves as the best kind of learning situation for investigation purposes.

Summary Assessment on Stages

It should be pointed out that American psychologists, enamored of behavioristic methods, have looked with suspicion upon the observational approach of Piaget and case studies involving the study of his three children. Even the newer "clinical method" of Piaget's colleagues in Geneva has been criticized as overly verbal and understandardized.

As we have seen, developmental psychologists are becoming increasingly skeptical of the term "cognitive-developmental stage." Piaget's stages therefore may be inadequate to thoroughly explain cognitive development. The authors of this work believe that stages are useful in general ways to characterize broad changes occurring over time and as indicators of developmental shifts. Significant cognitive changes take place with age, are gradual in nature, and are also closely related to maturation and learning. There is much overlapping of abilities in different age groups. Evidence from a wide variety of studies leads to the following conclusions:

1. There is evidence of the sequential concepts involving the order of time.

2. The acquisition of conservation skills in the concrete operation stage of Piaget does not always occur in an invariant sequence and may in some instances occur earlier than Piaget found.

3. Faulty concepts, like incorrect concepts, develop out of the quality and opportunity of one's experiences.

4. A general pattern of development may be observed, especially of concepts of causality, though children differ in cognitive style.

5. Piaget has overemphasized the motor aspect of learning, and underemphasized the role of perception in development.

INTELLIGENCE

Variation in intelligence is thought to be based upon ability to learn, including the retention of what is learned, the complexity of response, and the utilization of the symbolic processes. There is little argument that the dog is more intelligent than the duck, the chimpanzee is brighter than the dog, and a human being has superior mental ability to the chimpanzee. Among people, however, differences are not so readily agreed upon. The deprived have lower measured intelligence scores (whether Stanford-Binet or the California Test of Mental Maturity) than the affluent; professional persons score higher on tests than nonprofessionals. It is also generally agreed that intelligence is an amalgam of heredity and environment and that intelligence scores are the function of differential

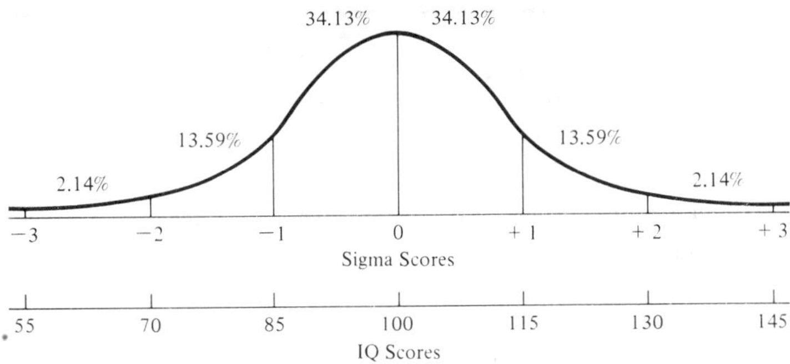

Figure 8.11 Normal curve distribution.

circumstances--conditions, health, motivation, culture, and maybe race.

Intelligence and Its Measurement

The written intelligence test provides a sample of what a person has learned in facts, from language use, and from insight into relationships. Intelligence has general meaning and is evident in the child through learning ability, acquisition, and application of the symbolic process. Intelligence is the overall adequacy of functioning in the physical, mental, and social aspects of everyday life. Wechsler (1960), a test developer, suggested that "intelligence is the aggregate or global capacity of the individual to act purposefully, to think rationally, and to deal effectively with his environment."

Alfred Binet conceived of intelligence as a unitary characteristic and regarded it as (1) directness of thought or ability to perform, (2) capacity to make adaptations, and (3) the ability to autocriticize (self-evaluate). The Binet test was the first intelligence test (1905) to have some validity. His first scale contained 30 problems designed to separate educable children from mentally retarded ones. The problems on this scale emphasized judgment, comprehension, and reasoning. By an assessment of how many problems could be solved by each age group, he was able to construct a graded scale or norms. This was an important step forward, because for the two previous decades investigators believed intelligence could be measured by physical characteristics such as visual acuity, coordination of sensory-motor activities, and response time.

Intelligence Quotient (IQ)

The term IQ was introduced by Stern in 1912 (Goodenough, 1949), who utilized the term M.A. (mental age) from Binet's ladder-like test to develop a formula for calculating intelligence. He reasoned that by dividing the chronological age (C.A.) into the mental age (M.A.), a relatively stable lifetime measurement of intelligence would result. A child of six with a mental age of nine would have, by dividing 9 by 6, an IQ of 1.5 (150). At age 12, assuming constancy of the mental age, 18 divided by 12 would produce an IQ of 1.5 (150). Later research did not support this linear relationship, however, so it was changed by Terman and others, who made 100 the quotient of his scale. The formula became MC/CA / 100 equals IQ. Multiplying by 100 would remove the decimal. The Stanford revision of the Binet Tests by Terman (1925) adopted a curve from the mean that is required to take in approximately 68 percent of the cases in a distribution (Figure 8.11).

EXAMPLES OF STANFORD-BINET TEST ITEMS

Age level	Representative item
2	Building a wall four or five blocks tall
3	Identifying pictures of common objects: tree, cat, dog, plate
5	What does the word *house* mean? *Car*? *Sister*?
7	In what ways are apples and oranges alike?
10	Repeating a six-digit sequence
14	Stating the analogies that exist between two concepts: cold and hot, long and short

Stanford-Binet Intelligence Scale

Lewis Terman, a psychologist at Stanford University, using Binet's test as a framework, made extensive revisions and published it in 1916. It has been revised twice, in 1937 and 1960, and was restandardized in 1972. This test is considered to be the model of intelligence tests. It is administered individually to children ranging in age from two to adolescence, and it also has a few generalized levels designed to accommodate adult intelligence.

The items for preschool children are somewhat different from those constructed for older children. The preschooler or mentally retarded child is asked to identify pictures, fold paper, or string beads; these tasks emphasize eye-hand coordination and perceptual discrimination. Older children are asked more direct questions, such as explaining proverbs, defining words, and solving problems. An eight-year-old would be expected to know the days of the week--for example, to know what day comes before Saturday. For representative test items see Table 8.2. The test is highly verbal, administered orally, and scored on the basis of a statistical table that compares one child's score with scores of other children of the same age (this is called a deviation IQ).

SUBJECTS ON THE WECHSLER ADULT INTELLIGENCE SCALE

Verbal	Performance
Information	Digit symbol
Comprehension	Picture completion
Arithmetic	Block design
Similarities	Picture arrangement
Digit span	Object assembly
Vocabulary	

Wechsler Tests

David Wechsler and his associates have developed a number of tests. Those currently in use are: the Wechsler Preschool and Primary Scale of Intelligence (WPPSI) (1967), the Wechsler Intelligence Scale for Children, revised (WISC-R) (1974), a new revision (1991) of the WISC incorporates more practical items and includes handicapped subjects, and the Wechsler Adult Intelligence Scale (1981). Each of these scales is based upon the belief that intelligence is composed of a number of abilities, each one measurable in separate subtests. Each score is divided into two parts: verbal and performance. Subtests of the WISC include object assembly (putting puzzles together), picture completion (picking out a missing part), vocabulary, and general information (see Table 8.3). Like the Stanford-Binet, Wechsler tests utilize a deviation IQ with an average score of 100. The WAIS was designed for use with adults--to yield an intelligence score and to diagnose abilities identifying weaknesses and strengths of an individual.

INTELLIGENCE TESTS

Individually administered tests	Group-administered tests (mainly verbal)
Entirely or largely verbal (use language in testing and also test language skills)	
All "Binet" tests, especially the Stanford-Binet	Cooperative School and College Ability Tests (SCAT)
Illinois Test of Psycholinguistic Abilities*	California Test of Mental Maturity (CMTT)**
The Merrill-Palmer Scales	Primary Mental Abilities Test (PMA)*
Peabody Picture Vocabulary Test	Differential Aptitude Tests (DAT)*
McCarthy Scales of Children's Abilities**	IPAT Culture Fair Intelligence Test
Wechsler's tests**	Lorge-Thorndike Intelligence Tests
Wechsler Intelligence Scale for Children (WISC-R)	Otis Quick Scoring Mental Ability
Wechsler Preschool and Primary Scale of Intelligence (WPPSI)	
Wechsler Adult Intelligence Scale (WASI)	
Nonverbal or "performance"	
Columbia Test of Mental Maturity	
Raven Progressive Matrices	
Pintner-Patterson Scale	
Leiter International Performance Scale	
Bender-Gestalt	
Wechsler's Tests (same list as above)**	
Goodenough-Harris Drawing Test	

*Yields multiple scores based on psycholinguistic or factor theory.
**Has nonverbal component.

Middle-aged and older adults who are in good health, continue to read magazines and newspapers, and are involved in a number of activities, tend to be able to score well on information, comprehension, vocabulary, picture completion, picture arrangement, and object assembly. They tend to do less well on digit symbol, arithmetic, and digit span.

Group Tests

IQ tests have proved to be accurate at predicting school success for a large group of children, even though minorities and others have protested their use. These tests, given to groups in a classroom or hall, are designed principally to conserve time and money, get a mass of data quickly, and to give a fair measure of assessment of ability to learn. One disadvantage of group testing as opposed to individual or clinical testing, such as in the use of the Stanford-Binet, is that the examiner cannot assess problems that would interfere with obtaining a fair sample of the child's ability. Such problems as nervousness, sickness, need for support, and an inappropriate setting could be altered or taken into account in an individual situation. Attempts to construct culture-free or culture-fair tests have been made, such as Raven's Standard Progressive Matrices, which relies on abstract diagrams rather than verbal items. Another attempt was made with the publication of the *Goodenough-Harris Drawing Test*. This test is less complex and asks only that children draw a picture of themselves, a woman, and a man. Many experts nevertheless believe that both are culturally laden; the Raven test depends somewhat on education, and the Goodenough-Harris Test depends on the importance of representational art in the subject's background (Liebert, et al., 1974). Some tests like the Otis Quick Scoring Test have a standard deviation (SD) of 10, which means the normal range of scores is between 90 and 110; whereas the Stanford-Binet has an SD of 16, providing a range of 84 to 116 for the normal; even though both represent in deviation IQs plus or minus 1 (sigma) or standard deviation.

Group tests, in addition to being efficient and economical, serve to ascertain special abilities as well as handicaps in children. Individually administered intelligence tests provide more in-depth information, but they are more expensive, require considerable time, and must be given by trained examiners who must be able to report accurately and completely what they have found. A list of the two types of tests is provided in Table 8.4. Normal distribution of IQs based on a large sample is shown in Table 8.5.

Intelligence and School Achievement

The correlation of IQ with school subjects ranges between .30 and .75, depending upon the subject. Reading and IQ have been found by Bond (1940) to have a correlation of .73. History and English have been found to have a corre-

DISTRIBUTION OF INTELLIGENCE TEST SCORES OF THE WAIS

IQ	Classification	Theoretical normal curve	Included actual sample*
130+	Very superior	2.2	2.6
120–129	Superior	6.7	6.9
110–119	High average	16.1	16.6
90–109	Average	50.0	49.1
80–89	Low average	16.1	16.1
70–79	Borderline	6.7	6.4
below 69	Mentally retarded	2.2	2.3

*The percents shown are for full scale IQ and are based on the total standardization sample (N = 1,880). The percents obtained for verbal IQ and performance IQ are essentially the same.

The gifted and talented are born not made--oh yeah!

lation with IQ of .59. In math, there is less dependence on verbal ability. IQ usually provides distributions that distinguish three groups: below average, average, and above average.* In individual cases and where scores fall at the dividing lines between the categories, defining levels is hazardous, for one's potential is the function of many conditions and circumstances. It is safe to conclude that intelligence test scores serve as a more valid basis for predicting scholastic success than predicting personality and social or vocational success.

Cattell's Types of Intelligence

Cattell suggested intelligence could be divided into two classes of abilities: fluid and crystallized. Fluid abilities are genetically related, while crystallized abilities are the result of cultural experiences that come from gradually accumulated knowledge, such as vocabulary, mathematics, and social reasoning. Fluid abilities, characteristically perceptual, decline over a period of time, paralleling changes in the sensory domain as a function of age. Performance measured as a relation between the two abilities, however, stays fairly constant from the teenage years to the 50s.

Gardner's Multiple Intelligence Theory

Howard Gardner (1983) has left the psychometric theory as proposed by Guilford and has postulated that there are at least seven distinct kinds of intelligence. Each kind of intelligence, according to Gardner, has its own argot and special symbols necessary for adequate functioning. He argues this thesis by saying some MRs are math savants and that some people lose their speech but not their musical talent. An intellectual profile should replace the IQ concept, according to the researcher. The types of intelligence Gardner has found are:

Interpersonal intelligence - deals with the complexities of interactions on a social level, such as with family, friends, schools, and bosses and co-workers.

Intrapersonal intelligence - self-knowledge and sense of self-worth and well-being experienced by persons "in contact" with their most inner feelings.

---

*One has to consider the standard error of the measurement. Standard error (SE) is the estimate of the amount by which a score differs from the hypothetical true score. On a retest (alternate test) an individual IQ score will vary up to 10 points. The formula for SE is:

Kinesthetic intelligence - intense awareness and control of bodily movements as exemplified by athletes and workers in dangerous jobs such as logging and construction.

Linguistic intelligence - ability to use language in all its subtle forms. This is the intelligence we test children on most often.

Mathematical intelligence - form of intelligence demanded for work on complex mathematical properties and problems.

Musical intelligence - gifted and ordinary children who are trained from early childhood display this type of talent.

Spatial intelligence - unique ability needed to design buildings, paint, and work in sculpture.

Gardner maintains that schools today place importance on mathematical and linguistic intelligences at the expense of the other five types. Schools need to emphasize all seven of these types to create well-rounded individuals capable of functioning in society. Critics such as Scarr (1985) say these types are simply talents.

Sternberg's Contextual Intelligence

Robert Sternberg (1984) has proposed that the quality and breadth of one's intelligence is best defined in terms of the context in which the behavior of an individual occurs. Some tribe members in Nigeria, given the names of fruits, animals, and tools and asked to sort them in a sensible manner, put the potato with the hoe because they order the objects by the functions they serve. When shown by Westerners how to sort the items, the natives say only stupid people do it that way (Cole, et al. 1971).

In effect, Sternberg (1985) believes that there are three facets to intelligence: componential, experiential, and contextual. A person might be considered highly intelligent in one area, such as having a high verbal ability (componential), but be perceived as limited because of a lack of social awareness (contextual). Componential intelligence involves three processes. (1) Meta components involve monitoring what we are doing, performance, the steps we undertake to organize a research paper, for example, or solve a physics problem. Knowing and acquisition involve the method of learning new material. Such thinkers do well on standardized and informal tests. (2) Experiential intelligence has to do with problem-solving abilities of creative thinkers who are successful at attacking a problem in several ways. They use cleverness, an ability to deal with novel situations, and expertise--the ability to process information automatically. (3) Contextual intelligence deals with a person's ability to get ahead in life through deft interpersonal manipulations of the environment. This type of intelligence is often mentioned by Sternberg as practical intelligence.

Feuerstein's Instrumental Enrichment

Reuven Feuerstein and associates have developed a program to teach thinking skills to children (Feuerstein, Rand, Hoffman, & Miller, 1980). This grew out of Feuerstein's notion that intelligence tests should be dynamic, testing what a child is capable of learning, instead of static, testing what a child knows at the time of taking the test. Feuerstein tested retarded Israeli children and found that many had potential to learn. He focuses on the "mediated learning," which is learning assisted by adults who sharpen, emphasize, elaborate, provide cues, and correct as they try to get the learner to solve and understand a problem. Feuerstein says that children who do poorly in IQ tests are careless thinkers in solving problems, often ignoring or discarding important clues. They are also impulsive, have poor spatial orientation, view problems in isolation, and fail to make proper inferences. The Feuerstein Instrumental Enrichment Program has over 500 pages of paper-

and-pencil exercises for teaching thinking through perceptual and cognitive skills. The program applies thinking skills to everyday events, and children are taught metacognitive strategies to monitor whether and in what depth they are learning the thinking skills.

Basis of Intelligence

Bayley (1970) says differences in mental abilities are attributable to heredity. Others argue that they are primarily environmental, with many scholars taking a position between these extremes. Correlates of mental abilities are impressive indicators of the rich complexity, still largely unexplored, of interactions among such variables as ability, motivation, attention span, emotional climate, environmental complexity, specific learning experience, and success and failure.

Bayley contends there is strong evidence that heredity operates to control the nature and level of mental abilities. The relationship with intelligence can be studied by the correlation between IQs of samples of groups. The results of over 50 studies representing 30,000 pairings of twins and non-twins are presented in Figure 8.12.

For the data summarized here, the heritability is .74. This does not mean that precisely 74 percent of intelligence is accounted for through heredity; however, it is an estimate. Due to differences in the type of data analyzed and method of calculation, the estimates of correlation have ranged from .45 to .87 (Jensen, 1973). The lower figure is based on the theory that a

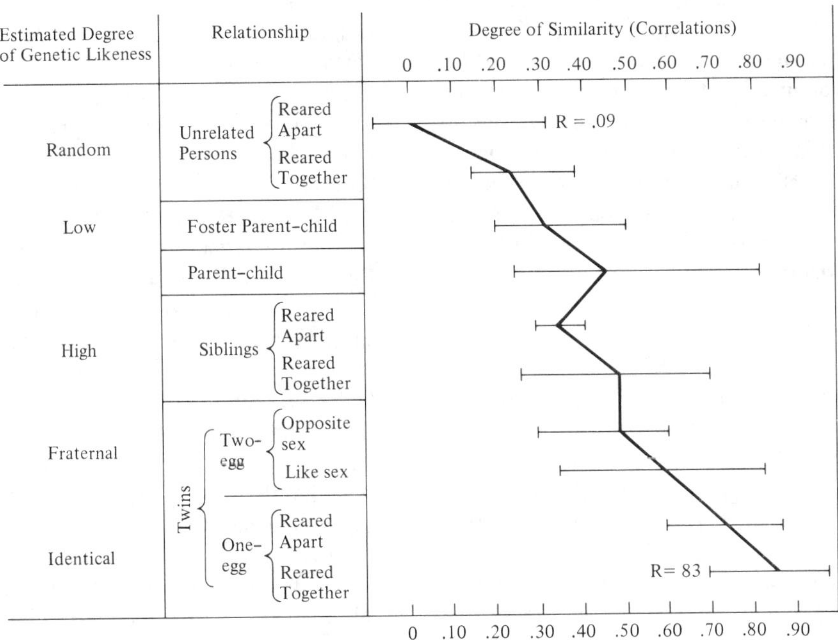

Figure 8.12 Relationships and intelligence. (*Source:* Erlenmeyer-Kimling & Jarvik, 1963. Copyright 1963 by the American Association for the Advancement of Science)

portion of variation in IQ score can be attributed to a variation in the genetic-environmental component. Parents contributing a certain gene influence their offspring by direct genetic components, but it should be remembered that heritability estimates apply to populations under specific circumstances and not to individuals. Also, it should be remembered that environmental conditions can be crucial. The metabolic disorder phenylketonuria (PKU) is genetically based; if not detected shortly after birth, mental retardation will result. A genetic trait can be significantly influenced by environmental circumstances, and while intelligence is a polygenic trait, it may still be radically affected by a single gene. An interaction between genetic (nature) and the environment (nurture) has been expressed by various researchers (Lindsey, Hall & Thompson, 1975).

In a study of children 5 to 11 years of age, Hsiu-Zu Ho and coworkers (1980) investigated the extent to which the genetic and environmental relationship changes during the course of development of cognitive abilities. Fifty-four identical twins and 33 same-sex fraternal twins were examined, utilizing a cross-sectional data analysis model known as Hierarchical Multiple Regression (HMR). Applying more specific cognitive tests found familial influences and the relative mixture of genetic and environmental influences on specific cognitive-abilities to remain stable during this period.

The Stability of Mental Growth

Long-term predictions of intelligence-test scores based on early scores are unreliable (Bayley, 1949). This was also shown by Jones (1954), who brought together and analyzed data from many studies. He found low correlations between scores obtained during the early years and scores at age 18. The correlations become increasingly higher at ages closer to 18. Lorge-Thorndike Intelligence Tests were administered by Eagle (1966) to 115 boys and 150 girls in the eighth grade who had previously taken the tests when they were in grades three or four. The results indicated that verbal IQ scores are more stable during the period from the third to the eighth grade than nonverbal IQ scores, and that the scores for girls were more stable than those for boys. Correlations on scores of the Primary Mental Abilities between 8 and 11 years by Meyer and Bendig (1961) show stability of academic abilities.

Earlier studies by Wheeler (1932) of Tennessee and Kentucky mountain children in an indigenous social setting indicated a decline in mental ability in children from ages 6 to 16. Other studies have confirmed this hypothesis (Skodak, 1939; Skeels, 1941). Jensen's and Inouye's study in Georgia found disadvantaged black children lost 13 IQ points from 5 to 18 years of age (1979). Regression in measured scores from 90 to 100 at 6 years of age, to 60 to 80 at 16 years of age, means losses of around 30 IQ points.

Optimal assistance to the underprivileged in early childhood has, however, resulted in dramatic increase in intelligence scores from earlier prognoses, as noted later in this chapter in the work of Heber (1977), Skeels (1966), and Klaus and Gray (1968). In other cases, attempts to enrich the educational lives of the deprived have failed to increase mental ability scores. In the Milwaukee experiment (Heber), massive amounts of assistance and funds were provided. Because of this it is highly unlikely that this will be universalized. It seems, though that early (ages one to three years) and persistent intervention materially helps develop mental skills. Recent studies by Scarr & Weinberg (1983) and Moore (1986) dealt with young black children being adopted by white advantaged families averaging 10 IQ points above the general population.

Investigators believe that most children are born with the potential to be normal. Based on this assumption, Bloom (1964) estimates that 50 percent of mature intelligence is reached by age four; consequently, an impoverished environment during the first four years will be quite detrimental to the child's intellectual development (see Table 8.6).

Cultural Impoverishment

An inadequate environment during childhood will adversely affect the development of intelligence to the extent that it can never completely overcome the ill effects, whereas an enriched environment will most likely accelerate its development (Bloom, 1964). "Almost all persons can learn if provided the appropriate prior and current conditions of learning" (Bloom, 1976). The early years are most critical, as shown by Bloom in Table 8.6. Willerman and coworkers (1970) found that retarded eight-month-old babies were seven times more likely to have low IQs by four years of age if they were from a lower socio-economic status. The physical aspect of development could account for some but not all of this difference. The major difference seems to be the early and systematic stimulation of the child by the parents. Nonetheless, it should not be overlooked that such physical care as diet, medical attention, and establishment of routines relative to sleep, play, and rest can help facilitate growth. Studies of culturally deprived children point to the following general conclusions:

1. The behavior that leads to social, educational, and economic poverty is socialized in early childhood--that is, it is learned.

2. The central quality involved in the effects of cultural deprivation is lack of cognitive meaning in the mother-child communication system.

3. Growth of the cognitive process is fostered in family control systems that offer and permit a wide range of alternatives of action and thought.

4. Growth is constricted by systems of control that offer predetermined solutions and few alternatives for consideration and choice.

Parent-Child Relationships

A study by Crandall and others (1964) showed that certain specific attitudes and behaviors of the parents toward their children's intellectual achievements were predictive of the children's academic test performance, while others were not. More significant relations were found between parents' attitudes and behaviors and their daughters' academic proficiency than occurred between these parents' attitudes and behaviors and their boys' performances. In particular, they noted that the more academically productive girls had fathers who more often praised and less often criticized their everyday achievements than did the less academically productive girls.

Interaction between mother and child is correlated with the child's IQ and school success.

HYPOTHETICAL EFFECTS OF DIFFERENT ENVIRONMENTS ON THE DEVELOPMENT OF INTELLIGENCE IN THREE SELECTED PERIODS

Age period	Percent of mature intelligence	Variation from normal growth in IQ units			
		Deprived	Normal	Abundant	Abundant deprived
Birth–4	50	− 5	0	+ 5	10
4–8	30	− 3	0	+ 3	6
8–17	20	− 2	0	+ 2	4
Total	100	−10	0	+10	20

Source: Bloom (1964).

Hess (1968) has shown in studies that mothers who give clear instructions and are consistently positive in reinforcing their children have youngsters with higher IQs than mothers who support to a lesser degree. Mothers who give explanations for directing courses of action including consideration of the children's feelings--"You'll hurt your cousin's feelings if you say that"--have children with higher IQs who do better in school. Parents who give explanations have generally higher intelligence (Freeburg & Payne, 1967) and consequently give more attention to teaching new words, pointing out inaccuracies, and putting pressure on children to do well.

Improving Cognitive Development

Goldstein and Myer (1980) studied cognitive and group differences in intelligence and noted the importance of developmental delay in the case of the learning disabled. The cognitive lag (delay) hypothesis views chronological age as a dependent variable; that is, behavior is not seen to develop as a function of children in the acquisition of basic cognitive skills. These investigators point out that low socio-economic black and white children do virtually the same as middle-class white children based on mental age scores. Standardized tests of intellectual development, through the use of chronological age norms, place a premium on rapid rates of development. The child with a mental age of six and a chronological age of five receives a much higher intelligence test score than the child with a mental age of six and a chronological age of seven, although both children may have the same intellectual competence, as measured by the Bender Gestalt Test. The lag implies that expectations from test scores of making an average score based on age alone are inappropriate. These investigators suggested (1) mainstreaming in a class with special attention to rates of progress in children, utilizing "mastery learning," such as suggested by Bloom (1976); (2) viewing behavior as a developmental level, not as the function of age; and (3) developing alternative methods for reporting test results on mental age scores and test items, profiles that would provide a more valid assessment of the child's intellectual strength and weakness.

Motivation and Intelligence

The child surrounded by poverty, many experts feel, will have the same desire to achieve as the child from the middle class. Even so, after serious attempts to equalize the motivational differences, performances on tests vary, as was found in the investigation of Lesser and coworkers (1965). In this experiment, boys and girls from four social classes and cultures were selected for study. Each class was represented by a lower status group and a higher (middle) status group. In each of the cultures (Jewish, Chinese, black, and Puerto Rican), the higher status group performed better than the lower status groups. Between the groups there were differences as follows:

Jewish children - higher verbal; lower reasoning and number.

Chinese children - low verbal; higher in reasoning, number, and space, with these about equal.

Black children - higher verbal; lower in reasoning, number and space.

Puerto Rican children - lower verbal; better in reasoning, number and space.

Ginsberg (1972) says these differences are not primarily ones of adequacy but rather of motivation. He suggests the use of Piaget-type tests as good indicators of motivation. His idea is summarized in the following quote from his work *The Myth of the Deprived Child*:

> In many fundamental ways poor children's cognition is quite similar to that of middle-class children. These are cognitive universals, modes of language and thought shared by all children (except the retarded and seriously emotionally disturbed) regardless of culture or upbringing. At the same time there do exist social-class differences in cognition. Yet the differences are relatively superficial and one must not make the mistake of calling them deficiencies or considering them analogous to mental retardation. (p. 14)

Sigler, Abelson, and Seitz (1973) have shown in two investigations that differences of as much as 10 to 15 points on standard IQ tests and like gains on the Peabody Picture Vocabulary Test may be due to motivation. Familiarization with the examiner; suitable, friendly conditions; and even the second testing improve the testing potential of the child. The authors would have to agree that motivation, cognitive styles, and personal styles are all important. Nevertheless, we agree with Ginsberg that Piagetian tests may come closer to testing basic motivational competencies, revealing differences between classes of children.

Sex Differences in Intelligence

There is no difference between boys and girls in overall ability on standard IQ tests. However, there are differences in specific areas. Boys are better at mathematical reasoning tasks, perform better on all measures of spatial reasoning, are more field independent and more analytic in cognitive style, are somewhat less verbal than girls, and generally do less well in school (Maccoby & Jacklin, 1974). Girls are better at learning languages, writing, English, and tasks requiring fine motor movement. Libsen and Golbeck (1980) found competence differences between boys and girls aged three, five, seven, nine, and eleven on Piagetian spatial tasks using "physical" or "nonphysical" versions of the horizontal and vertical to favor boys. Girls could be less motivated, and therefore performance is perhaps affected by lower expectations for success. Sex differences in language are usually attributed to the more rapid physical maturation of girls, although the early environment of the average boy is less conducive to language development than that of girls, and a greater difference exists for children from the lower social class.

On intelligence tests boys score over a greater range than do girls. There are more mental defectives among boys and as many gifted boys as girls. It is generally believed that girls do slightly better on intelligence tests, perhaps because of their linguistic skills. Girls, compared to boys of the same age, advance more rapidly in test intelligence, generally read earlier, and are ready for school at an earlier age. Girls, on the other hand, have been found to gain less than boys, judging by intelligence test scores, between adolescence and adulthood, with the brightest girls making the least gains (Bradway and Thompson, 1962). It should be noted, however, that until quite recently intellectual females were frequently not well accepted, so they may have hidden their abilities.

Racial Differences in Intelligence

It is generally known that inheritance is closely related to height, weight, personality, and intelligence. Black Americans score, as a group, 10 to 15 IQ points lower than white Americans. This fact is not debated, but how to interpret the difference is. The difference is not found among infants either for race or social class. In fact, black children exhibit somewhat faster motor development than white children.

School success is predicted by the IQ score in each group. Research by Jensen and Inouye (1979) on the cognitive ability of Asian-American (n=478), white (n=3, 174), and black (n=2, 518) children in grades two through six in California reveals little difference in memory among the races. On general intelligence the Asian-Americans scored 6 to 7 points higher than the American norms on the WISC full scale IQ, though they were from a lower socio-economic status than the whites. Lynn (1977), an English investigator, had findings consistent with these when the WISC was standardized for Japanese children.

The controversy of heritability of intelligence was given impetus with a statement by Jensen in 1969 in the *Harvard Review of Education*. The statement (made in reference to such special educational programs as Head Start) was that the failure of these programs was due to the innate variance in intelligence between blacks and whites. Jensen suggested that blacks score below whites in abstract problem-solving ability, but are equal or superior in memorization. He also recommended that educational programs be modified to take these differences into consideration.

Three investigators of the literature relative to racial differences in intelligence--Loehlin, Lindzey, and Spuhler (1975)--have summarized general aspects of this problem in the following manner:

1. The concept of racial difference in intelligence is largely demographic rather than biological; the differences in gene structures are in most cases far less between races than within them.

2. Estimates of heritability of intelligence differ, depending on the assumptions one makes. Jensen says .81 for the coefficient--others believe it is as low as .35. (This figure is known as the range of reaction, in this case .35-.81, meaning the broadest possible effect the phenotype has on the genotype. The effect of the environment on test scores of intelligence at .35 is much greater than that of heredity if true.)

3. Children born of interracial marriages have a higher IQ if the mother is white (Willerman, Naylor, & Myrianthopoulos, 1970). This suggests a maternal environment effect (prenatal and/or postnatal) rather than a genetic effect.

4. A study of illegitimate children conceived by U.S. servicemen and German women following World War II found no overall difference in average IQ between children whose fathers were black and those whose fathers were white. Since the children were raised in similar circumstances by German women, in comparable conditions of social status, and matched with age-mates in the same school classroom, the study gives credence to the idea that the environment is the major element in racial IQ differences (Eyferth, 1961). Since the characteristics of the fathers are unknown, the selectivity is therefore possibly unrepresentative, and the results cannot readily be interpreted.

Jensen's views opposing this position are stated in the work *Educability and Group Differences*, published in 1973. He maintains the isolation of racial populations from each other over many generations caused inevitable differences to accumulate in "gene pools," the racial reservoirs of inheritance. Jensen (1969) found this to be true when he studied the scores of all white and black siblings in the elementary schools of a racially mixed, medium-sized California community whose population was 40 percent black. Jensen found no convincing research to suggest that differences between blacks and whites are environmental, for he found the IQ differences between the races favoring white in the middle and upper classes with a larger variant (20 points) than among the poor. Jensen analyzed performance of children on all kinds of tests, even nonverbal and Piagetian, and found that differences still exist.

The critics of Jensen raise the question of the "range of reaction." The range of reaction is defined as the widest possible expression of any individual's genetic constitution in combination with the broadest possible manifestations of environment. An answer to this comes from Hunt (1969, 1972) and Dennis (1976, pp. 246-248), both using Piagetian tasks with children under five (in the Hunt study, children six to nine in the other tasks), which were translated into IQ scale. Each study found that various populations within the United States and among many cultures throughout the world differed by as much as 75 points. As Jensen sees it, given a normal distribution of intelligence with 80 percent heritability, the range of reaction in the United States is about 30 points from one end of the environmental scale to the other, but nowhere near 75. He insists that this 30-point range of reaction is enough to account for the spectacular success of Rich Heber's Milwaukee project. Heber has agreed with Jensen that intervention, raising IQs some 20 to 30 points, does not refute Jensen or the heritability theory. Assuming the same mean IQ of 80 for fathers and mothers, the children's normal (upward) regression to the population mean is coupled with the 30-point range of reaction, and the increase noted by Heber is accounted for adequately. The noted geneticist Dobzhansky (1973) says a person's genetic endowment establishes a range within which intelligence develops. Potential is there, for each level.

A study of minority test bias was made by Sandoval and Mulle (1980), when they asked 100 college students to judge 30 items from the Wechsler Intelligence Scale for Children--Revised (WISC-R) as to cultural prejudice. An item analysis of the WISC-R results showed half of the items to be more difficult for Mexican-Americans or blacks than for Anglo-Americans. The other half of the items, however, were of equal difficulty for children of all three groups. Three judges, from three different ethnic backgrounds (Anglo-American, black and Mexican-American), were asked to determine which items would be more difficult for a child from either a black or Mexican-American background as compared with an Anglo-American, and which would be of equal difficulty. The study indicated that the judges were not able to determine satisfactorily which items were more difficult for minority students. There was also no significant difference in accuracy between judges of the different ethnic backgrounds, showing the difficulty in validating bias in test items. A number of studies indicating racial difference in intelligence cannot be considered invalid on the basis of testing bias, but undoubtedly a need to argue for a comparison on mental age rather than chronological age exists. Whether heredity or nature means more depends upon the investigator, but the conclusions are largely inferential and often the arguments are about different assumptions.

Differences in Intelligence Due to Birth Order

Firstborn children, including only children, have on the average slightly higher IQs. Terman found among his sample of gifted children at the genius level that firstborns were in disproportionately greater number than would be expected by chance. Intelligence, among other variables, may be a product of how many brothers and sisters the child has (Zajonc & Markus, 1975). Intelligence declines with family size and in birth order with regularity.

Belmont and Marolla (1973) examined the birth order of 386,000 Dutchmen. The data taken from military records represented almost the entire male population of 19-year-old men in the Netherlands born between 1944 and 1947. To classify the men, the Dutch military had used the Raven Progressive Matrices, a nonverbal intelligence test that is relatively free of cultural bias. After examining the scores of the firstborn, second-born, and so forth, these investigators calculated the intelligence scores by occupational level, but the order of diminution was still invariant. The firstborn was the brightest and the last-born the dullest. Usually it is true that the firstborn receives undivided attention, resources, stimulation, and the chance to teach siblings when they arrive. According to a 1973 census (Chance, 1975), the average family size for blacks with children was 2.52, and for whites, 2.13. Only 2 percent of the white families had over six children, whereas 7 percent of black families fell in that category.

The differences in family size as suggested here could have an important effect on the average IQ and account in part for the disparity between the black and white races. Most experts acknowledge the part played by attention as an explanation of birth-order differences in intelligence; perhaps the dissipation in the health of the mother over the years of childbearing should also be examined as a possible cause. The uterus deteriorates, the placentas are less pliable and effective in giving oxygen and food to the fetus, and the neurological system developed from an older egg has become stale; these are all possible etiologies (origins). The spacing of children seems to help, for in this way adult attention is available at crucial times in development as from birth to two or three.

INTELLIGENCE AND SCHOOLING: COGNITIVE STYLES, GIFTEDNESS, AND CREATIVITY

Intelligence and Cognitive Styles

Many contemporary theorists contend that learning is essential for the development of cognitive structures and processes. Ausubel (1963) suggests:

> Cognitive structure refers solely to the stability, clarity, and organization of a learner's subject matter knowledge in a given discipline. The actual ideas and information embodied in this knowledge are "cognitive content." "Cognitive style" refers to the self-consistent inter-individual differences and idiosyncratic trends in cognitive organization and functioning. (p. 76)

For Wilkin and coworkers (1977) there are two major cognitive styles, field dependent and field independent. These differ in how they reflect the physical, social, and intellectual aspects of the environment. The intellectual, or cognitive difference is that field-dependent persons rely on external referents as guides in information processing, whereas field-independent persons put greater dependence in internal referents. Field-dependent persons are high in social sensitivity and social skills and low in restructuring skills and personal autonomy. Field-independent persons are high in cognitive restructuring and personal autonomy and low in social sensitivity.

Wilkin and coworkers (1977), from their investigations, suggest that it is reasonable to expect students' cognitive styles to influence their educational-vocational choices. Specifically, it is likely that relatively field-dependent people will show interest in, and do better in, areas that are primarily social in content, require interpersonal relations skills, and do not principally call for cognitive restructuring skills. Field-independent persons are likely to favor areas that emphasize cognitive restructuring skills, are primarily abstract and nonsocial in content, and tolerate an impersonal orientation. They tend to analyze the elements of a scene and focus on certain aspects, separating them from their backgrounds.

There is evidence that people we call field independent do significantly better at problems in which the essential element required for solution must be isolated from the content in which it is presented and used in a different kind of relation to the rest of the problem material. A study by Goodenough and Karp (1961), using factor analysis, was conducted with groups of 10- and 12-year-old boys as subject. The boys were given a special series of cognitive tasks, including perceptual and field-dependence tests and the subtests of the Wechsler Intelligence Scale for Children. Three main factors emerged: (1) verbal, (2) attention-concentration, and (3) the analytic. An analysis of the tasks presented by block design, picture completion, and object assembly suggests that they require the same kind of analytic functioning as do the perceptual tests. Apparently, children with either a field-dependent or field-independent way of perceiving are not significantly different in overall testing intelligence. But Morgan and Culver (1978) did find that field-independent college students had higher reading achievement than field-dependent students.

Kagan and Kogan (1970) identified, along other dimensions, three styles of intellectual preference among children. He called these styles categorical, descriptive, and relational. Categorical uses common class membership in combining stimuli (cat and mice are both animals); descriptive styles are formed on the basis of related physical attributes of stimuli (cat and mice both have four legs); relational strategies are working relationships among stimuli (cats are used to catch mice).

Robinson and Gray (1974), using the Iowa Test of Basic Skills and the Lorge-Thorndike Intelligence Tests with 258 grade-school boys and girls, investigated cognitive styles and learning. Illustration of the terms used to represent styles were as follows:

CATEGORICAL: Dog is to cat as chicken is to (pig).
a. feather b. eggs c. pig d. bark

DESCRIPTIVE: Chair is to legs as lamp is to (light bulb).
a. furniture b. light c. hand d. light bulb

RELATIONAL: Key is to lock as saw is to (board).
a. keys b. board c. tool d. teeth

This study indicated that standardized intellectual ability and school achievement tests are heterogeneous to sex when related to cognitive style requirements. Of the three modes, the descriptive style was the most important contributor in the prediction of school learning. For boys, relational style had a greater effect than categorical style. This style, however, accounted for more variation for girls than the rational mode. When the variance of verbal for girls is considered and when the nonverbal IQ was removed from the school-learning variance, this relationship was reduced. Based upon this study, preference of style and learning exist; the specific style and specific learning task, if identified, would enhance educational programs based on the mapping of cognitive styles of children.

Reissman (1966) suggested that there are observable differences, which he termed visual, aural, and physical styles. A summary of studies suggests that the auditory sense is superior to the visual when learners are young or illiterate. As age, literacy, and difficulty increase, the visual sense becomes better (Hartman, 1961; Raper, 1973). Black children of low socioeconomic status, however, utilize visual and motor learning over auditory and vocal learning (Stephenson & Gay, 1972).

Another aspect of cognitive style is reflectivity and impulsivity--the speed with which a child responds to problem solving. Differences have been noted as early as two years, but children tend to become more reflective with age (McCandless, 1977). The change in reflectivity as children grow older has been demonstrated by Kagan and Kogan (1970). Utilizing the Matching Familiar Figures Test, children were asked to select from six similar familiar figures the one that matched a standard figure presented separately from the rest. Reflectivity and impulsivity were rated according to how long it took the child to make a decision and whether or not the decision was correct. Between 5 and 12 years of age, children diminished the number of errors, but increased the decision-making time. Reflectivity increased with age. It may follow that impulsive children become less so but still remain more impulsive than reflective children, who may also increase in reflectivity. Reflective children do better at reasoning tasks and most schoolwork. They seem to be more creative and systematic in exploration. They also avoid physical risk taking and strange social situations. Reali and Hall (1970) compared the reactions of reflective and impulsive subjects to success and failure. Neither of these variables identified differences among the subjects.

Creativity

Lindzey, et al. (1975) conducted an investigation into the nature of creativity and found that highly creative persons possess the following attributes: flexibility, intuitiveness, perceptivity, originality, dedication, persistence, independence, moodiness, ingeniousness, unconventionality, eccentricity, dominance, self-centeredness, courageousness, assertiveness, extravertedness, and industriousness. Torrance (1965) reports that research has identified peaks of creativity in children at ages 4 1/2 and 9. He also reports valleys in the ability to think creatively at ages 3, 6, and 11. Gakhar and Joshi (1980) suggest that creativity exists in a framework of personality, temperamental and moral spheres, and intellectual traits.

Studies of creativity by Lehman (1964) show that young thinkers frequently demonstrate memorable creative achievements. He has collected a total of more than 200 significant attainments by individuals less than 21 years old. A high rate of creative productivity at an early age leads to the belief that creative youngsters should be identified early and given special training. Datta and Parlogg (1967) attempted to determine the kind of home in which the creative individual is likely to develop. The investigators noted that both creative young scientists and their equally bright but less creative controls describe their parents as moderately affectionate, nonrejecting, and high in encouraging intellectual independence. The creative subjects most often perceived both parents as furnishing a "no rule" situation in which the integrity and responsibility of the children were assumed rather than enforced in an authoritarian manner. Trowbridge and Charles' (1966) study showed that highly creative children had more self-direction and inner motivation, and used more free time alone reading, working, playing, and day-dreaming.

Creativity and Problem Solving

Davis and Houtman (1968) formulated and tested a strategy for creative problem solving through a four-step procedure: (1) clearly understanding the problem and stating it, (2) finding main types of solutions, (3) finding specific ideas for each main solution, and (4) choosing the best ideas. Figure 8.13 is a model of creativity and problem solving as suggested by Davis and Houtman.

Simbert (1971) identified a set of perceptual, cultural, and emotional blocks to creative problem solving. Perceptual blocks included:

1. Difficulty in isolating problems
2. Inability to define terms
3. Failure to distinguish between cause and effect
4. Difficulty in not investigating the obvious

Emotional blocks included:

1. Fear of making a mistake
2. Rigidity in thinking
3. Lack of drive
4. Lack of drive in carrying a problem through to completion
5. Desire of security

Klausmeier (1975) suggests three ways to foster creativity: encourage divergent production in many media, reward creative efforts, and foster a creative personality. For developing divergence, a teacher or parent can ask children or adolescents to try to draw a picture, write a poem, build a model, or learn to dance. When a project is completed by a child, praise and reinforcement should ensue, in order for the child to continue trying out ideas.

SCHOOLING AND INFORMATIONAL PROCESSES

It is in the school that children spend the most time learning about the world through social, emotional, intellectual, and even moral interaction with peers and adults. The middle-school years must be ones filled with successful encounters to bolster confidence and help

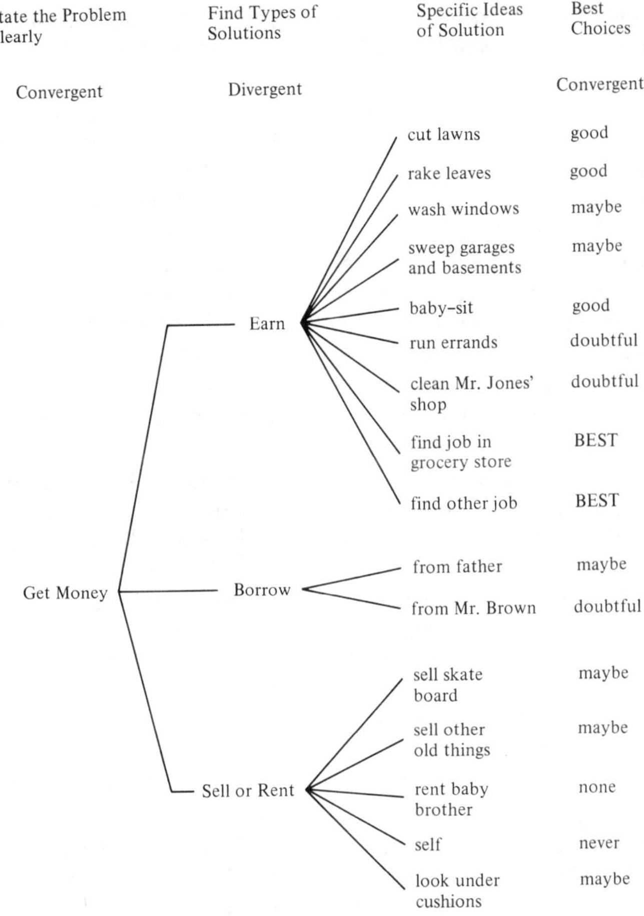

Figure 8.13 Steps in problem solving. (*Source:* Davis & Houtman, 1968)

develop a well-rounded and healthy child. There is mounting evidence, however, that American schools are failing at the task of teaching students both socialization processes and adequate concept attainment for real-world endeavors (Goldberg and Harvey, 1983). Miklos (1982) cited the National Assessment of Educational Progress (NAEP) data through 1981 indicating that elementary students are doing well in the basic skills but that older students show declining inferential comprehension skills. *The Reading Report Card: Progress Toward Excellence in Our Schools* (1985) describes trends in reading achievement over a 14-year period for students at ages 9, 13, and 17, using data from four national assessments over a decade. Although young readers seem to be achieving better in this decade than in the last, students seem to have difficulty in comprehending simple and complex relationships found in print. *The Writing Report Card: Writing Achievement in American Schools* (1987) indicates that students today, as measured in fourth, eighth, and eleventh grades, write only at a minimal level and have difficulty using critical thinking and organizational skills.

In a sample of the population at ages 21 to 25, Kirsch and Jungeblut (1986) describe children and youth who can read simple material with facility but cannot understand complex material nearly so well. *Learning to be Literate in America* (1987), which summarizes several NAEP surveys, cautions that schools need to help students learn to learn. All of these reports, published within a few years of each other, indicate that students experience difficulty with reading and writing skills such as critical thinking, drawing inferences, and applying what is read.

Goodlad, in *A Place Called School* (1984), comments on the "emotional flatness" in American classrooms. He observed students completing exercise after exercise without active involvement. He saw little opportunity for students to use knowledge in an active thinking environment. In his best-seller *Cultural Literacy* (1987), Hirsch attributes the problem to students' general lack of exposure to fundamental knowledge. Fortunately, there are some promising trends in American schools which pertain to teaching children at this age level. They will be described in the following section.

Cooperative Learning

There is a growing body of research to indicate that giving students opportunities to learn cooperatively in the classroom can enhance learning (Larson and Dansereau, 1986; Leal, Crays and Moetz, 1985; Palinscar and Brown, 1984; Johnson and Johnson, 1987). Cooperative learning aids young children in maintaining and generalizing study skills. One by-product of cooperative learning is that it may lessen such stress reactions as self-deprecation, lack of clear goals, disparagement, immature relationships with teachers, or pervasive depression (Gentile and McMillan, 1987). Most important, students mature as they discuss what and how material can best be learned. Students who work together also appear to have a higher regard for school and for the subjects they are studying, and are more confident and self-assured. Raniski and Nathenson-Mejia (1987) note that the cooperative classroom environment teaches social development, social responsibility, and concern for one another. Recently, Weinstein (1987) has suggested that cooperative learning strategies work in aiding student comprehension and retention because they fall into one or more of what she calls "categories of learning strategies," i.e., processes and methods useful in acquiring and retrieving information. Weinstein's five categories of learning strategies are:

1. Rehearsal strategies. The students act out and discuss information in groups in such a way that the discussion becomes a rehearsal of the new material to be learned.

2. Elaboration strategies. By retelling information learned, by generating questions in groups, and by writing about what has been learned, students are elaborating on what has been learned and enhancing new knowledge.

3. Organizational strategies. Anyone who has done committee work knows how much a group must be organized to reach a shared goal or implement a project. When working cooperatively, students learn to organize their time and their thinking about a topic.

4. Comprehension monitoring strategies. Children working cooperatively learn to monitor through listening, speaking, and writing how much they are learning about any given topic.

5. Affective strategies. Students learn to enjoy school more because of increased time in working with peers.

Teachers are using cooperative learning more often because they are seeing the benefits in increased productivity and less anxiety about learning.

Metacognition

The process of being reflective about oneself as a learner, of thinking about thinking and reasoning about what one does and does not know, is called *metacognition* (Babbs & Moe, 1983; Richardson & Morgan, 1990). Sternberg has called this knowing about knowing, rather than simply knowing about content to be learned (Sternberg & Powell, 1983). There is evidence that younger children are not cognizant of this very important skill; that is, they are not aware of the skills one utilizes to know and remember concepts (Flavell, 1982). Yet this skill is one that is needed to remember complex material found in junior high and high school textbooks. Children's metacognitive awareness develops into adolescence and even into early adulthood (Brown, et al, 1983). Although more research needs to be done in this important area, there is reason to believe that children and adults who practice this skill will have better awareness of, and success with, important cognitive tasks experienced in school.

Memory Strategies

Even though we have known for some time that short-term memory cannot be expanded to any significant degree, there is seemingly no limit to how far long-term memory can be expanded. Recent studies (Peters and Levin, 1986; Levin, Morrison and McGivern, 1986; Cohen, 1987; McDaniel, Pressley, and Dunay, 1987) have found that mnemonics training has been successful in a number of school contexts for aiding students in retention of material from the elementary years throughout high school. Mnemonic strategies work by relieving the burden on short-term memory through associating newly learned material with an already existing code in long-term memory. Memory training has much promise in schools for helping students better learn and retain information.

Computers and Learning

Computer technology is fast becoming a natural part of American life, both in the home and at school. Mason and Blanchard (1979) have suggested three uses of programmed materials available on computers:

1. Tutorial programs. These are self-contained materials that instruct students without the aid of an instructor.

2. Drill and practice. Instruction that is first presented by the teacher is supplemented by drill and practice exercises on the computer.

3. Programs with dialogue. Students must know how to "interact" with the computer by performing functions and routines for that purpose.

Computers have these two advantages: interaction between student and machine and immediate motivation for the student involved in learning. Surprisingly, however, many educational programs have not proven effective and children tire of repetitive programs once initial interest wanes. Because of this, advocates of computer learning have stressed learning that promotes discovery and creative methodology. Children can be taught to program material, create new endings to stories, solve problems in science and mathematics, and take part in analyzing complex structures and forms (Papert, 1980). Despite these new trends, often programming for middle childhood children seems too rote and too difficult for interest to be maintained for any length of time (Hawkins, et al., 1982). One promising area for computers is using word processing programs to teach writing and story construction utilizing a whole-language approach. Preschool children have been taught sequences of stories through placing graphic story elements in proper sequence (Foreman, 1985).

Children With Special Needs

A number of children in middle and later childhood manifest serious classroom difficulties in one or more areas of learning, yet cannot be thought of as mentally retarded or severely emotionally, physically, or socially disturbed. Children with *learning disabilities* are those with at least normal intelligence who exhibit problems in listening, thinking, reading, writing, spelling, and mathematics. Children with such learning disorders usually have difficulty in one or more of the following areas: motor control, perception, concentration on symbols, attention span, or memory (Myers and Hammill, 1976). They also tend to be hyperactive and impulsive, with frequent shifts observable in emotional mood.

What can be observed in the learning-disabled child is an often unusual way of receiving and perceiving information. Such children will often not be able to categorize information properly (Shepard, Smith and Vojir, 1983). At other times they take too broad a view of matter to be learned and are not able to concentrate on small sequences of learning (Geiger & Lettvin, 1987).

Placement of children into learning disabilities classrooms can have a profound effect on a youngster. The label may stigmatize a child, but good programs can have a profoundly beneficial effect for failing youngsters.

Policies for Handicapped Youngsters

Recently there has been a positive trend toward *mainstreaming* mildly and moderately handicapped youngsters under the auspices of Public Law 94-142. Handicapped children are taught in the regular classroom wherever possible, sometimes with the support of extra teachers and equipment. The federal requirement of educating such youngsters in the "least restrictive environment" has done much to gain acceptance for learning-disabled and retarded children. Such programs work, however, only where clear goal statements called Individualized Educational Plans (IEPs) are made and followed to support the overall classroom activities of the youngsters.

MORAL REASONING IN MIDDLE AND LATER CHILDHOOD

Children have to build a conscience or system of values. The child needs help to develop a moral code and principles. Classification of values, though important, is not enough to develop moral standards. But the relativity of values must be given attention. Educating people for democratic citizenship requires making value choices based upon moral standards (Hersh et al., 1979).

Learning to behave in ways approved by society is an important developmental task. In school the child is expected to distinguish broadly between right and wrong. By the time they reach adolescence, children should have a system of values and moral sensitivity designed to assist them in making moral decisions. Children sooner or later come to recognize that it serves their own interest to support the group's rules of conduct--the mores, laws, and customs of the community. For example, if children continue to violate the rules of tag by not admitting being tagged, the group will eventually not let them enter the game. Four essentials in a child's learning morality are as follows:

1. To be moral is to find out what the social group expects of its members. The mores are

spelled out for all group members in the form of regulations, laws, and customs. Certain acts are considered right or wrong because they further harm the group's welfare. Children learn that different groups--family, neighborhood, school, and the larger community--have rules and laws with varying penalties for breaking them.

2. To be moral is to have a growing conscience which acts as an internal control over one's behavior. The conscience is developed in children as they are conditioned and taught by parents, teachers, and other authority figures. Conscience is not simply conditioned anxiety, though approval of important persons depends at least partially on it. Internalized standards of conduct are a complex matter, requiring first environmental restrictions and finally personal self-control.

3. To be moral is to develop feelings of guilt and shame. Guilt is a kind of self-negation that children recognize when their behavior is at odds with accepted standards of conduct. Guilt is experienced only after certain prerequisites have been met: acceptance of standards of right and wrong, acceptance of an obligation to regulate one's own behavior, and feeling responsibility for others. In addition, it is necessary to possess sufficient self-critical ability to recognize that a discrepancy has occurred between one's behavior and one's internal standards of behavior. Shame serves to implement motivation in supporting correct or good deportment. Shame is usually defined as "unpleasant reactions of an individual to an actual or presumed negative judgment of oneself by others resulting in self-depreciation vis-a-vis the group" (Ausubel, 1955). Shame relies primarily on external judgment; sometimes it is associated with guilt. Guilt, on the other hand, rests on both external and internal sanctions.

4. To be moral is to have opportunity for interaction with members of the social group. Social integration plays an important role in moral development. It acquaints children with standards of approved behavior.

Lawrence Kohlberg (1972) believed we can teach moral judgment and behavior by presenting moral problems to young people, helping them to think effectively about these problems. This means suggesting higher levels of moral judgment and assisting children to develop ego strength that will support them at the level of individual and principle-based moral behavior.

We should recognize that at birth the child has no conscience and no scale of values. What is valuable is food, warmth, and comfort. Over a period of time children learn values and are taught to distinguish good from bad. One basis of conscience is punishment by parents--spankings, withholding of affection, combined with their love and regard for the child and the child's love and dependence on them. Another basis is the process of identifying with parents and taking on their roles. Children develop within themselves the warning and disquieting voice of conscience. From this time onward, they carry with them a moral controlling force wherever they go. It must be remembered that this conscience is built upon the model of parents, family, teachers, and peers of all kinds.

THEORIES OF MORAL DEVELOPMENT

Moral development in the past has been viewed as (1) a reclamation project, by those who believed the child was born in sin (an evangelical view); (2) starting out neither moral nor immoral (amoral) but as a clean slate (*tabula rasa* view of Locke) upon which experiences and training will write, determining whether children become moral or not; and (3) a pure innate circumstance that is corrupted by society (a Rousseauian view). Each of these views finds expression in the theories on moral development to follow: Social learning theory

	Stage I Constraint	Stage II Cooperation
	6-year-old	*12-year-old*
Viewpoint of child	Right and wrong is like black and white; role taking is limited.	Can role play, take another's place and point of view.
Intention	Consequences of an act is all that counts.	Intention dominates assigning guilt.
Rules	Rules are unalterable.	Rules made by people are changed by people.
Respect	Obey adult rules.	Respect for adults and peers leads to valuing others' ideas.
Punishment	The meaning of bad is connected with punishment.	Believes in milder punishment. Thinks reform can help and will assist the victim by compensation.
Justice	Intention and role taking are not used. Physical and moral law not separated.	Natural calamities are not confused with punishment.

and cognitive development theory, as illustrated through the views of Piaget and Kohlberg.

Social Learning Theory

In children moral development occurs in the same way that other learning takes place, from imitation of others, modeling and observation. Morality is culturally relative. The environmental influences on moral development are defined by quantitative variations in the power of reward, punishment, preachments, and modeling of conforming behavior by parents and other socializing agents. Morality is not a unitary trait like honesty or a single entity such as the superego. Social behavior (moral behavior) is a variable dependent upon the situation, as found in the classical study of honesty by Hartshorne and May (1928) and in Burton (1976), who found that the relationship between intelligence and honesty is less in the nonacademic situation and depends on the nature of the risk involved. Most actions lead to positive consequences in some situations and negative consequences in others, so that people develop sensitive discriminations and response patterns that cannot be generalized in all circumstance. When an action brings reward, children quickly adopt that type of response (Walters, Leat, & Mezei, 1963). Research by Rosenkoetter (1973) reveals that deviant models have a considerably greater impact upon children than honest models do.

Piaget's Stages in Moral Growth

Learning rules means establishing the morality of cooperation and agreement so necessary in democratic society. Going by the rules in time gives children insight as to why they have to be honest in supporting the rules and regulations. Piaget believes that middle childhood (ages 6 to 12) is the crucial period for learning the morality of cooperation. According to Piaget there are two stages in moral development: (1) morality by constraint, and (2) autonomous morality. In the first stage, parents and other authorities supervise children's conduct. Right and wrong are usually clear-cut with little reasoning involved. In the second stage (typically around 12), autonomous or cooperative morality develops through peer association. Young people who acquire a sense of justice understand why rules are important (often inventing new ones), have a concern for the rights of others, are willing to cooperate, favor equality, and practice give-and-take in human relationships (Piaget, 1965).

Kohlberg's Levels of Morality

The stages through which the moral development of children takes place have been outlined by Kohlberg in three levels: preconventional, conventional, and postconventional. Each of these levels contains two stages. Progress through them depends on the child's experience and education. The stages in moral development seem to exist in a number of different societies. Many people do not go beyond the second level of development (the law and order stage), and Kohlberg found that middle-class children move through the stages more rapidly than children from the working-laboring class. These are the levels and stages and their meanings based on Kohlberg (1976) descriptions:

Preconventional Level 1 (ages 4 to 10) In Stage 1, punishment and obedience, the child does not understand the conventions (rules) of society. Adults have more power so children always obey rules to avoid punishment. They avoid punishment to avoid censure, not out of respect for adults but out of fear.

In Stage 2 of the preconventional level--reciprocity--doing right is based upon the physical consequences of an action. Elements of fairness and sharing are there, but behavior is always interpreted in terms of a pragmatic way. Reciprocity is a matter of "you scratch my back and I'll scratch yours." Justice and gratitude are not involved, as the child conforms simply to obtain rewards.

Conventional Level II (ages 10 to 13) In Stage 3--the good-boy, good-girl stage, children behave well for that pleases or helps others and elicits approval. Children conform to avoid disapproval and dislike by others. In this stage there is much conformity to what the majority thinks or to an authority figure or the opinion of a person who counts. Behavior is now viewed by intention--"she means well"; this becomes important for the first time. One earns approval by being "good."

In Stage 4, law and order, fixed rules and maintenance of law and order are the principal motivators of behavior. Right behavior consists in doing one's duty, showing respect for law authority, and maintaining that the social order is good for its own sake. Individuals conform to avoid censure by authorities and the resulting guilt.

Postconventional Level III (ages 13 onward; or never) At Stage 5, the social contract stage, true morality is attained. Right action is defined in terms of general individual rights and standards that have been agreed upon by society. Individuals at this stage stress the legal point of view, but they recognize the possibility of changing laws after rational consideration of conflicts between human needs and the law. Free agreement and contracts bind people together where no laws apply. This is the official morality of the United States Constitution and government.

At Stage 6, the universal ethical principle stage, individual principles (conscience) guide behavior and conduct. People define right by the decision of their conscience through self-chosen ethical principles, such as justice, equality, or dignity, regardless of the law or opinions of others. These principles, once they are chosen, should be applied consistently. They are not absolute rules, such as the Commandments, but abstract ethical principles like the "Golden Rule," the *summum bonum* of Plato, or the Categorical Imperatives of Kant.

Development through these stages parallels one's intellectual growth. Research indicates that 10-year-old boys might be anywhere from Stage 1 to Stage 3 in moral development, and 13-year-old boys anywhere from Stage 2 to Stage 5. At 16, most boys are somewhere between Stages 3 and 5. Most persons, it is thought, never reach Stage 6. In examining the stages, it is obvious that the stages increasingly involve a wider community. In Stage 1 there is no consideration for others. At Stage 3, however, the orientation to morality is judged mainly by views of the immediate community of family, friends, and authority figures. With Stage 6 the entire world is brought into consideration in ethical decisions. A seventh stage has been added to these--religious transcendence--a religious morality of love and comprehensive view of justice. The hero models of Stage 7 include Dewey, Socrates, Tielhard DeChardin, and Martin Luther King, Jr. (Kohlberg, 1981).

Assessment of Theories

The universality of Kohlberg's stages remains to be demonstrated conclusively. Some say that Stage 5 corresponds to conservative legal philosophy whereas Stage 6 reflects traditional liberal, radical, and political reasoning (Hogan & Schroeder, 1981). They also contend that Kohlberg's theory is more a political manifesto than a scientific statement, with the reliability undefined, the validity of the measures unknown, and the reasoning still developed (p. 10). Gilligan (1977) has noted that the sample originally studied was all male. She cites studies to show that women have a tendency to use Stage 3 as their dominant mode of moral reasoning. Gilligan thinks apparent sex differences may reflect the current formulation of higher stages more than they would the failure to develop to these stages. Stress on abstract principles of justice may ignore personal and interpersonal issues, such as the conflict between caring for others and taking responsibility for one's own actions. Enright, Franklin, and Manheim (1980) suggest that throughout life people are faced with distributive justice--giving or receiving allowances, giving to charities and supporting others--more than with saving life through theft of a high-priced drug.

Sawin and Parke (1980), investigating empathy and fear as mediators of resistance to deviation in children, found a class of socialization--other-oriented induction--to be important in behavior control. The focus in this case is the implication of a child's behavior for other persons, which relies on empathy and role-taking processes for control. Induction relies on the child's cognitive ability to comprehend the interpersonal and situational advantages in controlling behavior for socialization, not just power assertion or love withdrawal.

Walker (1980) examined cognitive and perspective-taking prerequisites for moral development in children and is in agreement with Kohlberg's (1976) notion that they are necessary but not sufficient conditions for moral reasoning development. An assessment was made of the stage of development among fourth- through seventh-grade children, who were then exposed to moral Stage 3 reasoning in a brief role-playing situation. The results indicated that only those children who had attained the prerequisites of beginning formal operations (earlier proposed by Inhelder and Piaget--the reversal of relationships with inversion, that is, the negation of class) and perspective-taking made transitions to Stage 3.

It appears that moral development rests in part on each of the theories; although the development of morality comprises more than parental proscriptions (Kohlberg), identification with parent figures is significant in early development (Freud), as models and imitation of others are later (Bandura). In general the development of morality seems to follow sequences that parallel the cognitive groups (Piaget); nevertheless, the rate and ordering seem individually variant; unitary consciences do not exist; morality and prosocial behavior have strong situational components--somewhat dependent on age, intelligence, and sex, but more on group ideals and motivational factors. Learning enters into the moral development of children, but the method by which this is accomplished is complicated and not completely understood.

SUMMARY

The development of language in middle and later childhood enables children to interact with others and in time understand their perspective; the ability to communicate is most important to the development of cognition.

Piaget has offered a very complete description of the stages and structure of cognitive development. The development of the cognitive structure that accounts for growth involves the acquisition of schema through assimilation, accommodation, and equilibration. Cognitive development proceeds invariantly through major stages for middle and later childhood: pre-operational (ages 2 through 7), concrete operations (ages 7 through 11), and formal operational (ages 11 through 15). According to Bruner, cognitive growth is affected by (1) the external environment, (2) the child's acquisition of symbolic modes for representing, and (3) the child's ability to transform the world through manipulation of his or her environment. His stages in development are the enactive, the iconic, the symbolic, and the logical. Another theorist, Flavell, believes invariance in the stages of development represents a more accurate characterization of mental development than variance. He concludes: (1) stages are useful in a general approach but overlap, (2) sequential routes to maturity vary considerably among individuals, and (3) not all major cognitive acquisitions come from equilibration.

Significant cognitive changes take place with age. These are gradual in nature and are closely related to maturation and learning. There is much overlapping of the different age groups. A wide variety of studies seem to lead to the following conclusions:

1. There is evidence for the sequential, involving the order of time concepts.

2. The acquisition of conservation skills in the concrete operational stage of Piaget does not always occur in invariant sequence, and may in some instances occur earlier than Piaget found.

3. Piaget has overemphasized the motor aspect of learning and underemphasized the role of perception in cognitive development.

4. Faulty concepts, like incorrect concepts, develop out of the quality and opportunity of one's experiences.

5. A general pattern of development may be observed, especially in the development of concepts of causality.

6. Young children appear to have a preferred response characterized by a cognitive style. This is less pronounced in older children, as they seem to make greater use of a variety of responses.

Three factors in the cognitive domain affect learning efficiency at school--intelligence, special abilities, and previous experiences related to the learning tasks. Much controversy continues to exist about the nature and measurement of intelligence. The idea that intelligence as measured by tests was fixed and not subject to improvement prevailed during the early period of intelligence testing, although results from later studies disproved such a notion. Additional research revealed that although close genetic relationships tend to have somewhat similar patterns of mental growth, intelligence test scores are affected by environmental conditions. Longitudinal data collected from single individuals over a number of years show that there is a gradual and continual growth in mental abilities, with the various abilities maturing at different periods. However, the influences of an adverse environment during childhood cannot be completely overcome at a later stage.

Long-term predictions of intelligence test scores based on scores obtained during the preschool years are hazardous. Developmental curves for the different mental abilities show considerable variation, with leveling off of ability on most tests during the late teens or early 20s. However, certain longitudinal studies indicate an increase in information and vocabulary, with general abilities plotted on a curve plateauing in situations where environmental and occupational motivation is high and the use of divergence and convergence is required.

Some of the major influences affecting intellectual development are (1) an impoverished environment, (2) parent-child relationship, (3) lack of stimulation and motivation, (4) birth order, (5) endowment from heredity, (6) chronic or severe illness, and (7) sex. Most studies show that girls are slightly superior to boys in language development and the finer motor skills during the early years, with boys being ahead in spatial and mathematical abilities at adolescence.

School competencies were related including such informational processing areas as metacognition, memory strategies, and computer technology. Also discussed were children with special needs such as the learning disabled and handicapped.

Moral reasoning and development in middle and later childhood were discussed in terms of theories of Piaget, Kohlberg, and Social Learning Theory prevalent in the classic work of Hartshorne and May.

KEY WORDS

cognitive

conjunctive

disjunctive

relational

symbolic language

cognitive structure

reversibility

schemata

schema

assimilation

accommodation

contextual intelligence

spatial orientation

egocentricism

centration

conservation

seriation

classification

causality

iconic stage

mental age

intelligence

crystallized abilities

fluid abilities

experiential intelligence

attention span

impoverishment

deprivation

motivation

range of reaction

test bias

cognitive style

creativity

information processing

cooperative learning

metacognition

learning disabilities

mainstreaming

autonomous morality

REFERENCES

Ashton, P.T. Cross-cultural Piaget research: An experimental perspective. *Harvard Educational Review*, 1975, *45*:475-506.

Ausubel, D.P. *The Psychology of Meaningful Verbal Learning*. New York: Grune and Stratton, 1963, p. 76.

______. Relationship between shame and guilt in the socializing process. *Psychological Review*, 1955, *62*:378-390.

Babbs, P., and Moe, A. Metacognition: A key for independent learning from text. *The Reading Teacher*, 1983, *36*:422-426

Bayley, N. Consistence and variability in the growth of intelligence from birth to eighteen years. *Journal of Genetic Psychology*, 1949, *75*:165-196.

______. Development of mental abilities. In P. Mussen (ed.), *Carmichael's Manual of Child Psychology*. New York: Wiley, 1970, pp. 1163-1209.

Belmont, L., and Marolla, F.A. Birth order, family size, and intelligence. *Science*, 1973, *182*:1096-1101.

Bloom, B.S. *Human Characteristics and School Learning*. New York: McGraw-Hill, 1976.

______. *Stability and Change in Human Characteristics*. New York: Wiley, 1964.

Boden, M.A. *Jean Piaget*. New York: Viking, 1980.

Bond, E.A. *Tenth Grade Abilities and Achievements*. New York: Teachers College, Columbia University Press, 1940.

Boonsong, S. The development of conservation of mass, weight, and volume in Thai children. Unpublished Master's Thesis, College of Education, Bangkok, Thailand, 1968.

Bradway, K.S., and Thompson, C.W. Intelligence at adulthood: A twenty-five year follow-up. *Journal of Educational Psychology*, 1963, *53*:1-14.

Brainard, C.J. Stage, structure, and developmental theory. In G. Steiner (ed.), *The Psychology of the Twentieth Century*. Munich: Kindler, 1985.

______. *Piaget's Theory of Intelligence*. Englewood Cliffs, NJ: Prentice-Hall, 1978.

Branscomb, L., et al., *A Nation Prepared*. New York: Carnegie Forum on Education and the Economy, 1986.

Brown, A.L., Bransford, J.D., Ferrara, R.A., and Campione, J.C. Learning remembering and understanding. In P.H. Mussen (ed.), *Handbook of Child Psychology*, 4th ed., Vol. 3, New York: Wiley, pp. 77-166.

Bruner, J.S. Models of the learner. *Educational Researcher*, 1985, *14*:5-8.

_____. Early social interaction and language acquisition. In H.R. Schaffer (ed.), *Studies in Mother-Infant Interaction*. London: Academic Press, 1977.

_____. *Precursers of Cognitive Growth: Infancy*. Worchester, Mass.: Clark University Press, 1968.

Bruner, J.S., Goodnow, S.J., and Austin, G.A. *A Study of Thinking*. New York: Wiley, 1956.

Bruner, J.S., et al. Basic processes in children. *Monographs of SRCD*, 1963, *28*.

Burton, R.V. Honesty and dishonesty. In T. Lickons (ed.), *Moral Development and Behavior: Theory, Research and Social Issues*. New York: Holt, Rinehart and Winston, 1976.

Carey, S. Are children fundamentally different kinds of thinkers and learners than adults? In S.F. Chapman, J.W. Segal, and R. Glaser (eds.), *Thinking and Learning Skills*, vol. 2. Hillsdale, NJ: Erlbaum, 1985.

Case, R. A developmentally based theory and technology of instruction. *Review of Educational Research*, 1978, *48*:439-463.

Cattell, R.B. *Abilities: Their Structure, Growth, and Action*. Boston: Houghton Mifflin, 1971.

Chance, P. Race and IQ: A family affair? *Psychology Today*, 1975, *8*(8):40.

Circielli, V.G. Form of relationship between creativity, I.Q., and academic achievement. *Journal of Educational Psychology*, 1965, *56*:303-309.

Cohen, A.D. The use of verbal and imagery mnemonics in second language vocabulary learning. *Studies in Second Language Acquisition*, 1987, *9*:43-61.

Cole, M., Gay, J., Slick, J., and Sharp. D. *Cultural Concept of Learning and Thinking*. New York: Basic Books, 1971.

Crandall, V.R., Dewey, R., Katkovsky, W., and Preston, A. Parents' attitudes and behaviors and grade-school children's academic achievements. *Journal of Genetic Psychology*, 1964, *104*:53-56.

Cumeo, D.O. A general strategy for quantity judgments: The height and width rule. *Child Development*, 1980, *51*:299-301.

Dagenais, Y. Analyse de la coherence operatoire entre les groupements d'additional des classes, de multiplicatioin des classes d'addition des relations asymetriques. Unpublished dissertation, Universite de Montreal, 1973.

Dale, P.S. *Language Development: Structure and Function*. Hindsale, Ill.: Dryden Press, 1972.

Datta, L., and Parlogg, M.B. On the relevance of autonomy: Parent-child relationships and early scientific creativity. Paper read at the Seventy-Fifth Annual Convention of the American Psychological Association, 1967.

Davis, G., and Houtman, S.E. *Thinking Creatively: A Guide to Training Imagination*. Madison: Wisconsin Research and Development Center for Cognition Learning, 1968.

DeLemos, M.M. The developments of conservation in aboriginal children. *International Journal of Psychology*, 1969, *4*:255-269.

Dennis, W., as quoted in Jack Fincher (ed.), *Human Intelligence*. New York: Putnam, 1976.

Dobzhansky, T. *Genetic Diversity and Human Equality*. New York: Basic Books, 1973.

Duckworth, E. Either we're too early and they can't learn it or we're too late and they know it already; The dilemma of "applying Piaget." *Harvard Educational Review*, 1979, *49*(3).

Eagle, N. The stability of Lorge-Thorndike I.Q. scores between grades three and four and grade eight. *Journal of Educational Research*, 1966, *60*:164-165.

Elkind, D. Children's discovery of the conservation of mass, weight, and volume: Piaget replication study II. *Journal of Genetic Psychology*, 1961, *98*:219-227.

Enright, R.D., Franklin, C.C., and Manheim, L.A. Children's distributive justice reasoning: A standardized and objective scale. *Developmental Psychology*, 1980, *16*(3):193-202.

Erlenmeyer-Kimling, L., and Jarvik, L.F. Genetics and intelligence: A review. *Science*, 1963, *142*:1477-1479.

Eyferth, K. Leistungen verschiedener Gruppen Von Besatzung shindern in Hamburg Wecksler intelligence test fur kinder (HAWIK). Archiv fur die gesamte Psychologie, 1961, *113*:222-241.

Feldman, C.F., and Toulmin, S. Logic and theory of mind: Formal, pragmatic and empirical considerations in a science of cognitive development. In *Nebraska Symposium on Motivation*, vol. 23. Lincoln: University of Nebraska Press, 1975.

Feuerstein, R., Rand, Y., Hoffman, M.B., and Miller, R. *Instrumental Enrichment*. Baltimore: University Park Press, 1980.

Flavell, J.H. *Cognitive Development*, 2nd ed. Englewood Cliffs, NJ: Prentice-Hall, 1985.

_____. Structures, stages and sequences in cognitive development. In W.A. Collins (ed.), *Minnesota Symposia on Child Psychology*, vol. 15, ch. 2, 1-28. Hillsdale, NJ: Lawrence Erlbaum Associates, 1982.

_____. *Cognitive Development*. Englewood Cliffs, NJ: Prentice-Hall, 1977.

_____. *The Development of Psychology of Jean Piaget*. New York: Van Nostrand Reinhold, 1963.

Freeburg, N.E., and Payne, D.T. Parental influence on cognitive development in early childhood. *Child Development*, 1967, *38*:65-87.

Furth, H.B. Linguistic deficiency and thinking: Research with deaf subjects 1964-1969. *Psychological Bulletin*, 1971, *76*:58-72.

Gakhar, S., and Joshi, J.N. Creativity within a framework of personalogical context. *Psychology Studies*, 1980, *25*:48-57.

Gardner, H. *Frames of Mind*. New York: Basic Books, 1983.

Gelman, R. The developmental perspective on the problem of knowledge acquisition: A discussion. In S.F. Chapman, J.W. Segal, and R. Glaser (eds.), *Thinking and Learning Skills*, vol. 2. Hillsdale, NJ: Erlbaum, 1985.

Gentile, L., and McMillan, M. Stress and reading difficulties: Teaching students self-regulating skills. *The Reading Teacher*, 1987, *41*:178-178.

Gilligan, C. In a different voice: Women's conception of the self and morality. *Harvard Educational Review*, 1977, *49*:481-517.

Ginsberg, H. *The Myth of the Deprived Child*. Englewood Cliffs, NJ: Prentice-Hall, 1972.

Goldstcin, D., and Myer, B. Cognitive lag and group differences in intelligence. *Child Study Journal*, 1980, *10*(2):120-131.

Goodenough, D.R., and Karp, S. Field dependence and intellectual functioning. *Journal of Abnormal and Social Psychology*, 1961, *63*:241-246.

Goodenough, F.L. *Mental Testing: Its History, Principles, and Applications*. New York: Rinehart, 1949.

Goodlad, J. *A Place Called School*. New York: McGraw-Hill, 1984.

Hartman, F.R. Single and multiple channel communication: A review of research and a proposed model. *A-V Communications Review*, November 1961, *9*:235-262.

Hartshorne, H., and May, M.A. *Studies in the Nature of Character*, vol. 1: *Studies in Deceit*. New York: Macmillan, 1928.

Heber, R. Conversation with Director Heber of the Milwaukee Project on the completion of ten year follow-up study by F. R. Jones, June 1977.

Hersh, R., Paolitto, D., and Reimer, J. *Promoting Moral Growth*. New York: Longman, 1979.

Hess, R.D. Maternal influences upon early learning: The cognitive environments of urban preschool children. In R.D. Hess and R.M. Bear (eds.), *Early Education*. Chicago: Aldine, 1968.

Hirsch, E.D. *Cultural Literacy*. New York: Houghton Mifflin, 1987.

Hogan, R., and Schroeder, D. Seven biases on psychology. *Psychology Today*, July 1981, *15*(7).

Hsiu-Zu Ho, Foch, T.T., and Plomin, R. Developmental stability of the relative influence of gene and environment on specific cognitive abilities during childhood. *Developmental Psychology*, 1980, *16*(4):340-346.

Hunt, J.M. Has compensatory education failed? Has it been attempted? *Harvard Educational Review*, 1969, *39*:278-300.

_____. Heredity, environment, and class or ethnic differences. Paper presented to the 1972 Invitational Conference on Testing Problems, sponsored by the Educational Testing Service, Princeton, NJ, 1972.

Hyde, D.M. An investigation of Piaget's theories of development of number. Unpublished doctoral dissertation, University of London, 1959.

Jensen, A.R. *Educability and Group Differences*. New York: Harper & Row, 1973.

_____. How much can we boost IQ and scholastic achievement? *Harvard Educational Review*, 1969, *39*:1-123.

Jensen, A.R., and Inouye, A.R. Level I and Level II abilities of Asian, white and black children. U.S. Department of Health, Education, and Welfare, National Institute for Education, Washington, D.C., 1979.

Johnson, D.W., and Johnson, R.T. *Learning Together and Alone: Cooperative, Conjunctive, and Individualistic Learning*. Englewood Cliffs, NJ: Prentice-Hall, 1987.

Jones, H.E. The environment and mental development. In L. Carmichael (ed.), *Manual of Child Development*, 2nd ed. New York: Wiley, 1954.

Kagan, J., and Kogan, N. Individual variation in cognitive processes. In P. Mussen (ed.), *Carmichael's Manual of Child Psychology*. New York: Wiley, 1970, pp. 132-137.

Kaluger, G., and Heil, C.L. Basic symmetry and balance: Their relationship to perceptual-motor development. *Progressive Physical Therapy*, 1970, *1*:132-137.

Kirsch, I., and Jungeblut, A. *Literacy: Profiles of America's Young Adults*. Princeton, NJ: National Assessment of Educational Progress, 1986.

Klaus, R.A., and Gray, S.W. The early training project for disadvantaged children: A report after five years. *Monographs of the Society for Research in Child Development*, 1968, *33*(4).

Klausmeier, H.J. *Learning and Human Abilities: Educational Psychology*, 4th ed. New York: Harper & Row, 1975, pp. 138-159.

Kofsky, E. A scalogram study of classificatory development. *Child Development*, 1966, *37*:191-204.

Kohlberg, L. Stage and sequence: The cognitive-developmental approach to socialization. In D.A. Golsin (ed.), *Handbook of Socialization Theory and Research*. New York: Rand McNally, 1969.

_____. Moral stages and moralization: The cognitive-developmental approach. In T. Lickons (ed.), *Moral Development and Behavior: Theory, Research, and Social Issues*. New York: Holt, Rinehart and Winston, 1976.

_____. *The Philosophy of Moral Development*. New York: Harper & Row, 1981.

Kohlberg, L., and Mayer, R. Development as the aim of education. *Harvard Educational Review*, 1972, *42*:449-496.

Larson, C., and Dansereau, D. Cooperative learning in dyads. *Journal of Reading*, 1986, *29*:516-520.

Leal, L., Crays, N., and Moetz, B. Training children to use a self-monitoring study strategy in preparation for recall: Maintenance and generalization effects. *Child Development*, 1985, *56*:643-653.

Learning To Be Literate. Princeton, NJ: National Assessment of Educational Progress and the Educational Testing Service, 1987.

Lehman, H.C. Young thinkers and memorable creative achievements. *Journal of Genetic Psychology*, 1964, *105*:237-255.

Lesser, G.S., Fifer, G., and Clark, D.H. Mental abilities of children from different social class and cultural groups. Monographs of the Society of Research in Child Development, 1965, *30*(4): Whole No. 102.

Levin, J.R., Morrison, C.R., and McGivern, J.E. Mnemonic facilitation of text-embedded science facts. *American Educational Research Journal*, 1986, *23*:489-506.

Libert, R., Poulos, R., and Strauss, G. *Developmental Psychology*. Englewood Cliffs, NJ: Prentice-Hall, 1974.

Libsen, L.S., and Golbeck, S.L. Sex differences in performance on Piagetian spatial tools: Differences in competence or performance? *Child Development*, 1980, *51*:594-597.

Linzey, G., Hall, C., and Thompson, R. *Psychology*. New York: Worth, 1975.

Loehlin, J.C., Lindzey, G., and Spuhler, J.N. *Race Differences in Intelligence*. San Francisco: Freeman, 1975.

Lynn, R. The intelligence of the Japanese. *Bulletin of the British Psychological Society*, 1977, *30*:69-72.

Maccoby, E.E., and Jacklin, C.N. What we know and don't know about sex differences. *Psychology Today*, December 1974: 109-112.

McCandless, B.R., and Trotter, R.J. *Children: Behavior and Development*. New York: Holt, Rinehart and Winston, 1977.

McDaniel, M.A., Pressley, M., and Dunay, P.K. Long-term effect of vocabulary after keyword and context learning. *Journal of Educational Psychology*, 1987, *79*:87-89.

McDonald, F.J. *Educational Psychology*, 2nd ed. Belmont, CA: Wadsworth, 1965.

Meyer, W.J., and Bendig, A.W. A longitudinal study of the primary mental abilities tests. *Journal of Educational Psychology*, 1961, *52*:223-225.

Miklos, J. A look at reading achievement in the United States. *Journal of Reading*, 1982, *25*(8):760-762.

Mischel, W., and Mischel, H.N. A cognitive learning approach to morality and self-regulation. In T. Lickons (ed.), *Moral Development and Behavior: Theory, Research, and Social Issues*. New York: Holt, Rinehart and Winston, 1976.

Morgan, R., and Culver, V. Locus of control and reading achievement: Application for the classroom. *Journal of Reading*, February 1978, *21*:403-408.

Palinscar, A.S., and Brown, A.L. Reciprocal teaching of comprehension-fostering and comprehension-monitoring devices. *Cognition and Instruction*, 1984, *1*:117-175.

Peters, E.E., and Levin, J.R. Effects of mnemonic imagery strategy on good and poor readers' prose recall. *Reading Research Quarterly*, 1986, *21*:179-192.

Phillips, D.C., and Kelly, M.D. Hierarchial theories of development. *Harvard Educational Review*, 1975, *45*(3):351-375.

Phillips, J.L. *The Origins of Intellect: Piaget's Theory*. San Francisco: Freeman, 1969.

Piaget, J. *The Moral Judgment of the Child*. New York: Free Press, 1965.

_____. *The Origins of Intelligence in Children*. New York: International Universities Press, 1952.

_____. Piaget's theory. In P.H. Mussen (ed.), *Carmichael's Manual of Child Psychology*, vol. 1. New York: Wiley, 1970.

_____. *The Psychology of Intelligence*. Patterson, NJ: Littlefield, Adams, 1963.

Piaget, J., and Inhelder. *The Psychology of the Child*. New York: Basic Books, 1969.

Pulaski, M.A.S. *Understanding Piaget: An Introduction to Children's Cognitive Development*. New York: Harper & Row, 1971.

Raper, C.C. The relationship of socioeconomic status, sex and ability grouping to learning styles among eighth grade students. Unpublished master's thesis, Old Dominion University, Norfolk, Virginia, 1973.

Rasinski, T., and Nathenson-Mejia, S. Learning to read, learning community: Consideration of the social contexts for literacy instruction. *The Reading Teacher*, 1987, *41*:260-265.

The Reading Report Card: Progress Toward Excellence in Our Schools: Trends in Reading Instruction Over Four National Assessments, 1971-1984. Princeton, NJ: National Assessment of Educational Progress and Educational Testing Service, 1985.

Reali, N., and Hall, V. Effects of success and failure on the reflective and impulsive child. *Developmental Psychology*, 1970, *3*:392-402.

Richardson, J., and Morgan, R. *Reading to Learn in the Content Areas*. Belmont, CA: Wadsworth, 1990.

Riessman, F. Styles of learning. *NEA Journal*, 1966, *55*:15-17.

Robinson, J., and Gray, J. Cognitive styles as a variable in school learning. *Journal of Educational Psychology*, 1974, *66*(5):793-799.

Rosenkoetter, L.I. Resistance to temptation: Inhibitors and disinhibitors effects on models. *Developmental Psychology*, 1973, *8*:80-84.

Sandoval, J., and Mulle, M.P.W. Accuracy of judgment of WISC-R item difficulties for minority groups. *Journal of Consulting and Clinical Psychology*, 1980, *48*(2):249-253.

Sawin, D.B., and Parke, R.D. Empathy and fear as mediators of resistance to deviation in children. *Merrill-Palmer Quarterly*, 1980, *26*(2).

Scandura, J.M., and Scandura, A.B. *Structural Learning and Concrete Operations*. New York: Praeger, 1980.

Scarr, S. An author's frame of mind. *New Ideas in Psychology*, 1985, *31*:95-100.

Sigler, E., Abelson, W.D., and Seitz, V. Motivational factors in the performance of economically disadvantaged children on the Peabody picture vocabulary test. *Child Development*, 1973, *43*:294-303.

Simberg, A.L. Obstacles to creative thinking. In C.A. Davis and J.A. Scott (eds.), *Training Creative Thinking*. New York: Holt, Rinehart and Winston, 1971, pp. 119-135.

Skeels, M.H. Adult status of children with contrasting early life experience: A follow-up study. *Monographs of the Society for Research in Child Development*, 1966, *31*.

_____. Children with inferior social histories: Their mental development in foster homes. *Psychological Bulletin*, 1941, *38*:594.

Skodak, M. *Children in Foster Homes*. University of Iowa Studies of Child Welfare, 1939.

Smedslund, J. Concrete reasoning: A study of intellectual development. *Monographs of the Society for Research in Child Development*, 1964, *29*.

Stephenson, B.L., and Gay, W.O. Psycholinguistic abilities of black and white children from four SES levels. *Exceptional Children*, May 1972, *38*:705-709.

Sternberg, R.J. *Beyond IQ: A Triarchic Theory of Human Intelligence*. New York: Cambridge University Press, 1985.

_____. A contextualist view of the nature of intelligence. *International Journal of Psychology*, 1984, *19*:307-334.

Sternberg, R.J., and Powell, J.S. The development of intelligence. In P.H. Mussen (ed.), *Handbook of Child Psychology*, 4th ed., vol. 3: *Cognitive Development* (J.H. Flavell & E.M. Markman, eds.), New York: John Wiley, 1983, pp. 341-419.

Terman, L.M. *Genetic Studies of Genius*. Stanford, CA: Stanford University Press, 1925.

Torrance, E.P. *Rewarding Creative Behavior*. Englewood Cliffs, NJ: Prentice-Hall, 1965.

Trowbridge, N., and Charles, C. Creativity in art students. *Journal of Genetic Psychology*, 1966, *109*:281-289.

Uka, N. Sequence in the development of time concept in children of elementary school age. Ph.D. dissertation, University of California, 1956.

Verplank, W.S. *A Glossary of Some Terms Used in the Objective Science of Behavior*. Washington, DC: American Psychological Association, 1957.

Vygotsky, L.S. *Thought and Language*. Translated and revised by A. Kozulin. Cambridge, MA: MIT Press, 1986.

_____. *Mind in Society*. Cambridge: Harvard University Press, 1978.

_____. *Thought and Language*. New York: Wiley, 1962.

Wadsworth, B.J. *Piaget's Theory of Cognitive Development*. New York: McKay, 1979, pp. 10-112.

Walters, R., Leat, M., and Mezei, L. Inhibition and disinhibition of responses through empathatic learning. *Canadian Journal of Psychology*, 1963, *17*:235-243.

Wechsler, D. *The Measurement of Adult Intelligence*. Baltimore: Williman & Wilkins, 1960.

_____. *Wechsler Adult Intelligence Scale*. New York: Psychological Corporation, 1981.

Weikert, D.P., Rogers, L., and Adcock, C. The cognitive oriented curriculum. ERIC-NAEYE. *Publications in Early Childhood Education*. Urbana, ILL.: University of Illinois, 1971.

Weinstein, C.E. Fostering learning autonomy through the use of learning strategies. *Journal of Reading*, 1987, *30*:590-595.

Wheeler, L.R. The intelligence of East Tennessee mountain children. *Journal of Educational Psychology*, 1932, *23*:351-370.

Wilkin, H., Moore, C., Goodenough, D., and Cox, P. Field-dependent and field-independent cognitive styles and their educational implications. *Review of Educational Research*, Winter 1977a, *47*(2):1-64.

Wilkin, H., Moore, C., Oltman, P., Goodenough, D., Friedman, F., Owen, D., and Raskin, E. Role of field-dependent and field-independent cognitive styles in academic evolution: A longitudinal study. *Journal of Educational Psychology*, June 1977b, *69*(3):197-211.

Willerman, L., Naylor, A.F., and Myrianthopoulos, N.C. Intellectual development of children from interracial matings. *Science*, 1970, *170*:1329-1331.

Wohlwill, J., and Lowe, R. Experimental analysis of the development of conservation of number. *Child Development*, 1962, *33*:153-168.

Zajonc, R.B., and Markus, G.B. Birth order and intellectual development. *Psychological Review*, 1975, *82*:74-88.

PART IV

ADOLESCENCE: THRESHOLD OF ADULTHOOD TO MATURITY

Chapter 9

ADOLESCENCE: PHYSICAL AND INTELLECTUAL DEVELOPMENT

- ***Theories of Adolescence***
  - Freud - Psychoanalytic
    - Defense mechanisms
    - Stages
  - Erikson - Psychosocial
  - Piaget - Cognitive
  - Bandura - Social learning
  - Maslow - Humanistic
  - Havighurst - Cultural determinism
- ***The Adolescent Cohort***
  - Numbers
  - Cohesive forces
- ***Nutrition Needs of Adolescents***
  - Eating habits
  - Food requirements
- ***Health and Illness***
  - Physical changes
  - Contagious diseases
  - Deaths among adolescents
- ***Physical Development***
  - Sexual maturity
  - Developmental changes
  - Body shape and appearance
  - Anorexia and bulimia
  - Physical fitness
- ***Cognitive Development***
  - Piaget's theory
  - Informational processing - Sternberg

ADOLESCENCE--THEORETICAL ASPECTS, PHYSICAL AND INTELLECTUAL DEVELOPMENT

Adolescence is the period between childhood and adulthood. The line of demarcation is clearly defined from the onset of puberty, the beginning of adolescence. The entry into young adulthood is not so clear, however. It is rather a fusion of similarities that characterize later adolescence and early adulthood. Karl Garrison (1965), a psychologist and writer for 50 years in the psychology of adolescence, suggested, "the beginning of adolescence is to a marked degree a physical and physiological phenomenon, whereas the end of adolescence is mainly emotional-social." More recently, Conger and Peterson (1984) have described it as "beginning in biology and ending in culture." Certainly the basic aspect of early adolescence is physical and its latter part is completed with an emphasis on emotional control and socialization. Entry into the adult world of work and responsibility awaits.

Some writers have suggested that adolescence is a period when boys and girls have one foot in childhood and one foot in adulthood. This is fairly descriptive, as parents often say their youngsters want the privileges of adulthood and the responsibilities of the child. Perhaps this more appropriately details early (12 to 14) rather than later adolescence (17 to 20). Obviously, there is some variation in the interpreting of privilege and responsibility between parents and daughters/sons. We speak of the "generation gap," which many believe is partly a communication problem, but at the same time is partly a group subculture gap.

The world today is a complex society, whereas in past times and in simple societies the periods of life were closer together. One hundred years ago puberty came later, at age 15 or 16. At its onset most children had internalized the work world of their parents and indeed had already been launched into it. In our complex world, where change is very rapid due mainly to technology, fewer experiences are commonly shared by adults and children. So much has changed between the time of the parents' generation and the child's generation, few things that the parents have experienced have been experienced by the children, and vice versa. Strom (1969) expressed it as shown in Figure 9.1.

Children today have partially caught up with parents via television, the increased use of technology in schools and the universal advent of the computer. Communication remains a crucial aspect in bridging moral, social, and cognitive differences.

Part of the development to maturity can be addressed by looking at the categories in which the early adolescent finds himself by most accounts immature. The areas in which the adolescent ages 11 to 21 develop are: social and emotional, ethical, heterosexual, cognitive. Some of the aspects are seen in the following categories.

From (early adolescence)	To (later adolescence)
Social and Emotional Maturation	
Impatience and struggling for superiority	Patience and feelings of adequacy
Parental regulation	Personal control
Uncertainty about oneself	Self-acceptance and sociability
Copying others	Independence and self-esteem
Growth in Heterosexuality	
Awareness of sexual changes	Acceptance of sex identity
Association with members of same sex	Association with and liking for peers of opposite sex
Varied relationship with many	Selection of a possible mate for life
Cognitive Maturation	
Search for universal principles and final answers	Explanation of facts/theories needed
Truth accepted on basis of authority	Demand for substantial evidence before acceptance
Multiple interests and concerns	Some real consistent concerns
Ethical conduct	
Motivation of conduct via pleasure, etc.	Behavior based upon realistic aspiration and conscience
Lack of interest in ethical principles	Interest in humanistic and ethical principles
Conduct based on reinforcement	Behavior controlled by morality/ideals

THEORIES OF ADOLESCENCE

Scientific theories are important in three ways: (1) they help us describe in logical terms observable events that occur in adolescence; (2) they help us explain events that occur in a reasonable manner; and (3) they help us predict events about adolescence. For example, a theory should include hypotheses about the differential roles of peers and parents in the

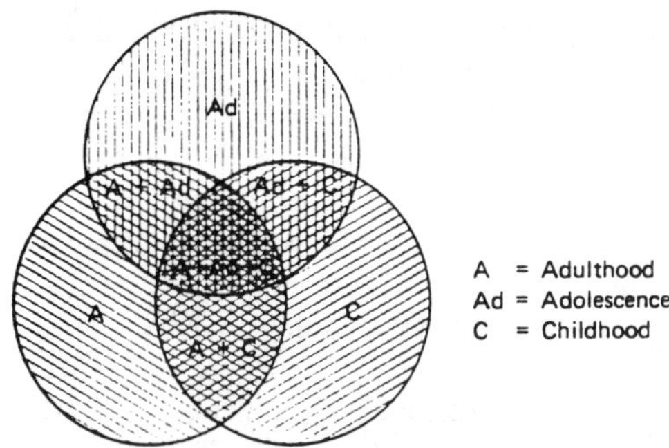

Figure 9.1 Life in a complex society--childhood, adolescence, adulthood. Adapted from R.D. Strom, *Psychology for the Classroom* (Englewood Cliffs, NJ: Prentice-Hall, Inc., 1969), p. 5.

development of youth. We will examine five theories: psychoanalytic (Freud), psychosocial (Erikson), cognitive (Piaget), social learning (Bandura), and humanistic (Maslow). The main framework of these theories has already been presented. Hence we will narrow their reference to the segment of life encompassing adolescence, which broadly covers the years from 11 to 21.

Psychoanalytic Theory

The focus of the psychoanalytic view begins with the later *latency* stage for the early adolescent. Earlier attention given to the genital area (phallic stage) is repressed, marking the onset of the latency stage. During this stage, the child concentrates on mastering the school and intellectual tasks fundamental for success in society. Much of the psychological energy is given to safe areas (group activities, games, school tasks), helping the child forget the difficult earlier period. At puberty's onset at 11 or 12, sexual interests are reawakened. Due to rapid physiological changes heralding puberty, adolescents often focus their thoughts on the body (principally the sex organs), the sensual, and the opposite sex. Freud believed that the first five years of life determined what the personality would be like during adolescence and in the adult years; i.e., the crucial stages are the oral, anal, and phallic (including the Oedipal and Electra complexes). When maladjustment occurs in youth, Freudians examine childhood experiences for the answers, for "as the twig is bent so grows the tree."

Adolescents are able to thwart strong impulses of the id by defense mechanisms such as *repression*, which provides a way for them to force tension-generating feelings out of the active mind into the subconscious. For sexual anxieties, *projection* is the usual method, putting the blame on a friend--"she's the one always thinking about sex, not me," although it may be very much on the person's mind. Young adolescents, when kidded about a girlfriend, may be embarrassed about it and vehemently deny it. This is *reaction formation*. Many youth use *sublimation* for anxieties. It is a sign of growing maturity, to make up for gaps in their lives (lack of money, status, dislike of school, a girlfriend, a nice family home or car, divorced parents). They may work hard at a job or on a project, study, or do volunteer work to compensate for these perceived shortcomings. They also use this escape to avoid thinking of sexual activities, masturbation, fantasies, etc. *Intellectualization* may be used. In such a case, the girl or boy re-channels worries into intellectual thought and terms. The coming fear of an operation, for instance, is handled by structuring a scenario of what will happen and then thinking of the steps routinely and matter-of-factly.

It was Freud's idea that all behavior, including personality aspects, are given impetus through unconscious drives. Sex as the unconscious determiner of behavior, albeit compelling, leaves something to be desired. Impressed by the views of Darwin, Bergson, Comte and others, Freud seems to have been mesmerized by emergent and species evolution, perhaps forgetting that human beings, like animals, do not live in a vacuum. Humans are nurtured in an environment both social and situational and it is the interaction of the physical and environmental that shapes the individual. We must look hard to find connections of early stages of Freud's theory and adolescent life. Certainly sex in its wider context--giving birth, recreational sex, the sensual aspects of drink, food, and creature comforts--covers many areas of life. Even so, a purely sexually oriented theory may fail to cover adequately adolescent life. Psychoanalytic derivatives--Oedipus complexes, castration, penis envy--are too disparate to qualify for discrete and easy scientific analysis.

Psychosocial Theory

Erikson is of the psychosexual persuasion but departs from Freud in several important ways. He thought that: (1) the childhood years were important in that he described adolescence as a time where the personality may be modified or changed; (2) the psychosexual stage, though very important, should not be given the dominant role in development; (3) cultural and social experiences play the major role in psychosocial theory; (4) ego processes are not totally controlled by the unconscious as in psychoanalytic theory; (5) adolescents are able to cope with the conflict between personality structures; and (6) identity formation characterizes adolescence with other developmental stages to follow--young adult to old age. Freud's stages abruptly end with the genital, which lasts until old age.

The stage of puberty heralds the onset of adolescence, paralleling the end of Erikson's fourth stage, initiative versus inferiority. This period parallels the elementary school period of six to twelve. The crucial aspect of this stage is competency, mainly focusing on school work and to some degree motor skills and coordination. If the child is not successful in school, he or she is going to feel inferior. The school building, peers, and family are constant reminders of this failure. The question then becomes what sort of compensation, what sort of defense mechanisms will be used to ease the pain of the suffering ego. Following this stage and during early adolescence the development of identity involves a number of issues that may be problematic. Erikson calls this stage *identity* versus *identity confusion* and sees this conflict as the social crisis or issue to be resolved. Although beginning in early adolescence, such a conflict may still be unresolved in the extended adolescent period (21 to 27). According to Erikson, the various developmental problems for the 12- to 15-year-old involve to some degree the following:

Early Adolescence

- Temporal perspective vs. time confusion
- Self-certainty vs. self-consciousness
- Role experimentation vs. role fixation
- Apprenticeship vs. work paralysis
- Identity vs. identity confusion
- Sexual polarization vs. bisexual confusion
- Leader and followership vs. authority confusion
- Ideological commitment vs. confusion of values

As adolescence continues by age 15 or 16, increasingly the girl or boy "tries on many hats," that is, experiments with role playing. They may commit themselves to a political group and submerge their identity in it, or become religiously oriented via conversion. These commitments may be a way to postpone or serve as a moratorium temporizing the question of identity. Even the "puppy love" or "being love" may be a reflection of or the shaping of identity. So the boy says to the girl, "Tell me what I can be," or the girl says to the boyfriend, "What do you think I could do?" This provides a mirror through which they can define themselves. This may be more important in early adolescence than the emotions that are generated or the physical or sexual feelings engendered.

Alternatively, youth at this period think time is forever and that they will "never get to be eighteen." They experiment briefly with new clothes or hairstyles or life views, only to have them swing radically in a different direction after a certain time. They often have a strong resolve to turn over a new leaf--"I'll get up early and cut the yard and trim the hedges as Mom and Daddy have insisted." After one attempt, however, they don't get up until 10 o'clock and are too sleepy to do chores. Or they may say, "I think I'll get a job at the record store." They get the job and three weeks later they either quit or are fired. When asked about it, "Oh! It wasn't what I thought it would be." They decide to run for a class office and then do nothing, ignoring the need to win votes, and ultimately are defeated. Having decided against leadership in this manner, they decide to be a follower. Logan Smith, writing in *Afterthoughts*, characterized this period when he said, "Don't laugh at a youth for his affectations; he is only trying on one face after another to find a face of his own."

The task or social competence to be learned in later adolescence has to do with intimacy and isolation. Later adolescence, principally those years 17 to 20, may be extended. Some writers speak of "extended adolescence," referring to those who in Erikson's terms have failed to come to grips with the work world and have not yet decided on an ethical or value system. They may be 26 or 27 years old, but have not transited to the adult world completely.

Many adolescents achieve a sense of identity in early adolescence and thereby escape from emotional upheavals. Their identity means they have found for themselves a meaning to life and see a continuity for "me" as an individual in the future. Intimacy often develops following identity, where adolescents find the capacity to commit to another person or others and develop the ability to continue the relationship even when it is difficult to do. Those with weak or diffused egos, because of uncertainty about self, cannot form close ties in relationships. Close relationships between boys and girls beginning in puberty are often not truly intimate but serve as a sounding board on what they think or how they feel. Such relationships give adolescents time to learn by interacting and sharing experiences with their friends. In middle adolescence (14 to 16) the individual relationships serve the purpose of providing the individual resolve. In later adolescence they help integrate the sexual function. This helps one young person unite with another. If adolescents lack an adequate view of self, they may isolate themselves from others by keeping their relationships on a formal basis. The struggle with sexual feelings may be experienced. As a result peers become very important for emotional rapport and support. The establishment of intimacy does not usually lead at this time to the sexual act, although expressions of considerable affection take place, such as pats on the back, hugging, etc. Most adolescents do not want sex completed, for they do not want to give up their independence or sense of idealism. The pressure of sexual desire is usually handled by most boys (70 percent had had sex by age 15 in the late 1970s) through masturbation and heavy petting and to a lesser degree by girls (45 percent had had sex by age 15 in the late 1970s [Dreyer, 1982]). By 20 (Waechter et al., 1985), 85 percent of the males and 60 percent of the females have engaged in masturbation. Fantasies and nocturnal dreams (wet dreams) also serve to reduce some tensions by both boys and girls, though fewer girls are involved. Sexual promiscuity, when it occurs, is usually an attempt to find an infantile relation rather than a mature psychosocial one.

In American society less emphasis is placed upon developing intimacy, probably because it is felt this will happen anyway. The culture is concerned about masturbation (generally viewed as bad), intercourse, and heavy petting by teenagers. Western society is concerned about the world of work almost exclusively. Hence we often do not understand youth's concern with the psychosocial and intimacy. Those youths who are independent and industrious are considered successful by adults. Adults may not have observed that many young people are unhappy even when they have competencies and jobs.

Cognitive Theory (Piaget)

The pubescent period begins around the time the child completes the concrete operation stage and is entering formal operations. In the concrete operational stage, one does not take into account the relative nature of phenomena. Adolescents at this stage have to perceive objects and events that are going to be thought about; sometimes thoughts about events are confused with the events themselves. In the formal operational stage, one can handle all types of abstract problems and think logically. That is, one can propose hypotheses and test them. This does not mean all adolescents of age 15 or 16 have reached this stage of thought. At times they cannot discriminate between personal interest and that of others. This is a reappearance from the pre-operational stage or the development of a new egocentrism. Elkind (1978) believes that adolescents see themselves as actors and other members of a group as the audience, thereby displaying their egotism. Lacking any natural stage, adolescents will manufacture their own, through loud talk or noisiness. They get attention for a while, but sometimes such loudness only builds adult ire. This tendency to create imaginary crowds is a product of egocentrism. It goes away gradually but often not until the young adult stage is reached.

Social Learning Theory

These theorists cover a wide range of thought based on Skinner, Bandura, and Mischel. Adolescent behavior is regulated, they believe, by three basic facts: reinforcement, punishment, and imitation or modeling. Skinner believed that you need to look at the overt behavior of adolescents, not the feelings and thoughts, for the latter only obfuscate the understanding of behavior. He maintained that operant conditioning helps to improve teenage behavior. Behavior, according to Skinner, is determined by its consequences--behavior followed by a positive stimulus, a reinforcement, is likely to recur. On the other hand, behavior followed by a negative stimulus (punishment) is not as likely to reoccur. If you reward the behavior you wish to see and provide no reward or a negative stimulus for what you do not want, this affects the actions of the adolescent. Behavior modification is often used with youth who have problems.

Problem reduction involves substituting acceptable patterns of behavior for those that are unacceptable. Contingencies are established to ensure that the desirable responses will be given and learned. This is accomplished through reinforcement, i.e., rewarding the acceptable behavior. Behavior modification experts think that adolescent emotional problems occur because the wrong arrangement of contingencies are made, ones that inadvertently reinforce the unacceptable behaviors. For example, when delinquents continue their negative, antisocial behavior it may be because they are paid off for their acts--material rewards, monies, drugs, and possessions--or perhaps are even given accolades and attention from their peers.

Cognitive Social Learning Theory

Contrary to the external reinforcement idea argued for by Skinner as the cause of behavior, Bandura believes adolescent achievement is a function of reaction to self, the reactions of others, and external effect. Trying to improve a theme that the teacher has returned for rewriting may stimulate the student to criticize his or her effort and strive for improvement. This is an example of the interest effect. Reciprocal control is a factor in adolescent behavior--self-produced consequences and personal performance standards and using reinforcement to control someone else's behavior will not always work. Bandura stresses that we are not weathervanes that forever turn in the direction that the wind blows. A conversation like the one below illustrates this:

Jack: Let's double-date with Carol and Jim.
Annabel: I understand they do a lot of parking and necking!
Jack: That doesn't mean we have to do it.
Annabel: What? The parking or the necking?
Jack: Ugh! Necking.
Annabel: I'll think about it.
Jack: Good!

Annabel has learned that she can control Jack and she uses this tact to temporize his plea. Jack is thinking that he is making progress, but recognizes that if he presses too hard, he'll be turned down, period! Adolescents exchange this sort of repartee with parents and peers all the time. It is a process in which one person tries to control the other's behavior. This is why Bandura says the perfect society as envisioned in Skinner's book, *Walden Two*, could never work.

Modeling, often called vicarious learning, accounts for much of adolescent behavior. Young people constantly watch others: peers, parents, relatives, TV stars, teachers. The girl watching her mother get compliments from her father for good meals may well try the same strategy on her brother or boyfriend. These theorists argue that if you tried to learn to cook a meal or drive a car via reinforcement (response-stimulus), the meal would never get cooked and the person would never learn to drive. They say such observation of models creates future behavior. Known as the continuity theory of modeling, it involves attention (viewing carefully), retention (remembering what they see and internalizing it at least somewhat), and finally providing incentive conditions. Having observed the model and encoded what has transpired, the adolescent makes use of it when appropriate. However, the value or reward of using what he or she has learned vicariously may provide too little of an incentive or reward, and hence is not acted upon. The label "mechanical mirror theory" has been associated with social learning theory, suggesting that individuals do not control their destiny but are controlled through the behavior they mirror in the environment.

Humanism

A third force (Humanists) believes that the ultimate aspect of development comes from internal impetus. Humanists focus on subjective experience and how adolescents interpret the world. They emphasize the uniquely human aspects of living--creativity and intentionality. Control of conduct, emotions, and thoughts in the adolescent is managed by conscious mental processes. Carl Rogers sees the adolescent as having two selves: the ideal self and the real self. The greater the distance between the two, the more chance for maladjustment. If significant persons--parents, peers, teachers and kin--give unconditional positive regard, there will likely be few significant adjustment problems. If, however, there is a gulf between the perceived self and real experience with others, social interaction may be affected. Anxiety and accelerated use of defense mechanisms often produce hostility. A non-threatening relationship with a person who accepts everything the youth says can bring about a clear focus and make the adolescent feel better about himself. Such a relationship can be the start of ensuring effective counseling and help.

Abraham Maslow, another humanist, constructed a theory of hierarchy of needs (see Chapter 1). The first two tiers, physical and safety needs, are satisfied by parents; if not, higher-order needs are not met. Following the biological needs, three psychological needs remain if self-actualization is to be achieved. These needs are (1) love, (2) esteem, (3) aesthetic and cognitive self-actualization. The love need is fulfilled by interaction with friends and developing love connections. Esteem needs are best met through success in school and college, through learning a skill, pursuing a profession or vocation, and engaging in behavior that elicits praise. Aesthetic and cognitive needs are met by engaging in exercises of appreciation of art, music, poetry, and philosophy. There is a continued need to read, to want to know and understand, that gives opportunity to reflect on life's meaning.

Self-actualization involves three factors. The first is perceptual efficiency, which allows for the forecasting of the future, analyzing problems, and lessening the negative impact of wishes, fears, and doubts. Spontaneity is another attribute, for it produces creativity but not perfection. Another aspect of spontaneity is "burgeoning out" what is potential in the person through "peak experiences," where the person at that level has moments of great intensity combined with clear perception of some seminal truth. Finally, self-actualized persons are categorized as having accepted themselves and others. They are democratic in their relationships with others and they have deeper personal interaction than most people, although these relationships are very selective.

Maslow did not pick adolescents to typify self-actualized people. (Three prominent examples were Eleanor Roosevelt, Thomas Jefferson, and Abraham Lincoln.) And it is a view by many theorists who accept this paradigm for development that most adults, after having achieved economic, professional, and vocational success, cease to strive for further development. Adolescents by nature of their general status--in school or beginning on a job--have not reached the ultimate in esteem and status, hence may not achieve the highest aesthetic and cognitive levels. Certainly needs for love and esteem are foremost, and in late adolescence love concerns have been negotiated and the basics for esteem have been provided through successful schooling and training.

These theories speak to different aspects of adolescent development. All are important in understanding the nature of growth for youth. Students, like the authors, will undoubtedly be eclectic in their approach. Many students like and understand the humanistic approach of Maslow. Typically they are unsettled about Skinner's approach--behavior is extensively controlled by the environment--although they recognize the effect of conditioning in their lives. They believe their lives have been shaped by modeling and imitation and accept the broad outlines of Freud--the psychic anatomy (ego, id, super ego)--and Piaget's cognitive construct--schema, assimilation, accommodation, and equilibrium--as it relates to organization and adaptation.

Aside from the theories presented above, cultural determinism affects the nature of adolescent development. In fact, some theorists such as Havighurst (1972) believe it largely determines the quality of development. Certainly society conveys approval and disapproval on the physical attributes of youth, their social propriety and moral impeccability. If a boy is mature in body beyond his years he may get the status usually reserved for a young adult. If he fails on a test, he may suffer the unhappy consequences of ridicule. A girl, on the other hand, who has matured beyond her years and looks at 13 like a 16- or 17-year-old, frequently gets salacious attention and often the assumption that she is programmed for early problems. She may dislike her early development, but parents are likely to be more strict with her than with others less mature. Generally, society approves when social customs, mores, and expectancies are met and it gives disapproval when they are not met. Development tasks for the young, middle, and older adolescents are presented here:

Early Adolescence

- Accept body changes
- Assert one's independence of adults
- Achieve acceptance in one's peer group
- Develop new intellectual skills

Adolescence

- Accept and adjust to a maturing body

- Accept one's sexuality as male or female
- Learn one's sex role
- Achieve acceptance in one's peer group
- Achieve some degree of independence from parents
- Develop mature behavior patterns

Late Adolescence
- Achieve independence from parents
- Develop a system of values and philosophy of life
- Establish a close personal affectional relationship with another
- Choose a life vocation
- Develop the skills and competencies required for future success

The Adolescent Cohort

Most authorities agree that the beginning of adolescence is puberty. The end of adolescence, as we pointed out earlier, is much less clearly defined. The term *adolescence*, from the Latin verb *adolescare*, means "to grow up," or to grow to maturity. By all accounts it is a significant period in the life of an individual. The current number of youth between the ages of 14 and 21 is nearly 29 million (Bureau of Census, 1988). If you add the 12- and 13-year-olds, there are approximately 35 million young people. Marriages are coming at a later time for the typical male and female. Fewer foreclosures for females on their future are therefore occurring from this cause. The number of marriages among 18- and 19-year-olds has dropped from 208 per 1,000 in 1960 to around 72.1 in 1985. The number of unwed mothers has greatly increased (Bureau of Census, 1988). The number of marriages in the 15-to-44 age range has dropped from 148 per 1,000 in 1960 to 99.0 in 1985. At that time unemployment of white males 16 to 19 was 16 percent, for Hispanics 24 percent, and for black males 39 percent. In 1986, 4.1 million youth, male and female, were employed, which is about 3.5 of every 10. The picture for drop-outs, however, is depressing, as of those who left school before graduation in 1985 (562,000), only 259,000 were employed in 1986 (Bureau of Census, Indicators of Youth, 1988).

Compulsory attendance laws, child labor legislation, and juvenile delinquency legislation have combined to give authorities more control over the adolescent. Though there is more leniency and discretion in dealing with youthful offenders, labor laws and unionism have contributed to making adolescence virtually a culture of its own. Age segregation, prolonged dependence, and mass media have helped to create a group of think-alike, do-alike, dress-alike youth. Even so, most investigators think it is not a period of Sturm and Drang (storm and stress) suggested by Hall (1916). Nor is it, as expressed by analyst Anna Freud (1949) and Peter Blos (1962), an inescapable period of turmoil due to a profound reorganization of adolescent emotional lives. Offer and Offer (1975) provide data that adolescence is not a uniquely stressful time. Dr. Anne Peterson of Pennsylvania State University (1987) reports a study examining the effects of school change, physical development, and home problems on early adolescents. The study reveals that more than 50 percent of her sample were almost trouble free, 30 percent of the group had intermittent problems, while 15 percent were caught in a "spiral of downward trouble and turmoil." Of these, boys usually reacted as being rebellious and disobedient, and girls were found to have more depressed moods.

As a rule, teenagers are not mature enough to adjust to the role demands of industrial jobs. The jobs that are available often tend to delay the opportunity for adolescents to fully realize their capabilities and are not intrinsically rewarding, although as pointed out earlier, 4.1 million adolescents do work, proving the importance to them of work and money. A need exists, the authors believe, to create new space for this age group, with new roles or changed roles that allow adolescents to reach their full potential by combining their idealism, enthusi-

Table 9.1 PHYSICAL CHANGES OF ADOLESCENCE

BODY SYSTEM	MALES AND FEMALES	MALES	FEMALES
Integumentary	Skin thickens, toughens Darkening of skin Sebaceous gland secretion increases (blocked sebaceous glands cause acne in 85% of adolescents) Sweat gland (apocrine and eccrine) secretions increase Pubic and axillary hair appears Extremity hair	Coarse facial hair	Soft, smooth texture; fine hair on cheeks, upper lip
Cardio-vascular	Heart size increases Pulse rate decreases	Pulse rate: Age 14--60-100/min. Age 16--55-95/min. Age 18--50-90/min.	Pulse rate: Age 14--65-105/min. Age 16--60-100/min. Age 18--55-95/min.
	Blood pressure decreases	Blood pressure: Age 16 Systolic mean--121 Diastolic mean--61	Blood pressure: Age 16 Systolic mean--121 Diastolic mean--61
	Blood volume increases Hemoglobin level increases White blood cell count decreases Sedimentation rate increases Platelet count increases		
Respiratory	Chest size increases Lung growth increases Respiratory rate decreases (16-18/min.) Respiratory volume, vital capacity increase		
Sense organs		Auditory acuity decreases	Auditory acuity increases Olfactory sensitivity increases
Height			
Growth (inches)		4-5	2-4
Average increase (inches)		4-12	2-8
Age at growth spurt		12-16	10-14
Age when growth ceases		18-20	16-17
Weight			
Total gain in pounds		15-60	15-55
Skeleton			
Age at peak height		14	12

BODY SYSTEM	MALES	FEMALES
Body Proportions	Thorax widens (lungs, heart, esophagus) Shoulder width increases Pelvis narrows Face lengthens Head proportion to total body length decreases (total cranial growth achieved before adolescence) Lower jaw increases Disproportions of early adolescence become proportional	Thorax narrows proportionally Shoulder width decreases proportionally Pelvis broadens Face lengthens Head proportion to total body length decreases (total cranial growth achieved before adolescence) Lower jaw increases Disproportions of early adolescence become proportional
Body Mass		
Muscle mass	Doubles (at 12-16 yrs); muscle strength increases	Muscle mass proportionate to general tissue growth; less increase in muscle strength than in boys
Fat distribution	Subcutaneous fat decreases Fat increases on the trunk	Subcutaneous fat increases Fat disposition more obvious: thighs, hips, buttocks, breasts

asm, and energy. The general scenario of the adolescent life may be depicted as suggested by Baldwin (1988):

> Age span: 11 through 17 years. This stage of growth begins in late fifth or sixth grade and typically ends at about the senior year of high school. During this time, your child joins a "tribe" of peers that is highly separate from the adult world. The peer group (tribe) clearly defines itself as a distinct subculture struggling for identity, with its own dress codes, language codes, meeting places, and powerfully enforced inclusion criteria.
>
> During these difficult years for both parent and child, the pronounced changes of puberty occur. The core struggle of the child is to become independent--and that means emotionally separating from parents and forging a new adult identity. Initial attempts are awkward and emotionally naive. In three areas, here's what the adolescent is like:
>
> a) Relationship to parents. Often suspicious and distrustful, the adolescent begins actively to push parents away and resists their attempts to give advice. Life is conducted in a secretive world dominated by peers. Sometimes rebelling, pushing limits, and constantly testing parental resolve are usual.
>
> b) Relationship to peers. The youth experiences emotionally intense "puppy love" relationships with members of the opposite sex and has "best friends" relationships with peers of the same sex. These relationships are often superficial, with undue emphasis placed on status considerations: participation in sports, attractiveness, belonging to an *in* group.
>
> c) Relationship to career/future. Largely unrealistic in expectations of the adult world, the adolescent sees making a good living--and getting the training required--as "no problem." Money made by working is often

spent on status items such as cars or clothes or just on having a good time. The future is far away.

PHYSICAL DEVELOPMENT

Most of the emphasis in the literature on development in the adolescent years deals with puberty. We would be remiss if we fail to point out some salient features of the broader nature of growth. A historical fact is that size, both in weight and height, has changed since the beginning of this century. Looking at girls and boys at 11 years of age in 1900, as compared with 1970, shows three or four inches of gain.

AVERAGE HEIGHT CHANGE IN GIRLS AND BOYS 1900-1970

	5-Year-Olds		9-Year-Olds		11-Year-Olds	
	Girls	Boys	Girls	Boys	Girls	Boys
1900	4'2"	4'2-1/2"	5'	5'	5'3-1/4"	5'3-1/3"
1970	4'4"	4'5"	5'4-1/4"	5'4"	5'5"	5'6"

(After Garrison, 1975.)

Paralleling these changes is the fact that puberty comes earlier for girls and boys. Some girls of 11 have given birth to babies in the United States, meaning that their pubertal entry was even earlier. A review of the changes in skin and hair, cardiovascular system, and respiratory and sense organs is presented below.

Nutrition is a very important aspect of adolescent life because of the tendency of many youth to forego breakfast and sometimes either lunch or dinner. For girls from 9 to 15 the caloric need is 2,500 calories per day; for boys 3,500 calories. The fast-food and pizza choice for many youth, along with snacking, needs to be figured in the total food consumption. A "Big Mac" contains 540 calories, the Quarter Pounder with cheese 520; a hamburger and orange juice 360; a "Big Mac," chocolate shake, and French fries is an estimated 1,100 calories. The daily suggested needs of adolescents are provided in Table 9.2.

The need for increased caloric intake parallels the body growth of early and middle adolescence. Weight gain is usually significant, with many youth, including girls, gaining 60 pounds during adolescence.

Height gains during adolescence may be up to 12 inches for some. Some girls may gain 8 inches, but they often average about 4 to 5 inches. Table 9.1 depicts a number of changes in physique: height, weight, skeleton, body proportions, and mass.

Health and Illness

One indication of the health status of youth is indicated in the examination of illness among youth. Polio has been virtually eradicated but AIDS is taking its place with 8,249 cases reported in 1985. Gonorrhea, syphilis, and tuberculosis have increased; however, in the 20- to 24-year group these continue to be more or less steady. The big increase comes from measles, with the apparent cause being lack of universal immunization during early childhood.

Deaths (1985) among 15- to 19-year-olds are caused mainly by automobile accidents (33.9 per 100,000) and homicides (39.9 males of all races per 100,000). Suicide posted a 17.3 rate for white males. This is an increase of 11 per 100,000 since 1960.

Sexual Maturity

Maturity of Girls Puberty is characterized by the development of the reproductive system. The entire process of sexual maturation requires about three or four years, but individual differences are wide. Sexual maturity comes earlier to girls. The onset of sexual maturity in girls is frequently abrupt, requiring immediate emotional, personal, and social adjustments. In boys this process is less sudden and adjustment problems more gradual. Girls who mature early may be disadvantaged in that they are often

Table 9.2 ADOLESCENT NUTRITION

Food Group	Servings Per Day	Average Size of Servings 10-12 Years	13-15 Years
Milk and cheese	4		
(1.5 oz cheese = 1 C milk)		1/2 - 1 cup	1/2 - 1 cup
Meat Group (protein foods)	3 or more		
Egg		1	1 or more
Lean meat, fish, poultry (liver once a week)		3-4 oz	4 oz or more
Peanut butter		3 Tbsp	3 Tbsp
Fruits and Vegetables	At least 4, including:		
Vitamin C source (citrus fruits, berries, tomato, cabbage, cantaloupe)	1 or more (twice as much tomato as citrus)	1 medium orange	1 medium orange
Vitamin A source (green or yellow fruits and vegetables)	1 or more	1/3 cup	1/2 cup
Other vegetables (potato and legumes, etc.) *or*	2	1/2 cup	3/4 cup
Other fruits (apple, banana, etc.)		1 medium	1 medium
Cereals (Whole grain or enriched)	At least 4		
Bread		2 slices	2 slices
Ready-to-eat cereals		1 oz	1 oz
Cooked cereal (including macaroni, spaghetti, rice, etc.)		3/4 cup	1 cup or more
Fats and Carbohydrates	To meet caloric needs		
Butter, margarine, mayonnaise, oils: 1 Tbsp--100 calories (kcal)		2 Tbsp	2-4 Tbsp
Desserts and sweets 100-calorie portions as follows: 1/3 cup pudding or ice cream 2 3" cookies, 1 oz cake, 1 1/3 oz pie, 2 Tbsp jelly, jam, honey, sugar		3 portions	3-6 portions

Cup = 8 oz or 240 ml.
Tbsp = Tablespoon (1 Tbsp = ca. 15 ml = ca. 1/2 oz).
Modified with Mildred J. Bennett, Ph.D., from "Four Food Groups of the Daily Food Guide," Institute of Home Economics, U.S.D.A., and Publication #30, Children's Bureau of the United States Department of Health, Education, and Welfare, 1987.

Table 9.3 NUMBER OF REPORTED CASES OF SELECTED DISEASES AMONG 15- TO 24-YEAR-OLDS: 1981 TO 1986

Disease and Age	1981	1982	1983	1984	1985	1986
Polio						
15 to 19	2	0	0	0	---	---
20 to 24	0	2	2	2	---	---
Measles						
15 to 19	466	279	382	676	842	1,159
20 to 24	128	92	163	204	251	304
Tuberculosis						
15 to 19	656	560	530	414	464	513
20 to 24	1,542	1,407	1,375	1,268	1,208	1,206
Gonorrhea						
15 to 19	243,432	235,086	220,385	210,530	218,821	215,918
20 to 24	374,562	363,135	340,378	329,476	341,645	337,711
Syphilis						
15 to 19	4,173	4,517	4,395	3,218	3,132	3,133
20 to 24	8,792	9,461	9,204	8,069	7,717	7,885
AIDS						
15 to 19	---	---	---	---	30	47
20 to 24	---	---	---	---	349	616

---Data not available. *Youth Indicators, 1988*. Bureau of the Census, Washington, D.C.

larger than the boys of their group, and their blossoming figures may attract envy from other girls as older boys vie for their attention. They may be embarrassed about being ahead of their peers; mothers often are more strict in disciplining these early maturing girls. This disadvantage may disappear when girls attend junior high school rather than schools organized with seventh and eighth grades as extensions of elementary schools. These mature seventh-grade girls may be more like typical eighth-grade, or even ninth-grade girls.

A first change in sexual development is the "bud" stage of breast development. This usually starts around ten years of age. The pigmented area around the nipple (the areola) becomes raised and the nipple is thrust forward. In some cases, the appearance of pubic hair precedes the bud stage, but this is not a significant sign of the adolescent spurt. Paralleling this is an expansion of the buttocks and hips due to the increase in fatty and supportive tissue. Underarm hair also becomes evident during this phase of growth (Katchadourian & Lunde, 1975). Figure

Table 9.4 ANNUAL NUMBER OF DEATHS AMONG 15- TO 19-YEAR-OLDS, BY AGE AND CAUSE OF DEATH: 1960 TO 1985

[Number of deaths per 100,000 persons in each specified group]

Age and cause of death	1960	1965	1970	1975	1980	1985
15 to 19 years old						
All causes	92.2	95.1	110.3	101.5	97.9	81.2
Motor vehicle accidents	35.9	40.2	43.6	38.4	43.0	33.9
All other accidents	16.8	16.5	20.3	19.0	14.9	10.3
Suicide	3.6	4.0	5.9	7.6	8.5	10.0
Males, white	5.9	6.3	9.4	13.0	15.0	17.3
Females, white	1.6	1.8	2.9	3.1	3.3	4.1
Males, all other races	3.4	5.2	5.4	7.0	7.5	10.0
Females, all other races	1.5	2.4	2.9	2.1	1.8	2.2
Homicide	4.0	4.3	8.1	9.6	10.6	8.6
Males, white	3.2	3.0	5.2	8.2	10.9	7.3
Females, white	1.2	1.3	2.1	3.2	3.9	2.7
Males, all other races	27.6	30.6	59.8	47.8	43.3	39.9
Females, all other races	7.0	7.1	10.1	14.6	10.1	9.4
Cancer	7.7	7.6	7.3	6.0	5.4	4.6
Heart disease	6.2	5.3	3.9	3.4	2.3	2.2
Pneumonia/influenza	2.8	2.1	2.1	1.5	0.6	0.5

Youth Indicators, 1988. Bureau of the Census, Washington, D.C.

9.2 shows the actions of sex hormones and the resultant development at puberty. Research by Tanner (1973) reveals that sexual maturation accompanied with increased skeletal size comes prior to the beginning thrust of sexual maturation (see Fig. 9.3).

The onset of puberty has been earlier for American girls for the past 100 years; however, little change has been observed over the past three decades. The first menstrual period can be expected between ages 10 and 17, with most girls experiencing their first period at 12 years of age (Tanner, 1972). In 1844 data on menarche for Norwegian girls revealed the average to have been 17; in 1940 it was just under 14. In 1865 Finnish girls had an average menarcheal age of 15.6; for American girls it has stabilized at around 12.8 (Zacharias, Rand & Wurtman, 1976). The typical girl is infertile until a year or so after menarche. Full sexual maturity and fertility are reached some time in the early or middle twenties.

Maturity of Boys

The foremost sign of puberty in males is the acceleration in the growth of testes and scrotum. This is followed by the growth of fine hair at the base of the penis. Between 13 and 16 the penis enlarges and lengthens, pubic hair increases, the scrotum continues to grow, the larynx enlarges, and the vocal cords double in length, sometimes causing jumps in pitch in the adolescent boy's voice. Mature sperm is not usually present in the ejaculatory fluid until a year or so after the accelerated penis growth. Nocturnal emissions are experienced, and semen propelled during sleep--often labeled wet dreams--occurs when boys are experiencing an erotic dream or their clothing or covering rubs against the penis.

The final and very important change for the adolescent boy is the appearance of facial hair. Although this is first seen as downy hair on the upper lip, especially near the corners of the mouth, it soon becomes darker and longer. Following this, fine hair appears on the side of the face near the ears. Somewhat later, coarse hair develops on the chin and lower cheeks. Hair on the chest and other parts of the body such as the back comes at still a later period, usually in the twenties.

Throughout the growing period there is a gradual darkening of the hair of the head, but at adolescence this becomes more marked. It is likely the darkening is due to an increase in adrenal androgens. There is also a distinct change in the shape of the hairline on the forehead as the individual begins to mature; this has been referred to as a secondary sexual character-

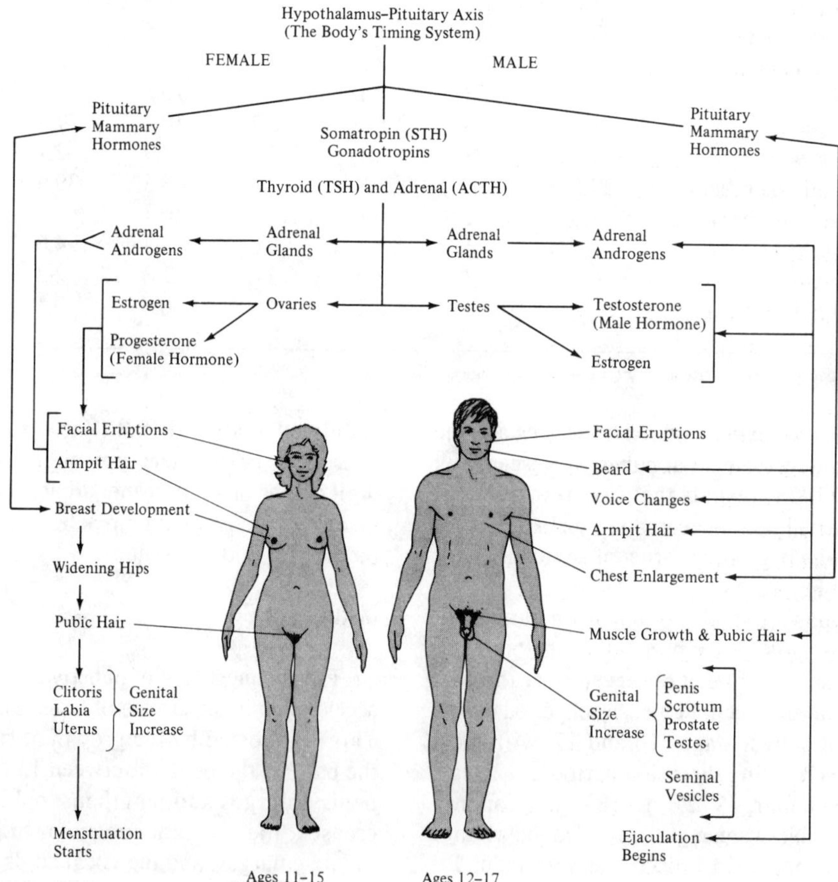

Figure 9.2 Sex hormones and development at puberty.

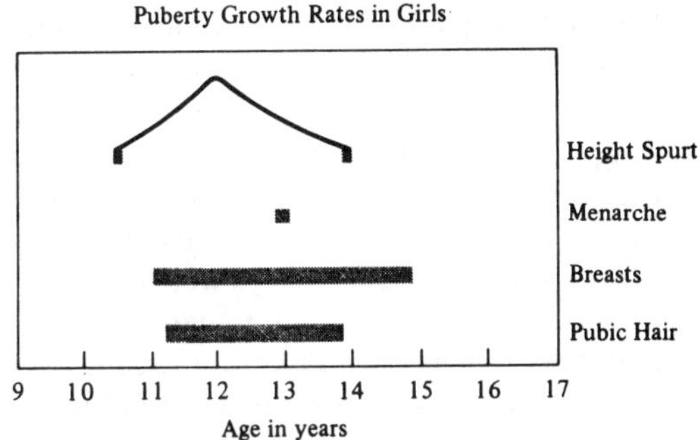

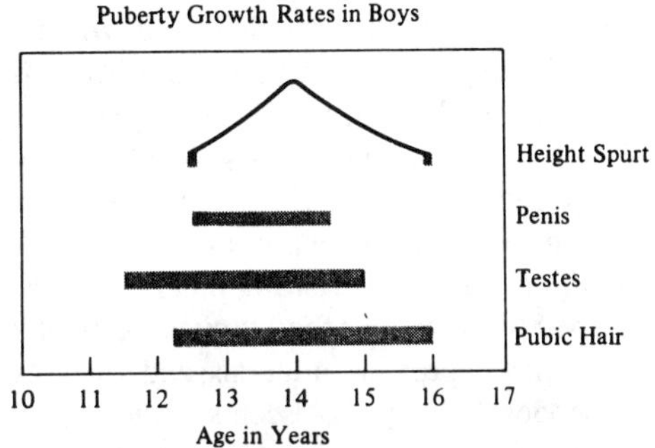

Figure 9.3 Puberty growth rates in girls and boys. (*Source:* Tanner, 1962.)

istic. The hairline of immature boys and girls follows an uninterrupted bowlike curve; in mature males the curved hairline is interrupted by a wedge-shaped recess on each side of the forehead.

Most young people advance in elementary schools in lock-step by common ages and hence are categorized by criteria that are standardized rather than individualized. The wide differential in maturation often makes it difficult for many children to measure up to ideal physical, intellectual, and social standards. The early maturing youngster has an advantage in meeting those ideals relating to attractiveness, height, athletic prowess, and so on. Adolescents get varying kinds of respect, attention, and value conferred upon them partially based upon their maturity. For the physically accelerated boy, this is positive. For the late maturing male, this is a disadvantage; often he develops negative self-concepts and the feeling of being isolated.

Important, though not directly connected with reproduction, is the development of secondary sex characteristics such as hair, which we have discussed, and skin glands. The three skin glands are the merocrine gland, the apocrine sweat gland, and the sebaceous gland. The merocrine and apocrine glands of the armpits become increasingly active during adolescence, even before the growth of axillary hair. Their secretion is fatty and has a pronounced odor that is usually not detectable in boys prior to puberty but becomes more noticeable during early adolescence. Among girls the apocrine sweat glands appear to undergo a cycle of secretory activity during the menstrual period, when larger volumes are produced. The sebaceous glands increase in size and activity during puberty, and this is thought to be closely associated with skin disturbances during adolescence. The size and activity of these glands are disproportionate to the size of the gland ducts, so that in puberty they frequently become clogged with dried oil and turn black as a result of oxidation with exposure to air. These plugged gland ducts are frequently referred to as *zits* or *blackheads*, and are most likely found on the chin and nose. The glands continue to function even though the opening has been blocked, and raised pimples then appear on the surface of the skin, much to the concern of the adolescent.

Although it is common among boys and girls in their teens, acne often has a detrimental emotional effect on youth. A study by Schachter and coworkers (1971) of 1,254 high school students found 69 percent of the boys and 58 percent of the girls had acne vulgaris on the face. This report found significant differences between those who had acne and those who did not have it. Those with acne enjoyed less social activity even though they received more help with grooming from their parents. Important factors that can aggravate an oily skin's tendency to acne are glandular disturbances, nervous tension, overwork, lack of sleep and irregular hours, dietary habits, and constipation (Michaelson, 1973). Although other cases are aggravated by chocolate, nuts, or some other specific food, the most important point about nutrition for the individual with an acne problem is to eat three nourishing meals each day with food from the four food groups, particularly those rich in proteins, minerals, and vitamins.

The view held by adolescents of their physical selves is significant for adjustment. When they depart from their peer group norms, they may face rejection or ridicule from their agemates. Because of this, many teenagers are preoccupied with their physical acceptability (Horrocks, 1976). Adolescent girls are sensitive to their body shapes, particularly their breasts, but also their nose, mouth, ears, and feet. Boys tend to compare and worry about their body size and muscles. They also tend to be troubled about small penises. Both boys and girls worry about skin blemishes, irregular teeth, and glasses or orthodontic braces. Weight is another concern of adolescents, principally of girls, who may also be resisting maturing or trying to get attention. In these weight watchers, dieting excessively can become a pattern difficult to reverse and eventually threaten life itself. This is called *anorexia nervosa* (Minuchin et al., 1978). Many are overweight, particularly in early adolescence; however, the rate of fat accumulation declines in both boys and girls during the growth spurt period. Self-concepts and identity are related to how adequate they perceive their bodies are. Positive acceptance of the physical self is an important step to maturity.

Body Shape and Physical Appearance

One of the markers of the period of early adolescence is concern with physical appearance and looks. Preoccupation with self characterizes both early and late adolescence. Much attention is given to how one looks and how one compares with the ideal. Some adolescents launch themselves into intense dieting, exercise programs, and various physical fitness schemes. It is important not to be overweight or underweight. Girls usually have a number of things they would change about themselves: less forehead, ears that don't protrude, bigger breasts, need to be taller. Boys would like to be larger, have wavy hair and to generally look better. Some boys even get into steroids to enhance their looks--to be more "macho" and have more muscle like heroes such as Rambo, Chuck Norris, etc. The three principal areas of concern are weight, height, and complexion for boys. Girls disdain being heavy basically because of social acceptance. Some 15 percent of adolescents are obese (20 percent over normal weight) (Kylylo, 1983). Besides appearance there are some immediate health risks involved. If weight is not controlled, other problems begin in a few years: cardiovascular, hypertension, elevated sugar, related endocrine problems. Many girls and some boys who try to reduce in a drastic way may find themselves with anorexia nervosa or bulimia.

Anorexia Nervosa and Bulimia

The numbers of adolescents, including some in extended adolescence (12 to 25), is estimated to be 26 million (American Psychological Association, 1986). Two percent develop the anorexic condition. Crisp (1980) estimates 1 percent of girls 16 to 18 are anorexic. The American Psychiatric Association defines the problem as a disturbance of body image, refusal to maintain normal body weight, and significant weight loss of 15 to 25 percent of normal (ideal) body weight. Anorexia nervosa means the loss of appetite as a result of nerves. This nervous condition stems from the fear of being overweight and losing the image girls have of what they should look like. Sometimes both very young girls (9 years of age) and older females up to 30 have this problem. Studies by Lachenmeyer and Munibrander (1988) of 1,250 girls from the ages of 13 to 19 found 13 percent of the group were significantly restricting their diets. They also examined eating disorders of males and females, revealing the data shown in Tables 9.5 and 9.6.

TABLE 9.5 Prevalence rates for eating disorders: Gender comparison. (Study I - low socioeconomic sample.)*

	Percentage		
	Female	Male	Total
Eating disorders			
Binge	51.8	49.7	50.0
Vomit	19.8	23.6	21.9
Binge and vomit	12.5	12.0	12.2
Clinical bulimia** (DSM-III)	9.7	5.7	7.6
Bulimia-1**	24.7	12.2	18.0
Bulimia-2**	12.5	5.7	8.8
Restricting	13.1	6.3	9.4
Laxatives	2.7	2.3	2.5
Diuretics	0.5	1.3	1.1
Diet pills	9.5	3.0	6.0

*Sample consisted of 328 females, 384 males, a total of 712.

TABLE 9.6 Prevalence rates for eating disorders: Gender comparison. (Study II - high socioeconomic sample.)*

	Percentage		
	Female	Male	Total
Eating disorders			
Binge	65.6	57.9	62.3
Vomit	22.6	22.5	22.6
Binge and vomit	14.6	15.3	15.0
Clinical bulimia** (DSM-III)	7.6	2.1	4.7
Bulimia-1**	4.5	0.4	2.7
Bulimia-2**	22.0	5.9	15.0
Restricting	13.6	3.4	9.3
Laxatives	4.0	6.0	4.9
Diuretics	5.0	5.5	5.3
Diet pills	16.6	6.4	12.2

*Sample consisted of 314 females, 235 males, a total of 549.

**Clinical bulimics meet all DSM-III criteria for bulimia. Bulimia-1 individuals meet all criteria except one. Bulimia-2 individuals meet all criteria except two.

Source: From "Eating Disorders in a Nonclinical Adolescent Population: Implications for Treatment" by J.R. Lachenmeyer and P. Munibrander, 1988, *Adolescence 23*(90), pp. 303-312. Adapted by permission of Libra Publishers, Inc.

Bulimia

Anorexia nervosa is characterized by not eating, which leads to the "skin and bones" condition. Bulimia, on the other hand, refers to recurrent episodes of binge eating typically followed by vomiting, the use of laxatives, etc., to purge the system of the food and drink. In the following five conditions, three must exist if someone is diagnosed as bulimic:

1. Consumption of high-calorie food during a binge.
2. Inconspicuous eating.
3. Abdominal pain, sleep, or self-induced vomiting following the eating binge.
4. Repeated attempts to lose weight via stringent diets, cathartics, diuretics, and self-induced vomiting.
5. Weight fluctuations.

The effect on the bulimic, who is often obese, is not usually a threat to life. However, a litany of consequences follow the individual who is caught up in this problem--dehydration, fluid shifts, electrolyte imbalance, hypoglycemic symptoms, malnutrition, gastrointestinal difficulties, laxative-related problems, insomnia, and neurological and endocrine problems. Greater numbers of boys are clinically bulimic than earlier thought to be the case; 5.7 percent of the lower socio-economic group and 2.1 percent of the higher group as seen in the Lachenmeyer and Munibrander survey were bulimic.

The bulimic among girls and sometimes older women (35 to 40) are unhappy with their bodies, are overly depressed, see themselves as overweight, and are often involved in alcoholism, drug use, overeating, and gambling. There is no simple solution to this problem. Sometimes bulimics are responsive to group therapy, individual psychotherapy, and counseling focusing on the reason for dieting (social and cultura). Treatment is generally more effective for girls under 18 years of age.

Physical Fitness

With all the emphasis on exercise in the past decade, one would believe that adolescent fitness is improving. But fitness data for 10- and 17-year-old girls and boys show no gains against 1958 records. In fact, girls of 17 years of age are only slightly more fit than 10-year-old boys (see Figure 9.4).

Some experts believe that there has never been a period when youth were so unfit. Access to health facilities, education, medical attention, and guidance are apparently not enough for a sizeable number of adolescents who are overweight. Many cannot do a push-up or a pull-up, and of those who can, many can do only two or three. Records of attendance reveal much absenteeism on the jobs and in schools, suggesting poor health habits resulting from uneven sleeping, eating, and exercise, and lack of a routine for keeping physically fit. Unfortunately, many youth have other problems, such as drugs, alcohol, delinquency, early pregnancies, and crime, that bear on the health issue.

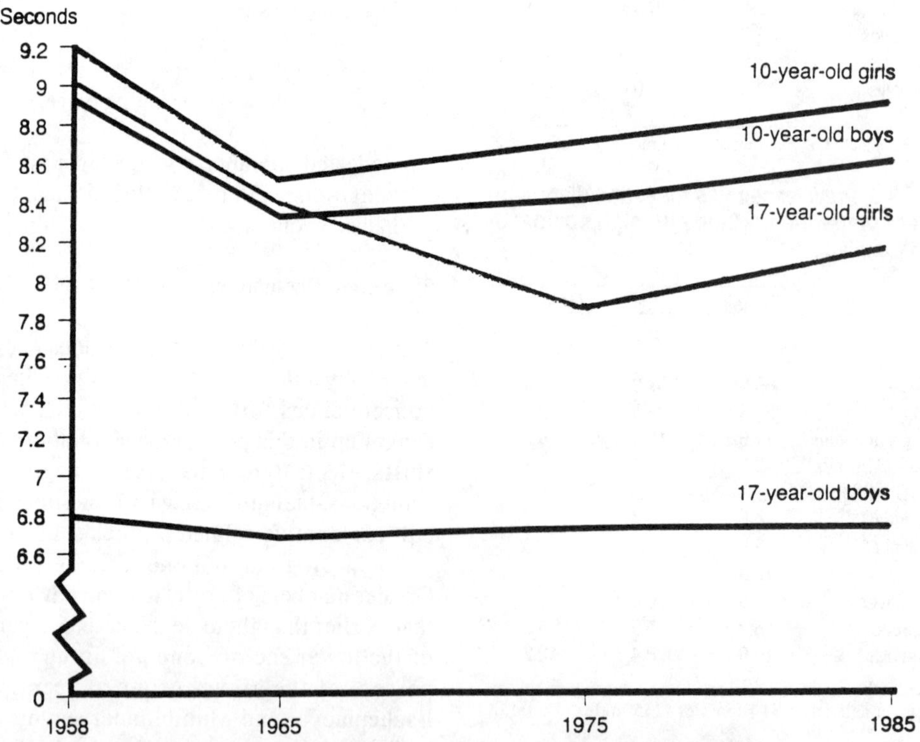

Figure 9.4 Seconds to complete the 50-yard dash in 1958, 1965, 1975 and 1985. (*Source:* U.S. Department of Health and Human Services, Office of the Assistant Secretary for Health, *The President's Council on Physical Fitness and Sports 1985, National School Population Fitness Survey*, and unpublished data.

Adolescents meet their peers--Fairfax USA and Shandong, China, interact in a teleconference.

COGNITIVE DEVELOPMENT

A number of adolescents enter the Piagetian formal operational stage in their early years (12 to 15), though some perhaps later. Piaget (1972) thought all youth reached this stage by age 20, if not through mathematical problem solving, or philosophical understanding, then through analogies or some type of apprenticeship. Piaget stated:

> ...they reach this stage in different areas according to their aptitudes and their professional specializations (advanced studies or different types of apprenticeship for the various trades); the way in which these formal structures are used, however, is not necessarily the same in all cases.

Some investigators (Fischer and Silvern, 1985) agree with Piaget; however, many believe that the entry into formal operations comes at a later time, perhaps beginning at 14 or even as late as 16. Kohlberg and Gilligan (1971) believed that perhaps as many as 50 percent of the adult American population do not reach this formal stage of thought. Piaget thought that brain maturity and development of social opportunity was such that this stage could be reached. However, he believed that even if neurological development was sufficient, the level would not be reached without stimulation and encouragement from the educational and cultural sectors of society. Epstein's (1974) examination of phrenoblysis noted that many researchers believe the brain increments continue until 15 to 17.

There are two attributes of formal thought: the adolescent has the ability to think about his own thought processes and is able to deal with complex problems involving reasoning. The second acquisition is the ability to imagine many solutions to a problem and to project many outcomes to an event. Increasingly adolescents not only deal with concrete things or events, but also have the capacity to think in logical and abstract terms.

The neopiagetian theorists, who have mainly discarded the stage-bound approach of Piaget, believe the child is much more capable than the preschooler described as pre-logical or preconceptual. These investigators talk about information processing where the pre-adolescent is beginning to have impressive classification and number skills.

Informational Processing

The definition of intelligence is a matter of conjecture by some theorists. For some intelligence is what we know; for others, our ability to know. Is it accumulated knowledge, is it the cognitive processes that give us that knowledge, or is it the practical application and use of knowledge? All are important. Critics of intelligence tests argue that most tests (and subtests) measure product (i.e., fact, information, rote items, etc., in various combinations) but ignore the process of intellectual behavior. Piaget suggests that these tests fail to measure the child's evolutional (qualitative) advance to new stages of thought. Many believe that process components such as memory, attention, problem-solving, and decision-making are necessary if we are to accurately judge mental and cognitive development. Robert Sternberg (1984) stated that five components of information processing might be measured separately. These components are:

1. Meta-components - the higher-order control processes that account for decision-making

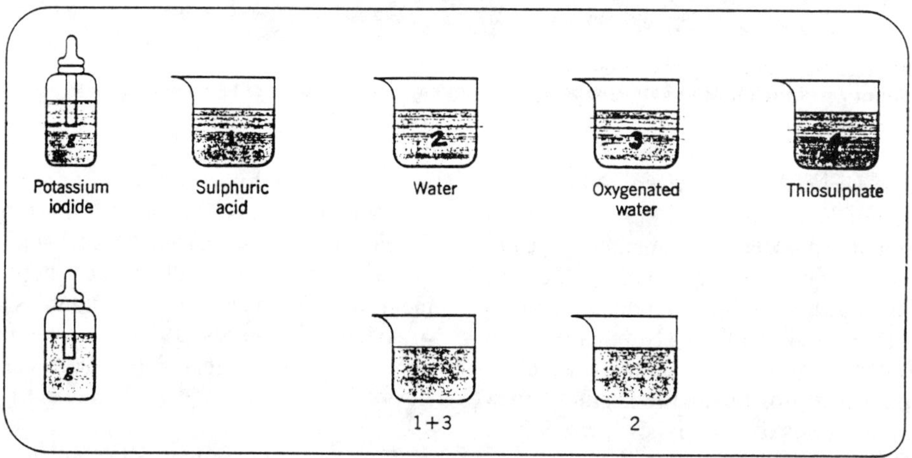

Figure 9.5 Piaget's yellow liquid experiment. A flask with a dropper in it, labeled *g*, contains potassium iodide. Four beakers contain colorless, odorless liquids, each of which is labeled with a number: 1 (sulphuric acid), 2 (water), 3 (oxygenated water), and 4 (thiosulphate). Two other beakers are presented to the subject. One contains 1 + 3 (sulphuric acid and oxygenated water); the other contains 2 (water). As the subject watches, the experimenter adds liquid from *g* (potassium iodide) to each of the two beakers by means of the dropper. The liquid in the beaker containing 1 + 3 becomes yellow. The subject is then instructed to reproduce the yellow color, using flask *g* and the beakers 1, 2, 3, and 4 as he or she wishes. The following combinations are logically possible in the experiment:

(1) g + 1	(6) g + 1 + 3	(11) g + 1 + 2 + 3
(2) g + 2	(7) g + 1 + 4	(12) g + 1 + 2 + 4
(3) g + 3	(8) g + 2 + 3	(13) g + 1 + 3 + 4
(4) g + 4	(9) g + 2 + 4	(14) g + 2 + 3 + 4
(5) g + 1 + 2	(10) g + 3 + 4	(15) g + 1 + 2 + 3 + 4

Combinations 6 and 11 produce the yellow liquid.

and planning. The ability to select a scheme for remembering is an example of this component.

2. Performance components - the process that carries out problem-solving.

3. Acquisition (storage) components - the facility of learning new material and information.

4. Retention (or retrieval) components - the process used to elicit information from the memory.

5. Transfer components - the process utilized to generalize information in one task to help with another task.

Cognition and growth of intelligence involve accruals of knowledge and development of information-processing components. Problem-solving is more efficient when the adolescent has a larger store of information and when it can be retrieved as it is needed. Coupled with their new-found abilities, adolescents believe in their omnipotence, basically because of the idealism engendered by the supremacy of thought. Youth believes that reason and logic can solve all problems and cannot admit that we do not have all the answers.

Children in the concrete operational stage cannot transcend the immediacy of the here and now. They cannot deal with the remote, the future, the hypothetical. In a verbal problem suggested by Jones (1985), "Jane is fairer than Susan, Jane is darker than Ross, who is the darkest of the three?" Children of 10 or 11 are likely to believe Jane and Susan are light complexioned. Susan is the lighter and Jane is between, therefore Ross is darker. Adolescents reason that Susan is darker than Jane and Jane is darker than Ross; therefore, Susan is the darkest.

In the classic experiment by Inhelder and Piaget (1958) involving five flasks of colorless liquid, the researchers asked subjects to produce a yellow liquid and they described the task as follows:

> The child is given four similar flasks containing colorless, odorless liquids which are perceptually identical. We number them: (1) diluted sulfuric acid; (2) water; (3) oxygenated water; (4) thiosulfate; we add a bottle (with a dropper) which we call *g*; it contains potassium iodide. It is known that oxygenated water oxidizes potassium iodide in an acid medium. Thus mixture (1 + 3 + *g*) will yield a yellow color. The water (2) is neutral, so that adding it will not change the color whereas the thiosulfate (4) will bleach the mixture [cancel out the yellow]. The experimenter presents to the subject two glasses, one containing 1 + 3, the other containing 2. In front of the subject, he pours several drops of *g* in each of the two glasses and notes the different reactions. Then the subject is asked simply to reproduce the color yellow, using flasks 1, 2, 3, 4 and *g* as he wishes.
>
> Children of ten or eleven typically take one flask (*g*--the flask with the potassium iodide) and adding liquid from it separately to each of the other flasks (1, 2, 3, and 4). When this fails to give the desired outcome, they tend to fall into a hit-or-miss pattern. They begin pouring liquid from one flask into another in a relatively aimless manner, hoping to stumble on the right combination by chance. If they find a correct combination, they stop their search, failing to appreciate that another combination is also possible (the two combinations that produce yellow liquid are *g* + 1 + 3 and *g* + 1 + 2 +3).
>
> Those adolescents in the stage of formal operations do the problem differently. They test all possible combinations in a systematic fashion. They, too, usually begin by adding the liquid from one flask (*g*) separately to the other flasks. But in contrast to younger children, they then proceed to combine the flasks three at a time and finally four at a time, arriving at the 15 possible outcomes. Formal operational thought closely parallels the kind of reasoning employed in the solution of scientific problems.

Piaget thought that children made the transition to the formal stage by becoming increasingly efficient in organizing and structuring input from the environment with concrete operational methods and that they come to see the inadequacies of this approach for solving problems in the real world with its gaps, uncertainties, and contradictions. Children lack the analytic ability to cope with the above-described liquid problem. Flavell (1969) attempts to specify the phases the child goes through to achieve formal operations. He distinguished between performance and competence. Competence is the underlying possession of some operation like that in the liquid experiment; performance is the ability to apply the operation to a particular task. Moshman (1977) has listed four steps in the formation of a new cognitive structure:

1. The individual fails at the task requiring a certain operation ability.

2. The individual is developing at the competence level and may solve any problem but better than chance depends upon the performance factors involved.

3. The operation is fully developed at the competence level but performance factors may still hinder its application to some tasks.

4. Performance factors no longer impede the successful application of the operation.

Not all adults develop to the formal operational level. Perhaps many of these are persons who would score less than average on a standardized intelligence scale. Cross-cultural studies have shown that some rural villagers in Turkey never seem to reach the formal stage (Douglas and Wong, 1977). Yet urban educated Turks (Kohlberg and Gilligan, 1971) do reach this stage. Indications are that full operational thinking may not be the general rule of adolescence (Elkind, 1975). In the next chapter we will discuss the adolescent relative to morality, sexuality, vocation, problems, and issues.

SUMMARY

The adolescent years are expanding ones. In the Western world adolescence begins as early as 11, close to the beginning of puberty, and continues until the early twenties, although some believe it may continue even longer. Three periods have been identified: early adolescence--emphasis is on physical change; middle--emphasis is on establishing peer relationships and friendships; and the latter period--the focus is on the social and emotional with the search for appropriate work a prominent feature.

Theories of adolescent development include the Freudian--suggesting physical drives and defense mechanisms to protect the ego give principal meaning to adolescent life; Erikson--believing the search for identity is the central coalescing factor in the life of youth; Piaget--emphasizing the growth toward and achievement of formal operations as crucial in building idealism of youth; and Skinner--believing adolescent behavior is regulated by reinforcement, punishment, and imitation or modeling. Bandura, a social learning theorist (cognitive) thinks youth's behavior is a function of their reaction to themselves, the reaction of others, and the external effect. However, humanist thought believes the major force of development comes from internal sources. Human beings are unique because they are creative and they have intentionality. Maslow, a representative of this point of view, thinks behavior is dominated by the hierarchy of needs, with physical ones dominating behavior until they are satisfied. When fulfilled psychological needs predominate, one is motivated by self actualization.

Adolescence is believed by many sociologists and psychologists to be a culture of its own, as teenagers develop their own language, use codes, wear special clothing, and share recreational interests. Though sometimes thought of as being in turmoil, most adolescents have little difficulty with the transit through the teenage years. On subjects like lifestyles, politics, and religion, they are in agreement with their parents. Disagreements come over friends, dating, drugs, schooling, and home responsibilities.

Health problems are significant: many adolescents are overweight and their eating habits are deficient. Concern over weight and good looks leads some, mainly girls, to become anorexic or bulimic. Physical development issues also affect the lives of youth. Sexual maturity occurs first in girls, with the menarche occurring as early as 11 or 12 years of age. The hypothalamus-pituitary axis accounts for timing of pubertal development. For girls, most pubertal changes occur between the years of 11 and 12; for boys, between the ages of 12 to 16. Causes of death during this period are largely those of accidents and suicides. Ignorance about sexually transmitted diseases is taking its toll. Only a minority of sexually active teenagers are utilizing contraceptive devices and many of these do so only on occasion. Physical fitness for most adolescents is a problem; many experts believe that never has youth been so unfit. Records from the U.S. Department of Health show no gains in 1985 against 1958.

Cognitive development shows great gains; most youth are in the formal stage by the end of this period. A few are in the concrete operational stage. The last incremental brain growth occurs between 15 and 17 years of age. Ability to solve abstract problems is in evidence. Informational processing involves meta components, performance components, acquisition components, retention components, and transfer components, which can be measured separately. These processes allow for an understanding of the basic parts of cognition and their measurement; they do not depend upon an accumulation of facts but indicate how intelligent operations solve problems efficiently.

KEY WORDS

acquisition components
anorexia
behavior modification
bulimia
cardiovascular
cognitive theory of modeling
Electra complex
extended adolescence
formal operation
heterosexuality
humanism
hypothalamus-pituitary axis
integumentary
intellectualization
latency stage
meta components
Oedipal complex
operant conditioning
performance components
phallic stage
prelogical
projection
repression
reaction formation
retrieval components
sublimation
transfer components

REFERENCES

American Association of Psychiatry. *DSM III: Diagnostic and Statistical Manual of Mental Disorders*, 3rd rev. ed. Washington, DC: The Association, 1987

American Psychological Association (APA). Eating disorders linked to family relations, study finds. (Press release). Washington, DC: Author, 1986.

Baldwin, B.A. Puberty and parents, Piedmont airlines. In *Human Development*, 1988-89. Guilford, Conn.: Duskin Publishing Group, 1988.

Bandura, A., and Walters, R. *Social Learning and Personality*. New York: Norton, 1963.

Blos, P. *On Adolescence: A Psychoanalytic Interpretation*. New York: Free Press, 1962.

Conger, J.J., and Peterson, A.C. *Adolescence and Youth: Psychological Development in a Changing World*, 4th ed. New York: Harper & Row, 1984.

Crisp, A.H. *Let Me Be*. New York: Grune & Stratton, 1980.

Douglas, J.D., and Wong, A.C. Formal operations: Age and sex difference in Chinese and American children. *Child Development*, 1977, *48*:689-692.

Dreyer, P.H. Sexuality during adolescence. In B.B. Wolman (ed.), *Handbook of Developmental Psychology*. Englewood Cliffs, NJ: Prentice-Hall, 1982.

Elkind, D. *A Sympathetic Understanding of the Child: Birth to Sixteen*, 2nd ed. Boston, 1978.

_____. Research on cognitive development in adolescence. In S.E. Dragastin and G.H. Elder, Jr. (eds.), *Adolescence in the Life Cycle*. New York: Wiley, 1975.

Epstein, H.J. Phrenoblysis: Special brain and mind growth periods, II Human mental development. *Developmental Psychology*, 1974, 7(3):207-217.

Erikson, E. *Identity, Youth and Crisis*. New York: Norton, 1968.

Fischer, K.W., and Silvern, L. Stages and individual differences in cognitive development. *Annual Review of Psychology*, 1985, *36*:613-648.

Flavell, J.H. *Cognitive Development*. Englewood Cliffs, NJ: Prentice-Hall, 1977.

Freud, A. *The Ego and Mechanisms of Defense*. London: Hogarth Press, 1949.

Freud, S. *New Introductory Lectures on Psychoanalysis*. New York: Norton, 1933.

Garrison, K., and Garrison, K.C., Jr. *Psychology of Adolescence*, 7th ed. Englewood Cliffs: Prentice-Hall, 1975.

Hall, G.S. *Adolescence*. New York: Appleton, 1916.

Havighurst, R.J. *Development Tasks and Education*, 3rd ed. New York: David McKay.

Horrocks, J.E. *The Psychology of Adolescence*, 4th ed. Boston: Mass.: Houghton Mifflin, 1976.

Inhelder, B., and Piaget, J. *The Growth of Logical Thinking*. New York: Basic Books, 1958, p. 108.

Katchadourian, H.A., and Lunde, D.T. *Fundamentals of Human Sexuality*, 2nd ed. New York: Holt, Rinehart and Winston, 1975.

Kohlberg, L., and Gilligan, C.F. The adolescent as philosopher: The discovery of the self in a postconventional world. *Daedalus*, 1971, *100*:1051-1086.

Lachenmeyer, J.R., and Munibrander. Eating disorders in the nonclinical adolescent population: Implications for treatment. *Adolescence*, 1988, *23*(90):303-312.

Maslow, A.H. *Motivation and Personality*, 2nd ed. New York: Harper & Row, 1970.

Michaelson, M. Acne is more than skin deep. *Today's Health*, 1973, *51*(2):14.

Minuchin, S., Rosman, B., and Baker, L. *Psychosomatic Families--Anorexia in Context*. Cambridge, Mass.: Harvard University Press, 1978.

Mischel, W. *Personality and Assessment*. New York: Wiley, 1968.

Moshman, D. Consolidation and stage formation in the emergence of formal operations. *Developmental Psychology*, 1977, *13*:95-100.

Offer, D., and Offer, J.B. *From Teenage to Young Manhood*. New York: Basic Books, 1975.

Piaget, J. Intellectual evolution from adolescence to adulthood. *Human Development*, 1972, *15*:1-12.

_____. *The Origins of Intelligence in Children*. New York: International Universities Press, 1952.

_____. Piaget's theory. In P.H. Mussen (ed.), *Carmichael's Manual of Child Psychology*, vol. 1. New York: Wiley, 1970.

_____. *The Psychology of Intelligence*. Patterson, NJ: Littlefield, Adams, 1963.

Peterson, A.C. Adolescent development. *Annual Review of Psychology, 39*:583-60.

Skinner, B.F. *The Behavior of Organisms: An Experimental Approach.* New York: Appleton-Crofts, 1938.

Smith, L. *Afterthoughts.* 1931.

Sternberg, R.J. (ed.) *Mechanisms of Cognitive Development.* New York: W.H. Freeman, 1984.

Strom, R.D. *Psychology for the Classroom.* Englewood Cliffs, NJ: Prentice-Hall, 1969, p. 5

Tanner, J.M. *Growth At Adolescence*, 2nd ed. Oxford: Blackwell, 1962.

_____. Growing up. *Scientific American*, 1973, *229*:30-43.

_____. Sequence, tempo and individual variation in the growth and development of boys and girls aged twelve to sixteen. In R.E. Grinder (ed.), *Studies in Adolescence.* New York: Macmillan, 1975, pp. 502-522.

U.S. Bureau of the Census. *Statistical Abstract of the United States.* Washington, DC: U.S. Government Printing Office, 1988.

U.S. Bureau of the Census. *Bureau of Census Youth Indicators*, 1988.

Waechter, E.H., Phillips, J., and Holady, B. *Nursing Care of Children.* Philadelphia: Lippincott, 1985.

Chapter 10

ADOLESCENCE: SOCIAL DEVELOPMENT--ISSUES AND PROBLEMS

ADOLESCENCE: SOCIAL DEVELOPMENT--ISSUES AND PROBLEMS

One way to examine the development of adolescence is to look at the expectations society has for its youth. The developmental tasks of Havighurst (1972) indicate the importance of social conforming for adolescents. The "tasks," though radically specific to the individual, will reflect the views of society and the subtle pressure pervasively exerted on its youth. The cultural expectancies (developmental tasks) of Havighurst are:

- to achieve new and more mature relations with age-mates of both sexes
- to develop the intellectual skills and concepts necessary for civic competency
- to prepare for a love relationship, marriage, and family

- to acquire a set of values and an ethical system to guide behavior
- to achieve socially responsible behavior
- to select and prepare for an occupation

Eugenia Waechter (1985) suggests many similar tasks for youth but categorizes them under early, middle, and later adolescence as follows:

Pre- and Young Adolescence

1. Develop readiness for and acceptance of body changes
2. Assert one's independence of adults
3. Achieve acceptance in one's peer group
4. Develop new intellectual skills

Adolescence

1. Accept and adjust to a maturing body
2. Accept one's sexuality as male or female
3. Accept and learn one's sex role
4. Search for and achieve a sense of identity
5. Achieve some degree of independence from parents
6. Develop mature behavior patterns

Later Adolescence

1. Achieve independence from parents
2. Develop a system of values
3. Establish a close affectional relationship with another
4. Choose a life vocation
5. Develop the skills and competencies required for success in one's chosen vocation

The life of young adolescents (11 to 14) will be dominated by physical changes, the growing importance of the group, and developing intellectual maturity. During the middle adolescence years (15 to 17), youth primarily develop an independence from adults (parents) and integrate into a peer group. Later during adolescence (18 to 21), they achieve identity, develop an ethical system, and decide about the future work world. The social impact on youth varies greatly, as do their achievement and adequacy in task development.

Most adolescents in America come through the critical years of 11 to 21 relatively untouched by the pitfalls. Having good schools, supportive parents, and effective local and community institutions help them grow to adulthood meeting the criteria of the "tasks," finding their way into the workplace, making commitments to families and friends, and assuming the responsibilities of citizenship. Many others under less than optimal conditions for healthy growth manage to become contributing members of the social order. Some achieve this status despite threats to their well-being that were virtually unknown to their parents and grandparents.

The Carnegie Corporation (Carnegie Corporation of America, Volume 35, Nos. 1, 2, Winter/Spring 1990) had this to say about the developing adolescent:

> there are other adolescents for whom poverty, racial prejudice, parental unemployment, family breakup, or disintegrated communities can mean the defeat of aspiration and hope. The obstacles in their path can impair physical and emotional health, destroy motivation and ability to succeed in school and jobs, and damage personal relationships and the chance to become an effective parent.

Certainly across all social groups, there are young people who drop out of school, commit violent or otherwise criminal acts, become pregnant, become mentally ill, abuse drugs and alcohol, attempt suicide, die or become disabled due to injuries from accidents. Unfortunately for many minority youth the options that were available at 11 or 12 fade by the time they reach 14 or 15. We will look at some of the developmental markers, the issues and problems for these and other young people.

The chief task of adolescence is to achieve identity. This psycho-social development includes the determination of a "sense of self," the role in which young people display their lives to others and society, the decision about work, and a value system upon which they can frame their larger life.

IDENTITY AND ITS SEARCH

Erikson alleges that the search and formation of identity is the principal task of adolescence. The formation of identity requires the ego to organize the individual's abilities, needs, desires, and mode of adapting to society. The search for identity may not end at the end of adolescence but continue throughout life; it may surface in confusion during the middle years, assume crisis proportion and eventually be the basis for reorganization of one's life. According to Erikson, at this time the conflict of identity and role confusion are the principal dangers to the youth. The issue of identity often continues to be temporized and with it the work and ethical system selection is delayed.

Some identity confusion in youth is normal, expressing itself in decisions about work and ethics, extreme self-consciousness about looks, and the sometimes overwhelming importance of peers. Intolerance and clannishness are defenses against identity confusion. Confusion is often exhibited by youth who regress into childishness to avoid conflicts or commit themselves impulsively to poorly thought out plans of action. Erikson does not believe that ideological commitment is an irrelevant defense mechanism. The time-out period provided by this psycho-moratorium allows the adolescent to focus on commitment that is personal and ideological. In fact the core of the identity crisis is the "virtue of fidelity," i.e., sustained loyalty, faith, and belonging--as to an idea, family, friends, ethnic group, religion, movement, or value.

Identity has several aspects to its nature. Marcia (1980) proposed four categories of status identity: (1) achievement identity; (2) foreclosure; (3) diffusion; and (4) moratorium. Three factors define the identities--presence or absence of a crisis, commitment to a selected occupation, and commitment to freely chosen values and ethics. Those who have achieved identity are ones who have passed through a crisis and are doing work of their own choosing. They also have framed a code of ethics by which they are trying to live. Those youths in the foreclosure mode are committed to definite occupations but their choices were made early and often heavily influenced by their parents. They generally made the transition to adulthood smoothly. The identity diffusion group is without direction; they typically have not decided what kind of work they will do or what sort of a value system they will organize their lives around. This type of status does not exclude crises or changes in direction, but there may be uncertainty as to work roles and morality. The final type of identity is moratorium, which may be seen in the adolescent or young adult. Young people in this situation have prolonged and unresolved crises--they cannot decide on work and/or values or about the thrust of their lives.

It is generally conceded that the achievement identity is the most socially desirable status. Marcia (1980) says that each status situation relates in some way to healthy and undesirable (pathological) dimensions. Trained observers in Northern Europe and Israel have consistently agreed upon individual statuses by observing behavior and attitudes exhibited by adolescents. The type of status also offers insight into the kinds of reactions adolescents have to anxiety, self-esteem, conflicts, and the bonds with parents.

Anxiety is a prevalent emotion for those adolescents who have many unresolved conflicts involving values, choices, and life's unpredictability. Those who foreclose rarely have anxiety. For them the issue is settled. They exhibit continuity and certainty. The variety of opportunities that exist now for girls in the occupational world preempts them from early foreclosures. According to Marcia (1980), males who foreclose have less self-esteem than males in moratorium; the foreclosure youth hold more authoritarian values and are closely tied to important others, usually kin. Members of the identity confusion group have frequently been rejected and detached from their parents, who may tend to provide little direction for their teenage children. The moratorium youth are often tied to their parents, yet have ambivalent feelings towards them, resenting their control but fearing their disapproval.

The identity achievement youth have a more even view of their parents. Unlike moratorium adolescents, they do not fear being abandoned to drift on their own. Girls and boys seem to differ in the degree of satisfaction in moratorium and achievement identity; males enjoy such status while females have considerable conflict in such roles. These conflicts tend to relate to career-family choices (Archer, 1985). In the secondary schools (grades 8-12) there are more individuals in the identity confusion and foreclosure status than the achievement and moratorium mode. It should be noted that the adolescent may have foreclosed in respect to sex role, yet be in the moratorium mode in terms of choosing an occupation. Also, the adolescent may have an indeterminate status regarding political ideas. Marcia (1980) characterizes the identity status as outlined below.

Having made a choice and/or a commitment, adolescents are more self-reliant, handle stress better, and set more realistic goals. If, however, the adolescent never reaches true identity status he may revert to an earlier status.

FAMILY AND PEER RELATIONSHIPS

One of the tasks for adolescents is to develop independence from their parents. This means sometimes countering suggestions from parents about clothes, friends, school work, recreation, and responsibilities at home. They often rebel against parental strictures and are restive under what they view as domineering control by parents. Despite the conflicts, however, parents and their children generally get along very well; for the most part teenagers agree with their parents on life styles, politics, religion, and value systems (Hill, 1987). Where there is conflict it centers around control of time, activities, and relations with friends and peers, with the adolescents' desiring increased freedom and the parents' wishing for more responsibility from them. Some mothers may feel that they are losing authority over their children, making the conflict particularly strong (Steinberg, 1987). The mother usually interacts with adolescents in the areas of household duties, leisure time, discipline, and other general activities. Fathers usually discuss problem-solving activities and general ideas more or less in a relaxed situation. Mothers, however, are more often busy with a number of family details and have the overall responsibility for the household. Therefore the mother may be fre-

IDENTITY STATUS

STATUS	CRISIS (Active Decision Making)	COMMITMENT (Acceptance of Politics)
Identity Diffusion	No crisis and no commitment, confused ethical and political beliefs--no decision on work.	
Foreclosure	No crisis.	Commitment determined from family views gathered from political, social, and religious issues. Work follows adult leadership.
Moratorium	Crisis, no commitments--period of exploration.	
Identity Achieved		Crisis is over--commitment is made, usually ethical system and Work issue are settled.

(*Source:* Marcia, 1980)

quently harried and give out information, directions, and mandates under pressure (Hausen et al., 1987).

As mentioned in the earlier chapter on parenting styles, the three categories affect the teenager. The authoritative parenting style seems to yield "normal and healthy" adolescent behavior. The sense of confidence and control allied with warmth provides a certain reassurance. Guidelines given by these parents usually provide some freedom to the creative and experimenting youth yet offer safety (Hill, 1987). The authoritarian parenting style, highly restrictive and inflexible, is most likely to stimulate considerable debate and conflict in the adolescent. This approach may account for early leaving of home by some adolescents and their radical departure from family norms for behavior. The permissive style of parenting encourages to a degree the independence of children and teenagers, as parents often seem aloof from their day-to-day affairs. Permissive parents may actually feel loving toward their children but rarely get involved in their decisions about school, friends, and work. These youth are sometimes rebellious, self-indulgent, impulsive, and socially inept.

Shifts in the family control equation occur during adolescence with sons acquiring more independence and mothers increasingly losing control, while the father-son relationship often remains about the same. By late adolescence sons often exceed their mothers' power. They remain, however, below the father in the family hierarchy. Most girls have a reproachment, usually by middle adolescence, with their mothers, becoming good friends, with the relationship offering interpersonal rewards (Wright and Keple, 1981).

Parent and Adolescent Communication

Major discussions and disagreements between teenagers and parents are usually over how teens use their time, their friends, clothes, school, smoking or drinking, and the time they come home at night. Some aspects of dealing with young people are provided by the National Institute of Mental Health (1981), as follows:

Parents can...

1. Give attention carefully to what your teenager is saying. Stop whatever you are doing--reading, television watching, other tasks--and focus on their talk.

2. Try to understand your teenager's point of view--speak calmly and be pleasant when you talk.

3. Keep the door open on the subject, don't belittle them by laughter or derision or shoot down their requests or ideas.

4. Encourage teenagers to discuss their ideas; don't put them down but offer your views honestly and matter of factly.

5. Help your teenagers to build confidence by encouraging them in activities they have chosen.

6. Welcome their participation in family decision making, compliment your teenagers frequently, and remember their need to challenge.

Teenagers should remember that their parents are not the enemy, but are usually vitally interested in their children. Parents also have needs, feelings, and they have their good and bad days because of the considerable responsibility involved with providing food, clothing, and shelter to the family. Because of this, adolescents should keep an open mind when talking with their parents. They need to share feelings concerning responsibilities both at home and at school. Finally, adolescents need to make good suggestions and slow criticisms and generally behave in a courteous manner in order to gain parental respect and win more family freedoms.

Youth and the Peer Group

The peer group includes at least three different sets of youth. The larger peer group may be a youth culture, as youth are segregated in high schools and colleges and may have their own agenda. Sociologists and psychologists see this group as a distinct one, with its own clothing, language, icons, entertainment, and styles. For boys, masculinity featuring athletic skills, risk taking, and physical mastery is important, along with defending one's honor. For girls, physical attractiveness, personal vivacity, skill in interpersonal relationships, and ability to exercise control over sexual encounters are important. Achievement of status is primarily obtained through presenting a "cool" and unflappable confidence in one's essential masculinity or femininity and by delivering a smooth performance in a variety of situations (Sebalk, 1984). Adolescents are often negative to "brains and bores"--those who work overtime at academics or at work/chores.

A second peer group is the "crowd." This group usually is limited to 15 to 30 adolescents who socialize together. Dunphy (1963, 1980) says there are two basic groups--the crowd and the clique. Usually the crowd is made up of several cliques (containing three to nine members). Cliques are formed by members who highlight a particular function, reputation, location, or ethnic identification. Sometimes they use names such as jocks, socialites, rocks, greasers, or tigers/bears. The third group is like the clique. In this type of group there may be three or four close friends who function as a small group and often live nearby each other.

Each group has different functions. The clique operates as a vehicle for visiting and talking; the crowd is the center of larger and more organized social activity, such as parties or dancing, which becomes the source of interaction between the sexes. Cliques, according to Dunphy, are usually identified by the leader's name, such as the Morty Smith or the Karen Nix group. The leader is most likely a person who has been a steady dater a long time, with positive personal attributes and material resources the group finds useful. Group formations among adolescents pass through five stages (Dunphy, 1963).

Stage 1: The pregroup stage. Composed of preadolescent friendship groups of individuals of the same sex.

Stage 2: Beginning of the crowd. Cliques of the same sex begin social interchange with the cliques of the opposite sex.

Stage 3: The crowd in structural transition. Members of opposite sex within the new group (combined cliques) begin to date, which marks the initiation of a new heterosexual clique. Members in this clique retain membership in the same-sex cliques.

Stage 4: The fully developed crowd. The transformation of group structure is completed as lower-status members of the same-sex clique become allied with heterosexual cliques. As a result of this the same-sex cliques are reorganized as groups composed of both sexes.

Stage 5: Beginning of crowd disintegration. Among late adolescents the crowd begins to disintegrate as cliques are formed that consist of couples who are engaged or dating regularly. The crowd often does not completely break up until somewhere in their twenties, when people form new interest groups, and when memberships are expanded to outside groups through college attendance, employment, marriage, and club affiliation.

Influence of Peers

The parent is not the only source of security for the adolescent; another source is peers.

Typical adolescents are conformists to their peers. Peers structure a framework of acceptable behavior patterns. Thus close identification with peers is an important source of security. It is with their peers that adolescents have opportunities to intimately share their problems and experiences. It is also from their peers that they are able to find sympathy and understanding. Through peers adolescents learn to cooperate and clarify their sex roles. Fischer and Bersani (1979) state that youth are free to drift into crime when they have few bonds with peers and institutions, bonds that would aid in forming higher self-esteem.

There is widespread agreement among students of developmental psychology that a rigid type of conformity characterizes early adolescence and diminishes in the later adolescent years. Both male and female adolescents, aged 13 to 14 and 18 to 21, were studied by Landsbaum and Willis (1971) concerning adolescent conformity. The result of their study indicates that younger adolescents, those termed "low-competency" subjects, when paired with "high-competency" subjects, displayed the most behavioral conformity. The data also offered evidence to support the view that younger adolescents are more vulnerable to the influence of peers than older adolescents. This may be observed among junior high school students, where a particular fad is followed by almost all the members of a group.

Lower-class peer groups frequently serve important status functions for adolescents who are disadvantaged according to criteria of society's institutions (schools, churches, businesses). Peer groups become the most important status points for such teenagers. Peer group norms and values stress for these youngsters achievement goals not easily attainable by the conventional norms and values of the larger society. For the lower-class youngster, therefore, the peer group is extremely important, and as Sherif and Sherif (1963, p. 91) point out: "The greater the importance to an individual member of a natural group...the more binding for him is participation in activities initiated by the group." It is out of this social framework that delinquency frequently arises.

Conformity to the peer culture is sometimes associated with good emotional and social adjustment. In a study by Langer (1954) designed to test this hypothesis, various clinical and social-psychological tests were administered to a sample of 600 school pupils from the 4th to the 12th grade, one-third of whom were Indian, one-third white Protestant, and one-third Spanish or Mexican. The results showed that, although conformity to peer-group behavior norms was positively correlated with emotional adjustment, deviance did not necessarily indicate maladjustment. There is some evidence that conformity is sometimes associated with feelings of adequacy, while lack of conformity may result from feelings of inadequacy or insecurity. Deviance from group behavioral norms leads to maladjustments mainly when such deviation separates the individual from the group, automatically cutting off an important source for the satisfaction of certain needs of the individual and perhaps producing an "isolate."

Various subcultures have been identified in high school and college. The high school subdivides into groups that Rice (1981) calls (1) the fun, (2) the academic, and (3) the delinquent. The college subculture subdivides as (1) the collegiate, (2) the academic, (3) the nonconformist, and (4) the vocational. Important in adolescent subcultures is clothing, which expresses identity, independence, or conformity to peer ideas; the automobile, which provides status and freedom and becomes the essence of sexuality for youth; and finally, money, which epitomizes the means of materialism. Another aspect of the adolescent culture is music, which serves to express what a youth thinks or to express what he or she would like to express. And nowhere is the nature of adolescence expressed more succinctly than in its language, often emphasizing slang expressions with their own special meanings. Such language serves to save time and elaborate explanations, to provide more precision than adult vocabulary would, and to serve group interests in terms of solidarity.

Peer Support

Peer and adolescent groups can provide positive roles in psychological and social development. As parental influence declines or is absent and the years of adolescence extend, the peer groups will become more important. Peer relationships provide opportunity for cross-sex and same-sex friendships and partnerships that are the forerunners of later mature friendships and mates. Boys and girls unable to get along with others in the play or work situation, or who do not know how to relate to their own sex group or the opposite sex, are likely to have problems later. Having a friend of the opposite sex to talk with about problems, fears, and future hopes is important. Kitwood (1980) interviewed 153 subjects in five urban areas in England in depth and found that youth placed a high value on "a friend." Parents in general seem to have difficulty discussing problems with their adolescents, particularly personal ones, because the air is often charged with differing emotions--love and hostility. Peers share, in many instances, the same experiences as their counterparts, therefore making it possible to be sympathetic and provide support for some adolescents who often face disapproval at home by highly rigid parents demanding inappropriate behavior for the time and place, and demanding inordinately good school achievement. Peer influence can be harmful where the need of status and security is such that it leads easily into delinquent acts, alcohol, and sex. The peer group does provide for most adolescents a positive proving ground for future interpersonal relationships, thereby paving the way for better adjustment with adults in friendships and cooperative enterprises. A study by Sullivan and Sullivan (1980) found that leaving home to live at college serves to increase young people's affection, communication, satisfaction, and independence in relation to their parents. The difficult task of being affectionate and achieving independence is accomplished. On the other hand, it was found that those who went to college at home did not improve their relationships.

Adolescent Use of Time

An examination of what youth does with its time provides some insight to what they feel is valuable. A survey of eighth graders in a 1988 study of 25,000 youth revealed that they spend 21.7 hours per week watching television, 5.6 hours doing homework, and 1.8 hours on outside reading. By way of contrast Asians spent 6.7 hours doing homework and black students in America spend 27.6 hours a week viewing television (Profile of the American Eighth-Grader, 1990).

Research by Csikszentmihal and Larson (1984) attempted to find out what adolescents do with their time, with whom do they spend it, and where and what they think about their activities. Seventy-five students in this study from Chicago's suburbs were hooked to a monitoring device which signaled every two hours, and the students then gave information as to their activities of the moment--where and with whom they were spending time. The location of activities were principally the following areas: home (41 percent), mainly in the bedroom, living room, or kitchen; the public arena (27 percent), mostly in a friend's home, at work, and/or in an automobile; and finally in school (32 percent), in the classroom and the cafeteria. Results revealed three general activity categories entitled productive (29 percent), maintenance (31 percent), and leisure (40 percent). The largest proportion of productive time was taken up with studying, working on the job, and classwork. Following this was maintenance, which involved chores, errands, eating, and transportation. Lastly, leisure involved socializing, watching television, and reading--all non-school activities.

Time spent with others included classmates 23 percent; friends 29 percent; family 19 percent; others 3 percent; and alone or with strangers 27 percent.

Summary information on when they were most happy revealed "when they were with friends"; "being with classmates" ranked second. "Being alone" ranked third. Half or more of their waking hours were spent with friends and other teenagers. All of these indicators point up the fact that peers are very important in the lives of the adolescent. A shift from dependency on parents to dependency on peers occurs before absolute independence is obtained (Steinberg and Silverberg, 1986). Peer groups change as children go through adolescence. Increasingly time is spent with friends rather than with those who are simply classmates. The groups grow larger and more complex. The intimacy of friendships increases, with adolescents' sharing more thoughts and feelings with others rather than simply engaging in activities (Gottman and Mettetal, 1987).

VALUES, MORALITY, AND RELIGION/MORAL DEVELOPMENT

Values are those things worth working for, saving for, and clinging to tenaciously. Things are valuable because of rarity (diamonds); custom (family dinner and discussion that follows); association and emotion (the father's gold watch that was given to a son at his death); and as a means of gaining control (protecting

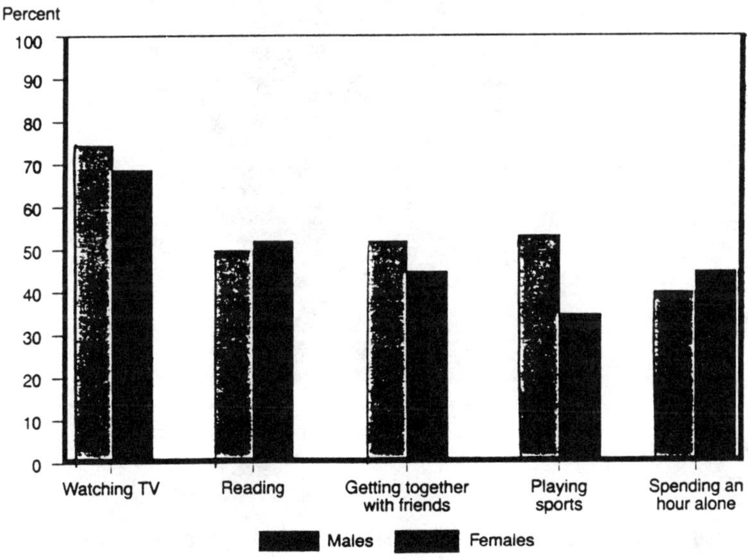

Figure 10.1 High school seniors' activities. (*Source:* U.S. House of Representatives, Select Committee on Children, Youth, and Families, *U.S. Children and Their Families: Current Conditions and Recent Trends, 1987.* University of Michigan, Institute for Social Reserach, *Monitoring the Future*, various years.

and supporting one's self, physically and psychologically).

Attitudes tend to be somewhat interrelated and consistent. They become loosely organized or related to larger structures or value systems, which are more permanent than are specific ideas. For example, an adolescent's attitude toward smoking, exercise, eating, drinking, drugs, adequate rest, and the control of disease will be reflected by his or her value system. Rokeach (1979) has described a value system as a hierarchically arranged set of values--that is, arranged in order of importance. Consciously or otherwise, each person develops established priorities of those behaviors, attitudes, or values that are important. The adolescent who shows little concern for most specific facets of health tends to place behaviors related to health low in a hierarchy of values.

Rokeach distinguished between terminal and instrumental values. Terminal values are ideals to strive for (goals); instrumental values are ways for achieving those ideals. The work of Rokeach (1979) reveals changes in values in every decade from late childhood to old age. Love, wisdom, and being logical were not as important as once thought; honesty was the most stable value chosen, ranking ahead of all other values from ages 11 to 70, emphasizing the importance of developing trust in children and youth. Values, then, furnish a linkage between emotions, attitudes, and thoughts or knowledge. When students studying about the problems faced by Abraham Lincoln as President of the United States are asked to consider their feelings about these problems, implicit or explicit, they are connecting knowledge and feelings.

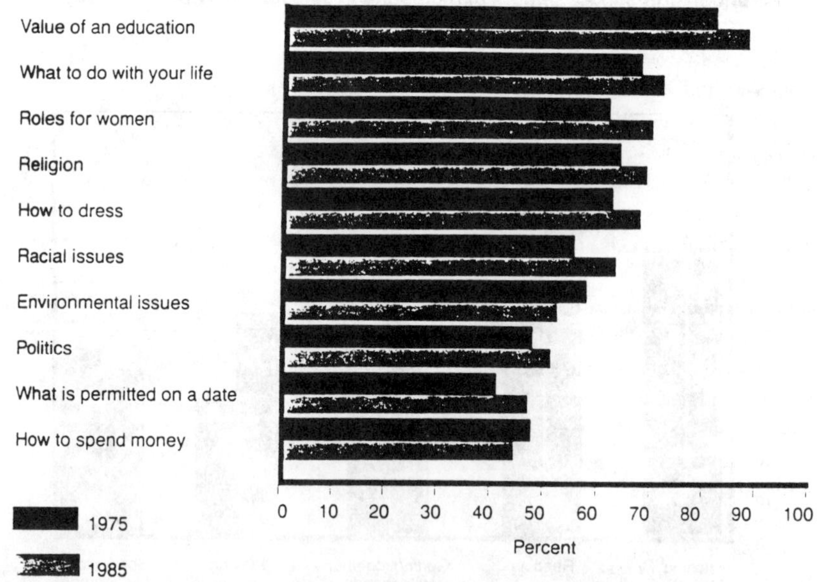

Figure 10.2 Attitudes compared to parents' views. (*Source:* University of Michigan, Institute for Social Research, *Monitoring the Future*, various years.

Bobby and Posterski (1985) found the percentages of adolescents 15 to 19 who selected values as "very important" to range as follows:

Friendship	92%
Being loved	88%
Freedom	86%
Success	81%
A comfortable life	79%
Privacy	70%
Family life	68%
Excitement	61%
Acceptance by God	41%
Recognition	41%
Being popular	22%

Obviously youth seem to favor the certainty of friendship and being loved over nebulous popularity.

Theories of Moral Development

There is substantial evidence that the growth in moral judgment and principles parallels that of cognitive development. Research by Kohlberg and Gilligan (1971) found that failure to develop high or principled moral reasoning is correlated with lack of a cognitive structure operating at the formal level (Piaget's stages are outlined in Chapter 7). In their study they found a majority (60 percent) of the subjects 16 years old or above were at the formal operational level, but only 10 percent showed the postconventional stage of morality. Some evidence exists to indicate that only a portion (10 percent of adult and adolescent middle-class Americans) reach the highest principled level in moral reasoning. Even fewer among the lowest socioeconomic class reach the highest level. There is also evidence that many more college-educated persons reach the highest level. In the Milgram experiment referred to earlier, 75 percent of the college students judged to be at the principled level of reasoning refused to shock the victim when ordered to do so by authorities; conversely, only 13 percent of those judged at the lower levels (preconventional and conventional) refused to administer the shock.

There is a clear relationship between age and Kohlberg's levels of morality, though a specific individual's moral development may not follow the age-grade pattern of development. This being the case, it follows, according to Piaget, that postconventional morality becomes possible only with adolescence and the development of formal operational thought. Kohlberg has found that most middle-class 10-year-old children (67 percent) are reasoning at the pre-conventional level, which consists of Stage 1 (punishment and obedience) and Stage 2 (behavior based upon rewards). By 13 the majority of these youths are at the conventional level, either Stage 3 (good boy, good girl) or Stage 4 (legalistic morality), to avoid censure of authorities. At 16, 35 percent of adolescents are at the postconventional level of moral reasoning, most at Stage 5 (morality determined by democratically accepted laws) rather than Stage 6 (morality based upon universals and individually accepted principles). Some fluctuations were noted at 20 and 24 years of age. Gilligan (1977) found women typically functioning on the conventional level. Turiel (1974) believes the retrogression discovered by some investigators in late adolescence and young adulthood can be accounted for by assuming that the subjects hold moral beliefs on particular issues. Consequently conventional morality is one of a number of alternatives they chose rather than a pragmatic approach not yet systematized in the final transition to postconventional morality. Figure 10.3 presents the varying percentages of each stage of morality from 10 to 24 years of age found by Kohlberg.

The universality of Kohlberg's stages remains to be demonstrated conclusively. Some say that Stage 5 corresponds to conservative legal philosophy whereas Stage 6 reflects traditional liberal, radical, and political reasoning (Hogan & Schroeder, 1981). They also contend that Kohlberg's theory is more a political

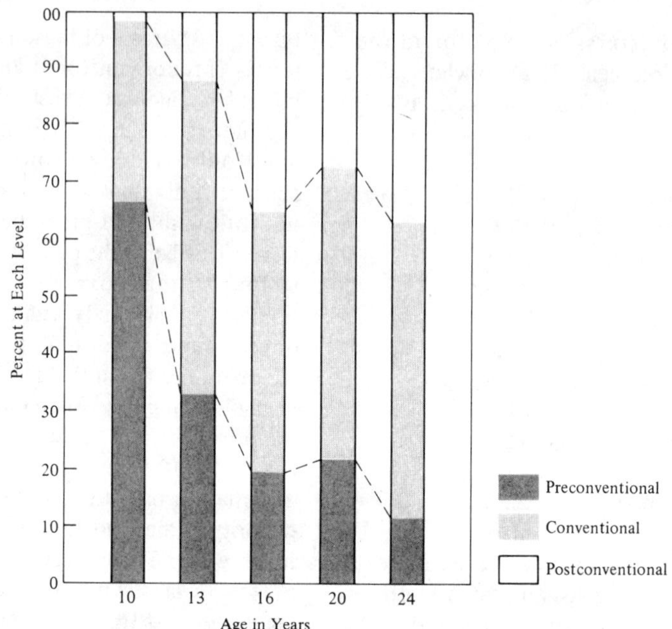

Figure 10.3 Levels of moral development by age. (*Source:* Kohlberg & Gilligan, 1971. Reprinted by permission of *Daedalus,* Journal of the American Academy of Arts and Sciences, *100,* 1971, Boston, Mass.)

manifesto than a scientific statement, with the reliability undefined, the validity of the measures unknown, and the reasoning still being developed (p. 10). Gilligan (1977) has noted that the sample originally studied was all male. She cites studies to show that women have a tendency to use Stage 3 as their dominant mode of moral reasoning. Gilligan thinks apparent sex differences may reflect the then-current formulation of higher stages more than they would failure to develop to these stages. Stress on abstract principles of justice may ignore personal and interpersonal issues such as the conflict between caring for others and taking responsibility for one's own actions. Gilligan (1988) says further those seeking justice organize relationships in terms of equality, symbolized by a balancing of the scales. For those valuing care the relationships connote responsiveness symbolized by a network. The typical woman focuses on care rather than abstract justice, hence the need for further modification of the levels of morality. Enright, Franklin, and Manheim (1980) suggest that throughout life people are faced with distributive justice--giving or receiving allowances, giving to charities and supporting others--more than with saving a life through theft of a high-priced drug, the example often used by Kohlberg.

Adolescents need to generalize broad values they often hold. It is probably true that since the early eighties the social and economic values of adolescents have become more conservative. They are increasingly concerned about personal well-being and financial success. They are less concerned about the welfare of others--the handicapped and society as a whole. Political liberalism has declined among youth as interest in individual success has grown. The impeccability or large institutions such as business, labor, the courts, the schools, and law enforcement has suffered partly due to the counterrevolution of the sixties and to greater knowledge of institutional operations and their fallibility as portrayed by the media in the 1970s and 1980s (Astin, 1987). At the same time interest in religion and church attendance has dropped over the past decade, particularly from 1980 as depicted by the following indicators (Table 10.1).

Religion and Youth

Western culture, like others, is oriented to religion. The adolescent growth period characterized by rapid physical and mental growth affects moral and spiritual development. The increased reflective element in the cognitive maturity of youth often leads to religious thoughts about faith, idealism, and life after death. The religious view of adolescents generally becomes more abstract and less literal and absolute. God is seen as a far-off abstract force rather than a man-like being with stern qualities. Religion offers several broad views about what takes place in adolescence. One suggests it is a time of conversion crisis, and another suggests it involves a religious identity crisis. Some religions emphasize adolescence as a period in which religious awakening takes place, while there is also some indication that it is a period of repudiation, at least in part, of religion as portrayed by the church.

Many youth are attracted to fundamentalist church groups (belief in the Bible and the necessity of being "born again" through faith in Christ) represented by Baptist, Methodist, Pentecostal, Church of God, Lutheran, and other churches, particularly in the rural South and Midwest. Youths who are among the higher socio-economic levels often attend formal churches like the Episcopal or Presbyterian, where the emphasis is usually on principles of moral life rather than dramatic conversions. These youths come into church membership through gradual developmental processes. Many believe religion in adolescence to be related to the larger identity crisis issue. In two studies, Hoffman (1970) and Podd (1972) suggest that the quest for identity is the search for a cause. Logan (1980) suggests that the ecology movement may, to some extent, be motivated by purist motives and adhered to with religious fidelity. The search involves questions that youth raise such as: Why am I here? What can I value? What can I believe? In this social context young people are looking for something to which they can devote themselves.

The view that religion is repudiated by many youths is seen to some extent in the church attendance of those in late adolescence and young adults (Jacquet, 1975). Adolescents

Table 10.1 RELIGIOUS INVOLVEMENT OF HIGH SCHOOL SENIORS: 1976 TO 1985

Religious Activity and Level of Interest	Percent of Seniors 1976	1978	1980	1982	1984	1985
Frequency of religious services attendance						
Weekly	40.7	39.4	43.1	37.3	37.7	35.3
1-2 times a month	16.3	17.2	16.3	17.4	16.2	16.6
Rarely	32.0	34.4	32.0	35.8	35.8	37.0
Never	11.0	9.0	8.6	9.6	10.2	11.1
Importance of religion in life						
Very important	28.8	27.8	32.4	28.4	29.7	27.3
Pretty important	30.5	33.0	32.6	33.0	32.6	32.4
A little	27.8	27.9	25.3	27.9	26.7	27.6
Not important	12.9	11.2	9.8	10.7	11.0	12.7

Source: University of Michigan, Institute for Social Research, *Monitoring the Future*, various years.

think the church is not doing its best to understand youth's ideas about sex (Yankelovich, 1974). They also feel the church does not afford the status to women and minorities that it should (Bengtson & Starr, 1975). It is generally known that Catholic youth disagree with their church's stand on birth control, marriage of priests, and traditionalism in the church service. The survey by Yankelovich (1974) gives indications that young people do not place emphasis on religion as a "very important personal value." Rokeach (1979), in his survey of terminal values (such as salvation) and instrumental values (such as education), concurs with this view. Using the Rokeach Value Survey Scale to study values in parochial and public schools, Brown and Lawson (1980) found only Catholic youth ranked salvation first; public school youth rated it 19th, and Friends and Episcopalians ranked it 17th on a list of instrumental values. The adolescent of today prefers religion that is based on fellowship and is unstructured and more personal than the institutionalized type found in formal church services.

The charismatic movement of recent years involves a variety of differing groups and offers shelter to many young people who are seeking direction in their lives, security, and completion of their identity. The disparate nature of these groups can be seen in an enumeration of some: Jesus People, Moon's Unification Church, Hare Krishna, Jesus Freaks, God's Forever Family, Jesus Boppers, Youth for Christ (predates the other groups), Crusade for Christ, and Christian YWCAs. The famous television evangelist Billy Graham was involved with the latter movements many years ago. The fact is that the fundamentalistic revival movement among youth (leaders: Edsin Orr, Phil Saint, Mel Trotter, Glen McBirnie, George Truett, and others) was observed in the 1930s and 1940s. The Jesus Movement, for one, is made up principally of youths in their late teens and early twenties from middle-class homes who have dropped out of school and are often alienated from society. Interviews of some members of this group by Balswick (1974) indicated that they came from all types of backgrounds and religions. Catholics and Jewish youth were found in disproportionate numbers. Many of these were former hippies, heavily into drugs and sex, while others were from anachronistic groups. Now some have joined the Jesus Movement, espousing love, peace, and happiness for all. Many young people once turned to ecological concerns when the Vietnam War ended. In the 1970s many communes of Jesus people still existed around the world, particularly in Europe and Southeast Asia (Balswick, 1974). The touchstone of these groups is the Bible; its use and quotations serve to unify groups and provide justification for group conduct and condemnation of society. They believe in Christ both as immanent and transcendent, in the second coming and the world's end, in the Holy Spirit living in each receptive person, in the efficacy of prayer, and in commitment to the cause. Youth are sustained by what some call getting "high" on Jesus or being moved by the spirit. They frequently utilize rock gospel music in their services. Many more religious groups, disparate in nature but organized as "ad hoc" assemblies, exist today reflecting religious values.

In summary it is safe to say that many young people have been influenced by the charismatic movement and that forms of worship have been altered due to these movements. Some clergymen have modified their ministry to accommodate the Jesus youth and street people. Though young people seem to be anti-church, they are not anti-religious but concerned with personal salvation as a way of solving the world's problems. Many of those involved are perhaps postponing solution of the identity crisis or seeking closure of it and use these sects as a way of adding meaning to their lives.

OPPOSITE-SEX INTERESTS AND DATING PATTERNS

One of the most significant adjustments, and a critical one for adolescents, is the development of sexuality. With the maturing of the endocrine gland system, particularly as related to sexual functioning, interest in the opposite sex increases dramatically. Biological growth and social pressures increasingly demand that adolescents come to resolve the problem of awakening sexual impulses. Sexual attraction and desire become a dominant force in their lives. Indeed the first intercourse is a milestone of considerable consequence for the individual. It has other connotations besides the act itself. For instance, it indicates a larger control over one's body, ability to enter an intimate relationship, freedom to a greater degree from parents, and a proclaiming of one's sexual identity.

The report of the Center for Disease Control (1991) indicates the sexual activity of female teenagers has soared in the past two decades. Surveying women 15 to 19 years of age, 25.6 percent have sex by the age of 15, whereas among 19-year-olds 75.3 percent have engaged in sex. In 1970 the corresponding figures were 4.6 percent for the 15-year-old; 48.2 percent for the 19-year-old. Among 17-year-olds the increase was from 32.3 percent to 51 percent. Sevgi Aral (1991), a sociologist with the Center for Disease Control, says of the results of the survey, "This is happening during a time when we are putting so much emphasis on public health messages regarding the risks of sexual activity because of the AIDS crisis." Among older adolescent women, particularly at the college level, an equalitarian, premarital sexual standard is replacing the traditional double standard. It is believed none the less that college students are more conservative in their sexual attitudes, choosing to have sex based upon emotional considerations and friendship and are not regarding sexual intercourse as a basis for marriage or engagement.

The new code for morality among young people involves the climate surrounding sexual intercourse; acceptability of sexual behaviors depends upon the emotional involvement of a couple. Under this view even petting of the couple is not approved if there is no feeling or love or strong affection.

Dating for a few boys and girls begins early. In a survey on dating by the National Institutes of Health (1974), by 12 years of age 10 percent of the boys had dated compared with only 7 percent of the girls (see Table 10.2). By age 13 girls passed the boys in numbers of dates and continued to do so until 17, the final year of the data collected. Dating is first seen as informal getting together of boys and girls at the home of one of the girls, where the parents usually serve as chaperons. The mother chaperons more often and may or may not directly monitor activities, which often include games, talking, story swapping, and sometimes dancing and having refreshments. In a study by Bernstein (1976) involving children in the fifth, sixth, and seventh grades, it was noted that interest in dating was noted by over 50 percent who acknowledged having a sweetheart. Also 87 percent of the seventh graders said they had experience with kissing. In research conducted by Jackson (1975) on the meaning of dating among nondaters aged 11 and 12 years, 58 percent of the girls said dating means to go out with the opposite sex; 35 percent of the boys

Table 10.2 YOUTHS WHO HAVE DATED BY AGE AND SEX

	Percent of youths who ever dated	
Ages	**Boys**	**Girls**
12 years	10.0	7.0
13 years	17.9	18.5
14 years	38.2	37.6
15 years	60.0	66.5
16 years	75.9	81.3
17 years	85.1	92.6

Source: National Institutes of Health (1975).

agreed. Eighteen percent of the girls said it meant to go out with a "special person"; no boys mentioned this but 18 percent of the boys said it was "fun." Another 18 percent said dating means going out without your parents.

As adolescents grow older, the dating pattern changes to one-on-one coupling and eventually to "going steady" by many. Some characterize steady dating as being with the other person at least twice a week on a regular basis. Adolescents, once they start to date, usually do so on an average of once a week. Typical activities for those who date are:

1. Movies, football, or basketball games
2. Concerts
3. Beach and/or swimming
4. Dances
5. Parties
6. Ice cream or drug store or pizza parlor
7. Parking
8. Home setting
9. Game establishments
10. School activities--plays, shows, etc.

Dating provides a number of functions, such as allowing members of the opposite sex to get together and explore compatibility, to terminate the relationship (early in the dating) without the loss of face, engage in sexual exploration and discovery within limits that are mutually acceptable, find companionship, engage in sympathetic problem sharing, and achieve status grading in which the individual is given higher status because of his or her date. Rice (1981) lists a number of reasons for dating:

1. Recreation
2. Socializing
3. Personal growth
4. Status grading
5. Providing a pleasant opportunity for companionship without responsibility of marriage
6. Sexual experimentation, satisfaction, or exploitation
7. Understanding and sorting of mates toward selection
8. Achieving intimacy

According to a number of studies (Allen & Eicher, 1973; Berg, 1975; Rice, 1981), the personal qualities most liked and disliked by teenagers are those listed in Table 10.3.

The popular date is one who can keep the ball rolling with banter and the typical "line." The line is an individual adaptation of a commonly accepted aspect of a young man's (or older man's) personality. Young men consciously practice, modify, and improve their lines. They even discuss their approaches and lines with other males. A girl will often parry the line as skillfully as she can, successfully creating greater interest in the boy and at the same time keep him from advancing too far in intimacy or involving herself too deeply emotionally. If the latter occurs, then the opportunity to have insight into his character to compare with others is precluded.

Unfortunately, as there are positive aspects of dating, there are also pitfalls. Many of the personal qualities that the dating system rewards are not those that lead to good marriages or partnership. The lines, the superficial bantering, and often the posturing and bragging are skills that do not lend themselves to sustained relationships in adulthood. Also the desire of the adolescent to be popular often results in the development of manipulative skills and serves to destroy interpersonal skills. Unsuccessful dating in our society is a powerful weapon of peer censure. The word that this girl will do this or that, that Bob has bad breath, that Jim is a lunk or a clod on a date, may mean the end of dating. An identity search by youth is complicated by the societal expectations of the dating system, where the biological and psychosocial adjustments create a difficult task for the individual. In steady dating, those with low self-esteem who are not socially accepted or popular frequently have regular partners to avoid being left out. For the younger adolescent dating does not usually lead to marriage, but it frequently leads to early sexual intercourse. Popular girls and boys usually date different individuals, and it places less responsibility on sexual controls, for very few youths copulate without dating a person frequently. Going steady is looked upon by many youths as a license for increasing sexual intimacy. The disadvantages of going steady are many; it may lead to early marriage and the birth of children, and the steady may become a drone, taking the date for granted. Further, it disrupts educational pursuits and creates economic problems.

As the adolescent grows older, the pressure to do serious dating increases. Group socialization or random dating becomes a stereotype that is to some degree stultifying. The biological aspect involving the sexual drives and curiosity reaches its peak (particularly for boys) during the late teen years. Teenagers have strong security needs, yet at the same time need to develop independence. Society does not provide for meeting these needs. Physical intimacy, however, does provide comfort and the easing of loneliness and may offer a sexual outlet that usually is increasingly satisfactory. Problems also come with increased or complete sexual intimacy. The interpersonal relationships are fraught with the struggle to find balance between persons, raising questions of who dominates the situation. There are also questions to be answered about love and exploitation, dependence and independence, anger and hostility. All have to be dealt with as the nature of sexuality is confronted.

ADOLESCENT PERSONAL PROBLEMS

In a study reported by Adams (1964), approximately 4,000 boys and girls from over 30 schools were asked to report their biggest personal problem. The boys and girls were also

Table 10.3 TRAITS LIKED OR DISLIKED BY ADOLESCENTS

Liked		
Appearance	**Social behavior**	**Character**
Good-looking	Outgoing, friendly	Kind
Feminine	Active	Sympathetic
Nice figure (girls)	Energetic	Unselfish
Masculine, good build (boys)	Has social skills	Generous
Neat, clean, clothes well groomed	Good sport	Cheerful
	Acts age	Optimistic
	Mature	Honest
	Good reputation	Sense of humor
		Cooperative
		Stable
		High ideals
Disliked		
Appearance	**Social behavior**	**Character**
Homely	Shy, timid	Cruel, bully
Poor figure	Passive	Quarrelsome
Sissy	Listless	Inconsiderate
Skinny	Loud, childish	Pessimistic
Sloppy	Bad reputation	A liar
Unclean	Poor sport	Can't take a joke
Clothes not suitable	Drip	Dirty mind
Physical handicap	Nonjoiner	Conceited
		Not reliable
		Domineering

asked to list what they thought was the greatest problem for other boys and girls of their age. The subjects ranged in age from 10 to 19. A review of the literature by Nicholson and Antill (1981) and a report of a study they undertook follows the general finding of the Adams study.

Problem areas and the percentages of personal problems of the Adams survey reported by each area for self and peers by the total group of boys and girls are presented in Table 10.4. Contrary to findings of many other studies, school problems were listed by a larger percentage of boys than girls. Girls listed more interpersonal and family problems than boys, while boys listed more problems related to sports, recreation, and finances. Both sexes see their peers as having fewer school problems and more interpersonal problems than they report for themselves. Otherwise, there was a close relationship between problem areas of self and of peers.

The Nicholson and Antill study shows the major problems to be (1) schooling and education, (2) social and interpersonal skills, and (3) home and family communication. This represents little change from the data reported by Adams in 1964. Six specific expectations derived from the later (1981) report are:

1. Girls will report more problems than boys.
2. Young adolescents report more problems than older adolescents.
3. Girls will report more social-interpersonal problems than boys; boys more problems concerning the future and finances.
4. Young adolescents will report more health and physical development problems; older youth more vocational problems.
5. Peer acceptance and masculinity will both be negatively related to the number of problems reported.
6. Femininity will be positively related to the number of problems reported.

Following the major pubertal changes, the pleasure of adolescence centers largely on discovering and learning more about members of the opposite sex. Since many school and extracurricular activities are coeducational, opportunities for girls and boys to have a variety of social interchanges exist. This allows them to learn the nature and interests of their sex counterparts. In the group-conscious middle adolescent years, positive impressions of the opposite sex stimulate affection and infatuation. This is often called "puppy love." It serves, besides providing experience, as a try-on

PERCENTAGE OF PERSONAL PROBLEMS REPORTED FOR SELF AND PEERS

Problem area	Self		Peer	
	Male	Female	Male	Female
School	35	23	21	14
Interpersonal	12	19	23	33
Maturity	2	3	2	7
Emotions	2	4	2	3
Work	6	5	7	6
Sports and recreation	4	2	5	2
Health	2	4	2	2
Ethical	1	2	1	2
Family	10	22	8	17
Habits	0	0	1	1
Finances	10	4	7	4
Unclassified	8	6	8	3
No answer	4	3	13	6
No problem	4	3	0	0

Source: Adams (1964).

identity by projecting one's diffused image on to the other person. Its reflection aids in the clarification of one's own identity. This probably accounts for the fact that much of this nubile love revolves around talking to each other and with the group. The typical adolescent will go through several such loves--even six or seven before marriage is not unusual. Associations are usually short-lived because the teenager is not socially or emotionally mature enough to sustain long-term intimate relationships. Many girls who are looking for romantic relationships mistake the interest of the boy in this situation, which is often purely sexual.

Clear-cut sexual urges appear first in boys. Early introduction to sexual arousal and orgasm comes through masturbation; the sexual urge is personal and organ-centered. Psychologically the sex hormones are nonspecific and the sex drive is undifferentiated before sexual habits are completely formed. When heterosexual yearnings begin, the principal urge is for companionship and the pleasant sensation of brief body contact such as in holding hands and dancing. Social and emotional warmth is desired by most postpubertal girls, as they want affection, affiliation, and love, but not primarily sex.

Love

In America love and romance are prerequisites for marriage. In some cultures, as among the Chinese and Japanese, they are regarded as irrelevant. Class, culture, health, and economics are more important. Many tribes in Africa and Asia insist that the notion of love is a disruptive influence in the lives of their people (Gluckman, 1955). Defining love is a difficult task. For adolescents it combines strong physical attraction, the desire to be with the loved object all the time, and deep psychological involvement (the awestruck state). Liebowitz (1983) claims that love has a unique chemical basis perhaps associated with phenylthylamine. In romantic attraction certain brain centers are believed to release great amounts of this substance, starting in motion a chain of neurochemical events that are much like an amphetamine high. Rubin (1973) found in surveying adolescents and young adults three components of romantic love: (1) attachment--the need to be with the loved person; (2) caring--the need to do almost anything for the loved person; and (3) intimacy--the need to tell one's sweetheart everything. Some adolescents, mainly those who are older, frequently fall in love following friendship and romance, get married, have children and remain with each other. For the most part many adolescent loves precede this stage. The difficulties that are inherent in romantic love are that the physical attraction is mistaken for lasting love. This leads to sexual activity which leads to pregnancy, creating disadvantages for the progeny and for the family, often a life of poverty.

Sexuality and Early Pregnancies

The sexual revolution of the 1960s and 1970s has been documented through many sources. Its meaning has been debated. Cobliner (1988) suggests that it has led to promiscuity and shallow relationships between casual acquaintances. He writes the following:

> sexual involvement between partners of the opposite sex has been sporadic, episodic, without commitment, and accompanied by a deliberate effort of both partners to suppress tender, romantic feelings and intimacy... sexual conventions clash with the fundamental urge to form human attachments; diminish and often shut out the experience of passion in sexual unions; and bring about inner turmoil that weakens self-confidence.

Still others as late as the mid 1970s were stating that young people were no more active than their parents had been, just more open and honest about sex. However there are data from national studies (Hayes, 1987; Hofferth, et al. 1987; Zelnick and Kantner, 1980) affirming that a dramatic change has taken place particularly among young women (U.S. Center for Disease

Control, 1991). Up until the early 1960s slightly over 7 percent of teenage girls reported having intercourse by age 16. By 1971, nearly 25 percent reported sexual unions. Data gathered by the Center for Disease Control in 1988 reveal 75.3 percent of teenage women had premarital sex. Data for males are sketchy; overall changes are less dramatic but consistent. Lueptow (1984) says clearly most young Americans do not regard the new morality as license for promiscuous thrill seeking. They appear to seek a sense of identity through an affectionate and emotionally involved form of physical intimacy. The research of Bobby and Posterski (1985) asked some 3,500 Canadian adolescents to respond to the statement: "If two people like each other do you think it is all right for them to have intercourse on the first date?" Twenty-two percent of the respondents said yes (19 percent boys, 3 percent girls). Next they were asked whether it is permissible to have sexual relations after a few dates. Fifty-one percent of the boys said yes, while only 33 percent of the girls said yes.

Differences regarding fantasies in male and female college students during sexual arousal were most likely to concern petting or intercourse with "one you love or are fond of" according to Miller and Simon (1980). Fantasies of sexual activity with strangers for whom they had no emotional attachment were ranked 79 percent for men but only 22 percent for females. Under experimental conditions with both sexes, greater sexual aggressiveness is generally observed in adolescent males, due in part to vastly greater increases in testosterone levels at puberty (Peterson, 1988; Katchadourian, 1985). The first sexual experience for teenage girls is most likely to be with a steady boyfriend three years older, whereas with boys it is often with a casual acquaintance a year older.

Masturbation

Of the total sexual outlet for adolescents, self-stimulation claims the largest share. Males masturbate more than females, reaching peak numbers at 16 or 17 years of age. By 19 years of age 85 to 90 percent of teenage males have participated in this form of sexual release. This is probably the same percent as the previous generation. Masturbation, however, is taking place more frequently among younger boys. Recent studies show that by 13 years of age 65 percent of boys have masturbated, compared to only 45 percent of 13-year-olds in a 1940 sample. Among girls there has been an increase at all ages. Thirty-three percent of girls by age 13 have masturbated, contrasting with earlier studies reporting only 15 percent. By age 20, 60 percent have masturbated as opposed to 30 percent in earlier studies (Kinsey, et al., 1953; Conger, 1980). Those who engage in sexual intercourse are three times as likely to masturbate than the sexually inexperienced.

The incidence of masturbation seems to have been effected largely by more tolerant attitudes, its universality and the mitigation of the idea that it is harmful. The act of masturbation is a part of normal development, and usually becomes a problem only when identified by parents as wrong or harmful. It can also be harmful if viewed as a deviation by the person practicing the behavior or if used as a substitute for some activity in which one feels inadequate.

Many contemporary educators believe masturbation is normal and healthy, helping people to learn how to give and receive sexual pleasure. It often provides a way to fulfill sexual desire without entering into a relationship for which one may not be ready (Barbach, 1975; LoPiccolo and Lobitz, 1972).

Homosexuality

Many teenagers have one or more homosexual experiences before the age of 15 (Dryer, 1982). Only 3 percent of the boys and 2 percent of girls make this their on-going practice, even though 15 percent of the boys and 10 percent of the girls have had a homosexual contact during adolescence. The incidence of homosexuality is alleged by Chilman (1983) to have been stable for the past 40 years. The fact that many homosexuals are more open in acknowledging their sexual preference and have sought to forward their rights often through demonstrations and parades means to some observers that their numbers have increased. Causes are attributed to genetic factors, hormonal imbalance, a family with a dominating mother and a weak father, and learning about sex from being seduced by a person of the same sex. Masters and Johnson (1979) and Durden-Smith & DeSimone (1982) believe interaction with environmental events and various hormonal circumstances cause homosexuality. The 1987 manual of the American Psychiatric Association classifies homosexuality as a disorder only when one has "persistent and marked distress about one's sexual orientation." The APA, then, has stopped calling homosexuality a "mental disorder."

Remabedi (1987), interviewing 29 anonymous homosexuals in Minneapolis, found the average age of becoming homosexual was 14. Eight of the subjects in this study felt physical and emotional attraction to other males as early as six years of age. Half felt they were influenced by negative family and environmental situations in early childhood. Six of the 29 subjects wanted to be heterosexuals, although their sexual preference was well-established. Many of the youths had serious problems. Eight dropped out of school due to their sexual orientation; 24 used illicit drugs, half had brushes with the law; and two-thirds of them had seen psychiatrists due to their sexual persuasion. One-third had been hospitalized for mental illness, all but one had contemplated suicide, and 10 had actually attempted it. Half of the number had sexually transmitted diseases. Seventy-nine percent classified themselves as homosexuals, while 21 percent said they were bisexuals. If this is representative of the wider sample of homosexuals, certainly this orientation is problematic. Remabedi (1987) contends that the younger homosexual males are probably at greater risk due to their physical and emotional immaturity.

A differing view suggests that homosexuality before puberty, from the psychoanalytic viewpoint, is considered normal, but after puberty indicates arrested development (Feibleman, 1974). Among college students (*Playboy*, 1976) in a national sample, 12 percent of the men and 4 percent of the women said they had at least one homosexual experience.

Bisexuality includes those individuals who are aroused by, and have sex with, both men and women; they may be heterosexual mainly and occasionally homosexual, or the reverse (Janda & Klinke-Hamel, 1980). There are no hard data on the incidence of bisexuality, and it was rarely mentioned in the literature 15 years ago. A study by Roesler and Deisler (1972) found that for youths to consider themselves homosexual, the following steps occurred: (1) engaging in early homosexual sex play, (2) seeking homosexual partners in adolescence, and (3) overtly participating in the gay world. On the average they found it took four years for youths to go from the first homosexual orgasm to the point of considering themselves homosexual. Many of these had visited a psychiatrist and contemplated suicide during the four years. The causes of homosexual orientation suggest the origins are disturbed family relationships, social learning, prenatal endocrine factors, or in some cases a same-sex living situation at a critical period of development (U.S. Department of Health, Education, and Welfare, 1978). Numerous organizations involving parents of gays (POG) exist, as do ministries to the gay community by the various churches.

Pregnancy and Contraception

The phenomenon of pregnancies among teenage girls is an ever growing problem. Even though sex education is nearly universally available, knowledge is lacking of condoms and other birth control devices. One must add to this the fact that there is a current lack of a cure for genital herpes and acquired immune deficiency syndrome (AIDS). Still, in the U.S. over a million girls 15 to 19 become pregnant. This represents over 10 percent of the entire age population of this group. Over 125,000 girls under the age of 15 become pregnant each year (Edelman, 1987). Older adolescents are twice as likely to use contraceptives even with the first intercourse than are girls of 15 (Shah and Zelnik, 1981). More than one-third of sexually active teenage girls become pregnant some time in their adolescent years (Jones, et al., 1986). According to 1985 records, about 40 percent of pregnancies were terminated by abortion while 40 percent gave birth. This accounts for the falling birth rate since 1970, though the birth rate for all unmarried teenagers has gone up. Some 10 to 15 percent of the number for abortions includes those girls who had miscarriages. Even in the pregnancies that occur postmaritally each year the problems encountered with adolescent pregnancies are more frequent than with older women. (See Chapter 3 for the risk to young adolescents giving birth.) The developed countries such as France, England, Sweden, and Norway, with the most open attitude toward sex also have the most effective formal and informal sex education programs, counseling, and contraceptive services for adolescents.

In the United States opponents of such preventive measures as sex education argue that these programs and other services encourage participation in sex by giving it status and tacit approval by school, health, and social services. Ironically 85 percent of American parents favor sex education. Fifty-eight percent of girls who had sex at 15 years of age had taken or were enrolled in sex education classes. Planned Parenthood Federation of America in 1986 reported on the use of birth control among sexually active teenagers, stating that nearly 60 percent of those youths interviewed who were between 12 and 17 years of age frequently or always used contraceptives. Many of the 35 percent who seldom used contraception had not had a comprehensive sex education program at school. Of those who had talked with their parents about birth control, sex, and pregnancy, 63 percent frequently or always used contraception. Those who talked with parents about sex and pregnancy but not birth control in nearly 60 percent of the cases did not use birth control. There is no evidence that sex education increases the incidence of sex among youth, but there is evidence that among sexually active youth those who have had sex education programs use effective birth control measures (Dawson, 1986).

Failure to Use Contraception

Among the major reasons teenagers do not use contraceptives were: (1) they thought they couldn't get pregnant because of the time of the month, their age, or the infrequency of intercourse; (2) contraceptives were not available when they needed them; (3) they felt that they did not control their lives and hence were fatalistic about the matter; (4) they believed contraception spoiled the spontaneity of the relationship; (5) they felt that if girls plan for use of contraception it appears they expect sex and it makes them too knowledgeable in a society that thinks boys should be the initiators of sexual relations. Another, lesser reason is that some girls wish to be pregnant (67 percent) as a means of holding their boyfriends, getting back at their parents, having someone to love and love them back, and finally to change the prospects of a dismal life (Chilman, 1983).

Help for Pregnant Girls

The number of infants born out of wedlock is rising. In the early 1980s, 39 percent of babies born out of wedlock were white while 90 percent of those born to black teenagers were in this category. Nine out of ten pregnant teenagers who bring their babies to term keep their infants.

Once the teenage mother realizes the demands placed upon her to care for an infant, she tends to leave it unattended for longer periods of time. Eventually such children are often placed in foster care programs and in many cases, particularly among black and Hispanic teenage mothers, the children are cared for by their grandparents. Many teenage mothers bear low-weight babies, have complicated pregnancies involving toxemia and anemia and deliveries that are prolonged; they are also more likely to bear children with neurological defects who die in the first year of life. Eighty-five percent of the boys who father children of teenage mothers abandon them. All too often little prenatal care is given or comes late in the pregnancies; many pregnant teenagers are very ill informed about health care generally and are slow to seek an examination.

Help for the unmarried pregnant teenager should be given as soon as possible. She needs to be assured of help and care and that she is capable of bearing and caring for an infant. In addition, she needs to know that she can express her fears, that she will continue to be attractive, and that life is not over, particularly where she is left out of school, bereft of counseling, and living away from her parents and kin. Many programs help pregnant girls stay in school, teach them job skills and parenting skills, and help them adjust. A number of high schools offer day care for the children of unmarried students to help them continue their schooling. Some programs offer parenting training for fathers (Buie, 1987). Training young people in parenting shows benefits for the child and mother. In a program reported by Field, et al. (1982), 80 low-income teenage mothers received training either though bi-weekly visits to their homes (utilizing a graduate student and aide) or by paid job training as a teacher's aide in the infants' nursery of a medical school. When compared with babies in a control group, the infants of both parent-training groups did better. Their babies weighed more and showed the most gains in growth. These mothers had fewer additional pregnancies. Also, more returned to work or school, and over time their babies showed the most progress.

It should be remembered that the teenager who becomes pregnant can have assistance, if not from her family or the father's family, then through social welfare agencies. Family and child organizations related to church groups often provide assistance. Adoption agencies may take infants from those mothers who cannot or do not wish to raise them. Social services in most areas assign a caseworker to each pregnant girl who comes to them. The caseworker provides vocational and educational guidance, public financial assistance, birth control information, and assistance in finding housing.

Rosen (1980), in a study of 432 females under 18, found 50 percent involved their mothers in pregnancy-resolution decision making. Educational facilities of school systems are usually offered to unmarried pregnant or married students in most states. Many urban centers have special facilities and programs for pregnant women. Some school systems, however, have policies that have not yet acknowledged court rulings; some have set times for termination of schooling after pregnancy, many shortly after the condition has been observed (Rice, 1981). Many special programs for the young pregnant teenager exist, such as the Edgar Allan Poe Schools in Baltimore; programs in Azusa, California; Emory University in Atlanta; and the Young Mothers Educational Development Program in Syracuse. The aim of these agencies is to provide a variety of support--medical, educational-vocational, contraceptive, and moral. In many places alternate schooling for pregnant teenagers and those with other problems has provided settings that are sympathetic, increasing youth self-esteem and satisfaction.

Sexually Transmitted Disease

Though not all sexually transmitted diseases begin with adolescents, it is during this time that youth should think about prevention. Many authorities think sex education should begin very early, perhaps by the primary grades. Venereal disease has spread dramatically over the past several decades, particularly among adolescents. Of the eight to ten million cases of STDs (Sexually Transmitted Diseases) each year in the United States, three out of four occur in the 15- to 24-year-old. The most common of these diseases is chlamydia, which causes infections of the urinary tract, the rectum, the cervix, and sometimes serious abdominal infection. Other diseases seen in increasing numbers are gonorrhea, genital warts, herpes simplex, syphilis, and acquired immune deficiency syndrome (AIDS).

AIDS is the most feared of all the diseases, leaving the immune system incapable of handling serious threats from pneumonia, cancers, and a variety of fatal diseases. The virus is transmitted through bodily fluids (blood and semen) and stays with the body for life, even though the person carrying it may show no signs of sickness. The symptoms may not appear for six months or in some cases as long as six or seven years. Most victims are homosexual or bisexual men, persons having many sexual partners, drug users who share needles, those receiving transfusions of blood or blood products, and infants who have been infected in the womb or during birth. Increasingly the disease is being spread in heterosexual populations. More than 90 percent of those diagnosed in 1981 as having AIDS have died (Blue Shield/Blue Cross reports, 1988). It is estimated that 1.5 million Americans are carriers; one-third of these will develop AIDS or a related condition (BCBSA, 1988). The number of cases predicted by 1991 is 270,000 to 300,000 (Center for Disease Control, 1987). Education has reduced somewhat the spread in the homosexual community, blood screening has reduced the risk of contraction by transfusion, and current efforts are being made to stop its spread among intravenous drug users.

Adolescents are vulnerable because of fearfulness to confide in parents about STD problems. Some believe the disease can be cured easily with penicillin. Also, some are on birth control pills, which do not block STDs, and they desire sex more than they fear disease. Therefore they postpone having treatment and are less likely to follow through with a treatment program. Table 10.5 lists the most common STDs, their etiologies, prognosis with treatment, and consequences. Adolescents and others who are sexually active can do a number of things to help themselves according to the Blue Shield/Blue Cross Association (1988). They name:

1. Know your partner - the more choosy you are the less is your likelihood of being exposed, particularly when you develop a close, caring relationship.

2. Have regular medical check-ups - This will provide you with an early indication of any STD problem.

3. Avoid exchanges of body fluids - Use a latex condom, do not allow secretions, blood from the partner to get into a cut or sore on your body.

Table 10.5 COMMON SEXUALLY TRANSMITTED DISEASES

DISEASE	NEW CASES IN 1986	CASES (%) M/F	CAUSE	SYMPTOMS: MALE	SYMPTOMS: FEMALE	TREATMENT	CONSEQUENCES IF UNTREATED
Chlamydia	4.6 million	60/40	Bacterial infection	Pain during urination, discharge from penis.*	Vaginal discharge, abdominal discomfort.*	Tetracycline or erythromycin.	Can cause pelvic inflammation disease. Leading cause of sterility in women.
Gonorrhea	1.8 million	60/50	Bacterial infection	Discharge from penis, pain during urination.*	Discomfort when urinating, vaginal discharge, abnormal menses.	Penicillin or other antibiotics.	Can cause pelvic inflammation disease or eventual sterility; also cause arthritis, dermatitis, meningitis.
Genital warts	1.0 million	40/60	Viral infection	Painless growths that usually appear on penis, but may but may also appear on urethra or in rectal area.*	Small, painless growths on genitalia and anus; may also occur inside the vagina without external symptoms.	Removal of warts	May be associated with cervical cancer; in pregnancy warts enlarged and may obstruct birth canal.
Herpes	500,000	40/60	Viral infection	Painful blisters anywhere on the genitalia, usually on the penis.*	Painful blisters on the genitalia, sometimes with fever and aching muscles; women with sores on cervix may be unaware of outbreaks.*	No known cure, but controlled with antiviral drug acyclovir.	Possible increase of cervical cancer.
Syphilis	90,000	70/30	Bacterial infection	In first stage, reddish-brown sores on the mouth or genitalia or both, which may disappear though the bacteria remain; in the second, more infectious stage, a widespread skin rash.*	Same as in men.	Penicillin or other antibiotics.	Paralysis, convulsions, brain damage, and sometimes death.
AIDS (acquired immune deficiency syndrome)	13,500	93/7	Viral infection	Extreme fatigue, fever, swollen lymph nodes, weight loss, diarrhea, night sweats, susceptibility to other diseases.*	Same as in men.	No known cure, but experimental drug AZT extends	Death, usually due to other diseases such as cancer.

*May be asymptomatic.
Source: Adapted from Centers for Disease Control, 1986; *Morbidity and Mortality Weekly Report*, 1987b.

4. Avoid anal and oral intercourse - This is a common route for transmitting and acquiring an STD.

5. Wash the genital and rectal areas before and after intercourse - use soap and warm water. Males should urinate after washing. Use of jellies, creams, and foams for contraception are recommended.

6. Practice good hygiene and learn the symptoms of STDs - Inspect the penis and outer genitalia, watch for discharge, sores, swellings, inflammation, blisters, etc. See the doctor immediately if you observe, feel, or know of problems.

7. Avoid persons known or suspected of having an STD or those having many sexual partners.

8. If you contract any STD inform all your sexual partners. They need to get medical help as soon as possible and in turn to inform their partners.

Teenagers are likely to believe that they are immune from STDs, "that it can't happen to me." They need to be counseled that anyone can get a disease. The U.S. Public Health Service has an AIDS hotline (1-800-342-AIDS) and also a hotline just for teenagers (1-800-234-TEEN).

Drugs and Adolescents

The overall rate of drug use among adolescents has dropped from 1979 to 1987 and perhaps continues to drop; it peaked in 1978 (Johnson, 1988). A drug culture in the United States has been developing for a number of years. The generation before the 1940s to the 1960s utilized drugs but the majority of them were alcohol and tobacco. The "baby boomers" heading into middle age are replacing them and using a variety of drugs. Nearly one-third of all prescriptions in the U.S. are diet pills and amphetamines or tranquilizers like Valium, which is now the most widely used drug in the nation. Table 10.6 shows the trends in drug use by adolescents.

Adolescents use drugs for a variety of reasons. First, youth are vulnerable to drugs because they are exceedingly curious about the world of adults, as glamorized in movies and television. Also, they are often too bold and oblivious to any shortcomings or dangers. The following are commonly given as reasons for drug use:

Example - The pervasive use by the population in general of many drugs such as alcohol, cigarettes, Valium, marijuana, and cocaine. The use is seen among the best of people, including government leaders, stars, athletes, professors, and clergymen. Caffeine and alcohol are common.

Peer Pressure - Use of drugs is less prevalent than it was in the 1960s. However the best way to determine who will use drugs is to ascertain if their best friend uses drugs. Out-of-school youth in socially disintegrating urban settings are at high risk due to pressure from their peers. Programs in schools are having a salutary effect on reducing social usage (Bachman et al., 1988).

Recreation - This is particularly a factor among senior high school and college youth--for example, drinking beer has been institutionalized by fraternities and sororities for business or fun. For many youth it is just the beginning.

Emotional Disturbance - The early users of drugs and alcohol acknowledge that boredom, peer rejection, anxiety, fear of failure, emotional isolation, and parental rejection have been handled through drugs.

Parent-Youth Problems - Parent-child relationships that are hostile, cold, and abrasive can

Table 10.6 TRENDS IN 30-DAY PREVALENCE AMONG CERTAIN DRUGS

	Percent who used in last thirty days						
	Class of 1982	Class of 1983	Class of 1984	Class of 1985	Class of 1986	Class of 1987	'86-'87 change
***Approx.* N =**	**(17700)**	**(16300)**	**(15900)**	**(16000)**	**(15200)**	**(16300)**	
Marijuana/Hashish	28.5	27.0	25.2	25.7	23.4	21.0	-2.4
Inhalants	1.5	1.7	1.9	2.2	2.5	2.8	+0.3
Inhalants Adjusted	2.5	2.5	2.6	3.0	3.2	3.5	+0.3
Amyl & butyl nitrites	1.1	1.4	1.4	1.6	1.3	1.3	0.0
Hallucinogens	3.4	2.8	2.6	2.5	2.5	2.5	0.0
Hallucinogens Adjusted	4.1	3.5	3.2	3.8	3.5	2.8	-0.7
LSD	2.4	1.9	1.5	1.6	1.7	1.8	+0.1
PCP	1.0	1.3	1.0	1.6	1.3	0.6	-0.7
Cocaine	5.0	4.9	5.8	6.7	6.2	4.3	-1.9
Crack	NA	NA	NA	NA	NA	1.5	NA
Other cocaine	NA	NA	NA	NA	NA	4.1	NA
Heroin	0.2	0.2	0.3	0.3	0.2	0.2	0.0
Other opiates	1.8	1.8	1.8	2.3	2.0	1.8	-0.2
Stimulants	13.7	12.4	NA	NA	NA	NA	NA
Stimulants Adjusted	10.7	8.9	8.3	6.8	5.5	5.2	-0.3
Sedatives	3.4	3.0	2.3	2.4	2.2	1.7	-0.5
Barbiturates	2.0	2.1	1.7	2.0	1.8	1.4	-0.4
Methaqualone	2.4	1.8	1.1	1.0	0.8	0.6	-0.2
Tranquilizers	2.4	2.5	2.1	2.1	2.1	2.0	-0.1
Alcohol	69.7	67.2	65.9	65.3	2.1	66.4	+1.1
Cigarettes	30.0	30.3	29.3	30.1	29.6	29.4	-0.2

U.S. Department of Health and Human Services, Washington, D.C.: National Institute on Drug Abuse 1988.

form the basis for drug use. Where parents are democratic, authoritative, and allow for gradual development, drugs most likely will not become a problem.

Escape From Pressure - Youth who feel burdened by responsibility placed upon them by parents or self-imposed are subject to the temptation of using drugs to reduce tension or escape boredom or pressure.

Alienation - Many adolescents are faced with economic difficulties, racial discrimination, physical problems, no parental guidance, and inadequate living conditions. They use drugs to escape the pain of their lives.

Some estimate there are as many as one million users of crack (cocaine) in America. Police crackdowns have little effect on the drug trade. Most treatment programs are overburdened, and their graduates have 50 percent recidivism (Lamar, 1988). With so many social problems demanding attention one wonders how the necessary effort for drug control and reduction can be accomplished. Without effective educational and employment programs, along with expanded prevention and treatment programs, an overwhelming number of urban youth will become criminals, addicts, and dropouts from life before they become adults.

Parents will have to become more aware of possible drug use by their children and become more responsible about their own behavior and the example they set.

IMPORTANT ISSUES IN ADOLESCENCE--VOCATIONAL, EDUCATIONAL, AND HELP TO DELINQUENT YOUTH, SUICIDES, AND RUNAWAYS

Working and Planning the Future

More young people, mainly those in high school, work part-time in the United States than in any other industrialized country. Currently 50 percent of high school seniors hold half-time jobs. Eighty percent of adolescents will hold a part-time job before they graduate (Greenberger and Steinberger, 1986). Adolescents like to do work outside of schools because it gives them a chance for greater freedom, allows them such concessions as staying out later, using the family car, purchasing things they wish to buy, gaining independence, providing an offset from boredom at school and home, finding out about the adult world, getting status, and finding adventure. The traditional value of working is found in the American "work ethic": to gain insight into the nature of work, to get along with people, to learn how to earn and manage money, and to become more self-sufficient.

As noted, few adolescents in other industrialized countries work. For one thing they have much more homework than the U.S. high school student, often doing schoolwork four or five hours each evening. They often go to school on Saturday and most parents review schoolwork with their children regularly. A survey revealed that one-third of U.S. students spent an hour or more on homework while another 40 percent said they spent no time at all on it (National Assessment of Educational Progress, 1981). The question can be raised whether the best and brightest of our young are spending too much time with part-time jobs that are relatively unproductive, while they ignore or do minimal work in school. Working does not seem to help adolescents organize their lives better and it adversely affects schoolwork when it approaches half-time hours. Many part-time jobs are menial and the money received does not seem to be worth taking the academic risks. For years the authors have listened to working students say they had to limit their study time on a test due to their outside work, complain that they couldn't finish an assignment on time because of work, or they had to miss class because it conflicted with a difficult work schedule. Of course we know that some students couldn't go to college without work to subsidize high tuition and board costs.

The types of jobs held by young women are: serving as aids in health and education, waitressing, working in fast food establishments, babysitting, and clerking. Typical jobs for males are bagging groceries, cutting grass, carrying newspapers, delivering pizza, and working as laborers, ticket takers, and fast-food preparers. These types of jobs lack continuity with adult work. They do provide some orientation to how business operates and how to get and hold a job.

Planning a Career

As the child matures and enters adolescence he or she goes through three stages (Ginsberg, 1951): the fantasy period, the tentative period, and the realistic period. In the fantasy period, children (usually in elementary school) choose high-status, exciting, and emotionally driven occupations. Time gives way to the tentative period, when the child is entering puberty and begins to use more realism in viewing occupations and careers. Through their high school years, children get increasingly more information on jobs and work. By the time they finish high school, adolescents in the realism stage are beginning to match their interests and abilities to specific kinds of careers. There is still con-

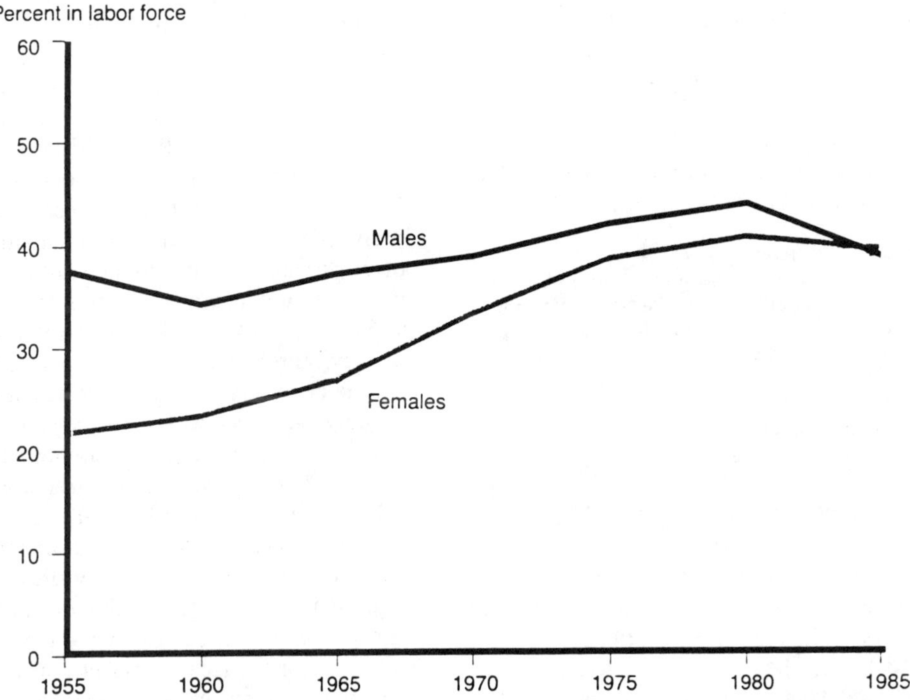

Figure 10.4 Labor force participation of 16- and 17-year-olds enrolled in school, by sex: 1955 to 1985. The labor force participation rate of 16- and 17-year-old male students showed little change during the 1955 to 1985 period. However, the rate for female students was significantly higher in 1985 than in the 1950s and 1960s. By 1985 about the same percentage of female as male students participated in the labor force. (*Source:* U.S. House of Representatives, Select Committee on Children, Youth and Families, *U.S. Children and Their Families: Current Conditions and Recent Trends, 1987.* U.S. Department of Labor, Bureau of Labor Statistics, *Handbook of Labor Statistics*, Bulletin 2217, June 1985.

siderable tentativeness in the choice of the older adolescent. Grotevant and Durett (1980) in a Texas study involving 6,000 high school seniors found that students showed a limited amount of knowledge about their first choice of occupation and about half were preparing to get less education than they needed in those fields. Fifty percent of the seniors hoped for a professional or technical career at a time when only 13 percent of the jobs were located in those fields.

Influences on careers come from various sources. Even part-time work provides some preparation for a career. The support of parents is the most important aspect in getting an education and pursuing a career of a particular kind. The higher the socio-economic class the more likely a son or daughter is to choose a higher status occupation or profession. Sons frequently follow the profession of their fathers. Daughters of working mothers have higher aspirations and achieve more than daughters of homemakers (Hoffman, 1979). Increasingly gender does not determine the direction women take in their work lives. It is well known that MBA classes are filled with women and freshman girls are enrolled in engineering and science in increasingly higher numbers. Ohio State University in 1945 had 15 percent of its freshman engineering class composed of women. In 1980 this doubled to 30 percent of the beginning class (Feldman, 1982). Girls entering non-traditional occupations usually have superior grades and standardized test results.

In any case, gender difference according to Papalia and Olds (1990) is not appreciable--

> the small differences in males' and females' abilities have no real psychological and educational implications. Particularly there is no reason for steering males and females toward different careers. Even if differences do exist, there is much overlap: some girls are better at math and science than boys, some boys are better writers and speakers than some girls.

The point is that interest and ability and not gender are the keys to work success. Certainly individuals will vary in wanting to work inside or outside, with people or without them, or with things or with ideas. Besides the above-mentioned aspects, however, the person must ultimately decide on a work direction based on his or her assessment. Many minority youth reflect their parents' ambitions for them and enroll in programs designed to reach their goals.

Vocational pursuits do relate to the adolescent search for identity. If the choice of a vocation or profession makes adolescents feel good about themselves and makes them feel that they can succeed, then identity is being crystallized. Others may believe their work doesn't make any difference. When significant others view the adolescent's work as having little prestige, the adolescents themselves are likely to be ambivalent about attaching their identity to this work and as a consequence may become tentative about settling their career choice. Obviously work helps to define one's identity. It relates to esteem, a value system, and the necessity to make a living. Idealism among youth generated in the 1960s and 1970s is falling, where 78.5 percent of male freshmen and 86 percent of female freshmen in 1969 picked developing a meaningful philosophy of life as important. By 1985 this had declined to 43 percent for both males and females. On the other hand, to "be very well off financially" gained from less than half in 1969 to three of every four male freshmen and two of every three female freshmen in 1985. Recent studies by the American Council on Education (1991) indicate "being well off financially" dropped for the second straight year after a 17-year rise

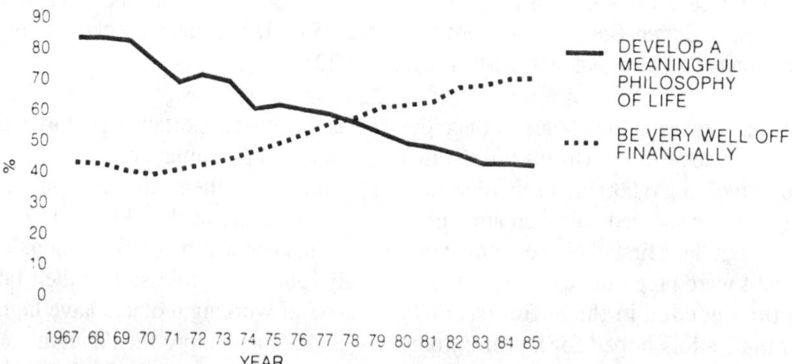

Figure 10.5 Changing life goals of freshmen, 1967-1985 (percentages). (Adapted from A.W. Astin, K.C. Green, and W.S. Korn, *The American Freshman: Twenty Year Trends.* Los Angeles Higher Education Research Institute, University of California at Los Angeles, 1987. By permission.

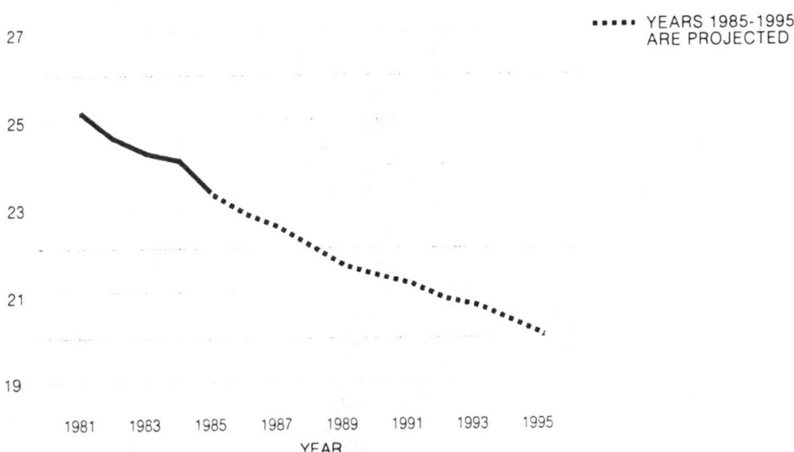

Figure 10.6 Youth in the civilian labor force aged 16-24 (in millions). (Adapted from Department of Labor, Bureau of Labor Statistics, 1986.)

from 39.1 percent in 1970 to 75.6 percent in 1987. Also, nearly 80 percent viewed racial discrimination as a major problem in America.

In the eighties, an opportunity for self-discovery held less attraction for youth than a strong career orientation. It is estimated only twenty million youth (16 to 24) will enter the labor force in 1995, due to the aging of the "baby boomers" and the decline in the rate of population growth.

Fewer youth from lower socio-economic backgrounds will attend college than those from higher socio-economic levels, and consequently will be handicapped in the job market. Among those 16 to 21 years of age seeking work and not in college, twice as many (28 percent) are likely to be high school dropouts as high school graduates (13.5 percent) (U.S. Bureau of Census, 1986).

An oversupply of college graduates is likely to continue through the 1990s. From 1970 to 1984 20 percent of college graduates took a job that did not require a degree. But there are occupations requiring a college degree that will not be overcrowded in the next five years, according to the data revealed in Figure 10.7. Still, the high-status, higher paying positions will require a college degree and in some cases a second degree (U.S. Department of Labor, 1986).

As expected, youth with less than a college degree will suffer higher unemployment rates. Many of the jobs that are available for the low-skilled with limited educations will be service types--delivery, fast food, laboring, and the like.

Education--Junior and Senior High School

The high school experience is the foremost factor in the lives of adolescents. The years in high school are marked by the structured curriculum, unstructured friendships and activities, social and athletic events interacting with mental and physical development in a setting where youth are increasingly treated as young adults. The principal agenda is social for most high school students. School is the place to meet friends, to share confidences and information, and to experience the widening world. Though organized mainly for academics, the high school is also called upon to teach sex education, family life education, drivers' train-

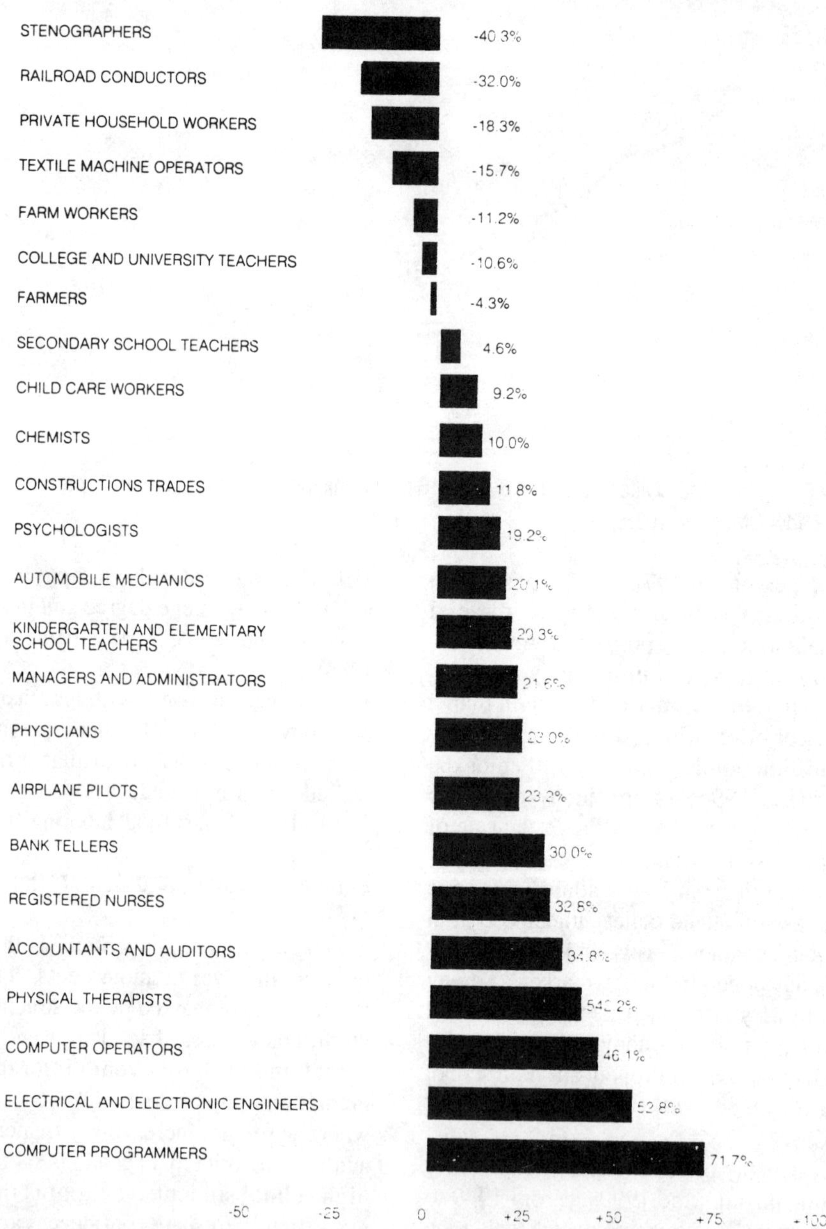

Figure 10.7 Job requirements and growth, 1984-1995. (Adapted from U.S. Department of Labor, Bureau of Labor Statistics. *Occupational Projections and Training Data, April 1986,* Bulletin 2251. Washington, DC: U.S. Government Printing Office, 1986.)

ing, vocational studies, technology, business, homemaking, health and physical education, citizenship, and drugs and alcohol education.

It is true that the National Commission on Excellence in Education (1983) gave poor marks to American schooling, stating that students in American schools 26 years earlier were better prepared. Many minority students, the report went on to say, were illiterate. Eighty percent could not write a persuasive essay and 65 percent could not solve a mathematical problem involving several steps. This failure was attributed to insufficient homework, too many electives, and the preparation of teachers in which the learning process is emphasized to an inordinate degree (Rock, et al., 1985). There were other aspects, however, not considered by the commission. For instance, the SAT score for 1951 combined for all girls and boys averaged 970; for 1985-86 it was 906, a drop of 64 points in 35 years. The 1951 group was very select, representing a class of only 50 percent of high school graduates. Nearly half of those did not go to college (Bent, et al., 1970). The ones that took the SAT were likely to be the very best students; in 1986 the public secondary schools were enrolling over 90 percent of students 14 to 17 years old, and most of these took the SAT in their junior and senior years. Most of these were graduating, with approximately 75 percent going on to higher education. Also the recent group included mainstreamed students with such learning difficulties as dyslexia, speech problems, emotional difficulties, and low mental ability. Many of these adversely affect the achievement levels reported. In summary, we are educating all the youth today, not just the select. If colleges of education have overemphasized the learning process, it is principally a reaction to the mainstreaming of special education students. The psychology of learning necessarily deals with differential learning abilities and informational processing that is likely to fit student capability, interest, and styles of learning.

Because of the pragmatic beliefs of government and the workplace, students often seek the largest payoff for the least amount of effort. Foreign students will continue to fill university science and engineering classes and most will become citizens of the United States. The authors rarely see Koreans, Taiwanese, Vietnamese, Pakistanis, Japanese, or Chinese in social science classes, because the payoff isn't great enough--they are not going to become teachers, social or criminal justice workers, health providers, or small business people. American youth do not study enough science and math as they should, but little can be done if they choose not to. What to do about it? On average, the citizen of today is better educated than in years past, when a fewer percentage graduated from college. Some hope exists for education and specifically for minorities, as shown in Figure 10.8.

There is evidence that parents who involve themselves closely in the schooling of their children help them achieve higher grades. Forehand, et al. (1986) found adolescents who got along with their parents and who were reasonably well adjusted obtained higher grades and behaved better in class.

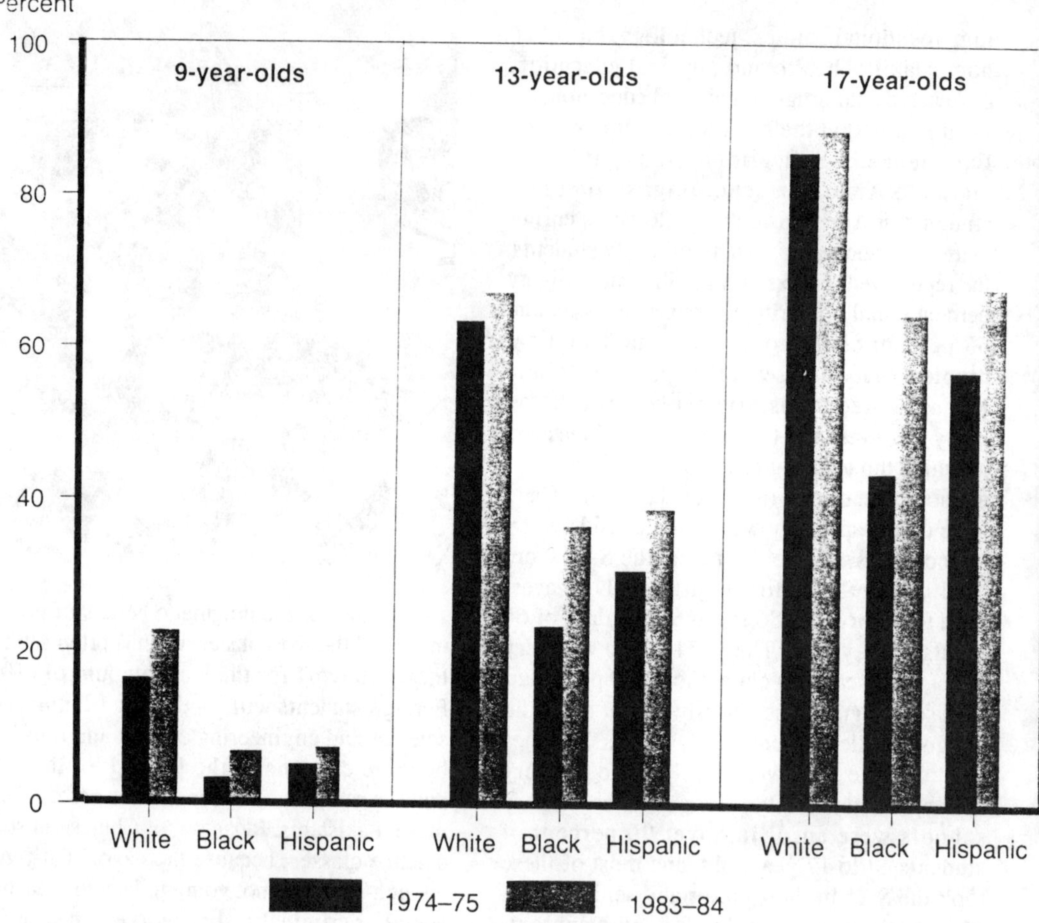

Figure 10.8 Percent of students reading at an intermediate level or higher, by age: 1974-75 and 1983-84. The percentage of students reading an intermediate level or higher rose for all 9-year-olds between 1974-75 and 1983-84. Reading proficiency improved significantly during this period for black and Hispanic students of all ages.

The effects of the transition from elementary school to high school are important because such a transition is often related to dropouts, adjustments, performance, and a feeling of anonymity. Research by Blyth, Simmons, and Carlton-Ford begun in 1983 as a five-year study found that children and youth who went to elementary schools organized with eight grades had fewer problems than those who went to elementary schools with six grades and junior high schools 7 to 9. They had their grades drop, participated in fewer extracurricular activities, felt alone and anonymous. Girls saw a drop in self-esteem. Since girls experience puberty earlier, begin to date earlier, have more stress on looks and personality, they may experience difficulty with change. Perhaps the breakup of old friendship patterns such as moving to a new house or the divorce of parents may impinge on girls at a vulnerable time. Attending the same school and remaining in the same home can be constants that provide a refuge and comfort that can be counted on to provide stability (Simmons, et al., 1987).

Currently the middle school movement is developing nationally purportedly to meet the needs of students at puberty. In this new concept, the traditional elementary school will end at grade five. The middle school will consist of grades six through eight (sometimes five to eight). It is uncertain whether this will lessen or actually create more adjustment problems in youth. Experts say the school will be designed to address the needs of the developing young adolescent, with fewer changes in class as the traditional junior high school, and will concentrate on each child's becoming academically effective. Special help in reading, math, counseling, etc., will be provided; also there will be opportunities for children to participate in a variety of interesting activities and explore creative and vocational opportunities. It remains to be seen what the results will be. Traditionally the largest number of dropouts usually occurs in the eighth and ninth grades during the transition to senior high or high school. The middle school concept may help this situation.

Dropouts

Over one-half million high school sophomores dropped out of school in 1980 and hadn't returned by 1982. Boys drop out more than girls, blacks more than whites. When socioeconomics are held constant, however, the black rate is better than whites; Hispanics are virtually equal to other races (Center for Educational Statistics, 1987). Youth drop out for a variety of reasons; among males--poor grades (36 percent); didn't like school (24 percent); being expelled (13 percent); and to help the family (26 percent); among girls--marriage and/or preg-

Table 10.7 PARENTING AND HIGH SCHOOL GRADES

	Self-Reported Grades			
Survey Item	Mostly A's	Mostly B's	Mostly C's	Mostly D's
Mother keeps close track of how well child does in school.	92%	89%	84%	80%
Father keeps close track of how well child does in school.	85%	79%	69%	64%
Parents almost always know child's whereabouts.	88%	81%	72%	61%
Child talks with mother or father almost every day.	75%	67%	59%	45%
Parents attend PTA meetings at least once in a while.	25%	22%	20%	15%
Child lives in household with both parents.	80%	71%	64%	60%

Note: This table, based on a survey of more than 30,000 high school seniors, shows the percentage of students with various grade averages who gave positive answers to each survey item. In each instance, the higher the grades were, the more likely the parents were to be involved with the child. *Source*: National Center for Education Statistics, NCES, 1985.

nancy (31 percent); "schooling is not for me" (31 percent); poor grades (30 percent); and a job (11 percent). Some investigators mention lack of motivation, part-time work, low self-esteem, little support from home, repeating a grade, disciplinary reasons, and low expectation and support from teachers (Rule, 1981).

Most dropouts find it hard to make it financially because most jobs require a high school education. The ranks of the unemployed are filled with dropouts. They are the last hired and usually the first fired and the jobs they perform are menial--factory work, laboring, baby-sitting, clerical, farm, and fast food work (Center for Educational Statistics, 1987). Large public school systems and the federal government have tried to help through such programs as Upward Bound. Upward Bound has been in existence since 1964. By 1988 some 80 percent of its graduates have entered four-year-colleges. These programs offer counseling, workshops on self-esteem, SAT help, tutoring for math and science, aids in technology, drug-abuse counseling, career planning, and help in applying for college. The program is expensive and though continually supported by Congress it does not have sufficient coverage to begin to solve the problem (Wells, 1988). The National Committee for Citizens in Education has established a dropout prevention center with a toll-free number (1-800-NETWORK) where a variety of information can be received on such topics as suspension, expulsion, reduction of grades, reinstatement, etc. Many more avenues will need to be explored and organized to prevent this national disgrace from growing. Beyond the problem of negative employment prospects for the dropout, many become delinquents, drifters, substance abusers, and criminals. This is likely to increase with fewer jobs available during the current economic turn-down.

Juvenile Delinquency

It is virtually impossible to define juvenile delinquency so that it applies to all areas of the United States. Standards and laws vary with different groups and in different states. However, generally we separate delinquents by the terms *status offenders* and *criminal offenders*. Status offenders are those who commit such acts as running away from home, being truant, and other minor offenses not considered criminal when committed by juveniles. Criminal offenders are those that commit such crimes as rape, murder, and robbery. Those under 18 will usually be tried by a judge and sentenced or given probation more lenient than for adult offenders. Some heinous crimes, i.e., murder and rape, may bring an adult trial and sentence.

The amount of damage caused by juvenile vandalism runs into the millions of dollars. In Virginia Beach and Norfolk, Virginia, contiguous communities of approximately 700,000, a current activity is to slash tires and break car windows. Several glass companies say half of their business comes from teenage vandalism (*Virginian Pilot*, January, 1991). More serious are the arrests of those under 18 years of age, and the actual number exceeds published reports, since many juvenile judges and court officials do not record them for the record. The causes for arrest among the under eighteen are seen in Figure 10.9.

It is hard to believe that youth under 18 commit one out of seven aggravated assaults and forcible rapes, even one of eleven homicides. If the 18 to 24 age group is included, the rate of assault and rapes is doubled and the rate of murders is quadrupled (U.S. Bureau of Census, *Statistical Abstract of the U.S.*, 1987, 107th ed.). Boys in the past decade were arrested four or five times more than girls, though recently the ratio has dropped to 3.5 to 1. Girls get in trouble for sexual activities, robberies, truancy, running away, and incorrigibility. Boys commit 90 percent plus of the violent offenses and account for 90 percent of the juveniles in correctional institutions (U.S. Department of Justice, 1988). Most of the rising number of women's offenses are in the areas of shoplifting and prostitution. This is

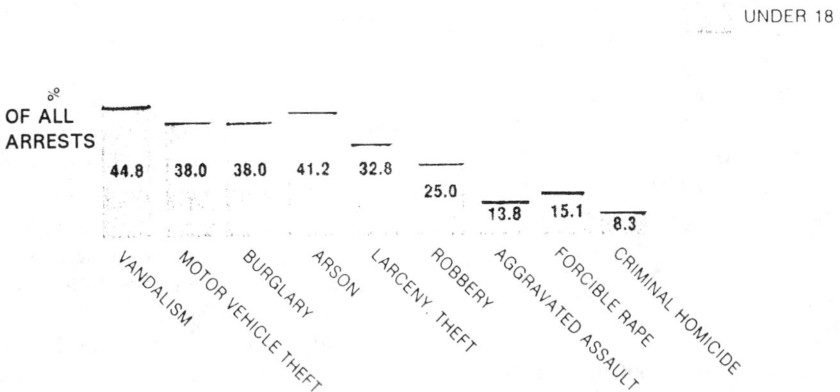

Figure 10.9 Arrests of persons under 18 years of age, as a percentage of all arrests. (Adapted from Federal Bureau of Investigation, *Crime in the United States*, annual; and U.S. Bureau of the Census, *Statistical Abstract of the United States, 1987* (107th ed.). Washington, DC: U.S. Government Printing Office, 1986.)

true particularly where drugs are involved, because additional money is needed to sustain chronic drug use. Often runaways from home and those rejected by parents or caretakers are introduced into sex for hire and stealing to pay for drugs and the basics of life.

Runaways are a type of delinquent, but in many cases these youth have been mistreated and abused physically and psychologically. In some cases the running away is a healthy response to an intolerable situation. More times than not the young person already carries psychological scars from previous mistreatment. In many instances agencies misbelieve or act too slowly. Often youth feel they cannot tell kin people or those from an agency about their problems. So they leave and typically go to large cities. New York has been a mecca for thousands. It is notable that recently so many runaway girls came from the Minneapolis area to New York City along Eighth Avenue that it was called the Minnesota strip. Young girls in such an environment often learn to be prostitutes.

One million young people run away from home each year (Garbarino, Wilson, and Garbarino, 1986). Half return in several weeks but, having gone once, they are more likely to go again, and if they return they face many adjustments. Family conflict and lack of communication are at the root of many runaways, though Janus, et al. (1987) reported 73 percent had been physically beaten and 51 percent had been victims of sexual abuse.

Although numerous groups and agencies are organized to help identify and assist the runaway, the House Committee looking into this suggests that only one-third of the one in twelve that are identified gets any attention (Janus et al., 1987). The NBC Monitor (1983) estimated that 5,000 youth are buried in unmarked graves each year because no one identifies or claims them. In New York City the Covenant House operates a center, known as "Under 21." This house is well known and does a creditable job; unfortunately it can help only a minuscule number of runaways. There are others: the Independence House, the Door, the Center of Alternatives in New York City, and many church groups and agencies in other urban cities. Unfortunately these are underfunded and lack staff and resources to do what is needed.

Causative Factors in Juvenile Delinquency

Factors involved in delinquency are complex and multivariate. Many of the kinds of problems involved are the same kind that relate to drug and alcohol use, maladjustment of youth, sexual promiscuity, emotional disturbances, and personality difficulties. We are going to list the categories of etiological factors under the social, biological, and psychological and discuss a number of aspects under each.

Social Factors

The social aspects that contribute to delinquency include the affluence of society, peer groups, the environment, class status, the family, cultural change, and school. The affluence of society is a contributor to delinquency. The availability of cars and the mobility of society, the propensity for spending money, the whirl of fun things to do such as sporting events, the theater, rock concerts, and partying, all contribute to lessening the control of adolescents' activities.

Peer Influence

The first use of drugs or alcohol and the first act of vandalism usually occurs with peers. Association with others reinforces each participant. Once started, the influence of peers provides support for delinquency. Where parents have been unable to establish communication or have been harsh in their judgments and actions, the peer group serves as a sympathetic audience and for some may become more significant than the family. The family also shares in the making of the delinquent. The broken and/or troubled home influences youth to become miscreant. According to Lambert (1972), the most important factor is that:

> many broken homes tend to be matriarchal in structure, thereby failing to provide the male adolescent with a suitable masculine figure with whom to identify. He then develops conflict over his sexual role, an obsessive concern with his masculinity, and his delinquent acts often function as a means of resolving this sexual role conflict (p. 164).

One study of over 5,000 juveniles showed that children from broken homes were twice as likely to be arrested for various offenses in proportion to the population (Chilton & Markle, 1972). There is also a greater tendency for lower-class parents to look to the police for help with their youth whereas middle-class parents turn to therapists (Chambliss, 1974).

Middle-class parents have their share of delinquent youth, particularly where there is little affection expressed, and where there is much activity with little time for talking with children and observing their day-to-day problems. The middle and upper classes often confer excessive freedom very early on their offspring; money, few home tasks, and idle time serve to contribute to boredom. Cogle, Tasher, and Morton (1982) recorded activities of the typical adolescent in a Louisiana study. They found adolescents spent one hour and five minutes per day in a variety of tasks. The distribution showed shopping involved about a fifth of the time (20 minutes), maintenance of the home (car, yard, and pets) 14 minutes, food preparation 11 minutes, housecleaning 10 minutes, dishwashing 6 minutes, and clothing care 1 minute. Girls spent more time than boys on every task but maintenance. This coupled with permissiveness in discipline sometimes leads to aberrant behavior.

Cultural Change

Youth, particularly those new to America or those who have moved to a large city, or lower class persons from rural or small town settings, have difficulties integrating into a new society. Youth often organize gangs in an effort to protect themselves and project their ethnicity. If they are from poor homes or have low paying jobs they usually live in a ghetto or at best a marginal neighborhood. Many minority youth are plagued, they feel, with an older generation that does not understand them or the cultural transition they must make. They often turn to their ethnic peers for support and protection. The radical change in values creates new demands to be someone, even a delinquent, to produce a sustaining self-image. Cultural change affects all youth but none so radically as recent arrivals to America.

Schooling Effects

The school environment is often detrimental to many youngsters. Where school programs are rigid and oriented to matriarchal control and values, male rebellion often follows; subsequently those rebelling are identified as troublemakers. Many youths, particularly males, who are rebellious in school or become so, frequently do not have the academic skills to succeed in the usual curriculum that allows only limited bilateral tracks, general or academic. It is interesting to note that much of the vandalism in society is directed at school buildings rather than warehouses or other structures. The aesthetic theory (Allen, 1987) of vandalism suggests among other aspects that youths take sheer enjoyment in destruction. Insensitive school administration, inadequate curricula, and perpetuation of dominant class values help pave the way for delinquency and perhaps provide reasons for "getting even."

Biological Factors

Biological determinants of delinquency are often considered minor. More attention, however, has been given to the following in recent years--heredity, health, neurological impairment, and maturation.

Heredity Genetic studies indicate that chromosome aberration, often involving an extra Y chromosome in the male giving him an XYY set, results in behavior characterized as aggressive, explosive, and undisciplined. A greater number than normally expected have been involved with criminality (Polini, 1970). Some investigators such as Sheppard (1974) believe that 25 percent of delinquency can be attributed to organic causes--endocrine problems, too little or too much insulin, hyperthyroidism, or other chemical reactions or imbalances.

Health Status For some time malnutrition has been linked to delinquency. The general state of physical health is important, for chronic problems involving diet, weight, sugar level, allergies, metabolism, and injuries may exist, which tend to affect an individual's homeostasis and therefore may contribute to antisocial behavior.

Neurological Impairment Pontium (1972) suggests that 15 to 20 percent of delinquents have neurophysiological dysfunction of the frontal lobe of the brain. It is believed by some that there is a link between the autonomic nervous system's responsiveness and criminality (Penner, 1982).

Recent studies completed by four Yale University researchers (Lewis et al., 1979) reveal that the more violent delinquents had greater frequencies of psychiatric symptoms such as paranoia, hallucinations, and delusions; and more neurological symptoms such as blackout spells, failing episodes, and psychomotor epilepsy. The extremely violent were found to have more serious problems in their medical histories, such as head injuries and physical abuse severe enough to damage the central nervous system (Lewis et al., 1988). Nearly all (98.6 percent) of the more violent youngsters had at least one neurological impairment. Thirty percent of the more aggressive group had grossly abnormal electroencephalograms or a history of grand mal epilepsy or both. None of the less violent youth had such symptoms. Seventy-five percent of the violent group and 33 percent of the less violent had been physically abused.

Maturation The physical and mental development of a teenager is very important. As a developmental task, youth need to accept their bodies. Ostrov (1979), utilizing the Offer Self-Image Questionnaire Scale in examining the differences between normal versus delinquent behavior, found on Scale 3 (body and self-image) a significant (.001) difference in adjustment. The view youth has of itself, particularly the very young and immature (12- to 15-year-olds), makes them vulnerable to group and older youth influence, thereby involving them in misdirected ventures.

Psychological Factors

Psychological factors are significant as a cause of delinquency Three principal ones are discussed here.

Troubled Home Life It has been established through many studies that fairly high correlations exist between delinquency and broken and disorganized homes, quarrelsome homes, and negligent homes (Offer, Marohn, and Ostrov, 1979). Consistent discipline, affection, and acceptance by families correlate with normalcy. Further validation of this comes from the Offer Self-Image Questionnaire Scale 7 (family relationships), in which he found highly significant differences (.0001) favoring the normal. Due to the type of family situation, youths may have trouble fitting into the mainstream or satisfying their social and emotional needs in the family, and they often join gangs that provide companionship and excitement but whose membership demands delinquent acts as an entrance requirement.

Poor Relations With Fathers Adolescent relationships with the father are important. Two studies involving 175 delinquent girls in the South (Georgia) and Southwest (Oklahoma) revealed that these girls were not close to their fathers, indicating that their fathers were cold, not loving, kind, or supportive, and that they perceived their fathers as rejecting. Another study by Miller (1980), designed as a search for gender-specific patterns in the self-reported involvement in 28 offenses utilizing 3,000 adolescents in a random sample, found the structure of delinquency essentially the same for boys and girls. Lang, in examining the problems of delinquent girls, found a major one to be the discipline in the home, which varied in extremes from harsh to permissive (Lang, Pampenfuks, & Walter, 1976).

Personality Difficulties Delinquency often is seen as a defense against the feeling of inferiority. Achievement is a significant goal of the adolescent and is often thwarted. Delinquents often view themselves as dumb or no good, and project poor self-images. Difficulty in learning social roles and having little control of impulsive behavior are involved. Offer, et al. (1979), whose research was mentioned earlier, examined the normal and delinquent on a scale of psychopathology and found the incidence to be significantly higher (.001) in delinquent youth. Depression and schizophrenia are problems of adolescents noted by Weiner (1970). Depression often accompanied by fatigue, hypochondria, and concentration difficulty leads to a rising number of suicides by adolescents (Curran, 1987). Low rates of recovery from schizophrenia are revealed by Weiner, who found 23 percent of hospitalized adolescents recovered, 25 percent improved, but 52 percent made little or no progress.

Significant psychological disturbances occur in adolescents. According to Graham and Rutter (1985), some 15 to 20 percent of youth have problems. The most frequently encountered are: anxiety reactions, depression, personality disorder, psychophysiological disturbances and psychoneuroses (some of these problems will be reviewed in the following pages). Delinquents are more likely than nondelinquents to be socially assertive, defiant, lacking in achievement motivation, hostile, suspicious, destructive, and lacking in self control (Farrington, et al., 1982). Some investigators maintain that delinquency may serve to improve self-esteem while some argue that delinquents continue to have negative self-concepts (Arbithnot et al., 1987). Jones & Swain (1977) found no significant difference between delinquency-prone junior high school boys and nondelinquency-prone bright boys (IQs of 115 and above). The delinquency-prone boys were, however, still in school. However, on the Karvaceus Delinquency Proneness instrument the typical delinquency-prone boy in the study scored high enough to theoretically be accepted in a Massachusetts Correctional Institution at the time of the study.

Prevention of Delinquency

The question as to how prevention can be effected must be addressed. One general answer is to transform society into a happy, productive one where no one goes unfed and unloved. Approaches to delinquency involving prison and correctional institutions obviously have not remedied the problems. Little ameliorative therapy involving education, psychological counseling, and vocational aid is given. Many attempts to affect the life of the delinquent have been made through study programs, family therapy, foster homes, youth workers, psychological assistance, and educational programs, but these have typically come too late to have much success. Phillips and coworkers (1973) reported on the success of small group homes, six to eight boys and two professional parents sharing living quarters. Interactions between youth and parents existed that were personal, frequent, and warm. One program reported was called "Achievement Place," whose results were compared with traditional training schools. In Achievement Place, boys were rewarded for assuming responsibility by receiving greater privileges. When compared with adolescents on probation or in the training school, the number of offenses was considerably reduced, school attendance was superior, and grades better. A number of Virginia cities (Norfolk, Portsmouth, and Richmond) have reported remarkable success with the small group home approach. The salient feature is the quality of the "parents."

Adverse social and economic conditions serve to generate delinquency. Broad attachment to urban blight and ghetto syndromes must be made that will give impetus to a large number of troubled and alienated youth. Blacks suffer the most and have considerably higher unemployment than whites; black adults have twice the unemployment rate of whites. Among youth 50 percent of nonwhite teenagers were out of work in 1986 compared to 20 percent of white (Bureau of Labor Statistics, 1987). The main job increase in the 1990s will be in low-wage, low-skill jobs, and in the service areas.

Massive assistance will be needed to begin to solve these problems, which are in a sense those fundamental to society itself. A pervasive climate of good will, concern for others, and improved educational programs must be initiated by society, along with utilizing the best of the small group home format and effective correctional institutional programs, as well as not permitting status offenders to be unnecessarily incarcerated. Two-thirds of the females and one-third of the males in the mid-seventies were in correctional institutions for status offenses (Wooden, 1976). Unfortunately the judicial system often fails to institutionalize adolescents who repeatedly commit serious crimes (Kaufman, 1979).

Behavioral methods offer greater promise than traditional approaches. Appropriate behavior controls that systematically reward good behavior with increased privileges and punish inappropriate behavior with loss of privileges are needed.

Some projects that offer greater success are found in institutions that focus on training in social skills as they relate to applying for a job, resisting peer pressure, personal problem solving, and planning (Sarason and Ganzer, 1973). If intervention efforts are going to succeed, changes in the child's and adolescent's home environment must take place. There is a need to start programs early in life, when the child and youth are part of a larger program of comprehensive psychological and physical care. Society, however, does not seem to have the inclination, the ways and means, or the will and toughness to understand that most of the problems of youth are related to drugs, delinquency, and failures of families.

Psychological/Physical Problems of Adolescents

Depression - involves sadness, temporary and often mild, in response to a specific life event or a seriously disturbing condition. In early adolescence young people are not likely to express their feelings openly and tend to deny self-critical attitudes. Older adolescents may mask depressive feelings with boredom, restlessness, hypochondriacal complaints, or acting out sexual aggressiveness or delinquent activity (Nicholi, 1988). Psychiatric disorders occur more frequently with boys before puberty but more with girls following puberty.

Psychological factors seem to be the basis of two kinds of depression. The first is seen in a feeling of emptiness--a vacuum likely to generate a high-anxiety state. The second kind is related to defeats suffered over a long period of time, where young people may have tried to solve a problem without success. They have few friends but intense ones. They are not understood--people fail to accept or understand them. A final precipitating event is the loss of a friend, a parent, or a love object (Curran, 1987). Some of these depressed adolescents try to kill themselves. They need therapy immediately when identified.

Anxiety Reactions - Those youth with acute anxiety may feel a sudden surge of fearfulness. They may be restless, feel dizzy, have head pains, difficulty sleeping, or nightmares (Nemiah, 1988). One factor involved may be the child-parent relationship. Therapy should begin as soon as possible while the symptoms can be discernible. To wait is to risk the problem's becoming a chronic one and giving impetus to withdrawal and ineffective school work. Physical evidences are vomiting, fatigue, diarrhea and pain.

Schizophrenia - This malady is rare until up to age 15, then accelerates rapidly. The incidence however, is only about 1 percent of the population. When full-blown it can be seen in peculiar speech, lack of contact with reality, poor emotional control, and failure to establish a relationship that has meaning; also conscious awareness of sexual and aggressive imagery. Vulnerability to schizophrenia is inherited; whether it develops depends on two factors--the ability of the child to withstand stress and the strength of the stress factor. The prognosis is that one-fourth recover, one-fourth will get better but suffer relapses occasionally. Fifty percent will make no progress and require residential care (Weiner and Elkind, 1972).

Psychotic Episodes - These exhibitions of psychotic behavior are different from schizophrenia. These behaviors show incoherence, delusions, and hallucinations, and have a sudden onset usually lasting a few hours or weeks. The causative factor is a severe psychosocial stressor--loss of a loved one or a life-threatening event. Psychological help and support from friends and family will help in alleviation. Mood swings can be expected and depression or lessening of self-esteem.

Other Problems - Children with eating or other problems need help and compassion from parents. The nature of help should come from the family physician who perhaps knows about the problem already. The physician can make a referral to either a psychiatrist or psychothera-

Table 10.8 1985 U.S. DEATH RATES (PER 100,000) BY AGE FOR ACCIDENTS, SUICIDES, AND HOMOCIDES COMBINED

	White		Black	
Age	Male	Female	Male	Female
15-24	111.8	32.3	132.8	29.4
25-34	98.8	25.1	186.5	40.4
35-44	80.6	25.3	175.1	36.5
45-54	77.1	27.4	147.9	33.1
55-64	85.4	30.6	145.5	36.6
65 and older	155.3	81.4	186.9	84.7

(Based on *Statistical Abstracts of the United States* [108th edition], p. 81, U.S. Bureau of the Census, 1988. Washington, DC: U.S. Government Printing Office)

pist. Many adolescents need one who has worked with young people and can establish rapport with them. The need for a valid diagnosis is essential for treatment.

Violence and Suicide Among Youth

Adolescence is a time when youths feel invulnerable. Bad things only happen to other people. Therefore risk-taking behavior, especially among males, is commonplace. This behavior is manifest in "playing chicken," adolescent rituals (usually associated with gangs), drug use and abuse, dangerous hobbies, and the racing of automobiles. Three and one-half more males than women die from accidents, suicide, and homicides, and more adolescents per 1,000 die from these causes than any age up to 55 years.

Many suicides are reported as accidents. Many may be accidents but some are tied to the subconscious motivation for the youth to kill himself. A few years ago some youths were experimenting with placing plastic bags over their heads, then pulling the open end tight around their neck and seeing how long they could go without breathing. A few deaths were reported from this exercise, mostly as accidents. However in some instances investigators from outside the family blamed the incidents on suicide. More men than women kill themselves, usually with firearms. Women more frequently commit suicide by poisoning. Table 10.9 shows suicide figures for ages 10 to 24.

Table 10.9 SUICIDE RATES (PER 100,000) IN THE UNITED STATES BY SEX, RACE, AND AGE GROUP FROM 1970 TO 1985

				Male						Female					
	Total			White			Black			White			Black		
AGE	1970	1980	1985	1970	1980	1985	1970	1980	1985	1970	1980	1985	1970	1980	1985
10-14	.6	.8	1.6	1.1	1.4	2.5	.3	.5	1.3	.3	.3	.9	.4	.1	.4
15-19	5.9	8.5	10.0	9.4	15.0	17.3	4.7	5.6	8.2	2.9	3.3	4.1	2.9	1.6	1.5
20-24	12.2	16.1	15.6	19.3	27.8	27.4	18.7	20.0	18.5	5.7	5.9	5.2	4.9	3.1	2.4

Source: Adapted from U.S. Bureau of the Census (1988), *Statistical Abstracts of the United States* (108th edition), 1987. Washington, DC: U.S. Government Printing Office, p. 82.

The causative factors relate to coping with one's own problems and concern with social problems. Rice (1981) notes that people who commit suicide:

1. Tend to come from disturbed family backgrounds.
2. Have no parental figure with whom to identify.
3. Have backgrounds of social isolation, making for vulnerability to a loss-of-love object.
4. Are often depressed.
5. Often exhibit symptoms of stress.
6. Often have poor impulse control, stemming from immature personalities.
7. Are likely to be subject to suggestibility.
8. Have extreme feelings of guilt or hostility toward self, often a component of suicide.
9. Cry for help or sympathy or attempt to manipulate others, often an indication of trying to cope and to receive help and not an attempt to finally end one's life.

A Final Word On Adolescence

Most young people pass through the years of adolescence without undue stress and dread but enter adulthood as effective citizens. Most do not get hobbled by drugs or sex, do not become pregnant, nor are they remanded to incarceration or drop out of school. Research by McSweeney and Jones (1991) revealed that idealism and future optimism characterizes the typical adolescent (19 to 21). Their study indicates that youth wish to get good jobs, hopefully working at an occupation that serves the community and nation in a salutary way.

The strengths of adolescents have been delineated by Otto and Healy (1966) as principally: health, intellect, special aptitudes, dependability, education, spiritual strengths, imagination and creativity, and social relationships. Most adolescents down-play their qualities or overlook them. Researchers (Papalia & Olds, 1990) suggest the following resources that adolescents possess:

1. Considerable energy, or drive, and vitality.
2. Idealism and a real concern for the future of this country and the world.
3. Exercising of their ability to question contemporary values, philosophies, theologies, and institutions.
4. Heightened awareness and perceptivity.
5. Courage and ability to take risks themselves or stick their necks out for others.
6. A feeling of importance.
7. A strong sense of fairness and dislike for intolerance.
8. Responsibility and reliability.
9. Flexibility and adaptation to change.
10. Openness, frankness, and honesty.
11. Above-average sense of loyalty to organizations and causes.
12. A sense of humor, which they often express.
13. An optimistic and positive outlook on life in general.
14. A seriousness of purpose and ability to think deeply.
15. A great sensitivity to, and awareness of, other people's feelings.
16. A sincere and ongoing search for identity.

SUMMARY

Extensive investigations and interest focusing on adolescence has made it one of the most researched periods in the life span. Writers such as Waechter identify three periods in adolescent life: pre- and young adolescence, adolescence, and later adolescence. There is little agreement on the end of adolescence but most authorities believe it starts at puberty and that its beginning centers on physical development and change whereas its ending centers on the social and psychological. The tasks of adolescence center on completing the competency of intellectual operations, acquiring a set of values, work orientation, and achieving mature relations with age-mates--of like and different sex along with developing interaction with a special person.

The formation of identity, a principal task for adolescence, requires the ego (Erikson) to organize the individual's abilities, needs, desires, and the mode for adapting to society. Marcia has identified four categories of the status of identity: achievement identity, foreclosure, diffusion, and moratorium. The factors that define the identities are the presence or absence of a crisis, commitment to a selected occupation, and commitment to freely chosen values and ethics. Those who have achieved identity have passed through a crisis and are doing or preparing for work of their own choosing. Those in the moratorium period are most closely tied to their parents; girls have more difficulty in this status than boys. Males who foreclose have more esteem than those who have yet to do so.

To some degree there is a struggle between families and peers for the attention and loyalty of youth. Despite the idea of generation gap and youth alienation, parents and their adolescents get along well. Most teenagers agree with their parents on life styles, politics, religion, and value systems. The conflict between them relates to their choice of friends, schoolwork, chores, dating, and drugs. As the teenager gets older, mothers lose some of their authority. Fathers, on the other hand, usually interact with their children on general ideas and problem-solving in a more or less relaxed atmosphere.

Parents, according to the National Institute of Mental Health, should give attention to the following things to improve their relations with their youth: (1) give careful attention to what they say, (2) try to understand the teenagers' point of view, (3) keep the door open on subjects and don't belittle, (4) encourage discussion of their ideas, (5) help build confidence by encouraging them in activities, and (6) welcome their participation in family affairs.

The peer group, according to many sociologists and psychologists, is a distinct group with its own clothing, language, icons, entertainment, and styles. Important for boys' credo is masculinity, athletic skill, risk-taking, physical mastery and defense of one's honor. For girls, priorities are physical attractiveness, personal vivacity, skill in interpersonal relations, and ability to exercise control over sexual encounters. Achievement of status is obtained by presenting a "cool" and unflappable confidence in one's sexual identity and delivering a smooth performance in a variety of situations. Three kinds of peer groups are the larger peer group, the crowd, and the clique, each smaller than the preceding one. Dunphy identifies five stages in the formation of the group: (1) the pregroup, (2) beginning of the crowd (a group of cliques of the same sex interact with the counterpart)--dating between cliques forms the crowd, (3) the crowd, (4) the fully developed crowd, and (5) the disintegration of the crowd where the couples formed earlier begin serious dating. Peers provide support, status, and are to some extent essential for good emotional and social adjustment according to Langer; however, one good friend can be as important as the clique.

Surveys show adolescent eighth graders watch television 21.7 hours a week, spending only 5.6 hours on homework and 1.8 hours on outside reading. This is much less than Asian youths who spend 6.7 hours on homework. Teenagers spend most of their time in their own bedrooms (41 percent), the public arenas (27 percent) (includes being at friends' homes or hangouts), and at school (32 percent).

The morality of adolescents parallels that of their cognitive stage; at 13 the typical youth is found at Kohlberg's conventional level, whereas at 16, 35 percent are at the level of moral reasoning. Friendships, being loved, and freedom are the most important values held by youth, as determined by a number of surveys. Most believe that the federal government, large corporations, and labor unions have not met their responsibility; on the other hand, many youths feel that universities, the national media, and churches have served society well.

Studies indicate that principal problems of adolescents concern schooling, interpersonal matters, the future, and the family. Lack of agreement with parents typically relates to dating, responsibilities at home and school, and drug use. On religion, politics, and family life-style there is usually agreement. Increasingly, youth issues relate to drug and alcohol use, delinquency, and sexual promiscuity. By all accounts the incidences of these have not slowed much in the past decade, reaching the point where major national efforts are now being expended to relieve some of the pressure of these problems, especially because of sexually transmitted diseases (STD). The incidence of AIDS goes on unabated. Teenagers know little about such diseases, and few use contraceptives. The most common disease is chlamydia, with over 4 million cases in 1986. Although 85 percent of parents favor sex education, many adolescents are denied such programs by conservative groups. There has also been an increase in teenage marriages, resulting in part from premarital pregnancy. Early marriages are fraught with difficulties, with high rates of divorce occurring particularly where partners are under 19 years of age.

Delinquency is said to have its etiology in social factors (peer groups, deprivation), biological factors (heredity, health, neurological impairment), and psychological factors (troubled home life, personality difficulties). The rise in juvenile delinquency has become a national problem. Research reveals that delinquents come from backgrounds of social and economic deprivation. The importance of male identification for the adolescent boy is emphasized by students of adolescent psychology. School failure is a serious problem for many adolescents and contributes to delinquency, drug addiction, and suicide, which has increased significantly. In 1988 suicide was the second leading cause of death for the 15-to-24 age group, 20 of every 100,000 in the United States. Only Norway, Canada, Australia, and Switzerland had more (*Statistical Abstract*, 1989-90). Crime has significantly increased among adolescent girls, paralleling the use of drugs and smoking. It is believed that there are serious implications for girls since they are more likely than adolescent boys to be misunderstood, judged by a different standard,and socially disapproved of. The widespread use of alcohol and other drugs, especially marijuana, has emerged as a serious problem to adolescent development. This problem, like that of juvenile delinquency, frequently appears among younger adolescents and is more widespread among boys than girls, though all types of juvenile crime are distributed among both sexes.

Increasing numbers of adolescents enter college; over 70 percent continue education after high school graduation. Research reveals that many of their occupational preferences are based on stereotypes. Investigators believe the development of the vocational task follows from the early life stage of childhood, ages 5 through 11, when fantasy characterizes the view of occupation--fireman, policeman--or the child identifies with the parents' work. From ages 11 to 18 a tentative selection stage begins, with choices made on the basis of likes and dislikes. Toward the end of this period adolescents make increasingly realistic choices under parental pressures and the impetus of high school graduation. A final realistic stage is beginning to work at a regular job. This relates perhaps more to lower-class than middle-class youth, where continued education takes place and final career stabilization occurs somewhere between 25 and 35 years of age. Youth from lower socio-economic classes seem to be unaware of the availability of counseling about opportunities for employment, the various aptitudes required, and the personal characteristics needed for different types of employment, as well as the barriers that foreclose employment. The majority of adolescent girls and young women are oriented to work and careers along with marriage and family. They like the idea of maintaining a good life that is afforded by two wage earners; many, therefore, will opt for career even within marriage. The principal orientation of youth toward work emphasizes that they desire jobs that include friendly, helpful co-workers; interesting work and opportunity to use their minds; results from their work that they can see; and finally, good pay.

KEY WORDS

acquired immune deficiency

bisexuality

charismatic movement

chromosome

developmental tasks

dyslexia

fantastic period

foreclosure

grand mal epilepsy

homosexual

identity

lesbianism

masturbation

moratorium

national risk

neurophysiological dysfunction

realism stage

schizophrenia

STD (sexually transmitted disease)

tentative period

REFERENCES

Adams, J.H. Adolescents' personal problems as a function of age and sex. *Journal of Genetic Psychology*, 1964, *104*:207-214.

Allen, C.D., and Eicher, J.B. Adolescent girls' acceptance and rejection based upon appearance. *Adolescence*, 1973, *8*:125-138.

Arbithnot, J., Gordon, D.A., and Jurkovic, G.J. Personality. In H.C. Quay (ed.), *Handbook of Juvenile Delinquency*. New York: Wiley, 1987, pp. 139-183.

Archer, S.L. Identity and the choice of social roles. *New Direction for Child Development*, 1985, *30*:79-100.

Astin, A.W., Green & Korn, W.S. The American freedman, twenty year treads. Los Angeles Higher Education Research Institute, University of California, Los Angeles.

Backman, J.G. An eye on the future. *Psychology Today*, July *21*:6-8.

Balswick, J. The Jesus people movement: A generation, 1974 interpretation. *Journal of Social Issues*, 1974, *30*:23-67.

Barbach, L.G. *For Yourself: The Fulfillment of Female Sexuality*. Garden City, NY: Doubleday, 1975.

Bent, R.K., Kronenberg, H.H., Broadman, C.C., et al. *Principals of Secondary Education*. New York: McGraw-Hill, 1970.

Berg, D.H. Sexual subcultures and contemporary heterosexual interaction patterns among adolescents. *Adolescence*, 1975, *105*:43-548.

Bergtson, V.L., and Starr, J.M. Contract and consensus. A generational analysis of youth in the 1970s. In R.J. Havighurst and P.H. Dreyer (eds.), *The Seventy-four Yearbook of the National Society for the Study of Education*. Chicago: University of Chicago Press, 1975.

Bernstein, A.C. How children learn about sex and birth. *Psychology Today*, 1976, *9*(8):34-35, 66.

Billy, R.W., and Posterski, D.C. *The Emerging Generation: An Inside Look at Canada's Teenagers*. Toronto: Irwin Publishers, 1985.

Blyth, D.A., Simons, R.G., and Canlton, Ford S. The adjustment of early adolescents to school transition. *Journal of Early Adolescence*, 1983, *3*(1-2):105-120.

Brown, N., and Lawson, R. Values in parochial and public 1980 schools: Alike or different? *Psychological Reports*, 1980, *47*:279-252.

Buie, J. Pregnant teenagers, new view of old solution. *Education Week*, April 1987, p. 32.

Bureau of Labor Statistics. Wives' and mothers' labor force activity include those with infants. *Months Labor Review*, 1986.

Carnegie Corporation of America, Vol. 35, Nos. 1 & 2, Winter/Spring, 1990.

Center for Disease Control, Sergi Aral, Atlanta, Georgia, 1991.

Chambliss, W.J. The state, the law, the definition of behavior as criminal or delinquency. In D.G. Glaser (ed.), *Handbook of Criminology*. Skokie, Ill.: Road M & Walley, 1974.

Chilman, C.S. Adolescent sexuality in a changing American society: Social & psychological perspectus. (NIH Publication No. 80-1426) Bethesda, MD: U.S. Department of HEW Public Health Science, 1980.

Chilton, R.J., and Marble, G.E. Family disruption, delinquent conduct and the effect of subclassification. *American Sociological Review*, 1972, *37*:93-99.

Cobliner, W.G. The exclusion of intimacy in the sexuality of the contemporary college-age population. *Adolescence*, 1988, *23*:127-136.

Cogle, F., Tasher, G., and Morton, D. Adolescent time use in household work. *Adolescence*, 1982, *17*(66):451-455.

Conger, J.J. A new morality: sexual attitude and behavior of contemporary, 1980 adolescents. In P.H. Mussen, J.J. Conger, and J. Kaden (eds.), *Reading in Child and Adolescent Psychology: Contemporary Prerequisites*. New York: Harper & Row.

Cross Blue, Shield Blue Association. *No-Nonsense AIDS Answers*. Chicago: Auther, 1988.

Csikzentmihalyi, M., and Larson, R. *Being Adolescent: Conflict and Growth in the Teenage Years*. New York: Basic Books, 1984.

Curran, D.K. *Adolescent Suicidal Behavior*. Washington, DC: Hemispheric Publishing Company, 1987.

Dawson, D.A. The effects of sex education on adolescent behavior. *Family Planning Perspectives*, 1986, *18*:162-170.

Dryer, P.H. Sexuality in adolescence. In B.B. Wolsman (ed.), *Handbook of Developmental Psychology*. Englewood Cliffs, NJ: Prentice-Hall, 1982.

Dunphy, D.C. The social structure of urban adolescent peer groups. *Sociometry*, 1963, *26*:230-246.

Durden-Smith, J., and DeSimore, D. The sex signals. *Playboy*, 1982, pp. 144-146, 226-242.

Edelman, M.W. *Families Imperil: An Agenda for Social Change*. Cambridge, Mass.: Howard University Press, 1987.

Enright, R.D., Franklin, C.C., and Manheim, L.A. Children's distributive justice reasoning: A standardized and developmental psychology. 1980 16/3 193-202, 1988.

Feibleman, J.K. The philosophy of adolescence. In Z.M. Contwell and P.M. Srajian (eds.), *Adolescence: Studies in Development*. Itasca, Ill., 1974, p. 74-98.

Feldman, R.D. *Whatever Happened to the Giving Kids: Perils & Profits of Growing Up Gifted*. Chicago: Chicago Review Press, 1982.

Field, T.M., Widmayer, S., Greenberg, R., and Stallen. Effects of parent training on teenage mothers and their infants. *Pediatrics*, 1982, *69*(6):703-707.

Fischer, B.J., and Bersoni, C.A. Self-esteem and institutionalized delinquent offenders: The role of background characteristics. *Adolescence*, 1979, *14*(52).

Forehand, R., Long, N., Brody, G.H., and Fareber, R. Home predictors of young adolescents' school behavior and academic performance. *Child Development*, 1986, *57*:528-1533.

Garbarino, J., Wilson, J., and Garbarino, A. The adolescent runaway. In J. Garbarino, C.J. Schellenbach, and J.M. Sebes (eds.), *Troubled Youth, Troubled Families: Understanding Families at Risk for Adolescent Maltreatment*. New York: Aldine D. Dryter, 1986, pp. 27-39.

Gilligan, C.F. In a different voice: Women's conception of self & morality. *Harvard Educational Review*, 1977, *47*:481-507.

Gottman, J., and Mettetal, G. Speculations about social and affective development-friendship and acquaintanceship through adolescence. In J.M. Gottman and J. Parker (eds.), *Conversations of Friends*. New York: Cambridge University Press, 1987.

Greenberger, E., and Steinburger, L. *When Teenagers Work*. New York: Basic Books, 1986.

Grotevant, H., and Durett, M. Occupational knowledge and career development in adolescence. *Journal of Vocational Behavior*, 1980, *17*:1971-172.

Hausen, S.T., Book, B.K., Houlihan, J., Powers, S., Wieiss-Pevoy, B., et al. Sex differences within the family: Studies of adolescence & operant family interactions. *Journal of Youth Adolescence*, 1987, *16*:199-220.

Havighurst, R.J. *Developmental Tasks and Education*, 3rd ed. New York: McKay, 1972.

Hayes, C.D. (ed.) *Risking the Future: Adolescent Sexuality, Pregnancy and Childbearing*, vol. 1. Washington, DC: National Academy Press, 1987.

Hill, J.P. Research on adolescents and their families past, present. *New Direction for Child Development*, 1987, *37*:13-32.

Hofferth, S.L., Kahny, J.R., and Baldwin, W. Premarital sexual activity among U.S. teenage women over the past three decades. *Family Planning Perspectives*, *19*:46-53.

Hoffman, L.W. Maternal employment. *American Psychologists*, 1979, *34*(10):859-865.

Hoffman, M.L. Moral development. In P.H. Mussen (ed.), *Carmichael's Manual of Child Development*, 3rd ed. New York: Wiley, 1970, pp. 276-277.

Jackson, D.W. The meaning of dating from the role perspective of non-dating preadolescents. *Adolescence*, 1975, *10*:123-126.

Jacquett, C.H. (ed.) *Yearbook American & Canadian Churches*. New York: Abingdon Press, 1975.

Janda, L.H., and Klinke-Hamel, K.E. *Human Sexuality*. New York: Van Nostrand, 1980.

Janus, M.D., McCormack, A., Burgess, A.W., and Hartman, C. *Adolescent Runaways, Causes and Consequences*. Lexington, Mass.: Lexington Books, 1987.

Johnson, L.D., O'Malley, P.M., and Bachman, C.J. *National Trend in Drug Use and Related Factors Among American High School Students and Young Adults (1975-1986)*. Rockwell, MD: U.S. Department of Health & Human Services, National Institute on Drug Abuse.

Jones, E.F., et al. *Teenage Pregnancy in Educationalized 198 Countries*. New Haven, CT: Yale University Press.

Jones, F.R., and Swain, M. Self concept and delinquency. *Adolescence*, Winter 1977, *12*(48).

Katchadourian, H.A. *Fundamentals of Human Sexuality*, 4th ed. New York: Holt, Rinehart & Winston, 1985.

Kaufman, I.R. Juvenile justice: A plea for reform. *New York Times Magazine*, 1979, 42-60.

Kohlberg, L., and Gilligan, C.F. The adolescent as philosopher: The discovery of the self in a postconventional world. *Dealdalus*, 1971, *100*:1051-1086.

Kilwood, T. *Disclosures to a Strange*. Longdon: Routledge & Regan Paul, 1980.

Kinsey, A.C., Pomeroy, W.B., Martin, C.E., and Gebhark, P.H. *Sexual Behavior in the Human Female*. Philadelphia: Saunder, 1983.

Lambert, B.G. *Adolescence, Transition from Childhood to Maturity.* Monterey, CA: Brooks/Cole, p. 164.

Landsbaum, J.B., and Willis, R.H. Conformity in early & late adolescence. *Developmental Psychology*, 1974: 334-337.

Lang, D., Pampenfuks, R., and Walter, J. Delinquent females' perceptions of their fathers. *The Family Coordinator*, 1986, *25*:475-481.

Langer, T.S. Normative behavior and emotional adjustment. Ph.D. dissertation. New York: Columbia University, 1954.

LaPiccolo, J., and Labitz, C. The role of masturbation in the treatment of sexual dysfunction. *Archives of Sexual Behavior*, *2*:163-171.

Lewis, D.O., Balla, D.A., Pincus, J.H., and Shannok, S.S. Psychobiological vulnerabilities to delinquency. Paper presented at the Association of Child Psychiatry meeting, October, 1979.

Liebowitz, M.R. *The Chemistry of Love.* Boston: Little Brown, 1983.

Logan, R.D. Identity, purity and ecology. *Adolescence*, 1980, XV(58).

Lomar, J.V. Kids who sell crack. *Time*, May 9, 1988, pp. 20-31.

Luepton, L.B. *Adolescents' Sex-Role and Social Change.* New York: Columbia University Press, 1988.

Marcia, J.E. Identity in adolescence. In J. Adelson (ed.), *Handbook of Adolescent Psychology.* New York: Wiley, 1980.

Masters, W.H., and Johnson, V.E. *Homosexuality in Perspective.* Boston: Little Brown, 1979.

McSweeney, J., and Jones, F.R. Survey of college and university undergraduate and graduate students and problems. Satisfactions and Failure Concerning Update from Psychology of Human Development, 1991. New York: Harper & Row, 1985.

Miller, P.Y. Female delinquency: fact & fiction. In Max Sugar (ed.), *Female Adolescent Development.* New York: Bunner/Mazel, 1980.

Miller, P.Y., and Simon, W. The development of sexuality in adolescence. In J. Adelson (ed.), *Handbook of Adolescence Psychology.* New York: Wiley.

National Assessment of Elementary Progress Reading, Thinking and Writing. Results from 1979-1980 assessment of reading and literature, Report No. 11-L-01m. Denver: Education Communication of States.

National Institute of Health. *National Health Survey*. DHEW Publication No. (HRA) 75-1629. Washington, DC: U.S. Government Printing Office, 1975.

National Institute of Mental Health (NIMH). *Plain Talk About Adolescence*. Washington, DC: U.S. Government Printing Office, 1981.

Nemiah, J.C. Psychoneurotic disorders. In A.M. Nicholi, Jr. (ed.), *The New Harvard Guide to Psychiatry*. Cambridge, Mass.: Harvard University Press, 1988, pp. 234-258.

Nicholi, A.M., Jr. The adolescent. In A.M. Nicholi, Jr. (ed.), *The New Harvard Guide to Psychiatry*. Cambridge, Mass.: Harvard University Press, 1988, pp. 637-664.

Nicholson, S.L., and Antill, J.K. Personal problems of adoelscents and their relationship to peer acceptance and sex role identity. *Journal of Youth and Adolescence*, 1981, *10*(4).

Offer, D., Marohn, R., and Ostrov, E. *The Psychological World of teh Juvenile Delinquent*. New York: Basic Books, 1979.

Ostrov, E., and Offer, D. Loneliness at adolescence: Correlation, attributions and coping. *Journal of Youth and Adolescence*, 1978, *12*:95-100.

Otto, H., and Healy, S. Adolescents and self perceptions of personality strengths. *Journal of Human Relations*, 1966, *14*(3):483-490.

Papalia, D., and Olds, S.W. *A Child's World*, 5th ed. New York: McGraw-Hill, 1990.

Parade Magazine. Profile of the American eighth-grades, 1990.

Penner, M.O. The role of selected health problems in the causation of juvenile delinquency. *Adolescence*, 1982, *17*(66).

Phillips, E.L., Phillips, E.A., Fixsen, D.L., and Wolf, M.M. Achievement place: Behavior shaping works for delinquents. *Psychology Today*, 1973, *7*:75-79.

Playboy. What's really happening on campus. 1976, *23*(10):128-169.

Podd, M.H. Ego identity status & morality--the relationship between two constructs. *Development Psychology*, 1972, *6*:497-507.

Polini, P. Chromosome phenotype-sex chromosome. In F.C. Fraser and V.A. McKuisick (eds.), *Congenital Malformations*. New York: Excerpta Medica, 1970.

Pontium, A.A. Neurological in some types of delinquency especially among juveniles. *Adolescence*, 1972, *7*:289-308.

Profile of American Eighth Graders. *Parade Magazine*, 1991.

Remabedi, G. Adolescent homosexuality. *Pediatrics*, 1987, *79*:331-337.

Rice, F.R. *The Adolescent*, 3rd ed. Boston: Allyn Bacon, 1981.

Rock, D.A., Ekstrom, R.B., Boerty, M.E., Hilton, T.K., and Pollack, J. Factors associated with decline of test scores of high school seniors 1972-1980. Washington, DC: Department of Education Center for Statistics, 1985.

Roesler, T., and Deisler, R. Youthful male homosexuality. *Journal of th eAmerican Medical Association*, 1972, *219*(8):1018-1023.

Rokeach, M.A. *The Nature of Human Values*, 2nd ed. New York: Free Press, 1979.

Rosen, R.H. Adolescent pregnancy decision making: Are parents important? *Adolescence*, 1980, *15*(57).

Rubin, K.H. Egocentrism in childhood: A unitary construct. *Child Development*, 1973, *44*:102-110.

Rule, S. The battle to stem school dropouts. *The New York Times*, 1981, pp. A1, B10.

Sarason, I.G., and Ganger, V.J. Modeling and group discussion in the rehabilitation of juvenile delinquents. *Journal of Counseling Psychology*, 1973, *20*:442-444.

Sebald, H. *Adolescence: A Social Psychological Analysis*. Englewood Cliffs, NJ: Prentice-Hall, 1984.

Shah, F., and Zelniah, M. Parent & peer influence of sexual behavior, contraceptive use and pregnancy experience of young women. *Journal of Marriage and the Family*, 1981, *43*:329-1948.

Sheppard, B.J. Making a case for behavior as an expression of physiological conditioning. In B.L. Kratoville (ed.), *Youth in Trouble*. San Rafael, CA: Academy Therapy Publications, 1974.

Sherif, M., and Sherif, C.W. *Reference Groups*. New York: Harper & Row, 1964.

Steinberg, L., and Silverberg, S.B. The vicissitudes of autonomy in early adolescence. *Child Development*, 1986, *57*:841-85.

Sullivan, K., and Sullivan, A. Adolescent parent separation. *Developmental Psychology*, 1980, *16*(2):93-99.

U.S. Department of Education. *Enrollment in Colleges and Universities, Fall 1985*. (Office of Educational Research & Improvement, Bulletin CS 87-313.) Washington, DC: Center for Educational Statistics, 1987.

U.S. Department of Health & Human Services. *Project Health and Statistical Fact Sheet*. Washington, DC: U.S. Government Printing Office, 1988.

U.S. Department of Health, Education, Welfare. *Hunt Special Report*, The U.S. Congress on Alcohol and Health. Washington, DC: U.S. Government Printing Office, 1978.

U.S. Department of Justice, Federal Bureau of Investigation, *Press Release on Crime, 1986*, July, 1987.

Virginia Pilot. Window smashing new vandalism trend. Norfolk, Virginia, January 1991.

Waechter, Eugenia H., Phillips, J., and Holaday, B. *Nursing Care of Children*. Philadelphia: J.B. Lippincott, 1985, p. 533.

Weiner, J.B. *Psychological Disturbance in Adolescence*. New York: Wiley-Interscience, 1970.

Weiner, J.B., and Elkind, D. *Child Development: A Core Approach*. New York: Wiley, 1972.

Wells, A.S. For those at risk of dropping out on endurance, a program that works. *The New York Times*, September 7, 1988, p. B9.

Wooden, K. *Keeping in the Playtime of Others*. New York: McGraw-Hill, 1976.

Wright, P.H., and Kepee, T.W. Friends and parents of a sample of high school juniors: An exploratory study of relationship, intensity, and interpersonal rewards. *Journal of Marriage and the Family*, 1981, *43*:550-570.

Yankelovich, D. *The New Morality: A Profile of American Youth in The 1970s*. new York: McGraw-Hill, 1974.

Zelnick, M., and Kanter, J.F. Sexuality, contraception, and pregnancy among young unmarried females in the U.S. Cited in I.L. Reiss, *Heterosexual Relationships*. U.S. Department of Health & Human Services Project Share, Rockville, Maryland, 1980.

PART V

BEGINNING ADULTHOOD

Chapter 11

THE YOUNG ADULT

THE PHYSICAL MODE
- ***Health Climate***
  - Problems
  - Exercise-Diet
  - Heredity

THE SOCIAL MODE
- ***Vocational Task***
  - Vocational stages and choices of work
  - Money and spending
- ***Historical Times and Change***
- ***Love, Life Styles, Marriage, and Family***
  - Success and benefits in marriage
  - Kinds of marriage
  - Styles in marriage and alternatives
- ***Parenthood***
- ***Satisfaction in the Life of Young Adults***
- ***Homemaker Responsibility***
  - Neighborhoods and community activity
- ***Social Tasks: Groups and Leisure***
- ***Marriage and Divorce***
- ***Remarriage***

THE PSYCHOLOGICAL MODE
- ***Stability of Personality***
- ***Values and Motives***
- ***Transitional Stages***
- ***Moral Development***
  - Theories
  - Values
- ***Young Adulthood and Cognitive Ability***

THE YOUNG ADULT

Establishing the precise moment when young adulthood begins is difficult. For a long period of time in the United States, legal status was reached at the age of 21. Today in our society the age of 18 has some legal status in that individuals can often vote, obtain a car license, and often purchase alcohol. But at 18 the young person is still a teenager by definition, and there are some people, including the authors, who have seen evidence of 25-year-olds who are functioning as extended adolescents. Pikunas (1976) says that:

> some have a strong desire to continue the life-styles of their peers despite the fact that chronologically they have reached the age of majority. A large number of young adults

> remain engrossed in typically adolescent activities and in other ways oppose what is conventional in adult society (pp. 315-316).

It is also recognized that many adolescent girls and some boys raised on farms who have maintained work schedules and shown maturity in supervising stock, cultivating crops, and other responsibilities may well be functioning at an adult level though only 17 or 18 years of age.

Another issue raised is the length of young adulthood. Obviously the answer to the chronological parameters of young adulthood is not agreed upon; many like 20 to 40 as a crude mark, with 40 beginning middlescence. Others like 18 to 35, while Buhler (1933), in her stage outline, suggests 15 to 25 as the adolescent years, 25 to 45 as the young adulthood period, and 45 or 50 as the start of middle adulthood. It seems certain that role plays a greater part in ascribing the functional age of people as they pass from the early adult years to middle age and later. Investigators such as Phillips and Kelly (1975) argue that hierarchical theories of development are suspect when they hold to invariant development through stages, because of the errant nature of experience. Nevertheless, developmental psychologists and life span researchers need an umbrella structure under which to theorize, investigate, and relate descriptions of behavior. Stages and phases may overlap, and we know aging as chronology is variant, for one may be 40 but have the cardiovascular system of a 60-year-old. The roles people play are often more important than a specific time period; but years do make understandable bench marks. Childbearing, for instance, is concluded for the average young woman by age 28; retirement comes in America to the typical person by age 65. Today the average age of retirement is 62. Most adolescents finish high school by 18, and most young adults are married by age 30. The fact that many significant things happen in the lives of people that are common to the experience of most allows us to examine how the times, experiences, and the self (heredity, values and work ethics, and personal styles) relate to human development.

Depicted below is a view of possible scenarios representing average physical, cognitive, motor, and social/personality aspects for those who are chronologically and legally adults (21, or 20 on the Jones model). Included here are the last phase of adolescence and the beginning

Table 11.1 TYPES OF LIFE SPAN DEVELOPMENT

Periods of Life	Physical	Motor	Cognitive	Psychosocial/Personality
Adolescence Late 17-19	Considerable muscle growth & strength, sexual maturity for boys.	Learns to dance, plays touch football, team member.	Completion of high school & starts college or work.	Develops emotional independence.
Adulthood Young 20-29	Physical maturity	Development of long-term interest in sports, golf, tennis, jogging, boating, hiking, camping, fishing, bicycling, swimming, walking, bowling.	Mastery of college work, technology or business skills. Adequacy in work life--economics decision making, ability to complete complicated forms--income tax, record keeping for insurance, mortgages & investments. Understanding of people, children and spouse. Knowledge of government, economic & social issues.	Developing economic independence & awareness of the community. Becoming one's own person and leadership roles.
Later Young 30-39	Weight gains, larger abdomen and thighs.			
Middlescence Younger 40-49	Waist expands, gains in weight. Arthritis onset for some. Hair recedes in men. Greyness occurs in both women and men.	Recreational varieties--traveling, visiting, games, swimming & walking.		Increase in status and responsibility in the community and in helping children become emancipated.

phases of the middle years. Some persons in the middle thirties may be characterized by the descriptions of persons 40 to 49. On the other hand, some who are 25 may still be in extended adolescence as regards values or work maturity.

MODEL OF ADULT DEVELOPMENT

The authors present a model by Jones (1980) that attempts to account for development and change in adult life. The elements of this theory are contained in three modalities--the psychological, the sociological, and the physiological--involving 10 components. The components (which are described more fully in the appendix) under the psychological modality are identity, role dimension, illusions, and perspective (philosophical and moral); under the sociological modality the components are developmental tasks, historical times, and reaction; and under the physiological modality they are change, stress (adaptation), and heredity. The modalities depicted in Figure 11.1 are not discrete entities but represent continuous change through the life span. They are presented in this manner in order to represent the varying impact of the components at differing times. For instance, stress (wear and tear) has perhaps less impact on young adults, generally, as the research of Selye (1976) has shown. In later life, when strength is failing, stress becomes a conclusive factor. Stages, phases, and times are indeterminant as precise chronological years. This model incorporates the ideas of many investigators and theorists: Erikson (1968), Havighurst (1972), Morris (1956), Freud (1933), Gutmann (1964), Gould (1978), Neugarten (1968), Selye (1976), Pressey & Kuhlen (1957), Levinson (1978), and others.

More recent investigators suggest the emphasis in understanding adult development is on the process; change is ongoing throughout the life span. These investigators (Baltes, 1979; Eichorn, et al., 1982; Neugarten and Neugarten, 1987; and Lener and Busch-Rossnagel, 1981) take the view that the transit through the adult years is a process of becoming.

The model in Figure 11.1 is fluid and ongoing, and is not invariant by periods. The three cubes are utilized to provide indications of possible change in the young-to-old adult continuum. It could have been easily presented as a tube flattened on the ends. It is the purpose of the authors to examine early, middle, and later adult life through the modalities and their components. The nature of development will relate to psychological, social, and physical characteristics at the various points in adult life. Information on adult life from recent investigations represents largely a "narrative" version of adult development. The disparate elements that forge development have not been completely isolated by research. The narratives do serve as guidelines (as in case studies and observations) and suggest aspects of development, as when Piaget (1963) ferreted out the compelling factors in adult development.

There is commonality of experience that affects everyone; these are normative influences and are graded and directed by age and history. Beyond this there are non-normative influences (Baltes, 1979). *Normative, age-graded influences* are biological and social changes that happen to the typical person at more or less predictable periods, such as puberty (10 to 14) or the menopause (42 to 52). An example of the social is normative age-gradual data for first-time marrying (15 to 30) and retirement (50 to 65).

Normative-history influences happen at intervals and include such events as depressions, epidemics, war, and social turmoil and pressures. These effects are general to a particular cohort confronting the historical circumstance. Introduction into a new and different culture often makes less of an impact. These events have meaning for life's development, for example, for Jews born in Germany in the 1930s or blacks born in Alabama at that time. The *non-normative events* that occur in the lives

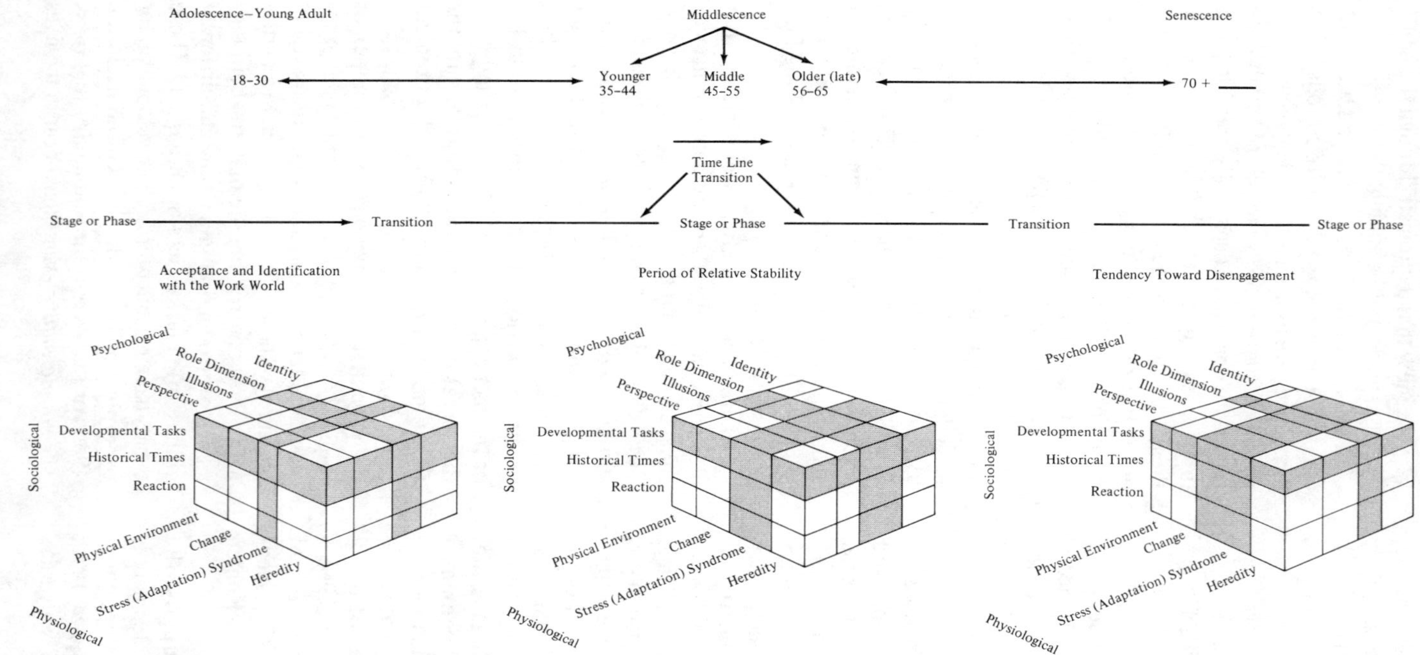

Figure 11.1 Theory of adult development.

of most people at differing times--they may be a divorce, re-marriage, illness, loss of job, chance encounters of an idea or an individual. These events may be critical, of course, but for some they do not occur. The chance meeting of a man and a woman who were friends in early life could result in a marriage that would completely change their lives. A woman could hear an idea about a possible career that would turn her psychological view of herself 180 degrees. Children and the older adult are more often affected by age-graded influences. If you're not six you can't enter the first grade or if you're 65 you may have to retire. On the other hand, adolescents and young adults are more often affected by historical influences--such as finding a job in economically depressed times and being called upon to enter a war, as in Korea in the early 50s, Vietnam in the 60s, or the Gulf War in the 90s. The war or draft, even National Guard experience can have a positive or negative effect upon your future. It could effect the postponement of education, marriage, having children, building a home, etc. On the other hand, a vacated position may give you a chance to secure a post you might never have had.

In the Jones theory these elements are components, each of which affects each individual in differing ways. The black strips represent a component in each of the modalities that has a strong likelihood of making a strong impact. Under the social component are developmental tasks for the young adult--economic competence, establishing a social network, and beginning a family, to mention a few. The job for the young adult who is still learning, has a larger impact than what would be the case in middle age. The middlescent individual has his or her own concerns but vocational and family tasks would be in the initial stages, not in the consolidation stage.

Under the *Physical Modality*, the stress component is depicted as being less than it is in middle age (the strip is broader) and much less than in older age, assuming physical and neurological characteristics are stronger in the young than the old. As for the *Psychological Modality*, role dimension is less (thinner strip) in the young adult years because young adults have not established themselves in their jobs or the community, and do not have the status of the middlescent individual. In the later years the role dimension usually diminishes as there is a tendency to disengage from work roles and other activities occur. It is argued that the components represent discrete and necessary elements that might be faced in the adult developmental pathway.

Non-normative influences can be seen in the psychological modality under identity and role dimension where a mid-life alteration of "what I am" or "what I should be" (ideal) modifies a life. The view of one's lifestyle--its inadequacy and/or incompatibility with a theme or idea--forces a change, sometimes radical, meaning a new job, new lifestyle, etc. Some of the thoughts about one's self, lifestyle and ideas often arise due to economic circumstances, changes in fortunes, perspective, values and physical liabilities. The *historical times*, a component in the Sociality Module, is noted as an ongoing concept that affects every generation, in some radical, individual, and often idiosyncratic way.

Age-grading may be seen in the theory under the social modality, where tasks are demanded by society in definitive age levels early in life. Even in adult life they are related, although with more flexibility. The 30-year-old (or even 20- to-30-year-old) is expected to have a job and in some measure is judged and categorized by it, whether by the community or the loan company or credit card issuer. The degree to which this affects a person is problematic but an impact is usually made that creates a reaction. Prevailing thought says that a woman should be married by age 30. The age-grade relates to role dimension in the psychological mode, as seen by society's standards of sobriety, deportment, etc. The sowing of wild oats is more acceptable for the 25-year-old than for the 55-year-old. The young are allowed to fail more often. What we have been saying is that the normative and the non-normative are clearly aspects of development in adulthood, but they are inextricably tied to other, larger aspects of development, i.e. the psychological, the social, and the physical. It is true that the effects of the non-normative, such as a long-lasting illness, can change irrevocably the stream of life. But this may affect a mere 10 percent to 20 percent of adults. Certainly 50 percent will divorce, but what impact, particularly for the young, will it ultimately have?

THE PHYSICAL MODE

The material on young adulthood (20 to 39) will utilize the pattern suggested by the model's three modalities--physical, social, and psychological. We will discuss the components and the subjects suggested under each of the modes, the environment, and changes due to heredity and stress.

The Health Climate

The natural strength of young adults is such that they are at the peak of their health; their ability to recuperate rapidly after strenuous exercise, to work or party through a night and still work effectively the next day, is well known. They miss fewer days from work than any other age group, whether from sickness, from minor causes as colds or respiratory problems, or from major illnesses such as cardiovascular conditions, neoplasms, or ulcers. Most have outgrown the childhood allergies, shake off colds easily and are rarely sick. The chief causes of death in this age group are accidents, suicides, and homicides. Three out of four men die as a result of accidents. Most of these are automobile related. Nearly 50 percent of the acute conditions experienced in young adulthood are respiratory, with the major chronic conditions being back problems, arthritis, hearing impairment (work conditions--construction, mining, trucking, etc.--are implicated), and hypertension. Hospitalizations are mainly concerned with childbearing, accidents, digestive problems, and genital tract diseases (U.S. Department of Health and Human Services, 1985).

The age of 35 represents the first time since infancy that the chief cause of death is physical illness. Race and gender are implicated in the death rates. Blacks are subject to more hypertension than whites and as a consequence develop more heart problems. The rate of homicide is greater for blacks than whites, and blacks have more deaths associated with drugs (U.S. Department of Health and Human Services, 1986). Men have a much higher death rate than women: for the 15 to 24 group, 141.2 deaths per 100,000 for men compares to 47.5

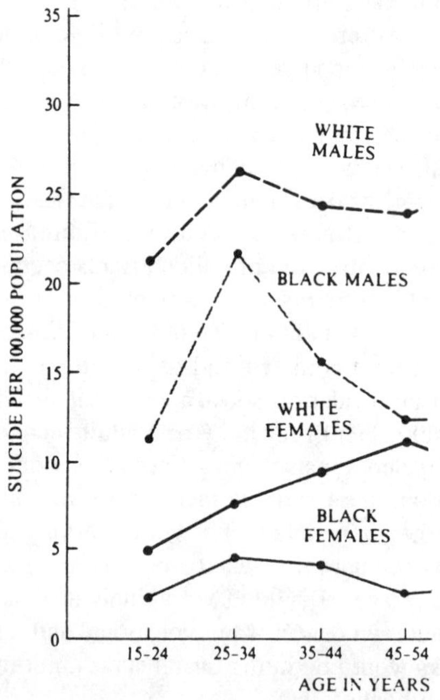

Figure 11.2 Suicide rates in the United States are markedly higher for white males than for any other group. (*Source:* U.S. Bureau of the Census, *Statistical Abstract of the United States: 1985*, 1984, Table 118, p. 79).

per 100,000 for women. Black men show 184.8 per 100,000; white men 135.0. Among those 25 to 34 years of age, black men and white men show 348.5 to 157.5 respectively per 100,000 deaths. Considering both sexes together, blacks and whites show 129.4 to 56.6 deaths per 100,000--over two to one difference of blacks over whites (Indicators, 1988).

Several aspects that relate to the health of young adults are important. The climate in which life is lived is affected in a singular way for this age group, mainly those 20 to 29, due to war, crime, drugs, occupation, and accidents.

War takes its toll from among those who have a very low natural death rate. People under 35 rarely die of natural causes. The low rate is due to the decline in heart and cancer deaths (U.S. Department of Health and Human Services, 1985). Beyond outright death in war, many more are affected by wounds or stress factors that require extensive rehabilitation. The young adult is more likely to be involved in drugs, smoking, and alcohol than older adults. They are more likely to be involved in accidents, crime, and delinquency--all of which make their lives more hazardous than those of others. Although the death rate is low for this group, many are impaired in accidents, incarcerated for crime, and institutionalized for drugs. In a study by Jones and Heinen (1979) it was found both among graduate students and the general population (with a combined *n*=600) that this sample under age 30 showed more stress, paranoia, and perceptual problems than those in their thirties or forties. Those in their thirties, though, had more responsibility than those in their twenties, and the forties' sample nevertheless had significantly better mental health. Of those in the twenties' sample, 40 percent (more men than women) had recognized problems of stress. Some things that would account for this were unsettled futures about jobs, marriage, children, etc. Those in the thirties were more likely to be settled on a career, were more likely to be married and still have energy to withstand the wear and tear of daily life. From the data presented below, the effect of certain factors indicates that until the period from 34 to 44, accidents and suicide are a larger cause of death than all the remaining factors combined. Even from this latter group, heart disease and cancer are not larger than accidental deaths and suicides. From Figure 11.3, only two in a thousand in the general population die from all factors and five of one thousand in the 45 to 54 group.

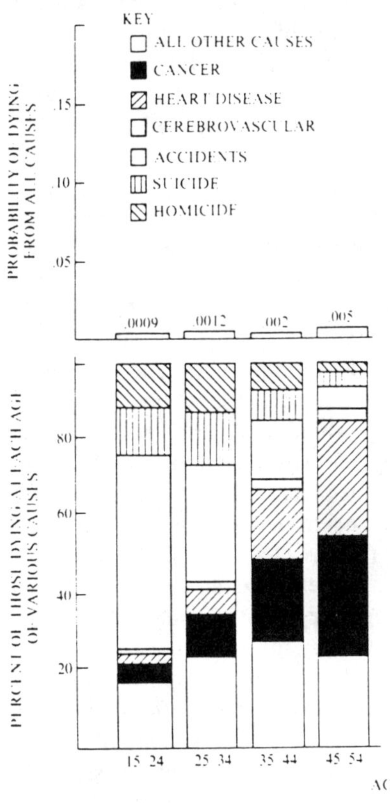

Figure 11.3 The upper part of this figure shows the probability of dying, for adults in each of a series of age groups, during 1983. The lower part of the figure shows what the people died of in 1983. Proportionately, many more young people die of accidents, suicide, and homicide, while beginning in the 45-54 age group, cancer and heart disease are the major causes of death. (*Source:* National Center for Health Statistics, *Monthly Vital Statistics Report, 1984*, 32(*13*).

Influences on Health

Women have lower death rates for all ages; men, though, have more illnesses and are hospitalized more often. This is accounted for through genetic protection afforded by estrogen and the presence of two X chromosomes. Women also see physicians more frequently about problems relating to pregnancy, menstruation, routine tests for cancer, etc., and as a consequence often get tests for sugar levels, thyroid, and blood pressure. As to which sex has the better health: women had a projected life span in 1990 of 80 years; men were expected to live an average age of 73 years (*Statistical Data Book*, 1980).

There are certain indirect influences on health such as environment, economics, education, gender, and marital status. Longevity, it is believed by some investigators, depends upon two factors--intelligence and heredity. Certainly research has shown the likelihood of developing high blood pressure and heart disease is greater among those who have not attended college. Findings from a national sample of nearly 5,700 persons from ages 18 to 64 found when such factors as age, sex, race, and smoking are controlled, the results favored the educated (Pincus, et al., 1987).

This does not equate good health with attending college, but there are factors that embellish a healthy life. The more educated usually have better resources for paying for preventive health measures, have better diet, understand the importance of health standards, tend to exercise more, eat more nutritiously, and develop more self-confidence, which translates into learning more effective ways of handling stress.

Marriage also affects health, with married couples usually living longer. Also support from the mate helps provide for regular sexual activity, more regulated and controlled lives, and the ability of couples to take care of each other. Single persons live less routine lives. This affects what and when they eat and sleep and all of their activities. In general they are more at risk whether through accidents, hospitalization, drugs, or transmission of disease. For women the menstrual cycle is an aspect of health, particularly in the years between 12 and 45. Although the cessation is occurring later, many women have had menopause before fifty. Estrogen may have long-term benefits for women, providing hormonal protection. Parlee (1983) found that the senses are effected by the menstrual cycle. Sight is the most acute at the time of ovulation. Hearing peaks at the beginning and again at the mid-cycle. Smell is most sensitive at the mid-cycle and sensitivity to pain is lowest just before the menstrual cycle. No change in cognitive functioning has been found. The effects of the Premenstrual Syndrome (PMS) are felt in some 20 to 40 percent of women, according to the American Council of Science and Health (1985). For these women symptoms may be tenderness of the breasts, anxiety, fatigue, headaches, acne, depression, and weight gain. The cause is not fully understood but may relate to biochemical and hormonal changes that come with the menstrual cycle. PMS is not likely to be suffered by very young females.

Exercise

If you don't use it you lose it. What else can explain men and women at 70 playing tennis, some competitively, and participating in marathons. The lungs, heart, and cardiovascular system all benefit from swimming, tennis, walking, jogging, and exercise routines at health spas or home; calories are cut, sleeping is better, anxiety is reduced, and there is a general euphoria that comes after vigorous exercise. Research by Jones (1991) indicates that again socioeconomics enters the picture--82 percent of lower-class recreation is sedentary--mainly television watching and card playing. Among the middle and upper classes these are 55 percent and 48 percent respectively. Of course having money is a factor, for it takes funds to play golf, have boats, go bowling, and have

Table 11.2 PERCENT OF POPULATION IN PHYSICAL EXERCISE, BY TYPE OF EXERCISE

	Regularly	Bicycle	Calisthenics	Jog	Weights	Swim	Walk
Male							
20-44 years	53	15	17	11	10	19	31
45-64 years	42	7	10	4	3	8	31
Female							
20-44 years	55	17	17	4	1	15	36
45-64 years	45	6	11	2	--	8	34

Source: U.S. Department of Commerce (1981).

equipment used in tennis, hunting, etc. Middle and upper classes have also been introduced to sports--golf, tennis, and boating, whereas some groups of children receive no chance to learn about sports and games unless from schools. But many schools are limited in this orientation. Table 11.2 reveals that most 20- to 44-year-old persons exercise regularly, with walking being the most often used exercise.

Grip strength (Figure 11.4) is less by the time a person reaches 40. The years from 20 to 40 are mainly peaks in the development of the physical body.

Heredity

Heredity plays an important role in health status via the predisposition to certain weaknesses and strengths. Problems carried forward from childhood, such as infantile paralysis, sickle cell anemia, cystic fibrosis, diabetes, single X chromosome in females, polydactylism, karotypes, and chromosome abnormalities are practical determiners of life's direction in general and vocations in particular. It has been estimated that the human central nervous system at age 30 contains approximately 20 billion neurons and that a decrement of about 0.8 takes place each successive year. In three decades, by age 60, the body loses approximately 25 percent of its neurons (Vogel, 1977). Vogel says that:

> longevity comes to him who carefully selects his ancestors. This is to say that we are physical and functional expressions of our deoxyribonucleic acid (DNA). Clearly, the human species is far from homogeneous in this constituent, since no two individuals are endowed with the same genetic information nor, for this reason, with the same biological potential. One concept suggests that all the biological systems are driven as by a mainspring (DNA), which is wound at birth and thus energizes life and establishes its timetable. Such a concept would suggest that longevity is predetermined solely by inherent genetic characteristics. However, it would be unrealistic to forget that the human organism exists in a generally adverse ecology to which neurons are responsive, and that the effects of the ecology are generally detrimental (pp. 232-233).

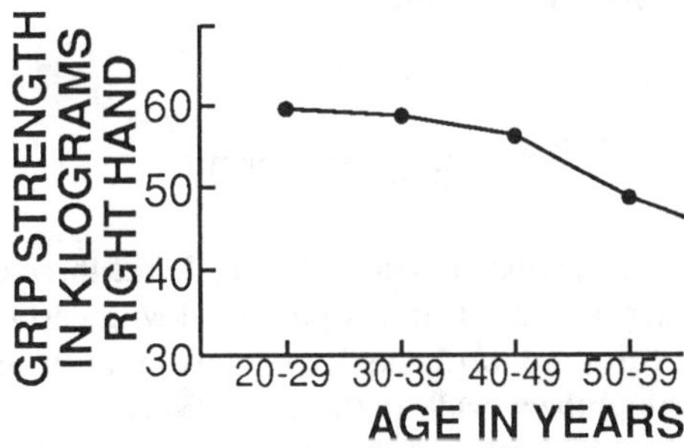

Figure 11.4 One of the consequences of loss of muscle tissue in adulthood is a loss of strength, such as these changes in grip strength in a group of men. Part of this loss of strength could also be the result of less use of the muscles, but that does not account for all of it. Muscle tissue is lost with age even among adults who do hard physical activity, or exercise regularly. (Adapted from Rossman, 1980, p. 128.)

Whatever the length of life, longevity is related to families as is the predisposition to heart, lung, and other problems. Also family related are the degree of intelligence applied to living standards and general health practices. The physical environment affects the length of life significantly. One can use as an example industrial towns with high levels of soot and other deleterious substances that precipitate lung diseases. Whether or not life is shortened by genetic constitution, some insight may be provided by comparing a single human biological event and a tree. An individual limb of a tree dies; nonetheless the remaining limbs of the tree are healthy. A lost leg or arm significantly affects the human organism, but perhaps very little the general life of the body. The inability to function in the physical mode (due to basic disability such as anemia, or a sickness induced partially by the environment, such as emphysema) may be as disturbing to an individual as its effects on one's role, one's identity, and perhaps ultimate success. Such difficulties, however, may be overcome through a societal setting that allows one to master the appropriate developmental tasks for one's level. A paraplegic, for example, can be rehabilitated, find employment, and perhaps even begin a family.

THE SOCIAL MODE

The period of young adulthood, like those of other periods of life, is presented with certain developmental tasks by society in cultures around the world. In the Third World there is little or no adolescent period, but childhood fuses into adulthood where work and adult responsibility are the expected characteristics of this time. In the Western world, particularly in the United States, marriage does not occur for most men until 25 and for women around 23. Economic responsibility may not be borne by the young woman or man. Indeed there may be considerable discretionary latitude in the demands of independence, community responsibilities, settling down, family and marriage, and general circumstances of their lives due to the cultural demands. Fifty years earlier the average age of marriage was much lower for men and women, affected by the historical times. Few persons went to college, marriage beckoned for the high school graduate, and the draft was waiting. The developmental tasks serve a "housekeeping" function in society, i.e., sorting people out, regulating their lives and activities, projecting certain moralities, setting standards for citizens, and providing expectancies in marriage. The "tasks" occupy the ground half-way between individual need and societal demand. The tasks are highly specific to a culture. Among Australian Bushmen selecting a career is meaningless. In our society, not all want to get married and many do not have children. The usually accepted tasks of young adulthood are:

- Developing a love relationship
- Learning to get along with a partner
- Beginning a family and becoming a parent
- Rearing children and making a commitment to home care
- Beginning a career or occupation
- Participating in community affairs
- Developing a relationship with a social group

The tasks are common and expected and failure to achieve a task does not indicate abnormality. However, in childhood and adolescence tasks sometimes elicit considerable censure and ribbing if they are not fulfilled. An example is the child of eight who cannot dress himself or the adolescent of eighteen who has never worked at any job or had a date. Failure in adulthood, as with children, means the unaccomplished task needs still to be learned and perhaps with more difficulty. Adults in society characterize those who don't work as "ne'er do well" loafers and those young adults who have yet to adequately learn the tasks as "nobodies," "no account," and the like.

Coleman (1974), who was interested in the transition from adolescence to adulthood, suggested the effective transition to adulthood is made when certain *self-centered skills* and *other-centered skills* were obtained. He categorized as self-centered skills those concerning mastery of work and occupation, self-management skills, consumer skills, and concentrated involvement skills (the narrowing of one's interest to a special endeavor). These skills make possible the attaining of economic independence, arriving at decisions involving wide choice, and succeeding in an undertaking. The other-centered skills involve social interaction skills, skills relating to the handling of others, and cooperative skills. These skills are useful in effectively dealing with different people in a variety of settings, assuming responsibility for those who are dependent, and working with others in shared projects.

The Vocational Task

One of the fundamental requirements for establishing maturity during the early adult years is achieving independence and responsibility. A major task in becoming independent requires having an occupation that allows for economic autonomy. People usually begin work as young adults in their hometown and they often marry persons who live near them. In the last several decades the most salient trend in the vocational preparation of youth entering adulthood is the fact that boys' and girls' interest in occupation and working is very similar. Nearly 60 percent of women are in the work force (55.4 percent in 1989, *U.S. Statistical Abstract*, 1988) and this figure will be higher by the year 2000. The Congressional Caucus for Women's Issues in 1987 revealed that one of every three economists, one of every four computer programers, one of every six mail carriers, and one of every two bartenders were women. Women educating themselves for professions has increased considerably over the past 10 years. Figure 11.5 shows dramatic changes in the number of women in veterinary medicine, with a jump of nearly 400 percent.

In broad categories of occupational employment, women in 1985 represented 45 percent of technical, sales, and administrative support (also clerical), compared to 19 percent for men. Women represented twice the percentage of men in service occupations, 18.5 percent to 9.5 percent, and in the managerial and professional specialties were nearly equal. Some disparities are revealed in Figure 11.6. Dramatic shifts in sales favoring women have taken place over the past 15 years in real estate, brokering, insurance, and establishment of small businesses.

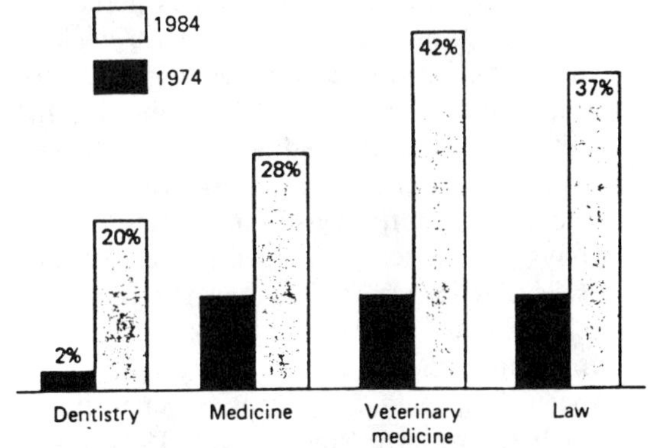

Figure 11.5 Percentage of women among graduate students pursuing advanced degrees in certain fields, 1974-1984. (*Source:* Associated Press, 1987.)

Occupational group	Males	Females
Managerial and professional specialties	24.7%	23.4%
Technical, sales, and administrative support (including clerical)	19.6%	45.5%
Service occupations	9.5%	18.5%
Precision production, craft, and repair (includes construction)	20.4%	2.4%
Operators, fabricators, and laborers	20.9%	9.1%
Farming, forestry, and fishing	4.9%	1.2%
Total	100.0%	100.1%

Figure 11.6 Employed persons by major occupational groups and sex. *Note:* Because of rounding, total for females is more than 100 percent. (*Source:* U.S. Department of Labor, 1985.)

Despite the fact that more women are in the work force than men, their pay is between 62 percent (Bureau of Census, 1986) to 70 percent (Congressional Caucus for Women's Issues, 1987) of that of men. Although bias in waging is a factor, those women entering the market for the first time often have little experience directly related to the job. The need to work to maintain a family without a father also means juggling the schedule, which is problematic. Many times managers, even if they are women, are concerned about the stability of the women working for the first time.

Gender differences exist in the pursuit of vocational aims. According to the SAT (Scholastic Aptitude Test) in 1987, 84 percent of those choosing engineering were boys, while 79 percent choosing teaching were girls. Girls chose foreign languages (80 percent), English (66 percent), health and allied fields (68 percent), social sciences and history (65 percent). Boys chose military science, architecture, physical science (70 percent), and computer science (65 percent). One thing is significantly changed from a decade or so ago: more girls are picking math as a major. Only slightly more boys chose math, 52 percent to 48 percent for girls (Newhouse New Service, 1987). It is certain that most females in college say they plan to work before and after marriage.

Vocational Stages and Choices of Work

Vocational values are extremely important in vocational selection and vocational stability. Work has different meanings and values for different people. It may be a source of prestige and recognition, an opportunity for service, a means of avoiding boredom, a basis for a sense of usefulness or worth, a source of creative expression, a means of satisfying a need for achievement, or simply a way of earning a living. The individual's self-concept will influence his selection of a vocation. The results of studies by Greenhaus (1971) indicated that individuals with high self-esteem tend to consider their own needs and relevant attributes in their satisfaction with their occupational choice, whereas those with low self-esteem tend to look toward external cues (hours, pay, conditions).

Several investigators have developed theories encompassed in stages of vocational life. One of these is Super (1963), presented as follows:

1. Growth Stage (1 to 14 years): Children develop self-concept. They play at various roles, occupations and work. These are usually unrealistic.

2. Exploration Stage (15 to 24): Teenagers explore and react to what they feel is a need and a demand by society to work. They examine their interests, capacities, values, and what is available to do. The educational decision is made by the end of this period or in some cases a tentative plan is constructed; usually work begins in this period.

3. Establishment Stage (25 to 44): Workers try to establish a permanent position for themselves in a job they like. Early in this period career and job securement may take place but stabilization occurs as 35 comes closer.

4. Maintenance Stage (45 to 64): The worker focusing on the present job tries to maintain the status quo.

5. Decline Stage (age 65 on): As physical and mental capacity decline work is adjusted to fit current abilities.

Havighurst (1964) deals with the acquisition of attitudes and work skills that put people into the work force. He offers these stages:

1. Identification (5 to 10): Children identify with mothers and fathers and the idea of working themselves.

2. Acquiring Habits of Industry (10 to 15): Students learn from school and chores the effort that is needed to succeed. They learn to prioritize work over school in some instances.

3. Identifying as a Worker (15 to 25): People choose an occupation and begin to prepare for it. They get some work experience that helps them choose and get started on a career.

4. Becoming a Productive Person (25 to 40): Adults perfect the skills required by their chosen career and move ahead in their work.

5. Maintaining a Productive Society (40 to 70): Workers are now at the high point of their careers. They begin to pay attention and give time to civic and social responsibilities related to the job.

6. Contemplating a Productive and Responsible Life (70 on): Workers are now retired and they look back on their careers as a contribution.

These theories are probably suited to the circumstances that existed several decades ago and may be applicable to only 50 percent of the people today. They may be less relevant to many persons in the complex, ever-changing society with its concomitant increase in the use of technology. People often hold several jobs before they make a major job commitment and some never really make a commitment at all. They also make major mid-career shifts, sometimes several (Okum, 1984).

Considerable influence is exerted on the young by parents who provide the sense of need. Also many of their interests and attitudes give impetus to vocational direction. Warm, loving families may provide the interest in occupations that promise to help children realize such esteem as was gained by their parents. *Self-concept*, as mentioned earlier, is another factor involving the selection of an occupation that matches their view of themselves. They may simply wish to find an occupation that will boost their ideas of a possible self and identity. The woman who is socially concerned, has much energy and some charisma may become a health and welfare employee or possibly enter into politics. The man who thinks he is bright and has verbal facility might go into the academic world as a professor.

Another aspect of vocational selection is seen in the trait theory. Holland (1973) developed a theory matching six personality traits with occupational traits.

These traits are: (1) realistic, (2) investigative, (3) social, (4) conventional, (5) enterprising, and (6) artistic. Someone exhibiting traits 3 and 4 might become a teacher, social worker, or hospital employee. Someone displaying traits 2 and 5 might become a researcher. Much research has been done on this approach, with the number of years in which the Strong Vocational Interest Blank has been used (Copyright 1933). It is now used in another but similar form as the Strong Interest Inventory distributed by the Consulting Psychologist Press, Inc. The six occupational themes remain the same as suggested by Holland; hence, he must have borrowed them from Strong. In any event many young adults who have been presented with the results of these inventories proceed to seek the training and education needed to fulfill the counseling suggestion.

Research on the Holland scale appears to back up his claims (Eberhardt and Muchinsky, 1984). Among men and women, ministers scored highest on the social scale, car salespersons on the enterprising scale, and engineers and physicians on the investigative scale. Investigators Benninger and Walsh (1980) found an interesting dichotomy between policewomen and policemen: female police scored highest on the social scale and male police scored highest on the realistic scale. In most occupations that are open to young adults of either gender, intellectual skills, education, family background, and personality traits play a significant role in the choice. However, one should be reminded that racial inequality has been so long taken for granted in this country, that in spite of affirmative-action legislation much more needs to be accomplished. In the past many more black women expected to work than white women--54 percent to 16 percent--and this difference is believed to still exist (Troll, 1985). It is obvious that the unemployment rates and wages are differential for blacks and whites. While there is a strong developing middle class of blacks, the question remains to be seen as to whether the current economic downturn will affect this positive trend in employment opportunities.

Employment prospects are discouraging when three or four trained persons compete for a single appropriate opening. On the other hand, some secure a position they are prepared for, such as a 25-year-old woman who had majored in distributive education but found she disliked this work. She finally began work as a secretary for an insurance company. Three years later, she has come to like her work and has been promoted to a supervisory role. An

Table 11.3 JOHN HOLLAND'S SIX PERSONALITY TYPES AND SIX WORK ENVIRONMENT TYPES

Type	Personality	Work Environment
REALISTIC	Aggressive, masculine, physically strong, low in verbal or interpersonal skills. Prefer mechanical activities and tool use, choosing jobs like mechanic or electrician or surveyor.	Demand for explicit, ordered, or systematic manipulation of tools or machines or objects animals.
INVESTIGATIVE	Thinking, organizing, planning, particularly abstract thinking. These people like ambiguous, challenging tasks, but are generally low in social skills. They are often scientists or engineers.	Demand for observation, creative symbol investigation of physical, biological, or cultural phenomena.
SOCIAL	Similar to extroverts. Humanistic, sociable, need attention. Avoid intellectual activity, dislike highly ordered activity. Prefer to work with people.	Demand for training, caring for, enlightening of, informing, or serving others.
CONVENTIONAL	Prefer structured activities and subordinate role; like clear guidelines. See themselves as accurate and precise.	Demand for systematic, ordered, precise manipulation of data, such as keeping records, filing, bookkeeping, organizing written material, following a plan.
ENTERPRISING	Highly verbal and dominating, like organizing and directing others; persuasive, high in leadership.	Demand for manipulating others, such as in sales of all types or other manipulation to further organizational goals.
ARTISTIC	Asocial, preference for unstructured, highly individual activity.	Demand for ambiguous, free, unsystematized activities to produce art or performance.

Source: Holland, 1973.

English teacher whose job was phased out due to lack of funds found work on a newspaper and now says she prefers this to teaching.

Graduates with liberal arts degrees will have trouble finding jobs; retraining may be a partial answer. Another may be taking a temporary laboring job, as did a Russian language major who is driving a truck while waiting to receive a call from the government offering him a job that will utilize his Russian. In the university setting, we find many liberal arts graduates serving as secretaries; some come to like it and advance to middle management positions or seek higher degrees. For some it is a holding pattern until something more appropriate appears.

The management of money is an important factor in achieving maturity. Despite the economic climate of the 1990s, young adults seem to have made little adaptation in terms of their material desires. They see eating out, owning a color television set, going to movies, and having an automobile as necessities.

Money and Spending

In 1984 the spending of young adults reflected the following as compared to a 1975 survey. (Youth Indicators, 1988):

1975 Plans	
Owning home	59%
Pension plan	57%
Savings account	54%
College degree	38%
Color TV	12%
Having a master's degree	12%

1984 Spending	
Food	15%
Housing	28%
Clothing	6%
Transportation	26%
Entertainment	6%
Education	5%
Other	12%

Having a car, being able to travel abroad, and having an air-conditioned home, although not listed above, were also rated above the color television and having a master's degree. Many couples, due to economic circumstances, have opted to forego having children. There are both married couples and singles who save by frequently taking their lunch to work, supplementing their diets with vitamins, and wearing old clothes at home and when shopping.

The following data (Figures 11.7 and 11.8) were obtained from the 1990-1991 United States Statistical Abstract (U.S. Government Printing Office). Presented are age distribution of the labor force, proportion of degree holders, change in broad occupational groups, and the projected rapid growth in some industries.

Fewer 16- to 34-year-olds will be in the work force in 2000 due to the fact that the baby boom group is getting older. The oldest "boomers" are 45 years old and in 1988 they represented 48 percent of the working force.

The industries and occupations that will grow more rapidly than others are presented below (Figures 11.9 and 11.10). Those industries providing services will account for nearly four out of five jobs by the year 2000 (*Occupational Outlook Handbook*, 1990-1991 Edition).

Women in the Work World

Women work, according to some, for the same reasons that men work--self fulfillment, consolidation of their identity, opportunity for self-direction, and economic benefits and security. The number of women, their level of pay, and the number of women workers with children, suggest the principal reason may be economic. Many women feel the drive to work outside the home partly due to the need for money and partly due to the emphasis on being fulfilled through work in the outside world. This latter impetus has been given by the feminist movement and especially the National Organization of Women. Nearly 60 percent of women are in the work force, many of whom

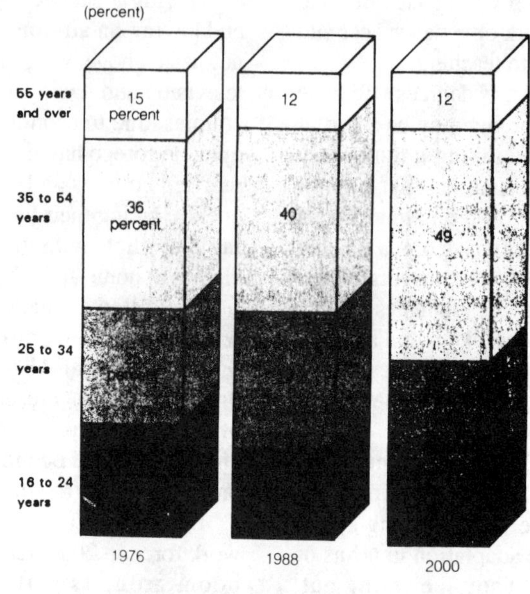

Figure 11.7 The age distribution of the labor force is changing.

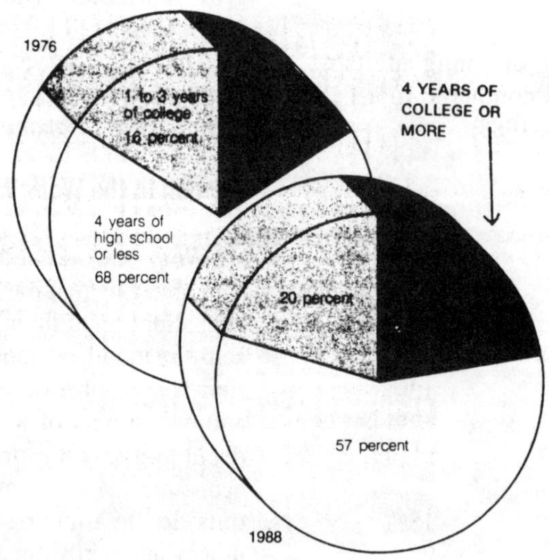

Figure 11.8 The proportion of workers with a college background has increased substantially since the mid '70s. College degree holders have increased 30 percent in 12 years.

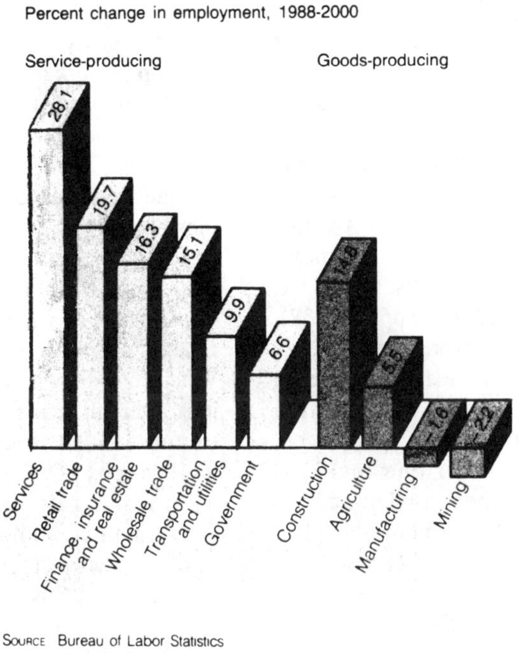

Percent change in employment, 1988-2000
Service-producing
Goods-producing
28.1
19.7
16.3
15.1
9.9
6.6
14.8
5.5
-1.6
-2.2
Services
Retail trade
Finance, insurance and real estate
Wholesale trade
Transportation and utilities
Government
Construction
Agriculture
Manufacturing
Mining
SOURCE Bureau of Labor Statistics

Figure 11.9 Some industries will grow more rapidly than others.

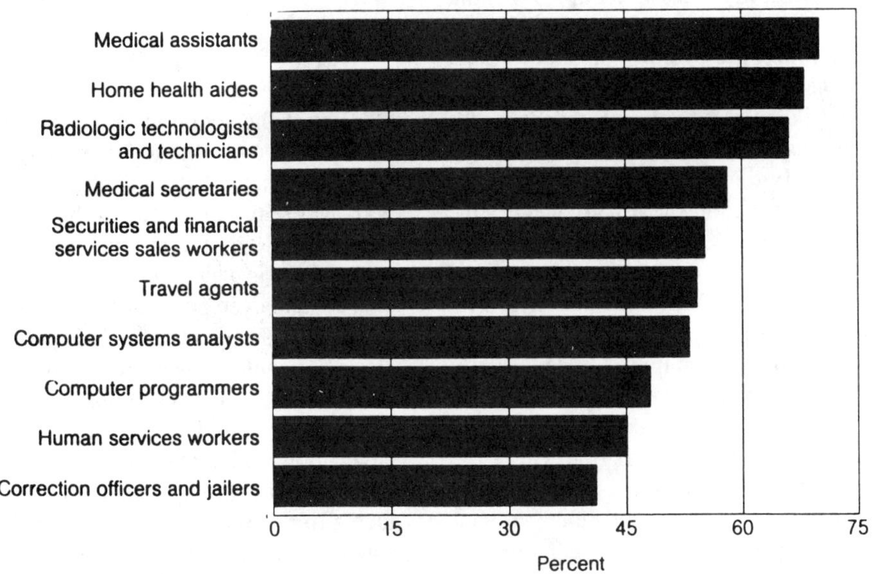

Medical assistants
Home health aides
Radiologic technologists and technicians
Medical secretaries
Securities and financial services sales workers
Travel agents
Computer systems analysts
Computer programmers
Human services workers
Correction officers and jailers
0
15
30
45
60
75
Percent
Source: Chart prepared by U.S. Bureau of the Census. For data, see table 646.

Figure 11.10 Projected percent change in employment for 10 fastest growing occupations: 1988 to 2000.

are divorced and in poverty status. The average number of children per family in 1990 was 1.9 children. The poverty level in 1987 for a family with two children was $6,951. Over 7 million white mothers and 3 million black mothers were caring for children, representing three out of seven of all families. U.S. Statistical Abstract shows the following percentages of female-headed families: blacks, 50.5; Hispanic, 53.1; and white, 27.4. (*Abstract*, 1990 pp. 424, 38). It seems apparent that many women work out of necessity and often these women have children under five. Fifty-one percent with children under three were working in 1987 (48 percent working with babies under one in 1985) (Census Bureau, 1988) as opposed to only 34 percent in 1975 (U.S. Department of Labor, 1987).

Despite the evidence that more young married couples are approaching equality in sharing the raising of children and dividing the household chores, women who work still do more than half of household chores if they have children. Certainly there are couples without children who both work, have good paying jobs, and seldom prepare evening meals at home. But with the typical couple, both of whom work and have children, it is the female who takes the major responsibility for child care--monitoring clothes and hygiene, schoolwork, sleeping, eating, etc. In addition she usually handles the family wash, cleaning and procurement of food and clothes purchases, in addition to social and community relations. Men sometimes help with shopping, dish washing or drying, babysitting, and cooking an occasional meal. Men usually do yard work, paint and make repairs, take care of the car(s), and sometimes pay the bills.

The dual-earner couple is one where the wife works at least 20 or more hours a week, with many women working full-time. Advantages accrue such as greater income, more self-fulfillment, providing a more equal relationship between husband and wife, greater sense of integrity for the woman, a closer relationship between a father and his children, and an embellished capacity for each partner to function and develop in work and family roles.

Conflict and stress abound for the woman in the mothering role. Do my children get enough attention? Am I meeting their needs? These are haunting questions for the woman. The man may be driven by his career, particularly if he is a professional and if he is in an occupation with long hours. He may feel guilty about not carrying his part of the load or angry because he resents extra assignments of work at home. Where children are involved someone has to look after child care, or if the children are older trusting to a "latch key" situation with its fearful implications. One thing is sure: this arrangement is not going to end, even though it is problematic for children's education, security, peer association, and orientation to drugs, sex, etc., because the benefits are too compelling. It allows the young couple to maintain two cars, purchase a home, take a vacation and have children in the first place.

THE HISTORICAL TIMES AND CHANGE

Part of the social modality is affected by historical events. In fact, these may affect not only the social but also the physical, such as in war, where devastation can be to objects or people. But more normative events are often social, such as depressions, epidemics, political chance, and even peace and tranquility. In the past such conditions as political philosophy affected people. The economic debacle of the 1930s changed the lives of many forever. More recently the Gulf War has had an effect. The new widow with a child had planned to devote her time to the raising of her child but must now face a life of work. Some work may demand education, it may cause frustration, loneliness, and may send the person into a completely changed world. A *reaction* to these circumstances isn't always bad, many turn out to be salutary. The young woman forced to fend for herself and child may find a job that fits her temperament, enlivens her life, and creates opportunity beyond which she never dreamed. The loss of a home or business due to a hurricane may force a man to reorient his future plans and draw on his inside resources and ingenuity to find a better life for himself and family. There are many of these success stories.

LOVE, LIFESTYLES, MARRIAGE AND FAMILY

Freud said the crucial element in maturity is the capacity to love and to work. Tolstoy, a contemporary of Freud, suggested that one can live life magnificently in this world if one knows how to work and to love. At one time only poets, romance writers, artists, and occasionally a philosopher talked or wrote about love.

One recent theory by the psychologist Sternberg that has received considerable attention involves three aspects of love--passion, intimacy, and commitment. In the developmental sense William Kroger believes there are four types of love; the first one "I love I," as seen in the child who only loves those who aid his well-being. The second type of love is projected self-love (I love me as seen in you). This case is found frequently with immature persons who see qualities of others that rightly or wrongly they attribute to themselves. Romantic love is a third type. In the western world marriage is usually based on this type, and most persons have been conditioned to believe that it is the highest form of love. The principal element of this love is passion and idealism. The final type of love is mature love, identified as the condition where each partner thinks only in terms of the other person's happiness--one's chief enjoyment is in giving, interacting, sharing, not expunging, getting, and possessing. By all accounts this type is rare; it is usually taken to distinguish love from mere attachment, liking, desiring, wanting, etc., as Freud used the term; although he said that love is the attachment and not the feeling. Freud's reasoning was that there may be feelings associated with attachment that are not always pleasant. Love in general can be romantic and lofty; on the other hand, it can be selfish and highly ego-centered. Some of our love makes us happy and provides a sense of fulfillment; other love keeps us constantly striving, feeling often times inadequate. Therefore, feelings associated with love are not dependable as the sole basis for life because they vary too much.

Sternberg (1986) formulated a theory of love in which he suggests there are three aspects or faces of love--commitment, intimacy, and passion. The three aspects can be visualized as the sides of a triangle. The larger the triangle, the greater the love. Intimacy is emotional closeness, sharing, communication, and support. Passion is motivational, physiological arousal, intense desire, which develops quickly and involves kissing, touching, hugging, making love. Commitment is cognitive; it starts with nothing and grows. It is first represented as short-term commitment in loving another, then it becomes long-term commitment to maintain that love as expressed by fidelity.

The shape of love based upon this theory says commitment is the cognitive component of love and is all that some couples seem to have remaining after intimacy and closeness have been lost and passion has died down. Intimacy is the emotional component of love. Some people can bare their souls to each other but show little in the way of commitment or passion. This is a characteristic of high-grade friendship. Passion, on the other hand, is the

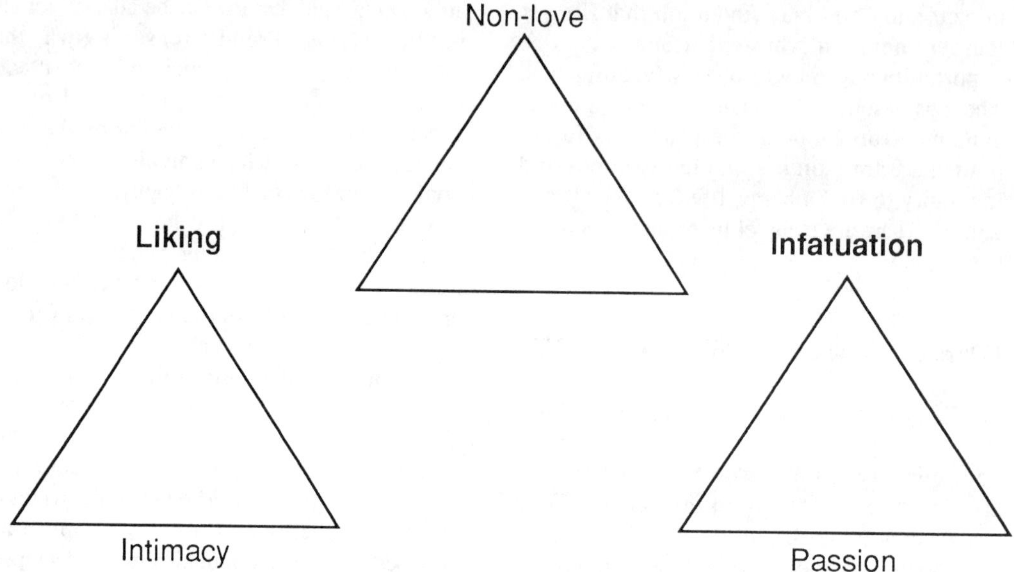

motivational component of love and often is primary in some love triangles. It might manifest in an affair or a fling in which there is little intimacy and even less commitment.

Triangles may be used to define various types of love, beginning with non-love. In this triangle there is no intimacy, commitment, or passion.

In liking another person, you have intimacy--you can talk to a person, tell them about your life and dreams; there is closeness and warmth but not passion or commitment. With infatuation there is only passion; it is adolescent-instant love upon seeing a dream girl or boy.

Empty love is frequently called cold love; there's no passion or intimacy. Whereas, romantic love often is portrayed as having passion and intimacy but not commitment (Romeo and Juliet type). This is like a summer affair that dies when autumn comes. Passion plus commitment is what Sternberg calls "fatuous love" (lacking reality). It's the Hollywood type of love--boy meets girl and marries her next week--the commitment is to the passion that's aroused but the emotional core necessary to sustain the commitment is not there.

Finally, there is companionate love, which is constructed of commitment and intimacy but

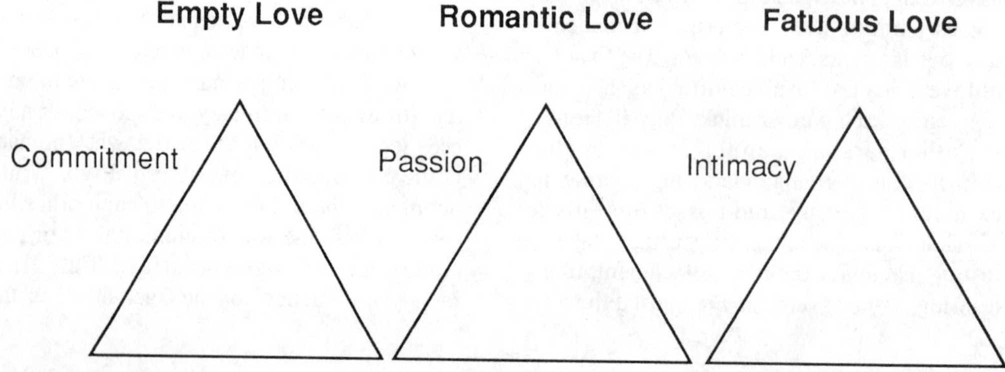

not passion. This is long-term friendship--the kind of committed love and intimacy seen in marriages in which the physical attraction has died. Consummate love is where the three forces are all there--passion, intimacy, and commitment. Sternberg says this achievement is nearly impossible--like keeping off weight after you have lost it. This love is possible only in very special relationships.

Companionate Love

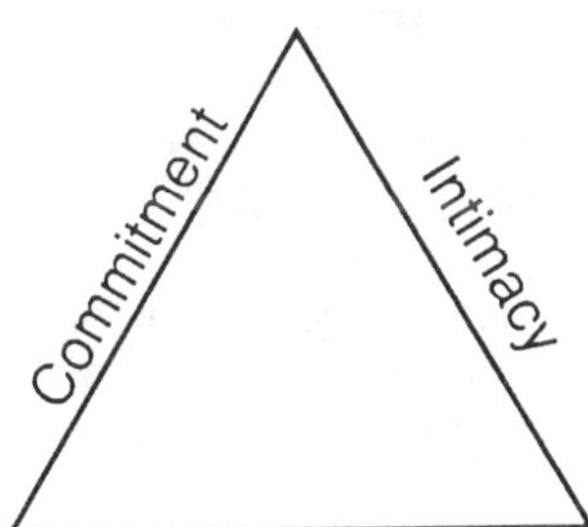

force is still there after the person or substance is gone. One thing is true, according to Sternberg: the consummate love involves couples who love each other more than anyone else.

Do opposites attract? Certainly it may be the stimulus to attract another's attention. But there is also the notion that we find someone in whom to reflect ourselves. There seems to be some self-love in selection for we can observe many similarities in persons who fall in love. These can be appearance, intelligence, warmth, popularity, or such family factors as socio-economic status, race, religion, or education. On the other hand a number of persons choose those who complement their lack of certain strengths. A man may, for instance, have to talk virtually non-stop in his work, so may value a woman who is quiet. Or the person who is mainly sedentary might enjoy someone who is vivacious and active. A study by Neiswender, Birren and Schaie (1975) based upon the examination of 24 couples described by people who knew them as "very much in love" found men and women experience love similarly. They found married love is qualitatively no different from unmarried love in realism, maturity, or idealism; older people love just as much as younger people. In fact, older couples seem to idealize their partners more. Sex is increasingly important from adolescence to middlescence, but becomes less important toward senescence. There seems to be three fundamental aspects of a relationship--the *emotional*--he

Consummate Love

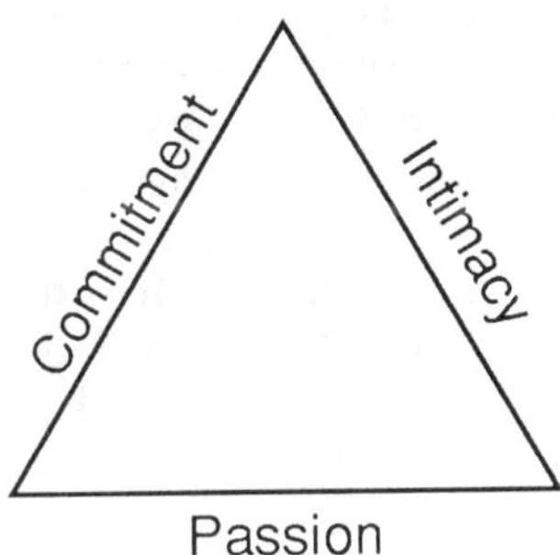

Many theorists believe women are better at achieving intimacy and value it more than men. If they fail to obtain the intimacy they desire from a man, they try to find it with women or another man. They establish close friendships and are able to say things they can't say to a man. This may account for the fact that women have a much more extensive network of support than does the average man--and his support is often principally from women.

Passion initially may be the positive force that drives people together. Though quick to develop, passion is also quick to level off. This negative motivational force, the one that works against the attraction, is slow to develop and slow to fade. The result is first an explosion of passion followed by habituation when the more slowly developing negative force begins. Like coffee, cigarettes, or alcohol addiction, increasing the amount of passion no longer stimulates the arousal that occurred earlier. When a person is dropped, he or she ends up much worse off--depressed, with withdrawal symptoms, irritable, with loss of appetite--the negative or she makes me feel complete; *verbal*--he or she confides in me and in a cognitive sense, respects my judgment; and *physical*--we touch and hold each other and have good sexual relations. Most authorities on marriage believe that the more balanced a couple is in sharing, giving, and taking, i.e., making equal contributions to a relationship, the more happy they will be. If the marriage is out of balance, such couples usually try to even it up by some changes. If they cannot do this then they may divorce. One must recognize that to have a perfectly complete marriage in every respect is probably impossible. But the spirit of fair play has to be there, contributing to harmony. Marriage is making a comeback from the low water mark of the 1970s, with 2 1/2 million marriages every year in the United States (Norton & Moorman, 1987).

Success and Benefits in Marriage

Some people may say they will never get married, but the fact is that at some time 95 percent do get married (Schuz & Rodgers, 1985). The largest group of singles account for 20 percent of the never-married (Bureau of Census, 1988). The first-time marrying age is 23.1 for women and 25.7 for men; 10 years ago it was 22.0 and 24.7. Marriage offers a number of benefits and it usually delivers happiness at least for a time. Obviously, however, with nearly one of two marriages ending in divorce, something is happening along the way to lessen significantly the happiness.

The benefits of marriage provide a systematic, socially approved way of raising children and continuing the race. Beyond this, marriage offers the following emoluments:

1. Economic benefits - division of labor, working and sharing unit.

2. Provision for sexual activity - usually exclusive rights and availability.

3. Steady companionship - secure source of friendship, affection, and partnership in many activities.

4. Emotional growth - mutual relationship and commitment to each other.

5. Affirmation of adulthood - provides status, helps settle the intimacy, isolate problems, and gives an identity.

These benefits are ideals that are met in many cases among couples, particularly among the recently married. However, divorce begins to mount by the third year and by the 10-year mark, the typical marriage ends in divorce. This trend has been relatively stable over the past 20 years (Bureau of the Census, 1988). The divorce rate has fallen slightly in the past few years, as has the marriage rate. See Figure 11.11 (U.S. Department of Health and Human Services, 1989).

Friendships and "going steady" in the adolescent years can lead to marriage. Sharing the intimacy often leads to sexual activity and/or commitment of selves. At its highest point sexuality has the quality of intimacy; at its finest level trust and devotion are also required. Before identity has been reached sexual union is usually dominated mainly by physical urging. Intimacy involves the possibility of being hurt by the rejection of one's love; some men who struggle with their identities will not take a chance. They may have multiple relationships without commitment. Men tend to fall in love more quickly than women, to be more satisfied with their mates' qualities, to be more romantic, but also to fall out of love more quickly (Hill, Rubin & Peplau, 1979). Women as a rule are more careful to pick spouses; they are usually more practical. The traditional marriage once gave the woman little choice about her occupation; however, with the women's movement has come greater equality in the job market, career orientations, and freedom.

Marriage has served two major purposes; first, in the traditional setting it has been a means to achieve certain individual and social ends. In this type of marriage, entered into by legal contract and ritualized by a ceremony, it

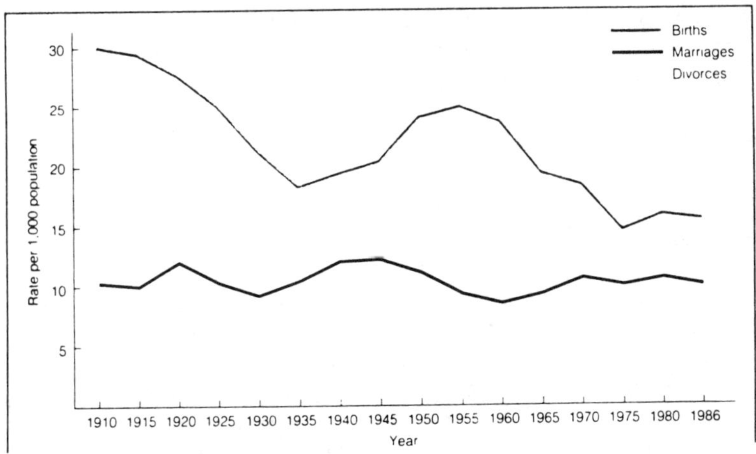

Figure 11.11 Changes in marriage, divorce, and birthrates per 1,000 population, 1910 to 1986. (From U.S. Bureau of Census, 1988, p. 59.)

has signaled full adulthood, has legitimized sexual monopoly and gratification, and has provided the opportunity to have progeny and to gain security and independence from parents. Expectations for men and women have been rather rigid and construed as such by the marriage contract. Society itself was protected by this type of marriage in that it helped to control sexual impulses and socialization of children, and to preserve customs and stabilize adult behavior, all of which were considered important by society (Dreyer, 1975).

The second purpose is to make marriage a terminal event. Dreyer (p. 221) says that "a growing number of young people seek to make it a terminal event, a type of hedonism, whereby new meaning is found in marriage by making it an approbation of personal identity, providing psychological intimacy, giving mutual pleasure, promoting personal growth opportunities, and offering transcendent relationships between two human beings." Some claim this approach is pleasure-oriented and egocentric, despite the brave talk about transcendence and permanency. The egocentrism of young adults is a characteristic of this period; marriage serves to clarify this even if it does not settle the identity issue.

People generally marry those they meet where they work, worship, live, or play. Murstein (1976) believes the filtering process in selecting a mate involves stimulus, values, and roles. The *stimulus* relates to the initial attraction involving propinquity and physical appeal. In the second stage the potential mate examines the *values* of the other. Likes and dislikes are discussed, as are goals and aspirations. Self-disclosure reveals the identities a person has. This is a necessary process that leads to intimacy. It represents a judgment about how much alike or different we are. Finally the potential mate asks what *role* will I play with this person? Will I be the leader, follower, or imitator and what are the family's expectations for my role? This may be an unresolved and difficult situation that confronts the couple after marriage, which may alter considerably their premarital views. The process of mating sometimes breaks down in marriage over role expectation. Another question might be whether chemistry plays a part in mate selection. Investigators agree that it probably does although how much and to what extent is unknown. Where the choice of mate differs radically from parental and sibling ideals, the parent can exert considerable pressure on their child. Such pressures can consist of outright ostracism, arguments, and statements that they will never accept the prospective spouse. They can cut off emotional and economic help, and be rude and unsociable when the potential spouse is present. Sullivan (1971) conducted research among parents who cited opposition to prospective spouses of their son or daughter, finding 81 percent used a variety of such obstructions to disrupt the relationship, and that they were successful in most cases.

Physicians frequently marry nurses; propinquity favors this, as when movie stars marry other stars or their promoters. Attraction involving the physical or personality is usually a requirement. Marriages often fail, and physical attraction cannot over a period of time overcome mismatches in personality or views about roles. Some couples survive, however, for they have developed similar views on a number of important subjects--religion, values and ethical systems, lifestyles, recreation and leisure, living conditions, future plans, education, and politics.

Americans believe in marriage; if they fail at it they will try again. When compared with unmarried persons of all ages married persons report higher levels of satisfaction and happiness. Important for both men and women are certain variables related to marital satisfaction. For men occupation followed by socio-economic status produces more happiness. Women who are older when they marry are happier. Male executives and professionals are more happily married than other men. Men in second marriages are also happier than women (Skolnick, 1981). Campbell et al. (1975) report young wives state they feel much less stress after marriage; men, though happy, said they felt more stress. Women apparently see marriage as an accomplishment and a source of security but men as a responsibility (Papalia and Olds, 1989). Education, personality, and intelligence matches are important in marital satisfaction. Social characteristics are important--highly social couples seem to do better at marital harmony (Skolnick, 1981).

Kinds of Marriages

A study of marriage was conducted by Cuber and Harroff (1965) of 211 upper middle class men and women who were highly successful professionals and had been married for at least 10 years and never contemplated divorce. From this sample, investigators isolated five types of marriages:

Conflicted-habituated The couple lived in a constant stormy atmosphere of domestic controversy. They apparently needed the discord, for they stayed together.

Devitalized This dull affair has no passion, little intimacy, but commitment (like Sternberg's Empty Love). Their lives are marked by sameness and habit though there was a time when it was different.

Passive-congenial This is a lifeless relationship also but unlike the devitalized was devoid of any earlier romance. It is emotionally barren. They stay together for social and economic reasons.

Vital The relationship is this marriage is important to both partners. There is a sharing of important experiences. Both partners are happy, devoting time to the marriage, but nevertheless retaining their individuality and autonomy.

Total These couples have a much greater commitment to the relationship and more intense agreement on everything. There is a total intimate sharing of all aspects of life.

In the 1990s some of these marriages will probably dissolve. There are trade-offs in marriage that may account for seeming stability. For the woman the husband's salary may be the off-setting factor even though there may be little or no sex life. The husband may perceive the wife is good with the children and cares for his parents. The prestige received by one spouse or the other sometimes is enough to keep them together. For the middle and lower middle class there would be fewer tradeoffs and for the lower class hardly any--they stay together because there is no escape. Women who leave with the children must for the most part live in reduced circumstances or near the poverty level. Most of the women in the Cuber and Harroff study did not work out of the home. This itself eliminates the stress of the regular work place and therefore is another trade-off. Today many singles can find companionship and sex outside of marriage and because most women now work, marriage is likely to bring them increased stress. The following represents some broadly defined ways of living together.

Styles of Marriage and Alternatives

In the traditional approach to marriage, the wife assumes the role of homemaker and the husband the major decision maker and breadwinner. This patriarchal style of marriage is still seen in some religious and ethnic groups. Most marriages are democratic in nature and based upon shared roles, affection, and companionship. In this style of marriage the husband usually takes the lead in decision making, though occasionally the wife may do so. An increasingly popular type of marriage is the egalitarian. In this kind of marriage there is a division of responsibility of fused roles--housekeeping, cooking, caring for children. Each partner has a career and contributes to the economic life of the home. In some situations the husband may be the principal housekeeper, contributing less to the financial needs of the home, while the wife has the principal career and does little cooking and caring for children, if there are any. In the open style of marriage the couple give each other wide freedom to pursue a variety of interests, even to having intense relationships with others of the opposite sex. Some of these types of marriages are handled by contract, which are typically renewable every few years, perhaps with some modification.

Remaining single A number of alternatives to marriage exist, the principal one being to remain single. One of three people remains single until around age 35. In 1986 22.2 percent of men in the 30 to 34 age range and 14.2 percent of women were single, for a total of 36.4 percent (Bureau of Census, 1986). Probably a third (12-14 percent) of this group are widowed or divorced. Some of these young adults want to keep as many options open for themselves as they can--that is, the freedom to move across the country, to travel, have varied experiences, change jobs, and savor being alone without the responsibility of husbands, wives, or children. Finally, others have a sexual orientation that may be lesbian or homosexual. Most women wish to marry prior to 30; after 30 some put their major energy into work and achieving economic independence. For the middle-class adult many opportunities for social and sexual life exist through ordinary means.

Ninety-five percent of Danish students, both males and females, report premarital sexual experience (Stevens-Long, 1979). By age 25, 82 percent of single women had premarital sexual intercourse; for men, the figure was 90 percent (Tanfer & Horn, 1985). In a 1982 survey (Simenaner & Carroll, 1982) which was a representative sampling of singles from the ages of 20 to 55, scientifically selected to reflect the demographic composition of the entire country, approximately three-quarters of single men and almost 90 percent of single women felt it was difficult or impossible to be meaningfully and sexually involved with more than one person during the same period of time.

Casual sex is found more often among older single people and among the recently divorced and separated. Stein (1976) interviewed 60 single men and women aged 22 to 62 and found a number of positive and negative aspects of being single. The advantages according to both sexes were career opportunity, self-sufficiency, sexual availability, exciting lifestyle, plurality of roles, freedom, autonomy, and varieties of experience. The negative aspects for both sexes were poor communication, sexual frustration, lack of friends, limited mobility, and limited availability of new experiences. Some of these reasons seem to overlap, suggesting that perhaps an assessment of being single depends upon one's age, the availability of companionship, and individual personality.

Homosexuality and Couples Kinsey's (1953) research indicates that at age 40, 37 percent of the males and 13 percent of the females have reached homosexual orgasm at least once in their lives. Among males aged 20 to 35, those who had exclusively homosexual experience ranged from 3 to 16 percent, and among females, 1 to 3 percent. A consensual figure suggests 10 to 12 percent for men and around 5 percent for women. About half of homosexual males live as couples compared with three-fourths of the females (Harry, 1983). The majority of gay couples place high value on equality or roles--sexual, economic, or decision making (Peplau, 1981). Relationships among homosexual male couples tend not to last long and to involve younger males. However, most of the data on this subject were gathered from bars and other places where the young are in the majority (Harry, 1983). The threat of AIDS has reduced promiscuity among homosexuals. Twenty percent of gay men and 33 percent of gay women have been married. Few men but most gay women are awarded custody of the children. After a divorce these women often establish a homosexual relationship. The children from these marriages do not usually become homosexuals, and when divorce or separation takes place in homosexual couples, children suffer as much as those in heterosexual families.

Divorced Singles Half of all divorces in America take place by the seventh year of marriage (Fisher, 1987). Over one million divorces a year occur in the U.S. Divorce is more likely among blacks and those who marry at an age under 20. Relatively high divorce rates exist for Protestants (Baptist, Methodist, Pentecostal, etc.) as opposed to Catholics and Jews (Glenn & Supancic, 1984). Other factors in divorce are socio-economic status, race, religion, and educational levels. Although there are considerable adjustment problems, economic troubles, and emotional problems surrounding divorce, marrying again seems to provide a cure of sorts for most. Considering the divorce process may take one to two years this is certainly fast. Some people suggest the only good divorce is when there are no children, little property and where both partners have a new love with whom to begin again.

Basically young divorcees are in transition. Often the divorced and remarried report more happiness in the second than in the first marriage (Benson-voder Ohe, 1984). The authors know couples who have been married twice and are now again contemplating divorce while at the same time projecting another marriage. Obviously the old saying "twice bitten, twice shy" doesn't always apply! Perhaps the experiences of people will make them less critical. They may have fewer expectations for euphoria and certainly, as they get older, more people are looking for better communication, caring, and support. Many single women undoubtedly wish to have a husband to support their children, otherwise their economic prospects are rather dismal. On average divorced mothers experience a 73 percent decline in their standard of living within the first year of divorce whereas their ex-husbands typically enjoy a 42 percent rise (Weitzman, 1985). The situation for children is not good, especially with their fathers. Two or more years after the divorce only one child in five ever stays overnight with the father. Half of all children of divorced parents have not seen their father in the past year.

Table 11.4 MAIN REASONS MEN AND WOMEN GIVE FOR DIVORCING

Reasons Women Give		Reasons Men Give	
1. Communication problems	70%	1. Communication problems	59%
2. Basic unhappiness	60%	2. Basic unhappiness	47%
3. Incompatibility	56%	3. Incompatibility	45%
4. Emotional abuse	56%	4. Sexual problems	30%
5. Financial problems	33%	5. Financial problems	29%
6. Sexual problems	32%	6. Emotional abuse	25%
7. Alcohol abuse by spouse	30%	7. Women's liberation	15%
8. Infidelity by spouse	25%	8. In-laws	12%
9. Physical abuse	22%	9. Infidelity by spouse	11%
10. In-laws	11%	10. Alcohol abuse by self	9%

Source: Summarized from "Perceived Causes of Divorce: An Analysis of Interrelationships," by M.D. Cleek and T.A. Pearson, 1985, *Journal of Marriage and the Family, 47*, pp. 179-191.

Divorced fathers contribute less to child care than before the divorce and unfortunately only one-third of all child-support payments are made (Ahrons & Wallach, 1986).

The reasons for divorce are charted in Table 11.4. Men in the long run are probably changed less than women by divorce, particularly if they keep their same job. Still they are stigmatized more at first because they usually move out of the home and the wife keeps the children. Most, however, marry again and if they are between 25 and 35 years of age actually will have greater income in the succeeding years.

Cohabitation Many people are cohabitating. At colleges this practice has become so widespread that considerable research has been done on it. Clearly a large number of single couples are living together on campuses across the country; and their attitudes, as well as those of their peers not living together, represent important trends in contemporary living patterns. Mackling (1983) says in a survey at Cornell University that one-third of the respondents shared accommodations with a member of the opposite sex. One of twenty-five couples in America cohabitate, whereas in 1975 this was one in forty. Also 2.2 million American couples were living together unmarried (U.S. Bureau of Census, 1986). In Sweden one of eight couples living together are not married (Tract, 1981).

The practice of unmarried cohabitation is not limited to any particular geographic area nor just to college youth. Noncollege youth have been investigated less, but evidence indicates that the number involved are significant. Cohabitation is fast becoming an established fact, and many small colleges have removed the strict visiting restrictions between males and females in dormitories.

Many people decide to live together for a variety of reasons including companionship, financial considerations, sexual relationships, understanding themselves, and clarifying what they want in a person for marriage. Educated women more than men cohabitate and are more likely to work than married women or the men they live with. More blacks than whites and more urban dwellers than rural cohabitate. Most young people think living together (usually for a period of two years) has advantages that outweigh the disadvantages. But a new problem is the increased litigation over common law marriage, or cohabitation, as referred to in some states, for living together has the force of a legal marriage. In many states cohabitation is illegal. In Europe little attention is paid to cohabitation, but in America implicit commitment of some type is involved in sharing living quarters outside of marriage. "Palimony" (alimony for an unmarried partner) is getting more legal attention in America. The courts are ruling, perhaps due to the impact of an eightfold increase of those under 25 cohabitating, that the couple define the obligation of the partners to support each other after they separate (Cherlin, 1979).

Group marriage This type of marriage is characterized by an agreement of three or more families (couples) who are married to join together. They share common living quarters, a division of work, social involvement, and sometimes sexual rights and responsibilities. There are economic advantages in these arrangements, in addition to the possibility of reducing isolation for women who are often alone or with children, due to the continuous presence of some of the group. Mutual support is one of the strong aspects that recommend this sort of arrangement; however, jealousy is a problem when it involves exchange of partners for sex. Most of these groups do not survive for a long period of time. Those couples married prior to the group association, however, usually survive the breakup of the group (Constantine & Constantine, 1977). In communal types of living there are sometimes married couples with children and some singles. The purpose of this arrangement is the desire to achieve intimacy within a larger family-like unit. It both offers some of the advantages and some of the disadvantages of the group marriage.

PARENTHOOD

Despite the problems of new marriages and lack of parenting skills, the honeymoon is quickly over when everyday chores begin in unending succession. The hygienic habits of the couple vary, and their tastes may be considerably different from what they would have believed. Despite everything if they have had good models and are patient, the marriage will develop on a positive basis. Issues to be settled are the distribution of power, roles, goals, size of family if any, social and recreational activities, and a host of other things previously mentioned. According to Reedy (1977), most happily married young couples who were asked about their relationship placed a high value on their ability to communicate openly and honestly and to express their sexual feelings with ease.

The median age for the first marriage of women is 22.5, for men 25.2 (Current Population Reports, 1983). Whether this will remain the case is doubtful, as the number of those choosing not to marry or to postpone marriage is increasing. Even choosing to have children out of wedlock by choice is not uncommon. Most married couples do have children, although the number has dropped to two per couple. An increasing number have decided not to have children at all or to have fewer children (Van Dusen & Sheldon, 1976). Research reinforces this trend by revealing that marriages are happier without children (Solnick & Solnick, 1971), and that the happiest period of marriage is the one before the children are born and after the children have left the home (Campbell, 1975). The economic resources and problems of successful child rearing are well known and undoubtedly serve to deter many from parenthood. On the other hand, countless numbers of marriages will begin with the premise (many undoubtedly fulfilled) that the promise of bonding, marital commitment, family, and children incorporates the ultimate in human living.

One professional group, known as the Group for the Advancement of Psychiatry (1973), has suggested that parenthood is developmental, following this four-phase direction:

1. Anticipation - Involves the discussion of parenting before the birth of a child; ambivalence is often expressed increasingly during the time of pregnancy about the responsibility of caring for the child.

2. Honeymoon - This is the period of novelty and learning. The baby is a toy, but it is a time of adjustment and learning new roles between parents and the child.

3. Plateau - This is the middle period of parental life, including the early years through the teenage period. Each step requires the parents to adjust and adapt their behavior to the child.

4. Disengagement - The period when the youth leaves home and the activity phase of parenthood ends. If the youth is handicapped, then their responsibility never ends. Many parents hang on to their children beyond their maturity, becoming permanently operational.

The couple who has never had children cannot fully recognize what is in store for them. There will be significant changes that Stage 2 (honeymoon) does not anticipate. Adjustments in setting priorities for money, duties, and family routines have to be made. Chronic tiredness may envelop the wife, her self-image may be lowered when she inspects her looks and body, sex life may be reduced, the father may feel neglected, and the parents may be overburdened by the cost of the first child.

It is obvious that many couples are not prepared for the role of parents. The difficulties that arise often create a crisis. Dating, courtship, and even cohabitation do little to acquaint couples with the demands of being parents. It is not unheard of for the immature male to be overwhelmed by the new problems and to leave the wife with a newborn child, if not permanently then for a period of time. The divorce rate is growing, as is the number of unmarried couples having children, creating a growing number of single-parent families among young adults. Where there are multiple children, the women must nearly always work, thereby increasing the burden on the family and child development. Many people consider it their right to have children without considering the cost or lack of parenting ability. Others produce children when the evidence strongly suggests they should not--when mothers are carriers of hemophilia or the parents are both diabetic or have other health problems that can affect the child. Classes and groups interested in parenting are greatly increasing; many of these, however, are those who wish to improve the information they already have. Many are wondering whether there will be a time when the government at the state or national level will impose some standard of fitness for procreation. It is a sensitive issue, but the attention given in family life courses in secondary schools as they are now handled is inadequate to improve parenthood, although undoubtedly the instruction reduces the number of out-of-marriage pregnancies.

SATISFACTION IN THE LIFE OF YOUNG ADULTS

A survey was conducted by McSweeney and Jones (1991) of 725 graduate and upper-division undergraduates at mid-Atlantic universities as to principal worries, goals, and satisfactions. This information was intended to update their 1979 survey. The researchers found that students' main worries were school completion and finances (jobs); their future goals were school completion and occupational success; and the most satisfying aspects of their lives were college work, family and children, and occupational success. The 1991 results were very similar to the 1979 survey in regard to principal worries, goals, and satisfactions, with an even greater percentage of the students in the latest survey emphasizing school completion as their biggest worry and future goal. Eighty percent of the 19- to 21-year-olds indicated school completion to be their biggest worry in 1990, compared to 62 percent of the age group in 1979. Sixty-eight percent of the 19- to 21-year-old group cited school completion as their future goal, compared with 36 percent in 1979.

Only 15 students among all groups indicated war as their biggest worry in 1991, while only four students in 1979 had cited this category as their biggest worry. The relative small number of students in the latest poll citing war as their biggest worry may be an indication that many students in October, 1990, did not think that the Middle East crisis would end in a war.

In each of the age groups in the current survey, a greater percentage of students cited family, children, and home as the most satisfying aspect of life. Seventeen percent of the 18- to 21-year-olds in the 1991 survey indicated family, children, and home, compared to 6 percent in 1979. A large percentage of this age group chose friendship as the most satisfying aspect as compared to 1979, 22 percent up from 14 percent. Only 65 students in the total survey cited love and sex as the most satisfying aspect of their lives. Only two of these respondents were over 30 years of age.

"Debt-free" in the future goal and "independence" in the most satisfying aspect of life were two new categories in the 1991 survey. These entries appear to support the major emphasis for most of the students on completing school, securing employment, and being financially independent.

From the beginning of adulthood until the early thirties, the typical American is faced with adjustment problems in different major life areas: work, community, and family. The fact that many of these problems seem to appear

	(n=276) age 19-21	(n-256) age 22-30	(n-110) age 31-40
	M F	M F	M F
Biggest Worry Now			
School completion	65-155	34-86	8-30
Financial (jobs)	12-46	28-62	11-28
War	2-5	2-2	2-1
Getting married	0-1	0-5	0-0
Occupational choice	4-5	3-5	0-0
Children (family)	0-5	1-2	3-4
Illness	0-0	0-1	0-3
Opposite sex (relations)	3-7	3-1	0-0
Marital problems	0-1	0-1	0-3
Job success	0-1	0-0	1-3
Moving	0-2	0-3	0-1
Social problems (crime, energy, and government)	2-2	2-0	2-0
Other dysgenic (time, personal assessment)	5-12	5-9	1-15
Future Goal Now			
School completion	57-130	30-73	12-47
Social improvement	0-0	1-0	0-0
Marriage	4-11	1-3	0-1
Having children	2-3	2-6	1-1
Vocational success	39-92	32-73	14-32
Good life (family life)	0-3	0-1	0-0
Marriage compatibility	1-2	2-1	0-0
Personal skills (sports, hobbies)	3-1	1-0	0-0
Others (don't know, travel, retirement, self-activity, spiritual)	1-4	2-2	0-3
Debt-free (money)	7-10	4-5	1-2
Most Satisfying Aspect of Life Now			
Family, children, home	4-42	15-34	13-36
Occupational success	6-10	4-14	11-18
Marriage	0-7	3-22	0-3
Love and sex	9-37	10-7	1-0
College work	15-47	13-27	2-10
Friendship	20-41	6-14	0-3
Athletic skills	5-3	3-0	0-0
Enhancement (sports hobbies)	10-15	6-13	1-2
Religion or church	1-6	3 8	1-2
Others (don't know, drinking, freedom, helping parents)	6-9	7-6	0-7
Health	3-7	4-3	0-4
Helping others	2-5	2-0	1-0
Independence	6-9	2-5	

Figure 11.12 Survey of worries, goals, and satisfactions.

simultaneously frequently creates confusion and conflicts. Even so these are happy years in the lives of most adults, covering the vesting stage, the greatest sexual satisfaction and highest energy levels for coping with stress and work.

Jones and Heinen (1979), studying maladjustment among graduate students and laypersons 20 to 49 (n=600) found less disturbance among the 30- to 39-year olds than among those in their twenties and forties. This was true whether they were graduate students or from the public at large (see Figure 11.12).

The incidence of maladjustment among those in their thirties was 25 percent, but for those in their twenties and forties it approached 40 percent. Those in their thirties participated in more activities (occupations, home, schooling, parental responsibility, number of children, community involvement) than did those in the other decades studied. Those in their thirties undoubtedly have adjusted to home, family, and occupational life, whereas those in their twenties have yet to finalize education in many instances and are unsure of their job prospects and future. Also, the decision of love partner relationships may be unresolved and the identity crisis may be still problematic. A study by Hock, Christman, and Hock (1980) found mothers who originally planned not to work but later decided to during the infant's first year had more unplanned pregnancies (55 percent to 26 percent) and were more discontented and less adaptive to change in plans than those mothers who held to their nonwork plans.

THE HOMEMAKER RESPONSIBILITY

Another developmental task for the young adult is establishing and managing a home, even if one is single or divorced. Most married couples have children, requiring at first all the attention of the mother and some of the husband. Many young mothers with occupations give them up until the children enter nursery school or kindergarten. Some never return to the job market. Mothers need to know how to manage the child-rearing routine and organize their own schedules. Mothers provide their daughters much advice about child managing and frequently give direct assistance. Schooling for parenting and rearing children is widespread and growing; the media also are giving greater attention to this.

Family life is typically built around the home. Its success usually depends upon how well it is managed--housekeeping, cleaning, preparing food, making repairs, and making the "home beautiful." Though many men participate in these activities, they are largely left to the woman even if she is employed away from the home. This is sometimes expressed as "man works from sun to sun but woman's work is never done." When men assist it is more likely with repairs, yard work, and the preparation of an occasional meal. Wives have been helped by labor-saving devices, but even so the wife with several children is often overworked, as she finds limited outlets for her personal growth, suitable leisure time, and creative activity. Even a short vacation can be a problem; however, in the book *Becoming Parents*, Youngner and Youngner (1980) suggest that parents leaving a nine-month-old infant for a week doesn't constitute emotional trauma. Where women with children wish to hold a job, they often find paying for a nursery or baby-sitters is prohibitive. Some divorced women with children have found a similar situation when they have tried to work, and consequently some have sought public assistance as an alternative. Most young married couples become efficient managers of their homes or apartments, the latter most likely their first dwelling. Working class women usually marry early, many of them having come from large families, through which some home responsibility has helped prepare them for many aspects of marriage. Many have children immediately, although some work for a while before having children to assist with the family finances.

Table 11.5 FACTORS ASSOCIATED WITH LIFE SATISFACTION AMONG ADULTS

	DEMOGRAPHIC VARIABLES
Income	Higher income is associated with higher life satisfaction but the effect appears to be relative rather than absolute.
Education	Higher educated adults are only slightly more satisfied; usually professionals are more satisfied.
Sex	No difference, although women may have higher highs and lower lows than men.
Work	Employed adults (including those employed as homemakers) are more satisfied than the unemployed, even when income is matched.
Married/Single	Married adults are more satisfied than unmarried. This difference is generally larger for men.
Parenthood	A zero or a slightly negative effect: Adults with children are sometimes found to be slightly less happy.
Religion	Adults who describe themselves as religious, or who say that religion is important in their lives, are more satisfied.
Life Events	The more "negative" life changes an adult has recently experienced, the lower the life satisfaction.
Goals	Adults who are committed to very long-term goals, with little short-term reward, are less satisfied than are adults whose goals are shorter term or less difficult to achieve.
	PERSONAL QUALITIES
Personality or Temperament:	
Extroversion	Extroverted adults are higher in life satisfaction than introverts.
Neuroticism	Adults high in neuroticism are less satisfied than those low on this personality trait.
Loss of Control	Those adults who feel they can and do control their own choices and opportunities are more satisfied than those who think they are mostly controlled by outside forces.
Amount of Social Interaction	Adults with more social contacts have higher life satisfaction than those with low levels of contact.
Quality of Social Interaction	Adults whose social interactions are more intimate and more supportive have higher satisfaction. This is especially true in marriage. If marital communication is poor, life satisfaction is adversely affected.
Health	Those adults with better self-perceived health are more satisfied than those who perceive themselves as ill or disabled. This is especially important in later years of adulthood.

Adapted from Diener, 1984, Campbell, 1981, and McSweeney and Jones, 1991.

Neighborhoods and Community Activity

Integration into the life of a community is necessary for achieving adult status. This means the assumption of responsibility indicative of growing altruism and concern for the wider world. Young adults are mobile when moving into a new community, but often lack the knowledge to begin to participate in adult organizations and community life. For this reason it is often difficult for the young adult to assume this responsibility (Havighurst, 1972). Part of the initial attempts to enter civic life comes from the neighborhood. Types of neighborhoods that exist explain the problems involved. Characteristics of neighborhoods have been categorized by Rogers (1979) as follows:

1. The parochial neighborhood is isolated from the larger community. The people here interact frequently, caring for their own, and feel they are essential parts of the network of neighborhood groups in the area.

2. The integral neighborhood is a radar-like network. The people have good jobs and many connections with other community groups. Unlike the parochial, which is turned in upon itself, residents are oriented to both their own and other neighborhoods.

3. The diffuse neighborhood has people who rely mainly on family groups more than they do on neighbors, with whom they interact little. They identify with the neighborhood because it is a good place to live but do not often associate socially with neighbors nor do they shape their lifestyles from them.

4. The stepping-stone neighborhood is like the integral neighborhood in that young adults who are upwardly mobile in work move quickly, usually after a year or two. They have many ways to facilitate integration of newcomers in a short time through neighborhood committees, the welcome wagons frequently characteristic of smaller cities and towns, parties, and neighbors' simply calling on them. In one such neighborhood newcomers contacted the neighbors in the block, stating they had stayed so brief a period in their last community they were determined to avoid this so they gave a get-acquainted party at their home (Hull, 1980). It turned out to be quite a success.

5. The transitory neighborhood, characteristic of communities containing many apartments and condominiums, includes people who have little in common with each other and, in fact, avoid any local associations and ties to the area. They identify with the neighborhood only with their residency, for they perceive that they will soon move away.

6. The anomic neighborhood exists in high-rise apartments and condominiums, where residents maintain their anonymity. Adults may socialize within the complex with a few people or attend a Christmas party, but other than attending a governing organization of the condominium, if there is such, there is virtually no contact. Residents of poorer anomic neighborhoods do not help each other, are distrustful of outside groups, and often view TV as a major social pursuit.

Participation in community life varies according to socio-economic class. Regardless of class, the young person is usually 25 or 30 before actively participating in community life, and many are older. Those in the middle class are strong supporters of civic or religious activity, even viewing it as a virtue. Many persons in the lower social-economic class put little faith in wider community activities such as town and citywide affairs, preferring instead labor unions, local social clubs, PTAs, churches, and fraternal orders. The neighborhood is the focus of activities rather than the wider community, and adults interact with others in informal rather than formal groups. Once in a while some from the working class (blue collar) will get elected to a school board or a city council or become a director in the union, allowing him or her the opportunity to become the leader beyond the home district. Some even become mayors of large cities.

Middle-class young people are more oriented to the community and participate in a variety of movements due to the models provided by their parents and their education. Many fathers get their sons into their civic clubs, place them on committees they chair, or suggest to their friends that their sons or daughters could help in a drive or activity. These groups allow for great numbers of volunteers. Not only do they serve the church as leaders and teachers, they organize Little Leagues and serve as coaches. They also become officers or chair committees in the PTA, in Scouting, and Boys and Girls Clubs. They head communities in the neighborhood and at the community level for heart, lung, cancer and other drives, political referendums, and fund raising for varying purposes. Professional women and men consider it their duty to give time and sometimes money to community activities. Numbers of these young people believe that it is good for their image and that it has positive effects on their work life.

The upper social class' view of community is not the same as that of the middle class. Although they give support, often financial, to causes, they are not sure of its value in terms of time spent. Many persons in this social class have access to facilities that the middle class wish their young people had. Upper class people may encourage their young to engage in activities because of their value in the middle years. A young person may be encouraged by older friends to run for the city council or even mayor. In prestigious law firms many think it is wise for some of their colleagues, usually young affiliates, to head up charity drives, to accept the chairmanship of an agency or program, and sometimes to run for political office or take a political appointment for a brief period of time.

THE SOCIAL TASKS: GROUPS AND LEISURE

Marriage severs many couples' ties with friends. The new status makes people mobile; it tends to separate singles from couples, and may accelerate interaction with the familial. Finding a congenial social group is an important task for the young adult. Many men drop bachelor interests as inappropriate or less important. Women often drop out of purely feminine associations, although those from the upper middle classes who completed college often maintain friendships over a lifetime. Basically the young adult couple is a new unit requiring affiliation with new groups and people. Young middle-class men may still play sports with informal groups.

Some working-class men often participate in similar activities but a great amount of their time is given to same-sex friendships existing before marriage. These men often go hunting or fishing together, play cards, go to car races, boxing matches, ball games,and male bars, and visit each other. The young woman of the working class typically finds her major social activities to center around other married women, family, and the church. This is the point where blue-collar young adults who are married are most likely to find common ground in their social life; however, 82 percent of this activity is sedentary (Jones, 1979). Middle-class couples, on the other hand, do many things together; they go to movies, parties, concerts, cookouts, camping, and swimming; go on vacations; play tennis; and go to sporting events--though 52 percent of this activity is sedentary. These couples usually have another couple or two who live nearby with whom they interact and share their recreation and leisure time.

Gordon, Gaitz, and Scott (1976) say that the most popular leisure activities in young adulthood are centered on home and family, visiting friends and family, watching television, gardening, reading, and enjoying hobbies. The young adult years are often filled with strenuous and exhausting physical activities: camping, hiking, skiing, hunting, and tennis. Many men like physical activity and pursuits that take them away from home. Women, on the other hand--though they spend much leisure time reading, improving their homes and gardening--are increasingly involved in activities formerly reserved for men.

MARRIAGE PROBLEMS AND DIVORCE

The problems that develop in marriage reflect several factors:

1) Dissimilarity of partners in age, social class, temperament, ethnic orientation, and intelligence.

2) Factors of economics as in the case where the marriage started with two wage earners and then unexpectedly the wife becomes pregnant. A succession of several children follows, preventing the spouse from returning to work and often militate against marriage survival.

3) Disparate views of the partner relative to philosophical perspectives, morality, lifestyles, and behavior such as chronic bizarre episodes, drinking bouts, overuse of drugs, and aberrant sexual activity.

4) Mental breakdowns and serious deterioration of health of the partners.

5) Interference by the partners' families.

6) The realization by the partners that marriage is just not the thing for them.

The three elements thought to be most important in sustaining a marriage are communication, sharing of interests, and cooperation. The third year of marriage is the point that many divorces take place. Research by Joseph Brayshaw (1962) reveals the order of problems for those married three years or less in contrast with those married 18 years or more.

THREE YEARS MARRIED OR LESS	EIGHTEEN YEARS MARRIED OR MORE
1. Sex	1. Ill health
2. Living conditions	2. Infidelity
3. Parental influence	3. Incompatibility
4. Ill health	4. Sex
5. Incompatibility	5. Parental influence
6. Infidelity	6. Living conditions
7. Income	7. Income

It is evident that the basic problems are the same, and although 15 or more years apart, only the order has changed. It is not surprising that problems with sexual adjustment lessen, as women begin to feel stronger sexual drives at 40, more like those of men of 20. The Hite Report (1981) revealed that some men reported they never had enough sex. Ill health, of course, can be mental or physical. Certainly many men and women are alcoholic by 35, and some are 30 to 40 pounds overweight with insufficient exercise, and therefore may be suffering from a variety of maladies that can damage a marriage. The early euphoria felt by women when they marry does not continue long, nor does the men's moderate happiness, who seem to feel more stress in marriage than women (Campbell, 1975).

Campbell (1975) reported that the happy glow seems to burst as couples have children. "For both men and women, reports of happiness and satisfaction drop to average, not to rise significantly until their children are grown and about to leave the nest (age 18)" (p. 39). For most couples, the birth of a child is a happy event, but one that puts a strain on their marriage. Couples with young children report feeling more pressure than any other group. Mothers, most of whom are between the ages of 25 and 34, carry the burden of child-rearing, and are under the greatest pressure and stress.

They are the most likely of any group of wives or husbands to describe themselves as feeling depressed and tied down by child-rearing responsibilities. They more frequently express doubts about marriage and often wish they were freed of the responsibilities of parenthood. The husbands also feel less satisfied with children, but they do not show the change of mood displayed by the wives, partly because they have never reached the high euphoric state the wives had reached earlier.

Men often have a more difficult time with divorce in the first phases (Chiriboga, 1982). Most men report being shocked by the divorce, since it is usually the wife who files for divorce (Kelly, 1982). Husbands are usually blamed for the problems, accept the blame, move out, and thereby find their social life disrupted (Kitson & Sussman, 1982). Although women are typically more distressed before the separation, men have more psychological and physical stress immediately after it (Bloom & Caldwell, 1981).

In the long run, however, women are much more seriously affected by divorce. The reasons are both social and economic. Women have fewer marriage prospects, find it more difficult to establish new relationships if they have custody of the children, and are at a major disadvantage financially. The financial problems of divorced women received considerable attention in the late 1980s as states passed laws to enforce child-support payments. Additionally, an ex-wife is not legally entitled to any of her former husband's Social Security benefits unless the divorce occurs after he has stopped working, nor does she share in pension or health benefits (Cain, 1982).

Remarriage

Most young adults who divorce remarry. Three-fourths of the women remarry and six of seven men remarry, most by the end of three years. Though often these marriages also do not succeed, many, particularly older persons, express greater satisfaction with marriage (Norton and Moorman, 1987). Although the United States has the highest divorce rate in the world, marriage is the preferred state of living although the rate of divorce has slowed. Still, over 1,000,000 divorces are finalized each year (Norton and Moorman, 1987).

THE PSYCHOLOGICAL MODE

Continuity and discontinuity characterize human life, particularly in the psychological realm involving identity, morals, philosophical perspective, illusions, and personality in general during the young adult years of 20 to 40. Some people who are 60 biologically may be only 45 socially and psychologically. Researchers have found greater consistency in adult life relating to the intellectual and cognitive areas--intelligence, cognitive styles, and self-concept. The greatest change comes from interpersonal behavior and attitudes.

Stability of Personality

Considerable research has been completed on the question of the nature of personality over the adult years. How much remains the same, how much changes, and what is due to structure, convention, motive, roles, locus of control, and general adaptability still needs to be researched and ascertained. Let us look anew at the theories of Maslow and Erikson and then compare Loevinger's ego development and Vaillant's theory of defense mechanisms. Erikson's social crises are faced by each individual--the young adult who must resolve the issue of intimacy versus isolation, and the young adult and middle-aged person who faces generativity or stagnation. The basic strengths that accrue during these periods are love and caring. Maslow's major focus was on the motivational orientation of people. There are two kinds of motives--deficiency motives (basic needs, i.e. food, safety, love and esteem, sleep, sex, etc.) and growth motives (discovery, understanding, and self actualization). Maslow believed only 10 percent of Americans reach their potential while 50 percent get love and 40 percent have their esteem needs met. Of course this is speculation, and indeed the true percentages may be less than this.

TABLE 11.6 Summary of Loevinger's Stages of Ego Development in Adulthood

STAGE	DESCRIPTION
Conformist	Obedience to external social rules; the child or adult identifies with welfare of the group, sex roles and inner life.
Conscientious-conformist	Separation of norms and goals; realization that acts affect others; transition level; self awareness seen as black and white; acceptance of individual differences increases.
Conscientious	Beginning of self-evaluated standards.
Individualistic	Recognition that the process of acting is more important than the outcome. Focuses on independence and dependence. Aware of inner conflict. Individual rules and ideals created about sex roles, marriage, and education.
Autonomous	Respect for each person's individuality; tolerance for ambiguity. Others are accepted on their own merit for what they are, no attempt to make them over.
Integrated	Resolution of inner conflicts. This stage is very rare, people transcend the conflict of the autonomous stage.

Loevinger's stages of ego development says that changes occur due to internal structural changes, changes in the way an individual experiences things, and changes in the relationship with people and the world. Like Erikson, Loevinger describes a movement from social roles and conventionality to individuality, autonomy, and awareness of the inner complexity of life. As persons develop in this scheme their autonomy scores on personality scales should go higher. The ego is the catalyst, the organizer, the integrator of our morals, values, motives, and cognitive processes. The ego is complex and influenced by personal experiences, providing the basic differences between individuals. The transition from one stage to another is dependent on biological and social changes creating the need for adaption. The final six stages that refer to adult development are described in Table 11.6.

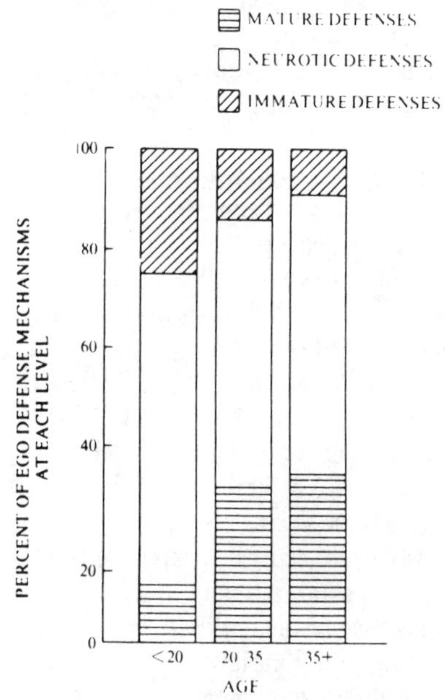

Figure 11.13 Percent of ego defense mechanisms at each level.

Vaillant took Erikson's stages as a basic framework and added a new stage he calls *career consolidation*. He places this stage before generativity versus stagnation, at sometime around 30 or 32 years of age. This is the period when the person is mastering a craft or skill, establishing competence and a reputation as a good worker. This focus of Vaillant's theory is on the nature of psychological adjustment to the problems and vicissitudes of life. The major form of adaptation is through defense mechanisms. These are outlined in Table 11.7.

Vaillant's theory does not rest on stages, although he accepted the framework of Erikson. It is a process of moving from less mature to more mature defense mechanisms. It is not achieved by all adults and no adult uses entirely mature mechanisms. Vaillant studied 100 subjects of the Grant Study of Harvard Men (covering from the late adolescent years and the early twenties to middle age at 50) and found that immature defenses decline with age. His data cast was of case studies with only a little statistical analysis. The data revealed the circumstances shown in Figure 11.13.

When Hahn (1976) analyzed the changes in individual Q sort items rather than in clusters of items she found decreases with age in defensiveness, fantasizing, and projection. The data drawn from the Grant Study of Harvard Men included those "relatively healthy and successful." Hence the nature of the sample may not have included as many in the neurotic category as in the rank and file.

Table 11.7 LEVELS OF DEFENSE MECHANISMS PROPOSED BY VAILLANT

LEVEL	DESCRIPTION
I. "Psychotic" Mechanisms	*Delusional Projection:* Frank delusions, such as delusions of persecution. *Denial:* Denial of external reality. *Distortion:* Grossly reshaping external reality to suit inner needs, including hallucinations, wish-fulfilling delusions (Prince Charming will find me any day now).
II. Immature Mechanisms	*Projection:* Attributing one's own unacknowledged feelings to others ("You're the one who's afraid, not me"). *Schizoid Fantasy:* The use of fantasy or inner retreat to resolve conflict. *Hypochondriasis:* Reproach toward others turned into complaints of physical illness. Often used to avoid making dependency demands directly, or to avoid complaining directly about being ignored. *Passive-Aggressive Behavior:* Aggression toward others expressed indirectly and effectively through passivity, or directed toward the self. *Acting Out:* Direct expression of an unconscious wish, but without acknowledging the emotion that goes with it. It includes delinquent behavior, but also "tempers."
III. "Neurotic" Mechanisms	*Intellectualization:* Thinking about wishes or desires in formal, emotionally bland terms and not acting on them. *Repression:* Memory lapses, or failure to acknowledge some information. Putting out of conscious memory. *Displacement:* Directing your feelings toward something or someone other than the original object (e.g., cuddling your cat when you really want to hold a lover). *Reaction Formation:* Behaving in a fashion directly opposite to what you would really (unconsciously) like to do (such as being exceptionally nice to a co-worker you detest, since you cannot acknowledge your hatred to yourself). *Dissociation:* Temporary, drastic modification of one's sense of character, such as a sudden devil-may-care attitude, periods of irresponsibility.
IV. Mature Mechanisms	*Altruism:* Vicarious but constructive service to others. *Humor:* Overt expression of ideas or feelings, but without discomfort, and without unpleasant effects on others (does not include sarcasm). *Suppression:* Conscious or semiconscious decision to postpone dealing with some impulse or conflict. *Anticipation:* Realistic expectation of future problem or discomfort, and planning for it. *Sublimation:* Indirect expression of some desire or need, but without loss of pleasure or adverse consequences (such as expressing aggression through sports). Instincts are channeled, rather than dammed up.

Source: Vaillant, 1977, p. 383-386.

Values and Motives

Veroff, et al., (1981) in the Michigan Survey Research Center Study of Mental Illness and Health, looked at the values in five categories by having his sample rank their first and second priorities (Figure 11.14). These were combined into five value orientations. The data that follow represent age divisions--21 to 39 and above 40. The younger group selected values reflecting sociability, hedonism, and self-actualization. The older group, however, revered moral respect and security. One should remember that the selections were projections not achievements. Research by Veroff, et al., (1984) from two large cross-sectional samples done two decades apart show women decline steadily from young adult to later adulthood in "affiliation" of seeking out or retaining emotional relations, while men's "hope for power" rises until mid-life then drops slightly for the first decade (1957) sample and hardly at all for the second decade group (1976). The motives were measured by the Thematic Apperception Test (TAT). The results provide some support for Maslow's views because there is a shift from afflictive needs to esteem needs, which are of a higher order.

The differences between young adults (20 to 39) and middle-age adults (40 to 69) on personality, values, and motives are characterized by the following statements. Typically the middlescent person will show increased levels of these indicators, except for flexibility, materialism, and hope for power among men.

1. Rising hope for power for men.
2. Higher levels of flexibility.
3. Inconsistency on nurturance/affiliation for women.
4. Low scores on generativity and ego integrity.
5. Premiums placed on material goals and getting things.
6. Low levels of humanitarian concerns.
7. Low levels of independence, autonomy; high levels of dependency.
8. Lower levels of cognitive contribution, self-confidence and openness to self.
9. Higher scores on immature defense mechanisms.
10. Toward the 40-year mark men will become

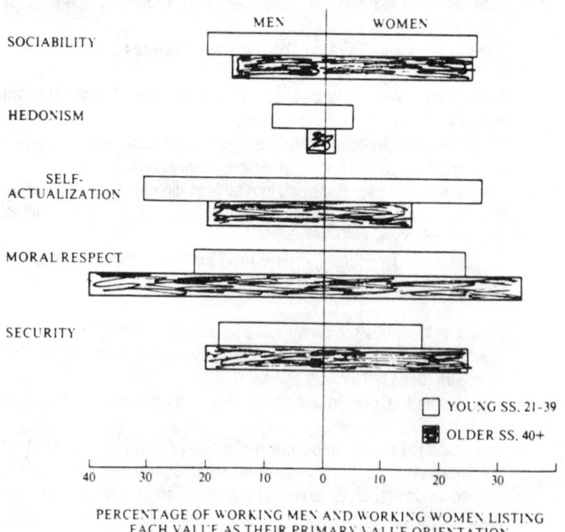

Figure 11.14 Percentage of working men and working women listing each value as their primary value orientation.

somewhat more nurturing and women more aggressive and involved with mastery of tasks.

Transitional Stages

Most life span psychologists agree that there are at least two transitions in young adult development. The first comes in late adolescence, the years 18 to 23, and involves both a personal identity search and a first attempt toward a vocation and settling on a value system. The second transition or phase occurs around 30 for many who examine their occupational, marital, and goal choices, and question their validity. A crisis is precipitated when they realize their goals or dreams will not be realized. This often leads to radical changes--in men, the changing of careers or divorce from their spouses, and in women the dropping of a career to become a housewife or the attempt at additional education and a new career. For many there is no crisis or transition, but a continuation of the earlier years of the mid-twenties when they first thought of themselves as adults, were working at an occupation, and establishing a family and/or a stable love life. This period is sometimes called the nesting period, and is characterized by the closeness of the couple, when sharing perhaps reaches its ultimate point. Levinson (1978) and others suggest that three transitions occur in the early adult years (16 to 34):

Ages 16 to 22: Youthful illusions about the adult world begin dissolving as young people become more peer-oriented rather than family-oriented. Emotions tend to be held inside and friendships are easily broken.

Ages 23 to 28: The young adult begins to reach out toward others and is busy mastering the world. Emotional extremes are avoided and commitments are rarely analyzed. Levinson sees this as a time for togetherness in marriage.

Ages 29 to 34: With the crisis stage generally hitting at age 30, adults are less confident, begin questioning their worth, and start finding life more difficult. An active social life starts downhill during this period, along with marital dissatisfaction. The spouse starts

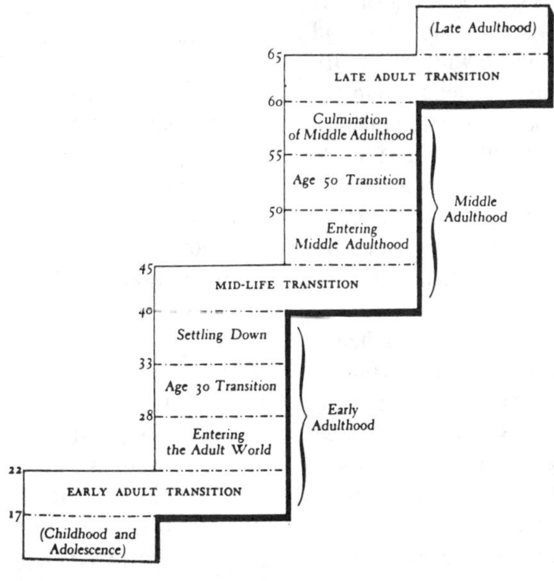

Figure 11.15

being viewed as an obstacle instead of an asset, and infidelity and divorce become more prevalent. Levinson detects a struggle among incompatible drives for order and stability, for total freedom, and for upward professional mobility.

Levinson believes as the young person pursues a dream, he or she may establish a mentor relationship. The mentor is ordinarily 8 to 15 years older (someone, perhaps, in his or her own stage of generativity) who takes the young person under a wing, and teaches, advises, sponsors, supports, and serves as a model for the young person. A mentor is often found in a work setting, but it could also be an older relative or a friend. Mentors are both parent figures and peers, and must be both if the relationship is going to work. The role of the mentor is to help the young person make the transition from reliance on the parents and their world to self reliance.

However, Levinson studies only men in arriving at transitional stages. Gould (1978) examined life histories and views of male and female psychiatric outpatients in seven age groups from 16 to 60 and over 500 nonpatients and found similar patterns in development and change. The sample was drawn principally from middle-class white males, and is therefore somewhat limited in value. Comparative studies involving large numbers of female subjects as well as a variety of cultures and socioeconomic levels are needed. Gould's theory is based on the social clock hypothesized by Neugarten, which defines the tasks of each period.

A stage theorist, Dimidjian, offers a theory directed to the adult development of women. She studied and interviewed in depth six professional women in their thirties and derived three stages much like those of Levinson's though his sample was male. Unlike Levinson's where men focused on careers, all six women, though committed to their work, placed the emphasis in their lives on a "special other." The special other was a child or heterosexual partner. The establishment of a life structure is the principal task of professional women in the early twenties to the thirties. Women are striving during this time for autonomy, self definition, and introspection.

TABLE 11.8 Summary of Gould's Theory and Characteristic Myths

Ages 16-22	Characteristic myth: I'll always belong to my parents and believe in their world.
Ages 22-28	Characteristic myth: Doing things my parents' way will bring results. If I become too frustrated or tired or am simply unable to cope, they will step in and show me the right way.
Ages 28-34	Characteristic myth: Life is simple and controllable. There are no contradictory forces within me. Our parents' values and now our values are to be examined for their use with our children.
Ages 34-45	Characteristic myth: There is no evil or death in the world. The sinister has been destroyed. If I have my parents, life will go on.
Ages 45-53	Characteristics: We are whoever we are going to be. We become less competitive and are more inner directed.
Ages 53-60	Characteristics: We continue on the path begun in the previous stage.

Dimidjian (1980) suggests three phases of transition for women:

Phase I - Early twenties: entering the adult world.

(1) Making attempts to form mutually supportive relationships with peers.

(2) Making attempts to establish an intimate, bonded relationship with a special other.

(3) Making attempts to define and train for a professional role.

Phase II - Early twenties to early thirties: a first life-structure.
(1) Establishing a life-structure that is anchored in the relational bond with the special other.
(2) Establishing a professional role that is internally valued as well as externally validated by academic or work setting.
(3) Experiencing an increasing push for autonomy, self-definition, and introspection.

Phase III - Early to mid-thirties: First crisis of adulthood.
(1) Intense self-examination takes place, redefining, delimiting, or extending the life-structure. The life-structure includes aspects of psychosocial development not fully addressed previously.

The process of transition is known. We see evidence in growing maturity, increased competence in our work and logic, changes in physical anatomy, identification of periods in the lives of people that affect the stream of development. Transitional periods have been identified by modal experiences--typical time for marriage, having children, children's leaving home and marrying, death of parents, and retirement. But a measure of passage is its ultimate complexity that we may have yet to fathom. Broadly speaking, in the transition from young adulthood to middle age something recognizable does occur. We become less dependent, less materialistic, less flexible, more generative, have more ego integrity, more concern for humanity, greater cognitive investment, and openness to self. With it all a definitive understanding of the process of transition is elusive. Still, we perhaps know enough to understand the impact of multiple variables; we know about synchrony and asynchrony in life's patterns. We also know about non-normative and normative effects and we know about emotional and personality emergence. All combine to allow us to plan and live more effective lives and to assist our children and others to do so.

Moral Development

Many adults do not develop to the final stage of moral maturity (Universal Principles), according to Kohlberg, which is a necessary condition but not sufficient to reach the formal stage of cognition (Piaget). Time is needed for reflection and, as Carol Gilligan (1982) has pointed out, women approach moral and ethical dilemmas from the viewpoint of responsibilities and caring. Women look for the solution that best suits the relationship with which they are dealing. Ethical and moral systems based upon caring for others, responsibility, and compassion are ignored. In Kohlberg's revision of his scales/scoring system, no sex differences were found (Pratt et al., 1984 and Walker, 1984). Girls and women can and do use moral reasoning based on principles of justice when they are presented with dilemmas in which that is the central focus.

Support for Kohlberg comes from longitudinal studies he and his colleagues had completed with an Israeli, Turkish, and American (Chicago) sample. The adolescents and young adults were interviewed a number of times over a period from 10 to 20 years. They were tested as teenagers and then rated once or twice over a period of 10 years (Colby, et al., 1983; Snarey, et al., 1985; Nisen and Kohlberg, 1982). The scores of the tests increased steadily even with the cultural differences in speed and movement through the stages. No subjects skipped a stage and only 5 percent regressed in stages. No one reached the sixth stage, as seen in the second figure.

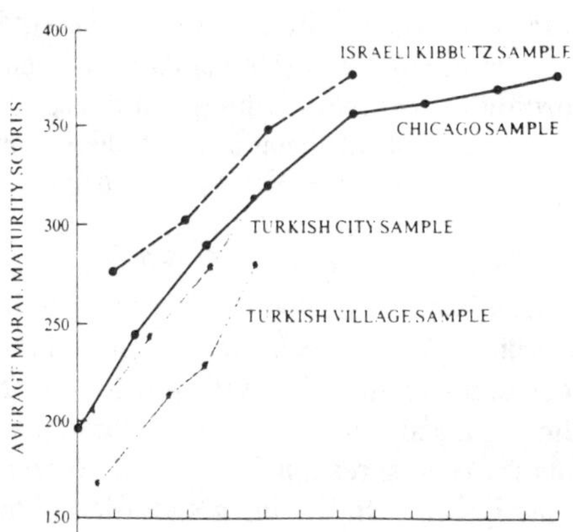

Figure 11.16 Moral progression with age.

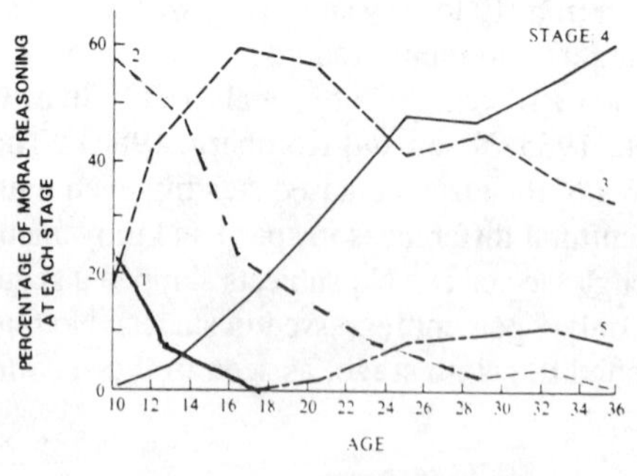

Figure 11.17 Time spent in each moral level.

Gilligan proposes the following stages of moral development for women:

STAGE	DESCRIPTION
Level 1: Orientation of individual survival	The woman concentrates on herself--on what is pragmatic.
Transition 1: From selfishness to responsibility	The woman realizes her connection to others and thinks about what would be the responsible choice in terms of other people and herself.
Level 2: Goodness as self-sacrifice	This conventional stage dictates sacrificing these wishes to what other people want--and will think of her. She is responsible for the actions of others; holding others responsible for her choices. She is in a dependent position--her indirect efforts to exert control often turn into manipulation, sometimes through the use of guilt.
Transition 2: From goodness to truth	She assesses decisions not on how others will react to them, but on her intentions and the consequences of her actions. She develops a judgment that takes her needs into account, and those of others. She wants to be "good" by being responsible to others, also wants to be "honest" by being responsible to herself. Survival returns as a major concern.
Level 3: Morality of non-violence	By elevation of the injunction against hurting anyone (including herself) to a principal that governs all moral judgment and action, the woman establishes a "moral equality" between herself and others therefore is able to assume responsibility for choice in moral dilemmas.

Source: Adapted from Gilligan, 1982.

Gilligan's response to the fact that many women have been categorized within the convention stage of morality was that their focus in a real situation or moral imperative is based upon the fact that they see the violence generated by inequitable relations. She says there is a need not only to discern and alleviate real trouble (local--neighborhood), but also there is the moral imperative to respect the rights of others (worldwide) and protect from interference their right to life and self-fulfillment. Kohlberg, in his studies of men, confirms that they "come to realize the limitations of a conception of justice which is blinded to real inequities of human life (p. 511)." They are more active and responsible in taking care of local concerns: this serves to correct the indifference of a morality of noninterference and leads to a consideration of the consequence of choice. In the classic case of Heinz's dilemma about whether or not to steal to obtain the drug his wife needs, the differences between levels of morality, it seems, are only philosophical viewpoints that separate men from women. Rights and responsibilities take place through a principled understanding of equity and reciprocity. For women, this mitigates the self-destructive potential of self-critical morality by stating that all persons have the right to care. For men the recognition of the need to care serves to provide a more balanced perspective.

To be judged at the highest moral level--the principled state--Heinz would have to steal the drug to effect a possible cure for his dying wife (see the description of Kohlberg's stages in Chapter 10). Many women who were judged by Kohlberg in his longitudinal study to be at Level 3 (the conventional stage) apparently saw the dilemma in terms of selfishness (if Heinz refused to steal the drug) or sacrifice (considering his status and limited means); the root of the matter being not simply the priority of life over property. The decision of many was to see the consequences of his action: to be put in jail, charged with a felony, and of less value to the sick wife, who might die anyway. In the collision of the two lives guilt is inescapable, but one life, it seems, can only continue at the expense of the other. An ethical principal utilized in a pragmatic fashion suggests there is as much maturity in moral reasoning as in accepting the principle but denying the actual consequences. Gilligan (1977) suggests the moral development of women proceeds from an initial concern with survival to a focus on goodness, and finally to a principled understanding of nonviolence as the most adequate rule for resolving moral problems (p. 525).

One could characterize Kohlberg's theory as one principally concerned with abstract justice, while Gilligan (who earlier worked with Kohlberg, much like Flavell and Piaget's relationship) suggests women see morality in terms of their responsibility to specific people and needs. We must take another look at the Level 6 stage that Kohlberg thought many college youth had attained. If one demands that someone must place himself or herself at risk, either economically (e.g., I sell my South African stock at a loss) or physically (e.g., I intervene in the clubbing of a peace activist or suffer castigation for a humanitarian cause) to attain Level 6, many people would not truly be at that level. Many college students, although they have demonstrated for a celebrated cause, do not exactly appear to be putting themselves at risk.

Without the notion of justice and fairness, how can we solve the problems of naked aggression? Without the idea that rehabilitation responsibilities will be enforced by the demands of justice, how do we know what is fair? It would appear that Gilligan's call for nonviolence is laudable. Just as important, compassion and care must be in evidence if there is to be a higher morality. As a universal one needs at some time to appeal to the lesser of the evil or greater of the good: hence the importance of justice.

Values

Rokeach (1979) found that love is not overwhelmingly important as a value for those in their twenties and thirties. He did, however, find that honesty was, and this suggests that basic to personality development and maturity is becoming increasingly truthful, first with oneself, and then with others, and that only then does caring develop. Implicit in development of personality is freedom--of movement, of spontaneity, of ideas to change work or other aspects of life.

McSweeney and Jones (1991) surveyed over 1,000 undergraduate and graduate students from the ages of 19 to 50 about their biggest worry, most satisfying present aspect of life, and future goals. Education ranked number one, making money was number two. Of 63 respondents that listed love, 44 were women and only one was aged 31 to 40. However, marriage and family were listed, proving that the romance factor for many had grown into broader aspects of love--companionship and caring.

Young Adulthood and Cognitive Ability

It is generally agreed that there are two kinds of intelligence--crystallized and fluid. Crystallized intelligence is learned information and the ability to remember it. Much of this comes from schooling, reading, and experience. Fluid intelligence is the process of perceiving relationships, forming concepts, reasoning, and abstracting, and is associated with changes over time. One thing is certain: fluid intelligence is greatest during young adulthood. Crystallized intelligence continues to grow if a person interacts with ideas, reads, keeps abreast of current news, and is in reasonably good health. Horn and Donaldson (1980) see changes in intelligence as shown in Figure 11.18, which notes that crystallized intelligence continues to grow while fluid intelligence decreases.

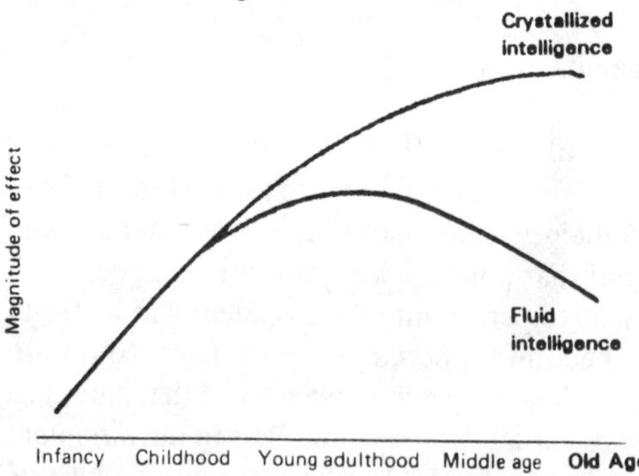

Figure 11.18 Magnitude of effect.

Schaie has proposed a five-step tier of stages of cognitive development, which in some ways is imposed on Piaget's stages. Riegel (1973) has argued for an additional Piaget stage he called the "dialectic" stage. We will discuss this later. Schaie contends that the purposes and ways to use knowledge and its meaning eventuate into the "wisdom of old age." Actual life experiences are important aspects of cognitive functioning. His theory for adults focuses on the cognitive needs of adults and their progression in the world.

1. Acquisitive stage (childhood and adolescence): Young people learn information and skills largely for their own sake and because of schooling, but hardly for participation in society. They do best on tests that give them a chance to show what they can do, although they have more meaning in their lives.

2. Achieving stage (late teens or early twenties to early thirties): The achieving stage occurs when youths no longer acquire knowledge for its own sake but have to use knowledge to achieve competence and independence. People do best on tasks that are relevant to the life goals they have set for themselves.

3. Responsible stage (late thirties to early sixties): People are concerned with long-range goals and practical, real-life problems that are likely to be associated with the responsibility they bear for their livelihood and family.

4. Executive stage (thirties or forties through middle age): People feel responsibility for societal systems (governmental, social, or business concerns) rather than just family units and have the need to integrate complex relationships on a number of levels.

5. Reintegrative stage (late adulthood): These people have less societal involvement and responsibility, and their cognitive functioning may be limited by physical changes--are more selective about the tasks they choose to do. The

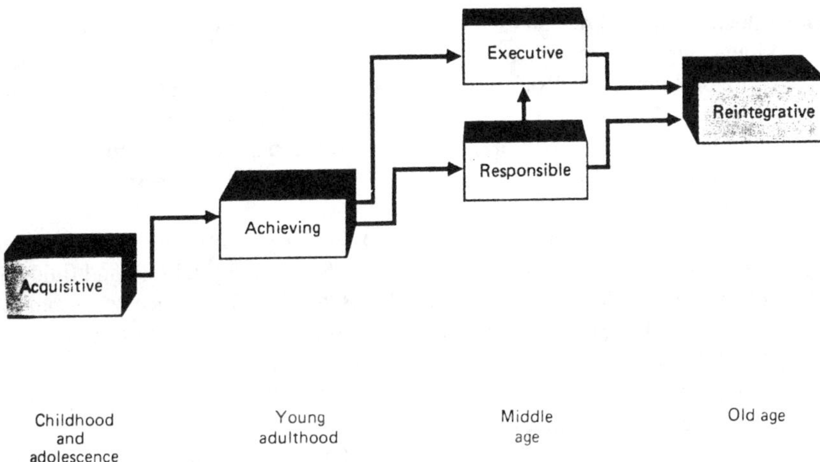

Figure 11.19 Stages of cognitive development in adults. (*Source:* based on Schaie, 1977-1978.)

purpose of what they do is important and they are less likely than before to bother with tasks that have no meaning for them.

The Schaie schemata appears as Figure 11.19. As for young adults aged 20 to 30, most would be in the achieving stage while the later young (30 to 39) by 40 perhaps would be in the responsible stage. Obviously traditional tests will do well in determining functioning intelligence--Stanford Binet and Wechsler Adult Tests will touch some aspects of the cognitive ability in dealing with complex societal and business concerns.

Riegel (1975) emphasizes the understanding of the contradictions that apply to achievement of adult cognitive development. He calls this dialectical thinking, perhaps after the philosopher Hegel (1972), who argued that societal, political, and philosophical change and thought took place through a dialectic process. This involved a thesis (the status quo); antithesis (the counter to status quo); and a modification of these positions, or compromise, which is the synthesis (bringing together the two sides or forces). For Riegel the dialectic is where an individual considers opposing thoughts and synthesizes them. An important aspect of the dialectical is harmonizing the ideal and the real. The practical (mundane) and the real serve as a dialectical correction to abstract formal thinking (the ideal). Ambiguity and contradictions in resolving issues--ethics, social implications, practical problems--are different from formal stage logic--in fact due to the many variables, are often much more complex. This is the strength of the adult's cognitive functioning. Gisela Labouie-Vief (1984) argues that the characteristics of mature adult thinking are commitment and responsibility. For her, cognitive development involves both the growth of logic described by Piaget and the growth of self-regulation into adulthood. Sternberg and Berg (1987) suggest a triarchic theory of adult cognition as seen below (Table 11.8).

I. Componential Subtheory

A. Metacomponents

1. Recognizing existence of a problem
2. Defining nature of the problem
3. Selecting lower-order components to solve problem
4. Selecting strategy into which to combine components
5. Selecting a mental representation upon which strategy acts

6. Allocating mental resources
7. Monitoring solution
8. Utilizing external feedback

B. Performance Components (partial list)

1. Encoding stimuli
2. Inferring relations between stimuli
3. Mapping higher-order relations between stimuli
4. Applying old relations to new stimulus domains
5. Comparing stimuli
6. Justifying selected solutions
7. Responding to stimuli

C. Knowledge-Acquisition Components

1. Selective encoding of information
2. Selective combining of information
3. Selective comparing of new to old information

II. Experiential Subtheory

A. Dealing with relative novelty
B. Automatizing information processing

III. Contextual Subtheory

A. Adapting to environment
B. Shaping environment
C. Selecting environment

It appears that the way Sternberg and Berg (1987) describe informational processing under the metacomponents is similar to many other theories of intellectual development ranging from later adolescence to adulthood. Typically IQ tests sample problem solving, abstractions, knowledge, and linguistics. This is componential in Sternberg's theory. To Sternberg these items do not reflect those behaviors which might relate to contextual intelligence through the application of experience in novel but real situations. Typical tests of intelligence do not measure the application of pragmatic intelligence and therefore underestimate the cognitive powers of many adults.

A summary of the intellectual aspects of the young adult is as follows:

1) Peak of intellectual ability between 20 and 35 in both crystallized and fluid intelligence.
2) Optimal performance on memory tasks.
3) Peak performance on laboratory tasks in problem solving.
4) Little change in speed and performance at 40.
5) Growth in "dialectics and contextual" intelligence.
6) Expanding crystallized intelligence at 35 to 40.
7) Overall the best period in adulthood for learning new material, understanding complex formulas, and solving logic problems.

SUMMARY

Adult change and development result from an interaction among the physical, the psychological, and the sociological factors at each period of life. There are numerous components of each of these modalities that are significant in the shaping of individual lives; the historical (normative and non-normative) and social times in which one lives, the nature of the cultural and physical environment, the accumulated stress and effect of heredity and change on the individual, and one's perspective, both philosophically and morally, on the natural world. The young adult years (young 20 to 29) and older or later young (30 to 39) comprise these times. The young adult is at the peak of health (accidents and suicides are the major causes of death among this group). Only at 35 is the chief cause of death physical illness. War takes its toll among those who have a very low natural death rate. However, the mental health of this group is often a pervasive problem. Many are reducing stress by exercise and more jog and play team sports than any other group.

The social aspect of life relates to responsible adulthood. It calls for the attainment of certain developmental tasks partially completed during adolescence--ego strength, sex-role attainment, marital or love-life adjustment, vocational adjustment, and possession of an ethical system and acceptance of a positive role in the neighborhood and community.

Achievement of the vocational task has been increasingly difficult for each generation. Vocational selection increasingly is concerned with relating traits of personality of individuals to occupational traits. Holland suggests six personality types and six work environment types. Research seems to back up the claims of this approach. Due to technological advancements there will continue to be a growing demand for education and training; some additional training may be required at different periods of the individual's life. Fewer 16- to 34-year-olds will be in the labor force due to the passage into middle age of the baby boomers. The values an individual stresses in selecting a vocation will be influenced by the socioeconomic class to which the person belongs, although there is evidence that class lines may not be as rigid today as formerly.

Professional workers seem to get more satisfaction from their work, and partially because of their training, are least likely to change occupations. Most change occurs in unskilled workers and those in white-collar occupations that demand little special training. The unskilled are perhaps least likely to find their jobs challenging and/or interesting. Their satisfaction results from extrinsic rewards in the form of paychecks, vacations, and the like.

Marriage occurs usually among equals in social status who live nearby and are approximately the same age. Sternberg's triangle of love--intimacy, passion, and commitment--increasingly becomes the standard. Many women are often ambivalent about combining jobs and marriage. Women make up nearly 60 percent of the work force; many have children at home. Nine out of ten will work outside the home at some time in their lives. A high discrepancy in certain personality traits between husbands and wives contributes to marital discord, along with economic and sexual factors. The birth of a child does not usually dispel such discord. The unmarried in our society are increasing and are often faced with difficult social and psychological problems; however, with new freedom and tendency to forego marriage for a few years, more are establishing themselves as singles or cohabitating, opting to explore many facets of life--travel, education, a variety of jobs, and styles of living outside traditional marriage. Many couples are deciding not to have children. Some evidence exists to suggest these are the happiest couples. In some cases vocational success or a career is a substitute for marriage.

With increased leisure time, young adults, even among working youth, give careful consideration to how weekends, evenings, holidays, and vacations are to be spent. Many youth of both sexes in their twenties and early thirties like thrilling experiences and vigorous outdoor activities. Middle-class adults spend 52 percent of their time in sedentary activities, and lower-

Looking each other over is a major young college adult pastime.

class adults 82 percent. This is probably decreasing because of the emphasis in schools and communities on lifetime sports.

Although young adulthood is characterized by pulling up roots and making a start on one's own life, it is also a time of quandary in trying to create a stable life. Even though the incidences of maladjustment and personality problems are high for young adults, still there are a number of generally stable aspects of the personality. Many satisfactions in life exist, including school completion and family and vocational success. Factors associated with satisfaction include extraversion, good health, and religion. Many personality variables carry forward from childhood into adulthood, such as spontaneity, sex-typed activity, and achievement. Differences among the sexes appear in dependence, behavior disorganization, and heterosexuality.

As many as two or three phase transitions take place in the young adult, the first upon entering adulthood at 18 to 22, and the second around 30 to 34, where reappraisals occur, often forcing dramatic change in the life pattern. During the earlier period many young adults come to Kohlberg's principled level of morality. Some investigators believe there is a major shift between 23 and 28, a time when many marriages dissolve.

Intellectual skills that are fluid are at their highest points around ages 25 to 30; crystallized intelligence climbs until the sixties, as does physical strength, both combining to form a protective bulwark against the frustrations and problems in establishing maturity. Positive factors in the second-half development of the young adult (30 to 39) are noted, such as achieving ego identity, freedom in personal relations, depth of interests, the humanizing of values, and increased caring for others. Schaie and others believe the executive and responsibility stages in adult intelligence are required increasingly by adults for success.

KEY WORDS

normative events

non-normative events

historical times

DNA

trait-theory

empty love

fatuous love

demographic variable

stepping-stone neighborhood

anomic neighborhood

transitional stages

conventional stages

psychological modality

physiological modality

sociological modality

consummate love

conflict-habituated marriage

devitalized marriage

passive-congenial marriage

parochial neighborhood

transitory neighborhood

defense mechanism

intimacy versus isolation

triarchic theory of cognition

REFERENCES:

Ahrons, C.R., and Rodgers, R.H. *Divorced Families: A Multidisciplinary Developmental View.* New York: Norton, 1987.

American Council on Science and Health. *Premenstrual Syndrome,* (pamphlet). Summit, NJ: Author, 1985.

Baltes, P.B. Life-span developmental psychology: Some converging observations of history and theory. In P.B. Baltes and O.G. Brim, Jr. (eds), *Life-Span Development and Behavior*, vol. 2. New York: Academic Press, 1979.

Bloom, B.L., and Caldwell, R.A. Sex differences in adjustment during the process of marital separation. *Journal of Marriage and the Family*, 1981, *43*:693-701.

Brayshaw, A.J. Middle-aged marriage: Idealism, realism and the search for meaning. *Marriage and Family Living*, November 1962.

Cain, B.S. The plight of the grey divorcee. *New York Times Magazine*, December 12, 1982, pp. 89-90, 92, 95.

Campbell, A. *The Sense of Well-Being in America: Recent Patterns and Trends.* New York: McGraw-Hill, 1981.

Campbell, A. The American way of mating: Marriage is children only maybe. *Psychology Today*, May 1975, *8*(6):17-41.

Campbell, A., Converse, P.E., and Rodgers, W.L. *The Quality of American Life: Perceptions, Evaluations and Satisfactions.* New York: Russell Sage Foundation, 1975.

Cherlin, A. At issue--Cohabitation how the French and Swedes do it. *Psychology Today*, 1979, *13*(4).

Children Today. Youth attitudes. 1975, *4*(6):14-15.

Chiriboga, D.A. Adaptation to marital separation in later and earlier life. *Journal of Gerontology*, 1982, *37*:109-114.

Colby, A., Kohlberg, L., Gibbs, J., and Lieberman, M. A longitudinal study of moral development. Monographs of the Society for Research in Child Development, 1983, *48*(1-2), Serial No. 200.

Coleman, J.S. *Youth: Transition to Adulthood.* Chicago: University of Chicago Press, 1974.

Congressional Congress for Women's Issues. *The American Woman.* Washington, DC: Author, 1987-1988.

Constantine, L.L., and Constantine, J.M. Sexual aspects of group marriage. In R.W. Libby and R.N. Whitehurst (eds.), *Marriage and Alternatives: Explaining Intimate Relationships.* Glenview, Ill.: Scott, Foresman, 1977, pp. 186-194.

Current Population Report. *Population Characteristics: Marital Status and Living Arrangements, March 1982.* Washington, DC: U.S. Government Printing Office, May 1983, Series T-20, No. 380, p. 2

Diener, E. Subjective well-being. *Psychological Bulletin*, 1984, *95*:542-575.

Dryer, P.H. Sex, sex roles, and marriage among youth in the 1970s. *Youth*, 74th Yearbook of the National Society for the Study of Education, Part I. Chicago: University of Chicago Press, 1975, pp. 194-223.

Eichorn, D.H., Clausen, J.A., Haan, N., Honzik, M.P., and Mussen, P.H. (eds.), *Present and Past in Middle Life.* New York: Academic Press, 1982.

Erikson, E. *Identity, Youth and Crisis.* New York: Norton, 1968.

Farley, F., and Davis, S. Personality and sexual satisfaction in marriage. *Journal of Sex and Marital Therapy*, 1980, *6*(1).

Fisher, H.E. The four-year itch. *Natural History*, 1987, *96*(10):22-33.

Freud, S. *New Introductory Lectures on Psychoanalysis.* New York: Norton, 1933.

Gilligan, C. *In a Different Voice: Psychological Theory and Women's Development.* Cambridge, Mass.: Harvard University Press, 1982.

Gilligan, J. In a different voice: Women's conceptions of self and of morality. *Harvard Educational Review*, 1977, *47*(4):481-517.

Glenn, N.D., and Supancic, M. Thc social and demographic correlates of divorce and separation in the United States: An update and reconsideration. *Journal of Marriage and the Family*, 1984, *46*:563-575.

Gordon, C., Gaitz, J., and Scott, J. Leisure and lives: Personal expressivity across the life span. In R.H. Binstock and E. Shanas (eds.), *Handbook of Aging and the Social Sciences.* New York: Van Nostrand Reinhold, 1976, pp. 310-341.

Gould, R. *Transformation: Growth and Change in Adult Life.* New York: Simon & Schuster, 1978.

Greenhaus, J.H. Self-esteem as an influence on occupational choice and occupational satisfaction. *Journal of Vocational Behavior*, 1971, *1*:75-83.

Gutmann, D.L. An explanation of ego configuration in middle and later life. In B.L. Neugarten and associates (eds.), *Personality in Middle and Later Life*. New York: Atherton Press, 1964.

Group for the Advancement of Psychiatry. Reported in Papalia and Olds (eds.), *Human Development*. New York: McGraw-Hill, 1978.

Haan, N. Change and sameness. *International Journal of Aging and Human Development*, 1976, *7*:63.

Harry, J. Gay male and lesbian relationships. In E.D. Macklin and R.H. Rubin (eds.), *Contemporary Families and Alternative Lifestyles: Handbook on Research and Theory*. Beverly Hills, CA: Sage Publications.

Havighurst, R.J. *Developmental Tasks and Education*, 3rd ed. New York: David McKay, 1972.

_____. Stages in vocational development. In H. Borrow (ed.), *Man in the World at Work*. Boston: Houghton Mifflin, 1964.

Hill, C.T., Rubin, Z., and Peplau, L.A. Breakups before marriage: The end of 103 affairs. In G. Levinger and O. Moles (eds.), *Divorce and Separation: Context, Causes and Consequences*. New York: Basic Books, 1979.

Hite Report. New York: Knopf, 1981.

Hock, E., Christman, K., and Hock, M. Fathers associated with decisions about return to work in mothers of infants. *Developmental Psychology*, 1980, *16*(5):535-536.

Holland, J.L. *Vocational Preference Inventory* (VPI), Palo Alto, CA: Consulting Psychology Press, 1975.

Horn, J.L., and Donaldson, G. Cognitive development II: Adulthood development of human abilities. In O.G. Brim and J. Kagan (eds.), *Constancy and Change in Human Development*. Cambridge, Mass.: Harvard University Press, 1980.

Jones, F.R. *Understanding the Middle Years*. Unpublished manuscript, 1991.

Jones, F.R., and Heinen, J.R.K. *Stress and Mental Health of Graduate Students and Non-Graduates by Age and Educational Levels*. Washington, DC: U.S. Department of Health Education, and Welfare, Institute of Education, Document ED 159 499.

Jones, F.R., and McSweeney, J. Worries, goals and satisfactions of students. *U-News*, Norfolk, Virginia, June 21, 1978.

Kelly, J.B. Divorce: The adult perspective. In B. Wolman (ed.), *Handbook of Developmental Psychology*. Englewood Cliffs, NJ: Prentice-Hall, 1982.

Kinsey, A.C., Pomeroy, W.B., Martin, C.E., and Gebbard, P.H. *Sexual Behavior in the Human Female*. Philadelphia: Saunders, 1953.

Kitson, G.L., and Sussman, M.B. Marital complaints, demographic characteristics and symptoms of mental distress in divorce. *Journal of Marriage and the Family*, 1982, *44*:87-101.

Labouie-Vief, G. Intelligence and cognition. In J.E. Birren and K.W. Schaie (eds.), *Handbook of the Psychology of the Aging*, 2nd ed. New York: Van Nostrand Reinhold, 1985.

Lerner, R.M., and Busch-Rossnagel, N.A. *Individuals as Producers of Their Development*. New York: Academic Press, 1981.

Levinger, G. Stability in marriage. *Journal of Marriage and the Family*, 1965, *27*(1).

Levinson, D. *The Seasons of a Man's Life*. New York: Alfred Knopf, 1978.

Loevinger, J. *Ego Development: Conceptions and Theories*. San Francisco: Jossey-Bass, 1976.

Macklin, E.D. Nonmarital heterosexual cohabitation: An overview. In E.D. Macklin and R.H. Rubin (eds.), *Contemporary Families and Alternative Lifestyles: Handbook on Research and Theory*. Beverly Hills, CA: Sage Publications, 1983.

McSweeney, J., and Jones, F.R. Survey of worries, goals and satisfactions in graduate and non-graduate students on the east coast. In Press. *Psychology of Human Development*, Kendall Hunt, 1991.

Morris, C. *Varieties of Human Values*. Chicago: University of Chicago Press, 1956.

Murstein, B.I. *Who Will Marry Whom? Theories and Research in Marital Choice*. New York: Springer-Verlag, 1976.

Neiswender, M., Birren, J., and Schaie, K.W. Age and the experience of love in adulthood. Paper presented at the annual meeting of the American Psychological Association, Chicago, Ill., 1975.

Neugarten, B. Adult personality: Toward a psychology of the life cycle. In Neugarten (ed.), *Middle Age and Aging*. Chicago: University of Chicago Press, 1968.

Neugarten, B.L., and Neugarten, D.A. The changing meanings of age. *Psychology Today*, 1987, *21*:29-33.

Newhouse News Service. Sex still a factor in student job goals. *Chicago Sun-Times*, September 1987, p. 37.

Nisan, M., and Kohlberg, L. University and variation moral judgment: A longitudinal and cross-sectional study in Turkey. *Child Development*, 1982, *53*:865-876.

Norton, A.J., and Moorman, J.F. Current trends in marriage and divorce among American women. *Journal of Marriage and the Family*, 1987, *49*(1):3,14.

Okum, B.F. *Working With Adults: Individual, Family and Career Development*. Monterey, CA: Brooks/Cole, 1984.

Papalia, D.E., and Olds, S.W. *Human Development*, 4th ed. New York: McGraw-Hill, 1989.

Parlee, M.R. Reproductive issues, including menopause. In G. Baruch and J. Brooks-Gunn (eds.), *Women in Midlife*. New York: Plenum, 1984.

Peplau, L.A. What homosexuals want in relationships. *Psychology Today*, 1981, *15*:28-38.

Phillips, D.C., and Kelly, M.E. Hierarchical theories of development in education and psychology. *Harvard Educational Review*, 1975, *45*(3):351-375.

Piaget, J. *The Psychology of Intelligence*. Patterson, NJ: Littlefield, Adams, 1963.

Pikunas, J. *Human Development: An Emergent Science*. New York: McGraw-Hill, 1976.

Pincus, T., Gallahan, L.F., and Burkhauser, R.V. Most chronic diseases are reported more frequently by individuals with fewer than 12 years of formal education in the age 18-24 United States population. *Journal of Chronic Diseases*, 1987, *40*(9):865-874.

Pressey, S.L., and Kuhlen, R.B. *Life Span Development*. New York: Harper & Row, 1957.

Reedy, M.N. Age and sex differences in personal needs and the nature of love: A study of happily married young, middle-aged and older couples. Unpublished doctoral dissertation, University of Southern California, 1977.

Reigel, K.F. The dialectics of human development. *American Psychologists*, 1976, *31*:689-700.

Riegel, F.R. Dialectic operations: The final period of cognitive development. *Human Development*, 1973, *16*:346-370.

Schaie, K.W. The Seattle longitudinal study: A 21-year exploration of psycholometric intelligence in adulthood. In K.W. Schaie (ed.), *Longitudinal Studies of Adult Psychological Development*. New York: The Guilford Press, 1983, pp. 64-135.

Scholastic Aptitude Test Educational Testing Service, Princeton, NJ, 1991.

Schulz, D.A., and Rodgers, S.F. *Marriage, the Family, Personal Fulfillment*, 3rd ed. Englewood Cliffs, NJ: Prentice-Hall, 1985.

Selye, H. *The Stress of Life*, 2nd ed. New York: McGraw-Hill, 1976.

Simenaner, J., and Carroll, D. *Singles: The New Americans.* New York: Simon & Schuster, 1982.

Skolnick, A. Married lives: Longitudinal perspectives on marriage. In D.H. Eichorn, J.A. Clausen, N. Haan, M.P. Honzik, and P.H. Mussen (eds.), *Present and Past in Middle Life.* New York: Academic Press, 1981.

Snarey, J.R., Reimer, J., and Kohlberg, L. Development of social-moral reasoning among kibbutz adolescents: A longitudinal cross-cultural study. *Development Psychology*, 1985, *21*:3-17.

Solnick, A., and Solnick, O. (eds.) *Family in Transition.* Boston: Little Brown, 1971.

Statistical Abstract of the United States, 1982-1983. Bureau of the Census, Department of Commerce. Washington, DC: U.S. Government Printing Office, 1982.

Statistical Data Book, United States Statistical Abstract. Washington, DC: Government Printing Office, 1990.

Stein, P.J. Being single: Bucking the culture imperative. Paper presented to the 71st annual meeting of the America Sociologist Association, September 3, 1976.

Sternberg, R.J. *Science Digest*, April 1985, pp. 60, 78-79.

Sternberg, R.J., and Berg, C. What are theories of adult intellectual development theories of? In C. Schooler and K.W. Schaie (eds.), *Cognitive Functioning and Social Structure Over the Life Course.* Norwood, NJ: Ablex, 1987.

Stevens-Long, J. *Adult Life.* Los Angeles: Mayfield, 1979.

Strong Vocational Interest Blank, Stanford University Press, Stanford, CA: 1933. Distributed by the Consulting Psychologist Press, Inc. Revision, 1974.

Super, D.E. *Career Development: Self Concept Theory.* New York: College Entrance Examination Board, 1963.

Tanfer, K., and Horn, M.C. Contraceptive use, pregnancy and fertilization patterns among single American women in their 20s. *Family Planning Perspectives*, 1985, *17*(1):10-17.

Troll, L.E. *Early and Middle Adulthood*, 2nd ed. Monterey, CA: Brooks/Cole, 1985.

U.S. Bureau of the Census. *Statistical Abstract of the United States. Households, Families, Marital Status, and Living Arrangements, March 1986: Advance Report.* Current Population Reports, Series P-20, No. 412. Washington, DC: U.S. Government printing Office, 1986.

U.S. Bureau of the Census. *U.S. Statistical Abstract 1988.* Washington, DC, 1989.

U.S. Bureau of the Census. *U.S. Statistical Abstract 1986*. Washington, DC, 1987.

U.S. Department of Commerce, Bureau of the Census. *1981 Statistical Abstract of the United States*, 102nd ed. Washington, DC: U.S. Government Printing Office.

U.S. Department of Health and Human Services. *Health, United States, 1985*. Publication No. PHS 86-1232. Washington, DC: U.S. Government Printing Office.

U.S. Department of Health and Human Services. *Health, United States, 1986, Prevention Profile*. DDH Publication No. PHS 87-1232. Washington, DC: U.S. Government Printing Office.

U.S. Occupational Outlook Handbook, 1990-1991 Edition. U.S. Government Printing Office, 1990.

U.S. Statistical Abstract. Washington, DC, 1990. U.S. Government Printing Office 1990-1991.

Vaillant, G.E. *Adaptation to Life*. Boston: Little, Brown, 1977.

Van Dusen, R.A., and Sheldon, E.B. The changing status of American women: A life cycle perspective. *American Psychologist*, 1976, *31*:106-116.

Veroff, J., Dovan, E., and Kulka, R.A. *The Inner American: A Self-Portrait From 1957 to 1976*. New York: Basic Books, 1981.

Vogel, F.S. The brain and time. In E.W. Busse and E. Pfeiffer (eds.), *Behavior and Adaptation in Late Life*, 2nd ed. Boston: Little, Brown, 1977, pp. 232-233.

Walker, L.J. Sex differences in the development of moral reasoning: A critical review. *Child Development*, 1984, *55*:677-691.

Weitzman, L.J. *The Divorce Revolution: The Unexpected Social and Economic Consequences for Women and Children in America*. New York: Free Press, 1985.

Youngner, S., and Youngner, M. Becoming parents (Jaffe and Viertel), a book review. *Journal of Sex and Marital Therapy*, fall 1980, *6*(3).

Youth Indicators. *U.S. Statistical Abstract*, 1988. Washington, DC: U.S. Government Printing Office, 1988.

PART VI

MIDDLESCENCE AND THE LATER YEARS

Chapter 12

MIDDLESCENCE: THE IN-BETWEEN YEARS

MIDDLESCENCE: THE IN-BETWEEN YEARS

Middlescence represents the years in between those of the young adult and those of the later adult period. The word *middlescence* is used here to encompass those years roughly from 40 to 50. Forty is half of the projected life expectancy of a female baby born in 1991 (*World Fact Book*, 1990). As we noted in Chapter 11, the authors consider the middle years of middlescence to be 50 to 59, and the older years of middlescence 60 to 69.

Classifying people into stages and divisions may relate to class perceptions, chronology, or appearances, but it is more a matter of role that determines one's functional category.

Some have called the middle-aged generation the "Command" generation or the "Take Charge" generation. In fact, they claim the world would bankrupt itself if they were eliminated. Their voting records are better than those of younger adults, their attendance on the job is better, and--representing only a third of the population--the age group 40 to 65 earns more than half the money (Rakstis, 1970). Bernice Neugarten (1964) in her book *Personality in Middle and Late Life* says, "Middle-aged men and women are the norm bearers and the decision makers of our society. And while they live in a society which may be oriented toward youth, it is controlled by the middle-aged."

The middle years (40 to 50) is a period that represents the prime of life. Many psychologists are saying it is the best time of life, taking into consideration a number of broad factors, such as status, family, life satisfaction, community leadership, and achievement. At 40 health is generally good. There are crises confronting many during this period--most do not have mid-life crises (Neugarten, 1980)--but it is also the time of life during which curiosity, creativity, and comprehension can be given freer play than ever before. The individual at the midpoint in life is not encumbered by considerations of vocational training nor limited by the sense of inexperience that normally afflicts youth.

The positive aspect of middle adulthood according to Erikson (1968) is "generativity as opposed to stagnation." People whose lives have been characterized by generativity are productive in their work, have stimulating avocations, wide interests, and make continuous contributions to their families and communities. Others have stagnated, just going through the motions in their work, and may be apathetic toward their family and community or have given up completely. Where individuals have accomplished the cultural tasks, called by Havighurst "developmental tasks" (discussed later in the chapter), they usually have achieved a sense of self-realization by middle middlescence (50 to 59). They are more open, caring, and autonomous (Loevinger, 1976). An examination of the changes and problems of middlescence will follow the same format as the preceding chapter on the young adult, beginning with the physical mode. A summary of developmental aspect in middle age follows.

Middlescence	PHYSICAL	MOTOR	COGNITIVE	PSYCHOSOCIAL/ PERSONALITY
Younger 40-49	Waist expands, gains in weight. Arthritis onset for some. Hair recedes in men. Greyness occurs in both women and men.	Recreational varieties--traveling, visiting, games, swimming & walking.	Understanding of people, children and spouse. Knowledge of government, economic & social issues.	Increase in status and responsibility in the community and in helping children become emancipated.
Middle 50-59	Menopause in women. Lessening of potenia in men. Onset of diabetes for some.	Lessening of active sports--travel & vacations. Bicycling, walking.	Crystallized intelligence increases--fluid intelligence decreases.	General happiness for most men and women, many are grandparents.
Later 60-69	Most people have a chronic health problem. 30% of weight is fat for women & men. Many people exercise regularly.	Increase in sedentary activities. Card and game playing. Gardening and sewing, some play golf or tennis.	Recall more difficult. Likes games and puzzles.	Emotional maturity. Retirement for many. Part-time work for some. Defensive styles shift from neurotic to mature ones for coping.

THE PHYSICAL MODE

Health

Individuals monitor their bodies more frequently in the middle years than in early adulthood; consequently, they are aware of and sensitive to changes. These years are characterized by obvious changes in the way the body operates and appears. The most significant outward change relates to weight gain, which occurs in terms of means for both men and women from the mid-twenties forward to the sixties. For men, becoming bald-headed and losing hair color, accompanied by wrinkles beginning to show on the face, are physical markers of aging. The skin, once stretched tightly over the body, begins to loosen. Cuts heal less quickly than in earlier years, and the increase in discolored skin, particularly in fair-skinned persons, begins to appear. The body after vigorous exercise gets stiff sooner than before, and muscles that were underused sometimes ache. By the end of middlescence individuals have lost a small proportion of their height; strength declines slowly, about 10 percent from the ages of 30 to 60. The loss of strength that occurs is usually in the legs and back; increasingly, men and women in their forties and fifties try to lift less and attempt to get help for heavy objects. Exercise is a help in retaining muscle strength, and for those few who have had large losses of strength in their twenties, a training program can be of help. Many adults maintain their muscle tone until they are 70 (Timiras, 1972). There is a significant loss of muscle tissue (actual muscle cells) over the adult years, with the most rapid decline occurring after age 50 (Rossman, 1980). There is some indication that the greatest loss is in so-called "fast twitch" muscle fibers, which are the ones primarily involved in rapid bursts of speed or strength (such as sprinting), with slower loss in "slow twitch" fibers, which are involved in prolonged activity (such as jogging) (Ostrow, 1984). The major effect of this loss of fibers is a reduction in physical strength. It is important to emphasize that all muscles show these changes, including the muscles of the diaphragm and chest used for breathing, and those of the bladder, used for elimination.

Biological Markers

A biological marker for women is menopause (cessation of the menstrual cycle and the ability to have children), as the climacteric (time of hormonal, physical, and psychological change in men) is for the male. For the male this change is less dramatic and noticeable. Hormonal level changes occur for both sexes. Women at the time of menopause lose estrogen and progesterone; in men testosterone drops off gradually during middlescence. According to Masters and Ballew (1965) both sexes generally tend to become "neuter." They have more sex hormonal balance, with less masculine and feminine hormone (androgen and estrogen levels) and greater hormone levels of the opposite sex being produced, such as androgen in women. These researchers say that women by 50 years of age and men by 60 years of age reach this balance. Masters and Ballew caution, however, that there are great individual differences. Many women are only slightly affected by menopause, although some have difficulty with the onset of hot flashes, nervousness, and headaches. Final cessation of the menses takes place between 48 and 52 (Berger & Nostesegian, 1976). Many women do not know what to expect, and counseling is often recommended (Rogers, 1979). As many as one-third consult physicians (Katchadourian, 1987).

As the metabolic rate decelerates, the control of weight is more difficult, particularly in American society, where food and drink in the middle years become a chief way of socializing. People who are overweight, drink, smoke, have high levels of cholesterol, and exercise little are more subject to heart attacks. Fat increases from 25 onward and the average American is overweight (Novak, 1972).

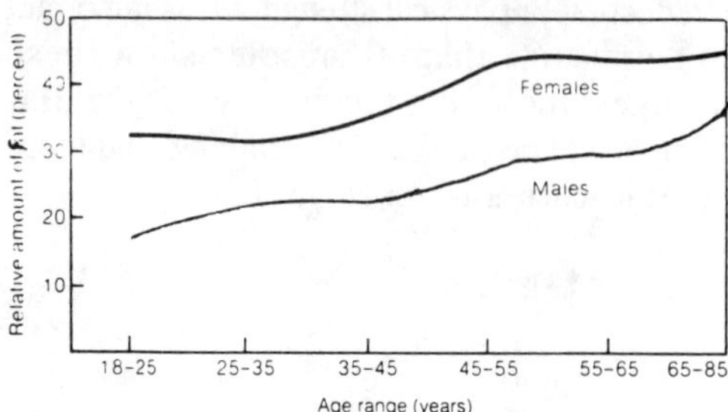

Figure 12.1 Relative amount of fat. (Adapted from Novak, 1972.)

The main causes of death during the middle years are cardiovascular problems, cancer, and respiratory disease. Other diseases such as diabetes, chronic bronchitis, asthma, and hay fever do not increase consistently after 45 or 50 (Kimmel, 1974). Verbrugge (1975) states that the major chronic diseases for women are arthritis, rheumatism, osteoporosis, hypertension with heart involvement, and nervous conditions. For men the major problems are lower-extremity impairment, back and spine impairment, visual impairment, and diseases of the heart. Two of five by the age of 45 have one of these conditions; by age 50 almost everyone has some chronic health problem (Hunt & Hunt, 1974).

There are several significant changes in bones associated with age. First, bone marrow (in which blood cells are made) gradually disappears in arms and legs and becomes concentrated in the bones of the trunk. Second, calcium is lost from the bones, making them more brittle and porous, a process called osteoporosis. As a consequence, bone fractures increase markedly in frequency after about age 45 in women and 75 in men (Lindsay, 1985). Osteoporosis is far more likely to be severe in women, particularly postmenopausally. The loss of ovarian hormones that is part of the menopausal process (which we will describe shortly) seems to be one of the causal factors, but diet and lifestyle also make a difference. The major known risk factors are listed in Table 12.1.

Third, changes in the bones of the joints, resulting primarily from the wear and tear of years of body movements, appear to be virtually universal. When such changes become marked, they are called osteoarthritis (Rossman, 1980).

TABLE 12.1 Risk Factors for Osteoporosis

Factor	Incidence & Effect
Race	Whites have higher risk than other races.
Gender	Females have higher risk than males.
Weight	Those who are light for their height have higher risk.
Timing of Climacteric	Women with early menopause, or those who have had their ovaries removed, are at higher risk.
Family History	Those with family history of osteoporosis have higher risk.
Diet	Diet low in calcium and high in caffeine and/or alcohol leads to higher risk.
Lifestyle	Sedentary lifestyle associated with higher risk.
Number of Children	Women who have borne many children are at higher risk.

Source: Lindsay, 1985

Women consult physicians more often than do men (Fisher & Greenberg, 1979). Women are more health conscious and they tend to live longer (Papalia & Olds, 1989). For a three-year period the frequency of visiting for young adult females showed a mean of 2.68 per year against 1.20 a year for men. No significant discomfort between the sexes was found, but women reported more throat and urinary symptoms than men.

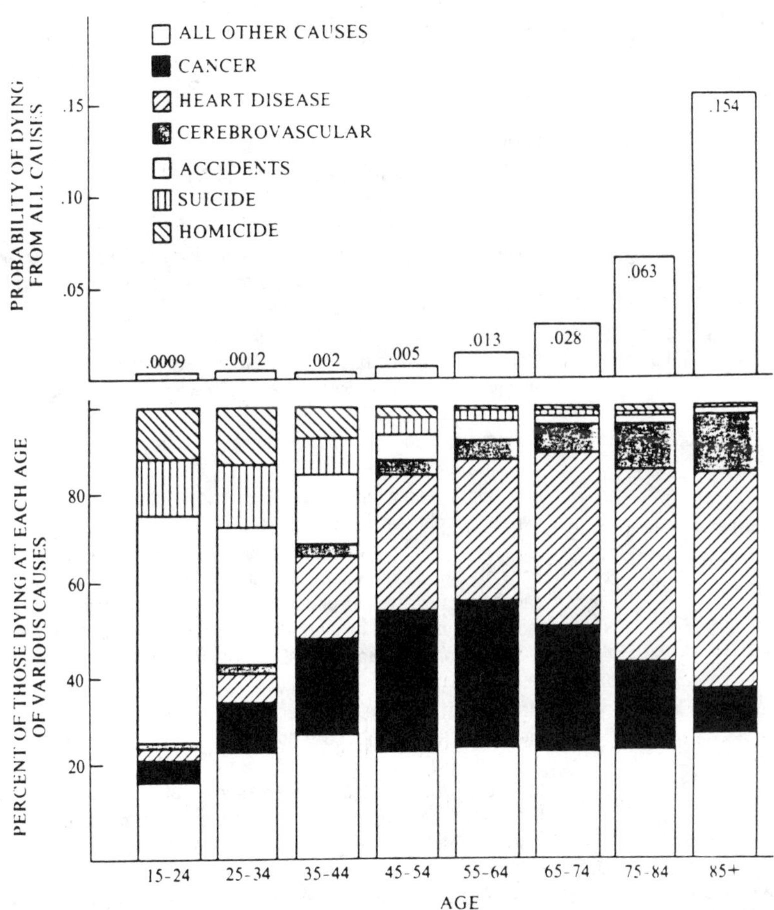

Figure 12.2 The upper part of this figure shows the probability of dying, for adults in each of a series of age groups, during 1983. The lower part of the figure shows what the people died of in 1983. Proportionately, many more young people die of accidents, suicide, and homicide, while beginning in the 45-54 age group, cancer and heart disease are the major causes of death. (*Source:* National Center for Health Statistics, *Monthly Vital Statistics Report, 1984*, 32(*13*).

Heart disease remains the largest killer, with cancer second. Rates of both of these diseases are down, which can be attributed to greater concern for diet, exercise, and life styles relative to heart conditions. Cancer rates have dropped considerably below heart fatality rates due to early detection. Most cancers diagnosed from 1960-63 show 10 percent to 20 percent declines in comparison rates to those diagnosed in the period 1973 and 1980. Types of cancer evident in these percentages are uterus, testis, melanoma of skin, breast (10 percent), bladder, Hodgkin's disease (30 percent), uterine cervix (9 percent), colon (7 percent), and rectum (10 percent). Even ovary (5 percent), brain (4 percent), and stomach (4 percent) cancers were evident (National Cancer Institute, 1983). Lifestyles relating to various diseases are presented below. It should be noted that the environment is a crucial element in cancer, with many scientists believing that 80 percent of cancers result from environmental carcinogens.

Table 12.2 DISEASE CONDITIONS AND LIFESTYLES

DISORDERS/DISEASE	LIFESTYLE FACTORS
Diseases of the heart and circulatory system	High fat, highly refined carbohydrate diet, high salt; overweight; sedentary lifestyle; cigarette smoking; heavy drinking, alcoholism; unresolved, continual stress; personality type.
Strokes	Sedentary lifestyle; low fiber, high fat or high salt diet; heavy drinking, alcoholism (which contribute to atherosclerosis, arteriosclerosis, and hypertension, risk factors for cerebrovascular accidents).
Osteoporosis and dental and gum diseases	Malnutrition--inadequate calcium, protein, vitamin K, fluoride, magnesium and vitamin D; lack of exercise; immobility; for women, low estrogen.
Lung diseases such as emphysema	Cigarette smoking; air pollution; stress; sedentary habits.
Obesity	Low caloric output (sedentary), high caloric intake; high stress levels; heavy drinking, alcoholism; low self-esteem.
Cancer	Possible correlation with personality type; stress; exposure to environmental carcinogens over a long period of time; nutritional deficiencies and excesses; radiation; sex steroid hormones; food additives; cigarette smoking; occupational carcinogens (for example, asbestos); viruses; reduced immunity.
Dementia and other forms of memory loss	Malnutrition; long illness and bed rest; drug abuse; anemia; other organ system disease; bereavement; social isolation.
Sexual dysfunction	Ignorance (the older individual and society at large); societal stereotypic attitudes; early socialization; inappropriate or no partner; drug effects (for example, antihypertensive drugs); long periods of abstinence; serious disease.

Adapted from Weg, R. Changing physiology of aging. In D.W. Woodruff and J.E. Birren (eds.), *Aging: Scientific Perspectives and Social Issues*, 1983, p. 274, Monterey, CA: Brooks/Cole

Mental and Emotional Health

These terms are sometimes used interchangeably. There are several basic aspects of mental health: independence, ability to accept reality and to handle feelings of hostility, ability to adjust to a variety of experiences, respect for the rights of others, and ability to keep the emotions under control and feel comfortable with oneself. The incidence of mental disturbance is not known precisely; there are data to suggest, however, that the number in the general population is large. There are approximately 400 state and county mental hospitals, besides many private mental health centers, which alone accounted for nearly 7 million patient-care episodes in 1975.

Using the Hoffer-Osmond Diagnostic Test (providing a perceptual score and depression, paranoia indications), Jones and Heinen (1979) found the incidence of disturbance among volunteer graduate students and laypersons (n=600) aged 20 to 49 to be on the order of 40 out of 100. Those in their twenties were the most disturbed; the incidence of maladjustment dropped off to 25 percent during the thirties (the differences were significant at the .01 level), only to rise again in the forties, with women then having the highest incidence of problems. The male subjects on average were more disturbed in their twenties and thirties than women. The group of male graduate students with the best mental health according to the instrument utilized were those in medicine; among 25 male subjects none was judged maladjusted. The portrait of women characterized as disturbed was as follows:

1) More likely to be the twenties or forties.

2) More often employed in sales and clerical work, or as professionals and housewives.

3) Under more stress than men at that time.

4) More likely to choose mother as the most significant person in their early life.

5) Less likely to describe their present life as very satisfactory.

6) Twice as likely to be black than white.

7) Likely to be changing jobs or beginning a new career.

8) More often sick than men generally and women categorized as normal.

9) Usually visited a clinical psychologist or psychiatrist less frequently than men generally and women classified as normal.

10) More likely to be single or divorced than women categorized as adjusted.

Men who were disturbed had similar portraits, except that they had less stress, less sickness, fewer visits to psychiatrists, and were more likely to be white-collar workers in management. For women, with new stresses stemming perhaps from changing role expectations, the settling of the issue of identity and problems with establishing themselves could account in part for this. Though younger women possess youth and curiosity, they still find these strengths are not sufficient bulwarks against anxiety and tension in making a start on their adult lives. Judged by this research, women in their thirties, although they had more responsibility than women in their forties and participated in more activities, still evidenced less maladjustment and stress. Perhaps by 30 they have adjusted to their life pattern (home, spouse, job), have set goals, have completed or nearly completed their education, and remain physically strong enough to battle the distractions and dream of a better future. By contrast, women in their forties reflecting upon their condition have unfulfilled goals and a great amount of responsibility. They see their strength diminishing, their lives shortening, and dimmer prospects for some future euphoria. Attempts to cope in the competitive workplace lead to alcohol abuse for many and accompanying depression.

An interesting finding of this study (Jones & Heinen) was that among maladjusted males (n=100), not one picked his father as the most significant person in his life. On the other hand, of those judged normal, 42 percent of the men chose their mothers, while another 42 percent chose their fathers.

In a study by HEW (1956) on first admissions to mental hospitals in New York State, it was found that the age with the highest incidence of admission for males was 35 to 44; the years 25 to 34 were high for females. A more recent figure suggests approximately the same finding, except that the incidence of disturbances requiring hospitalization are up in more categories--four times greater in 1975 than in 1955 for admission involving patient-care episodes (National Institute of Mental Health, 1980). Depression is a pervasive and universal problem for both men and women. Role changes demand adjustment for both sexes. The current social, economic, and political climate is not likely to help stabilize fears and encourage confidence. Most persons with personality difficulties will not enter institutions. Many find that with their work, the help of counseling, and support of their families, they can lead lives stable enough to allow functioning at a fairly adequate level.

The Environment and the Effects of Crowding

Though the terms are often used interchangeably, *crowding* is a psychological experience, whereas *density* is a physical one. Both are factors in changing one's life. In some populations both have killed people--like the Indians who were placed upon reservations; they have caused the spread of contagion, and the riots of the 1960s and early 1970s in the ghettos were attributed in part to crowding. In the 1970s sociologists and psychiatrists at London's Bedford College (Levi, 1971) interviewed a random sample of 220 women in Camberwell, a working class district in South London with a population density roughly twice that of London. One-third of the women were found to seek psychiatric help or had symptoms of psychological disorders. However, in Hong Kong there are districts with 2,000 persons per acre with low disease rates, a low rate of mental illness, and less serious crime than in America. Perhaps, as Epstein (1981) points out, the problems may center on management of the environment and the commonality of goals of people in high-density areas like Hong Kong. In the 1960s researchers in the midtown Manhattan study, which was conducted by psychologists and sociologists of Cornell University Medical School, studied 2,000 residents of New York City between 59th and 96th Streets--an ethnically and economically diverse area in which the average population density ran to 600 people per acre, four times that of the city's central core as a whole and 100 times that of the city's more lightly settled sections. Four out of every five people surveyed had symptoms of psychiatric disorders; one of four had neuroses severe enough to disrupt their daily lives. When compared with citywide averages, midtown had twice as much suicide, accidental death, tuberculosis, and juvenile delinquency, and three times as much alcoholism. The study did not attempt to establish the causative factor in these cases as crowding, but suggested that it is related to crowding as in the case of crime--its rate and cause of stress paralleling the difficulties of people (Time-Life Books, 1976). Troll and Fisher (1978), studying 1,660 Manhattan residents between the ages of 20 to 59, found that mental health decreased with age. Twenty years later about half the respondents were found and interviewed when they were between 40 and 79 years of age. Remarkably, men stayed the same and women improved in mental health. Troll (1985) believes that more advancement opportunities of the 1960s and 1970s might have accounted for the improvement, giving subjects more of a chance to improve and adapt.

More evidence that tends to support Fisher and Troll concerning depression among older adults was revealed by the research of Holzer, et al. (1985), presented below (Figure 12.3).

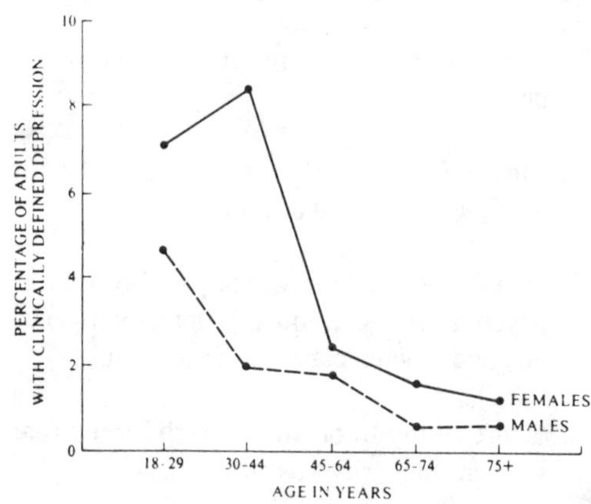

Figure 12.3 Percentage of adults with clinically defined depression.

The elderly, we suppose, were not included in the samples identified above. Most of the nursing homes, and to some degree institutions, would have those over 60 and not primarily those between 40 and 60. Also, nursing home care could be perceived as better than living alone.

Suicide as an indication of depression is much higher for white males than for other groups, showing dramatic rises after the typical retirement age of 65. Retirement "blues" perhaps offer an explanation, as work for most men has been the centerpiece of their lives. Most men also have one or more chronic health problems by the time they reach 65. On a positive note, researchers have noted that the suicide rate has been cut in half since 1940 (McIntosh, 1985).

Suicide rates for both black and white males are high, indicating adjustment among women may be superior to men, due in part to the fact that many are continuing to be supported by a network of friends when they enter into a new role. Many men see no transition into a role equal to that of the workplace. They are also likely to be in poorer health than the typical woman although women show a greater advance of depression. Depression is pervasive and probably the number one problem in mental health. Development of avocations, hobbies, exercise, and the cultivation of support groups and friends will alleviate some of the problems.

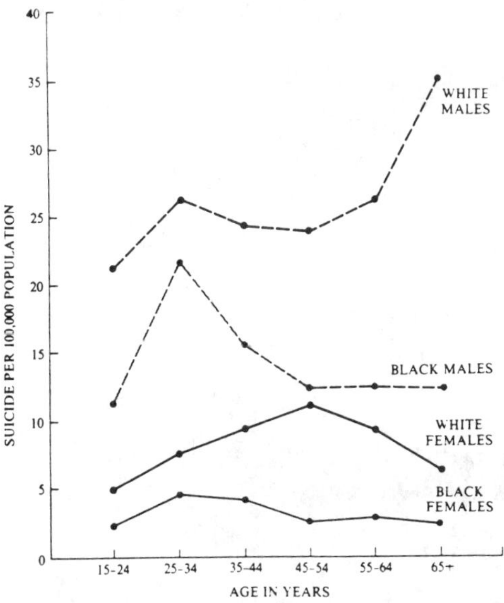

Figure 12.4 Suicide among adults. (*Source:* U.S. Bureau of Census, 1985.)

THE SOCIAL MODE

The middle years have one common denominator for all: they are years when lives are in change. Although life is different in degree for each, there are certain fundamental tasks that are essential if the passage to the later adult years is to be assured. Havighurst (1972) suggested that the middle years (30 to 60) are also the time when society makes its maximum demands upon people--family, the community, and the broader society seeking leadership

Developmental Task

The developmental tasks of this time arise from the changes within the body, from environmental pressures, and from the impetus given by the individual to fulfill his or her aspirations and goals. The significant tasks for the middlescent are as follows:

1) Helping children become responsible and happy adults.
2) Achieving adult social and community responsibility.
3) Maintaining performance in one's occupational career.
4) Relating to one's spouse as a person and equal.
5) Developing leisure-time pursuits.
6) Accepting the physical and mental changes of middle age.
7) Adjusting to the aging and death of parents.

As the adolescent years are the period for learning, and the young adult years the time for beginnings, the middle years are for productivity and consolidation. The middlescent provides the stability, leadership, and care for society's continuance. Whereas the twenties are a time for making commitments and achieving intimacy, and the thirties are a time for giving depth to love relationships, family, and one's occupational pursuit, the forties and fifties are a time of consolidating one's effort. Appraisal frequently takes place at this time, and this evaluation sometimes leads to change of lifestyle, love commitment, occupation, and the reordering of priorities. Often these concerns contrast sharply with the tasks outlined previously. This midlife transition is acknowledged by Levinson (1978), Dimidjian (1980), Loevinger (1976), and Gould (1978), and its significance, particularly for those who feel this is their last chance to make old dreams come true or initiate new ones, is a crucial one.

Cultural Demands

It is difficult for a person to achieve all the tasks prescribed by our culture. Helping children to achieve a responsible, happy, mature adult status demands that parents understand their own development and emotions in order to allow the freedom needed by adolescents to achieve independence. The ability of parents to provide guidance implies a willingness to be firm and fair, being neither oversolicitous nor overpunitive; this allows youth to develop emotional freedom (Duvall, 1971). Parents must provide good models for youth, and consequently they need to be good homemakers, good providers, good citizens, and cooperative in helping children develop their plans.

Many feel that achieving adult social and civic responsibility is not important. For instance, many working men are not interested in social and political problems, nor many times are the women of this age interested in social and civic life (Havighurst, 1972). Agreement among people on ideals and goals is important for the civic health of a democracy; the national life depends upon responsible citizenry. Many of the reform movements in America have been stimulated by civic organizations and community concern. Middle-class women have typically been involved in these groups as a major interest. When women are released from childrearing many begin to take on new jobs and commitments, some to fill the void left by the children and others to continue an earlier social-civic interest.

Many feel it is important in our culture to obtain a home and have enough financial stability to live comfortably. It is true that most men and some women attain their highest status and income during the middle years. Many women

Working together.

return to the work force after their child-rearing period is over, usually as a supplement to the family income in order to help put their children through college, to improve their homes, or to use their time satisfactorily. Often disturbing to middlescent tranquility is the fact that a number of men change their jobs between the ages of 40 and 60. This means beginning again in a new career, and is often very difficult. There may be difficult physical requirements for such jobs as construction, security work, police work, and fire fighting. Or there may be psychological limitations due to excessive noise, tedious paperwork, and the need for exactness in an occupation. Also, retraining or additional education is required in many instances. Many retired Army and Navy officers, for instance, enter college and go into teaching (Jones, 1990). Opportunity exists for many in urban centers to provide counseling and training through the public school systems. Provision for entry into a variety of occupations is made through evening classes, vocational and technical centers, as well as through community colleges. Technological advances will necessitate the phasing out of some workers, and hence there is a requirement for the middle-aged and others to retrain themselves.

Leisure

An adult task for the middlescent is developing leisure-time activities. Many already have enough such activity. There are those who have increasing amounts of time but have developed few leisure-time pursuits. These new activities will differ from early adult ones, principally in that they are not basically physically oriented but sedentary. People, however, should not forget the value of physical exercise or games even if they are middle-aged. Many will take up crafts at this period of time, as available time is more abundant with the pressures of child care, business, or professions lessening. Authorities believe that each individual needs a hobby, recreational pursuits, and activities that will provide sources of pleasure for the coming years.

A problem at this time is that many couples in the middlescent years have difficulty relating to each other. The man who is absorbed in his work during the early part of his adult life may often neglect to provide the attention to his wife that she needs, particularly if she has remained in the home. Men need to learn to be more sensitive and tender with women, while women would benefit from the adoption of such heretofore masculine traits as courage, adventuresomeness, and enterprise (Montagu, 1968). Men, too, need the support of their wives in the middle years as goals of the earlier years remain unfulfilled and appreciation for vocation is being reserved for younger men. What helps is development of leisure pursuits that can be shared.

Many women during the middle years, according to Bernard (1975), become strongly feminist and more aggressive, which is likely to disturb the husband. He may find that he has to adjust to a different type of person after years of marriage. Frequently women become more interested in leadership roles and social problems and become more adventuresome, as Montagu (1968) suggested they should be. Men need to understand this development and provide support. Where conflicts arise over roles, discussion of the issues and developing satisfying leisure pursuits, some of which can be shared, will serve to improve the communication between the partners.

Many women need understanding and the feeling that they are worthwhile during the physical changes that occur during menopause. Increasing numbers of women are having mastectomies and hysterectomies, and although most are successful dealing with the emotional trauma, the ordeal requires considerable support by husband and children.

In a stratified sample of 1,441 persons Gordon, et al. (1976), found the following as to forms of intensity in leisure activity.

TABLE 12.3 Qualitatively varying forms of leisure activity (expressive primacy in personal activity), according to intensity of expressive involvement.

Intensity	Forms of Leisure Activity
Very high	SENSUAL TRANSCENDENCE Sexual activity Psychoactive chemical use Ecstatic religious experience Aggression, "action" (physical fighting, defense or attack, verbal fighting) Highly competitive games and sports Intense and rhythmic dancing
Medium high	CREATIVITY Creative activities (artistic, literary, musical, and so on) Nurturance, altruism Serious discussion, analysis Embellishment of instrumental (art or play in work)
Medium	DEVELOPMENTAL Physical exercise and individual sports Cognitive acquisition (serious reading, disciplined learning) Beauty appreciation, attendance at cultural events (galleries, museums, and so on) Organizational participation (clubs, interest groups) Sightseeing, travel Special learning games and toys
Medium low	DIVERSION Socializing, entertaining Spectator sports Games, toys of most kinds, play Light conversation Hobbies Reading Passive entertainment (as in mass-media usage)
Very low	RELAXATION Solitude Quiet resting Sleeping

(Adapted from Gordon, Gaitz, and Scott, 1976)

Here are some selected activities and participation among men and women over the life span revealed from the Gordon, et al., study (Figure 12.5). It is interesting to note that cooking as an activity increases for men and decreases for women beginning around forty-five years of age. Leisure and recreation by social class in the middle years is presented below, suggesting greater need for exercise (Jones, 1991).

TABLE 12.4 Leisure Participation by Class

	Upper Class	Middle Class	Lower Class
Team Sports	2%	2%	2%
Individual Sports (Tennis, Golf, Bowling, Jogging)	30%	20%	10%
Hobbies	20%	23%	5%
Sedentary (Cards, Televiewing)	48%	55%	82%

According to Aristotle, the attainment of leisure is the purpose of everything we do. The balance of life even in old age should be an even three-part balance--work, learning, and play (Bolley, 1979).

Changes and Responsibilities in the Middle Years--The Middle Man Function

Accepting the changes that come in middlescence is a challenge. Physical and mental changes are significant. The ability to memorize and do rapid calculations is recognizably impaired. Lapses in memory and slower reactions to some kinds of verbal questions or statements are a problem. The heavier physical body and loss of muscle tone and agility create psychological problems that often bring depression. Most changes have to be accepted and adjusted to while others, given some attention, can be changed with a specific program, such as a diet or new leisure pursuits.

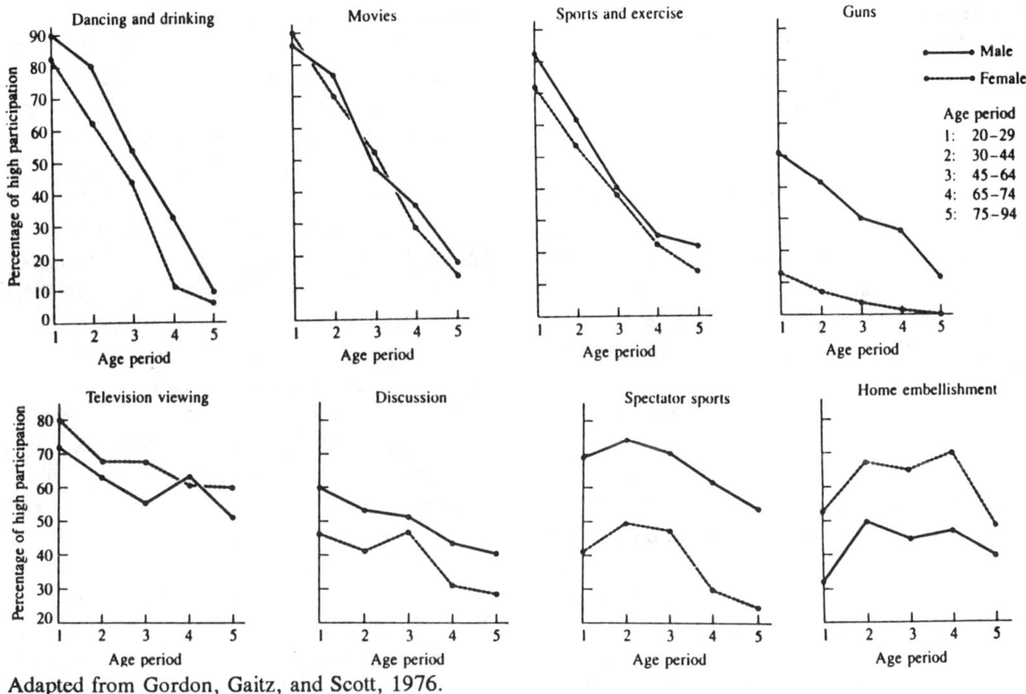

Adapted from Gordon, Gaitz, and Scott, 1976.

Figure 12.5 Selected activities among men and women over the life span.

Mr. and Mrs. In-Between

A final task of the middlescent is one that involves playing *the role of a middle-man.* The middle-man function is the task of helping to emancipate teenage children and at the same time caring for aging parents. This is superimposed on an additional problem of forwarding one's own interests. Most persons feel an obligation to care for their parents, yet neither elderly parents nor their children seem to want to live together. If the economic circumstances are limited and the health of older persons precarious, then living together may be a necessity. Some advantages accrue to the middlescent couple when the parents live with them, since the parents often have excellent rapport with young children and provide assistance with household duties. Looking after the children on occasions is a benefit, and some grandparents also contribute financial help to the family.

Within the American society there are considerable differences among the classes as to how to deal with older parents. On the one hand, older persons with upper-class status usually retain their high status until their demise and frequently live alone. They tend to maintain an active interest in family affairs, business, and church. On the other hand, in the middle class there is often considerable hostility between the generations; only seldom does this involve money, but it relates many times to the unresolved parent-child conflicts that surface when the generations live together (Havighurst, 1972). Often the first instance of older parents' need of their middlescent children is during the continued sickness and/or death of their spouse. Roles of the older parents and the middle-aged child often reverse at this point, when the children assume part or all of the caretaking role from their parents. Children's assistance varies from economic aid, transportation, sharing holidays and travel, and doing some chores and providing gifts for them. When parents have a disabling health problem and cannot or will not live alone, then a decision is imperative. Most often the daughter is the responsible caretaker and the parent a mother (Troll, 1986). Usually this situation is superimposed on newly formed freedom experienced when the children are on their own or in high school or college. The love, money, and energy spent on a parent can create conflict between duty and the needs of the middlescent. Whether to have a housekeeper in the parents' home, to send parents to a nursing home or a relative's home, or bring them into the middlescent family's home, is a crucial consideration requiring patience and fortitude. If the parents are brought into the home of the middlescent child who has older children or even younger ones, the logistics involved in the maintenance of life as usual, establishing the rule of order, and providing respect for each person demands great skill. Where the relations with parents in the early years have been good and the middlescent's expectations and feelings about the necessary adjustment are realistic, this task can be less awesome. In time it may become for many a rewarding experience. Counseling from family service agencies can be of considerable assistance in making a decision and during the transitional phase of relocation.

There is less evidence that lower-class families have these difficulties, although financial problems are the rule. In some instances the grandmother lives with her daughter, allowing the daughter to work while she does the housework and tends to the child care. If the grandmother or father receives social welfare benefits, the effect may facilitate the adjustments required by the family.

Middle-Age Parenting Roles

Two tasks exist for the middlescent parents: (1) relating successfully with their children and helping to emancipate them into the adult world, and (2) adjusting to their absence. The first of these tasks is difficult, for the demands of maturing young persons necessitate that they become independent of their parents. Increasingly, parents have to compromise at least partially on matters that involve their children's friends, styles of dress, vocational interests, leisure time, and personal tastes. Parents assisting children with choices through discussion and by example will serve to inculcate their values and still allow the children to have autonomy. However, even when children have married and have marital troubles, many parents cannot stay out of the arguments, thereby often complicating the situation. Remaining silent is a complex decision, particularly when physical violence is evident or when situations exist involving drug use, multiple infidelity, refusal to work, or criminal activity.

Guttmann (1964) believes that men become more passive and women become more protective and aggressive in this period. Rosenberg and Farrell (1976) have suggested that the mother's role in nurturance and aggression is important to the family's emotional life, and that in time "she pushes her husband from the

Middlescence and socialization.

stage and seems to draw strength from his decline" (p. 163). Among middle-class men there is less authoritarianism during this period. Men of the lower class, however, often abdicate any decision about their children to their wives, particularly when the children have surpassed them in education. Many mothers of all classes, perhaps less in the upper class, serve as confidants to their daughters and sometimes to their sons. Daughters typically view their fathers as models of maleness and some their mothers as models of femaleness. There is considerable research to support the view that parents in their prime of life generally continue to give their children more than they get from them (Aldores, 1987; Troll, 1986).

Postparenthood

The postparental family is new in America; only in the last decade or so have many parents (both) survived the marriage of their youngest child. This means that many middlescent couples are "childless" before they are 60. Women especially have found less marital satisfaction during the early years of childbearing and reached the lowest point just prior to the last adolescent child leaving home (Rollings & Feldman, 1970). On the average, men are 54 and women are 51 when the last child is married. When this occurs the quality of life frequently rises, as more time is left for self, and family resources once committed to educating and caring for children can be used for travel, redecorating, clothes, and entertainment. For many this is only a brief period, since grandparenting soon begins. The feeling of continuity with the future generation, emotional satisfaction, and the idea of being young again through the children were mentioned as positive aspects of grandparenting in a study by Neugarten and Weinstein (1964). Types of grandparenting are as follows:

Traditional: The *formal kind* of grandparent leaves the role of parent to their children and offers special treats on occasion to the grandchildren.

The *surrogate* parent is usually a grandmother who takes care of a child or children at the parent's request and is likely in the home while the mother works.

The *endowed wisdom and special skills* kind of grandparents see themselves as authorities in some aspect of teaching skills.

Informal: The *funseeker* is a grandparent who plays with the children simply to have fun, and usually both the young and old enjoy this.

The *distant-figure style* represents grandparents who relate to the child only on special occasions such as birthdays, holidays, and religious festivals. This type is found among younger or older grandparents--that is, those of 55 to 60 or 75 to 80.

When children leave home during the middle years it creates an "empty nest" syndrome for some women, causing them to seek jobs or other activities. Grandparenting will fill a void for many. Stevens-Long (1979) reports that a number of studies suggest high levels of satisfaction among women who have entered employment after their children were grown. These women still have time for grandparenting.

Marriage

The satisfaction that comes to marriage by persons in the middle years is judged from divorce statistics, questionnaires, interviews, studies utilizing case histories from psychologists and psychiatrists, and studies of socioeconomic status. Marriages are reported to be at their best in the beginning, when general euphoria exists, and again later after about 20 years, when the last children have left home.

As Blood and Wolfe (1960) report, many marriages erode in time. They studied 700 couples, interviewing husbands and wives separately, finding serious erosion had taken place in most marriages after 20 years.

The role expectations that each spouse has of the other determines to a great extent marital satisfaction. Udry (1971) believes that the role expectation of the man and woman should not vary much if the marriage is to be satisfactory. Many forces precipitate role changes and expectations of marriage roles: the women's movement in its various forms, including college and university courses in women's careers, women studies, and psychology; discussion groups on consciousness raising, awareness, and self-confidence; opportunities for women to pursue formerly male-dominated professions; and greater freedom of expression in society; as well as the increase of women in the work force.

Marriages are perhaps most idyllic when the husband has a self-concept that harmonizes with that of his father and the father of the wife. The wife's view, it is assumed, has been internalized from the model of her father. Some believe that marriages must be equal to be healthy and satisfactory. Rapoport and Rapoport (1975) think that this is overdrawn; they contend that the marriage should be equitable rather than trying to have roles be equal. They say people will shift and change at various periods in life, so that the load of household chores, child care, and leadership in family matters will be shared. Resistance to adjustment and role change comes from ingrained traditional views derived from earlier socializations. O'Reilly (1980) expresses this in the statement, "in the end we are all housewives" (p. 69). She says that regardless of a women's career role, those of food server and comforter are the most pervasive. Inequalities are further characterized by West (1982), who reports that men in conversation with females interrupt 96 percent of the time. If men interrupt men, it is criticized as a violation of their rights, but if men interrupt women, it is viewed as inconsequential.

The establishment of equitable decision-making roles requires a change in the notion of feminine and masculine sex stereotypes. An aspect of this problem is expressed by Rapoport and Rapoport (1975, p. 430) by the following questions:

> ...is the man who does not like to sew on buttons expressing a free inclination to have his dislike respected as an individual taste, just as many of his wife's individual tastes should be expressed, or is he responding to sex typing? Conversely, is the women who cannot change a fuse, or who cannot handle financial accounts, only expressing personal inclinations, or is she tied to sex-role binds?

Barbara Forish (1978), on the other hand, says:

> ...women have been programmed to please men. To develop masculine skills, withstand the social pressures that surround working women, sustain interrole and intrarole conflicts many working women experience, these are formidable barriers. Women are frightened of losing the approval of the men upon whom they base their self-evaluation (p. 294).

Satisfaction in Marriage

Unfortunately so many marriages result in divorce that investigators are looking at why couples do not break up. Certainly most suggest the following reasons: (1) the marriage is satisfactory, (2) although no love exists, there are sufficient trade-offs, (3) there is no escape (insufficient help to initiate and carry-through a divorce), (4) lack of emotional strength and courage to both plan and complete the divorce, (5) parents, kin, and friends will not allow it, and (6) an upswing in marriage occurs (children leave, communication improves, or some nagging problems are solved). It is believed that marriage follows a U-shaped cycle, with the early years or the beginning of the U representing the euphoria and nesting period in early marriage; the bottom of the curve represents the middle years with heavy responsibilities; then

Table 12.5 STAYING TOGETHER

MEN	WOMEN
My spouse is my best friend.	My spouse is my best friend.
I like my spouse as a person.	I like my spouse as a person.
Marriage is a long-term commitment.	Marriage is a long-term commitment.
Marriage is sacred.	Marriage is sacred.
We agree on aims and goals.	We agree on aims and goals.
My spouse has grown more interesting.	My spouse has grown more interesting.
I want the relationship to succeed.	I want the relationship to succeed.
An enduring marriage is important to social stability.	We laugh together.
We laugh together.	We agree on a philosophy of life.
I am proud of my spouse's achievements.	We agree on how and how often to show affection.
We agree on a philosophy of life.	An enduring marriage is important to social stability.
We agree about our sex life.	We have a stimulating exchange of ideas.
We agree on how and how often to show affection.	We discuss things calmly.
I confide in my spouse.	We agree about our sex life.
We share outside hobbies and interests.	I am proud of my spouse's achievements.

Adapted from Lauer and Lauer, 1988.

after the children leave home marriage satisfaction increases in the later years (Gruber, Baldini and Schaie, 1986). Lauer and Lauer (1985), in surveying over 300 happily married couples, found the reasons they gave for marriages holding together were quite similar. Sexual compatibility, once thought to be a crucial aspect of marriage, was far down on the list of women and not much higher on the men's. Table 12.5 reveals the most significant reasons given for staying together.

It must be remembered there are many aspects of marriage, such as child-rearing, the home, financial stability, sexual relations, companionships, recreation, social life, status, and opportunities for personal growth. If certain aspects of marriage are lacking, they may often be counterbalanced by other aspects like a spouse's being a good provider, being good with the children, or being "like my parents." When viewed in this manner, marriages may last longer, as couples take a more comprehensive assessment of their lives. This can serve to improve communications about their lives including social activities, work, home management, financial concerns, and values, both in the short- and long-term variety. Figure 12.6 gives a graphic depiction of the stability of marriage.

Divorce and Afterward

The alternatives to traditional marriage are to remain single, get a divorce, participate in a group marriage, or have an open-type marriage. The latter two are apparently not very real alternatives to conventional marriage, judged by the number of persons involved in these types. Apparently, they are too fragile and too hazardous for consideration by the traditional majority (Rogers, 1979). Increasingly, greater numbers of people are staying single longer, and at the same time more are divorcing and remaining single. Changes in the view of divorce and the sheer numbers involved have effected differences that no longer make it difficult to participate in society's mainstream. Greater permissiveness in sexual mores and ability to establish emotional and financial independence allows for many people an unentangled freedom of lifestyle and from responsibility. Most divorced men in this country are between 35 and 44, with the 45-to-54 age group second; for women the 45-to-54 group is first, followed by the 35-to-44 age group. Even when one is divorced as late as in their mid-fifties the typical person remarries, although for older middle-aged women (45 to 64) it is more difficult.

The reasons why almost half of all marriages will end in divorce in 1991 when in 1900 only 1 marriage in 14 did, can be summarized as follows: (1) the change from a rural to urban way of life, (2) change in the status of women, (3) grounds for divorce becoming more numerous and less stringent (such as the use of cruelty, incompatibility, constructive desertion, and no-fault divorce), and (4) loss of values that reinforced the principle of lifelong monogamy.

Factors Involving Divorce

Divorce for many middlescent couples, unlike the young adults who obtain no-fault divorce, requires a court disposition for dissolvement. Principally because they own more property and because of the feeling of stigma of being divorcees, women are often motivated to get a complaint making the husband the offending party. Grounds and petition for divorce usually occur under the following grievances: cruelty, desertion, chronic drunkenness or drug abuse, adultery, imprisonment of the spouse, lack of support, and insanity.

The nature of divorce is complex and it does not occur overnight. Many varied factors interact, as suggested by Levinger and Moles (1979), on the stability of marriage. There are two features to this scheme (Figure 12.6): on one hand, external support and internal attractions tend to keep marriages together and, on the other hand, external attractions work against marriage. If the supports are indeed commanding enough in terms of the internal attraction, then the marriage will be healthy. If the internal attractions are insufficient, then the marriage may stay together because of such external factors as legal barriers, children, or career needs. When the external attractions to escape marriage become strong enough, then the emotional ties to marriage will be broken. If the

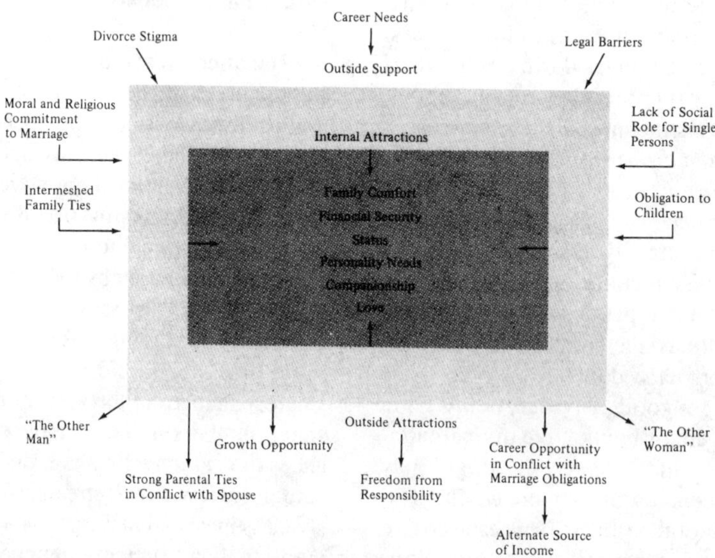

Figure 12.6 Factors in the stability of marriage. (*Source:* Levinger, 1965.)

impetus from these stimuli--the attraction of another man or woman, growth opportunities, and so on--is continued, then divorce is inevitable.

No matter how desirable relief from a poor marriage is, divorce usually does not occur without problems. Only in a few situations will the promise of euphoria outweigh the guilt, anguish, legal matters, effects on others (especially children), and numerous adjustments. Two such situations are where one or both spouses have a love relation awaiting fulfillment, or where fear exists for personal safety. Many persons, particularly women, when considering future loneliness may give up the idea of divorce or rejoin their spouse if they have separated. Men, when they reflect on the fact that the wife has looked after their children, the home, social life, food, and clothing often decide to return to the spouse. Hof and Dwyer (1982) have utilized value analysis as a tool for examining obstacles and to explain the current behavior of married couples as individuals. They have added to the cost-award analysis a new element they call perception of risks. This element is introduced into the marriage scenario to raise the issue of what might be lost with change--security, status, children, affection, and so on. This type of analysis has been found to add an aspect to the decision about married problems that is frequently overlooked.

Divorce for women in their middle years is usually more difficult than for men, because women have fewer resources. Economically, there is less emotional and psychological support outside the home and a reduced chance of getting married again. If middle-aged women have young children when they attempt to enter the job market, the prospects for success are cloudy. When marriages have continued for a long period, 20 to 30 years, divorce creates difficulty in adjustment--lingering unhappiness, bitterness, and even depression are often the result (Chiriboga, 1982). Eventually the economic status of men who continue to work rises as women's typically falls.

Remarriage

The chances of establishing a romantic connection and finding a marriage partner are much easier for men than for women, who must compete with younger women for a new partner (Whiting, 1984). Since physical attraction is the standard of desirability in our society, women past 55 and 60 will have little chance of finding a husband and even some difficulty in finding a person with whom to have an intimate relationship (Katchadourian, 1987). On a positive note, Furstenberg (1987) found in his studies that women are about as well off when they do marry the second time as the first. Men report happiness at the same level of the first marriage and women only slightly less so (Glenn and Weaver, 1977). Black women have less chance of remarrying while the more educated of both races have a better chance to do so. Happiness and satisfaction in marriage are not age related.

Stress and Divorce

Holmes and Rahe (1976) examined stress in the lives of 5,000 subjects from the United States, Canada, Europe, and Japan and were able to rank life events according to stress. The highest stress value for a life event was 100 life change units for the death of a spouse; the next two events were divorce (73 LCUs) and separation (65 LCUs)--all higher than a jail term (63 LCUs). The rate of deaths among divorced people due to alcoholism, drug abuse, and suicide parallels this assessment. Sometimes people can avoid divorce by consulting a marriage counselor or minister who is trained in dealing with such problems.

In 1972 Rahe found among 400 subjects involved in stress that those reporting less than 150 life change values in the past year remained healthy but those who scored 300 or above were likely to have a significant physical or mental health problem in the ensuing year. A number of other stress conditions might be coupled, particularly if children are involved, such as change in work hours, change in school, residence, living conditions, social activities, etc., all adding to stress and pushing the LCU units to 150 or beyond.

Work Life and Career Adjustment

Work is the most pervasive, common factor in the lives of adults. Its social meaning identifies persons as adults. Through work people are recognized in that they are needed by others and are a part of the social fabric. Kaplan and Tausky (1972) epitomize the place of work in America when they say:

> in the United States it is a bluntly and ruthlessly public fact that to do nothing is to be nothing and to do little is to be little. To be unemployed, especially a man, is to be a social outcast whose very membership in American society is suspended (p. 469).

Since this is true, it is understandable that most of the hard-core unemployed wish to work and if possible to get off welfare (Kaplan & Tausky, 1972). Work is the glue that holds life together; it has been recognized by mental health authorities as making it possible for those with personality difficulties to survive outside of institutions, for work provides a structure through which they can function and can gain stability.

A study by Entine (1974) of 37 "career dropouts" aged 35 to 55, who chose voluntarily to leave successful white-collar jobs or professional careers, found most of these people were dissatisfied with the concept of work in a career system as the means to personally rewarding employment. They had varied conflicts with their employers, were bored, and felt put upon by the work they did, feeling it was meaningless. After quitting and taking new jobs and positions, they were happy, although for most it meant harder work, less prestige, and smaller

Rank	LIFE EVENT	Mean Value (life-change units)
1	Death of spouse	100
2	Divorce	73
3	Marital separation	65
4	Jail term	63
5	Death of close family member	63
6	Personal injury or illness	53
7	Marriage	50
8	Fired at work	47
9	Marital reconciliation	45
10	Retirement	45
11	Change in health of family member	44
12	Pregnancy	40
13	Sex difficulties	39
14	Gain of new family member	39
15	Business readjustment	39
16	Change in financial state	38
17	Death of close friend	37
18	Change to different line of work	36
19	Change in # of arguments w/spouse	35
20	Mortgage over $10,000	31
21	Foreclosure of mortgage or loan	30
22	Change in responsibilities at work	29
23	Son or daughter leaving home	29
24	Trouble with in-laws	29
25	Outstanding personal achievement	28
26	Wife begins or stops work	26
27	Begin or end school	26
28	Change in living conditions	25
29	Revision of personal habits	24
30	Trouble with boss	23
31	Change in work hours or conditions	20
32	Change in residence	20
33	Change in schools	20
34	Change in recreation	19
35	Change in church activities	19
36	Change in social activities	18
37	Mortgage or loan less than $10,000	17
38	Change in sleeping habits	16
39	Change in number of family get-togethers	15
40	Change in eating habits	15
41	Vacation	13
42	Christmas	12
43	Minor violations of the law	11

amounts of money. There is an alienation outside of work. Vocational educators and counselors need to give attention to helping individuals find satisfying types of work that will embellish their lives. Nestor (1980), a counselor reporting on women 35 to 65, found such women contradicted age stereotypes in utilizing courage and ingenuity to find satisfactory work outlets.

The existential movement's coloration of today's world is having an effect on the ways of defining achievement. For most of the 20th century, work has been judged successful if it brought material things--homes, cars, clothes, vacations, and so on. However, recently the benchmark of success was often evaluated by criteria involving quality of work, the effect of the work on self-fulfillment, and freedom relating to the job. Forty percent of adults interviewed in 1974 by Yankelovich said they would take economic risks to improve the quality of their lives. Rogers (1979) lists five factors accounting for a new work ethic: (1) new ways of defining success, (2) a change in employee-employer relationships, (3) less anxiety over economic matters, (4) the belief in the right to have a job, and (5) loss of faith in the "cult of efficiency." Many older workers have had as their chief motivation economic security, but many younger middlescent men 35 to 45 among the middle class are concerned about what the job does to them and their self-fulfillment. Kohn (1980), writing about job complexity and adult personality, suggests that among 50 separate dimensions of occupation--such as flow of work, relationships with coworkers and supervisors, pace of work, and fringe benefits--that "substantive (basic) complexity of work is the single most pervasive and important element for men's and women's psychological functioning." The lower class worker is demanding better working conditions and fringe benefits, some of which have to do with the quality of life. Their interests have been focused on survival needs, but this is changing through increased education and information from unions and cooperative organizations.

Yankelovich (1974) found that work, beyond economic functions, structures time, provides a context for relating to other people, offers an escape from boredom, and sustains a sense of worth. Among males aged 55 to 64, 74.3 percent were actually in the labor force in 1980, though by 1990 this is projected to drop to 69.9 percent; for women 41.9 percent were in the labor force in 1980, growing to 42.3 for 1990 (Morrison, 1982).

When workers rate job satisfaction, 89 percent like it a great deal as compared with 33 percent who say their work is just a job (Giese, 1987). In 1985 during any given week, 4.7 percent of the workers in the U.S. took some unscheduled time off from work. In Europe 7.7 percent took time off from work, the Netherlands 5.4 percent, Canada 11.6 percent, England 11.8 percent, and France 5.9 percent. Also, in other countries like those above workers get longer holidays (Church, 1987).

Job Discontent and Problems

Discontent with work is often expressed by high rates of absenteeism and job mobility, slowdown in production, wildcat strikes, and even sabotage. Related also to job dissatisfaction is the use of alcohol and drugs in coping with work problems. Pressure on the job has been linked to heart attacks, ulcers, rheumatism, and mental disease (Upjohn Institute, 1973). A report by that institute involving a cross-sectional survey of white-collar workers including professionals, found that only 43 percent would choose voluntarily to do the same work; among blue-collar workers only 24 percent would do so. Job satisfaction is associated with opportunities to share in decision making, to use their own judgments, and to be allowed to accept problem-solving challenges independently. Having a sense of self-respect, opportunity to perform in challenging significant work and achieve personal growth, is basic to satisfaction.

Women Workers

Although figures vary as to the percent of women in the labor force, between 1980 and 1990 the number of women in the work force is expected to increase 60 percent, even though unemployment affects women first (U.S. Department of Labor, 1982). Among women with children 6 to 17, 50 percent are employed outside the home (Rogers, 1979). A new study by the Census Bureau shows that there are 5.9 million families, or 12 percent of all U.S. families, in which women earn more than their husbands (*U.S. News & World Report*, 1984). As pointed out in the previous chapter, 9 of 10 women will hold employment outside the home at some time in their lives. Many women will reenter or enter for the first time into the job market, even though it requires further education during the middle years. Many do this because they need the money, many to receive satisfaction of achievement that sometimes is lacking in housework, and many for self-fulfillment. In a study of work among mothers of preschoolers 51 percent said they would work even if the husband's earnings were sufficient for economic maintenance. Some 56 percent of the mothers of older children said they would do the same (Popenoe, 1976).

PSYCHOLOGICAL MODE

Change in the middle years has long been an absorbing topic for many researchers. Normative changes occur in some general ways that are observable in the later middle years around 55 as noted by Guttman (1977). Men perhaps are less masculine and more nurturing and passive, and women are more concerned with active mastery, tending to become more forceful, domineering, managerial, and independent. Others believe that gender roles are more a fusion of androgyny than switching male and female roles of earlier times. Nevertheless, change occurs that is recognized as Lord Tennyson wrote in the Princess, "In the long years liker must they grow; the man be more of a woman, she of man." Certainly psychological change affects personality--the lessening of strength, some mellowing and less aggression for men.

Personality and Change

Evidence from research generally supports the notion of stability in personality, but since personality is complex and variegated some change shows itself. Epstein (1980) and Finn (1986) found contradictions to status quo continuation of personality in midlife. Stability marks many attributes of personality such as cognitive style, intelligence, and self-concept, but less so interpersonal relationships, behavior, and attitudes (Mischel, 1969). Kelly and Connely (1987), investigating personality constancy as part of a longitudinal study on marriage, examined subjects 20 years apart with the final sample representing 86 percent of the originals in the study (300 subjects). Of 38 variables measured no change was evidenced in 20; some change was revealed in 18, but not substantial. The most consistency occurred in vocational interests and values; self-ratings were moderately consistent; attitudes toward marriage, religion, entertaining and the like were least consistent. Mischel (1969) suggests that stability over time may well be the case with personality even though there is variability from one situation to another.

Woodruff and Birren (1972), followed up a 1944 study of college students that utilized the California Test of Personality 25 years later and found that men and women described themselves in virtually the same words they had used earlier. In the follow-up on the Berkeley and Oakland studies the youths were assessed at the beginning of their teens and later in their thirties and forties, on 90 personality items. Scales found statistically significant correlations, though they differed individually in personality over time. Costa, et al. (1986), at the Gerontological Research Center in Baltimore have examined individual scores over time on standardized self-report personality scales, finding considerable continuity. Assertive 19-year-olds were likely to be assertive at 40; neurotics were likely to be complainers throughout life. A mellowing does occur and most of the subjects dropped a few standard points on tests of temperament and personality.

Whether cultural changes are responsible for changes in men more than maturational factors is questionable, according to Helson and Moane (1987). They note men over 50 had become more tolerant, cooperative, meditative and less forceably masculine, and women increased in confidence and coping skills. Some of the male traits were thought to be associated with acceptable patterns for middlescent and older men.

Women Change

There may be a relation between Levinson's stage of "becoming one's own man" and the developmental stage in women identified by Droge's study (1982) and the theory by Dimidjian (1980). Women in their late thirties begin to identify themselves in a broader context--the dreams of women in their thirties was to incorporate both career and marriage, according to Droge's study. Dimidjian, in her study of professional women in their thirties, found that career interests were the most important aspect of their lives. They also identify the importance of a "special other." Women seem to have difficulty in middle life--they enter work later and have, if single or divorced, more difficulty in finding a mate.

Troll suggests two interesting ideas which she identifies through the use of two Greek mythological characters--Cassandra and Tantalus. Cassandra was the Trojan princess who was worried and agitated, not unlike many middle-aged women of today. Troll says that today's women is a "worrier par excellence; since birth she is tuned in to the feelings of others--her family (their woes), her children's and their husbands' problems." She wonders if she gives them enough attention. Later she wonders if her children's marriages are good and if they are turning out right. The Cassandras of today worry about their husbands and their jobs, their grown children's values, and finally their own fulfillment. The second character--Tantalus--was forever reaching for something beyond his reach, good things seemingly close at hand. The middle-class woman believes that she can capture the dream of a career or resume old pursuits after years of being a housewife. She finds she cannot make up the years lost to the family. These elements certainly appear in the lives of the middlescent woman particularly among the middle class. It would appear that women make changes in career and family commitment due to age rather than a desire for greater expression. Divorce often occurs for many when the children leave home, when a shift in values may occur in the late forties or early fifties. Real modifications made by women are usually healthy, for these adventurers escape the middle-age blues and typically show high self-esteem (Papalia and Olds, 1989). To associate women with the Levinson stages is not appropriate except as a general comparison, for in that study only men were involved. The major aspects of women's lives are the birth of their children, the launching of them into the work world, and the post-parental period. Women are oriented first to their families, then to careers and self-fulfillment. Men usually are oriented to career and later to family and nurturance.

Middle Crisis or Transition

Many think that a crisis or major adjustment occurs between the years of 35 and 50, with the majority of researchers suggesting between 40 and 50. Jacques (1967) suggests 35; Gould (1972) thinks 35 to 42 are the transitional years, and questions are resolved between 43 and 50. Levinson noted that the midlife transition peaks in the early forties. Neugarten and Weinstein (1964) believe the crisis comes in the fifties. It also might be regarded as part of the shift to retirement and older age. There is no dispute that change and crisis do occur. In examining the literature concerning the life span, a consensus suggests that many persons have three transitional periods, not counting adolescence: one in early adulthood, perhaps at 28 to 34; one in middlescence, 39 to 49; and one on the eve of the later years, around 60 to 70. Roles people play are the important element in their lives. Although years provide markers that mean something in the broad sense, the roles are different for some, as evidenced by the healthy 93-year-old woman still driving who, when asked when middle-age begins, replied "60" (Jones, 1976).

Descriptions of the crisis vary from a re-evaluation of one's life pattern to an acknowledgment of a decrease in life's satisfactions and the ability to cope. Some believe stress is likely to accompany a serious midlife crisis, but Costa and McCrae (1980) looked at stress in men 30 to 35 and found young men had more stress than older men. This result was documented by Jones and Heinen (1979). Long and Porter (1984) found major readjustments among some women served to be exhilarating and to many desirable. Bee (1988) thinks there may be crises among educated white males but few among the general population. In fact, she labels it a "myth." Steinberg and Silverberg (1988) found that the women in their study who were dissatisfied with life were often concerned about identity but not typically involved in crises. Certainly change must take place along with adjustment. The psychoanalytic perspective, forever true to its calling, suggests that part of the middle-age phenomenon, "the phantom self," has origins in childhood (Perry, 1989) and even the evolution of defense mechanisms to more mature ones relate to adjustments from earlier problems (Vaillant, 1977). Hence for the psychoanalysts a unique crisis does not exist outside of an earlier formation. So for them time, circumstance, age, or other variables are not critical aspects of the midlife crises.

McGill (1980) believes the midlife crises will affect considerably more than 25 to 33 percent of men between the ages of 40 and 60 now thought to be involved in this development. Neugarten and Datan (1973) believe there is no general crisis during the middle years. There are still others whose life is positive and productive with little need for radical change or apathy. The transition from one period to another is smoothly made, perhaps by quiet dialogues with oneself.

Also Lowenthal and Chiriboga (1973), who studied middle-aged couples in San Francisco, found no evidence of midlife crisis. There were those in the study who had serious problems which to the investigators appeared to be a continuation of early ones. Relief was expressed by most of the couples when their last child left home. When asked to name the significant turning points in their lives, they reported completing school, getting their first jobs or advancements in their work, getting married, and having children. Some of the women, but none of the men, noted beginning to date, meeting their future mates, having an affair, separating because of illness or death, moving, getting a divorce, and leaving home. More of the women than the men perceived these events negatively, but women reported more stress than men. According to Bernard (1973), the sex difference may result in the unacceptability for men to admit anything is wrong with their mental health, or it may be that women's life roles are less healthy. Based upon subjects in a recent study, Lowenthal and Chiriboga (1973) believe that adult reaction to stress can be predicted from earlier lifestyles.

In summary, the midlife crisis seems identifiable by many, but others simply see it as adjustment. Its positive significance is that it calls for reflections and questioning that often lead to the creation of a new version of oneself and insights that were unavailable at earlier times. Seen at its worst, the crisis issues (work life, divorce, health change) may not be allowed to surface and be resolved in terms of growth for the individual. In such a case it may result in destructive reaction formation, hostility, and conflicts involving both the person in crisis and others closely related (Dewald, 1981).

Personality Development and Adjustments

Although there is disagreement among life span psychologists as to precisely when various significant changes or crises occur, there is general agreement that the personality is not forever fixed in childhood or early adulthood. They also agree that, despite change in physical and intellectual abilities, which in the aggregate represent losses, such losses are offset by the possibility of positive personal growth. The egocentric nature of personality development in the adolescent and young adult gives way to becoming nurturing, extrinsically oriented, and less self-concerned. Osherson (1980) focuses on three aspects of maturation in midlife: (1) increased learning about self and ability to have internal dialogue about one's experience, (2) increased recognition of the complexity of self and others, and (3) a greater capacity for autonomous choice and decision making in one's life.

Robert Peck (1968) has described personality in the middle years in terms of four psychological developments basic to effective adjustment through these years.

1) Valuing wisdom over physical strength. The knowledge people have gained over the years helps let them make wise choices and

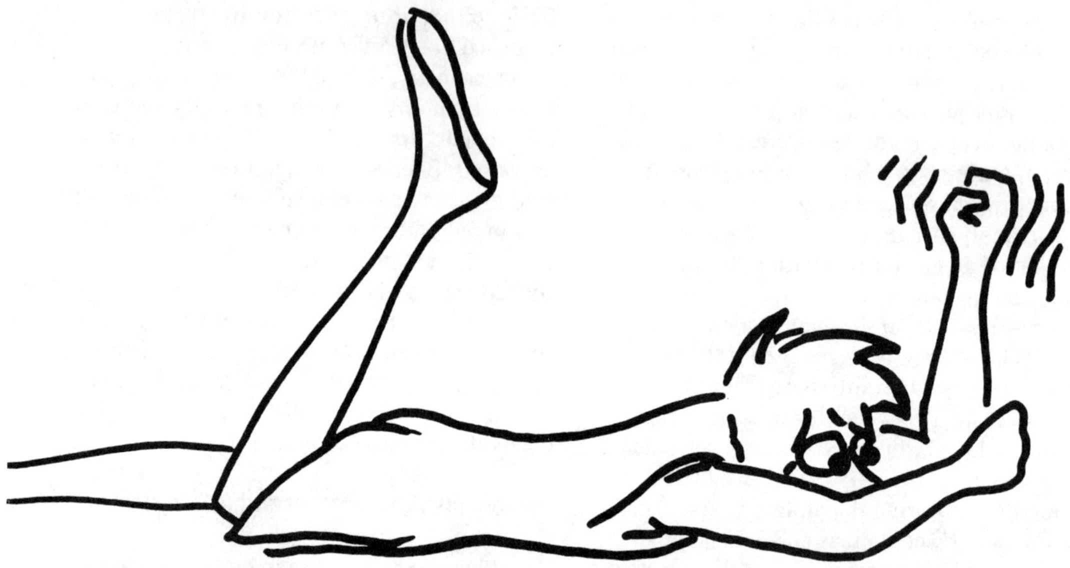

Temper tantrums occur in this age group with distressing frequency

compensates for declining physical strength and looks.

2) Valuing socializing over sexualizing. Friendship and trust and support in interpersonal relationships mean more than sex.

3) Valuing cathetic flexibility over cathetic impoverishment. Cathetic emotional flexibility is crucial because the deaths of spouses, parents, and friendships during the middle years require considerable adjustment.

4) Valuing mental flexibility over mental rigidity. The key in middle age is adaptation. New solutions are needed. Flexibility helps balance past experience.

By 60 years of age many women are trying to adjust to widowhood. Bahr and Harvey (1980) found that among the newly widowed, education and income correlate, suggesting that widows with lower levels of education and income have poorer morale and therefore need to be given special attention from counselors and supporters. These views by Peck are extensions of those of Erikson concerning his stage of generativity versus stagnation.

Personality Patterns

We dealt with characteristics of the personality that were stable in Chapter 6--research by Kagan and Moss (1962) indicating that the personality variable that correlated the highest with childhood rating and adult rating was achievement, with sex-typed activity following next. Kelly (1955), who investigated personality change through using self-rating on 38 variables over a 20-year period, found nonsignificant differences in the early and late average scores. Woodruff and Birren (1972) found people tend to think more changes have occurred than have. In measuring personal and social adjustment the subjects (at the age of 45) in this study were asked to respond to the early personality test again as they remembered they had before. The remembered scores were lower than the original ones, suggesting that they were better adjusted 25 years earlier than they thought. Comparing scores of this group when they were 20 and the scores at 45 years of age, there was no significant difference, suggesting that age affects personality in only a few broad ways. Personality is thought to be predictable due to genotypic continuity, and changes in behavior do not necessarily indicate instability in personality. Nonetheless, earlier traits in the adolescent may be reversed from dependent and happy to become independent and unhappy. Change may occur, but it would be in the same direction for all individuals of a particular type (Livson, 1973). Few of these types of studies have been done. Most are phenotypic (obvious traits), which examine the extent that particular traits, disposition, and skills are stable over different times of measurement (Livson, 1973). Generally, cross-sectional studies support the view that personality traits are stable; but if subjects are matched for socio-economic level, education, cultural background, and marital status, evidence of change emerges (Neugarten & Hagestad, 1977). Phenotypic continuity is seen in Table 12.6 which looks at the Berkeley subjects at midlife.

A more recent analysis of the Berkeley data by Haan, et al. (1985-1986), using Q-sorts identified six patterns or components of personality. These patterns stated in continuum form are: self confident-victimized (comfort with oneself and belief in acceptance); assertive-submissive (direct and aggressive style of life); cognitively committed (intellectual and achievement orientation); outgoing-aloof (the social enjoyment of others); dependable (controlled-productivity); and warm-hostile (interpersonal giving and support). It was found that orderly positive progression through development was observed for all of the personality components except assertive-submissive, where women particularly regressed from assertiveness highs in their early forties to a more submissive stance by 54 to 61. From cognitive theory the perception of life and change is important. Many women who are frustrated cannot break out of their homebound situation. Therefore, they may indeed adopt submissiveness to curry favors within the family (husband and demanding teenaged children) instead of assertiveness in terms of outside employment and careers, education, etc., as can some middle and upper middle class women. Control is another factor in their condition. Control may be limited to mundane family routines. The view of the coming of menopause or other experiences probably affected these scores. Typically, by 60 years of age assertiveness among men and women is less evident as is the cognitively committed aspect paralleling both mental and physical change. The patterns in men and women follow.

Values and Change

In middle age most people have a system of values that serve to provide ready-made answers for most of life's problems and successes. It is important, however, that these are held as general guidelines and bases for making tentative decisions, since some entirely new adjustments will be required during this period. New issues and problems arise constantly during the middle years, demanding flexibility and the investment of energy in new people. Those that are unable to do this vegetate, or in Erikson's terms, *stagnate*. The ability to try out new things, to discuss new ideas, and to stay alert to change in one's surroundings and the wider

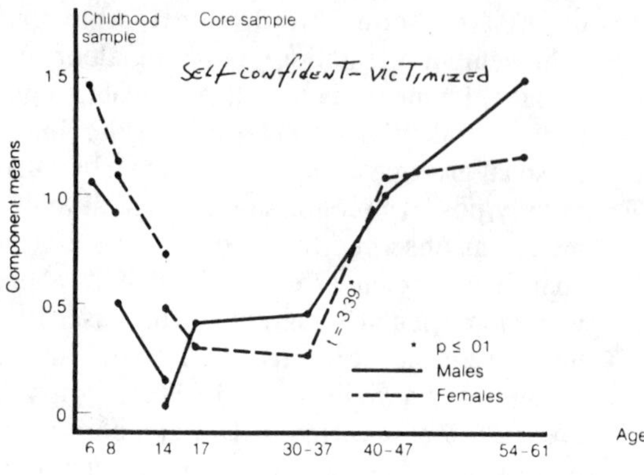

Figure 12.7

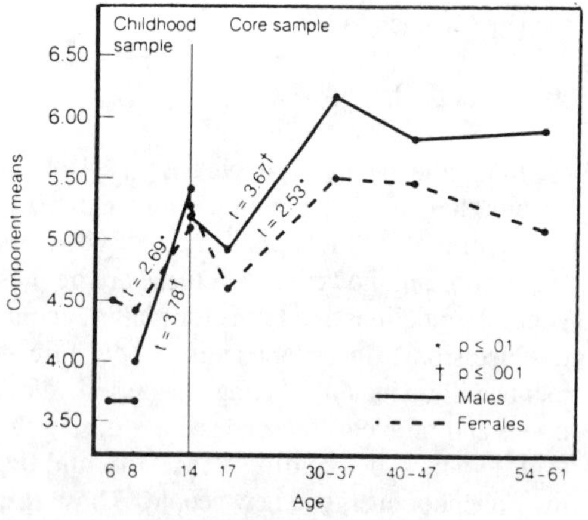

e. Average scores for dependable

Figure 12.8

a. Average scores for self-confident-victimized

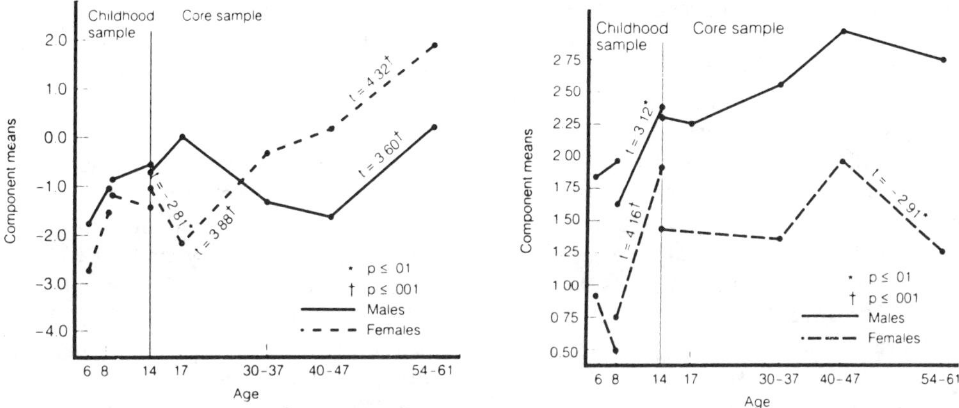

Figure 12.9 (After Haan.)

world, is important for successful living as one grows older. Some people have faced these problems earlier in life, and mature adults have made successful emotional adjustments to them.

Rokeach (1979), in a cross-sectional longitudinal study of values over the life span (the entire sample was composed of some 2,500 subjects), found that significant changes in values occurred over the life span in 30 to 36 instrumental and terminal values. Rokeach stated, "The general impression gained from an inspection of the data reveals one of continuous value change from early adolescence through old age with the presence of several generation gaps rather than just one" (p. 246). The three most important terminal values across the life span were world at peace, family security, and freedom. Peace was number one for those in their forties and fifties. Among instrumental values, loving shows the most clear-cut linear relation to age. It begins as second in importance among 11-year-olds and declines to 14th for people beyond 70. Honesty is the most stable of all the 36 values, its composite ranking being first for all age groups without exception. Salvation, a Christian value, ranked high among older people, but had little status among Jews and among people who held no religious beliefs. Organizing the values into development patterns, the cluster representing freedom, happiness, social recognition, courage, honesty, and self-control showed little fluctuations with age. If values change (Rokeach found they were significant for age), one can then argue for personality changes. Some become more rigid, others more flexible.

Self-Confidence and Self-Concept

Self-confidence grows in the early adult years and continues to increase in the forties (Vaillant, 1977). Gutmann (1975) believes people begin to concentrate in the middle years on thought and feelings instead of actions and events, becoming less confident that they can control their lives by their own actions. Among middle-aged men (Bardwick, 1971), the source of self-esteem is found in the success of their work. On the other hand, Livson (1973) found that married women who typically function successfully in their fifties fall into two categories. Both had developed stable personality styles by the time of adolescence, but followed different routes to psychological development. The first type were traditional, conventional, sociable, and nurturant. These women transited easily into middlescence by finding satisfaction in their families and children. The second type were career-oriented and unconventional. They were doers instead of socializers from their earlier years. As 40-year-olds, they were depressed and irritable in many cases, but with their children gone they resumed their intellectual and career interests.

Perhaps the broadest changes that occur in the middle years, as indicated from the studies of Gutmann (1975) and Eisdorfer and Lawton (1973), take place between the ages of 40 and 60. Between these years a number of events occur. At the beginning of this period, the pervasive view of younger middlescent persons is that they can control their environment; they are still aggressive and positive in achieving certain goals, particularly the women. On the other hand, those at the latter end of this period, when judged by projective tests in which the subjects viewed and interpreted scenes representing situations involving middlescent people, found greater passivity among men and a lessening of active mastery, and for women, increases in those over 55. Four components of self-concept indicate male and female differences (Figure 12.10). Conversely they possess greater nurturance than earlier. In women assertiveness is the rule, with egocentrism developing into a larger dimension than found in younger women. The change in the physical organism, particularly the reduction in androgen and estrogen hormones, as noted by Masters and Ballew (1965), parallels somewhat the role

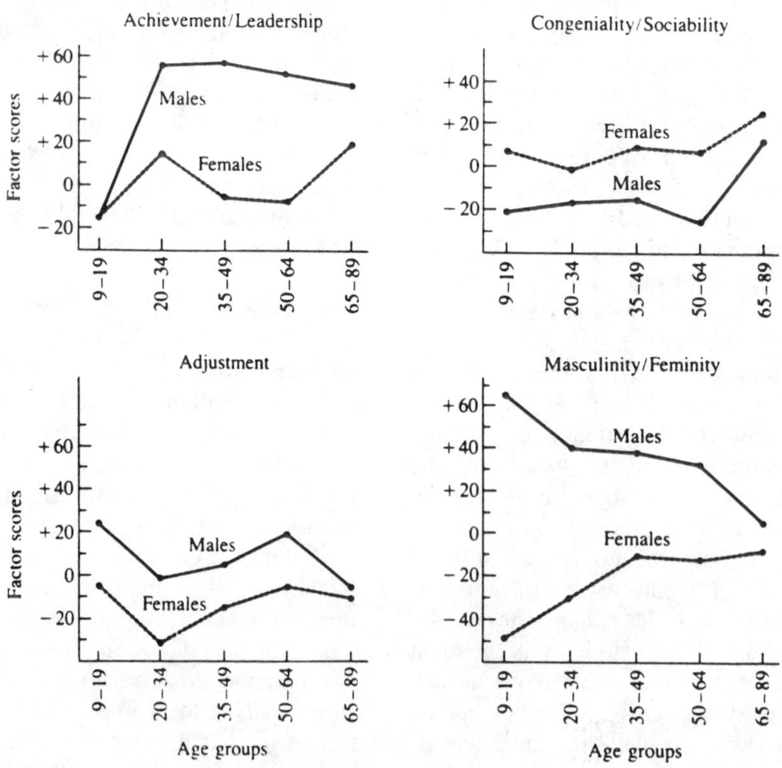

Figure 12.10 Sex and age differences in four components of the self-concept. (*Source:* Monge, 1975.)

reversal for men and women. The cleavage between sex roles obviously declines partly as a function of disuse of critical life events, with child-bearing over, married or love companionship issues usually settled, and the "fires of youth" diminished. Change in personality is likely over the years. Studies reveal correlations of only .30 to .50 on earlier traits when the subjects are in their forties. However, if we assume the .50 figure as a reasonable one, this represents only 13 percent better than chance for cross-prediction purposes (efficiency of prediction formula $E = 1 - \sqrt{1-R^2}$), suggesting that for some considerable change occurs.

Middlescent--self-involved.

Coping with Stress

Persons and various social groups adjust to stress in different ways. In a study of some 300 managers ("Only married men need apply," 1976), two groups were identified as high and low stress types. The high stress groups were characterized as excessively competitive, aggressive, hostile, and unconcerned with anything other than their work. Their way of dealing with stress was to work harder, while low stress men typically used five coping mechanisms: (1) building resistance by regular sleep and good health habits, (2) keeping work separate from other activities, (3) getting exercise, (4) talking things over at work with their peers, and (5) taking breaks physically from a situation when necessary. The researchers thought that the differences between the two types were "working harder" or "working smarter," with the former constantly working to overcome the problems and the latter relaxing through a change of pace that allowed them to organize their work more effectively under calmer conditions.

General Adaptation Syndrome

Stress created enough damage over the years to be a large contributor to heart attacks, ulcers, and numerous other difficulties. Emotional stress can be described as a condition involving tension, frustration, or conflict. Anxiety may or may not be present. Prolonged stress, as we

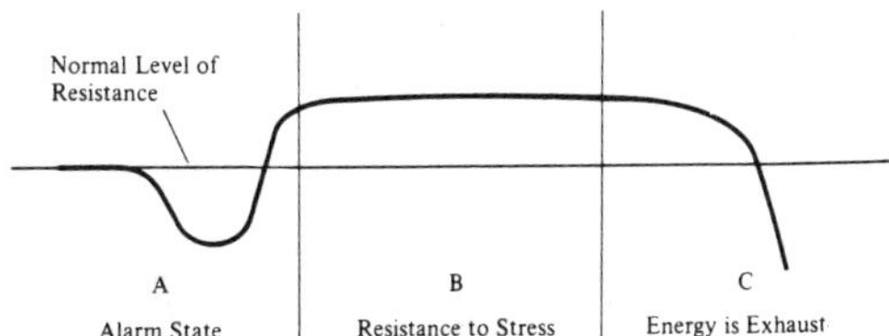

Figure 12.11 Theory of human stress.

indicated, can have severe, damaging effects on both physical and emotional health. Following the theory of Hans Selye (1976), the General Adaptation Syndrome (GAS) involves the physical manifestations of stress. The three stages involved in the GAS are as follows:

1. The alarm reaction. The body mobilizes its defense mechanisms (avoidance, repression, regression, sublimation, and so on). If the stress continues for some time, the next stage is entered.

2. Resistance to stress. The person maximizes his or her ability to withstand the stressor. This may continue for months, depending on the strength of the person and the amount of rest he or she can secure during this maximum resistance effort. This stress puts considerable strain on the organism's resources, so that psychosomatic disorders often occur. Under chronic duress, the third stage is likely to be reached.

3. Exhaustion. In this stage devitalization sets in, and the power to fight the stress is effectively lessened. All body functions are weakened, and the internal resources for dealing with the problem are virtually nil. If this stage is continued long, energy is exhausted and death ensues.

Stressful events that precipitated the onset of psychosis were examined by Bowers and coworkers (1980). These investigators studied 45 men and women aged 30 to 59 over time and had three independent specialists rate the charts for the events associated with the onset of psychosis. Table 12.7 indicates the results by category of stress, items, and incidence.

Stress on the Job, Unemployment and Burnout

Occupational stress is a common occurrence. It occurs when people are in jobs they do not like or low-status jobs that consist of highly repetitive or emotionally connected work, such as in health care, factories, personnel service, and fast food, etc. The biggest work-related stressor is no work at all. The worst circumstance is unexpected loss of a job. Two significant aspects are involved here: the loss of income and the loss of self esteem (Voydanoff, 1983). Many persons laid off from their employment develop health problems they never had before--high sugar levels, heart problems, hypertension and eating difficulties (Perrucci and Targ, 1984). Being able to put the job loss in perspective helps, as does the support of family and friends. If the loss allows for new opportunity and is seen as a challenge, its effects will be mitigated. Those in lower socioeconomic levels who lose their jobs will have more problems, for they often lack intellectual and technical skills that make them employable.

Burnout is characterized by emotional exhaustion on the job and the feeling that one cannot accomplish any more. Burnout is especially common among people in the helping professions--teaching, medicine, social work, and police work, and it often strikes those who are the most dedicated. They get frustrated in trying to help people as much as they would like (Jones, 1991). Vacation, relaxation, exercise, and a job change are helpful. Stress on the job, whether or not it results in burnout, often involves the following:

- Low pay
- Work quotas
- Lack of recognition and promotion
- Long hours, few breaks
- Lack of support and an unsupportive boss
- Unclear job responsibilities
- Repetitive work
- Difficulty with home management and the job
- Sexual harassment
- Lack of input and ways to express frustration

Category	Items
Medical stresses	Termination of therapeutic medication; use of provocative drugs (stimulants, hallucinogens, steroids); physical illness, surgery, disability; pregnancy or abortion; childbirth.
Stress associated with loss or threatened loss of a supportive relationship	Termination of professional therapeutic relationship; death of a family member; death of a close friend; loss of love relationship (nonmarital) or threatened loss; recent move; change or threatened change in other close relationship (parent, sibling, adult son or daughter); severe illness in family member or close relationship.
Stress associated with role change demand	Concern over nonmarital status, increased intimacy demand in love relationship; midlife role change demand; midlife role change in spouse; retirement.
Stress associated with marriage or parenting	Overt marital discord; marital divorce or separation; guilt over extramarital affair; marital estrangement (without overt discord or separation); problem with phase-appropriate emancipation of children; other child-rearing problem (i.e., limit setting); excessive intrusion in marriage by parent or in-law.
Stress associated with vocational or financial problems	Threatened or actual decrease in vocational or economic status; job loss; threatening increase in vocational status; actual or feared loss of financial support; legal problems.

Events	Percent of total group
Physical illness, surgery, disability	24
Change or threatened change in other close relationship	21
Overt marital discord	18
Recent move	16
Actual or feared loss of financial support	14
Job loss	13
Severe illness in family member or close relationship	13
Intrusion in marriage by parents or in-laws	11
Discontinuation of therapeutic medication	11
Problem with phase-appropriate emancipation of children	11

Source: Bowers and coworkers (1980).

Intelligence and Intellectual Functioning

Views of intelligence and intellectual ability have changed in the past decade or so. There is evidence that when middle-aged persons are in good health and engaged in activity requiring mental ability, they show wisdom that comes from experience and a logical faculty equal to that of the younger adult. People perhaps cannot remember as well as they once could; even so, much of this is caused by fear that significant losses have occurred. Verbal skills and reasoning for the middlescent are likely to be better, as people accumulate information and their vocabulary increases (Birren, 1976). The ability to organize and process visual material, such as finding a single figure in a complex one, improves in the middle years. Normally, people will remain as they were in early adulthood or improve in intellectual functioning. Difficulties, where they exist, have to do with nonverbal skills, such as motor skills, speed of response, certain mathematical operations, and memorizing nonsense syllables or digit symbols (Botwinick, 1977). Physical and mental difficulties will interfere with intellectual ability, but it functions in many areas, continuing without decline until the age of 60.

Researchers find that between 45 percent and 60 percent of people maintain a stable level of performance into their seventies on tests of fluid and crystallized intelligence, other than in the areas mentioned above. A few people (10 to 15 percent) increase in their performance by the time they reach their sixties. A few decline in work fluency, some increase in verbal meaning and inductive reasoning, which does not seem to drop any more than other abilities (Schaie, 1983). Denney and Palmer (1981), using 84 adults 20 to 79 in playing the game "Twenty Questions," found that those in their middle years did more poorly than the younger adults. Subjects were also posed such practical problems as: What do you do if you are trapped in your car in a blizzard? Your basement is flooded, how do you handle it? You bought an appliance and it stopped working two weeks after purchase, what recourse do you have? On these types of questions the middlescence subjects did the best of all the age groups.

Information processing is utilized in a different way by middle-age people than younger adults. In very early adulthood (19 to 23) continuing from adolescence, the focus is on acquisition of skills, reasoning abilities, acquisition of information, and problem solving. As adults begin occupational life, have families, and function in the community, they must apply knowledge previously obtained to the real world, which involves social as well as theoretical cognitive skills. These are elements in intelligence not typically measured in the usual I.Q. tests. In middle age, with competence assured, leadership roles and responsibility call for executive ability as one works with community organizations. The Schaie model, presented in the chapter on the young adult, describes this graphically. Riegel (1976) emphasizes the dialectic aspects of adult thinking. The dialectic harmonizes the ideal and the real life situations. Ambiguity and contradictions in resolving issues--ethics, social implications, practical problems--are different from formal stage logic. Sternberg and Berg (1987) have as one part of their triarchial theory *Contextual Subtheory*, which emphasizes adaptation to environment, shaping of environment, and selection of the environment. All of these require maturity and experience in order to negotiate a workable resolution.

Abilities--Fluid and Crystallized

A number of earlier studies of intellectual ability among middle-aged and older adults by Wechsler (1972) suggest decline in cognitive ability to be the function of age. Wechsler recognizes differences in intelligence as fluid (native ability) and nonfluid or crystallized intelligence, which is based principally on formal education. The assumption is that, as the body ages, the nervous system is impaired in terms of the speed with which it processes information, the mind becomes less efficient, and the memory bank less accurate. A study of Lachman, Lochman, and Thronesbery (1979) on metamemory (knowledge of memory stored) utilizing three groups with mean ages of 20.58, 49.92, and 68.92, investigated memorial accuracy and efficiency. The researchers found metamemorial function holds up well to at least an average of 68 years in volunteer subjects. Memory for specific complex reading information may deteriorate, but not much among educated and active adults.

Wechsler believes such abilities as vocabulary skills, verbal reasoning, and object assembly increase with age until around 60 or so; whereas abilities that "don't hold"--speed of reasoning, memory ability, and learning of new material--in brief, the ability to reorganize one's perceptions--are affected. Horn (1980) postulates that fluid intelligence peaks earlier, while crystallized abilities peak later and may be more persistent. Figure 12.12 represents the relationship of these types of intelligence and their combination.

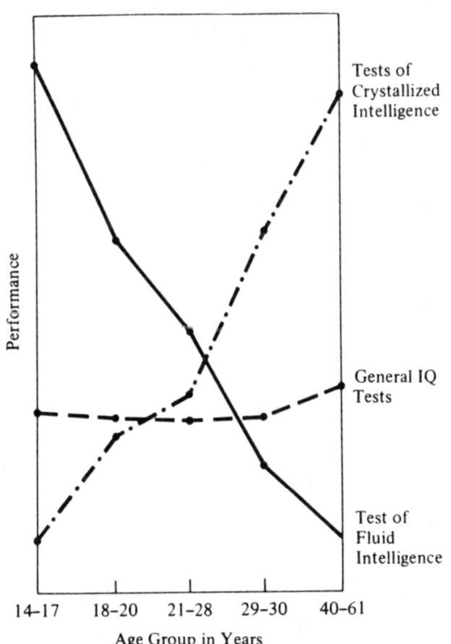

Figure 12.12 Fluid and crystallized intelligence.

Variations in intellectual functioning are perhaps greatest among middlescent persons, except perhaps in the older age group. Those people with high ability as young adults are likely to be more outstanding in this respect, particularly where the environment has been stimulating and they have maintained good health and had opportunities to utilize their ability. Much of the rigidity or caution complained of in people over 55 or 60 results from lack of recognition that they have greater numbers of experiences and associations upon which to draw, and this serves to inhibit quick reaction in solving new problems. Creativity is often high in a number of middle-aged persons. Dennis (1966) found that persons in their forties were generally more productive in science, humanities, and artistic creativity than in other decades.

Papalia (1972), utilizing Piagetian tests of cognitive functioning, found high levels of conservation ability in adults aged 30 to 64, with the highest overall performance being among the 55- to-64-year-old group. Many persons never reach the formal operational stage of Piaget's cognitive development. Tomlinson-Keasey (1972) examined formal operational use among sixth-graders, college women, and middle-aged women and found that college girls of around 20 years of age did the best, with 67 percent doing work at the formal operational level; middle-aged subjects were next with 54 percent. It is thought that education and experience have much to do with this ability.

To say that abilities decline based upon cross-sectional data can never be validated unless one knows that abilities were possessed in earlier times. Longitudinal studies will increasingly yield new information; preliminary results suggest caution--and that we should not underestimate the intelligence of middle-aged people.

SUMMARY

What happens in the development of the middlescent is complex. It starts with what one brings to the middle years in terms of personality development, physical and mental health from the young adult years, and the effect of culture as it was transmitted by the socioeconomic circumstances of the times. Change, then, is seen as a function of an interaction of the physiological, sociological, and psychological modalities with variant components having differential effects. The middle years, called middlescence by the authors, in general encompass the years from 40 to 69. The early middlescent years are from 40 to 49, the middle years 50 to 59, and the later middlescent years 60 to 69. Using 69 rather than 65 for the upper limits of middle age is created by the revised estimate of longevity. In 1990 eighty years is projected for the female infant; also 65 attached to retirement is no longer a good marker for that as average age in the United States is 62, though the years to be lived in retirement have lengthened.

The important thing about adult life categorizations is that they principally relate to role rather than chronology. Markers in the middle years are represented by the biology, social activities, mental ability, health, vocational concerns, emancipation of children from the home, and adjustments. Reappraisal of life is a usual occurrence among people during the in-between years. The effects of self-examination and environmental concerns frequently force people to face the reality of whether to stagnate or be productive. This confrontation may be called a crisis. When the crisis is resolved, it may result in changes, not infrequently in new vocational pursuits, divorce and remarriage, and lifestyle and roles perhaps are slightly reversed for men and women. Mid-life crises according to Neugarten are uncommon. Women become, according to Gutmann, more aggressive in taking leadership roles, and men become more nurturant and take more passive roles.

In dealing with the physical modality, gradual change in the organism takes place, characterized by some losses in sensory ability, muscle tone and strength, and sex hormones. The principal significance for women is the period of menopause ending childbearing ability; this is often accompanied by a number of usually minor discomforts. Men experience heart attacks in greater numbers than women, though in both groups two out of five have chronic health problems by the time they are 45 years of age. Both men and women experience deceleration of the metabolic rate, muscle cell loss, weight gains, and have bone marrow loss particularly in the upper middle years 60 to 69. More women than men experience emotional and personality difficulty, based upon clinician and health authority reports; however, more men commit suicide than do women. First admissions to a mental hospital for women were found to be highest in the age group 25 to 34; for men the highest incidence was in the group 35 to 44. Depression, created in part by stress and frustration, is a pervasive problem for the middlescent of both sexes. Job stress is pervasive, often causing burnout, often involving low pay, little input, and difficulty with home management. Heart disease and cancer are the leading cause of death for both. The physical environment becomes an increasingly critical factor in the life of adults--its red tape, noise, pollution levels, crowding, and ecology.

The sociological mode has its impact upon adults. The cultural expectations of society, as seen in the developmental tasks, affect the direction of one's life--achieving social and community responsibility, stability in the occupational career, relating to one's spouse as a person, and accepting changes of middle age. Erikson's social crisis suggests stagnation of productivity characterizations in middle years 50 to 60.

Middlescent persons generally have their highest status during this period; they also typically have their greatest responsibilities. Many men and women change their occupations, and women often find employment after the years of child-rearing, again or for the first time. Serving the "middle-man function" in the middle years becomes an exclusive problem in this period for a man or woman or both if they have children. On one hand, they are assisting their children to become emancipated from the home; on the other hand, they have growing responsibilities in caring for their aging parents. Often the life pattern must be changed to accommodate this situation. Forwarding their own interests simultaneous to a caretaking role often creates difficulty for the individual in harmonizing these diverse concerns.

Family patterns have changed in recent years; fewer than half of the households have a mother, father, and children together. Many children live with one parent, and many couples, by the time of middle age, have opted not to have children. The postparental family is new in America. In the intact family, many husbands and wives as parents are surviving beyond the time when their last child leaves the home. Grandparenting is becoming a more usual pattern than in yesteryear, representing the traditional kind or a more informal type.

Marriage satisfaction is found most often before children are born and after they leave the home. Many middle-aged persons will divorce and remarry, with the failure rate about the same as in the first marriage. Marriages seem to survive longer when expectations of the couples match the realities of their life and make each other their best friends. Effective communication between couples is a basic attribute of a successful marriage. Divorce is highly stressful, second in stress only to the death of a spouse, to which it is tantamount in many ways and is likely to interface with their work and health problems. Men find work in the in-between years very significant to their self-images and happiness; women increasingly desire to get the same rewards out of work that men wish to have, and many women are reentering educational programs to qualify for better paying positions. Most satisfaction from work comes in the professions, probably due to the fact that they can control much of the direction of their work and organize its facilitation. Unemployment is difficult to handle for middlescent men generally and for some women who have always worked. Working class, blue-collar people suffer the most from unemployment and, even if working, often feel they are manipulated and have little mobility to move to a better life through higher-level jobs.

Although it is difficult or in some cases impossible to separate psychological aspects of life from the social and even the physical, we speak of mental life as an entity, recognizing that it relates to the physical and social aspects of life. It is evident that in the lives of many persons dramatic changes take place, life is viewed differently at different times, and everyone has to make adjustments throughout life.

Effective personality adjustments according to Peck are based upon:

1) Valuing wisdom over physical strength.

2) Valuing socializing over sexualizing.

3) Valuing cathexis flexibility over catholic impoverishment.

4) Valuing mental flexibility over mental rigidity.

The problems that come during transitional periods--noted by some experts as being in the late 20s, again in the late 30s or early 40s, and at retirement and widowhood--sometime force a crisis situation. The crisis, if it occurs in the middle years, involves usually an assessment of one's life, marriage, work, lifestyle, and if widowed beginning a new life. Above these it often involves a reassessment of one's value with honesty and integrity becoming increasingly important.

In general mental abilities decline from 40 to 70 in most. The principal change is in fluid intelligence (native ability, reaction speed) as opposed to crystallized intelligence (ability to deal with concepts, etc.) which mainly accrues from formal education. This type of ability may even grow after 50 in some persons. Verbal skills and reasoning for the middlescent are likely to be better. The ability to organize and process visual material, such as finding a single figure in a complex one, improves in the middle years. Physical and mental difficulties will interfere with intellectual ability, but it functions in many areas well, continuing without decline until the age of 60. It should be remembered that information processing is utilized in a different way by the middle aged with the emphasis on executive functioning (solving current problems) than developing further the kinds of acquisitions of knowledge dealt with by Piaget.

KEY WORDS

middlescence

generativity

stagnation

estrogen

testosterone

androgen

osteoporosis

postparental

cathectic flexibility

general adaptation syndrome

occupational stress (burnout)

fluid intelligence

crystallized intelligence

executive ability

REFERENCES

Ahrons, C., and Wallasch, L. The relationship between former spouses. In D. Perlman and S. Duck (eds.), *Intimate Relationships: Development, Dynamics, and Deterioration*, Beverly Hills, CA: Sage Publications, 1983, pp. 269-296.

Baltes, P.B., and Schaie, K.W. Aging and IQ: The myth of the twilight years. *Psychology Today*, 1974, *7*(10):35-40.

Baltes, P.B. Life-span developmental psychology: Some converging observation of history and theory. In P.B. Baltes and O.G. Brim, Jr. (eds.), *Life-Span Development and Behavior*, vol. 2. New York: Academic Press, 1979.

Benninger, W.B., and Walsh, W.B. Holland's theory and non-college degree-working men and women. *Journal of Vocational Behavior*, 1901, *17*:81-88.

Birren, J.E. Aging: The psychologist's perspecive. In R.H. Davis (ed.), *Aging: Prospects and Issues*. Los Angeles: University of Southern California Press, 1976, pp. 16-28.

Bloom, B.L., and Caldwell, R.A. Sex differences in adjustment during the process of marital separation. *Journal of Marriage and the Family*, 1981, *43*696-701.

Botwinick, J. *Aging and Behavior*. New York: Springer, 1973.

______. Intellectual abilities. In J.E. Birren and K.W. Schaie (eds.), *Handbook of the Psychology of Aging*. New York: Van Nostrand Rheinhold, 1977, pp. 580-605.

Brayshaw, A.J. Middle-aged marriage: Idealism, realism and the search for meaning. *Marriage and Family Living*, November, 1962.

Buhler, C. Der Menschliche Lebenslaufs Psychologishes Problem Hirzel, 1933.

Cain, B.S. Blight of the grey divorcees. *New York Times Magazine*. December 12, 1982, pp. 89-90, 92, 95.

Campbell, A. The American way of mating: Marriage is children only maybe. *Psychology Today*, May 1975, *8*(6):17-41.

______. *The Sense of Well-Being in America. Recent Patterns and Trends*. New York: McGraw-Hill, 1981.

Cherlin, A. At issue--Cohabitation how the French and Swedes do it. *Psychology Today*, 1979, *13*(4).

Children Today. Youth's attitudes. 1975, *4*(6):14-15.

Chiriboga, D.A. Adaptation to marital separation in later and earlier life. *Journal of Gerontology*, 1982, *37*:109-114.

Colby, A., Kohlberg, L., Gibbs, J., and Lieberman, M. A longitudinal study of moral judgment. *Monographs of the Society for Research in Child Development*, 1983, *48*:Whole No. 200.

Coleman, J.S. *Youth: Transition to Adulthood*. Chicago: University of Chicago Press, 1974.

Congressional Caucus for Women's Issues. *The American Woman 1987-1988*. Washington, DC, 1987.

Constantine, L.L., and Constantine, J.M. Sexual aspects of group marriage. In R.W. Libby and R.N. Whitehurst (eds.), *Marriage and Alternatives: Explaining Intimate Relationships*. Glenview, Ill.: Scott, Foresman, 1977, pp. 186-194.

Denney, N.W., and Palmer, A.M. Adult age differences on traditional and practical problem-solving measures. *Journal of Gerontology*, 1981, *36*(3):323-328.

Diener, E. Subjective well-being. *Psychological Bulletin*, 1984, *95*:542-575.

Dreyer, P.H. Sex, sex roles, and marriage among youth in the 1970s. *Youth, 74th Yearbook of the National Society for the Study of Education, Part I*. Chicago: University of Chicago Press, 1975, pp. 194-223.

Eberhardt, B.J., and Muchinsky, P.M. Structural evaluation of Holland's hexagonal model: Vocational classification through the use of biodata. *Journal of Applied Psychology*, 1984, *69*:174-181.

Eichorn, D.H. The institute of human development studies, Berkeley and Oakland. In L.F. Jarvik, C. Eisdorfer, and J.E. Blum (eds.), *Intellectual Functioning in Adults*. New York: Springer, 1973, pp. 1-6.

Eichorn, D.H., Clausen, J.A., Haan, N., Honzik, M.P., and Mussen, P.H. (eds.), *Present and Past in Middle Life*. New York: Academic Press, 1982.

Eisdorfer, C., and Lawton, M.P. (eds.) *The Psychology of Adult Development and Aging*. Washington, D.C.: American Psychological Association, 1973.

Erikson, E. *Identity, Youth and Crisis*. New York: Norton, 1968.

Farley, F., and Davis, S. Personality and sexual satisfaction in marriage. *Journal of Sex and Marital Therapy*, 1980, *6*(1).

Fisher, H.E. The four year itch. *Natural History*, 1987, *96*(10):22-33.

Freud, S. *New Introductory Lectures on Psychoanalysis.* New York: Norton, 1933.

Gilligan, C. *In a Different Voice: Psychological Theory and Women's Development.* Cambridge, Mass.: Harvard University Press, 1982.

Gilligan, C., Ward, J.V., and Taylor, J.M. *Mapping the Moral Domain.* Boston: Harvard University Press, 1988.

Gilligan, J. In a different voice: Women's conceptions of self and of morality. *Harvard Educational Review*, 1977, *47*(4):481-517.

Glenn, M.D., and Supanicic, M. The social demographics correlates of divorce and separation in the United States. An update and reconsideration. *Journal of Marriage and the Family*, 1984, *46*:563-575.

Gordon, C., Gaitz, J., and Scott, J. Leisure and lives: Personal expressivity across the life span. In R.H. Binstock and E. Shanas (eds.), *Handbook of Aging and the Social Sciences.* New York: Van Nostrand Reinhold, 1976, pp. 310-341.

Gould, R. *Transformation: Growth and Change in Adult Life.* New York: Simon and Schuster, 1978.

Greenhaus, J.H. Self-esteem as an influence on occupational choice and occupational satisfaction. *Journal of Vocational Behavior*, 1971, *1*:75-83.

Group for the Advancement of Psychiatry. Reported in Papalia & Olds (eds.), *Human Development.* New York: McGraw-Hill, 1978.

Gutmann, D.L. An explanation of ego configuration in middle and later life. In B.L. Neugarten & Associates (eds.), *Personality in Middle and Later Life.* New York: Atherton Press, 1964.

_____. Parenthood: A key to the comparative study of the life cycle. In N. Datan and L.H. Pinsberg (eds.), *Life Span Developmental Psychology: Normative Life Crises.* New York: Academic Press, 1975, pp. 167-184.

Haan, N. Personality organization of well-functioning younger people and older adults. *International Journal of Aging and Human Development*, 1976, *7*:117.

Harry, J. Gay male and lesbian relationships. In E.D. Macklin and R.H. Rubin (eds.), *Contemporary Families and Alternative Lifestyles: Handbook on Research and Theory.* Beverly Hills, CA: Sage Publications, 1983, pp. 216-233.

Havighurst, R.J. Stages of vocational development. In H. Borow (ed.), *Man in a World of Work.* Boston: Houghton Mifflin, 1964.

_____. *Developmental Tasks and Education*, 3rd ed. New York: David McKay, 1972.

Hill, C.T., Rubin, Z., and Peplau, L.A. Breakups before marriage: The end of 103 affairs. In G. Levinger and O. Moles (eds.), *Divorce and Separation: Context, Causes and Consequences.* New York: Basic Books, 1979.

Hite Report. New York: Knopf, 1981.

Hock, E., Christman, K., Hock, M. Fathers associated with decisions about return to work in mothers of infants. *Developmental Psychology*, 1980, *16*(5):535-536.

Holland, J.L. *Making Vocational Choices: A Theory of Careers.* Englewood Cliffs, NJ: Prentice-Hall, 1973.

Horn, J.L, and Donaldson, G. Cognitive development II: Aduthood development of human abilities. In O.G. Brim and J. Kagan (eds.), *Constancy and Change in Human Development.* Cambridge, Mass.: Harvard University Press, 1980.

Jones, F.R. Making the most of the middle years. Unpublished manuscript, 535 pages, 1991.

Jones, F.R. Model of adult development, 1980. In *Psychology of Human Development.* New York: Harper & Row, 1985.

Jones, F.R., and Heinen, J.R.K. Stress and mental health of graduate students and non-graduates by age and educational levels. Washington, DC: U.S. Department of Health, Education and Welfare, Institute of Education, Document ED 159499.

Katchadourian, H. *Fifty: Midlife in Perspective.* New York: Freeman, 1987.

Kelly, J.B. Divorce: The adult perspective. In B. Wolman (ed.), *Handbook of Developmental Psychology.* Englewood Cliffs, NJ: Prentice-Hall, 1982.

Kinsey, A.C., Pomeroy, W., Martin, C.E., and Gebbard, P.H. *Sexual Behavior in the Human Female.* Philadelphia: Saunders, 1953.

Labouie-Vief, Gisela. Logic and self-regulation from youth to maturity: A model. In M.L. Commons, F.A. Richards, and C. Armon (eds.), *Beyond Formal Operations: Late Adolescence and Adult Cognitive Development.* New York: Draeger, 1984, pp. 158-159.

Lachman, J., Lochman, R., and Thronesbery, C. Meta memory through the adult life span. *Developmental Psychology*, 1979, *15*(5): 543-551.

Lerner, R.M., and Busch-Rossnagel, N.A. *Individuals As Producers of Their Development.* New York: Academic Press, 1981.

Levinson, D. *The Season's of a Man's Life.* New York: Alfred Knopf, 1978.

Mackling, E.D. Nonmarital heterosexual cohabitation: An overview. In E.D. Mackling and R.H. Rubin (eds.), *Contemporary Families and Alternative Lifestyles: Handbook on Research and Theory.* Beverly Hills, CA., pp. 49-74.

Masters, W.H., and Ballew, J.W. The third sex. In C.B. Vedder (ed.), *The Problems of the Middle Aged.* Springfield, Ill.: Thomas, 1965.

McSweeney, J., and Jones, F.R. Survey of worries, goals, and satisfactions among undergraduate and graduate students. 1991 unpublished date and in the *Psychology of Human Development*, 2nd ed. New York: Harper & Row, 1985.

Morris, C. *Varieties of Human Values.* Chicago: University of Chicago Press, 1956.

Murstein, B.I. *Who Will Marry Whom? Theories and Research in Marital Choice.* New York: Springer-Verlag, 1976.

Neugarten, B. Adult personality: Toward a psychology of the life cycle. In Neugarten (ed.), *Middle Age and Aging.* Chicago: University of Chicago Press, 1968.

Neugarten, B.L., and Neugarten, D.A. The changing meaning of age. *Psychology Today*, May 1987, *21*:29-33.

Newhouse Service News. Sex still a factor in student job goals. *Chicago Sun-Times*, September 25, 1987, p. 27.

Nisan, M., and Kohlberg, L. Universality and variation in moral judgment; A longitudinal and cross-sectional study in Turkey. *Child Development*, 1982, *53*:965-876.

Norton, A.J., and Moorman, J.E. Current trends in marriage and divorce among American women. *Journal of Marriage and the Family*, 1987, *49*(1):3-14.

Occupational Outlook Handbook, 1990-1991 edition. U.S. Department of Labor. Washington, DC: U.S. Government Printing Office, 1991.

Okun, B.G. *Working With Adults: Individual, Family and Career Development.* Monterey, CA: Brooks & Cole, 1984.

Papalia, D.E., and Olds, S.W. *Human Development*, 4th ed. New York: McGraw-Hill, 1989.

Parlee, M.B. Menstrual rhythms in sensory processes: A review of fluctuations in vision, olfaction, audition, taste, and touch. *Psychological Bulletin*, 1983, *93*(3):539-548.

Peck, R. Psychological development in the second half of life. In B. Neugarten (ed.), *Middle Age and Aging.* Chicago: University of Chicago Press, 1968.

Peplau, L.A. What homosexuals want in relationships. *Psychology Today*, 1981, *15*:28-38.

Phillips, D.C., and Kelly, M.E. Hierarchical theories of development in education and psychology. *Harvard Educational Review*, 1975, *45*(3):351-375.

Piaget, J. Intellectual evolution from adolescence to adulthood. *Human Development*, 1972, *15*:1-12.

Pikunas, J. *Human Development: An Emergent Science*. New York: McGraw-Hill, 1976.

Pincus, T., Callahan, L.F., and Burkhauser, R.V. Most chronic diseases are reported more frequently by individuals with fewer than 12 years of formal education in the age 18-64 United States population. *Journal of Chronic Diseases*, 1987, *40*(9):865-874.

Pratt, M.W., Golding, G., and Hunter, W.J. Does morality have a gender sex, sex role and moral judgment in young, mature, and older adults? *Human Development*, 1984, *26*:277-288.

Reedy, M.N. Age and sex differences in personal needs and the nature of love: A study of happily married young, middle-aged and older couples. Unpublished doctoral dissertation, University of Southern California, 1977.

Riegel, K.F. The dialectics of human development. *American Psychologist*, 1976, *31*:689-700.

_____. Toward a dialectic theory in development. *Human Development*, 1975, *18*:50-64.

_____. Dialectic operations: The final period of cognitive development. *Human Development*, 1973, *16*:346-370.

Rogers, D. *The Adult Years*. Englewood Cliffs, NJ: Prentice-Hall, 1979.

Scholastic Aptitude Test. College Entrance Examination Board, American College Testing Program, *High School Profile Report, 1987*. College Entrance Examination, *On Further Examination, 1977*, and *National Report on College-Bound Seniors, 1987*.

Schulz, D.A., and Rodgers, S.F. *Marriage, the Family and Personal Fulfillment*, 3rd ed. Englewood Cliffs, NJ: Prentice-Hall, 1985.

Selye, H. *The Stress of Life*, 2nd ed. New York: McGraw-Hill, 1976.

Simenaner, J., and Carroll, D. *Singles: The New Americans*. New York: Simon & Schuster, 1982.

Skolnick, A. Married lives: Longitudinal perspectives on marriage. In D.H. Eichorn, J.A. Clausen, N. Haan, M.P. Honsik, and P.H. Mussen (eds.), *Present and Past in Middle Life*. New York: Academic Press, 1981.

Snarey, J.R., Reimer, J., and Kohlberg, L. Development of social-moral reasoning among kibbutz adolescents: A longitudinal cross-cultural study. *Developmental Psychology*, 1985, *21*:3-17.

Solnick, A., and Solnick, O. (eds.) *Family in Transition*. Boston: Little Brown, 1971.

Stein, P.J. Being single: Bucking the culture imperative. Paper presented to the 71st annual meeting of the American Sociological Association, September 3, 1976.

Sternberg, R.J. A triangular theory of love. *Psychological Review*, 1986,pp. 119-135.

Sternberg, R.J., and Berg, C. What are theories of adult intellectual development theories of? In C. Schooler and K.W. Schaie (eds.), *Cognitive Functioning and Social Structure Over the Life Course*. Norwood, NJ: Ablex, 1987.

Stevens-Long, J. *Adult Life*. Los Angeles: Mayfield, 1979.

Strong, E.K., and Campbell, D.P. *Strong Vocational Interest*. Stanford, CA: Stanford University Press, 1933.

Super, D.E. *Career Development: Self-Concept Theory*. New York: College Entrance Examination Board, 1963.

Tanfer, K., and Horn, M.C. Contraceptive use, pregnancy and fertility patterns among Americans in their 20's. *Family Planning Perspective*, 1985, *17*(1):10-19.

Tomlinson-Keasey, D. Formal operations in females from eleven to fifty-six years of age. *Developmental Psychology*, 1972, *6*(2).

Troll, L.E. *Early and Middle Adulthood*, 2nd ed. Monterey, CA: Brooks/Cole, 1985.

U.S. Bureau of the Census. *Marital Status and Living Arrangements*, March 1983. (Current Population Reports: Population Characteristics. Series P-20, No. 389) Washington, DC: U.S. Government Printing Office, 1984.

U.S. Chamber of Commerce, Bureau of Census. *Statistical Abstracts of the United States*, 102nd ed., 1981

U.S. Department of Health and Human Services. Publication No. PHS 87-123. Washington, DC: U.S. Government Printing Office, 1986.

U.S. Department of Health and Human Services. Publication No. PHS 86-1232. Washington, DC: U.S. Government Printing Office, 1985.

U.S. Statistical Abstract. Published in the U.S. Bureau of Labor Statistics, Bulletin 2307 and unpublished data. Washington, DC: U.S. Government Printing Office, 1988.

United States Statistical Abstract, Washington, DC: U.S. Government Printing Office, 1991.

United States Department of Labor, U.S. Bureau of Census. Current Population Reports, Series P-20, Nos. 432 and 433, and Series P-60, Nos. 161 and 162. *Employment and Earnings January.* Washington, DC: U.S. Government Printing Office, 1988.

Vaillant, G.E. *Adaptation to Life.* Boston: Little, Brown, 1977.

Van Dusen, R.A., and Sheldon, E.B. The changing status of American women: A life cycle perspective. *American Psychologist*, 1976, *31*:106-116.

Veroff, J., Douvan, E., and Kulka, R. *The Inner American: A Self-Portrait From 1957-1976.* New York: Basic Books.

Vogel, F.S. The brain and time. In E.W. Busse and Pfeiffer (eds.), *Behavior and Adaptation in Late Life*, 2nd ed. Boston: Little Brown, 1977, pp. 232-233.

Walker, L. Sex differences in the development of moral reasoning. A critical review. *Child Development*, 1984, *55*:677-611.

Youngner, S., and Youngner, M. Becoming parents (Jaffe and Viertel), a book review. *Journal of Sex and Marital Therapy*, Fall 1980, *6*(3).

Youth Indicators. U.S. Department of Labor, Bureau of Labor Statistics. Conmer Expenditure Survey: Interview Survey, 1982 and 1984. Bulletins 2225 and 2267, 1988.

Youth Indicators, U.S. Statistical Abstract, 1988.

Chapter 13

THE LATER ADULT YEARS

LATER ADULTHOOD: PHYSICAL AND MENTAL HEALTH, SOCIAL AND PERSONAL ADJUSTMENT

It is difficult to say when middle age leaves off and old age begins, for as we have pointed out it is primarily a matter of role. People play various roles as the result of certain factors that bear on their lives: the physical, social, and psychological. The 60- to 65-year old who participates in a variety of activities will have a different reaction to questions about aging than will the person who is incapacitated or leads a sedentary life. The former will feel little change from when he or she was 50. The latter perhaps sees life as more constricted and the environment as threatening. This view often comes to those in their 60s and 70s. It is true that generally we can predict fairly accurately people's ages by looking at them. However, characterizing adequately a person's status in living must include his or her ability to work, to adjust, and to participate in community life. Middlescence (middle age) may be a negative word to those in the in-between years, but, unlike the older person, they do receive credit for doing most of the work and paying the bills of society. Older persons in ancient times were shunned in society; an exception was China. In primitive cultures historically the aged were abandoned; unfortunately, advanced technological societies have also shown an attitude of disregard for the aged.

However, the growing number of older persons in Western society and the greater financial protection afforded them through Social Security and insurance programs have combined with their growing political influence to improve their status in the 1990s. The American Association of Retired Persons is a strong advocacy organization for older Americans. In 1991 there are over 30 million Americans over 65 years of age. This represents over 12 percent of the population. And although most of the myths about the old are not true or only partially true, distorted views still persist. When researcher Babladelis (1987) asked a number of students at one of the California state universities about older people, they estimated 30 percent were old (the term "old" should apply to those 60 and above) and were reluctant to spend time with them. Although society is getting older the old are getting younger. According to Horn and Meer (1987) the habits of the 70-year-old today approximate those of the 50-year-old 25 years ago in both activity and attitudes.

There are a number of myths about growing old. As we have suggested above, many people equate age in chronological terms with physical health. "You're as old as you feel" is appropriate and true more times than not. A number of myths have been circulated that relate only tangentially to the process of growing old. Some myths that have been perpetrated are as follows:

1. The elderly population as a group live in nursing homes, hospitals, and homes for the aged. The truth is only 1.5 percent who are 65 to 74, 7.1 percent from 75 to 84, and around 23 percent of those 85 and over do so (U.S. Bureau of the Census, *Current Population Reports*, 1983).

2. Most of the elderly are chronically sick and bedfast. The truth is that only 8 percent who live at home are bedfast. Another 5 percent are seriously incapacitated, while 11 to 16 percent are restricted in mobility. About 35 of each 100 persons of all ages are injured per year, but only 21.4 of the elderly (Turner, 1982). Forty percent do not see a physician from one year to the next (Shanas et al., 1968). In a 1980 survey of those over 65, only 8 percent of men and women categorized themselves as being in poor health (U.S. Department of Commerce, 1983).

3. Senility is a natural accompaniment of old age. The term is often used to describe dementia and is not a medical diagnosis but a general term for many symptoms. The most common dementia is Alzheimer's disease, which represents 6 to 8 percent of the older population. A total of 15 percent of Americans over 65 are demented (Davies, 1988). The truth is that senility does not occur invariably, and when it does it is not beyond help. Much deterioration formerly blamed on aging is now known to result from illness, drugs, alcohol, depression, glandular problems, nutrition, and circulatory difficulties. The brain does not necessarily deteriorate with advancing age. Learning ability and IQ (crystallized) may even increase with age, depending upon one's interest, activity, and health (Galton, 1979; Lachman, Lochman, & Thronesbery, 1979; Schaie, 1983).

4. Most older persons are in poor health and develop colds, flu, and the like very easily. The National Public Opinion research (1985) found 38 percent over 65 said they were in good health, the same as the 55-to-64 group: only 15 percent said they were in poor health compared to 14 percent among the 55-to-64 age group. Persons over 65 have some advantages in health over the younger adult in that they have fewer colds, flu infections, and acute digestive prob-

lems. When acute illness does strike older persons, restrictions are greater; yet on the average they lose only 10 days a year for sickness (AARP, 1986).

5. Most people over 65 are in financial difficulty. The truth is only 15 percent of the elderly report that "they do not have enough money to live on." In 1981, 9 million persons depended on Social Security for their sole support; many were under 65 (Hildreth, 1981). Exter (1987) says that the 65 and older group are three times better off than 30 years ago and more of them own their own home (75 percent) than other age groups; only 12.6 percent are below the poverty line, whereas 14 percent of the rest are below it and they pay less tax (U.S. Census Bureau, 1985).

These are just a few of the myths that abound. McKenzie (1980), looking at a number of other myths, such as the elderly's being inflexible, unproductive, lonely, cranky, more religious, sexless, and serene, found they need considerable qualifying to approach validity. Since the population is graying, perhaps considerably more data on the status of the older persons will become available, and the probability exists that many other stereotypes about the old will be eliminated. The stereotypes gain credence because of societal expectations that reinforce the mythologies of aging. These mythologies have come from earlier times in this century when being 60 was considered old and 75 ancient. Some authorities like Bernice Neugarten have a classification of 55 to 70 as the young-old, with middle-old being 65 to 75, and the old-old representing those over 75. This seems increasingly less than an appropriate grouping and the authors believe this should be pushed 10 years beyond her classification. As of 1990 the female neonate had a life expectancy on average of 80 years (*World Data Book*, 1991).

Though much of the study of gerontology is directed to the positive aspects of aging, consideration of the biological decline is also inevitable; the bodily systems deteriorate in both structural and functional aspects. Accident proneness increases as physical coordination declines. Biological errors, non-cycling cells, and metabolic disturbances add to the problem. Cognitive decline is perhaps most often observed in memory; metamemory (knowing about remembering) holds up well to about 70, for compensation occurs through the use of imagination (Lachman, Lochman, & Thronesbery, 1979). The meaning of self helps the old person preserve ego integrity. This will be discussed in the section on the psychological modality. Preceding this will be a discussion of the biological and sociological modalities.

THEORIES OF AGING

The biological process of aging is usually associated with a decline of efficiency that eventually leads to death. Some biologists define aging as a progressive loss of functional capacity after an organism has reached maturity (Garn, 1979); still others divide loss in functioning into primary and secondary aging. Primary aging refers to the biological process and is usually thought of as being rooted in heredity. The processes involved are inborn and inevitable, detrimental changes that are time-related though independent of stress, trauma, or disease. Various aging processes are not recognizable in all people, and those that are present do not progress at the same rate. Secondary aging refers to disability that results from stress or chronic disease.

Busse (1977) has identified several biological theories of aging, which are as follows:

1. Exhaustion theory. This early theory rests on the assumption that a living organism contains a fixed store of energy similar to that of a battery.

2. Biological genetic programming. This theory maintains that there is a built-in longevity that allows for the organism to mature and live long enough to ensure the raising of offspring. The usual life span is all that can be expected due to the complex nature of the body chemistry (Comfort, 1976).

3. Mean time to failure. This theory incorporates the engineering concept that failure is embedded in every machine, including the human organism. Parts can be replaced, but barring replacement for every part, failure will at some time ensue (Hayflick, 1980).

4. Accumulation of copying errors. According to this view, life is eventually terminated due to the fact that cells develop errors in replication, and this reproduction of errors reduces the metabolic efficiency and interferes with the capacity to repair (Lumpkin et al., 1986).

5. Stochastic theory. This is a probabilistic theory involving "hits" that occur when something alters a chromosome. Radiation can make a hit. Szilard (1977), the atomic scientist who advanced this theory, believed every animal cell carried a load of faults. A fault is a congenital absence of one of the genes essential to cell function. A cell functions or operates when one of a pair of genes continues to work, but when members of a pair of essential genes are incapable of functioning, the cell dies.

6. Composite theory. This approach considers aging to be fundamentally an increasing probability of development of a degenerative disease. As people age they become increasingly susceptible to degenerative diseases. Also, as people get older they develop all of the diseases (degenerate) but at different rates. The disease that plays the major role in one's demise is a matter of chance (Rowe & Kohn, 1987).

7. Auto-immune mechanisms. This view holds that the immune systems over time change so that they alter the body's natural defense against infection and begin to attack normal cells. Normal cells have lost the ability to transmit the proper message, and consequently appear to be foreign to the body. Alterations in the DNA molecules of the cells occur that impair cell functioning (Glenister & Williams, 1987; Schmeck, 1982).

The major social theories of aging are the disengagement, activity, and social exchange theories.

The disengagement theory (Cumming & Henry, 1961) views aging as a progressive process of physical, social, and psychological withdrawal from the world at large. On the physical level people reduce their activity and focus on conserving their energy. On the social level they drop membership in many clubs and organizations, attendance at parties, various affairs, and relate to an ever-smaller group of people, which facilitates in time a peaceful death as social ties are reduced to a minimum. Psychologically the aged become less concerned with the outside world and larger issues of politics and business. This theory assumes not only withdrawal by the individual but a withdrawal of society from the aged person and a gradual transfer of their functions to younger persons. Many theorists such as Maddox (1969) and Palmore (1975) refute this theory. Babchuck, et al. (1979), studying older people (65 and up) in a midwestern community of 35,000, found little drop in affiliations. Palm Coast, Florida, a community of 30,000, finds retirees anything but retired (many work at jobs still in their 70s and 80s, and nearly all are active in church clubs and recreation (Johnson, 1991).

The activity theory (Havighurst, Neugarten, & Tobin, 1968). This theory is suggested as an alternative to the disengagement theory, and suggests that older persons except for certain biological and health changes are similar to middle-aged persons. The lessening of social interaction is the function of society's withdrawal, not the desire of the aged. The healthy aging person is one who stays active and resists the shrinkage of his or her social world. Also, these theorists admit some disengagement takes place after 60 or 65. The healthy older person maintains fairly stable levels of activity (Neugarten & Neugarten, 1987).

The social exchange theory (Dowd, 1984). According to this view people enter social relationships because they desire rewards from them--financial gain, recognition, love, security, social approval, and social gratitude. In seeking such rewards they have negative, unpleasant experiences (effort, fatigue, embarrassment) or they are forced to abandon some positive experiences in order to pursue more rewarding activities. When they have little to offer in order to maintain status and they cannot keep up with mainstream midlife activities, they tend to disengage themselves from society. Older workers are finally retired to make way for younger workers. The promise of Social Security and Medicare are the remaining rewards for the old. Technological societies tend to undermine the values of knowledge and experience of older persons. Although these factors shed light on the elemental exchange theory, it falls short of explaining the aging situation.

The modernization/technological theory. This view assumes that in former times (preindustrial) older people had greater status due to their accumulated knowledge and control of land and business. Traditional societies offered more standing to the old. This position argues that in modern industry, etc., older people are given lower-level jobs and have less control. Japan is an exception in that the Japanese venerate the elderly. Their orientation to filial piety and ancestor worship has reduced the economic impact of aging (Palmore & Maeda, 1985). The elements of exchange, a key feature of the modernization theory, is important in pointing to the effects of technology on the stations in society held by the old. However, the invention of the sewing machine and the spinning machine, for instance, actually improved the status of many older workers relative to the development of the cottage industry. With this industry the old could make yarn and sew piece-goods in their own homes. As a result, they were able to develop greater financial stability and recognition (Quadagno, 1982). Obviously, the economic system does affect the status of the elderly but does not explain some features of the social aspects of aging (Ishii-Kuntz & Lee, 1987).

Exit theory. Blau (1973) theorized that when people lose their core roles--those involving family, jobs, their husbands or wives, or status--remaining socially useful is seriously undermined. A status role can be an officer in a club, a church deaconship, or a volunteer in a charity organization. For some, however, the loss of children to adulthood or death of a spouse allows time to participate in social activities for which they didn't have time before. The Duke Longitudinal Studies dealing with life satisfaction of the elderly indicate no overall social loss from their work or family (Palmore, 1976).

The Psychological Theories

These theories usually are based upon personality and developmental theories (see Chapter 11 for the authors' theory). Personality theories consider the innate needs and forces that motivate behavior as they are modified by the physical and social environments. The developmental theories of personality take into account the organismic changes in the growing child, interaction with the mother, and so on. The study of personality in old age may be accompanied by considering possible alteration in the physiological processes of the elderly person and the interacting relationship that exists between the environment and the individual. The effects of these interactions influence psychological functioning and sometimes account for deterioration in mental abilities and personality problems--psychosis, senility, and so on.

A number of investigators, such as Neugarten and Hagestad (1977), in exploring the patterns of personality in middle and late life have found some significant differences between 40-year-olds and 60-year-olds. The 60-year-olds see the environment as more complex and dangerous. Older men seem more receptive than younger men to nurturing and sensual promptings. Also, according to Neugarten, older women become more comfortable with their own aggressiveness and egocentricity. Reichard, Livson, and Peterson (1962), in studying personalities of 187 men aged 55 to 84, were able to classify them into five major categories according to their adjustment. The five divisions were:

1. The mature were constructively adjusted, having accepted themselves, their weaknesses and strengths, and their past lives. Most were free of neurotic conflicts and had close personal relationships.

2. Rocking-chair men (dependent) had high levels of acceptance but were passive and were dependent on others and saw the later years as freedom from obligation.

3. The armored (defensive) relied on defense mechanisms to cope with negative emotions. Although usually well adjusted, they were rather rigidly maintaining active life patterns.

4. The angry (hostile) were often bitter, poorly adjusted, and expressed their unhappiness in an aggressive manner, blaming others for their difficulties, and were easily frustrated.

5. Self-haters blamed themselves for their failure and were usually depressed, viewing old age as a catastrophe.

The activity theory of aging believes that the maintenance of activities is important to most people as they draw sustaining satisfaction, self-esteem, and health from them. In a study by Maddox (1963) involving the activities and attitudes of 127 aged subjects observed over a 20-year period, it was found that there were no significant overall decreases in activities or change in attitudes among men, while among women some decrease was noted. Most support for disengagement theories comes from cross-sectional surveys rather than longitudinal data, which means if studies of this type were available they might produce contrary evidence. Rutzen (1980) says most older people cannot readily be regarded as disengaged on most measures of disengagement. The process is probably not inevitable and inexorable in its progression; social disengagement should be viewed separately from primary relationships. Busse (1977) found that some reduction in activities or attitudes resulted in compensating increases in other activities.

Extension of Life Span

An extension of life is probably tied to reduction in mean temperature of the atmosphere, limiting intake of food, and improving the ecology, the genetic system, and lifestyles. It is likely that improvement will probably be effected over a period of decades. Fries (1980), a medical researcher, believes the length of life is fixed; in 2045 the plateau level will be reached, when the average will be 85 years. According to Hayflick (1980), most cells may reproduce about 50 times, but two kinds of animal cells escape this pattern: cancer and germ cells. Cultures from human embryonic lung tissue regenerates about 15 times before dying. There is almost a perfect correlation between the normal life span and the number of times culture taken from this tissue regenerates (Cristofalo & Hayflick, 1985). If human beings could understand the common mechanism involved they could possibly reset the biological clock. Environmental factors such as traumatic life experiences also alter longevity. Also, according to Busse (1977, pl. 23), the concept "that such experiences may differently influence the span of men as opposed to women" has not been given a great deal of attention. Busse says that by comparing the age of death in male and female identical twins, when each has died of natural causes, greater variation exists in the age of death in identical male twins than female twins. Therefore, one of the identical male twins has been exposed to a more hostile environment or accumulation of traumatic events than the other twin.

As the ranks of the aging grow, so will some terminologies develop to differentiate the aged--that is, the young-old, the middle-old, and the advanced elderly of 85 and beyond. The authors suggest 70 to 79 for the young-old; 80 to 89 for the old and 90-plus for the old-old. Older people, like the middlescent when viewed functionally, will not readily fit into chronological age brackets. However, the elderly view aging negatively both in themselves and in life in general. Their own stereotypes of aging are like those of other people, so they speak of others their own age as "old fogies," although they consider themselves to be all right (Moore, 1975). As Bernard Baruch said, "Old age is always 15 years older than I am."

Research on old persons' perception of age has shown that, as people grow older, they think old age begins later and later. Even some 80-year-olds think they are young (Rosow, 1974). Obviously, there is a cleavage between self-image and that held by others. Some people talk about age in terms of the manner in which people think, what they call psychological flexibility. Others suggest there is social age, physical age, and developmental age. We will examine next the physical and biological aspects of aging.

THE PHYSICAL MODE

Aging is a matter of differential effects upon the body. A man's hair can still be dark, but his vocal cords atrophied so that the voice is high-pitched and without the deeper resonance of earlier years. Kalish (1975) says it well when he suggests that "a man of 70 may retain a perfectly smooth, unwrinkled face, a full head of black hair, and a heart performing like that of a man in his 50s while his renal functioning may be like that of an 80-year-old." As interesting as this is, it does not provide us with a general view of the aging organism. Major research undertaken by Nathan Shock (1962) yielded some estimates of the ability of the human body to function gauged against the 30-year-old. According to his projections, the 75-year-old man has 56 percent of his original brain weight; his vital capacity--including the lung's ability to hold air, the time required to get the heart down to normal after exertion, and so on--is approximately 56 percent. His maximum work rate is 70 percent of his former benchmark ability. About two-thirds of the original number of nerve trunk fibers remain; however, 90 percent of his original nerve conduction velocity still exists. Weight and skeletal losses occur as aging proceeds, and in general this is good, as it serves to accommodate the aging heart and less effective cardiovascular system. People shrink in size due to the fact that the discs between their spinal vertebrae atrophy. The bones, however, become more porous, and broken bones are a source of major concern for the elderly. Women have higher rates of injury from falls than men, though the death rate is higher for men (Hogues, 1982). Following menopause, because of osteoporosis--a thinning of the bone--some women develop a "widow's hump." Women should take calcium supplements along with their regular diets to aid the skeletal system to keep its strength. A hip fracture may mean the end of mobility without assistance, and, since the marrow in the bones accounts for the red blood cells, the ability of the body suffers greatly in its attempt to sustain homeostasis and life in general. Tooth and gum problems are common. Most people over 65 years of age

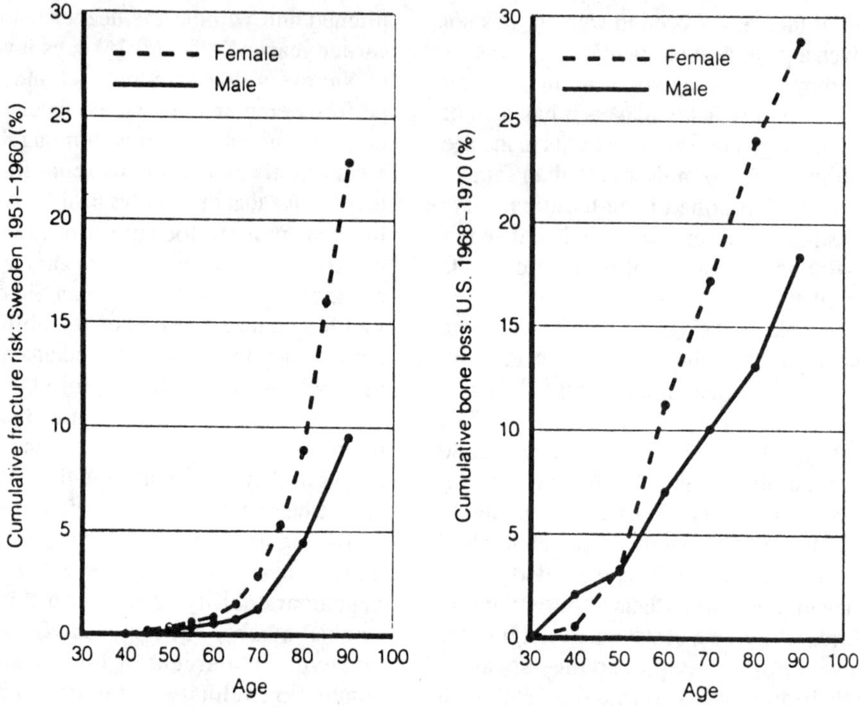

Figure 13.1 Cumulative fracture risk and bone loss curves. The cumulative fracture figure is about 10 percentage points lower than the cumulative bone loss figure. (*Source:* "Bone Loss and Aging" (p. 43) by S.M. Garn, 1982, in R. Goldman and M. Rockstein (eds.), *The Physiology and Pathology of Aging*, New York: Academic Press.)

have lost all or most of their teeth (Bromly, 1974).

Rahe and Arthur (1974) studied the effects of aging on swimming performance. They have concluded that swimming performance in aging athletes in excellent condition is primarily affected by pulmonary function, and decreases by roughly 1 percent per year from approximately 25 years up to the age of 59. This age was the last age included in the study. The authors noted considerable differences among the men in that some approaching the age of 60 were breaking a minute for the 100-yard freestyle, a time that 15 years prior was a good time for high school swim teams. Of course, improved methods play a part in this performance. Still, that this can be done at all is promising and suggests what is in the offing as it continues. Jeremy Gaines, 72-year-old of Chesapeake, VA, ran the 100 meters in 14 seconds in the Virginia Golden Olympics in 1984. Although not a state record, this was only 2 seconds off the first Olympic Games' record in Athens, Greece (1896) (12 seconds - 100 meters).

As physiologist Shock (1962) has pointed out (see Figure 13.2) the heart pumps only 65 percent as much blood at age 75 as at age 30. The brain receives 80 percent as much blood, but the kidneys only 42 percent as much. Maximum oxygen declines by 60 percent; since oxygen is needed to combine with nutrients for the release of chemical building blocks and energy, the older person on the average has less staying power and lower reserves of strength. However, some 60-year-old men are as strong as some 20-year-old men. The same is true of women. Measures of the same kind of sample as those taken by Shock in 1962, 30 years later would undoubtedly reveal less decrements in physiological performance.

Sensory, Perceptual, and Motor Abilities

Sensory abilities age, like other aspects of the body, in varying fashion. Many at 70 have little or no impairment in seeing but cannot hear. Generally, however, there is on the average a lessening of sensitivity in hearing, vision, touch, and perhaps smell and taste. During the middle years most people develop farsightedness, though this tendency usually stabilizes at about age 60. By 65 people have other visual problems. They are likely to have 20/70 vision or less; perception of depth is more of a problem, as are color perception and ability to see in the dark (Bell, Wolf, & Bernholz, 1972). The retina cannot accommodate for sufficient light nor assist in recovering from glare exposure (Timiras, 1972). The lens becomes less transparent with age (Klein & Schieber, 1985). Peripheral vision, depth perception, and color vision in the dark become poorer (Botwinick, 1978). Relief from some of these problems is offered by replacing the cloudy lens for a plastic one in the case of cataracts. That vision losses are accumulative can be judged by the number of older persons who are blind. Over 50 percent of the legally blind are over age 65 (White House Conference, 1972). Half of the accidental deaths of those 65 years or older are caused by falls because, according to Hogue (1982), they cannot perceive hazards or respond effectually.

Hearing, Smell, and Taste

Hearing deficiencies are common among older persons. The older the adult, the poorer the perception of high-frequency sounds (Dibner, 1975). It is difficult for many older people to follow a conversation when there are competing or background noises from radios, television sets, or crowds talking around them. Even though vision problems affect nearly everyone by the age of 70, hearing impairment is more pervasive, as hearing affects 13 percent between the ages of 65 and 74, whereas 26 percent of those over 75 years of age. Of an estimated 5 million with serious hearing loss in the United States, 55 percent are over 65 (Kalish, 1975). Men are affected to a greater degree than women, mainly in lost sensitivity to

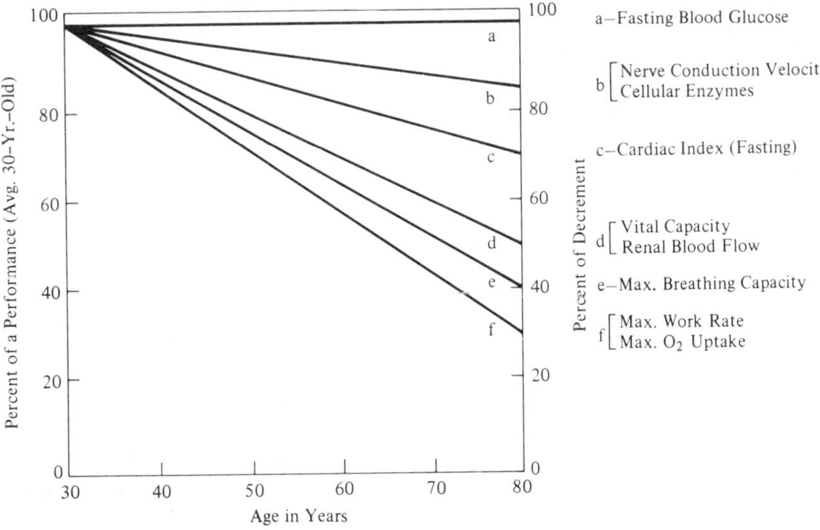

Figure 13.2 Age decrements in physiological performance. (*Source:* Shock, 1962.)

higher tones and among different sounds (Belsky, 1984). Part of the problem is loss of hair cells in the inner ear. Hearing aids are available that reduce the background noise for those not afflicted with a physical change causing impairment of the auditory receiver.

Smell and taste are difficult to determine; some studies suggest less sensitivity to sugar and salt taste and a slight loss in the number of taste buds from age 20 to 70 (Dibner, 1975). In time, atrophy of the olfactory bulb, the organ found at the base of the brain which is responsible for smell perception, accounts for this (Bromley, 1974).

General body sensitivity diminishes over time, although people are more sensitive to touch but have less tolerance to hot and cold. Some older people report no pain after contracting such diseases as peritonitis or pneumonia. Botwinick (1984) believes some people are less sensitive to pain, though there are marked variations. Maintenance of homeostasis is a frequent problem, and along with this is the reduced sensitivity of tactile senses, especially in the hands and feet. There is little evidence to show that perception of pain, heat or cold lessens (Dibner, 1975). This follows the morphology of development and decline in that the extremities are the last to be fully developed and the first to decline. The vestibule senses, which relate to posture and balance of the skeletal system, lose some ability, undoubtedly accounting for many falls of the old and complaints of dizziness (Rodstein, 1964). Sleep at night changes little, although its quality, judged by more frequent waking periods, is reduced as interruptions occur more often for toilet trips and cover changes (Thompson & Marsh, 1973). The older person should rest more frequently and lie down more often. However, exercise and activity would provide more oxygen, strength, and generally better functioning of the body precluding some naps and resting (Salthouse, 1985). Many should have a nap or two a day in addition to the night's sleep, one in the late morning and another in the afternoon.

Sensory-Motor Abilities

Psychomotor performance declines during the adult years; muscle strength diminishes from the twenties onward; speed of response and reflexes, although yielding slowly through the years, do diminish. Digital reaction remains

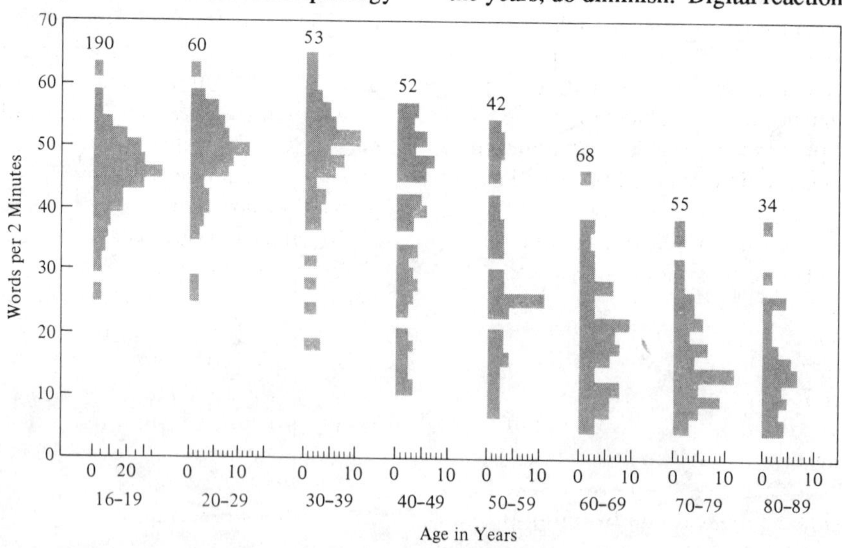

Figure 13.3 Age differences in writing speed. (*Source:* Birren & Botwinick, 1951.)

on a plateau until nearly 60, foot reaction remains on a plateau to 40, and pursuit reaction drops rather precipitously after 30 (Miles, 1931). Handwriting is a complex skill, learned through practice over a long period of time. Birren and Botwinick (1951) found that the speed of handwriting slows down with advancing age. Figure 13.3 indicates that the range of differences are wide, but even so those in their sixties to eighties could do half as well in writing speed as those in their forties. The range of those in their eighties is equal to the range of those 70. So if we talk about reaction time we should note wide variation among people.

Slowness in processing formation and decreased efficiency in sensory-motor coordination create a condition with motor skills not conducive to driving safely. Data reveal that people over 65 have a disproportionate number of accidents, usually relating to improper turning and the inability to see and to determine speed. Drivers over 70 have been characterized as "very similar to teen-age drivers" relative to their high accident rates (Zylman, 1972). This results in death in the 75 to 84 group twice as high as the 15 to 24 group, although the injury rate is much lower (Hogue, 1982). The best explanation for the general age-related slowing of behavior does not involve peripheral processes (peripheral processes relate to sensory and motor function), but is related to changes in the central processes--the slowing down of the cycle time, the time required for neural activity (nerve conduction, etc.) (Salthouse, 1985).

There is a positive note concerning the losses suffered in psychomotor ability. It is increasingly believed that physical exercise throughout life, particularly in the early middle years onward, diminishes losses in speed, stamina, and strength. In addition, basic functions of the body, such as circulation and breathing, continue at higher levels of efficiency than otherwise expected (Bromley, 1974). Following a physical conditioning program perhaps indicates that many of the effects we associate with aging result more often from the lack of using our bodies and requiring them to perform more vigorously than from the years on the calendar. Fries (1980) states "if loss of reserve function represents aging in some sense, then exercising an organ presents a strategy for modifying the aging process" (p. 133).

Sex Behavior in Older Age

Contrary to the notion that there is little sex among the aging past 60, research reveals that some older persons even into their nineties enjoy having sex. Society has placed a taboo upon sex for the older citizen, perhaps growing out of the Victorian age. American humor reinforces the idea that the years past 60 are sexless. Some comments are "Definition of old age: the time in life when a man flirts with girls but can't remember why"; or "The sexual life cycle of man: tri-weekly, try weekly, try weakly"; or the quote from Puner (1974): "Young men want to be faithful and are not. Old men want to be faithless and cannot." Eda LeShan, the development psychologist, says, "having started my adult life feeling guilty about sex, I'll be damned if I'll end my days feeling guilty about too little" (AARP, 1991).

The notion that sex is good for the young but lecherous for the old is another. Pfeiffer (1977) reported that a number of investigators have commented on the difficulty of obtaining subjects for a study clearly labeled sexual in nature. Even physicians complain that information on sex upsets their patients. Not until about 1960 did the physical part of sex become recognized by the scientific community as a normal element in the lives of older people (Breeher, 1984). There is a small but growing body of information on the subject, coming principally from the Kinsey studies, from those of Masters and Johnson, and more recently from the Duke University publications on the natural history of sexual behavior in old age.

Of the subjects studied by Kinsey, there were 106 men and 56 women over 60 years of age. Considering the large total sample (14,084 men and a similar number of women), this group was vastly underrepresented. Many analyses in their works do not include the aged at all. Suffice it to say this limited evidence reveals that 20 percent of those men who were 60 were impotent; this had increased to 75 percent among those who were 80 years of age. Among females, while noting a gradual decline in activity from 20 to 60, it was suggested that this was the product of the aging process in the male (Kinsey, 1953, p. 353). Kinsey and his colleagues further observed that in contrast to men, single and postmarital females had rates of sexual activity that were far below those of their married counterparts.

The initial Masters and Johnson report (1966) revealed that men past 60 were slower than younger men to be aroused sexually, slower to develop erection, slower to effect intromission, and slower to achieve ejaculation. Physiological signs of sexual excitement, the sexual flush, and increased muscle tone were less obvious than in younger subjects. Findings paralleled those for women; physical response to sexual stimulation noted by breast engorgement, nipple erection, sexual flush over the breasts, and so on, were diminished among those women who had had regular sexual activity. Masters and Johnson interviewed 133 men above the age of 60 (52 were above 70), concluding that male sexual responsiveness wanes as men age. They place an emphasis on the role of monotony in determining declining sexual activity. Busse (1977) questions why this should be more important in advanced age than earlier in life. Masters and Johnson do not explain this, but do conclude that men who have had a high sexual "output" during their younger years are likely to continue to be sexually active in their older years. Of the women interviewed by these investigators, 54 were above age 60, and 17 were above 70. On the basis of this sample they say that the capacity for sexual intercourse with orgasmic response is not lacking in older women. At 60, one of four men are affected by impotence; at 80 three of four. They are probably less related to age than heart problems, circulatory disease, diabetes, or some types of surgery or medication (Solnick & Corbit, 1983).

Longitudinal Studies of Sexuality

The Duke Longitudinal Study, begun in 1954 at their Center for the Study of Aging and Human Development, investigated 254 subjects. Ranging in age from 60 to 94 years, divided approximately equally between men and women, they were seen repeatedly at three-year intervals. Over the years a number of subjects dropped out due to illness, death, and moving from the area. Remaining besides singles were 31 intact couples, providing an opportunity to cross-validate the information provided by each marriage partner. From the longitudinal data two major conclusions were drawn: (1) sexual interest and coital activity are evidenced in many persons beyond 60, and (2) the patterns of sexual interest and coital activity differ substantially for men and women of the same age. Eighty percent of the men who were not impaired in health or in intellectual and social functioning reported continuing interest in sexual matters. Ten years later the proportion of those still sexually interested had not declined significantly.

Of women whose health was not impaired and whose intellectual functioning was good at the start of the study, only about one-third reported continuing sexual interest. This proportion did not change greatly over the next 10 years. Only a fifth of these same healthy women reported at the start of the study that they were still having sexual intercourse regularly. Data from the Kinsey (1953) and the Duke Study (Pfeiffer, Verwoerdt, & Wang, 1969) agreed that only a third of the women reported strong sexual feelings in their younger years. Kinsey also reported total sexual outlet among all age groups to be at lower levels for women.

Sexual Activity

A possible explanation of the sexual outlet is the interest and activity differential among men and women. Beyond this is the fact that the onset of menopause has a negative influence on sexual interest in some women. The data from the Duke study indicate that the median age of cessation of intercourse occurred nearly a decade earlier in women than in men--that is, 60 for women and 68 for men (Pfeiffer, et al., 1968). A majority of the wives attributed this to their husbands, with the men in general agreeing with them. It seems likely that some older men are obtaining sexual gratification by masturbation and from sources other than their wives. While the Duke study (Busse, 1977) showed gradual decline in sexual interest and activity with increasing age, the longitudinal study revealed that 20 to 25 percent of the men, but only a small percentage of the women, had rising sexual interest and activity with advancing age. The investigators involved in this study believe there is no basis for the idea that "you can wear the body out." The contrary seems true. Persons who have been very active in their younger years tend to continue their sexual lives into the latest decades of their lives (Pfeiffer & Davis, 1972). Table 13.1 presents results of a study of the frequency of sexual intercourse among older persons. Elderly widows and widowers interested in dating or marriage are often urged by family and friends to give up the idea. Provision for privacy is often lacking; therefore solitary sexual acts are foreclosed.

Interruptions of sexual activity due to illness need not always be permanent whether the illness is physical or psychological. For instance, the myocardial infarction, in the physical category, and depressive reaction in the psychological, are types of problems that interrupt intercourse. These, according to Masters and Johnson (1970), need not be permanent, for once the myocardial infarct has healed there is no reason (unless the impairment is so great that even limited exercise must be foregone) why the patient should not return to regular sexual activity. Relative to depressive reaction, when it has been treated, the patient should be told that his or her decline in sexual activity was an expression of the depressive reaction, not of advancing age.

FREQUENCY (IN PERCENT) OF SEXUAL INTERCOURSE IN LATER LIFE

Group	Number	None	Once a month	Once a week	2–3 times a week	More than 3 times a week
Men						
46–50	43	0	5	62	26	7
51–55	41	5	29	49	17	0
56–60	61	7	38	44	11	0
61–65	54	20	43	30	7	0
66–71	62	24	48	26	2	0
Total	261	12	34	41	12	1
Women						
46–50	43	14	26	39	21	0
51–55	41	20	41	32	5	2
56–60	48	42	27	25	4	2
61–65	44	61	29	5	5	0
66–71	55	73	16	11	0	0
Total	231	44	27	22	6	1

Source: Pfeiffer, Verwoerdt, and Davis (1972, p. 1264). Copyright 1972, The American Psychiatric Association. Reprinted by permission.

Illness Patterns Among the Aged

Contrary to popular myths, one characteristic of older persons is that they are less often affected by acute illness than are younger people. However, when such illness occurs, it leads to a greater number of days of restricted activity than illness in the younger adult. Table 13.2 provides the number of acute illnesses per 100 persons per year, by age.

Even though the aged, those over 65, have more days of restricted activity, it is still less than for children under 5 (see Table 13.3). Also data from HEW (1973) reveal that approximately 15 percent of those aged 45 to 65 are hospitalized every year, compared with 25 percent of those over 65. Older people are probably in better health than is generally known due to gains in education, health care, and support.

TABLE 13.2 Number of acute illnesses per 100 persons per year, by age

Age	Number of illnesses
Under 5	372
5-14	290
15-24	239
25-44	204
45-64	144
65+	109

Source: National Center for Health Statistics (1974, p. 22).

TABLE 13.3 Days of restricted activity associated with acute illnesses per 100 persons per year, by age

Age	Days of restricted activity
Under 5	1,151
5-14	896
15-24	833
25-44	883
45-64	928
65+	1,092

Source: National Center for Health Statistics (1974, p. 23).

Based upon data obtained by the U.S. Department of Health and Human Services (1988), the following shows a number of selected chronic conditions in those aged 65 to 74 and those over 75, per 1,000 people.

TYPE OF CONDITION

Problem	Ages 65-74	Ages 75 & up
Type: Genito-urinary, endocrine		
Diabetes	91.9	108.5
Goiter or thyroid problem	23.8	29.1
Migraine headache	21.3	20.1
Kidney trouble	28.8	39.3
Bladder disorders	29.5	53.0
Disease of prostate	26.7	22.6
Type: Circulatory Conditions		
Heart disease	250.0	319.4
Ischic heart	120.9	154.4
Heart rhythm disorders	74.7	60.7
High blood pressure (hypertension)	385.2	409.2
Varicose veins of lower extremities	76.2	71.9
Hemorrhoids	70.2	64.1
Type: Respiratory Conditions		
Chronic bronchitis	62.9	55.4
Asthma	46.4	36.3
Hay fever or allergic rhinitis sans asthma	72.4	67.2
Chronic sinusitis	168.6	170.7
Emphysema	44.5	32.7
Type: Skin and musculoskeletal conditions		
Arthritis	443.3	540.1
Gout	28.5	39.6
Trouble with bunions	31.9	46.7
Trouble with dry itching skin	27.7	38.4
Trouble with in-grown toenails	39.6	57.8
Trouble with corns and calluses	39.7	54.4
Type: Impairments		
Visual	69.3	136.3
Cataracts	84.3	233.2
Glaucoma	29.1	58.5
Hearing impairment	244.2	378.4
Tinnitus	83.2	88.3
Deformity or orthopedic impairment	158.4	195.7
Back	93.0	115.1

Lower extremities	75.5	107.4
Upper extremities	13.8	18.1
Type: Selected digestive conditions		
Ulcer	42.9	30.0
Hernia or abdominal cavity	46.5	84.8
Frequent indigestion	43.3	35.6
Enteritis or volitis	11.2	46.2
Diverticula of intestines	41.9	42.7
Frequent constipation	51.2	83.9

Arteriosclerotic heart disease is the most important cause of death in the elderly in all age ranges--65 to 74, 75 to 84, and 84 and up--with cerebral and subarachnoid hemorrhage second. Although neoplasm is among the highest 20 causes of death among the aged with increases at every age, lung cancer is the exception, dropping from age 65 onward. The death rate for emphysema remains relatively constant.

Age	Number of illnesses
Under 5	372
5–14	290
15–24	239
25–44	204
45–64	144
65+	109

Source: National Center for Health Statistics (1974, p. 22).

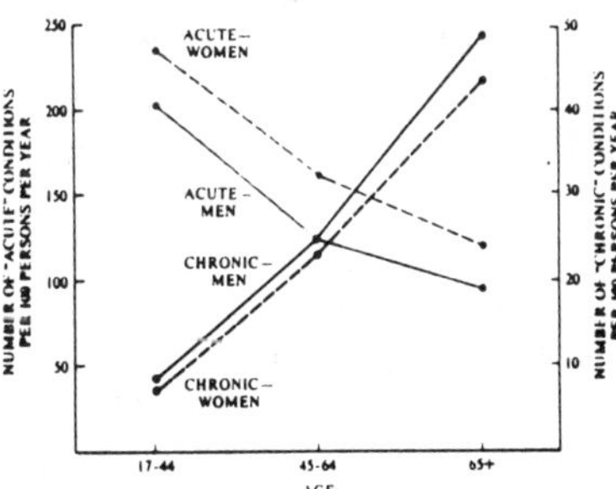

Figure 13.4 The number of acute (short-term) illnesses tends to go down with age, while the number of chronic illnesses goes up. These particular figures, from 1978, are typical of health patterns in the United States in recent years. (*Source:* National Center for Health Statistics, *Vital and Health Statistics*, Series 10, No. 130.)

Health Status

Health for the elderly is frequently a fragile state of affairs: a delicate balance is maintained and a minor illness can lead to major consequences. For instance, aspirin prescribed for a patient with arthritic pain can cause a flare-up of a peptic ulcer, or a diuretic prescribed for mild congestive failure may cause a painful onslaught of gout. Minor changes can create difficulty; because of this, physicians exercise caution in altering routines, drug usage, and activities of their aged patients. The acute illnesses of the elderly are not unique, for in general the chronic illnesses and causes of death are similar to those in the middle years (National Center for Health Statistics, 1974). Chronic disease is common among the aged, but usually results in only mild limitations in everyday functioning. The poor delivery of health care to the aged has more profound effects than do the illnesses that seem directly attributable to aging (Estes, 1977).

THE SOCIAL MODE

Only in the past two decades have investigators examined the nature of the social setting and the relationships that exist among older people in society. Among the various age cohorts the elderly have had a low priority. The aged typically have held higher status in agricultural societies than in industrial ones. This needs some further analysis, however, for high status in many hunting and agricultural societies meant for the aged merely relief from work, becoming advisors to tribes, and not being allowed to go hungry, as among Kaffir men (Holden, 1971). In modern society older people are better cared for. There is some evidence that while employment, occupational, and education status of the aged relative to younger people has declined substantially in several industrial societies, this may be leveling off or reversing itself in the most advanced nations, such as the United States and Canada (Palmore & Manton, 1974). Whether the aged are accorded high or low status, the average old person has to adjust to new conditions and new tasks the same as do young adults. The nature of the tasks, however, do differ.

The Developmental Tasks for the Older Person

Havighurst (1972) suggests that the development tasks for later maturity differ in only one fundamental respect from those of other periods: they involve disengagement from some of the more active roles of middle age and leave open the decision to initiate new activities and participate in such new roles as grandparenting, new employment, membership in retired citizen groups, or volunteer work. Perhaps a minority accept disengagement from active roles with grace, but most older persons react by entering other activities. Great effort is expended to hold onto their mental faculties, their biological strength, and their economic achievements. The social area provides the best opportunity to continue or even improve the quality of life by social group membership, part-time work, church participation, and kinship relationships. The tasks of this period are more personal than the earlier ones. The major task in life is to clarify, deepen, and accept one's own life and to use a lifetime of experience with personal change or loss to an advantage.

The following is a list of Havighurst's Development Tasks, slightly abridged:

1) Adjusting to changing physical strength and health;
2) Adjusting to retirement and less income;
3) Adjusting to the ill health and/or death of the spouse;
4) Establishing affiliation with one's own age group;
5) Adapting a social role in a flexible way; and
6) Establishing satisfactory living arrangements.

Many of these are appropriate, many are not depending upon the individual situation. Certainly everyone will experience loss of strength and probably health. But many will have resources to deal with various needs and many will not suffer a loss in standard of living, for there will be fewer expenditures unless catastrophic health problems arise.

Slightly fewer than half will face the death of a spouse. Adaptation to a social role has already been accomplished and affiliation with one's own age group usually is handled years before one is 70. Havighurst's idea is that from a psychological standpoint the older person is discouraged from trying to stay with a younger cohort group--their lack of energy and money may relegate them to an inferior station. On the other hand, if they participate in the older age group, socialization is easily facilitated and opportunities exist for participation and leadership roles. Living circumstances have typically been ongoing so require no drastic changes. Of 32 million Americans over 65, only 4 million or so are in nursing homes.

Erikson characterized the task of late adulthood as one of maintaining integrity and forswearing disparagement. This may be too general and too amorphous. It is true that one understands integrity as the sense that life is worthwhile and has purpose. Peck (1968), who enlarged on the social crisis of Erikson for the middle years, also offers three tasks for the later years. He suggests that life is not over and there are things to consider and do. After all, many people at 65 or 70 are going to live 20 or more years. Peck says three developmental aspects await the older adult:

1. Ego differentiation versus work-role: The task is to develop new interests--to shift our attention from our former jobs to avocations and other aspects of living--gardening, our spouses, maybe part-time or volunteer work, creative

activity--so that we keep our sense of being and perspective.

2. Body transcendence versus body preoccupation: If we live long enough more pain and disability are likely, hence we should elevate the mind over the body, emphasizing the importance of mental activities--family and other social activities, projects, conversation with friends--all of which take the mind off our ailments and problems.

3. Ego transcendence versus ego preoccupation: The thought is abhorrent that we will at some point stop thinking, imagining, and wondering. Everyone must live to the fullest until they die. When preoccupied with when or how we will die, living will be diminished unnecessarily. Hence living the good life is the best preparation for leaving it.

ADJUSTMENT TO RETIREMENT

The most fundamental factor in the lives of middlescent men and women is their occupation. In America, if the job is lost many older people feel life is lost. For with employment one receives status, social interaction, financial rewards, and--perhaps most fundamental of all--a belief that one is important. Where inadequate sources of money affect retirement, it militates against broadening one's social and avocational life and may even reduce one's activity, such as causing one to drop out of a club because of the dues. It is typically viewed by many economic advisors that an adequate retirement means that one owns a home and will have accumulated, through Social Security, pension funds, and savings, money equal to about two-thirds of that required in the average years of middle adult life. Eventually, working-class persons may suffer less than the middle-class, because they receive higher Social Security benefits relative to their former wages. But few of these have private pension funds, and of those who are unmarried 87 percent are poor--mostly widows (Morrison, 1982, p. 165). It is also suggested that one have a next egg of several thousand dollars for emergency purposes, but inflation increasingly cuts into retirement funds. Since many women are now working with full pension benefits and at better rates of pay, the situation is not all bleak. Though the final outcome for an individual is unknown, certainly more persons will be covered by some kind of insurance that is calculated to change as the value of the dollar does. They will also have available Medicare, Medicaid, and social agency assistance (*Social and Economic Characteristics of the Older Population*, Current Population Reports, 1979). Since the recent changes in the federal law (1978) allowing people to work until they are 70, some states, such as Virginia, do not have laws mandating retirement by 70 for state employees. Even so the National Center for Health Statistics asked 55-to-74-year-olds (both working and retired persons) about their ability and desire to work. Most could perform the basic tasks: bending over, kneeling, climbing stairs, carrying 10 to 25 pounds, etc. Six of ten indicated they had no problem with the work. Asked if they would go back to work, 12 percent of those who retired for reasons other than health expressed interest in going back to work. In fact some businesses have tried to woo retirees back to work with good incentives with little success (*Wall Street Journal*, July 9, 1987, p. 29).

	Percentage of Men Employed Full-Time or Part-Time	*Percentage of Women Employed Full-Time or Part-Time*
60 and 61	65.7	38.6
62 to 64	44.3	27.7
65 to 69	23.6	13.0
70 and older	10.3	4.2

Figure 13.5 Percentages of men and women employed full or part time. (Based on data from Bureau of Labor Statistics, 1987.)

Many work, some part time, after 70. Figure 13.5 shows the percentage involved in 1986.

Working part time is one way of easing into full retirement. Nearly 40 percent of men and women work until 70 (*Wall Street Journal*, 1987). Typically research shows that men and women, when they have enough resources to maintain a stable living, are satisfied in retirement. Those who do not have sufficient funds are unsatisfied.

Satisfactions in Retirement

The picture frequently presented of happy retirees in utopia-like settings is not in harmony with scientific studies bearing on the adjustment of the retiree. Retirement is frequently a time of uncertainty, loneliness, and anxiety, affected by increasing separation from active participation in social and world affairs. Therefore, 50 percent of older workers and retirees who have no private pension plan typically do not have access to retirement education (Morrison, 1982).

Lohmann (1980), studying three groups of elderly (n=259), utilizing a variety of adjustment scales, with over 60 nursing home residents, home-bound and "community" aged, found that the white community cluster and females had the highest degree of satisfaction and adjustment. Greater control and therefore activity obviously benefits the life of the community aged. Anatharaman (1980) found in studying older Hindus (Barbalore City), 59 men and 59 women aged 59 to 73, that respondents staying with their families were better adjusted than those staying in institutions. The perceived loss of control is apparently important in adjustment and satisfaction, as indicated in a study of elderly women by Fawcett, Stonner, and Zepelin (1980), who reported that the lack of external control (belief in controlling influence of others) promotes good morale to the institutionalized elderly. Life satisfaction was inversely related to perception of the institutional constraint and, in fact, was its most powerful determinant.

According to McGee and Wells (1982) men view retirement as a threat to their traditional identity. Housework is not acceptable to them as a substitute, and most did not share these tasks any more after than before retirement. Women are affected by their husband's retirement in that they suffer a loss of freedom, privacy, and a reduction in their social network. These investigations suggest that for some older women the chance to again nurture their husbands will offset the fact that their children have gone. Certainly younger cohorts of women, a majority of whom will have had jobs, will as they progress to old age come to retirement with a different perspective and problems.

Transitions to Retirement

Retirement, according to Robert Atchley (1976) comes in phases:

1. Pre-retirement - Some years before people stop working they think of retirement in vague terms, but concern for the present overshadows the future.

2. Near retirement - This period involves making plans for the new period in people's lives, which is generally viewed positively. They work out the major details and recognize work will stop.

3. Honeymoon period - Immediately following retirement euphoria reigns-- new-found freedom brings excitement, and opportunities abound for doing what retirees didn't have time for before.

4. Disenchantment - Life settles into a routine--time and boredom are too plentiful. People have an emotional let-down and some may try to find work at least part-time.

5. Reorientation - Emotional and social adaptation depend principally on people's disillusionment. They try to find things to do, new people in non-work areas.

6. Stability - People come to grip with themselves and retirement, arriving at choices for a comfortable and orderly lifestyle.

7. Termination - Retirement is ended either by disability, which makes the person immobile or limited, or by death. With the former, people lose their autonomous status.

Some of these phases are not in sequential order, and many persons do not go through the disenchantment and reorientation stages. Successful aging means contentment and happiness; the opposite side of this is misery and despair. One of the chief underlying factors in happiness is moderately good health--being mobile, able to care for oneself, and having a clear mind. Of course, reasonably good economic conditions are needed to exist (see Figure 13.6). Many widowers find they have to pay for many services that their wives formerly provided (cleaning, food preparation, etc.), therefore have less money.

This 1985 outlook was optimistic--higher Social Security taxes and fewer benefits in the 1990s may have affected these views for the 55-to-65 and over-65 age groups. Many are taxed heavily on their Social Security benefits and pay more for fewer services from Medicare and Medicaid.

Retirement--The Use of Time

While the work life has increased, the period of retirement has also increased one-half or more, for many up to 25 years. This creates a special problem for retirees, for they must, in some cases, adjust to a life of retirement or leisure for which they are usually poorly prepared. Time is a peculiar thing: we strive to reduce hours and years of work, and when we have done so, we do not know what to do with the free time. Those who have shown creativeness, resourcefulness, and individualism during past crises may be expected to face with greater security the sudden change resulting from retirement. This knowledge should contribute to or produce more favorable attitudes toward retirement. The innovative mode of adaptation, therefore, should be associated with greater prevalence of positive attitudes.

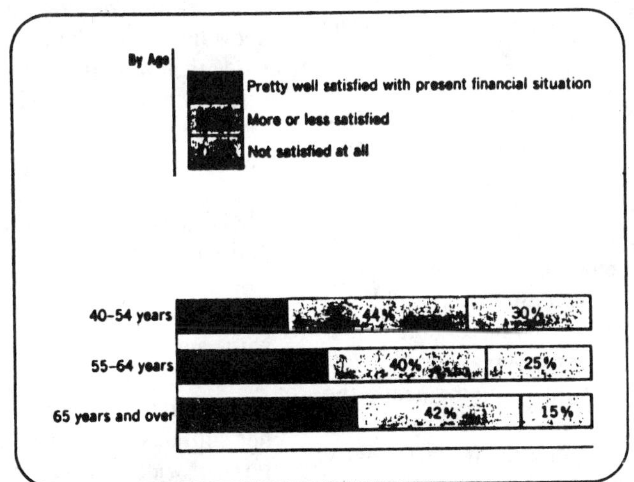

Figure 13.6 How Americans 54 to 64 and 75 and over view their finances. (*Source:* Adapted from the surveys by the National Opinion Research Center, General Social Surveys, 1982, 1983, and 1985 combined. *Public Opinion*, February/March 1985, p. 34.)

TABLE 13.4 Mean Activity Score by Age Category (1962)

Age*	Mean Score
60-64	29.2
65-69	28.1
70-74	27.1
75-79	27.7
80 and over	25.2

*n=250.
Source: Maddox and Eisdorfer (1962).

Adjustment to the Loss of a Spouse

Over half of the women over 65 in the United States are widowed. Three times as many women as men experience the shock and trauma of losing a spouse (Figure 13.7). In 1986, 65.5 percent of the total male population were married, 2.6 percent were widowed, and 6.6 percent were divorced. Among females 60.5 percent were married, 12.4 percent widowed, and 8.9 percent divorced. In 1986, 22.5 percent of men over the age of 75 were widowed, while 67 percent of women in the same age bracket were widows.

It is common to hear the expression by widows in their seventies "once your husband dies old age sets in quickly." In 1986 there were more than 11 million widows over 18 in the United States. The chances of becoming a widow at age 65 is one in two, at 85 it is three in four (U.S. Bureau of the Census, 1988). Some believe it is easier to become a widow in old age than when one is younger; however, grief is grief, and more of the old need support from their spouses than do younger widows. The younger widow usually has children close by and a larger support group at hand. Additionally, in the younger women's group the likelihood of remarriage is a possibility, and the long-term effects on morale are not usually found. Where the older widows or widowers have no children and are in poor health the loss of a spouse can be devastating (Lopata, et al., 1982).

The death of a spouse is a major psychological problem. Adjustments involve a whole range of issues--moving in with relatives, moving to a smaller home or apartment, moving to be near kin perhaps in other states, going to a nursing home, remarrying, deciding whether or not to work, deciding whom to confide in. The changing life will require learning new ways. New learning is difficult enough without the other distractions.

Death of a spouse and close friends or kin produces for the aged painful forms of isolation, as disruption of the social structure is radically affected. If the spouse dies, then disorganization of lifestyles creates vast problems of reorganization in one's life. One heartbroken man who had been married for 47 years confessed after his wife had died: "I hardly know how much of my feeling is sheer selfishness, not having her wait on me in the many little ways that I had come to take for granted" (Rogers, 1979, p. 350). The death of a spouse means the loss of a sexual relationship, the loss of a significant person with whom one has shared work, companionship, and leisure (Parkes, 1972).

Unfortunately there is little information from reliable research on widowers. We do know that the death rate of widowers over 45 is twice that of married men. It should be noted that over half of all men between 46 and 65 who are widowed remarry usually after three or four years (Cleveland & Gianturco, 1976).

Social Opportunities of Widows and Widowers

Our information about the social relationships and lives of widows is more abundant. One source, Lopata (1973), studied a number of widows living in metropolitan Chicago. From her subjects she was able to delineate three types of widowhood through the extent of their involvement in different types of social relationships. One of the types included women who had superior educations and were from the middle class. These women were highly in-

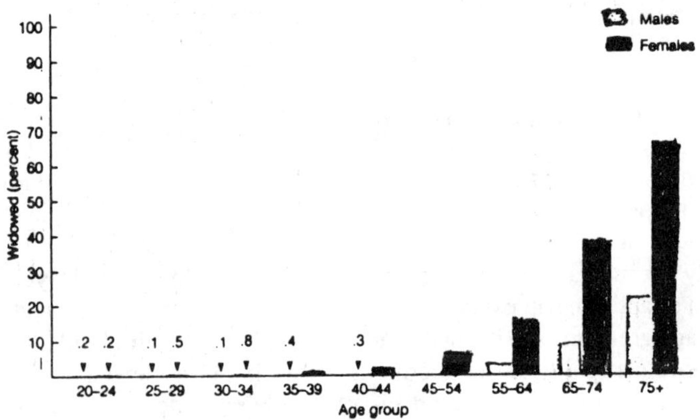

Figure 13.7 Percent of people widowed by age group and sex.

volved in being wives to their husbands; they assigned many roles to them as persons, fathers, and partners in leisure-time and other activities. Widowhood left the women of this group with a greater disorganized self-identity and life. On the other hand, they had more resources through which to form a new lifestyle once the "grief work" (acknowledging the death and lamenting it) was completed.

At the other end of the continuum were women from the lower socio-economic working classes who lived in ethnic neighborhoods, who belonged to sex-segregated worlds and were closely involved with kin and neighbors as friends. Following the death of their husbands, they received considerable support from this network of women friends with whom they had been intimately associated.

A third type was categorized by Lopata as being somewhat in between the other types. This group involved women who play many roles, a number of which did not include the husbands. The adjustment to widowhood tended to vary with the degree to which their social relationships were integrated with those of their husbands. The most important long-term negative consequence has been found by the research of Harvey and Bahr (1974) to be socio-economic loss rather than the fact of widowhood. Many of the widows in the Lopata study maintained their own homes rather than moving in with kin or married children. Only 10 percent chose to do otherwise; the others wanted the independence of being in their own households.

It is generally thought that when widowed people can have the help of a close friend who is supportive and will listen to the "talking out," or of a caring family, it greatly assists the transition to a new stable life. If they have anticipated the death, as in chronic illness, this usually makes the grieving and adjustment period shorter. Being socially marooned is a problem; many persons categorize the widow or widower differently; they may not know how to act or they feel pain over the loss, or they are afraid to get involved in being responsible for the person, or they may not wish to think about their own mortality. Nevertheless the result is the same: isolation. Religious faith and a church connection or philosophical belief helps many people along with friends, perhaps new ones, and finding another identity.

Since there are many more widows (8 to 1) than widowers there is no dearth of companionship, support, and care for these men. Many marry within a year of their wife's death. In a study of couples 60 years of age or older, Vinich (1978) found that those married two to six years were very happy in their marriages.

Maintenance of Social Relations and Family Ties

Gerontologists have emphasized the positive aspects of aging, suggesting that persons at 65 or 75 can have considerable social influence and exercise leadership roles. Reasonable health, if maintained by diet and medical care, usually preempts senility for most. The view of Havighurst (1972) in establishing an explicit affiliation with one's age group misses its mark, for among the older adults this can be accomplished just by existing or doing nothing positive. The task should emphasize having a continuing wide range of interrelationships with young adults and the middle aged, in addition to their own age group. There may be age grading for certain social functions and games. It may be the 75-year-old does not wish to play singles in tennis or make a quick trip 500 miles away to see a football game or go on a short vacation with a 50-year-old group. Certainly 75-year-old people probably will be more comfortable with persons of like age.

Grandparenting

Ninety-four percent of older people with children are grandparents and the chance of being a great-grandparent increases with age: Of those over 80, three-fourths are great-grandparents. On average women are a grandmother by 50; men grandfathers by 52 (Troll, 1983). They have been portrayed as white-haired, genial, wearing glasses, and lavishing gifts and attention on their grandchildren. The grandfather is often viewed as a male grandmother. College students, when asked to provide an image of their grandparents, often see little difference in them (Hess and Markson, 1980). Today's grandparents (those in the middle and upper classes) are not those of yesteryear--they are healthier, wealthier, more active, and better educated. They may conform to a category such as those reviewed in Chapter 12; the most common relationship they enjoy with grandchildren is companionship style. Grandparents do not baby-sit often, they do not discipline; they may play or watch television with the kids,

Characteristics of elderly person	Same house-hold	Daily	3–4 per week	Children's frequency of contact 1–2 per week	1–2 per month	2–4 per year	Annually or less	Total	Number of children*
Marital status									
Married	5.3	11.6	4.8	26.1	21.7	20.3	10.1	100	207
Widowed, single, divorced	1.6	22.9	9.4	29.9	11.5	16.2	9.4	100	314
Age									
75–9	4.0	13.5	7.6	28.1	18.1	19.9	8.9	100	327
80–4	2.2	23.0	7.4	27.4	12.5	19.3	8.2	100	135
85+	0.0	32.8	6.3	26.6	7.8	11.0	15.6	100	64
Sex									
Male	5.6	18.6	6.8	20.3	14.7	22.0	11.8	100	177
Female	1.7	18.1	7.7	31.5	15.7	16.9	8.3	100	349
Social class									
Professional, managerial	(4.3)	(17.0)	(12.8)	(23.4)	(7.1)	(21.3)	(6.4)	100	47
Skilled, non-manual	1.3	13.9	6.3	24.1	12.7	31.6	10.1	100	79
Skilled manual	4.9	18.9	6.7	22.6	19.5	16.5	11.6	100	164
Semi-skilled and unskilled	1.8	19.6	6.7	34.7	13.8	16.0	7.6	100	225
Disability									
None	7.1	20.0	5.9	34.1	14.1	8.3	10.6	100	85
Slight	1.0	17.6	8.8	14.7	24.5	25.5	7.9	100	102
Minor	2.9	14.7	5.9	32.4	14.8	22.8	6.6	100	136
Appreciable	4.5	18.8	7.1	33.0	12.5	12.5	11.6	100	112
Severe	0.0	18.5	11.1	22.2	13.0	22.3	13.0	100	54
Very severe	(0.0)	(27.0)	(8.1)	(24.3)	(8.1)	(21.6)	(10.8)	100	37

*Total number of children of elderly people in the sample.

Figure 13.8 (a) Frequency of contact and (b) proximity between persons aged 65 and older and their children, by age. (From U.S. Bureau of the Census, 1988, p. 36.)

even take them on trips and keep them sometimes. But today's grandparents want freedom and fulfillment to use their leisure as they wish and have close, not constant, association with their grandchildren. Grandparents are certainly good for the young--they provide another source of support, a confident, a mentor, or an advocate, and they provide insight about one's family and its workings. Among middle and upper classes, grandparents often are the principal resource enabling the grandchild to attend camp, have music lessons, a car, and a college education. In times of crisis (divorce, illness, financial) they may be able to do what is necessary and helpful (Cherlin & Furstenberg, 1986).

Grandparents in the lower middle class often baby-sit regularly, either looking after their grandchildren at their home or going to their children's home. Among lower-class grandparents, they frequently live with one of their children and are often considered parents, making decisions, cooking meals, and disciplining their grandchildren. Of course, they are sometimes only in their thirties and forties, having had their children in their teens and early twenties, with their children repeating this pattern. The grandparenting role is not clearly defined, often mediated by the middle generation some of whom disagree with their parents' views, etc. The roles of grandparents generally depend upon inclination, personality, economics, geography, health, and the implicit and explicit ideas of the parents (Datan, et al., 1987).

To the older person the family often provides the greatest satisfaction, beginning after the children leave home, and their grandchildren are not their chief responsibility, and continuing into later years (Rollings & Feldman, 1970). Divorce rates among older couples are very low. Even so, the aged couple is often faced with new problems due to less money. There are problems with living arrangements, moving to smaller quarters, relationships with children, and health difficulties. As they age, elderly parents tend to move closer to rather than farther from their children.

The data below represent a British sample taken from Sheffield, England, a metropolitan center much like a mid-size American city such as Cincinnati. It is utilized here because it focuses on elderly persons, those above 75, excluding the young-old of Neugarten (1968) and the five years of Jones, who extends this category until 79 (Chapter 11).

A number of older parents cannot support themselves and have to rely upon children to supplement their sources of income or assume the entire responsibility of support. Two-thirds reported they received support from their families mostly by money. Another third depend upon children or other relatives for help with housework, meals, visits to the doctor, shopping, and travel. The older people are, the more likely they are to live with a child. Sometimes this is a grandchild now in the twenties or thirties. Twenty-eight percent of older people live with a middlescent child, usually a daughter, and this percentage increases with age. It is higher for women than for men (Shanas et al., 1986). Studies of the family interaction of elderly people in America show that, irrespective of social class, they are more likely to ask their daughters than their sons for help (Shanas et al., p. 113). Daughters are the principle providers of expressive support, in the form of contact, and are also the principle providers

Table 13.5 FREQUENCY OF CONTACT BETWEEN DIFFERENT GROUPS OF ELDERLY PEOPLE AND THEIR CHILDREN (%)

	CHILDREN'S FREQUENCY OF CONTACT								
Characteristics of elderly person	Same house-hold	Daily	3-4 per week	1-2 per week	1-2 per month	2-4 per year	Annually or less	Total	Number of children*
Marital Status									
Married	5.3	11.6	4.8	26.1	21.7	20.3	10.1	100	207
Widowed, single, divorced	1.6	22.9	9.4	29.9	11.5	16.2	9.4	100	314
Age									
75-79	4.0	13.5	7.6	28.1	18.1	19.9	8.9	100	327
80-84	2.2	23.0	7.4	27.4	12.5	19.3	8.2	100	135
85+	0.0	32.8	6.3	26.6	7.8	11.0	15.6	100	64
Sex									
Male	5.6	18.6	6.8	20.3	14.7	22.0	11.8	100	177
Female	1.7	18.1	7.7	31.5	15.7	16.9	8.3	100	349
Social Class									
Professional and managerial	4.3	17.0	12.8	23.4	7.1	21.3	6.4	100	47
Skilled, non-manual	1.3	13.9	6.3	24.1	12.7	31.6	10.1	100	79
Skilled manual	4.9	18.9	6.7	22.6	19.5	16.5	11.6	100	164
Semi-skilled and unskilled	1.8	19.6	6.7	34.7	13.8	16.0	7.6	100	225
Disability									
None	7.1	20.0	5.9	34.1	14.1	8.3	10.6	100	85
Slight	1.0	17.6	8.8	14.7	24.5	25.5	7.9	100	102
Minor	2.9	14.7	5.9	32.4	14.8	22.8	6.6	100	136
Appreciable	4.5	18.8	7.1	33.0	12.5	12.5	11.6	100	112
Severe	0.0	18.5	11.1	22.2	13.0	22.3	13.0	100	54
Very severe	0.0	27.0	8.1	24.3	8.1	21.6	10.8	100	37

* Total number of children of elderly people in the sample.

(Qureshi & Walker, 1989). Daughters may be closer to mothers and fathers than sons, though this is not clear. Daughters are likely to hold a less valued job if they must quit it, and daughters are thought to be more nurturant. Family-help patterns vary to some degree with social class. The size of the middle-class family is usually smaller, and the elderly are less likely to be dependent upon their children for help or actually live with a member of the family. This does not mean, however, that aged parents within any social class are physically separated from their children. Shanas (1967, p. 265) points out from his review of marriage trends that the immediate household of the old person differs by whether he is of white-collar or working-class backgrounds in Britain and the United States and by whether he is of these or of agricultural background in Denmark. However, if an old person has children and there is no child in his household, one of his children is likely to live in the immediate vicinity. White-collar parents are the most likely of all parents to be at some distance from their nearest child, but even the great majority of these persons live close enough to an adult child to ask for help if needed.

Friendships

A study reported by Roscow (1964) included 1,200 older people, middle- and working-class residents of several hundred Cleveland apartment buildings. The apartments varied in the proportion of older tenants. Thus the buildings were apartments classified into the following groups: normal (1 to 15 percent aged households); concentrated (33 to 49 percent); and dense (over 50 percent). The study revealed that first, regardless of density, age-grading is even stronger in the working class than in the middle class, which has somewhat more flexibility in intergenerational friendships within the age group.

Havighurst (1972) suggests that the following types of housing arrangements provide the best solution for aiding the elderly in this task: (1) small villages or communities in warm climates designed for old people; (2) housing units designed for older people in various parts of the city; (3) apartment units in single-family residences, designed for two or three families; (4) cooperative housing projects for older people with communal eating, laundry, and other facilities; and (5) homes for the aging for

Table 13.6 PERCENTAGE OF ELDERLY PEOPLE LIVING IN DIFFERENT TYPES OF HOUSEHOLD

			JOINT HOUSEHOLDS			
Age, sex and marital status	Lone person	Couple	Single person + other(s)	Married couple + other(s)	Total	Number
Age						
75-79	44.0	41.7	11.4	3.0	100	168
80-84	60.5	21.0	9.9	6.2	100	81
85+	65.1	18.6	16.3	0.0	100	43
Sex						
Male	28.0	54.8	9.8	7.6	100	93
Female	62.8	22.1	13.5	1.5	100	199
Marital Status						
Single person	56.5	4.3	34.8	4.3	100	23
Married	--	90.3	1.0	8.8	100	103
Widowed, divorced or separated	83.6	--	16.4	0.0	100	165
All Elderly People	51.6	31.7	12.9	3.9	100	306

those with no family and/or limited ability to care for themselves. The social service and domicile needs of the elderly (Table 13.8) have been projected by the British Department of Health, Social Security as being approximately 25 percent of the population (Little, 1980). This represents part of the guidelines for local authority social services' 10-year development plan 1973-1983, Circular 35/72.

TABLE 13.8 Residents of Nursing Homes

White	92%
Elderly	90+
Predominantly women	73
Widows or widowers	62
No immediate family or friends regularly visiting	50
Partially disoriented	30
Chronic brain changes	25
Previous stroke victim	15

Source: "Nursing Homes," *Mayo Clinic Health Letter* (Rochester, Minn: Mayo Clinic, 1987).

There is a widespread trend in all industrial societies for fewer elderly people who have children to live with them. In 1962 Shanas and her colleagues found that just over two-fifths of single, widowed, and divorced people aged 65 and over were living alone (Shanas et al., 1968, p. 156). For those living with children the proportions varied between one-third and one-half depending on the number and sex of the children. According to Qureshi and Walker (1989), a significantly higher proportion of elderly people lived with their children in Britain (42 percent) than in Denmark (20 percent) or the USA (28 percent). More recent research has found that joint households consisting of elderly people living with their children are an increasingly rare phenomenon, a finding that appears to be common to all industrial societies (Fengler, Danigelis, & Little, 1983, p. 358).

Differences in living arrangements do not necessarily imply differences in the experience of loneliness, and neither does living alone mean that old people do not remain in close contact with their children and other relatives.

Only 1.4 million lived in nursing homes in 1981. Table 13.9 follows.

The extent that other needs are met (75 and over) is seen in Table 13.10.

THE PSYCHOLOGICAL MODE

The separation of the psychological and the physical cannot be accomplished entirely satisfactorily. Many of the etiological factors in the mental disturbance of the older persons are directly related to the physical body. In this case we will deal with the aspect of the body that relates to the mind, examining personality difficulties, identity and self-concept, and mental abilities.

Personality, Identity, and Self-Concept

Although there is a lack of information on psychological development of the aged, the research that we have suggests that what happens in old age grows out of the middle years. Where persons have successfully solved the basic crises during the earlier adult years--the bimodal problems referred to by Erikson (1963) as intimacy versus isolation and generativity versus stagnation in the middlescent years--unsullied transition to aging is ensured. Having settled the crises in favor if intimacy and generativity, they are now prepared to resolve the crisis of ego integrity versus despair by passage into a status of high ego integrity. When one reaches this point, integrity is the principal aspect that provides solidarity in life and prepares one to maintain a way of life against various adversities. Ambiguities about life are resolved and the peaceful end of life is accepted. Integrity, though a general concept, refers to being true to oneself, when the person has maintained solidarity of beliefs, morality, and goals, resulting in a well-ordered life. Nehrke, Hulicks, and Morganti (1980) studied 99 domiciliary residents from a Veterans Administration hospital who were divided into three age groups, 50 to 59, 60 to 69, and 70 up, on the measures of life satisfaction, locus of control and self-concept. The investigators found support for Erikson's psychosocial crisis of ego integrity versus despair. The older subjects had resolved the crisis to a greater degree than the younger subjects, even though they had been there longer. Perhaps the younger group was concerned with stagnation of middlescence and the problem of producing.

Adults whose lives were marked by considerable isolation had found it difficult when they were younger to harmonize their personalities and the emotional-affectional components of their lives with others. During middlescence many were unproductive and therefore more likely to view their aging lives with despair. Considerable ego damage has therefore accumulated; their unstable emotions have likely gener-

Table 13.9 NEED FOR/RECEIPT OF CARE AND ASSISTANCE

	No Difficulty		Some Difficulty		Cannot Perform		
ACTIVITY	Received assistance	Did not receive assistance	Received assistance	Did not receive assistance	Received assistance	Did not receive assistance	Number*
Washing all over	0.3	80.3	4.6	6.3	8.3	0.0	300
Getting in/out of bed	0.0	83.7	1.7	11.6	3.0	0.0	301
Going up/down stairs	0.4	56.9	1.9	34.8	0.7	5.2	267
Cutting toenails	3.0	41.9	7.3	18.8	27.1	2.0	303
Heavy shopping	8.0	25.0	17.7	11.3	37.3	0.7	300
Light shopping	5.9	57.2	4.5	4.8	27.5	0.0	269
Preparing/cooking hot meals	27.5	50.5	7.0	4.9	10.1	0.0	287
Heavy laundry	13.7	34.1	16.3	7.4	28.5	0.0	270
Light laundry	8.6	64.5	4.7	5.5	16.8	0.0	256
Heavy housework	13.7	22.9	17.0	9.8	29.1	1.0	306
Light housework	12.9	67.1	4.9	5.6	8.7	0.7	286
Decorating	7.7	9.1	14.0	2.5	59.6	7.0	285
Gardening	5.2	35.1	16.6	9.0	30.8	3.3	211

* Numbers differ because answers to some questions included the categories "I don't know how to" (e.g., cook a meal), or "no facility" (e.g., garden). Adapted from Qureshi & Walker, 1989, p. 71.

ASSESSED NEED AND CURRENT PROVISION OF DOMICILIARY AND OTHER SOCIAL SERVICES FOR POPULATION AGED 65 AND OVER

Services	Assessed need per 1,000 elderly	Proportion of need currently met (percent)
Domiciliary nursing*	25	100
Meals-on-wheels*	27	40
Laundry service*	20	20
Home aid**	28	10
Occupational therapy	18	15
Physiotherapy	27	70
Chiropody (hand and feet treatment)	115	70
Social day care	17	20
Day ward care	4	10

*Weekly.
*Biweekly.
Source: Little (1980, p. 74).

ated evidence of delusions, hypochondria, and often serious disturbances marking senility.

Most older persons, even with declining health and strength, do not show dramatic changes in personality (Neugarten & Neugarten, 1987). Longitudinal studies show that people who are happy, emotionally stable, and have ego strength as young adults are usually well-adjusted in their later years (Mussen et al., 1982). Nor is the self-concept more negative; most older people view themselves as positively as younger people. Those who have been successful and affluent tend to have more positive self-concepts than those in institutions (Caspi & Elder, 1986). Many older persons are pleasantly surprised with their later-year lives (Horn & Meer, 1987). A 13-nation international survey on human values and well-being over the adult lifespan found more contentment, satisfaction, and stability among over 50 than in younger adults (Butt & Beiser, 1987).

Values of the Older Person

Rokeach (1979) investigating values held among people ranging in ages from 11, 15, 17, and each of the decades onward to 70 plus, found they varied considerably. The most important common value, whether terminal or instrumental, was honesty for each age group. Integrity is, in a sense, honesty, and is crucial in the lives of aging persons. Among 36 values identified by Rokeach were mature love and salvation (terminal values). Mature love showed the most clear-cut linear relation to age. It began as second in importance with the 11-year-olds and declined to 14th for people beyond 70. Salvation had an extremely low priority throughout adolescence, ranking near the bottom; it increased slightly during the college years onward; but by the sixties it dropped inexplicably to 10th. Perhaps solidarity in life's purpose and its integrity are the most important elements in the older person's life, and when this exists death is rather an afterthought, not the main event.

Although Neugarten (1977) suggests that most people continue their personal styles in relating to the world from middle age into their later years, some studies indicate greater plasticity in women than in men. The adult longitudinal studies of Maas and Kuypers (1974) suggest change characterizes women more than does consistency in lifestyle and personality. Ryff and Baltes (1976) suggest that values--instrumental to terminal value continuum--might be applied to adult development and aging. They argue that Erikson (1968) implied a sequence from instrumentality (initiative, industry) to terminality (generativity, integrity). Gutmann

(1964), though focusing on men, posits a sequence in earlier adult life characterized by control of the outer world affairs (alloplastic mastery) but eventuates to an internal, self-oriented emphasis (autoplastic mastery).

Research by Ryff and Baltes (1976), utilizing the Rokeach Value Survey in a modified form, examined the value transition in women, thereby testing the instrumentality-terminality sequence hypothesis. Women in middlescence averaged 43.1 years in age; the older women in the study averaged 70.4 years. They were asked to rate the 18 instrumental and terminal values of the Rokeach scale both from the retrospective and the prospective view. The results indicated that middlescent women were more instrumentally oriented than were older women when they applied a retrospective judgment. The middle-aged women indicated they would be more terminally oriented in a prospective view of being an older person. The findings in this study, though cross-sectional in nature, are buttressed by the consistency in prospective, retrospective, and concurrent assessment.

Differences among the aged are considerable, as a study by Ahammer and Baltes (1972) indicates. They asked adolescents, adults, and older people how desirable were the affiliative, achieving, nurturing, and autonomous at their own ages. Being affiliative was believed more desirable by the adolescents and older persons than by the middlescent. The middlescent, on the other hand, was more concerned about achievement than the young or the old. All of the groups thought autonomy and nurturance were equally desirable. When these groups were asked to report what the other generations are like, misconceptions were consistent in that older adults were misjudged on aspects of self-concept that remain the same across the generations.

It is conjecture but certainly getting older does not convey being more honest. Even so older adults eschew friendship, sharing, intimacy--all related to honesty. No longer does the older person need or desire to be completely pragmatic or a moral relativist but wants most of all to have integrity.

CARING FOR HEALTH AND HEALTH PROBLEMS

Sickness and Long-Term Care

One out of five older persons spends some time in a long-term care facility--a mental hospital, convalescent or nursing home, or other institution (Kastenbaum & Candy, 1973). While those over the age of 65 make up nearly 30 percent of the patients in public mental hospitals and 11 percent of those in private mental hospitals, they account for only 2 percent of all patients seen in psychiatric outpatient clinics (Goldstein, 1968). Part of this may depend upon the types of psychiatric disorders they have--organic or functional. The organic represents senile brain disease, cerebral arteriosclerosis, and the functional psychoses, neuroses, and so on. Studies of Leighton and coworkers (1963) and Srole and coworkers (1978) indicate that the proportion of persons who have any degree of mental illness does not increase significantly with age. However, among those suffering from psychiatric difficulties requiring hospitalization, the proportion increases greatly with advancing age. The major cause is organic psychosis (a physical cause) rather than functional (no known physical cause) psychosis. In the age group 65 to 74, more than half of the persons in mental hospitals have a functional problem, whereas among those over 75 the ratio is reversed.

Women in general and members of the white race are more likely to be institutionalized than men and nonwhites. Blacks are hospitalized less than one-third the rate usually found in the general population, which suggests that their families make greater commitment to their care or they are importuned by economics and prejudice (Kastenbaum & Candy, 1973). Aging itself does not necessarily eventuate into senility. Aging is senescence (growing old); that is, related to chronology, but senility means a substantial loss of organic and functional integration that is associated with the reduction of physical and cognitive operational ability. Most older people are not generally in poor health. However, changes in the physical organism occur with aging that increase the possibility of the development of chronic illness (Levin, 1971).

It is thought that most older people are in emotional good health, although paradoxically there is a relatively high incidence of mental illness, due in part to the increase in multiple life stresses and in part to organic brain disorders. Few of the elderly receive treatment. Only 2 percent in psychiatric clinics are over 60, and 4 to 5 percent of those over 65 are visiting community health centers (Butler & Lewis, 1973). Many old persons do not recognize that problems such as depression can be treated. The view is also held by many middle-aged and older adults who feel that psychiatrists and psychologists are interested only in the young, rich, and beautiful (Schofield, 1974).

Health Service and Health Problems

Most elderly people are in fair to good health, though most have at least one chronic problem--diabetes, arthritis, hypertension, impairment of the hips, legs, back, or spine (AARP, 1986). Those over 65 report fewer colds, acute digestive problems, flu, and headaches than younger people. When acute illness does strike the later adults there are more restricted days involved than for the younger person. Loss of teeth, which occurs among most elderly, affects nutrition: because eating is difficult they may forego eating important foods or the necessary quantity. Common problems associated with poor nutrition range from dementia, drug-nutrient interactions, to depression and involve the social factors of living alone, alcoholism, and insufficient outside activity and exposure to sunlight.

Mental and Behavioral Problems

Confusion, forgetting, and personality change are often coupled with old age. Called dementia and/or senility, its etiology is often physical--lack of proper diet, health care, and sympathetic interaction. Dementia is not inexorable (15 percent can be reversed), even though some three million are affected (AARP, 1987). While some cases are irreversible, others can be reversed with treatment. Alzheimer's disease, a neurological illness affecting the cerebral cortex, is a degenerative brain disorder that affects about 6 percent. Those suffering with this disease can't remember even their own names, they lose their intelligence, and cannot control their bodily functions. The main early symptoms are loss of memory, inability to play simple games, and outbursts of extravagance. Alzheimer's origin is cloudy: it was once thought to be mainly inherited, but some believe it stems from a biochemical deficiency or a viral infection. A number of new drugs have been tested and used to improve memory, and the use of fetal brain tissue has been tried. Drugs relieve irritation and depression or provide a transit to improved sleep, but no real cure is in sight (Cohen, 1987).

Other problems that can be reversed are over-medication and depression (this often creates disorganization, absent-mindedness, and disinterest in the outside world). Some aged persons do not recognize that they can be treated and are fearful that if they go to a clinic the cost will be exorbitant or they will be suspected of being crazy. Metabolic diseases, infectious disorders, anemia, low thyroid, and head injuries can be cured or substantially alleviated if they are correctly diagnosed (AARP, 1987).

Functional and Organic Disorders

Functional illness is thought to be principally emotionally related, although it may be genetically based, accounting for 30 to 40 percent of those hospitalized. The major categories of these types of illness are as follows:

1. Psychotic disorders, which are "thought disorders" referred to as late-life schizophrenia or senile schizophrenia. Most of these cases are those of long standing.

2. Affective or mood disorders, which are seen in behavior characterized by depression or anger frequently brought about by the death of a loved one, retirement, or children leaving the home.

3. Paranoid condition, in which older people convince themselves someone is persecuting them. A frequent complaint is that "the neighbors are talking about me or laughing at me."

4. Neurotic states, in which people are very anxiety-laden but their personality is still fairly well integrated, though depression is a common problem.

5. Hypochondriasis, which represents an anxious preoccupation with one's body in part or as a whole. This problem is a way for the older person to solve a psychological problem. Escape from personal failure into the sick role, used somewhat by all ages, is most common among the old. Anxiety and depression over the loss of prestige, security, retirement, and so on, may be shifted to one's body.

6. Personality difficulties, which are defects in the personality that have usually occurred over a long period of time.

Depression, the psychiatric disorder most frequently associated with successful suicide in old age, crosses many of the types of mental problems noted above. Many more young persons attempt suicide than accomplish it. The ratio is about 7 to 1. Among the old, the number attempting suicide nearly equals the number effecting it (Benson & Brodie, 1975). The young who attempt suicide frequently do so with anger or to bring people to terms, but the old actually intend to die. Suicide among white men increases precipitously after 50 (see Table 13.11) perhaps, as suggested by Butler (1975), because they have the most to lose in status, income, and so on, and therefore can handle the loss less well.

Organic mental illness is caused by some defect of brain tissue function. About 65 or 70 percent of major mental illnesses are organic in nature. Although half of these problems are acute and are reversible, the other half become chronic. The reversible and acute brain syndromes may be caused by congestive heart failure, malnutrition, anemia, strokes, drugs, alcohol, infections, or injuries. Many afflicted with acute brain syndrome die from depletion of energy or disease. Those surviving the crisis period often make good recoveries.

The chronic brain syndromes are generally the basis of what is usually called senility. Two types predominate: (1) senile brain disease (senile psychosis), which is associated with degeneration of the cells in the brain, and (2) cerebral arteriosclerosis, which exists where hardening of the blood vessels causes a blockage of oxygen and nutrients to the brain. When damage occurs, it is irreversible. It is thought that heredity and the social environment have an effect here. Most older persons do not receive help with their problems. Society tolerates the mental aberrations of the old. Gerontologists have repeatedly made the point that the alleged "senility" of many of the old could be erased if they were given proper respect by the general population, good diets, and medical treatment, along with a pleasant and stimulating environment. According to the Bureau of Census, 15 to 20 percent of the elderly have symptoms of mental illness. Of those cases, 16 percent may be due to depression and another 5 or 6 percent to senile dementia. The rate of admission of the elderly to mental health services is 7 percent against 16 percent for the general population. Nursing homes have a high number of the mentally ill among their elderly patients.

Nursing Homes and Other Alternatives

Increasingly the children of older parents are resisting taking them into their homes. Qureshi and Walker (1989) say 28 percent in America, though this is thought to be dropping. Many cannot because of lack of room, jobs, or other economic commitments; others will not let this affect their homes and children for various idiosyncratic reasons--but many of these will pay for care. A poll of 1,230 young to the young-old by Public Opinion (Dec.-Jan. 1986) found that the older the children were the less they believed their home was the place for their elderly parents who could no longer take care of themselves. Of the 25- to 34-year-olds 46 percent agreed whereas 53 percent disagreed. The 45- to 54-year-old group had only 33 percent agreeing; for the 55- to 64-year-old group only 31 percent and only 26 percent of the 65 and older agreed. Obviously by 65 many have their own health and financial problems. There are also many alternatives for the children other than nursing homes, which creates considerable guilt among many. Today with the assistance of pensions and Social Security, many of the elderly can pay for care. Nursing homes house only 2 to 5 percent at any given time but 23 percent of the 85-and-older group. Most homes are privately operated and have proprietary interest as their major purpose. Many patients or healthy elderly are placed in small rooms, fed standardized, high-carbohydrate diets, and watch television in a common room. Many homes are wards for the elderly and dying. Government legislation (Medicare and Medicaid) have cast nursing homes in the role of hospitals. They are consequently bureaucratic in operation, and physicians and nurses control the daily activities. They impose medical solutions on a variety of social problems. Many of these "patients" could be cared for in day care, by visiting nurses, or through "meals on wheels" services, etc. In Europe the long-term care in institutions is usually under government sponsorship, with local public control operating in accordance with national guidelines. In any event, among American nursing homes one-third failed to meet the minimum standards for receiving Medicare and Medicaid in late 1987. Some alternatives to nursing homes are as follows:

1. <u>Adult day care</u> - providing care typically from 9 a.m. to 5 p.m. Often these centers will monitor cardiovascular problems, nutrition, medication, and some therapy. They have exercise and other programs and provide snacks. Some children could handle this arrangement.

2. <u>Home care</u> - the elderly live in their homes and caretakers visit to provide light cleaning,

give medicine, prepare meals, or arrange to have them delivered.

3. Temporary assistance - available on a four-hour minimum in a number of cities. The aides are sometimes nurses and all helpers are required to have nursing care experience. This form of care is expensive.

4. Intermediate care facility - requires a month-long stay or more. Usually provides semi-private rooms and a variety of therapies--physical, speech, etc. Professionals closely supervise the medicine taken.

5. Rehabilitation centers - mostly operated on an out-patient basis. Costs run to over $100 a day. Such centers provide help with use or re-use of arms, legs, etc. They are useful for those caring for their elderly at home.

Ideal nursing homes should be attractive, lively, home-like and allow the elderly a chance to participate in decisions about the operation of the home. They should also allow interaction between men and women and privacy for their dating and sexual activity. They should offer a full range of social, therapeutic, and rehabilitative services. They should offer stimulating services (Kaynor-Jones, 1982). A study in a Connecticut nursing home by Langer and Roden (1976) found the elderly who were told to be responsible for changing things they didn't like and to decide how they spent their time, as opposed to a control group who were told the staff would do everything for them, showed greater happiness and were more active, alert, and involved. The others became weaker and more disabled. Alfred Adler has said control over one's fate is essential for mental health.

Mental Ability and Learning

Baltes and Schaie (1974) and Schaie (1983) believe that "general intellectual decline in old age is largely a myth" (p. 35). Although younger adults will generally not concede this, many intellectual abilities hold up fairly well with age. As was pointed out in Chapter 12, much of the view about consistent drops in intelligence has been drawn from cross-sectional data rather than from longitudinal studies. They have often focused on fluid intelligence and have disregarded the consistency in crystallized intelligence and the emergence of peaks at varying ages in adult life. Eisdorfer (1977) reports that the members of the American Psychological Association's Task Force on Aging proposed that a major portion of the variance attributed to age differences in past cross-sectional studies be more properly assigned to differences in ability between successive generations; that is, differences in education, health, nutrition, and so forth. This suggests that differences between younger adults and older persons in ability reflect a variety of conditions, such as neurological deterioration, physical limitations, physiological factors (health condition), speed, test anxiety, motivation, self-defeating attitudes, cautiousness, poor problem-solving techniques, lack of continuous intellectual activity, and the phenomenon of terminal drop. Terminal drop exists with all ages; that is, test scores drop precipitously as death nears. Jarvik and coworkers (1962) initially discovered this in their research with the old. Since more old die than young, more of the aged exhibit terminal drop.

Cognitive Difficulties

There are a number of cognitive difficulties associated with advancing age. Piagetian tasks, in particular conservation of volume and space, are reversed in old age. Perceptual difficulties which relate to poor vision could also play a significant part here. Studies such as Looft (1972) suggest that old people are more egocentric than young adults. We usually note egocentricity in the child, that is, inability to recognize other possibilities or viewpoints, recognizing that it is replaced when socialization develops. Since the elderly are increasingly isolated, this may bring on egocentricism. However, those who are egocentric in nonsocial circumstances tend to retain the ability to communicate with other people when there is a reason to do so.

In problem-solving tasks older persons take much longer time to complete them, but their accuracy when judged against the young adult was not significantly (statistically) different. In the famous conservation of column experiment of Piaget (two identically filled glasses are poured into a third differently shaped glass, usually taller and thinner), where children were asked which glass had the most liquid, the two- to seven-year-old, in the pre-operational stage of their intellectual development being perceptually demonstrated, usually said the taller glass held more liquid. Papalia and Bielby (1974) found the old more like the child than the middlescent in performing this task. Older persons are likely to do poorly on problem solving where they need to discover some information and then utilize it in order to solve a problem. Flexibility seems to be a specific deficit among the old in shifting from one kind of solution to another. Symbolic interchanges are also difficult for the aging, although on recognition they frequently do well (Botwinick, 1966).

Perceptual Processes and Memory

There is evidence from many sources that there is a slowness of perceptual processes, memory, and learning behavior with advanced age. It seems that the more complex the behavior and the higher the level of the nervous system involved, with age comes a greater slowness in the response (Birren, 1974).

Perception. A variety of studies have yielded differences with age in perceptual abilities. This is clearly illustrated in the case of vision, with flicker fusion thresholds increasing with age; that is, a flickering light is seen as a continuous light at a lower frequency by older subjects than by younger subjects. Results of studies by Kline (1972) show that in order to be perceived as a single stimulus, the minimum exposure time of the initial stimulus was longer for the older subjects. Birren (1974) states: "One is left with dual phenomena in which the excitation corresponding to the initial stimulus takes a longer time to reach the maximum effectiveness as well as to decay, as shown by a longer marking interval" (p. 811). If poor sight and hearing prevent a person from perceiving the information correctly, it will not be stored in the memory. This is a problem of the young also. The old, learning from lectures, tapes, and records as with languages, music, speech, and general teaching, are handicapped due to the inability to hear higher tones. According to Shock (1962), 45 percent of men over 60 have a loss of 45 decibels for tones about 3,520 cycles per second. These are the higher sounds we make in speech, and include sounds such as *s*, *sh*, and *ch*.

Memory. Birren (1974) concludes that memory as well as the perceptual processes are likely influenced by a slowing in the central nervous system processing. Concerning results of studies by Johnson (1973) and Robertson (1972), Birren points out that the largest difference in memory function is in retrieving information rather than in its storage. Recovery of information from long-term storage is best done by recognition rather than by total recall. Johnson's studies showed that cued recall benefits most of the older subjects, as was confirmed by Lachman, Lochman, and Thronesbery (1979), with metamemory studies. The results of Robertson's studies indicate that older subjects retain but frequently permit this material to intrude as inappropriate associations. Birren states, "The proposition being favored here is that the primary change is in speed of neural events which influences memory" (Birren, 1974, p. 811).

Botwinick (1973) states that progressive memory loss does not necessarily accompany old age, although memory loss is found in increasing proportions of the aged. Some of the elderly population have good memories. Some aspects of memory are differentially affected by aging; age-related decreases are greater for recall tasks than for recognition tasks (Craik, 1977). Memory losses have several general causes relating to encoding new information, loss of information, and retrieval of information. Loss of stored information may be due to deterioration in the memory traces or perhaps retrieval cues that stimulate recall being proactively less effective (Posner, 1967; Tulving & Pearlstone, 1966). Studies of aging twins by Jarvik and Kato (1970) observed that in some older people the proportion of cells missing one or more chromosomes (hypodiploid cells) was very high, going up to 25 percent or more. The high frequency of hypodiploid cells among the aged ranging from 77 to 93 years was related not to chronological age as such but to impaired mental functioning, including learning and memory. Faulty retrieval may mean breakdown in the strategies by which stored information is recalled (Reese, 1976). Certainly if people have learned little, they will have little to recall.

Learning. If perceptual processes and memory are slowed as a result of aging, then we might presume that learning would likewise be slowed. Learning and memory are inextricably interwoven, as researchers study one to understand the other. Thus considerable research has been conducted relative to the pacing of learning of the aged. The results suggest that older subjects would profit from longer intervals between stimuli to elicit a response (Eisdorfer et al., 1963, 1965). Birren (1974) states:

> In learning experiments the issue may be discerned as to whether older subjects want more time or need more time. Given the interpretation that they are cautious and seek more certitude before they respond, they want more time. Taking the interpretation that the central processing time is limited, then they need more time. In the case of perceptual and memory processes it would appear to the writer at least that the older individual needs more time rather than wants more time (p. 812).

Crystallized and Fluid Intelligence

Horn believes fluid intelligence is more crucial to cognitive functioning than is crystallized intelligence. Crystallized intelligence is the accumulation of information and experience and typically rises until the sixties and seventies where people are healthy, and stay active and involved in life. It is argued by Schaie and Baltes that though some abilities decline, mainly fluid (reaction time, memory etc.) others crystallized (recognizing synonyms, word fluency, vocabulary) increase up to 50 years of age. The long-term studies of Schaie and his colleagues tested 50 subjects per year (half women, half men) at five-year age intervals every seven years; the original subjects were tested and new subjects added. By 1984 500 subjects had been tested. The following represents their findings:

1. Variability in subjects - One-third of those over 70 do better on intelligence tests than the average young. Healthy adults do not experience any significant loss of mental ability until their sixties.

2. Multidirectional changes - Fluid intelligence begins to decline in the thirties because neurological losses affect response time, but the decline is not due to ability.

3. Environmental aspects - Patterns of maturity among cohorts shows up as with the young, the more recently people have lived the more education they have and the more exposure to information. Health is typically better as jobs more often depend on cognition rather than physical labor.

4. Associated sensory and physical - Hearing and vision problems are common; particularly hearing among men. Those easily fatigued have

high blood pressure, etc. Those who have fewer neurological problems do best. Old people in cross-sectional studies may be influenced by terminal drop (the sudden drop in intellectual functioning shortly before death). Time limits affect older persons' performance greater than the young, as speed of response is much slower.

Studies (Blackburn et al., 1986) that examined the effect of training, practice with 70-year-olds, and social support giving pre- and post-tests (using similar material that was practiced) have found that of the three groups all but the control showed gains in their intelligence. The three groups were a control, which received no assistance; the first experimental group, with formal training in figural relations involving a fluid type test; and the second experimental group, which was self-taught, i.e. they were given no formal training. Apparently the opportunities to work out their own solutions worked better than learning rules, because this group did the best. It is believed late adulthood need not be a time of mental decline if people are motivated and assisted in putting forth the extra effort in enhancing their intellectual prowess (Dixon & Baltes, 1986).

If one views the kind of adult intelligence that is most important according to Schaie (1983) as being executive functioning and responsibility along with wisdom, the healthy working adult loses only in speed but is much brighter than the young in practical intelligence and effective functioning (Dixon & Baltes, 1986). In the mechanics of intelligence certainly there is decline, as much of this is fluid. But in the pragmatics of intelligence and the application of accumulated specialized skills, knowledge and wisdom grow until late adulthood. This dual-process model is supported by Schaie and his colleagues.

Indications of recent findings of Wilkie and Eisdorfer (1978) show that elderly women perform differently from older men and do not show performance loss during learning. Forgetting among older women is related to their tendency to associate with too many factors in their environment (Boyarsky & Eisdorfer, 1973).

The research of Botwinick and Siegler (1980) involved the testing of four age groups (60 to 63, 64 to 67, 68 to 71, and 72 to 75) in the first year of their cohort and in the last year. The data utilized were from the Wechsler Adult Intelligence Scale (WAIS). When the data were examined cross-sectionally and longitudinally, no significant age differences were found in the cross-sectional comparisons. Statistically significant age differences were found with the longitudinal comparisons, albeit small.

New understanding and research on the impact of physical health and the social surroundings will serve to extend the intellectual skills for increasingly longer periods of time. James Birren (1980) says:

> Cognitive and social behaviors in later adulthood may have resulted from forces of selection, e.g., counterpart theory (biologically based later-life changes are associated with early-life characteristics subject to pressures of selection) and the survival advantage which later life behaviors, such as wisdom, may confer upon younger members of the family or tribe (p. 33).

SUMMARY

Our modern scientific and technological advancements have helped create a large population (32 million) of people over 65 years of age who are no longer needed on the labor market. New legislation allows most to work until 70 years of age. The aging at 65 are in the last of their middlescent years (later middle years 60 to 69), though some researchers like Neugarten call them the young-old (55 to 70). Many, particularly paid executives, professionals, and those running successful businesses, do not wish to retire even at 70. Most working-class persons are usually happy to retire unless they have insufficient resources upon which to live.

People whose lives have been less successful and frustrating are often resentful in retirement and have adjustment problems. Persons with well-rounded or passive personalities adjust better to retirement. The angry, defensive type of person functions adequately if there are enough activities to keep him or her occupied.

There are a number of theories of aging, both biological, social, and psychological. The biological emphasizes genetic aspects, environmental factors, defects in the replication of vital cells, general exhaustion, and loss of effective immune systems. The theory of disengagement, a social theory of aging, suggests that persons as they age withdraw socially, psychologically, and physically (they reduce their activities) from society, and that society withdraws from them. The activity theory is offered as an alternative to the disengagement theory; it affirms that old people, some biological and physical changes aside, are like the middle-aged, and do not desire to withdraw from society. The social change theory states that people enter social relationships because they seek rewards, and the aged are no different. However, the elderly are vulnerable in society because they have less and less to offer in exchange for favors, and hence may lose status.

Besides these theories there are personality and development theories. Personality theories are based upon physical and mental changes in people as they interact with the environment and the individual. They emphasize the control of frustration and the use of defense mechanisms. Developmental theories emphasize the interaction adults have with society that affects the psychodynamic nature of their lives. Support, lifestyles, health, stress, and family play significant parts in determining the quality of life for the elderly.

Aging, no matter which theory one subscribes to, has biological, psychological, and social implications. Many myths about old age abound, such as that most older people are chronically ill, senile, living alone, and in financial difficulties. These are largely false. It is true that the aged suffer progressive losses in time in terms of brain function, maximum work rate, and the time required to get the heart to normal after exertion. Vision and hearing are poorer and handwriting proficiency erodes. Nevertheless, the aged are living longer, have greater economic resources through pensions and Social Security, and are more effective politically than ever before. Individual differences in aging are apparent. There are significant social class variations; however, lifelong behavior patterns determine the way individuals adapt to problems they face over the life span. The aged have developmental tasks like those of older adult periods: to face the loss of a spouse, to adjust to chronic illness, to move to smaller places and often to locations far from their original homes, to maintain family ties and social relationships, and to adjust to their own demise.

Interaction with members of the family and friends continues throughout this period of life. Age-grading of friendships is stronger in the working class than in the middle class. Technological changes have produced important problems related to retirement, with the notion that disengagement from work leads to unhappiness. Some retirees adapt to retirement more readily than others. This can best be accounted for by the nature of the work from which they retire and the personalities of the retirees. The attitude of the worker is an important indicator of his or her adjustment to retirement.

There is no single pattern of retirement suitable to all workers. Perhaps education for aging must become a new feature of our society, with some preparation for retirement in the fourth decade of life. Any program that is to be successful must take into consideration the basic psychological needs of the aged.

Changes in cognitive functioning are evident, particularly in fluid intelligence (reaction time, mazes, etc.) but less among those who are healthy and involved with people and the community. In crystallized intelligence where experiences and information gathered over the years remain there is perhaps less. Losses in brain cells and size occur, but the peripheral processes are not at fault in the slower response time of older people: this is principally the function of disease and nerve conduction. Where learning activities have practical meaning and purpose older people show they can learn. Cross-sectional studies (Horn) as opposed to longitudinal studies (Baltes, Schaie) show greater losses in cognitive ability among the old. It is believed that when the baby boom generation becomes the old, it will show gains over the elderly of the past, due to better general education, health care, and the redefinition of the later years.

The key to the later years is the general manner in which the middle-aged person has maintained Erikson's generativity as opposed to stagnation, has reasonably good health, has developed Peck's ego differentiation, has had a reduction in the work role, and has been able to transcend the body fixation and the "end of life" preoccupation. Where this is true despair will be minimal and integrity enhanced. Many of the old will become models for others, towers of strength, and will be venerated.

KEY WORDS

senescence

senility

crystallized intelligence

fluid intelligence

social exchange

autoimmune theory

mean time to failure

biological genetic programming

disengagement theory

activity theory

stochastic theory

osteoporosis

vital capacity

peripheral processes

endocrine system

genitourinary

ischic heart disease

arteriosclerotic heart disease

arthritis

emphysema

ego differentiation

body transcendence

ego transcendence

meals on wheels

terminal values

instrumental values

intermediate care

hypochondriasis

REFERENCES

American Association of Retired Persons (AARP), When the mind falters: Medical sleuths, caring professionals may find simple and reversible cause. *AARP News Bulletin*, 1987, pp. 6-7.

_____. *A Profile of Older Americans.* Washington, DC: Author, 1986.

_____. *A Profile of Older Americans Brochure.* Washington, DC: Author, 1986.

_____. Elderly prefer neighbors of same age, survey indicates. *AARP New Bulletin*, June 1974.

Adams, R.G. Friendships and aging. *Generations*, 1986, *10*(4):40-43.

Ahammer, I.M., and Baltes, P.H. Objective versus perceived age differences in personality: How do adolescents, adults and older people view themselves and each other? *Journal of Gerontology*, 1973, *27*:46-51.

Anatharaman, R.N. A study of institutionalized and noninstitutionalized older people. *Psychological Studies*, 1980, *25*(1):31-33.

Atchley, R.C. *Social Forces and Aging: An Introduction to Social Gerontology*, (4th ed.), Belmont, CA: Wodsworth, 1985.

Babchuck, N., Peters, G.R., Hoyt, D.R., and Kaier, M.A. The voluntary associations of the aging. *The Gerontology*, 1979, *34*:579-587.

Babladelis, G. Young persons' attitudes toward aging. *Perceptual and Motor Skills*, 1987, *65*:553-554.

Ballweg, J.A. Resolution of conjugal role and adjustments after retirement. *Journal of Marriage and Family Living*, 1967, *29*:277-281.

Baltes, P.B., and Schaie, P.B. The myth of the twilight years. *Psychology Today*, 1974, *7*(10):35-40.

Bell, B., Wolf, E., and Bernholz, C. Depth perception as a function of age. *Human Development*, 1972, *3*:77-82.

Belsky, J.K. *The Psychology of Aging: Theory, Research, and Practice.* Pacific Grove, CA: Brooks/Cole, 1984.

Benson, R.A., and Brodie, D.C. Suicide by overdose of medicines among the aged. *Journal of American Geriatric Sociology*, 1975, *23*.

Birren, J.E. Translations in gerontology--from lab to life: Psychophysiology and speed of response. *American Psychologist*, 1974, *20*(1):808-815.

_____. Progress in research on aging in the behavioral and social sciences. *Human Development*, 1980, *23*:33-45.

Birren, J.E., and Botwinick, J. The relation of writing speed to the senile psychoses. *Journal of Consulting Psychology*, 1951, *15*:243-249.

Blackburn, J.A., Papalia, D.E., and Foye, B. "Fluid ability training: Comparison of treatment procedures." Papers presented at the annual meeting of the American Psychological Association, Washington, DC, 1986.

Blau, Z.S. *Old Age in a Changing Society*. New York: New Viewpoints, 1973.

Botwinick, J. Cautiousness in advanced age. *Journal of Gerontology*, 1966, *21*.

_____. *Aging and Behavior*. New York: Springer, 1973.

_____. *Aging and Behavior*, (3rd ed.). New York: Springer-Berlag, 1984.

Botwinick, J., and Siegler, J. Intellectual ability among the elderly: Simultaneous cross-sectional and longitudinal comparison. *Developmental Psychology*, 1980, *16*(1):49-53.

Boyarsky, R.E., and Eisdorfer, C. Forgetting in older persons. *Journal of Gerontology*, 1972.

Brecher, E., and The Editors of Consumers Report Books. *Love Sex, and Aging: A Consumer Union Report*. Boston: Little, Brown, 1984.

Bromley, D.B. *The Psychology of Human Aging*, (2nd ed.). Middlesex, England: Penguin Books, 1974.

Busse, E.W. Theories of aging. In W.E. Busse and E. Pfeiffer (eds.), *Behavior and adaptation in late life*. Boston: Little, Brown, 1977.

Butler, R.N. *Why Survive?* New York: Harper & Row, 1975.

Butler, R.N., and Lewis, M.I. *Aging and Mental Health: Positive Psychosocial Approaches*. St. Louis: Mosby, 1973.

Butt, D.S., and Beiser, M. Successful aging: A theme for international psychology. *Psychology and Aging*, 1987, *2*:87-94.

Caspi, A., and Elder, G.H., Jr. Life satisfaction in old age: Linking social psychology and history. *Psychology and Aging*, 1986, *1*:18-20.

Cohen, G.D. Alzheimer's disease. In G.L. Maddox (ed.), *The Encyclopedia of Aging*, pp. 27-30. New York: Springer, 1987.

Conklin, F. Should retired women live together? *NRTA Journal*, 1974, *25*:19-20.

Cox, H. The motivation and political alienation of older Americans. *International Journal of Aging and Human Development*, 1980, *11*(1).

Cristofalo, V.J., and Hayflick, L. Basic biological research in aging: An overview. In G.L. Maddox and E.W. Busse (eds.), *Aging: The Universal Human Experience*. New York: Springer, 1985.

Cumming, E., and Henry, W. *Growing Old*. New York: Basic Books, 1961.

Datan, N., Rodeheaver, D., and Hughes, F. Adult development and aging. *Annual Review of Psychology*, 1987, *38*:153-180.

Davies, P. Alzheimer's disease and related disorders: An overview. In M.K. Arohnson (ed.), *Understanding Alzheimer's Disease*, pp. 3-14. New York: Scribner, 1988.

Dibner, A.S. The psychology of normal aging. In M.G. Spencer & C.J. Dorr (eds.), *Understanding Aging: A Multidisciplinary Approach*. New York: Appleton-Century-Crofts, 1975.

Dixon, R.A., and Baltes, P.B. Toward life-span research on the functions and pramatics of intelligence. In R.J. Sternberg and R.K. Wagner (eds.), *Practical: Nature and Origins of Competence in the Everyday World*. New York: Cambridge University Press, 1986.

Dowd, J.J. Beneficence and the aged. *The Journal of Gerontology*, 1984, *39*:102-108.

Dowd, J.J., and LaRossa, R. Primary group contact and elderly morale: All exchange power analysis. *Sociological Social Research*, January 1982, *66*(2).

Eisdorfer, C. Intelligence and cognition in the aged. In E.W. Busse and E. Pfeiffer (eds.), *Behavior and Adaptation in Late Life*. Boston: Little, Brown, 1977.

Eisdorfer, C., et al. Stimulus exposure time as a factor in serial learning in an aged sample. *Journal of Abnormal Psychology*, 1963, *67*.

Erikson, E.H. *Childhood and Society*. New York: Norton, 1963.

_____. *Identity, Youth, and Crisis*. New York: Norton, 1968.

Estes, E.H. Health experience in the elderly. In E. Busse and E. Pfeiffer (eds.), *Behavior and Adaptation in Late Life*, 2nd ed. Boston: Little, Brown, 1977.

_____. Health experience in the elderly. In E. Busse and E. Pfeiffer (eds.), *Behavior and Adaptation in Late Life*. Boston: Little, Brown, 1969.

Exter, T.G. Where the money is. *American Demographics*, 1987, *9* (March): 26-32.

Fawcett, G., Stonner, D., and Zephehn, H. Locus or control, perceived constraint, and morale among institutionalized aged. *International Journal of Aging and Human Development*, 1980, *11*(1).

Fengler, Daniegelis, and Little, 1983, p. 358.

Fries, J.F. *Aging, Natural Death, and the Compression of Morbidity*. New England: Penguin Books, 1974.

Fromm, E. Psychological problems of aging. *Child and Family*, 1967, *6*(2):78-88.

Galton, L. *The Truth About Senility--And How to Avoid It*. New York: Crowell, 1979.

Genevay, B. Intimacy as we age. *Generations*, 1986, *10*(4):12-15.

Goldstein, M.S. Medicare and care of mental illness. *Health Insurance Statistics*, HI-4, March 7, 1968. Washington, DC: U.S. Department of Health, Education, and Welfare Social Security Administration, Office of Research and Statistics.

Gran, S.M. From notes by F.R. Jones, June 2, 1979, University of Michigan Center for Human Development.

Harvey, C.D., and Bahr, H.M. Widowhood, morale, and affiliation. *Journal of Marriage and the Family*, 1974, *36*(1):97-106.

Havighurst, R.J., Neugarten, B.L., and Tobin, S.S. Disengagement and patterns of aging. In B.L. Neugarten (ed.), *Middle Age and Aging*. Chicago: University of Chicago Press, 1968.

Hayflick, L. The cell biology of aging. *Scientific American*, 1980, *242* (January):58-65.

Hess, B.B., and Markson, E.W. *Aging and Old Age. An Introduction to Social Gerontology*. New York: Macmillan, 1980.

Hildreth, J.M. The battle to save social security. *U.S. News & World Report*, July 1981.

Hogue, C.C. Injury in late life. I. Epidemiology. *Journal of American Geriatrical Society*, 1982, *30*(2):1983-190.

Holden, W.C. *The Past and Future of the Kaffin Races*. London: W.C. Holden, 1971.

Horn, J.C., and Meer, J. The vintage years. *Psychology Today*, 1987, *21* (May):76-84.

Horn, J.L., and Donaldson, G. Faith is not enough: A response to the Baltes-Schaie claim that intelligence does not wane. *American Psychologist*, 1977, *32*:369-373.

Ishii-Kuntz, M., and Lee, G.R. Status of the elderly: An extension of the theory. *Journal of Marriage and the Family*, 1987, *49*:413-420.

Jarvik, L., Kallman, F.J., and Falek, A. Intellectual changes in aged twins. *Journal of Gerontology*, 1962, *17*:289.

Johnson, Olie. Century 21 agent, former Dean of the School of Business, Old Dominion University, Norfolk, Virginia. Conversation with the author, March 17, 1991.

Kalish, R.A. *Late Adulthood: Perspectives on Human Development*. Monterey, CA: Brooks/Cole, 1975.

Kastenbaum, R., and Candy, S. The 4% fallacy: A methodological and empirical critique of extended care facilities population statistics. *Aging and Human Development*, 1973, *4*:15-22.

Kasyer-Jones, J.S. Institutional structures: Catalysts of or barriers to quality care for the institutionalized aged in Scotland and the U.S. *Social Science Medicine*, 1982, *16*:935-944.

Kinsey, A.C., et al. *Sexual Behavior in the Human Female*. Philadelphia: Saunders, 1953.

Klein, D.W., and Schieber, F. Vision and aging. In J.E. Birren and K.W. Schaie (eds.), *Handbook of the Psychology of Aging*, 2nd ed. New York: Van Nostrand Reinhold, 1985.

Lachman, J., Lochman, R., and Thronesbery, C. Metamemory through the adult life span. *Developmental Psychology*, 1979, *15*(5):543-551.

Langer, E., and Rodin, J. The effects of schocie and enhanced personal responsibility in an institutional setting. *Journal of Personality and Social Psychology*, 1976, *34*(2):191-198.

Larson, R., Mannell, R., and Zuzanek, J. Daily well-being of older adults with friends and family. *Psychology and Aging*, 1986, *1*(2):117-126.

Leighton, D., et al. The character of danger: Psychiatric symptoms in selected communities. *The Stirling County Study of Psychiatric Disorders and Sociocultural Environment*, vol. 3. New York: Basic Books, 1963.

Leshan, E. Life over sixty. *American Association of Retired Persons*, Washington, DC, 1991 (April), *32*(4):20.

Leven, M. *Older Americans: Special Handling Required*. Washington, DC: National Council on Aging, 1971.

Little, V. Assessing the needs of the elderly: State of the art. *International Journal of Aging and Human Development*, 1980, *11*(1).

Lohmann, N. A factor analysis of life satisfaction, adjustment and morale measures with elderly adults. *International Journal of Aging and Human Development*, 1980, *11*(1).

Looft, W. Egocentrism and social interaction across the life span. *Psychological Bulletin*, 1972, *78*(2):73-92.

Lopata, H., Heinemann, G.D., and Baum, J. Loneliness: Antecedents and coping strategies in the lives of widows. In L.A. Peplau and D. Perlman (eds.), *Loneliness: A Source Book of Current Theory, Research and Therapy*. New York: Wiley, 1982, pp. 310-326.

Lopata, H.Z. Living through widowhood. *Psychology Today*, 1973, *7*(2):86-92.

Lowenthal, M.F., Thurnher, M., Chiriboga, D., and Associates. *Four Stages of Life*. San Francisco: Jossey-Bass, 1977.

Lumpkin, C.K. Jr., McClung, J.K., Pereira-Smith, O.M., and Smith, J.R. Existence of high abundance antiproliferative RNAs in senescent human diploid fiborblasts. *Science*, 1986, *232*:393-394.

Maas, H.S., and Kuypers, J.A. *From Thirty to Seventy*. San Francisco: Jossey-Bass, 1974.

Maddox, G.L. Activity and morale: A longitudinal study of selected elderly subjects. *Social Forces*, 1963, *41*.

_____. Retirement as a social event in the United States. In J.C. McKinney and F.T. deVyver (eds.), *Aging and Social Policy*. New York: Appleton-Century-Crofts, 1966.

_____. Disengagement theory, a critical evaluation. *Gerontologist*, 1969, *4*:80-83.

Masters, W.H., and Johnson, V.E. *Human Sexual Inadequacy*. Boston: Little, Brown, 1970.

Masters, W.H., and Johnson, V.E. *Human Sexual Response*. Boston: Little, Brown, 1966.

McGee, G., and Wells, K. Gender typing and androgyny in later life. *Human Development*, March-April 1982: 116-138.

McKain, W. A new look at older marriages. *The Family Coordinator*, 1972, *21*:61-69.

McKenzie, S.C. *Aging and Old Age*. Glenview, Ill.: Scott, Foresman, 1980.

Miles, W.R. Measures of certain human abilities throughout the life span. *Proceedings of the National Academy of Science*, 1931, *17*.

Moore, P. What we expect and what it's like. *Psychology Today*, 1975, *9*(3):29-30.

Morrison, M.H. *Economics of Aging: The Future of Retirement*. New York: Van Nostrand Reinhold, 1982.

Nehrke, M., Hulicks, L., and Morganti, J. Age differences in life satisfaction and self concept. *International Journal of Aging and Human Development*, 1980, *11*(1).

Neugarten, B.L., and Hagestad, B. Age and the life course. In R. H. Binstock and E. Sharp (eds.), *Handbook of Aging and the Social Sciences*. New York: Van Nostrand Reinhold, 1977.

Neugarten, B.L., and Neugarten, D.A. The changing meanings of aging. *Psychology Today*, 1987, *21* (May): 29-33.

Palmore, D., and Maeda, E. *The Honorable Elders Revisited: A Revised Cross-Cultural Analysis of Aging in Japan*. Durham, N.C.: Duke University Press, 1985.

Palmore, E. Predicting longevity. *Gerontologist*, 1969, *9*.

_____. Review of Irving Roscow, socialization to old age. *Social Forces*, 1976, *55*:215-216.

Palmore, E., and Manton, K. Modernization and status of the aged. *Journal of Gerontology*, 1974, *29*(2).

Papalia, D., and Bielby, D. Cognitive functioning in middle and old age adult: A review of research based on Piaget's theory. *Human Development*, 1974, *17*:424-443.

Peck, R.C. Psychological development in the second half of life. In B.L. Neugarten (ed.), *Middle Age and Aging*. Chicago: University of Chicago Press, 1968.

Pfeiffer, E. Sexual behavior in old age. In E. Busse and E. Pfeiffer (eds.), *Behavior and Adaptation in Late Life*. Boston: Little, Brown, 1977.

Pfeiffer, E., and Davis, G. Determinants of sexual behavior in middle and old age. *Journal of American Geriatric Sociology*, 1972, *20*(4).

Pfeiffer, E., Verwoerdt, A., and Davis, G. Sexual behavior in middle life. *American Journal of Psychiatry*, 1972, *128*(10).

Pfeiffer, E., Verwoerdt, A., and Wang, H.S. Sexual behavior in aged men and women. I. Observations on 254 community volunteers. *Archives of General Psychiatry*, 1968, *19*:753.

Puner, M. *To the Good Long Life: What We Know About Growing Old*. New York: Universe Books, 1974.

Quadagno, J.E. *Aging in Early Industrial Societies*. New York: Academic Press, 1982.

Qureshi, H., and Walker, A. *The Caring Relationship*. Philadelphia: Temple University Press, 1989.

Rahe, R.H., and Arthur, R.J. Effects of aging upon U.S. masters championships swim performance. *Journal of Sports Medicine and Physical Fitness*, 1974, *14*.

Reichard, S., Livson, F., and Peterson, P.G. *Aging and Personality*. New York: Wiley, 1962.

Rokeach, M. *The Nature of Human Values*, 2nd ed. New York: Free Press, 1979.

Rollings, B.C., and Feldman, H. Marital satisfaction over the family life cycle. *Journal of Marriage and the Family*, 1970, *32*:20-28.

Rosow, I. Long concentrations of aged and intergenerational friendships. In P.F. Hansen (ed.), *Age With a Future. Proceedings of the Sixth International Congress of Gerontology, Copenhagen, 1963*. Philadelphia: Davis, 1964.

Rowe, J.W., and Kahn, R.L. Human aging: usual and successful. *Science*, 1987, *237*:143-149.

Rutzen, S. The social distribution of primary social isolation among the aged: A subculture approach. *International Journal of Aging and Human Development*, 1980, *11*(1).

Ryff, C.D., and Baltes, P.B. Value transition and adult development in women: The instrumentality-terminality sequence hypothesis. *Developmental Psychology*, 1976, *12*(6):567-568.

Salthouse, T.A. Speed of behavior and its implications for cognition. In J.E. Birren and K.W. Schaie (eds.), *Handbook of the Psychology of Aging*, 2nd ed. New York: Van Nostrand Reinhold, 1985.

Schaie, K.W. The Seattle longitudinal study: A twenty-one year exploration of psychometric intelligence in adulthood. In K.W. Schaie (ed.), *Longitudinal Studies of Adult Psychological Development*. New York: Guilford Press, 1983, pp. 64-135.

Schaie, K.W., and Willis, S.L. Can decline in intellectual functioning be reversed? *Developmental Psychology*, 1986, 22:223-232.

Schofield, W. *Psychotherapy: Purchase of Friendship*. Englewood Cliffs, NJ: Prentice-Hall, 1974.

Schemeck, H.M. Jr. Mysterious thymus gland may hold the key to aging. *New York Times*, January 1982, pp. 17-18.

Shanas, E. *The Health of Older People: A Social Survey*. Cambridge, Mass.: Harvard University Press, 1962.

Shanas, E. Family help patterns and social class in three countries. *Journal of Marriage and the Family*, 1967, *29*(2).

Shanas, E., Townsend, P., Wedderbrun, N., Friis, H., Milhoj, P., and Stehouwer, J. (eds.). *Old People in Three Industrial Societies*. New York and London: Atherton and Routledge & Kegan Paul, 1968.

Shock, N.W. The physiology of aging. *Scientific American*, January 1962, *206*:110-120.

Solnick, R.E., and Corby, N. Human sexuality and aging. In D.S. Woodruff and J.E. Birren (eds.), *Aging: Scientific Perspectives and Social Issues*, 2nd ed. Pacific Grove, CA: Brooks/Cole, 1983.

Srole, L., and Fischer, A.K. (eds.). *Mental Health in the Metropolis: The Midtown Manhattan Study*. New York: McGraw-Hill, 1978.

Sussman, M.B. Family life of old people. In E. Shana & Binstock (eds.), *Handbook on Aging*, 1977, Ch. 9.

Szilard, J. Quoted in E. Busse and E. Pfeiffer (eds.), *Behavior and Adaptation in Late Life*, 2nd ed. Boston: Little, Brown, 1977.

Thompson, L., and Marsh, G. Psychological studies on aging. In C. Eisdorfer and M.P. Lawton (eds.), *The Psychology of Adult Development and Aging*. Washington, DC: American Psychological Association, 1973.

Timiras, P.S. *Development Physiology and Aging*. New York: Macmillan, 1972.

Treas, J. Aging and the family. In D.S. Woodruff and J.E. Birren (eds.), *Aging: Scientific Perspectives and Social Issues*. New York: Van Nostrand, 1975, pp. 92-108.

Treas, J., and Van Hilst, A. Marriage and remarriage rates among older Americans. *Gerontologist*, 1976, *16*:132-136.

Troll, L.E. Grandparents: The family watch-dogs. In T.H. Brubaker (ed.), *Family Relationships in Later Life*. Beverly Hills, CA: Sage, 1983.

Turner, B.F. Sex-related differences in aging. In B.B. Woman (ed.), *Handbook of Developmental Psychology*. Englewood Cliffs, NJ: Prentice-Hall, 1982.

U.S. Bureau of the Census. Census of housing, 1970 Subject Reports. *Housing for Senior Citizens*. First report HC (7)-2, Washington, DC: U.S. Government Printing Office, 1983.

U.S. Bureau of Census. Current Population Reports, Series No. 128. *America in Transition: An Aging Society*. Washington, DC: U.S. Government Printing Office, 1983.

U.S. Bureau of Census. *Current Population Reports*, 110th ed. Washington, DC: U.S. Government Printing Office, 1990.

U.S. Bureau of Census. *Statistical Abstracts of the United States, 1987*, 108th ed. Washington, DC: U.S. Government Printing Office, 1988.

U.S. Bureau of Census. *Statistical Abstracts of the United States, 1985*. Washington, DC: U.S. Government Printing Office, 1985.

U.S. Department of Commerce, Bureau of the Census. Current Population Reports, Series No. 128. *America in Transition: An Aging Society*. Washington, DC: U.S. Government Printing Office, 1983, p. 15.

U.S. Department of Health, Education, and Welfare. *Facts on Old Americans*. Washington, DC: U.S. Government Printing Office, 1973.

U.S. Department of Health and Human Services (USDHHS). *HHS*, June 21, 1988.

U.S. Public Health Service. *Vital Statistics of the United States, 1970. 2. Mortality*. Rockville, Maryland, 1974.

Vinick, V. Remarriage in old age. *Family Coordinator*, 1978, 27(4):359-363.

Wall Street Journal. Out of retirement. July 9, 1987, p. 29.

White House Conference on Aging and Blindness. *Special Concerns Session Report*. Washington, DC: U.S. Government Printing Office, 1972.

Wilkie, J., and Eisdorfer, C. Verbal learning performance among old men and women. *Journal of Gerontology*, 1978.

Chapter 14

LIFE'S COMPLETION

- ***Children and Youth Face Death***
  - The dying child
  - Adolescent death
  - Young adult
  - Middlescent view of death
  - Later adulthood
- ***Theory of Death and Dying***
  - Kubler-Ross theory
  - Stages
- ***Bereavement and the Grieving Process***
  - Disbelief
  - Yearning
  - Depression
  - Recovery
- ***Special Issues Regarding Death***
  - Euthanasia
  - Suicide
  - Death education
  - The hospice
- ***Reflection on Life***
- ***Experiencing Death***

LIFE'S COMPLETION

Ideally people having a full and long life die surrounded by their closest friends and family. Frequently, however, the circumstances are not always the best. Most often the situation and the time are not the most desirable. And although every adult expects to die someday, they expect it to happen when they are old, and such is not always the case. Children, adolescents, young adults, and the middle aged die.

Dying with dignity, near people who care, is an ideal end to anyone's lifetime. It is what we can help make possible for others and eventually for ourselves. Death is a topic that must be a concern for students of adult years, for at some time in this period there will be a vital need for knowledge in the arrangements of caring for the dying spouse, parent, kinsman, or someone else. Unpleasant, morbid perhaps, but part of life. And life lived to the fullest takes the sting out of death, as Nikos Kanantzakis writes in his *Report to Greco*--"For this was my greatest ambition; to leave nothing for death to take--nothing but a few bones."

Sociologists have given a lot of time and energy to studying the way we have ritualized our behavior. These rituals are significant in reducing our tensions. But until recently little has been done to help the dying patient emotionally. Doctors Glaser and Strauss in their book, *Awareness of Dying*, describe the elaborate system that many hospitals used in the past to withhold information from patients, particularly the information that they were dying. Indications were that doctors made short, infrequent visits, friends and family became emotionally distant, and they wore make-believe masks. One study showed that nurses took twice as long to answer the rings of dying patients as they did of those who were not terminally ill. Of course, from medical school onward, the mission of the physician is to extend life. But people often want to know they are dying so this revelation will bring their loved ones closer to them. The practice of avoiding dealing with death has changed in the last decade as medical schools have become more concerned with ethics and death. The growth of the Hospice movement and media and educational attention paid to such issues as the right to die, euthanasia, suicide, artificial maintenance of life, and healthy dying are bringing death out of the closet. The issue of death is faced by professionals and lay persons alike more openly and honestly.

Death was not a stranger to our great-grandparents. Then people were not taken off to hospitals but died at home surrounded by those they had known and loved all their lives. The senior author's grandparents died under these conditions. Death, especially from contagious diseases, struck all ages, children to the elderly. In fact over a hundred years ago during plague or national disaster, death rates reached 40 percent (Lofland, 1986); in addition, one-third of all babies died in infancy. Half of all children died before their 10th birthday. Death was not a remote event at all. Now death rates are typically below 9 percent and infant mortality only around 1 percent. Associations with death are fewer and less frequent.

Today we recognize that there are at least three aspects of death. *Physical* or *biological* death (although its legal definition may vary) typically means the cessation of bodily function--the heart has stopped for a time and brain waves and electrical activity are nonexistent. The *social* factors involve those customs and mores centered on the rituals of mourning and the legal aspects of inheritance. The *psychological* elements concern the nature of acceptance of death, people's emotional reactions, and their coping mechanisms.

Children and Youth Face Death

Kubler-Ross (1976) believes nearly all patients (certainly those sick for a length of time) know they are dying, including children. The clues come from doctors, nurses, and loved ones. Dying patients may even set up traps for those around them and, noting the contradictions, draw their own conclusions.

The Dying Child

Children who are terminally ill usually are not told they are dying. Many professionals who have cared for dying children believe that most children (above five or six years of age) lying in bed seriously ill are worrying about death and wish for someone to help them talk about their fear. Research by Myra Bluebond-Langer (1977) suggests that terminally ill children are aware of the fact that they are dying and that they become aware through these stages.

THE INFORMATION GETTING PROCESS

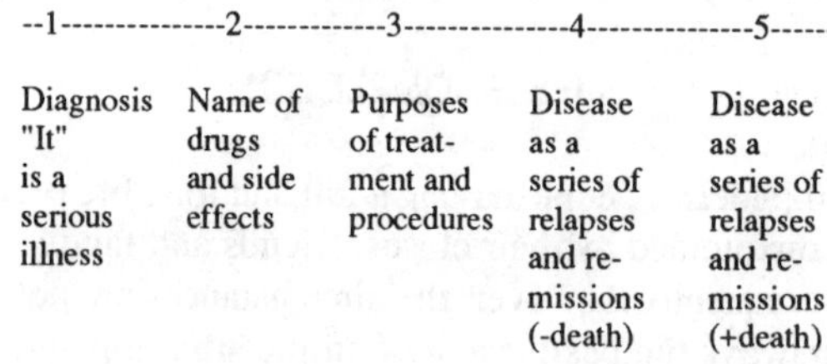

Ms. Bluebond-Langer (1977) suggests that leukemic children's acquisition of knowledge is a long process, and even if they do not know the name of the disease, nevertheless learn its serious nature early. If another child with leukemia dies, then the child remaining changes his or her view of self somewhat along this line.

SELF CONCEPT CHANGE

----------1-----------2-----------3----------4-----------5-------

Well	Seriously ill	Seriously ill but will get better	Always ill but will get better	Always ill but will never get better	Dying

Very young children believe death is reversible; sometime between five and seven children generally come to understand death is permanent. Some believe that teachers and parents, or others if they are lucky, never die. They also think the dead can think and feel (Speece and Brent, 1984). Children from lower socio-economic families connect death with violence, whereas those from middle-class families associate it with disease. Having a pet or caring for a plant and eventually observing its death can be useful in providing a natural way to learn about life's ending (Bluebond-Langer, 1977).

Adolescent Death

At a time when young people value their physical prowess and looks above everything, the prospect of death seems shocking and debasing. They are often shamed by the thought of their body's being unhealthy. They are frequently very resentful; at a time when the struggle for independence and self-concept is most important, they feel the growing years have come to nought. They say, "I must have been very bad to deserve this." They naturally resent and envy the carefree, fun-filled lives of their peers. Professional health personnel have the most difficult time in dealing with dying adolescents, who have greater maturity than younger children, hence recognize sooner their condition. Some adolescents still in the egocentric stage view death in highly romanticized ways. The brave are fearless in the face of death, and their concern with identity pushes them to think not *how long* they will live but rather *how* they will live, like the movie hero John Derek--"I want to live fast, die quick and leave a beautiful memory." Their stages of dying are much like those of adults, although many try to cover up their feelings and put the best face on it for the sake of friends and loved ones.

Young Adults

The early adult years are filled with completing education, getting started with a job, and beginning a marriage, and perhaps having children. The prospect of death is frustrating, for young adults know they can't fulfill their life and their dreams. Sometimes they turn to rage or go on benders. They often make very poor patients for hospital care. Of course hospital employees are usually young themselves, so the denial of life to the young adult seems particularly poignant to them and is a constant reminder of their own mortality. Like all adults, the young do not tend to consider their own deaths. Even among those in their middle years, most do not have wills or plans about their deaths, and certainly few young adults have wills (Kastenbaum, 1977).

Middlescent View of Death

Certainly this group has considerable contact with death, for usually they bury their grandparents and parents and also experience the demise of friends, associates, kin, and others. However, perhaps of all groups, the middle aged are most fearful of death--they may have more commitment to life than any other group: the young have hardly begun, the older group has nearly finished the course, but they have children to emancipate, the elderly to look after, and the final completion of their own lives. The chance that they might not get it done is troubling.

Later Adulthood

Older persons in general are not as worried and are less anxious about the ends of their lives. They have subliminally been aware of life's end for a long time. They have cried for their dead loved ones and lamented their own demise (Bengtson, et al., 1975). Those who have had meaningful lives are usually better able to handle the prospect of death than are those still concerned with the meaning of their lives. Certainly many people facing their own deaths, if their lives have been stable and they are elderly, have no special preoccupation with it. Many very sick people have heavy medication so may not be aware of impending death. Many physicians believe that a natural anesthetic keeps people from recognizing the moment of dying.

There is a *terminal drop* (Jarvik, 1962) in psychological functioning shortly before death, i.e. anywhere from a year to two weeks before. Usually there is less cognitive ability, less introspection, and more docility. Stages of death and dying have been identified by Kubler-Ross (1975). Most authorities on death agree that dying persons go through some of these stages, if not all.

Theory of Death and Dying

Kubler-Ross (1975) contends that there are five emotional stages in dying. Frequently the spouse, parents, and even children or brothers and sisters of the dying person go through some of the steps which follow.

1. Shock and denial. This is one way the person wards off an overwhelming situation and takes time to develop a defense. It is a healthy way of confronting the initial news, saying "I can lick it."

2. Then denial changes to "Why me?" or "Why my child?" Frequently people will scream at God or blame Him and become envious of the young and healthy. If people in this stage can express their rage without being judged, they can often feel enough release to begin the next stage.

3. This stage is the bargaining stage, "If you give me one more year I'll be a good Christian," or "Let me live until the children finish school or get married." Burt Reynolds played the part of a man in this stage in the movie, "The End," by promising God a generous tithe to let him escape from drowning as he attempted suicide. However, the nearer he got to shore, the less he was interested in sharing his money with God. Bargaining represents the recognition that time is limited and life is finite.

4. The fourth stage is depression-- realistic depression. The truth has irrevocably dawned--people need to cry and grieve for the loss of their own life. This is very normal behavior. Many times loved ones go through this stage with the dying person.

5. In the acceptance stage peace is made with the self and then the final moment of death is neither frightening nor painful. When I asked my personal friend and surgeon a few years ago whether most patients at the point of death realized it, he replied, "No, in most cases." Of course not all dying patients reach this final stage of acceptance or go through all the emotions of these stages or in the order suggested by Kubler-Ross.

Some investigators say people go through a "dying trajectory"--the interval between realization of death and death. The trajectory may be weeks or months; for the old dying trajectory is leisurely and less intense. Anxiety and use of defense mechanisms mark the usual trajectory called the acute state; that is, when death is near. A second aspect is the chronic stage, where people recognize their plight but hope to get well. In the final stage, the terminal, the hope for recovery is given up and anxiety fades and the person accepts death. The dying are affected by their cultural heritage, environmental circumstances, gender, personality, and developmental level.

Kastenbaum (1977) believes that in general the Kubler-Ross stages have value but may be too narrow, for they may not take into account sufficiently the kind of disease the person has. The disease may affect pain, length of the terminal period, mobility, and lucidity. Also medical personnel who view the stages may be encouraged to categorize the patient in a certain stage; i.e., his or her outbursts are due to the anger stage. It may be, some believe, that the anger relates to a real problem (Kastenbaum and Costa, 1977), not the alleged anger stage.

Bereavement and the Grieving Process

"It is sweet to mingle tears with tears; griefs, where they wound in solitude, wound more deeply." The above was said by Agamemnon to Seneca in the first century, A.D.

Bereavement is the state of loss of a loved one or friend by death. Grief is what Seneca was talking about; it involves the anguish, sorrow, and troubled thoughts people have over a death. Mourning represents the ways people show their grief--the Shakespearian actor William Booth fell on his wife's grave on numerous occasions, when restrained he would say, "This is what is left of her in me." The importance of grieving, mourning, and going through the rituals--visitations, funeral services, memorials, visit to the cemetery, and discussions of the life of the deceased--are important ways of mitigating the distress and the psychologically debilitating aspects of death.

The grieving process usually involves four stages, according to Parkes (1972), as follows:

1. Disbelief - it may involve shock and perhaps denial and the loss of appetite, weeping, anguish, and being numb.

2. Yearning - the bereaved person longs to be with the deceased and is thinking about him or her constantly; they may hallucinate about the deceased.

3. Depression - this may occur later in some but it generally indicates a person is beginning to adjust to the loss. The apathy is a method for controlling multiple stimuli of foreboding thoughts of doom.

4. Recovery - reconciliation has begun, grief can be recalled through happy occasions, such as holidays and trips.

Anticipatory grief is usually observed when the death of a loved one is pending. Many people grieve and cry a lot and sometimes, when the actual death occurs, cannot cry or lament. They may yearn and be depressed later, but the healing process is probably accelerated by this, though not always (Doka, 1985).

Special Issues Regarding Death

A number of issues have become subjects of debate in the past several decades, such as euthanasia, right to die, and suicide. There is generally no debate about the use of the hospice, although the development of private-home facilities has raised some conversation about the protocol of releasing patients to families, etc.

Euthanasia

Many people have a great fear of becoming "vegetables," being held captive in limbo between life and death. The fact that patients suffer no pain is not enough, some people contend, but those suffering terminal illness should be able to select the manner they exit from life. A prominent woman known to one of the authors had terminal cancer. She planned a special occasion to honor her death. She invited her friends to a brunch, hired an orchestra, and bid each person a personal good-bye. Later in the day she overdosed herself and died. Most of her friends were sympathetic.

Jackson and Younger (1979) claim medicine has a special responsibility not to cause death, even in cases where treatment is just keeping

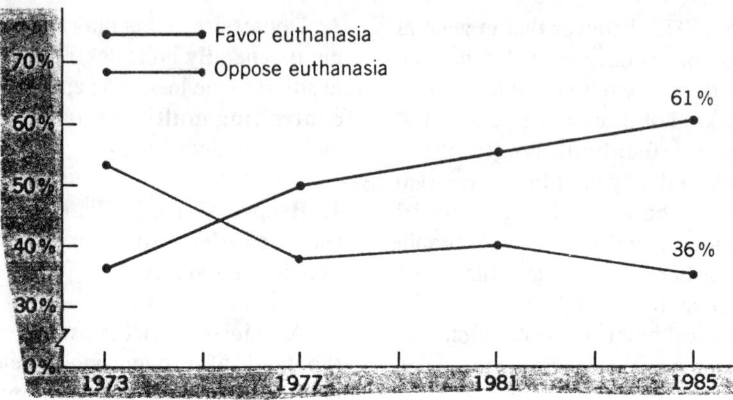

Figure 14.1 Percent who favor euthanasia.

the person alive, and the family requests withdrawing support. The fact is that many hospitals and physicians on their own have often hastened death by increasing dosages or withdrawing supports. Growing sentiment exists for euthanasia as indicated in Figure 14.1. This has occurred over a 12-year period.

The Control

Controlling death raises what many think are pertinent questions about the "right to die a good death." Do we, Shneidman (1976) asks, rob individuals of a dignified death if we artificially maintain their life systems beyond the point where they can regain consciousness? Do we prolong life because we fear death, even though the patients themselves may be at peace and ready to die? These questions have been given great attention in recent times. The "living will" prepared by the Euthanasia Education Council is shown in Figure 14.2. It has the effect of assuring the individual some control of his or her life in the last days of life. Many people believe that patients should be allowed to come to terms with the truth of their condition, and they should have some control over things that happen to them, such as the amount of medication to be taken and even the decision to leave the care facility and be taken home. The patient should not receive psychologically abrasive treatment; being swept along without any self-control is probably a simpler way but it is not dignified. The hospice is a positive idea where genuine humane support is the practice and where persons are allowed a choice of domiciliary in the final days of life. This treatment may sometimes contribute to an earlier death, however, as the surroundings can accent the hopelessness of the patient's situation.

Suicide

One of the most difficult situations that people can possibly have to deal with is the suicide of a spouse, parent, or child. It is usually baffling, leaving many unanswered questions and adding burdens far beyond the cases of those who die from illness. Very few people are able to handle this situation with any detachment, for it is not just that we have suffered a loss but that the deceased left us the message of our ultimate failure in dealing with them.

That many sick and aged wish to die is undoubtedly true, as witnessed by the death of Nicholas A, a lonely 78-year-old Polish immigrant who writes a sad letter home, concluding with this paragraph:

> "I am sick and tired of the constant enemas I get, and my stomach hurts, and my left hand can't lift anything. It seems I will remain a cripple, and if with such health one has to suffer (and my left side hurts very much), in order not to be a burden to anyone, I decided to do away with myself."

He was later found dead by a bullet discharged from a gun held in his one good hand. The philosophical and ethical questions about whether suicides such as the following should always be prevented have received comparatively little attention.

1. Suicides carried out for the good of some cause, such as religious or military heroism. An example is the driver of the truck that crashed into an embassy in Lebanon. (He was a martyr to the Moslems.)

2. Those carried out as a reaction to what appears to be a hopeless, painful, or debilitating situation, as in terminal illness. The death of Hemingway might fall into this category.

3. Those in which circumstances are not desperate, but in which the individual is no longer receiving the pleasure from life that he wants, and so makes the decision to die.

4. The so-called love pact suicide, where the double death is seen as having some aesthetic value, possibly being an expression of love, beauty, or dedication. The "star crossed" lovers' death of Romeo and Juliet is an example.

Although the ancient Stoics of Greece and Rome upheld the right to suicide, the Christian Church, beginning with the writings of St.

TO MY FAMILY, MY PHYSICIAN, MY LAWYER, MY CLERGYMAN
TO ANY MEDICAL FACILITY IN WHOSE CARE I HAPPEN TO BE
TO ANY INDIVIDUAL WHO MAY BECOME RESPONSIBLE FOR MY HEALTH, WELFARE OR AFFAIRS

Death is as much a reality as birth, growth, maturity, and old age—it is the one certainty of life. If the time comes when I, ______________________________ can no longer take part in decisions for my own future, let this statement stand as an expression of my wishes, while I am still of sound mind.

If the situation should arise in which there is no reasonable expectation of my recovery from physical or mental disability, I request that I be allowed to die and not be kept alive by artificial means or "heroic measures". I do not fear death itself as much as the indignities of deterioration, dependence, and hopeless pain. I therefore ask that medication be mercifully administered to me to alleviate suffering even though this may hasten the moment of death.

This request is made after careful consideration. I hope you who care for me will feel morally bound to follow its mandate. I recognize that this appears to place a heavy responsibility upon you, but it is with the intention of relieving you of such responsibility and of placing it upon myself in accordance with my strong convictions, that this statement is made.

Signed ______________________

Date ______________________

Witness ______________________

Witness ______________________

Copies of this request have been given to ______________________

____

____

____

Figure 14.2 Living will.

Augustine in the *City of God*, suggested suicide is never justified because, for the Christian, hope always exists. With some moderation, suicide has been generally viewed thusly until this day by the Church.

The actual number of suicides in America is estimated to be 30,000 to 100,000 per year (men commit suicide two to three times more than women, though women attempt it three to five times more than men). This is less, perhaps, than the number killed in automobile accidents; nonetheless, a significant number of capable persons are lost, and the potential number of suicides looms exceedingly large. The suicide rate among older white men is higher than any other group. It is lowest among elderly black women. Many suicides among the old are associated with depression. Methods range in effectiveness from 91.6 percent for gunshots and 78 percent for carbon monoxide to 4.1 percent by cutting (poisons and drugs were 23 percent and 11.5 percent respectively). It is estimated that for every completed suicide there are 10 times as many attempts. If we take the figure of 50,000 for a yearly toll and multiply it by 10, we arrive at a half million persons per year; in one decade this would mean 5 million persons. The presence of this vast number of people who wish to kill themselves becomes slightly awesome.

Who are potential suicide victims? The Metropolitan Life Insurance Company in a statistical bulletin listed the causes of suicide for one year in Detroit. Among women's suicides, 50 percent related to domestic difficulties, 20 percent ill health, and 10 percent love affairs. For men 40 percent ill health, 30 percent domestic affairs, and 3 percent love affairs.

People who are depressed are candidates for suicide. Those who talk about suicide frequently do it. Suicides are often psychologically damaged personalities confronted by a bad situation--health problems, loss of friends, parents, or support. Persons with low self-esteem and those with little optimism are vulnerable.

Support in the crisis situation is crucial. "Crisis hot-lines" are available for help. Assistance from trained counselors is important. Many ministers and social workers have special training in this area. Candidates for suicide must constantly be told that they are cared for and loved, but this must be demonstrated if possible, not just verbalized.

Death Education

Some claim death should be taught in public schools and elsewhere; others feel it's not the business of the school. Some schools introduce the subject of death even in early childhood classes, and courses are offered in some high school seminars. It is believed by some educators that it is important for people to explore the attitudes toward death and to know about the manner in which various cultures handle it. The emotional aspects of those who are confronted with death are also important. A number of goals are suggested for death education, among them are the following:

1) To help children grow up with as few death-related anxieties as possible.

2) To help people see death as a natural end to life.

3) To help people feel comfortable around the dying and treat them humanely and intelligently until the end.

4) To help health-care professionals and others get a realistic view of their responsibilities to the dying.

5) To understand and be able to help a suicidal person.

6) To assist consumers in becoming knowledgeable about funeral services and the economic issues involved in death.

7) To make dying as positive an experience as possible and convey the importance of care and support as well as being sensitive to the wishes and needs of the dying person.

The Hospice

In recent times the hospice movement has grown tremendously. Norman Cousins in his 1979 work, *The Anatomy of an Illness*, said that a hospital is no place for a person who is seriously ill. Hospitals are set up to treat acute illnesses, not the terminally ill. The dying patient needs relief from the constant, often needless tests and treatment. The hospice is a special facility, a family-centered setting where these patients can go. In these settings the professionals--doctors, nurses, social workers, family, psychologists, clergy, and friends--combine their efforts to make the last days of the patient as comfortable and pleasant as possible. Typically, in the hospice facility there is a family room with a T.V., card table, and books are available. Cooking facilities are close by, generally away from the bedroom, and each patient has a private toilet. This sort of arrangement is home-like to encourage family to spend a lot of time there. The climate is designed to facilitate the best possible circumstances for easing the patients' pain and helping them to cope with their impending demise. Many types of these programs exist--some are connected with regular hospitals and some are privately operated, and the cost is not usually exorbitant.

Reflecting on Life--Its Recollections and Review

Old memories are better than yesterday's happenings for the aged. When life is near its end, the old, as Aristotle said in the *Rhetoric*, "live by memory rather than hope, for what is left to them of life is but little compared to the long past." Time can be embellished by imagination. The rough places are blunted and blurred in memories that the three-dimensional present could never rival. Butler (1971) suggests that a review of one's life is a part of nearly all of the elderly's experience in completing their life span. It serves to help them cope with unresolved conflicts, provides insight through reflection of the significance of their lives, and helps prepare them for the acceptance of death. For some, however, this process of life review brings intense guilt, self-deprecation, and despair. Pollock (1981), a psychiatrist, believes that in the elderly, reminiscence has a special therapeutic benefit. He says memory can be used to rescue people, places, and events from insignificance. Some relief comes through the cathartic expression of feelings and loneliness. Many, for the first time, inform their families about things that happened in their earlier lives. Butler (1963) has said concerning this that undisclosed themes of great value may emerge, changing the quality of a lifelong relationship. Revelations of the past may allow a new intimacy, turn a deceit into the truth; they may sever long-term bonds, or make hatreds out of chronic antagonisms.

The review usually happens without obvious causes. Many believe the review process may be elicited by a crisis that involves retirement, the loss of a spouse, or one's own impending death. It is thought that the life review is an important element in a person's overall adjustment to death and is an ongoing aspect of psychological adjustment and personality development. This does not mean that a new type of euphoria develops among the old, for Lieberman and Coplan (1970) found that those a year or less from death show poorer cognitive ability, lower introspective orientation, and a more docile self-image on personality tests than those three years away from death. Researchers Palmore and Cleveland (1976), of Duke University's Center for the Study of Aging and Human Development, found among their subjects less evidence of terminal drop than reported by other researchers.

Experiencing Death

There is a question as to what can be experienced in death. This is a question apart from religious and theological views. For to experience a thing one must have a living brain and sensory apparatus. In this sense death is not a part of life. Nevertheless we do experience, by thought, our future deaths, and certainly no one comes to middle age without grieving and lamenting his or her own death countless times. From early childhood onward we are constantly subliminally aware of our death, as well as every other person's mortality. Some philosophers contend that we knew nothing about our lives before our birth; it gave us no conscious pain or suffering. How, then, can the end of life concern us in the same sense? We are caught in a time frame--birth to death--and we do not see the boundaries of our life. As the philosopher Wittgenstein (1889-1951) in *Tractatus* (1922) says, "We cannot see beyond the boundary of our visual field; it is more correct to say that beyond the boundary of our visual field we do not see." We can cross the great gulf only through the leap of faith that religious tradition suggests we utilize. But for now our task is to fulfill the promise of life and strive to reach our potential in "human development."

SUMMARY

Death was not a stranger to our great-grandparents. Then people were not taken off to hospitals, but died at home surrounded by those they had known and loved all their lives. The senior author's grandparents died under these conditions. Death, especially from contagious diseases, struck those from all ages, children to the elderly. In fact, over a hundred years ago during the plague or national disaster, death rates reached 40 percent, and one-third of all babies died infancy. Half of all children died before their tenth birthday. Now death rates are typically below 9 percent and infant mortality only around 1 percent. Associations with death are fewer and farther between.

Today we recognize that there are at least three aspects of death. The physical or biological (although its legal definition may vary) typically means the cessation of bodily function--the heart has stopped for a time and brain waves and electrical activity are nonexistent. Euthanasia supporters argue for the right of self determination in controlling the time and setting of death. The social factors involve those customs and mores centered on the rituals of mourning and the legal aspects related to inheritance. Mourning is the way people show their grief; four stages have been identified: the disbelief stage, with shock and numbness; yearning, where people long to be with the deceased; depression-apathy; and recovery-reconciliation, where grief is recalled through happy occasions.

The psychological aspects of dying have been addressed in part by theories of death and dying of Kubler-Ross, Shneidman, and others. The stages are shock and denial: "No, not me" is a healthy way of confronting the realization of death, followed by "I can lick it." The next stage is the "Why me?" period, where denial turns to rage. The third stage is bargaining: "God, if you give me time to see my child through graduation I'll accept it." This is the beginning recognition that life is limited. The next stage is depression, the realization that life is over, and the final stage follows when peace is made within one's self. Some do not go through this final stage or others; if people have a long termination, this affects their transition. Most authorities believe even children, except the very young, go through some of these stages and even if not told of their impending death, realize its presence.

The right to death, the manner of termination of life, suicide, life support removal, and control of death have been the subject of debate and legal adjudication. Cut-clear procedures have not been established, living wills have been overturned as the courts try to adjudicate these issues and the medical profession attempts to ferret out its obligations and responsibilities.

Death education, being offered increasingly in schools and colleges, is designed to reduce anxieties concerning death among children and youth, and to help provide information to a variety of people. Such education seeks to determine the health-care and medical professions' responsibilities to the dying, to help consumers become knowledgeable about funeral cost, etc., and to make the dying experience as positive as possible. The hospice idea has grown due to the need for appropriate settings for the dying. Teams of professionals assist the dying to be comfortable and to reduce the harassment to a minuscule amount.

Older persons, having lived successful lives, become models for others, the reservoirs of wisdom, and transmitters of a valuable heritage to their families. Having lived well and long, their ego integrity allows them to see life--though they exit in death--continuing in their children.

KEY WORDS

the dying trajectory

euthanasia

terminal drop

hospice

living will

life review

death work

thanatology

stages of death

demise

REFERENCES

Bengtson, V., Cuellar, J.A., and Ragan, P. Group contrasts in attitudes towards death: Variation by race, age occupational status and sex. Paper presented at the annual meeting of the Gerontological Society, Louisville, KY.

Bluebond-Langer, M. Meanings of death to children. In H. Feifel (ed.), *New Meanings of Death*. New York: McGraw-Hill, 1977, pp. 47-66.

Butler, R.N. *Why Survive?* New York: Harper & Row, 1975.

_____. The life review. *Psychology Today*, December 1971, *5*:49-51f.

_____. The life review: An interpretation of reminiscence in the aged. *Psychiatry*, 1963, *26*.

Doka, K. Expectation of death, participation in funeral arrangements, and grief adjustments. *Omega*, 1985, *15*(2).

Glaser, B., and Strauss, A.L. *A Time for Dying*. Chicago: Aldine, 1968.

Jackson, L.D., and Younger, S. Patient autonomy and "death with dignity." *New England Journal of Medicine*, 1979, *301*:404-408.

Jones, F.R. Making the most of the middle years. Unpublished manuscript, 1991.

Jarvik, L., Kallman, F.J., and Falek, A. Intellectual changes in aged twins. *Journal of Gerontology*, 1962, *17*:299.

Kastenbaum, R. Temptations from the ever after. *Human Behavior*, September 1977, *6*:28-33.

Kastenbaum, R., and Costa, P.T., Jr. Psychological perspectives on death. In M.R. Rosenzweig and L.W. Porter (eds.), *Annual Review of Psychology*, vol. 28. Palo Alto, CA: Annual Review Inc., 1977.

Kubler-Ross, E. *On Death and Dying*. New York: Macmillan, 1969.

_____. Coping with the reality of terminal illness in the family. In E.S. Shneidman (ed.), *Death: Current Perspectives*. Palo Alto, CA: Mayfield, 1976, pp. 138-162.

Lieberman, M.A., and Coplan, A.S. Distance from death as a variable in the study of aging. *Developmental Psychology*, 1970, *2*:71-84.

Lofland, L.H. When others die. *Generations*, 1986, *10*(4):59-61.

Palmore, E., and Cleveland, W. Aging, terminal decline, and terminal drop. *Journal of Gerontology* 1976, *31*:76-81.

Parkes, C.M. *Bereavement.* New York: International Universities Press, 1972.

Pollock, G.H. Aging or aged: Development or pathology. In *The Course of Life*, vol. 3, *Adulthood--A Aging Process.* National Institute of Mental Health, Washington, DC: U.S. Government Printin Office, 1981.

Shneidman, E.S. Death work and stages of dying. In E. Shneidman (ed.), *Death: Current Perspectives* Palo Alto, CA: Mayfield, 1976.

Speece, M.W., and Brent, S.D. Children's understanding of death: A review of three components of death concept. *Child Development*, 1984, *55*:1671-1686.

Wittgenstein, L.J. *Tractatus.* Logico-philosophicus, London, 1922.

APPENDIX

Three Modalities That Seem To Be Relevant at Each of the Major Periods of Adult Life in Understanding Development

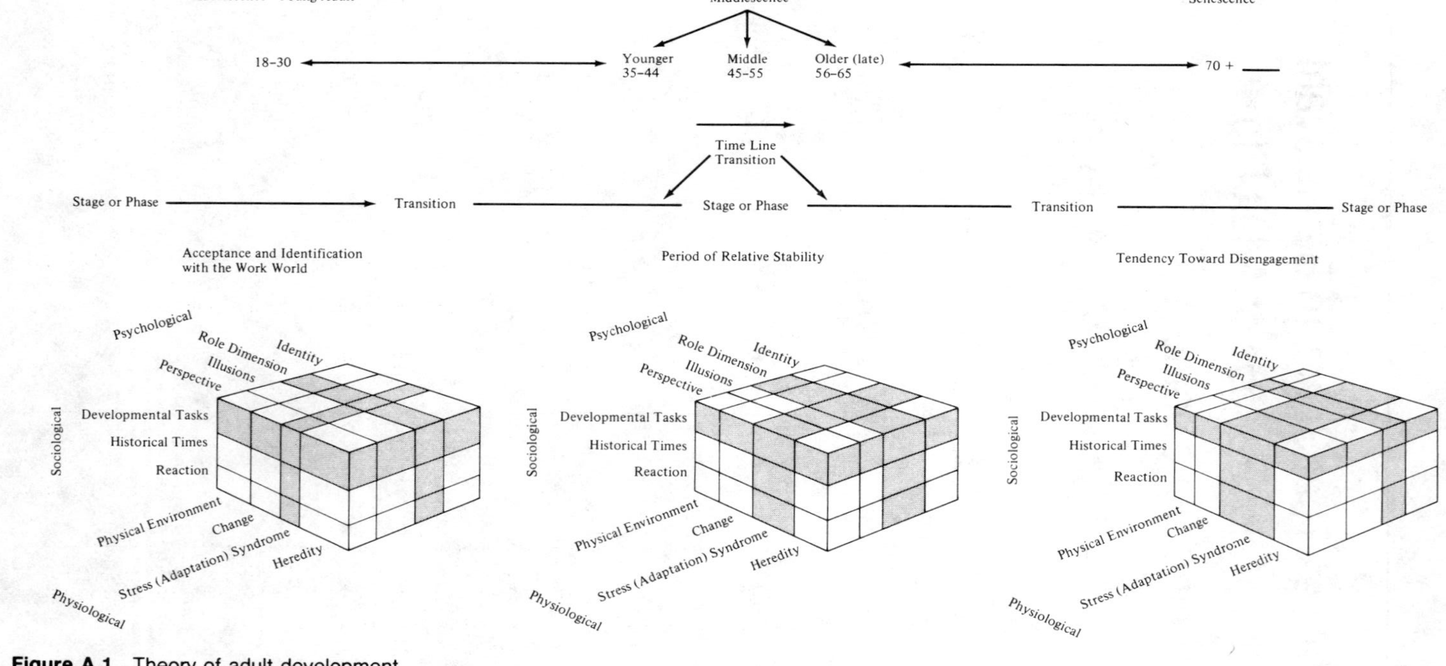

Figure A.1 Theory of adult development.

THREE MODALITIES THAT SEEM TO BE RELEVANT AT EACH OF THE MAJOR PERIODS OF ADULT LIFE IN UNDERSTANDING DEVELOPMENT

Psychological	Sociological	Physiological
1. Identity	1. Developmental tasks	1. Physical environment
2. Role dimension	2. Historical time	2. Change
3. Illusions (psychoanalytic)	3. Reaction	3. Stress
4. Perspective (philosophical)		4. Heredity

YOUNG ADULT

Descriptive Components of Each Modality

Psychological	Sociological	Physiological
1. *Identity* (the view as to who and what we are) Becoming an independent agent; maximizes alternatives and opportunities Oriented to a family and/or a love relationship Becomes compatible with the work ethic and community responsibility Identity crystallizes, composed of inner and outer reflection 2. *Role dimension* (the characteristics and settings of how we display our lives, life-styles, and so on) Father-husband-lover-worker-leader-follower-homemaker Mother-wife-lover-worker-homemaker-leader-follower Introvert-extrovert-conservative-expansive	1. Developmental tasks Cultural expectancies from mundane world *Adolescence* Preparing for an occupation Courtship and experimentation Developing skills for civic competency, acquiring a set of values, and so on *Young adult* Getting started in an occupation Love relationship and/or marriage Having civic and social responsibility, and so on 2. Historical time (the nature of world and society at a particular time and place) Periods of economic difficulty Social upheaval War and devastation Peace and tranquility	1. *Physical environment* Ecological problems Weather shifts and patterns Floods, fires, hurricanes, earthquakes, droughts 2. *Change* (major shifts determining direction of development) Homeostatic variance (endocrine imbalance) Weight gain or loss Structural defects Maladies and Accidents 3. *Stress* (resistance capabilities both physical and mental—general adaptation syndrome) Eustress—stimulation and thrill Mental/personality difficulties Demands of the ego for risk taking and arousal states

YOUNG ADULT (*Continued*)

Psychological	Sociological	Physiological
Type A or B personality Theoretical/practice Sex orientation and/or vacillation 3. Illusions (fantasies, beliefs, and fairy tales that envelop us) Psychodynamic balance of psychoanalysis parts—thrust of ego in controlling moral dictates and biological urges. The beliefs of childhood No death while parents live Happiness in the end if we mind and love our parents 4. Perspectives (philosophical views) Our view of the constructed world (nature of reality) Our place in the cosmic scheme of things Beliefs about truth and morality	3. Reaction (mode of response or adjustment with varying constraints tasks/times) Accommodation Surrender Transcendence	4. *Heredity* (the given physical anatomy and concomitants) Proclivities for strength, health, and long life. Proclivities for intelligence and/or talents and propensities Negative physical and mental aspects.

MIDDLESCENT ADULT

Descriptive Components of Each Modality

Psychological	Sociological	Physiological
1. *Identity* (the view as to who we are and what context we reflect) Concern for children and/or family Greater sense of self-control and confidence usually exists than in young adulthood—men assume more responsibility for personal problems and use maturer strategies for coping with them, women	1. Developmental tasks Cultural expectancies from mundane world Assisting teenage children to become responsible adults Achieving adult social and civic resonsibility Maintaining satisfactory work performance Developing adult leisure activities	1. *Physical environment* Ecological problems Weather shifts and patterns Floods, fires, hurricanes, earthquakes, droughts 2. *Change* (major shifts determining direction of development) Homeostatic variance (endocrine imbalance)

often assume greater leadership roles in community or work world

Continuity and change effects of identity—midlife crises often herald new occupations, effects family and change in love relationships

Socializer rather than sexualizer in personal relations

Generativity versus stagnation

2. *Role dimension* (the characteristics and settings of how we display our lives, life-styles, and so on)
   - Father-husband-lover-worker-leader-follower-homemaker, sex-orientation
   - Mother-wife-lover-worker-homemaker-leader-follower, sex orientation
   - Middleman function served between the generations
   - Type A or B personality, introvert–extrovert
3. Illusions (fantasies, beliefs, and fairy tales that envelop us)
   - Psychodynamic balance of psychoanalytic parts
   - Modified beliefs of childhood with the death of parent/parents and others
   - Religious and conversion experiences
   - Reconstructed dreams or disillusionment
4. Perspectives (philosophical views)
   - Our view of the constructed world (nature of reality)
   - Our place in the cosmic scheme of things
   - Beliefs about truth, values, and morality

Relating to one's spouse as a person

Adjusting to physiological changes

Adjusting to aging parents and their demise

2. Historical time (the nature of world and society at a particular time and place)
   - Periods of economic difficulty
   - Social upheaval
   - War and devastation
   - Peace and tranquility
3. Reaction (mode of response or adjustment with varying constraints tasks/times)
   - Accommodation
   - Surrender
   - Transcendence

Weight gain or loss

Structural defects

Chronic illness and diseases

Accidents

3. *Stress* (resistance capabilities both physical and mental—general adaptation syndrome)
   - Eustress—stimulation and thrill
   - Mental/personality difficulties
   - Demands of the ego for risk taking and arousal states
4. *Heredity* (the given physical anatomy and concomitants)
   - Proclivities for strength, health, and long life
   - Proclivities for intelligence and/or talents and propensities

OLDER ADULT

Decriptive Components of Each Modality

Psychological	Sociological	Physiological
1. *Identity* (the view as to who we are and the context we reflect) Harmonizing successes and failures and retrospective review Ego integrity versus despair Integration of beliefs, general views, motives into an accepted order and understanding of one's life Despair in life, projecting a life poorly lived, lacking order, goals unachieved, life is viewed as too brief and unfair	1. *Developmental tasks* Cultural expectancies from mundane world Adjusting to decreasing physical strength and health Adjustment to retirement and reduced income Acceptance of the death of a spouse Participation in activities of a suitable age group Finding and adjustment to social roles in a flexible manner Establishment of satisfactory physical living arrangements	1. *Physical environment* Ecological problems Weather shifts and patterns Floods, fires, hurricanes, earthquakes, droughts Change in living accommodations and neighborhood
2. *Role dimension* (the characteristics and settings of how we display our lives, life-styles, and so on) Level of participation in social, community, religions activities Parents-grandparents, widow-widower, lover, leader-follower, worker, homemaker Engaged-disengaged, passive-active Personality continuum and aspects, introverted–extroverted, interiorization vs. exteriorization Family and remarriage Independence and dependence Head of the clan, purveyor of wisdom	2. *Historical time* (the nature of world and society at a particular time and place) Periods of economic difficulty Social upheaval War and devastation Peace and tranquility	2. *Change* (major shifts determining direction of development) Homeostatic variance (endocrine imbalance) Weight gain or loss Structural defects Sensory losses Maladies and accidents Chronic illness and disease
3. Illusions (fantasies, beliefs, and fairy tales that envelop us)	3. Reaction (mode of response or adjustment with varying constraints tasks/times) Accommodation Surrender Transcendence	3. *Stress* (resistance capabilities both physical and mental—general adaptation syndrome) Chronic insecurity and fear Mental/personality difficulties
		4. *Heredity* (the given physical anatomy and concomitants) Proclivities for strength, health, and long life. Proclivities for intelligence and/or talents and propensities Negative physical and mental aspects.

- View of life, death, the future as colored by the process of aging
- Psychodynamic balance or imbalance, evidence of paranoia, depression, neurosis, distortion
- Beliefs of childhood

4. Perspectives (philosophical views)
   - Our view of the constructed world (nature of reality)
   - Our place in the cosmic scheme of things
   - Beliefs about truth, values, and morality

GLOSSARY

accommodation The process of shifting or enlarging usual modes of thinking, or schema, in order to encompass new information or experiences.

achievement tests Tests designed to measure how much mastery a person has in specific academic skills.

Acquired Immune Deficiency Syndrome (AIDS) An incurable and fatal sexual disease, transmitted through the exchange of body fluids.

adaptation Piaget's term for the cognitive processes through which a person adjusts to new ideas or experience. Adaptation takes two forms, assimilation and accommodation.

Addison's disease A malady due to a disease of the superadrenal glands which results in an anemic emaciated condition.

affective domain Encompasses all of one's emotional aspects: feelings, longings, values, motivations, aspirations, frustrations, and identifications. Includes one's internal responses to external events.

albinism Congenital lack of pigment in the skin, eyes, and hair.

allele One of a pair of genes affecting a trait. When alleles are identical, an individual is homozygous for a trait; when alleles are dissimilar, the individual is heterozygous.

American Psychological Association (APA) A professional organization made up of psychologists with various specialties (for example, developmental, clinical, and physiological psychologists). The APA publishes psychological journals, holds annual conventions, and sets standards and ethics for testing, research, training, and psychotherapy.

amniocentesis Prenatal medical procedure by which a sample of the amniotic fluid is withdrawn and analyzed to determine the presence of certain birth defects.

amniotic fluid The liquid, contained within the amnion, that cushions the growing fetus.

amphetamines A stimulant that affects the central nervous system, producing irritability, anxiety, and rapid heartbeat. Two types of chemicals are dexedrine sulfate (speed) and methamphetamine (meth).

anal stage Sigmund Freud's term for the second stage of psychosexual development (occurring during infancy), in which the anus becomes the main source of bodily pleasure.

androgens Male hormones.

androgynous Capable of expressing both masculine and feminine behaviors and attitudes.

anorexia nervosa A rare illness in which a person refuses to eat and consequently starves. Most victims are adolescent girls.

Apgar scale A quick assessment of a newborn's heart and respiratory rate, muscle tone, color, and reflexes judged on a scale of 1 to 10. This simple method is used to determine whether a newborn needs immediate medical care following birth.

aptitude tests Tests that are designed to measure potential, rather than actual, accomplishment. Intelligence tests are the aptitude tests most commonly used in childhood.

arthritis Inflammation of the joints. When moved, considerable pain often ensues. Most people eventually suffer some degree of this affliction.

assimilation Piaget's term for the inclusion of new information into already existing categories or schemes. For example, a person may eat a new food and be unable to name it, but may nevertheless be able to guess by its taste, smell, or texture that it is, say, a fruit. In this way a new object is placed in the preexisting category "fruit."

attachment An affectional bond between a person and other people, animals, or objects that endures over time and produces a desire for consistent contract and feelings of distress during separation.

audiogenic A genetic condition involving hearing produced by sound.

authoritarian parenting Obedience-oriented parenting type where self-regulation and development of independence is of low value and a dogmatic approach is the rule.

autonomic nervous system A division of the peripheral nervous system that regulates smooth muscle--that is, organ and glandular activity.

autonomous Independent of external control; self-regulating or unaffected by learning.

autonomous moral reasoning Kohlberg's term for the highest stages of moral reasoning, in which the person follows universal principles, realizing that the rules of society can be broken. (Also called postconventional, or principled, moral reasoning.)

autonomy versus shame and doubt According to Eriksonian theory, the second critical alternative of personality development. Between 18 months and 3 years, the child develops a sense of autonomy (independence, self-assertion) or the feeling of doubt and shame.

autosomal dominant inheritance Pattern of inheritance in which a specific gene is dominant; that is, if it is inherited, it manifests itself in the individual.

autosomal recessive inheritance Pattern of inheritance in which a trait appears only if an individual has inherited two genes for it, one from each parent. If the individual inherits only one gene for the trait, it will not appear in the individual but may be passed on to children.

babbling Extended repetition of a combination of sounds such as *ba, ba, ba*. Babbling begins at about 20 weeks of age.

Babinski reflex A normal, neonatal reflex that causes the child's toes to fan upward when the sole of the foot is stroked.

behaviorism A theory of psychology that holds that psychologists should study observable behavior rather than hypothesize about inner motives or unconscious needs. Behaviorism is also called learning theory, because it maintains that most human behavior is learned, or conditioned, rather than inborn.

biological theory of aging View that aging is rooted in heredity, a process that accounts for progressive loss of functional capacity after maturity.

blastocyst Fluid-filled sphere resulting from cell division of the zygote.

blastula The human organism about one week after conception (in this form it is a hollow sphere consisting of more than a hundred cells).

bulimia An eating disorder where a person goes on binges of heavy food consumption and then purges the food from the body by laxatives or self-induced vomiting.

carriers Individuals who possess recessive genes as part of their genotype (total genetic makeup) rather than their phenotype (outward appearance). A carrier can pass on a recessive gene to his or her children, but unless the child inherits the same gene from both parents, the child will usually not develop the characteristic.

case history The research method in which the scientist reports and analyzes the life history, attitudes, behavior, and emotions of a single individual in much more depth than is usually done with a large group of people.

centration The focusing of attention on one aspect of a situation or object to the exclusion of other aspects. Young children, for example, have difficulty realizing that a mother is also a daughter, because they concentrate, or center, on one role to the exclusion of others.

cephalocaudal development Growth proceeding from the head downward (literally, from head to tail). Human growth, from the embryonic period throughout childhood, follows this pattern.

cephalocaudal principle Principle that development proceeds in a head-to-toe direction; upper parts of the body develop before lower parts do.

cerebrontonia A personality type whose temperament is typified by having quick reaction, being a loner, sleeping poorly, having a rigid carriage, and being socially inhibited. Correlates with the ectomorphic body type.

childhood schizophrenia An emotional disturbance that can develop during early or middle childhood. Its symptoms include an unusual difficulty with social play, conversation, and emotional expression.

chordate A phylum of the animal kingdom that includes human beings, fish, animals, and so on.

chromosome The microscopic particles found in every human cell that carry the genetic material transmitted from parents to children, determining their inherited characteristics.

circular reaction Jean Piaget's term for an action that is repeated because it triggers a pleasing response. An example of a circular reaction would be a baby shaking a rattle, hearing the noise, and shaking the rattle again.

clarification of values A means of exploring the basis for holding values and helping children and others in forming values. It is not the teaching of a set of values.

classical conditioning A procedure in which conditioned reflexes are established by the association of one stimulus with another stimulus that is known to cause an unconditioned reflex. Also known as Pavlovian conditioning or respondent conditioning.

classification The sorting of objects into categories or classes, as in sorting foods according to whether they are fruits, vegetables, or dairy products.

clinical study A study consisting of in-depth interviews and observations. It can be controlled or can be varied for each subject.

cognitive development That domain of human development involved with thought processes vital to perception, communication, memory, and reasoning.

cognitive dissonance Conditions that set up discordance in the individual. A person is motivated to reduce the dissonance through changes in behavior or cognitive mediation.

cognitive domain Encompasses all those aspects involved in perceiving, interpreting, organizing, storing, retrieving, coordinating, and using stimuli received from one's internal and external environments.

cognitive theory The theory that the way people understand and think about their experiences is an important determinant of their behavior and personality.

cohabitation Living together and maintaining a sexual relationship without being legally married.

concrete operational stage Third stage of Piagetian cognitive development (from 7 to 11 years), during which children develop logical, but not abstract, thinking.

conditioning The process of learning that occurs either through the association of two stimuli or through the use of positive or negative reinforcement.

conservation Used by Piaget to indicate the ability of a child to know that two objects which were equal will remain equal if nothing is added or removed.

control group In research, a group of subjects who are similar to the experimental group on all relevant dimensions (for example, sex, age, educational background) but who do not experience special experimental conditions or procedures.

conventional morality Kohlberg's term for the moral reasoning, in which social standards are the primary moral values.

convergent thinking A type of thought aimed at finding a single, logical solution to a problem.

coordination of secondary schema Fourth substage of Piaget's sensorimotor stage, characterized by simple problem solving based upon previously mastered responses.

correlation The degree of association or relationship between two variables. A statistical measure the magnitude of which varies between -1.0 and +1.0.

correlation coefficient The numerical expression of how closely two sets of measurements correspond. Correlation coefficients range from +1.00 (perfect positive correlation) to -1.00 (perfect negative correlation).

critical period Any period during which a person is especially susceptible to certain harmful or, in some instances, beneficial influences. During prenatal development, for example, the critical period is usually said to occur during the first eight weeks, when the basic organs and body structures are forming and are therefore particularly vulnerable.

cross-sectional research Research involving the comparison of groups of people who are different in age but similar in other important ways (such as sex, socioeconomic status, level of education). Differences among the groups--as, for instance, between a group of 12-year-olds and a group of 15-year-olds--are presumably the result of development rather than some other factor.

crystallized intelligence Ability suggested by Cattell and Horn which relates to recall of stored information influenced by education and cultural circumstances. This area of intelligence includes reasoning, comprehension, and spatial perception. It usually increases with age.

deep structure Noam Chomsky's term for the underlying rules of grammar and inherent meaning in each language. According to Chomsky, a child's ability to understand this structure is innate (understanding, for example, that different sentence structures indicate either a statement or a question).

defense mechanisms Behavioral or thought patterns that distort one's feelings or perceptions in order to avoid unbearable inner conflicts. In psychoanalytic theory the ego is thought to institute these defenses when a real or imagined threat is perceived.

deferred imitation The ability to recreate an action, or mimic a person, one has witnessed some time in the past. Infants are usually first able to do this between 18 and 24 months of age.

dependent variable The variable that measured changes correspond to changes in the independent variable. In psychological experiments the dependent variable is often a response to a measured stimulus.

depressants Psychoactive drugs (Valium, metrobamate, and the like) that tend to reduce arousal.

deprivation The state of being without something that is considered necessary for normal development.

depth perception The awareness of the distance between oneself and an object. Before depth perception develops, infants reach for objects that are far too distant to grasp.

deterministic The view that human values, attitudes, behaviors, and emotional responses are determined by past or present environmental factors.

developmental psychology The branch of psychology that scientifically studies the changes in behavior, personality, social relationships, thought processes, and body and motor skills that occur as the individual grows older.

developmental task A growth responsibility, positioned between an individual need and a societal demand, that arises at a certain time in the life cycle of an individual. The successful accomplishment of a developmental task builds a foundation for potential success in subsequent tasks.

disengagement theory A view that aging is a process of progressive physical, social, and psychological withdrawal from the world at large.

disequilibrium Piaget's term for the state of conflict that results from the inability to integrate new information into existing schemes.

displacement A defense mechanism in which a less threatening object or person is substituted for the actual source of anger or anxiety.

divergent thinking A type of thought aimed at finding several correct solutions to the same problem.

dizygotic twins Simultaneously born offspring who develop from two separate zygotes, each the product of a different sperm and ovum. These twins are therefore no more similar genetically than any other two children born to the same parents.

DNA (deoxyribonucleic acid) Molecules possessing hereditary information that determines the makeup of cells.

dominant gene A gene that exerts its full phenotypic effect in the offspring regardless of whether it is paired with another dominant gene or with a recessive gene.

double helix The pattern of chromosomes, discovered by Watson and Crick, that are in the shape of a twisted ladder. A sugar alternates with phosphate to form the sides of the ladder. The sides are combinations.

Down's syndrome A genetic abnormality caused by the presence of an extra (a 47th) chromosome. Individuals with this syndrome have round faces, short limbs, and are underdeveloped physically and intellectually.

drive reduction theory Motivated sequence of behavior, can best be explained as moving from an aversive state of heightened tension (drive) to a level of reduced tension, which is the goal of the sequence.

dyslexia A specific learning disability involving unusual difficulty in reading in children who have otherwise normal capacity to learn.

echolalia Stage of prelinguistic speech that occurs at around 9 to 10 months; characterized by imitation of sounds of others.

eclampsia A serious disease that can occur during the last weeks of pregnancy. If not promptly treated, it can cause fetal brain damage and even death of the child and mother.

ecological approach A perspective of developmental psychology that emphasizes the impact of society, culture, physical setting, and other people on the development of each individual.

ectomorph A body type that is characterized by tallness, thinness, and fragility.

ego As conceptualized by Freud, the rational, reality-oriented part of the personality.

egocentrism Thought processes that are governed solely by one's own point of view. In the egocentrism of early childhood, many children believe that other people think exactly as they themselves do.

Electra complex The female version of the Oedipus complex. According to psychoanalytic theory, at about age 4 girls have sexual feelings for their father and accompanying hostility toward their mother.

embryo The human organism from about two to eight weeks after conception, when basic body structures and organs are forming.

embryonic disk The thickened cell mass from which a baby develops.

enactive representation First stage of Jerome Bruner's cognitive theory, in which the child represents ideas, objects, and events through physical action.

endocrine gland A ductless gland that secretes its hormones directly into the blood stream, and assists in body regulation and growth. Some of these glands are pituitary, thyroid, gonads, and adrenals.

endometrium The lining of the uterus.

endomorph A body type characterized by a round, soft, and fat body.

equilibrium Piaget's term for the stage of mental balance achieved through the assimilation and accommodation of conflicting experiences and perceptions.

erysipelas An acute febrile (feverish) disease associated with local inflammation of the skin and subcutaneous tissue caused by homolytic streptococcus.

estrogen Hormones that are produced primarily by the ovaries and regulate sexual development in puberty. Although boys' adrenal glands produce some estrogen, it is chiefly a female hormone.

euthanasia The act of painlessly putting to death a person with an incurable disease.

exhaustion theory Biological theory of aging based on the assumption that the human being has a fixed store of energy for living.

exocrine gland Gland whose secretions are expelled through ducts to the outside of the body, such as the sebaceous glands.

exosystem Term used by Bronfenbrenner to mean the interplay among the major social structures which have an impact on the individual, such as government and the media.

experimental group In research, a group of subjects who experience special experimental conditions or procedures.

experimental study Study that manipulates one or more variables (independent variables) and examines the effect of the manipulations on other variables (dependent variables). Experimental studies have highly controlled procedures and, therefore, can be replicated by the same or other researchers.

factor analysis A statistical method that allows one to compute the number of factors required to account for the intercorrelations among the scores on the tests making up a battery. Where tests have very high correlations, one test will be sufficient as they test the same thing.

fallopian tube The tube that conveys eggs from the ovary to the uterus; fertilization occurs here.

fetal alcohol syndrome A congenital condition characterized by a small head, abnormal eyes, malproportioned face, and retardation in physical and mental growth, that sometimes appears in children whose mothers overused alcohol during pregnancy.

fetology The study of the fetus, its environment and care.

fine motor skills Skills involving small body movements, especially with the hands and fingers. Drawing, writing, and tying a shoelace demand fine motor skills.

foreclosure Erikson's term for premature identity formation, in which the young person does not explore all the identities that are available.

formal operational thought Piaget's term for the last period of cognitive development, characterized by hypothetical, logical, and abstract thought. This stage is not reached until adolescence, if at all.

fluid intelligence Ability broadly based upon motor speed, induction, and memory (according to Cattell and Horn), which reaches its peak during adolescence or early adulthood.

galactosemia Inability of an individual to be able to digest and utilize milk.

gene The basic unit of heredity, carried by the chromosomes. Genes direct the growth and development of every organism.

general adaptation syndrome Term used by Hans Selye to indicate the adjustment of a person to stress in its various forms, enjoyable and harmful.

generativity versus stagnation According to Eriksonian theory, the seventh critical alternative of personality development, characterizing midlife. The mature adult is concerned with establishing and guiding the next generation, or else feels stagnation (personal impoverishment).

genital stage Freud's term for the last stage of psychosexual development, in which the primary source of sexual satisfaction occurs in an erotic relationship with another adult.

genotype Actual genetic composition of an individual; may differ from the phenotype because of the possession of recessive genes.

geriatrics Branch of medicine concerned with aging and the elderly.

germinal stage First stage of pregnancy (fertilization to two weeks); characterized by rapid cell division and increasing complexity.

gerontology Study of the elderly and of the process of aging.

gestation period The total period of time from conception to birth; 266 days on the average.

gestalt An event that occurs through a single formed pattern (configuration), not through a summation of separate physical, psychological, or biological elements such as reflexes or sensation. Gestalt psychology is now subsumed under field theory.

grasp reflex The closing of a neonate's fingers in reaction to an object, such as a pencil, placed in the palm of the neonate's hand.

gymnosperm X-carrying sperm.

habituation A process whereby a particular stimulus becomes so familiar that physiological responses initially associated with it are no longer present. For instance, a newborn might initially stare wide-eyed at a mobile, but gradually look at it less often as habituation occurs.

hallucinogens Psychoactive drugs that usually produce hallucinations that involve misinterpretation of imaginary experiences as actual perceptions.

hemophilia Tendency, usually hereditary, to bleed profusely even from slight wounds.

heterosis Increased vigor for growth frequently displayed by crossbred animals or plants.

heterozygous The condition in which cells contain different genes for the same trait. The dominant gene will determine the appearance of the trait.

holophrases A single word that is intended to express a complete thought. Young children (usually about 1 year of age) use this early form of communication.

homosexual A person whose sexual orientation is toward the same sex. For females, *Lesbian* is the equivalent term.

homeostasis Tendency for an organism to maintain within itself relatively stable conditions of temperature, chemical composition, blood pressure, and so on. It has been utilized to indicate balance and control in a psychological sense.

homeostatic model A paradigm for relating the theory of antisocial and prosocial behavior to the stable self-image.

homozygous The condition in which cells have matching genes for a trait.

hospice Specialized facility for the terminally ill patient with the usual support systems. Unlike regular hospitals they emphasize informality and humaneness.

hypothalamus A part of the brain that produces hormones that regulate many aspects of physiological development.

iconic thought Jerome Bruner's term for the mode of thought in which images or words are believed to possess the same qualities as the people or objects they represent.

id As conceptualized by Freud, that part of the personality containing primitive, unconscious sexual and aggressive impulses.

identification A defense mechanism through which a person feels like, or adopts the perspective of, someone else. Children identify with their parents for many reasons--one of them, according to psychoanalytic theory, to cope with the powerful emotions of the Oedipus (or Electra) complex.

identity (1) As a Piagetian term, the principle of logic that states that a given quantity of matter remains the same if nothing is added to or subtracted from it, no matter what changes occur in its shape or appearance. (2) Erikson's term for a person's sense of who he or she is as a unique individual. The main task of adolescence, according to Erikson, is the establishment of the young person's identity, including sexual, moral, political, and vocational identity.

identity confusion Erikson's term for the experience of a young person who is uncertain what path to take toward identity formation, and therefore becomes apathetic and disoriented. Also called identity diffusion.

imprinting Innate, instinctual, rapid form of early learning that occurs during a critical period in an organism's development.

independent variable The variable under experimental control with which the changes studied in the experiments are correlated. In psychological experiments the independent variable is often a stimulus, responses to which are under study.

industry versus inferiority The fourth of Erikson's eight "crises," in which the school-age child busily masters many skills or develops a sense of incompetence.

infancy That period of life before a child is able to communicate through speech, usually from birth until 18 months or 2 years. Also called *babyhood.*

information processing A cognitive conception of learning describing how a person attends to storing, coding, and retrieving information.

infrahuman Below human level, such as the primates.

initiative versus guilt The third of Erikson's eight "crises" of psychosocial development. During this stage, the preschool child begins, or initiates, new activities--and sometimes feels guilty as a consequence.

instrumental aggression Fighting over an object, a territory, or a privilege. Examples include quarreling over a toy, a seat at the front of the classroom, or a chance to wash the blackboard.

instrumental-terminality sequence hypothesis Used by Rokeach and others to indicate types of values. The instrumental are those valued because they help in getting something. Terminal are final goals like peace and salvation.

integrity versus despair Erikson's eighth stage of development, in which elderly people evaluate their lives to decide if they have fulfilled their potential and made a lasting contribution to their family or community.

intelligence quotient (IQ) Mathematical score computed by dividing an individual's mental age by chronological age and multiplying by 100: IQ = MA/CA x 100.

intimacy versus isolation Erikson's sixth stage of development, in which young adults seek other people to share their lives with, or become isolated.

isolette Incubator type of support facility that controls the oxygen, humidity, and temperature, mainly designed for neonates. Some isolettes are constructed to allow weighing the baby in the incubator.

juvenile delinquency Violation of the law by a person under 18 years of age. Trial is usually held in juvenile court with the view in mind to rehabilitate the offender.

karyotype A chart on which photographs of chromosomes are cut out and arranged according to size and structure. Demonstrates chromosomal abnormalities.

Lamaze method A technique of childbirth that involves breathing and relaxation exercises during labor.

language acquisition device (LAD) Noam Chomsky's term for an infant's inborn ability to acquire language according to a relatively stable sequence and timetable.

latency Freud's term for the period between the phallic stage and the genital stage. During latency, which lasts from about age 7 to 11, the child's sexual drives are relatively quiet.
law of pragnanz (goodness) Law stating that people will strive for equilibrium and homeostasis.
locus of control The perceived location of the control over an individual's life. It can be internal, as when people believe they control their own life, or it can be external, as when people believe their life is controlled by others.
longitudinal research A long-term study of the same people that is designed to measure both changes and continuity in behavior and personality over time.
LSD Chemical substances from lysergic acid, the most prominent of which is LSD. In the normal person it produces symptoms similar to those of schizophrenia.
macrosystem Term used by Bronfenbrenner to indicate the prevailing pattern of culture or subculture such as economic, social, legal, and political systems.
mainstreaming The practice of putting handicapped and exceptional children in regular classrooms whenever possible to broaden their environment.
marasmus A disease that afflicts infants suffering from severe malnutrition. Growth stops, body tissues waste away, and eventually death occurs.
masturbation Titillation of the penis in males, and in females usually the clitoris, until an orgasm is reached.
maturation Changes in the body or in behavior that result from the aging process, rather than from learning. The child's ability to babble certain sounds at age 6 months and the loss of the front baby teeth at about 6 years are examples of changes that result from maturation.
meiosis The special process of chromosome duplication and cell division that occurs only in the gametes (the reproductive cells). Meiosis produces new cells, sperm or ova, each containing (in humans) only 23 chromosomes.
menarche A female's first menstrual period. May not produce fertile ova.
menopause The end of menstruation usually occurs during middle age; it is accompanied sometimes by physical symptoms and emotional reactions.
mesomorph A body type characterized by more than average musculature.
mesosystem Term used by Bronfenbrenner to indicate the interaction between the settings in which the person develops--for the child, home, school, and community.
metabolism Breaking up or breaking down of protoplasm within an organism; chemical changes that affect nutrition.
metamemory The ability to use and explain techniques that aid memory.
methadone (or dolophine) A chemical substitute for the natural opiates, used in medicine as pain relievers.
microsystem Term used by Bronfenbrenner meaning interaction of the person and the environment in the immediate setting.
middle childhood That period of life, usually from about ages 6 to 11, when a child is ready for the more systematic learning that occurs in elementary school.
middlescence Roughly those years between young adulthood and old age. For some 30 to 55 or 35 to 65, for others 40 to 60; also a function of the role people exhibit.
midlife crisis Turmoil precipitated by the review and reevaluation of one's past, typically occurring in the early to middle 40s.

mnemonics Memory devices that make the task of memory easier, mainly to-be-remembered information. Word association and acrostics are examples.

modeling The patterning of one's behavior after that of someone else. New responses can be learned, and old ones modified, through modeling.

monozygotic twins Two offspring who began development as a single zygote (formed from one sperm and one ovum) that subsequently divided into two zygotes. They have the same genetic makeup, are of the same sex, and look alike.

moratorium Erikson's term for the informal pause in identity formation that allows young people to explore alternatives without making final choices. For many young people, college or military service provides such a moratorium.

moro reflex A reflex most easily elicited during the infant's first three months of life that consists of a thrusting out of the arms in an embrace-like movement when the baby suddenly loses support for the neck and head.

morphemes The minimal units of meaning in a language, consisting of phonemes that are combined to form basic words, prefixes, and suffixes.

motor skills Those abilities that involve body movement and physical coordination, such as walking and reaching.

multifactorial characteristics Those abilities or qualities that are determined by the interaction among several genetic and environmental influences. Characteristics such as intelligence, personality, and talent are multifactorial.

multiple intelligence (after Howard Gardner) A theory suggesting intelligence may be one of seven multiples (kinesthetic, linguistic, math-logical, etc.) identified on neurological, pathological, and other bases, loosely connected by different systems.

multiple regression A statistical procedure using multiple correlations to predict future behavior.

myelin A white, fatty substance that covers some nerve fibers.

neonate Newborn infant up to 4 weeks of age.

neuromuscular Pertaining to the structure and functions of both nerve and muscle.

object permanence The concept that objects and people continue to exist even when they cannot be seen. This concept develops gradually between 6 and 18 months of age.

Oedipus complex In psychoanalytic theory, both the sexual desire that boys in the phallic stage have for their mother and the associated feelings of hostility they have toward their father. This complex is named after Oedipus, a character in ancient Greek legend who unwittingly killed his father and married his mother.

operant conditioning Learning in which a response continues to be made because it has been reinforced.

oral stage According to Freudian theory, the psychosexual stage of infancy (first year), characterized by reception of gratification in the oral region. Feeding is the major situation in which gratification occurs.

organismic model View of humanity that sees people as active agents of their own development; focuses on qualitative changes and sees development as discontinuous.

ossification The hardening of cartilage into bones--a natural process as a child grows.

ova (*singular*, **ovum**) The reproductive cells of the human female, which are present from birth in the ovaries.

ovulation The process (usually occurring two weeks after the beginning of each menstrual period) in which an ovum (egg) matures, is released by the ovary, and enters one of the fallopian tubes.

oxytocin A hormone that is sometimes administered to a pregnant woman to induce labor, or to strengthen uterine contractions.

parallel play Play in which two or more children simultaneously use similar toys in similar ways but do not interact.

penetrance The ability of a gene to manifest itself in the phenotype of an individual who carries it.

penis envy Freudian concept that the female envies the penis and wants one of her own.

period of the embryo The time from approximately the second to the eighth week after conception, during which the rudimentary forms of all anatomical structures develop.

period of the fetus The time from two months after conception until birth. In a full-term pregnancy this period lasts seven months.

period of the ovum The first two weeks after conception, during which rapid cell division occurs.

permissive family style Parents whose child-rearing values one's self-expression, self-reliance, and self-regulation.

phallic stage The third stage of psychosexual development, according to Freud, in which the penis, or phallus, is the focus of psychological concern as well as of physiological pleasure.

phenotype Observable characteristics of a person; may vary from the genotype.

phenylketonuria (PKU) A genetic disease, now easily detected, in which the individual is unable to properly metabolize protein. If left untreated, mental retardation and hyperactivity result.

phobia An irrational fear. Many phobias have specific names, such as claustrophobia (fear of enclosed places), aquaphobia (fear of water), and agoraphobia (fear of open spaces).

phonemes The basic vowel and consonant sounds that exist in a language.

phrenoblysis The investigation centered on the growth and shape of the human skull.

physical modality Term used by Jones to represent one mode of three (social, physical, and psychological) that interact to account for adult development. The physical mode components are physical environment, change, stress, and heredity.

pituitary gland A gland in the base of the skull that produces hormones that regulate growth and trigger the biological changes of puberty.

placenta An organ made up of blood vessels leading to the bloodstreams of both the mother and fetus and having membranes to prevent mixture of the two. These membranes serve as screens through which oxygen and nourishment pass to the fetus and wastes pass from the fetus to the mother to be excreted through her system.

pleasure principle In Freud's theory, the wish for immediate gratification of one's needs. This is the principle by which the id operates.

polygenic inheritance The interaction of many genes to produce a particular characteristic. For example, skin color, body shape, and memory are all polygenic.

postconventional stage of moral development According to Kohlberg, the third and most advanced level of moral development; involves observation of self-accepted moral principles rather than the principles of others.

preconventional morality Kohlberg's term for the first stages of moral reasoning, in which the person's own welfare is paramount and the customs or mores of society are relitively unimportant.

preeclampsia A disease of pregnancy most common during the last trimester. Early signs are high blood pressure, sudden weight gain due to water retention, and protein in the urine. If left untreated, it can develop into the sometimes fatal disease eclampsia. (Also called toxemia.)

preoperational thought Jean Piaget's term for the second period of cognitive development. Children in this stage of thought, which usually occurs between the ages of 2 and 7, are unable to grasp logical concepts such as conservation, reversibility, or classification.

primary circular reaction Jean Piaget's term for infants' repeated actions that involve their bodies (such as sucking the thumb or kicking the legs).

progesterone Female sex hormone produced by the ovaries, which assists the uterus in preparation for pregnancy and the breasts in preparation for lactation.

projection A defense mechanism in which one attributes one's own undesirable thoughts or actions to someone else.

prosocial behavior Ways of responding to others with sympathy, helpfulness, cooperativeness, protecting, and giving.

proximo-distal development Growth proceeding from the center (spine) toward the extremities (literally, from near to far). Human growth, from the embryonic period through childhood, follows this pattern.

psychoanalytic theory A theory of psychology, originated by Sigmund Freud, that stresses the influence of unconscious motivation and drives on all human behavior.

psycholinguistics The psychological study of the acquisition and use of language.

psychological modality Term used by Jones to represent one mode of three (social, physical, and psychological) that interact to account for adult development. The psychological components are identity, role dimension, illusions, and perspective.

psychosexual stages Freudian theory of developmental stages characterized by the area where erotic feelings are organized.

psychosis A severe emotional disturbance characterized by a loss of contact with reality.

psychosocial stages The eight stages of developmental conflict in Erikson's theory of personality development.

psychosomatic illness Physical sickness that has a psychological cause.

puberty The period of early adolescence characterized by rapid physical growth and the attainment of the physiological capability of sexual reproduction. Puberty usually begins at about age 10 or 11 for girls, and 11 or 12 for boys, although there is much variation caused by genes and nutrition.

rapid eye movements (REMs) Eye movements in the final stage of sleep that occur during dreaming. The movements are measured by attaching small electrodes above a person's eye.

rationalization Making unacceptable thoughts or behaviors more acceptable by attributing to them a socially acceptable explanation.

reaction formation A defense mechanism through which a person overreacts in one direction to deny his or her feelings in the opposite direction. For instance, a couple getting a divorce, in order to deny the feelings of love they still have for each other, contend that their spouse is deceitful and cruel.

readiness The level of development reached by an individual that allows him or her to profit from a learning experience.

reality principle According to Freud, the ego's guiding principle, which tries to mediate the demands of the id and the rules of society in order to find the most rational and productive course of action.

recessive gene A gene that affects the expression of a particular phenotypic characteristic only when it is not paired with a dominant gene.

reflective Descriptive of a learning style that involves pausing to think and weighing all alternatives before choosing an answer to a question.

reflex An automatic response, such as an eye blink, involving one part of the body.

regression A defense mechanism in which an individual, under stress, will temporarily revert to a more immature form of behavior (such as bed-wetting by a 12-year-old).

reinforcement Anything (for example, food, money, a smile) that increases the likelihood that a given response will occur again. For example, giving a child a warm hug for being polite will increase the chances that that behavior will be repeated.

repression A defense mechanism which, according to Freud, is characterized by unconscious rejection of anxiety-producing situations.

respondent conditioning (involuntary) A type of learning in which a previously neutral stimulus becomes a conditioned stimulus through repeated pairings with an unconditioned stimulus such as food.

response A behavior (either instinctual or learned) following a specific cue. (See *stimulus.*)

reversibility Used by Piaget to indicate the ability of the child to bring an operation back to its original starting point (such as a clay ball made into a hot dog being made back into a ball).

reward-cost matrix A scheme (decision base) for indicating the cost or reward of antisocial or prosocial behavior.

Rh disease A condition (also called erythroblastosis) that occurs when antibodies produced by the mother's blood cause damage to the fetal blood supply. This disease can now be prevented.

Rho GAM An anti-Rh immunoglobulin used to counteract incompatible blood from the Rh-negative mother.

rites of passage An anthropological term for any ritual that marks the transition from one stage of life to another. The initiation ceremonies at puberty are one example of a rite of passage; weddings and funerals are others.

rooting reflex A normal neonatal reflex that helps babies find a nipple by causing them to turn their heads toward the stimulus and start to suck whenever something brushes against their cheek.

rubella (German measles) A virus which, if contracted during pregnancy, can cause the fetus to develop serious handicaps, among them blindness, deafness, and autism.

schema Piaget's term for a general way of thinking about, or interacting with, ideas and objects in the environment.

schemata A term of Piaget that refers to the structure of framework into which one's experiences are integrated.

schizophrenia A common form of severe mental illness (psychosis) signified by illogical thinking and emotional response.

secondary circular reaction Jean Piaget's term for infants' repetition of actions to produce responses from objects or people (such as squeezing a rubber duck or laughing while playing with an adult).

secondary sexual characteristics Sexual features other than the actual sex organs, such as a man's beard or a woman's breasts, that are used to distinguish male from female.

self-concept A person's sense of himself or herself as a separate person, with particular characteristics. The development of this sense of self begins at birth, but only between 1 and 2 years of age can children truly differentiate themselves from others.

senescence Old age, literally growing old.

sensorimotor intelligence Jean Piaget's term for the first stage of cognitive development (from birth to about 2 years). Children in this stage primarily use the senses and motor skills (grasping, sucking, and so on) to explore and manipulate the environment.

seriation Ability to sort stimuli into categories according to characteristics (for example, color or shape).

sex-linked genes Genes that are carried either on the X or Y chromosome exclusively. Sex-linked genes account for the fact that certain genetic diseases or characteristics are more likely to occur in one gender than in the other.

sex typing A process through which children acquire attitudes and behaviors appropriate to their culture for members of their sex.

sexual abuse A type of maltreatment in which the victim (often children) is forced to submit to sexual exploitation from looking and words to intercourse due to the abuser's status or physical superiority.

sexually transmitted disease (STD) Venereal diseases passed on by sexual activity such as chlamydia, gonorrhea, genital warts, herpes, etc.

sickle-cell anemia A genetic blood disease, common among black Americans, that can cause fatigue, swelling of the joints, and sometimes death.

social exchange theory A social theory of aging that suggests that as people age they have little in the way of favors to offer others and are increasingly vulnerable; therefore, they tend to withdraw from society.

social learning theory The theory that learning social traits (such as aggression or generosity) occurs through imitation of, and identification with, other people.

social modality Term used by Jones to represent one mode of three (social, physical, and psychological) that interact to account for adult development. The social mode components are developmental tasks, the historical times, and reaction.

somatotonia A personality type in which temperament suggests a restless, noisy, aggressive, adventuresome, active person; correlates with the mesomorphic body type.

stages of dying Phrase coined by Kubler-Ross indicating the steps one goes through in dying: shock and denial, anger, bargaining, depression, and acceptance.

statistical significance The trustworthiness of an obtained statistical measure as a statement about reality--for example, the probability that the population mean falls within the limits determined from a sample. It refers to the reliability of a statistic finding. Acceptable levels are 1 out of 100 (.01) or 5 out of 100 (.05). Says nothing about the findings value.

stepping reflex A reflexive reaction in which a neonate appears to be walking when held vertically with feet against a hard surface and moved from side to side.

stimulants Psychoactive drugs that increase arousal, such as coffee, dexedrine, and methamphetamine.

stimulus An external condition or event that elicits a bodily response or prompts a particular action. For example, the sight or aroma of an appetizing meal is a stimulus to which the response is usually starvation.

stochastic theory Biological theory of aging which is probabilistic as to the number of "hits" of radiation or whatever that will produce faulty genes.

sublimation According to Freud, a defense mechanism characterized by rechanneling of uncomfortable feelings.

sucking reflex The natural tendency of an infant to suck when an object such as a finger or nipple is placed in the infant's mouth.

sudden infant death syndrome (SIDS) The sudden death of an apparently healthy infant (usually between the ages of 2 and 4 months). The immediate cause is that the infant stops breathing; the underlying cause is not known.

superego Freud's term for that part of the personality that contains the conscience, including the internalization of moral standards set by one's parents.

surface structure Noam Chomsky's term for the particular vocabulary and rules of grammar that differ from one language to another. The surface structure is distinct from the deep structure of language, which includes the general rules that are shared by most languages.

symbolic function The ability to use words and images to represent objects and actions. This ability, which children usually acquire around age 2, makes it possible to remember the past, imagine the future, and deal with the present with more reflection and imagination. The third stage of cognitive development of Jerome Bruner in which the child uses language to relate to the real and abstract.

taxonomy of educational objectives A way of classifying learning objectives, whether cognitive, psychomotor, or effective.

teratogens External agents, such as viruses, drugs, chemicals, and radiation, that can cross the barrier of the placenta and harm the embryo or fetus.

tertiary circular reactions Jean Piaget's term for the repetition of certain actions with slight variations each time (such as hitting a drum with a stick, and then with a pencil or a hammer). Tertiary circular reactions occur during the fifth stage of sensorimotor intelligence (usually between 12 and 18 months of age).

testosterone Hormones that are produced primarily by the testes, that regulate sexual development in puberty. Although girls' adrenal glands produce some testosterone, it is chiefly a male hormone.

thalidomide A mild tranquilizer--now banned--that when taken early in pregnancy prevented normal formation of the fetus' arms, legs, and ears.

third stage of labor The expulsion of the placenta after a child is born.

tonic neck reflex An infant's reaction to having his or her head turned sharply to one side--extending the arm and leg on the same side and flexing the arm and leg on the opposite side.

toxemia A poisoning of the blood.

transductive reasoning A term of Piaget that refers to a preoperational child's tendency to use associative reasoning rather than induction or deduction.

transformational grammar A term used by Chomsky to suggest that through preverbal, intuitive rules an individual turns deep structure into surface grammar (the spoken or written).

trauma A serious condition of the body, psychic or physical, due to a wound or mental shock.

trophoblast The outer cells of the blastula. These cells later form the four membranes (the yolk sac, amnion, allantois, and chorion) that protect and nurture the embryo and fetus.

trust versus mistrust Erikson's term for the infant's basic experience of the world as either good and comfortable or as threatening and uncomfortable. Early caregiving experiences usually mold the child's viewpoint. This is the first of Erikson's eight stages of development.

ultrasound Method of scanning the womb for detection of the fetal outline to determine whether the pregnancy is progressing normally.

value clarification An approach designed to assist children in the forming of values and placing them in perspective.

visceratonia Personality type of an individual in which temperament is alleged to indicate a friendly, comfort-loving person with slow reactions, who sleeps well and has a relaxed carriage. Correlates with the endomorphic body type.

visual cliff A laboratory device that consists of a ledge with an apparent drop of several feet that actually is covered by a sheet of transparent glass. Very young children will not venture beyond the end of the ledge even when coaxed by parents, a refusal that demonstrates early development of depth perception.

vital capacity The air-holding capacity of the lungs.

withdrawal Avoiding an anxiety-producing situation; a common defense mechanism in children.

XO (Turner's syndrome) A genetic abnormality occurring in females who inherit one rather than two X chromosomes. It results in incomplete sexual maturation and usually mental retardation as well.

XX The chromosomal pair that determines that a zygote will develop into a normal female. This combination results when an ovum (which always carries an X chromosome) is fertilized by a sperm carrying an X chromosome.

XXY (Klinefelter's syndrome) A group of genetic disorders present in males who inherit an extra X chromosome. This syndrome prevents the development of secondary sex characteristics.

XY The chromosomal pair that determines that a zygote will develop into a normal male. This combination results when an ovum (which always carries an X chromosome) is fertilized by a sperm carrying a Y chromosome.

XYY A genetic abnormality present in males who possess an extra Y chromosome. Men who have this disorder are generally taller and may be more prone to antisocial behavior than the norm.

zone of proximal development From Vygotsky, the difference between what children can do on their own (actual development) and what they can do with a tutor (potential development).

zygote The one-celled organism formed from the union of a sperm and an ovum.

NAME INDEX

C

D

E

N

O

P

Y

Z

SUBJECT INDEX

D

E

F

X

Y

Z